P9-DCL-138

Introduction to Advertising and Promotion

An Integrated Marketing Communications Perspective

Introduction to Advertising and Promotion

An Integrated Marketing Communications Perspective

Third Edition

George E. Belch   **Michael A. Belch**

San Diego State University

IRWIN

Chicago • Bogotá • Boston • Buenos Aires • Caracas
London • Madrid • Mexico City • Sydney • Toronto

©RICHARD D. IRWIN, INC., 1990, 1993, and 1995

All rights reserved. No part of this publication may be
reproduced, stored in a retrieval system, or transmitted,
in any form or by any means, electronic, mechanical,
photocopying, recording, or otherwise, without the prior
written permission of the publisher.

Sponsoring editor:	Nina McGuffin
Senior developmental editor:	Andy Winston
Marketing manager:	Jim Lewis
Project editor:	Paula M. Buschman
Production manager:	Ann Cassady
Cover designer:	Keith McPherson
Cover illustrator:	Rick Smith
Interior illustrator:	Keith McPherson
Art studio:	Electronic Publishing Services, Inc.
Manager, graphics and desktop services:	Kim Meriwether
Compositor:	Publication Services, Inc.
Typeface:	10/12 Ehrhardt MT
Printer:	Von Hoffman Press, Inc.

Library of Congress Cataloging-in-Publication Data

Belch, George E. (George Edward)
    Advertising and promotion : an integrated marketing communications
perspective / George E. Belch, Michael A. Belch. – 3rd ed.
      p. cm. – (The Irwin series in marketing)
    Rev. ed. of: Introduction to advertising & promotion. 2nd ed.
c 1993.
      Includes index.
      ISBN 0-256-13696-3 ISBN 0-256-13697-1 (international students ed.)
      1. Advertising.   2. Sales promotion.   3. Communication in
marketing: I. Belch, Michael A. II. Belch, George E. (George
Edward).   Introduction to advertising & promotion.   III. Title.
IV. Series.
HF5823.B387   1995
659.1—dc20   94–22646

Printed in the United States of America
1 2 3 4 5 6 7 8 9 0 VH 1 0 9 8 7 6 5 4

To Mom and Dad
and
To Jessica, Gayle, Derek, and Danny—
A special dedication for putting up with us

Preface

ⓐ THE CHANGING WORLD OF ADVERTISING AND PROMOTION

Nearly everyone in the modern world is influenced to some degree by advertising and other forms of promotion. Organizations in both the private and public sector have learned that the ability to communicate effectively and efficiently with their target audiences is critical to their success. Advertising and other types of promotional messages are used to sell products and services as well as to promote causes, market political candidates, and deal with societal problems such as the AIDS crisis and drug abuse. Consumers are finding it increasingly difficult to avoid the efforts of marketers, who are constantly searching for new ways to communicate with them.

Most of the people involved in advertising and promotion will tell you that there is no more dynamic and fascinating a field to either practice or study. However, they will also tell you that the field is undergoing dramatic changes that threaten to change advertising and promotion forever. For decades the advertising business was dominated by large, full-service Madison Avenue–type agencies. But now these agencies must change if they hope to survive into the 21st century.

The threats come from all sides—clients demanding better results from their advertising and promotional dollars; lean but highly creative smaller ad agencies; sales promotion and direct marketing firms who want a larger share of the billions of dollars companies spend each year promoting their products and services; consumers who no longer respond to traditional forms of advertising; and new technologies that may reinvent the very process of advertising.

At the 1994 annual meeting of the American Association of Advertising Agencies, Allen Rosenshine, chairman and CEO of BBDO Worldwide, said, "Companies basically and fundamentally no longer accept on faith the value of conventional advertising placed in conventional media." Keith Reinhard, chairman and CEO of DDB Needham Worldwide, noted that the large agencies "have finally begun to acknowledge that this isn't a recession we're in, and that we're not going back to the good old days."

There are numerous examples of the dramatic changes sweeping the advertising industry. Coca-Cola has recently taken most of the responsibility of creating commercials for what may be the world's best known brand away from McCann-Erickson, its agency and marketing partner for the past 40 years, and given it to a high-powered Hollywood talent firm with no previous advertising experience, Creative Artists Agency. In the past several years the advertising culture has been shaped more by small agencies such as Wieden & Kennedy in Portland, Oregon, urging consumers to "just do it" than by any of the New York–based mega-agencies.

In addition to redefining the role and nature of their advertising agencies, marketers are changing the way they spend their promotional dollars. Spending on sales promotion activities targeted at both consumers and the trade has surpassed advertising media expenditures for years and continues to rise. In a recent article titled "Agencies: Change or Die," Joe Cappo, *Advertising Age* senior vice president, wrote, "What is happening in the advertising industry right now is a massive revolution that is changing the rules of marketing. This revolution is taking place not only in the United States, but in all affluent countries where advertising and media are well developed."

A number of factors are fueling this revolution. The audiences that marketers seek, along with the media and methods for reaching them, have become increasingly fragmented. Advertising and promotional efforts have become more regionalized and targeted to specific audiences. Retailers have become larger and more powerful, forcing marketers to shift money from advertising budgets to sales promotion. Marketers expect their promotional dollars to generate immediate sales and are demanding more accountability from their agencies. Many companies are coordinating all their communications efforts so they can send cohesive messages to their customers. Many advertising agencies have acquired, started, or become affiliated with sales promotion, direct marketing, and public relations companies to better serve their clients' marketing communications needs.

This text will introduce students to this fast-changing field of advertising and promotion. While advertising is its primary focus, it is more than just an introductory advertising text because there is more to most organizations' promotional programs than just advertising. The changes discussed above are leading marketers and their agencies to approach advertising and promotion from an integrated marketing communications (IMC) perspective, which calls for a "big picture" approach to planning marketing and promotion programs and coordinating the various communication functions. To understand the role of advertising and promotion in today's business world, one must recognize how a firm can use all of the promotional tools to communicate with its customers.

TO THE STUDENT: PREPARING YOU FOR THE NEW WORLD OF ADVERTISING AND PROMOTION

Some of you are taking this course to learn more about this fascinating field; many of you hope to work in advertising or some other promotional area. The changes in the industry have profound implications for the way today's student is trained and educated. You will not be working for the same kind of communication agencies that existed 5 or 10 years ago. If you work on the client side of the business, you will find that the way they approach advertising and promotion is changing dramatically.

Today's student is expected to understand all of the major marketing communication functions: advertising, direct marketing, sales promotion, public relations, and personal selling. You will also be expected to know how to research and evaluate a company's marketing and promotional situation and how to use these various functions in developing effective communication strategies and programs. This book will help prepare you for these challenges.

As professors we were, of course, once students ourselves. In many ways we are perpetual students in that we are constantly striving to learn about and explain how advertising and promotion work. We share many of your interests and concerns and are often excited (and bored) by the same things. Having taught in the advertising and promotion area for a combined 30-plus years, we have developed an understanding of what makes a book in this field interesting to students. In writing this book, we have tried to remember how we felt about the various texts we have used throughout the years and to incorporate the good things and minimize those we felt were of little use. We have tried not to overburden you with definitions, although we do call out those that are especially important to your understanding of the material.

We also remember that as students we were not really excited about theory. But to fully understand how advertising and promotion work, it is necessary to establish some theoretical basis. The more you understand about how things are supposed to work, the easier it will be for you to understand why they do or do not turn out as planned.

Perhaps the question students ask most often is, "How do I use this in the real world?" In response, we provide numerous examples of how the various theories and concepts in the text can be used in practice. A particular strength of this text is the integration of theory with practical application. Nearly every day an example of advertising and promotion in practice is reported in the media. We have used many sources, such as *The Wall Street Journal, Business Week, Fortune, Marketing & Media Decisions, Advertising Age, AdWeek, Business Marketing,* and *Promo,* to find practical examples that are integrated throughout the text. We have spoken with hundreds of people about the strategies and rationale behind the ads and other types of promotions we use as examples.

Each chapter begins with a vignette that presents a practical example of advertising and promotion or other interesting insights. Every chapter also contains a number of boxed **IMC Perspectives** that present in-depth discussions of particular issues related to the chapter material and show how companies are using integrated marketing communications. **Global Perspectives** are presented throughout the text in recognition of the increasing importance of international marketing. **Ethical Perspectives** focus attention on important social issues and show how advertisers must take ethical considerations into account when planning and implementing advertising and promotional programs.

We have included more than 350 advertisements and examples of numerous other types of promotion, all of which were carefully chosen to illustrate a particular idea, theory, or practical application. Please take time to read the chapter openings and IMC, Global, and Ethical Perspectives, and study the diverse ads and illustrations. We think they will stimulate your interest and relate to your daily life as a consumer and a target of advertising and promotion.

TO THE INSTRUCTOR: A TEXT THAT REFLECTS THE CHANGES IN ADVERTISING AND PROMOTION

Our goal in writing the third edition of this text was to focus on the many changes that are occurring in the advertising industry and how they influence promotional strategies and tactics. We have done this by continuing with the *integrated marketing communications perspective* we introduced in the second edition. More and more companies are approaching advertising and promotion from an IMC perspective, coordinating the various promotional mix elements with other marketing activities that communicate with a firm's customers. A recent study found that an overwhelming majority of marketing managers believe IMC can enhance the effectiveness and impact of their marketing communications efforts. Many advertising agencies are also developing expertise in direct marketing, sales promotion, event sponsorship, and other areas so they can meet all of their clients' integrated marketing communication needs—and, of course, survive.

The text is built around an integrated marketing communications planning model and recognizes the importance of coordinating all of the promotional mix elements to develop an effective communications program. Although media advertising is often the most visible part of a firm's promotional program, attention must also be given to direct marketing, sales promotion, public relations, and personal selling.

This text integrates theory with planning, management, and strategy. To effectively plan, implement, and evaluate IMC programs, one must understand the overall marketing process, consumer behavior, and communications theory. We draw from the extensive research in advertising, consumer behavior, communications, marketing, sales promotion, and other fields to give students a basis for understanding the marketing communications process, how it influences consumer decision making, and how to develop promotional strategies.

While this is an introductory text, we do treat each topic in some depth. We believe the marketing and advertising student of today needs a text that provides more than just an introduction to terms and topics. The book is positioned primarily for the introductory advertising, marketing communications, or promotions course as taught in the business/marketing curriculum. It can also be used in journalism/communications courses that take an integrated marketing communications perspective. In addition to its thorough coverage of advertising, this text has chapters on sales promotion, direct marketing, personal selling, and publicity/public relations. These chapters stress the integration of advertising with other promotional mix elements and the need to understand their role in the overall marketing program.

◉ ORGANIZATION OF THIS TEXT

This book is divided into seven major parts. In Part I we examine the role of advertising and promotion in marketing and introduce the concept of integrated marketing communications. Chapter 1 provides an overview of advertising and promotion and its role in modern marketing. The concept of IMC and the factors that have led to its growth are discussed. Each of the promotional mix elements is defined and an IMC planning model shows the various steps in the promotional planning process. This model provides a framework for developing the integrated marketing communications program and is followed throughout the text. Chapter 2 examines the role of advertising and promotion in the overall marketing program, with attention to the various elements of the marketing mix and how they interact with advertising and promotional strategy.

In Part II of the text we cover the promotion program situation analysis. Chapter 3 describes how firms organize for advertising and promotion and examines the role of ad agencies and other firms that provide marketing and promotional services. We discuss how ad agencies are selected, evaluated, and compensated as well as the changes occurring in the agency business. We also consider whether responsibility for integrating the various communication functions lies with the client or the agency. Chapter 4 covers the stages of the consumer decision-making process and both the internal psychological factors and the external factors that influence consumer behavior. The focus of this chapter is on how advertisers can use an understanding of buyer behavior to develop effective advertising and other forms of promotion. In Chapter 5 we discuss the concepts of market segmentation and positioning and their role in the development of an advertising and promotional program.

Part III of the text analyzes the communications process. Chapter 6 examines various communication theories and models of how consumers respond to advertising messages, while Chapter 7 considers source, message, and channel factors. These first three sections of the text provide students with a solid background in areas of marketing, consumer behavior, and communications that are important to promotional planners and against which specific advertising and promotional planning decisions can be made and evaluated.

In Part IV we consider how firms develop goals for their integrated marketing communications programs and determine how much money to spend trying to achieve them. Chapter 8 stresses the importance of knowing what to expect from advertising, the differences between advertising and communication objectives, characteristics of good objectives, and problems in setting objectives. Chapter 9 discusses methods for determining and allocating the promotional budget.

Part V of the text examines the various promotional mix elements that form the basis of the integrated marketing communications program. Chapter 10 discusses the planning and development of the creative strategy and advertising campaign and examines the creative process of advertising. In Chapter 11 we turn our attention to ways to execute the creative strategy and some criteria for evaluating creative work. Chapters 12 through 15 cover media strategy and planning and the various advertising media. Chapter 12 introduces the key principles of media planning and strategy and examines how a media plan is developed. Chapter 13 discusses the advantages and disadvantages of the broadcast media (TV and radio) as well as issues regarding the purchase of radio and TV time and audience measurement. Chapter 14 considers the same issues for the print media (magazines and newspapers). Chapter 15 examines the role of support media such as outdoor and transit advertising and some of the new media alternatives.

In Chapters 16 through 19 we continue the IMC emphasis by examining other areas of the promotional mix. Chapter 16 looks at the rapidly growing area of direct marketing, in which companies communicate directly with target customers to generate a response or transaction. Chapter 17 examines both consumer-oriented sales promotion and programs targeted to the trade. Chapter 18 covers the role of publicity and public relations in IMC as well as corporate advertising. Basic issues regarding personal selling and its role in promotional strategy are presented in Chapter 19.

Part VI of the text consists of Chapter 20, where we discuss ways to measure the effectiveness of advertising and promotion, including methods for pretesting and posttesting advertising messages and entire campaigns. In Part VII we turn our attention to special markets, topics, and perspectives that are becoming increasingly important in contemporary marketing. Chapter 21, on business-to-business marketing, examines how advertising and other forms of promotion are used to help one company sell its products and/or services to another firm. In Chapter 22 we examine the global marketplace and the role of advertising and other promotional mix variables in international marketing.

The text concludes with a discussion of the regulatory, social, and economic environments in which advertising and promotion operate. Chapter 23 looks at industry self-regulation and regulation by governmental agencies such as the Federal Trade Commission, as well as the regulation of sales promotion and direct marketing. Advertising's role in society is constantly changing, and our discussion would not be complete without a look at the criticisms that are often made against it, so in Chapter 24 we consider the social, ethical, and economic aspects of advertising and promotion.

CHAPTER FEATURES

The following features in each chapter enhance students' understanding of the material as well as their reading enjoyment.

Chapter Objectives

Objectives are provided at the beginning of each chapter to identify the major points that should be learned from it.

Opening Vignettes

The vignettes provide a practical example or application or discuss an interesting issue that is relevant to the chapter. These opening vignettes are designed to create interest in the material covered in the chapter.

IMC Perspectives

These boxed items feature in-depth discussions of interesting issues related to the chapter material and the practical application of IMC. Each chapter contains several of these insights into the world of integrated marketing communications.

Global Perspectives

These boxed sidebars provide information similar to that in the IMC Perspectives, with a focus on international aspects of advertising and promotion.

Ethical Perspectives

These boxed items discuss the moral and/or ethical issues regarding practices engaged in by marketers and are also tied to the material presented in the particular chapter.

Key Terms

Important terms are highlighted in boldface throughout the text and listed at the end of each chapter. These terms help call students' attention to important ideas, concepts, and definitions.

Chapter Summaries

These synopses serve as a quick review of important topics covered.

Discussion Questions

Questions at the end of each chapter give students an opportunity to test their understanding of the material and to apply it. These questions can also serve as a basis for class discussion or assignments.

Four-Color Visuals

Print ads, photoboards, and other examples appear throughout the book. More than 450 ads, charts, graphs, and other types of illustrations are included.

CHANGES IN THE THIRD EDITION

We have made a number of changes in the third edition to make it as relevant and current as possible as well as more interesting to students.

- **A Stronger Emphasis on Integrated Marketing Communications** The third edition puts an even stronger emphasis on approaching the field of advertising and promotion from an integrated marketing communications perspective. We continue to focus on how the various elements of an organization's promotional mix are combined to develop a total marketing communications program that sends a consistent message to customers. The first chapter examines the factors that have contributed to the increased attention to IMC on both the client and agency side. Chapter 3 focuses on other communication agencies, such as sales promotion and direct response firms. More attention is also given to setting objectives for IMC programs (Chapter 8) and measuring their effectiveness (Chapter 20).

- **IMC Perspectives** New boxed items focus on specific examples of how companies like Eveready, Apple Computer, and Southwest Airlines, as well as advertising agencies such as Leo Burnett, are using integrated marketing communications. The IMC Perspectives also address interesting issues related to advertising, sales promotion, direct marketing, and personal selling.

- **New Chapter Opening Vignettes** All of the chapter opening vignettes in the third edition are new and were chosen for their currency and relevance to students. They include insights into how companies like Kellogg, Coca-Cola, Compaq, Acura, Hewlett-Packard, and Nestlé as well as organizations such as Major League Baseball use advertising and other IMC tools.

- **New and Updated Global and Ethical Perspectives** Most of the boxed items focusing on global and ethical issues of advertising and promotion are new; those retained from the second edition have been updated. The Global Perspectives examine the role of advertising and other promotional areas in international markets. The Ethical Perspectives discuss specific issues, developments, and problems that call into question the ethics of marketers and their decisions as they develop and implement their advertising and promotional programs.

- **Contemporary Examples** The field of advertising and promotion changes very rapidly, and we have tried to keep pace with it. Wherever possible we have updated the statistical information presented in tables, charts, and exhibits throughout the text. We have reviewed the most current academic and trade literature to ensure that this text reflects the most current perspectives and theories on advertising, promotion, and the rapidly evolving area of integrated marketing communications. We have also updated most of the examples and ads throughout the book. *An Introduction to Advertising and Promotion* continues to be the most contemporary text on the market, offering students as timely a perspective as possible.

- **Concise Writing** In response to requests from instructors and students, we have reduced the length of the text by nearly 100 pages. The third edition has been carefully edited to make the writing style tighter and more concise. In making these changes, we were careful not to reduce relevant content or the many examples that are such a popular feature of this text. However, students will find the writing in the new edition more active, direct, and succinct and thus easier to read.

SUPPORT MATERIAL

A high-quality package of instructional supplements supports the third edition. All of the supplements have been developed by the authors to ensure their coordination with the text. We offer instructors a support package that facilitates the use of our text and enhances the learning experience of the student.

Instructor's Manual

The instructor's manual is a valuable teaching resource that includes learning objectives, chapter and lecture outlines, answers to all of the end-of-chapter discussion questions, transparency masters, and further insights and teaching suggestions. Additional discussion questions are also presented for each chapter. These questions can be used for class discussion or as short-answer essay questions for exams.

Manual of Tests

A test bank of more than 1,500 multiple-choice questions has been developed to accompany the text. The questions provide thorough coverage of the chapter material, including opening vignettes and IMC, Global, and Ethical Perspectives, and are categorized by level of learning (definitional, conceptual, or application).

Computerized Test Bank

A computerized version of the test bank is available to adopters of the text.

Four-Color Transparencies

Each adopter may request a set of 100 four-color acetate transparencies that present print ads, photoboards, sales promotion offers, and other materials that do not appear in the text. A number of important models or charts appearing in the text are also provided as color transparencies. Slipsheets are included with each transparency to give the instructor useful background information about the illustration and how it can be integrated into the lecture.

Video Supplements

A video supplement package has been developed specifically for classroom use with this text. The first video contains nearly 100 commercials that are examples of creative advertising. It can be used to help the instructor explain a particular concept or principle or give more insight into how a company executes its advertising strategy. Many of the commercials are tied to the chapter openings, IMC and Global Perspectives, or specific examples cited in the text. The video includes commercials for Infiniti and Porsche automobiles, Compaq computers, Taster's Choice coffee, Chips Ahoy! cookies, and Continental Airlines. A number of international commercials are included, as well as those used in public service campaigns for such organizations as the American Indian College Fund and the Partnership for a Drug-Free America. Insights and/or background information about each commercial are provided in the instructor's manual written specifically for the videos.

The second video contains longer segments on the advertising and promotional strategies of various companies and industries. Among the segments are an examination of the cola wars, which focuses on the ongoing marketing and advertising battle between Coke and Pepsi, highlights of several promotions that won the 1994 Reggie Awards (given each year to the best sales promotion campaigns), and case studies of the integrated marketing communications programs used by Southwest Airlines, and Sprint to introduce its new voice-activated FONCARD.

⦿ ACKNOWLEDGMENTS

While this third edition represents a tremendous amount of work on our part, it would not have become a reality without the assistance and support of many other people. Authors tend to think they have the best ideas, approach, examples, and organization for writing a great book. But we quickly learned that there is always room for our ideas to be improved on by others. A number of colleagues provided detailed, thoughtful reviews that were immensely helpful in making this a better book. We are very grateful to the following individuals who worked with us on the first two editions. They include Lauranne Buchanan, *University of Illinois;* Roy Busby, *University of North Texas;* Lindell Chew, *University of Missouri, St. Louis;* Catherine Cole, *University of Iowa;* John Faier, *Miami University;* Raymond Fisk, *Oklahoma State University;* Geoff Gordon, *University of Kentucky;* Donald Grambois, *Indiana University;* Stephen Grove, *Clemson University;* Ron Hill, *American University;* Paul Jackson, *Ferris State College;* Don Kirchner, *California State University, Northridge;* Clark Leavitt, *Ohio State University;* Charles Overstreet, *Oklahoma State University;* Paul Prabhaker,

Depaul University, Chicago; Scott Roberts, *Old Dominion University;* Harlan Spotts, *Northeastern University;* Mary Ann Stutts, *Southwest Texas State University;* Terrence Witkowski, *California State University, Long Beach;* Robert Young, *Northeastern University.*

We are particularly grateful to the individuals who provided constructive comments on how to make this edition better: Chuck Areni, *Texas Tech University;* Lee Bartlett, *Brigham Young University;* Timothy A. Bengston, *University of Kansas;* Wendy Bryce, *Western Washington University;* John Charnay, *Woodbury University in Burbank, California;* Ernest F. Cooke, *Loyola College in Maryland;* Michael Cotter, *Grand Valley State University;* Robert Erffmeyer, *University of Wisconsin-Eau Claire;* Laurence Feldman, *University of Illinois at Chicago;* Nancy Frontczak, *Metropolitan State College of Denver;* Eric Haley, *The University of Tennessee;* Suzette Heiman, *University of Missouri;* Jean A. Husby, *Chippewa Valley Technical College;* Ronald B. Kaatz, *Northwestern University;* Stephen Kresky, *Brown Mackie College;* Tina M. Lowrey, *Rider College;* Peter M. Lynagh, *University of Baltimore;* Kenneth G. Mangun, *Roosevelt University;* Mary Ann McGrath, *Loyola University-Chicago;* Anita M. Olson, *North Hennepin Community College;* Nancy Pennington, *Minnesota School of Business;* Srivatsan Ramachandran, *Northwestern State University of Louisiana;* Joel Reedy, *University of South Florida;* Brad Sago, *School of Business-Anderson University;* Stanley V. Scott, *University of Alaska, Anchorage;* Don Shomwell, *Florida State University;* Jack Siegrist, *Monmouth College;* Penny M. Simpson, *Northwestern State University;* Richard E. Stanley, *Middle Tennessee State University;* Carl Stark, *Henderson State University;* Mary Ann Stutts, *Southwest Texas State University;* Clint Tankersley, *Syracuse University;* Chuck Tomkovick, *University of Wisconsin-Eau Claire;* Thomas W. Taylor, *University of Georgia;* Sandra Young, *University of North Texas.*

We received valuable comments and ideas from the reviewers of the third edition: Terry Bristol, *Oklahoma State University;* Robert H. Ducoffe, *Baruch College;* Robert Gulonsen, *Washington University;* and Denise D. Schoenbachler, *Northern Illinois University.*

We would also like to acknowledge the cooperation we received from many people in the business, advertising, and media communities. This book contains several hundred ads, illustrations, charts, and tables that have been provided by advertisers and/or their agencies, various publications, and other advertising and industry organizations. Many individuals took time from their busy schedules to provide us with requested materials and gave us permission to use them.

Several practitioners helped make this book more practical and realistic by sharing their insights and experiences. We would like to acknowledge the input of

David Kennedy of Wieden & Kennedy, Richard Brooks of Phillips-Ramsey, Inc., Bruce Goerlich of D'Arcy Masius Benton & Bowles, Inc., Carol Zerweist of Whirlpool Corp., Melanie Jones of KNBC-TV, Ethan Orlinsky of Major League Baseball, and Rebecca Holman.

A manuscript does not become a book without a great deal of work on the part of a publisher. Various individuals at Richard D. Irwin have been involved with this project over the past several years. We are particularly grateful to Rob Zwettler for believing in us and having the faith to champion this book and help make it such a success. We could never overlook all the work done by Eleanore Snow that helped make the second edition so successful and set the stage for this revision. Our editor on the third edition, Nina McGuffin, provided valuable guidance and was instrumental in making sure this was much more than just a token revision. A special thanks goes to Andy Winston, our developmental editor, for all of his efforts and for being so great to work with. Thanks also to Paula Buschman for once again doing a superb job of managing the production process.

We would like to acknowledge the support we have received from the College of Business at San Diego State University. Dean Allan Bailey has provided us with an excellent working environment and has been very supportive. We also want to thank Sandy Behe for all of her help and the great job she did on the library research, and Charlotte Goldman for her assistance in getting many of the ads that appear throughout the book.

On a more personal note, a great deal of thanks goes to our families for putting up with us over the past few years while we were revising this book. Gayle, Danny, Derek, and Jessica have had to endure the deviation from our usually pleasant personalities and dispositions for a third time, and once again we look forward to returning to normal. Finally, we would like to acknowledge each other for making it through this ordeal a third time. Our mother will be happy to know that we still get along after all this—although it's getting a little tougher.

George E. Belch
Michael A. Belch

Contents in Brief

Contents

Chapter *1*

An Introduction to Advertising and Promotion

Chapter Objectives

● To examine the promotional function and the growing importance of advertising and other promotional elements in the marketing programs of domestic and foreign companies.

● To introduce the concept of integrated marketing communications (IMC) and reasons for the increasing importance of this perspective in planning and executing advertising and promotional programs.

● To introduce the various elements of the promotional mix, consider their role in an IMC program, and examine how various marketing and promotional elements must be coordinated to communicate effectively.

● To introduce a model of the IMC planning process and examine the various steps in developing a marketing communications program.

Kellogg's and NBC Match Cereals with Stars

It is not uncommon for cereal companies to show a picture of a celebrity on a package to help capture consumers' attention and convey a certain image for the brand. For years General Mills has used Michael Jordan and other star athletes on the front of Wheaties boxes to help position the brand as the "breakfast of champions." Recently Kellogg Co., the nation's largest cereal maker, has shown how this concept can be leveraged into a successful integrated marketing communications program. In 1993, Kellogg Co. entered into a fully integrated marketing alliance with NBC to develop a wide range of marketing programs and promotions that involved matching consumers of specific cereal brands with the network's shows.

Stars of six popular NBC shows—"Seinfeld," "Wings," "Blossom," "The Fresh Prince of Bel-Air," "Saved by the Bell: The New Class," and "The Tonight Show with Jay Leno"—appeared on boxes of Kellogg's cereals. NBC and Kellogg Co. considered factors such as a show's rating, audience demographics, and Q scores of the stars (a measure of a celebrity's popularity among various demographic groups) to see which most closely resembled the profile of a given cereal's customers. For example, research showed that "Seinfeld" viewers tend to be adults who eat more of Kellogg's Low-Fat Granola, so the series' four leading cast members appeared on this brand's box. "Saved by the Bell: The New Class" was coupled with Kellogg's Rice Krispies because of the brand's high teen appeal, while Kellogg's Crispix cereal was paired with "The Tonight Show with Jay Leno" based on research showing that many adults eat the brand as a late-night snack. Other pairings included "Wings" cast members with Kellogg's Frosted Bran cereal; "Blossom" with Kellogg's Corn Flakes; and "The Fresh Prince of Bel-Air" with Kellogg's Raisin Bran.

Kellogg kicked off the integrated marketing program in August 1993 with in-store displays in 30,000 supermarkets promoting "Breakfast around the World." The basis of this promotion was a contest where consumers who watched the premiere of 10 new NBC shows could win a family vacation to international destinations plus a year's supply of Kellogg's cereal.

The second phase of the promotion began in October with an emphasis on the six returning NBC series featured on Kellogg's cereal boxes. In addition to featuring the series' stars and the NBC peacock logo, the boxes offered consumers a chance to order specially produced premiums. For example, the Kellogg's Low-Fat Granola box premium offered an official "Have Breakfast with Seinfeld" cereal bowl, which played off the main character's reputation for being a cereal aficionado. Other premium offers included a "Blossom" telephone and "Saved by the Bell" trading cards, "Fresh Prince" jersey, and "Tonight Show" T-shirt designed by Jay Leno. Various boxes also carried cutout characters, fun facts and profiles, and a national sweepstakes promotion offering a chance to win a trip to Hollywood to have breakfast with the cast of the programs. The integrated marketing program continued throughout the fall with strong network, radio, magazine, newspaper, and in-store advertising support.

Both Kellogg and NBC viewed the partnership as a success. NBC's vice president of marketing estimated that the boxes featuring the stars generated over 1 billion impressions for the network's shows. He viewed the boxes as mini-billboards that appeared in the most uncluttered promotional environment of all—people's homes. Kellogg Co. saw the partnership as an excellent integrated marketing program which matched well with the company's branding strategy, had strong consumer appeal, and created excitement and high participation levels among retailers.

Sources: Cyndee Miller, "Research Guides NBC, Kellogg in Matching Granola with 'Seinfeld,'" *Marketing News*, Sept. 1993, p. 18; Joe Mandese, "NBC and Kellogg Co-Star," *Advertising Age*, July 19, 1993, pp. 1, 32; "NBC and Kellogg Unveil Groundbreaking Partnership: 'Breakfast around the World' Kicks Off Largest-Ever Network/Advertiser Marketing Campaign in August," *Kellogg's News Release*, July 19, 1993.

he opening vignette illustrates how the roles of advertising and promotion are changing in modern marketing. In the past, marketers such as Kellogg Co. often relied primarily on advertising through the mass media to promote their products. However, many companies are taking a new approach to marketing and promotion: they integrate their advertising efforts with a variety of other communication techniques such as sales promotion, direct marketing, publicity and public relations (PR), and event sponsorships. They are also recognizing that advertising and other forms of promotion are most effective when they are coordinated with other elements of the marketing program.

The Kellogg's/NBC promotional effort is an example of how marketers are using an integrated marketing communications approach to gain competitive advantage. A number of communication tools were used to promote Kellogg's cereals and NBC programs. Advertising was done through a variety of media, and sales promotion techniques such as couponing, contests, and premium offers were used. Both NBC and Kellogg generated publicity for the promotion through press releases and other public relations activities. The promotion was also carried to the point of purchase with in-store displays and specially designed boxes.

In addition to having strong consumer appeal, the promotion generated support from retailers and gave them an extra incentive to display the six Kellogg's brands. The Kellogg's/NBC alliance also shows how marketers are partnering to take advantage of joint promotional opportunities.

The Kellogg Co. and NBC, along with thousands of other companies, recognize that the way they must market their products and services is changing rapidly. The fragmentation of mass markets, the explosion of new technologies, economic uncertainties, and the emergence of global markets and competition are all changing the way companies approach marketing as well as advertising and promotion. For many organizations, developing marketing communications programs that are responsive to these changes is critical to their success. Advertising and other forms of promotion will continue to play an important role in their integrated marketing programs.

THE GROWTH OF ADVERTISING AND PROMOTION

Advertising and promotion are an integral part of our social and economic systems. In our complex society, advertising has evolved into a vital communication system for both consumers and businesses. The ability of advertising and other promotional methods to deliver carefully prepared messages to target audiences has given them a major role in the marketing programs of most organizations. Companies ranging from large multinational corporations to small retailers increasingly rely on advertising and promotion to help them market products and services. In market-based economies, consumers have learned to rely on advertising and other forms of promotion for information they can use in making purchase decisions.

Evidence of the increasing importance of advertising and promotion comes from the growth in expenditures in these areas. In 1980, advertising expenditures in the United States were $53 billion, and $49 billion was spent on sales promotion techniques such as product samples, coupons, contests, sweepstakes, premiums, rebates, and allowances and discounts to retailers. By 1993, an estimated $139 billion was spent on local and national advertising, while sales promotion expenditures increased to more than $177 billion![1] Companies bombarded the U.S. consumer with messages and promotional offers, collectively spending more than $6 a week on every man, woman, and child in the country—nearly 50 percent more per capita than in any other nation.

Promotional expenditures in international markets have grown as well. Advertising expenditures outside the United States increased from $55 billion in 1980 to $170 billion by 1993.[2] Both foreign and domestic companies spend billions more on sales promotion, personal selling, direct marketing, event sponsorships, and public relations, all important parts of a firm's marketing communications program.

Global Perspective 1-1
The New Global Consumer

For many years, multinational companies have focused most of their attention on the industrialized and highly developed markets of the United States, Japan, and the countries of Western Europe. Relatively stable economies and high disposable incomes of the nearly 700 million consumers living in these countries will continue to make them important to marketers. However, markets in these industrialized countries are struggling to awaken from the economic slumber that has slowed their growth. The United States and Western Europe have been mired in recession for the past five years, while Japan nervously jiggles its bursting bubble economy. Moreover, demand for many products peaked in these countries as most basic needs were met. As the CEO of a large package-goods firm told his new product development staff, "An important rule to remember about the developed world is that nobody really *needs* anything anymore."

While many markets in developed countries are mature, this is not the case in most of the world. According to the World Bank, 77 percent of the world's population lives in what are known as developing areas. A planet full of consumers, from Eastern Europe's struggling new capitalists to the youthful and increasingly affluent middle class of South America and the striving countries of the Pacific Rim, are waiting impatiently for everything from blue jeans to washing machines and automobiles. Astute marketers recognize that these developing countries represent the greatest growth opportunities most companies will ever know.

The world's largest markets are developing in Asia. With 1.2 billion people and a rising per capita income, China will become Asia's largest consumer market after Japan by the year 2000. In the 1980s, Chinese consumers were looking for television sets, refrigerators, and washing machines. In the 90s, they want VCRs, telephones, and motorcycles. Estimates of India's middle class range from 100 to 300 million, and the number of consumers with money to spend on branded products is growing rapidly. The Southeast Asian countries of Indonesia, Malaysia, Thailand, and Singapore have young populations who are enthusiastic purchasers of many products.

Opportunities in Eastern Europe are also immense. The region is as populous as Western Europe, and its 300 million consumers are starved for basic products that are taken for granted by Westerners: hamburgers, pizzas, telephones, washing machines, and refrigerators. Whirlpool Europe is achieving sales growth averaging 6 percent a year in Eastern Europe—three times the rate in Western Europe.

Accompanying the rapidly growing economies of these developing countries is a tremendous demand for high-quality, branded products. Bausch & Lomb, maker of Ray Ban sunglasses, has been selling the coveted eyewear to Indonesia's

middle class for $50 to $100 (more than American consumers will pay for like models). In China, Gillette recently introduced Oral-B toothbrushes at 90¢ (versus the average local price of 10¢). If the company can achieve just a 10 percent market share, it will sell more toothbrushes in China than in the United States.

Advances in technology, travel, and communications are turning the world into a global consumer village, and people everywhere want to be part of it. Along with the higher standard of living that quality products can deliver, consumers want international brands that possess the cachet advertising has helped create. They want to be part of the Pepsi generation, wear the united colors of Benetton, and view the world through their Ray Ban sunglasses. More than ever before, global marketers interested in growth will be there to give them what they want.

Sources: Bill Saporito, "Where the Global Action Is," *Fortune* Special Issue, Autumn/Winter 1993, pp. 63–65; Rahul Jacob, "Asia, Where the Big Brands Are Blooming," *Fortune*, August 23, 1993, p. 55.

The tremendous growth in expenditures for advertising and promotion reflects in part the growth of the U.S. and global economies.[3] For example, Global Perspective 1–1 discusses how expansion-minded marketers are taking advantage of growth opportunities in various regions of the world. The growth in promotional expenditures also reflects the fact that marketers around the world recognize the value and importance of advertising and promotion. Promotional strategies play an important role in the marketing programs of companies as they attempt to communicate with and sell their products to their customers. To understand the roles advertising and promotion play in the marketing process, let us first examine the marketing function.

@ WHAT IS MARKETING?

Before reading on, stop for a moment and think about how you would define marketing. Chances are that each reader of this book will come up with a somewhat different answer, as marketing is often viewed in terms of individual activities that constitute the overall marketing process. One popular conception of marketing is that it primarily involves sales. Other perspectives view marketing as consisting primarily of advertising or retailing activities. For some of you, market research, pricing, or product planning may have come to mind.

While all these activities are part of marketing, it encompasses more than just these individual elements. The American Marketing Association, which represents marketing professions in the United States and Canada, defines **marketing** as

> the process of planning and executing the conception, pricing, promotion, and distribution of ideas, goods, and services to create exchanges that satisfy individual and organizational objectives.[4]

Effective marketing requires that managers recognize the interdependence of such activities as sales and promotion and how they can be combined to develop a marketing program.

Marketing Focuses on Exchange

The AMA definition recognizes that exchange is a central concept in marketing.[5] For **exchange** to occur, there must be two or more parties with something of value to one another, a desire and ability to give up that something to the other party, and a way to communicate with each other. Advertising and promotion play an important role in the exchange process by informing consumers of an organization's product or service and convincing them of its ability to satisfy their needs or wants.

Not all marketing transactions involve the exchange of money for a tangible product or service. Nonprofit organizations such as charities, religious groups, the arts, and colleges and universities (probably including the one you are attending) receive millions of dollars in donations every year. Charitable organizations often use ads like the one in Exhibit 1–1 to solicit contributions from the public. Donors generally do not receive any material benefits for their contributions; they donate in exchange for intangible social and psychological satisfactions such as feelings of goodwill and altruism.

The Marketing Mix

Marketing facilitates the exchange process by carefully examining the needs and wants of consumers, developing a product or service that satisfies these needs, offering it at a certain price, making it available through a particular place or channel of distribution, and developing a program of promotion or communication to create awareness and interest. These four Ps—*product*, *price*, *place* (distribution), and *promotion*—are elements of the **marketing mix**. The basic task of marketing is combining these four elements into a marketing program to facilitate the potential for exchange with consumers in the marketplace.

The proper marketing mix does not just happen. Marketers must be knowledgeable about the issues and options involved in each element of the mix. They must also be aware of how these elements can be combined to provide an effective marketing program. The market must be analyzed through consumer research and this information utilized in developing an overall marketing strategy and mix.

The primary focus of this book is on one element of the marketing mix: the promotional variable. However, the promotional program must be part of a viable marketing strategy and coordinated with other marketing activities. A firm can spend large sums on advertising or sales promotion, but it stands little chance of success if the product is of

@ **EXHIBIT 1-1**

Nonprofit organizations
use advertising to solicit
contributions and support

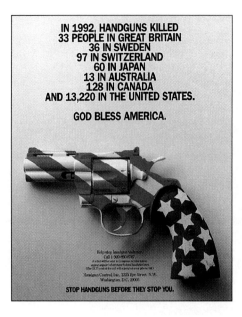

poor quality, is priced improperly, or does not have adequate distribution to consumers. Marketers have long recognized the importance of combining the elements of the marketing mix into a cohesive marketing strategy. Many companies also recognize the need to integrate their various marketing communication efforts, such as media advertising, direct marketing, sales promotion, and public relations, to achieve more effective marketing communication.

@ **INTEGRATED MARKETING COMMUNICATIONS**

In past decades, many marketers built strong barriers around the various marketing and promotional functions and planned and managed them separately, with different budgets, different views of the market, and different goals and objectives. These companies failed to recognize that the wide range of marketing and promotional tools must be coordinated to communicate effectively and present a consistent image to target markets. In the 1990s, many companies are moving toward **integrated marketing communications (IMC)**, which involves coordinating the various promotional elements along with other marketing activities that communicate with a firm's customers.[6]

The American Association of Advertising Agencies defines integrated marketing communications as

> a concept of marketing communications planning that recognizes the added value of a comprehensive plan that evaluates the strategic roles of a variety of communication disciplines—for example, general advertising, direct response, sales promotion, and public relations—and combines these disciplines to provide clarity, consistency, and maximum communications impact.[7]

Advocates of the IMC concept, such as Don Schultz of Northwestern University, argue for an even broader perspective that considers all sources of brand or company contact that a customer or prospect has with a product or service.[8]

Integrated marketing communications calls for a "big picture" approach to planning marketing and promotion programs and coordinating the various communication functions. It requires firms to develop a total marketing communications strategy that recognizes how all of a firm's marketing activities, not just promotion, communicate with its customers. Consumers' perceptions of a company and/or its various brands are a synthesis of the bundle of messages they receive (such as media advertisements, price, direct marketing efforts, publicity, sales promotions, and type of store where a product is sold).

For example, a high price may symbolize quality to customers, as may the shape or design of a product, its packaging, brand name, or the image of the stores in which it

⊚ EXHIBIT 1–2

A distinctive package and brand name help communicate a quality image for a product

is sold. Vanderbilt perfume is one product that uses a distinctive package and brand name as well as a high price to connote a quality, upscale image that is reinforced by its advertising (Exhibit 1–2). Although the product is available in mass retail outlets, its positioning is premium as reflected in the package as well as the price.

Integrated marketing communications seeks to have all of a company's marketing and promotional activities project a consistent, unified image to the marketplace.

The Growing Importance of Integrated Marketing Communications

There are a number of reasons why marketers are adopting the concept of integrated marketing communications. One fundamental reason is that marketers recognize the value of strategically integrating the various communication functions rather than having them operate autonomously. By coordinating their marketing communication efforts, companies can avoid duplication, take advantage of synergy among various communication tools, and develop more efficient and effective marketing communication programs. Advocates of IMC argue that it is one of the easiest ways a company can maximize the return on its investment in marketing and promotion.[9]

The integrated marketing communications movement is also being driven by changes in the ways companies market their products and services. The main reason for the growing importance of the IMC approach is the ongoing revolution that is changing the rules of marketing and the role of the traditional advertising agency.[10] Major characteristics of this marketing revolution include:

- A shifting of marketing dollars from media advertising to other forms of promotion, particularly consumer and trade-oriented sales promotions. Many marketers feel that traditional media advertising has become too expensive and is not cost effective. Also, escalating price competition in many markets has resulted in marketers pouring more of their promotional budgets into price promotions rather than media advertising.
- The fragmentation of media markets, which has resulted in less emphasis on mass media such as network television and more attention to smaller, targeted media alternatives such as direct mail and event sponsorships.
- A shift in marketplace power from manufacturers to retailers. Consolidation in the retail industry is resulting in small local retailers being replaced by regional, national, and international chains. These large retailers are using their clout to demand promotional fees and allowances from manufacturers, which often siphons monies away from advertising. Moreover, new technologies such as checkout scan-

EXHIBIT   1–3

Elements of the
promotional mix

ners provide retailers with information on the effectiveness of manufacturers' promotional programs. This is leading many marketers to shift their focus to promotional tools that can produce short-term results, such as sales promotions.

- The rapid growth and development of database marketing. Many companies are using computers to build databases containing customer names; geographic, demographic, and psychographic profiles; purchase patterns; media preferences; credit ratings; and other characteristics. Marketers are using this information to target consumers through a variety of direct-marketing methods, such as telemarketing and direct-response advertising, rather than relying on mass media through traditional advertising.
- Changes in media buying practices. Many companies are taking media buying inhouse or are turning to independent media buying services that offer discounted rates. Those who have kept media buying with their advertising agencies are demanding reduced commissions and more accountability. They are also telling their agencies to consider less expensive alternatives to mass media advertising.

This marketing revolution is affecting everyone involved in the marketing and promotional process. Companies are recognizing that they must change the ways they market and promote their products and services. They are selling to customers who are increasingly price sensitive and less likely to respond to creative advertising through the mass media. Nestlé, IBM, Sprint, Microsoft, Nike, and many other companies have adopted the IMC approach, and research shows that its use will continue to spread.[11] IMC Perspective 1–1 discusses how Apple Computer used integrated marketing communications to help introduce the Newton line of personal digital assistant devices.

The marketing revolution has had even greater impact on traditional advertising agencies. Many agencies have responded to the call for synergy among the various promotional tools by acquiring PR, sales promotion, and direct marketing companies and touting themselves as IMC agencies that offer one-stop shopping for all of their clients' promotional needs.[12] Some agencies became involved in these nonadvertising areas to retain their clients' promotional dollars and have struggled to offer any real value beyond creating advertising. However, most agencies recognize that their future success depends upon their ability to understand all areas of promotion and help their clients develop and implement integrated marketing communication programs.

A successful IMC program requires that a firm find the right combination of promotional tools and techniques, define their role and the extent to which they can or should be used, and coordinate their use. To accomplish this, those responsible for the company's communications efforts must understand the role of promotion in the marketing program.

**The Role of
Promotion**

Promotion has been defined as the coordination of all seller-initiated efforts to set up channels of information and persuasion to sell goods and services or promote an idea.[13] While implicit communication occurs through the various elements of the marketing mix, most of an organization's communications with the marketplace take place in a carefully planned and controlled promotional program. The basic tools used to accomplish an organization's communication objectives are often referred to as the **promotional mix** and include advertising, direct marketing, sales promotion, publicity/public relations, and personal selling (Exhibit 1–3). In this text, we will also view direct marketing as a major

IMC Perspective 1–1
Apple Uses IMC to Launch Newton

For nearly two decades Apple Computer, Inc., has been the innovation leader in the personal computer market. Apple brought affordable computing to the masses in the late 1970s with the Apple I and II PCs. In 1984 the company set a new standard for personal computers with the introduction of the Macintosh, which was promoted as "the computer for the rest of us." In 1991 Apple introduced the PowerBook line of notebook computers, which became an instant hit and generate over $1 billion in annual sales.

Apple recognizes that it must continue to innovate and stay ahead of the rapidly changing personal computer market. According to Apple's former chairman, John Sculley, computers, telephones, television, and other electronic products are on a collision course that will create an entirely new generation of products and industries. A major part of Apple's corporate strategy is to develop products that will move the company beyond PCs and into the digital revolution market where computers, communications, consumer electronics, and entertainment converge.

The first step in this new strategy came with the introduction of Apple's widely publicized Newton line of personal digital assistant devices. The first Newton product was the Newton MessagePad, a hand-held computer that can recognize handwriting and combines an electronic memo pad and calendar with faxing and paging functions. To launch the Newton MessagePad, Apple used a major integrated marketing communications campaign combining media advertising, point-of-purchase displays and materials, publicity and PR, direct marketing, trade shows, and other promotional efforts.

Apple unveiled the Newton with a gala event at the Macworld Expo computer trade show in August 1993. It had used only limited advertising because awareness was already extremely high as a result of the massive publicity the product was receiving. As Newton reached national distribution, Apple began an ad campaign created by the BBDO Worldwide agency utilizing television, print, and outdoor media. The "Newton intelligence" banner campaign promoted the MessagePad and laid the groundwork for the Newton product concept by educating people about the new technology.

Apple also hired CKS partners, an unconventional agency led by a trio of former Apple managers, to work on a variety of promotional tasks for the Newton including packaging, point-of-purchase displays, in-store posters, and brochures. BBDO and CKS work closely together to ensure that the communication efforts for the Newton are integrated. Apple's marketing communications manager said BBDO gets customers into the store, while CKS helps close the sale. A major part of CKS's strategy is a point-of-purchase kiosk that allows shoppers to take a 90-second interactive demonstration tour of the Newton MessagePad. CKS also developed a flip-book for the display that offers handwriting tips for using the Newton.

Apple's initial advertising and promotional efforts for the Newton target primarily business and professionals, since the company believes the device will find a home in this market before becoming a hot consumer item. Many experts think the Newton line may help Apple in its quest to bring leading-edge computer technology to the masses. As it does so, Apple will continue to use a marketing communications strategy that integrates the various promotional efforts designed to help turn shoppers into Newton buyers.

Sources: "Apple's Future," *Business Week*, July 5, 1993, pp. 22–27; Bradley Johnson and Alice Z. Cuneo, "Here's Newton, but No Ad Blitz," *Advertising Age*, Aug. 2, 1993, pp. 3,30; Jan Baben, "Apple Fills Up Its Marketing Cart," *Business Marketing*, Sept. 1993, pp. 12–14.

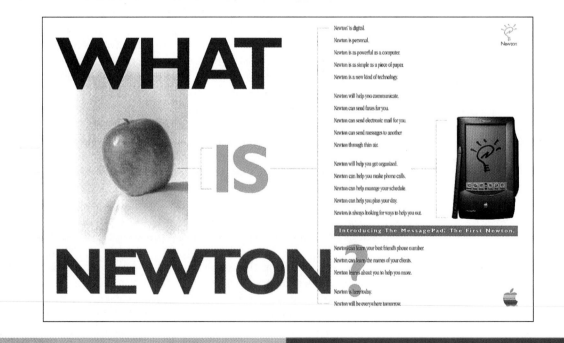

promotional mix element marketers can use to communicate with their target markets. Each element of the promotional mix plays a distinctive role in an integrated marketing communications program and may take on a variety of forms, and each has certain advantages.

THE PROMOTIONAL MIX

Advertising

Advertising is defined as any paid form of nonpersonal communication about an organization, product, service, or idea by an identified sponsor.[14] The *paid* aspect of this definition reflects the fact that the space or time for an advertising message generally must be bought. An occasional exception to this is the public service announcement (PSA), whose advertising space or time is donated by the media.

The *nonpersonal* component means advertising involves mass media (e.g., television, radio, magazines, newspapers) that can transmit a message to large groups of individuals, often at the same time. The nonpersonal nature of advertising means there is generally no opportunity for immediate feedback from the message recipient (except in direct-response advertising). Therefore, before the message is sent, the advertiser must consider how the audience will interpret and respond to it.

There are several reasons why advertising is such an important part of many marketers' promotional mix. First, it can be a very cost-effective method for communicating with large audiences. For example, during the 1992–93 television season, the average 30-second spot on prime-time network television reached nearly 12 million households. The cost per thousand households reached was just $8.37.[15]

Advertising can also be used to create images and symbolic appeals for a company or brand, a capability that is very important for companies selling products and services that are difficult to differentiate on functional attributes. For example, advertising for Marlboro cigarettes uses the cowboy and "Marlboro country" advertising theme to create a masculine image (Exhibit 1–4). This image has helped make Marlboro one of the leading brands of cigarettes in the world.

Another advantage of advertising is its ability to strike a responsive chord with consumers when other elements of the marketing program have not been successful. Popular advertising campaigns attract consumers' attention and can help generate sales. For example, in 1986 the California Raisin Advisory Board launched its dancing raisins campaign, which featured the Claymation characters performing their now famous conga line routine to the sound of "Heard It Through the Grapevine." The dancing raisins commercials have remained a consistent favorite among consumers and have helped boost raisin sales by more than 20 percent. Exhibit 1–5 shows a more recent spot from this campaign, designed to promote the versatility of raisins.

Popular advertising campaigns can also sometimes be leveraged into successful integrated marketing communication programs. IMC Perspective 1–2 (see page 14) discusses how Eveready has done this with its popular Energizer bunny campaign.

Direct Marketing

In **direct marketing,** organizations communicate directly with target customers to generate a response and/or a transaction. Traditionally, direct marketing has not been considered an element of the promotional mix. However, because it has become such an integral part of the IMC program of many organizations and often involves separate objectives, budgets, and strategies, we view direct marketing as a component of the promotional mix.

Direct marketing is much more than direct mail and mail-order catalogs. It involves a variety of activities, including direct selling, telemarketing, and direct-response ads through direct mail and various broadcast and print media. Some companies, such as Tupperware, Discovery Toys, and Encyclopaedia Britannica, do not use any other distribution channels, relying on independent contractors to sell their products directly to consumers. Companies such as L. L. Bean, Lands' End, and The Sharper Image rely heavily on direct marketing and have been very successful through their direct-mail and phone-order business. Dell Computer became one of the fastest-growing computer companies in the world by selling a full line of personal computers through direct marketing (Exhibit 1–6, page 15).

@ **EXHIBIT 1–4**

Marlboro became a
leading brand of cigarettes
by developing a masculine
image for the product

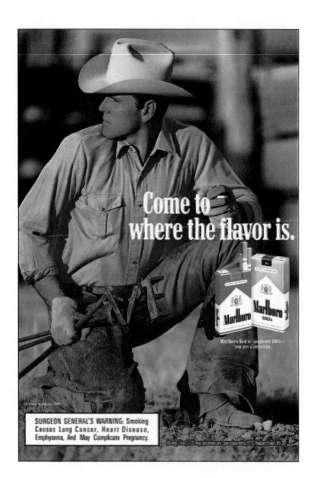

Direct-marketing tools and techniques are also being used by companies that distribute their products through traditional distribution channels or have their own sales force. Direct marketing plays a big role in the integrated marketing communication programs of consumer products companies and business-to-business marketers. These companies spend billions of dollars each year to call customers directly and attempt to sell them products and services or qualify them as sales leads. Marketers send out direct-mail pieces ranging from simple letters and fliers to detailed brochures and videotapes to give potential customers information about their products or services. Direct-marketing techniques are used to distribute product samples or target users of a competing brand of a product or service.

Sales Promotion

The next variable in the promotional mix is **sales promotion**, which is generally defined as those marketing activities that provide extra value or incentives to the sales force, distributors, or the ultimate consumer and can stimulate immediate sales. Sales promotion is generally broken into two major categories: consumer-oriented and trade-oriented activities.

Consumer-oriented sales promotion is targeted to the ultimate user of a product or service and includes couponing, sampling, premiums, rebates, contests, sweepstakes, and various point-of-purchase materials (Exhibit 1–7, page 15). These promotional tools encourage consumers to make an immediate purchase and thus can stimulate short-term sales. *Trade-oriented sales promotion* is targeted toward marketing intermediaries such as wholesalers, distributors, and retailers. Promotional and merchandising allowances, price deals, sales contests, and trade shows are some of the promotional tools used to encourage the trade to stock and promote a company's products.

Sales promotion expenditures in the United States reached $177 billion in 1993 and accounted for more promotional dollars than advertising.[16] Among many consumer

EXHIBIT 1–5 The Dancing Raisins commercials have helped boost sales of California raisins

package-goods companies, sales promotion is often 60 to 70 percent of the promotional budget.[17] Many companies have switched the emphasis of their promotional strategy from advertising to sales promotion. For example, over the past several years, the H. J. Heinz Co. cut its advertising expenditures by nearly 43 percent while allocating nearly all of its increased marketing spending to trade promotions.[18]

Promotion and *sales promotion* are two terms that often create confusion in the advertising and marketing fields. As noted, *promotion* is an element of the marketing mix by which firms communicate with their customers and includes all the promotional mix elements we have just discussed. However, many marketing and advertising practitioners

IMC Perspective 1–2
Eveready Builds a Successful Integrated Marketing Communications Program around Its Popular Bunny

One of the most successful advertising campaigns in recent years has featured the Eveready Battery Co.'s Energizer bunny. The Energizer campaign, which began in 1989, was built around the concept of parody commercials. The pink, drum-thumping Energizer bunny barges across the screen, interrupting spoofs of clichéd pitches for products such as flavored instant coffee, pretentious wines, deodorant soaps, and nasal sprays. Over the past five years the bunny has appeared in more than 25 parody spots, entertaining consumers and helping deliver the key point: that Energizer batteries are long-lasting and, like the bunny, "keep going and going."

The Energizer bunny commercials have been among the most popular on television and have received numerous creative awards. More importantly for Eveready, the bunny campaign helped halt Energizer's decline in market share and significantly increased sales. However, the Energizer bunny campaign is more than just great advertising—Eveready has leveraged it into a very effective integrated marketing communications program.

Eveready has used the popularity of the bunny campaign to generate support from retailers in the form of shelf space, promotional displays, and other merchandising activities. Consumer promotions such as in-store displays, premium offers, and sweepstakes use the pink bunny. Pictures of the bunny appear on Energizer packages to ensure brand identification and extend the campaign's impact to the point of purchase. Eveready also extended the integrated approach to tie-ins with sports marketing and sponsorships. For example, the Energizer bunny delivered the first pitch of the 1992 season at the home opener for all 24 major league baseball clubs. As part of the deal, Energizer sponsored the season-long radio broadcasts for all of the clubs. The ad's popularity has led to enormous publicity that has contributed to awareness of the Energizer brand name and helped make the bunny a pop culture icon.

To keep the campaign fresh and fun and guard against wearout, Eveready had its advertising agency, Chiat/Day, develop new creative executions for the bunny commercials. The new commercials, which began running in the fall of 1993, feature the evil Supervolt Battery Co. employing the wicked witch of the west and King Kong to snare its nemesis, the Energizer bunny. For the next several years, consumers are likely to see these charged-up foes' futile attempts to stop the bunny. The ads, along with Eveready's successful integrated marketing program, will probably keep Energizer sales going and going and going.

Sources: Julie Liesse, "How the Bunny Charged Eveready," *Advertising Age*, April 4, 1991, pp. 20, 55; Julie Liesse, "Opening Day and the Bunny Goes Up to Bat," *Advertising Age*, April 6, 1992, pp. 1, 37; "Charged-Up Foes for Bunny," *Advertising Age*, Oct. 11, 1993, p. 3.

ENERGIZER   MONUMENT VALLEY, UTAH. 5:32 P.M. STILL GOING. NOTHING OUTLASTS THE ENERGIZER.

@ **EXHIBIT 1-6**

Dell Computer relies on direct-response advertising to market its personal computers

@ **EXHIBIT 1-7**

Coupons are a popular consumer-oriented sales promotion tool

use the term more narrowly to refer to *sales promotion* activities to either consumers or the trade (retailers, wholesalers). In this book, *promotion* is used in the broader sense to refer to the various marketing communication activities of an organization.

**Publicity/
Public Relations**

Another important component of an organization's promotional mix is publicity/public relations.

Publicity

Publicity refers to nonpersonal communications regarding an organization, product, service, or idea that is not directly paid for or run under identified sponsorship. It usually comes in the form of a news story, editorial, or announcement about an organization and/or its products and services. Like advertising, publicity involves nonpersonal communication to a mass audience, but unlike advertising, publicity is not directly paid for by the company. The company or organization attempts to get the media to cover or run a favorable story on a product, service, cause, or event to affect awareness, knowledge, opinions, and/or behavior. Techniques used to gain publicity include news releases, press conferences, feature articles, photographs, films, and videotapes.

An advantage of publicity over other forms of promotion is its credibility. Consumers generally tend to be less skeptical toward favorable information about a product or service when it comes from a source they perceive as unbiased. For example, the success (or failure) of a new movie is often determined by the reviews it receives from film critics, who are viewed as objective evaluators by many moviegoers. Another advantage of publicity is its low cost, since the company is not paying for time or space in a mass medium such as TV, radio, or newspaper. While an organization may incur some costs in developing publicity items or maintaining a staff to do so, these expenses will be far less than for the other promotional programs.

Publicity is not always under the control of an organization and is sometimes unfavorable. Negative stories about a company and/or its products can be very damaging.

Public relations

It is important to recognize the distinction between publicity and public relations. When an organization systematically plans and distributes information in an attempt to control and manage the nature of the publicity it receives and its image, it is really engaging in

EXHIBIT 1–8

Advertising is often used by companies to enhance their corporate image

a function known as public relations. **Public relations** is defined as "the management function which evaluates public attitudes, identifies the policies and procedures of an individual or organization with the public interest, and executes a program of action to earn public understanding and acceptance."[19] Public relations generally has a broader objective than publicity, as its purpose is to establish and maintain a positive image of the company among its various publics.

Public relations uses publicity and a variety of other tools, including special publications, participation in community activities, fund-raising, sponsorship of special events, and various public affairs activities, to manage an organization's image. Organizations also use advertising as a public relations tool to enhance their image. For example, Exhibit 1–8 shows a corporate ad for State Farm Insurance Companies.

Traditionally, publicity and public relations have been considered more supportive than a primary part of the marketing and promotional process. However, many firms have begun making public relations an integral part of their predetermined marketing and promotional strategies. PR firms are increasingly touting public relations as a communications tool that can take over many of the functions of conventional advertising and marketing.[20]

Personal Selling

The final element of an organization's promotional mix is **personal selling**, a form of person-to-person communication in which a seller attempts to assist and/or persuade prospective buyers to purchase the company's product or service or to act on an idea. Unlike advertising, personal selling involves direct contact between the buyer and seller, either face to face or through some form of telecommunications such as telephone sales. This interaction gives the marketer communication flexibility; the seller can see or hear the potential buyer's reactions and modify the message accordingly. The personal, individualized communication in personal selling allows the seller to tailor the message to the customer's specific needs or situation.

Personal selling also involves more immediate and precise feedback because the impact of the sales presentation can generally be assessed from the customer's reactions. If the feedback is unfavorable, the salesperson can modify the message. Personal selling efforts can also be targeted to specific markets and customer types who are the best prospects for the company's product or service.

PROMOTIONAL MANAGEMENT

In developing a promotional strategy, a company combines the promotional mix elements, balancing the strengths and weaknesses of each, to produce an effective promotional campaign. **Promotional management** involves coordinating the promotional

@ **EXHIBIT   1-9**

Business-to-business marketers often use advertising to build awareness

mix elements to develop a controlled, integrated program of effective marketing communication. The marketer must consider which promotional tools to use and how to combine them to achieve the organization's marketing and promotional objectives. Companies also face the task of distributing the total promotional budget across the promotional mix elements: What percentage of the budget should they allocate to advertising, sales promotion, direct marketing, and personal selling?

Companies consider many factors in developing their promotional mix, including the type of product, the target market, the decision process of the buyer, the stage of the product life cycle, and its channels of distribution. Companies selling consumer products and services generally rely on advertising through mass media to communicate with ultimate consumers. Business-to-business marketers, who generally sell expensive, risky, and often complex products and services, more often use personal selling. Business-to-business marketers do use advertising to perform important functions such as building awareness of the company and its products, generating leads for the sales force, and reassuring customers about the purchase they have made (Exhibit 1–9).

Conversely, personal selling also plays an important role in consumer product marketing. A consumer goods company retains a sales force to call on marketing intermediaries (wholesalers and retailers) that distribute the product or service to the final consumer. While the company sales reps do not communicate with the ultimate consumer, they make an important contribution to the marketing effort by gaining new distribution outlets for the company's product, securing shelf position and space for the brand, informing retailers about advertising and promotion efforts to users, and encouraging dealers to merchandise and promote the brand at the local market level.

Advertising and personal selling efforts vary depending on the type of market being sought, and even firms in the same industry may differ in the allocation of their promotional efforts. For example, in the cosmetics industry, Avon and Mary Kay Cosmetics concentrate on direct selling, whereas companies such as Revlon and Max Factor rely heavily on consumer advertising. Firms also differ in the relative emphasis they place on advertising and sales promotion. Companies selling high-quality brands use advertising to convince consumers of their superiority, justify their higher prices, and maintain their image. Brands of lower quality, or those that are difficult to differentiate, often compete more on a price or "value for the money" basis and may rely more on sales promotion to the trade and/or consumers.

The marketing communications program of an organization is generally developed with a specific purpose in mind and is the end product of a detailed marketing and promotional planning process. We will now look at a model of the promotional planning process that presents the sequence of decisions made in developing and implementing the IMC program.

THE PROMOTIONAL PLANNING PROCESS

As with any business function, planning plays a fundamental role in the development and implementation of an effective promotional program. Those individuals involved in promotion design a **promotional plan** that provides the framework for developing, implementing, and controlling the organization's integrated marketing communication programs and activities.

Promotional planners must decide on the role and function of the specific elements of the promotional mix, develop strategies for each element, and implement the plan. Promotion is but one part of, and must be integrated into, the overall marketing plan and program.

A model of the IMC planning process is shown in Exhibit 1–10. The remainder of this chapter presents a brief overview of the various steps involved in this process.

Review of the Marketing Plan

The first step in the IMC planning process is to review the marketing plan and objectives. Before developing a promotional plan, it is important to understand where the company (or the brand) has been, its current position in the market, where it intends to go, and how it plans to get there. Most of this information should be contained in the **marketing plan,** a written document that describes the overall marketing strategy and programs developed for an organization, a particular product line, or a brand. Marketing plans can take several forms but generally include five basic elements:

1. A detailed situation analysis that consists of an internal marketing audit and review and an external analysis of the market competition and environmental factors.
2. Specific marketing objectives that provide direction, a time frame for marketing activities, and a mechanism for measuring performance.
3. A marketing strategy and program that include selection of target market(s) and decisions and plans for the four elements of the marketing mix.
4. A program for implementing the marketing strategy, including determining specific tasks to be performed and responsibilities.
5. A process for monitoring and evaluating performance and providing feedback so proper control can be maintained and any necessary changes made in the overall marketing strategy or tactics.

For most firms, the promotional plan is an integral part of the marketing strategy. Thus, the promotional planners must know the role advertising and other promotional mix elements will play in the overall marketing program. Also, the promotional plan is developed similarly to the marketing plan and often uses its detailed information. Promotional planners focus on information in the marketing plan that is relevant to the promotional strategy.

Promotional Program Situation Analysis

After the overall marketing plan is reviewed, the next step in developing a promotional plan is to conduct the situation analysis. In the IMC program, the situation analysis focuses on those factors that influence or are relevant to development of a promotional strategy. As with the overall marketing situation analysis, the promotional program situation analysis will include both an internal and an external analysis.

EXHIBIT   1–10   An integrated marketing communications planning model

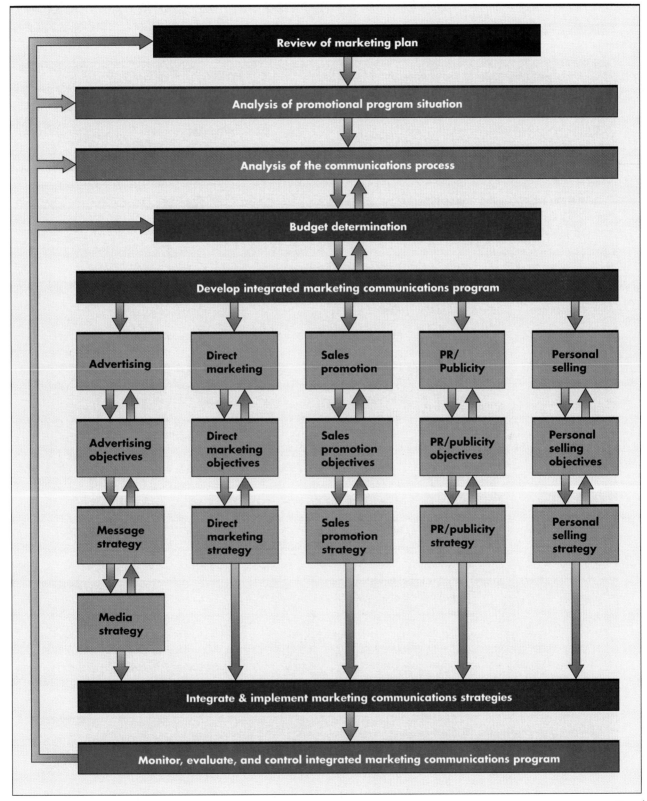

continued

Review of marketing plan
    Examine overall marketing plan and objectives
    Role of advertising and promotions
    Competitive analysis
    Assess environmental influences

Analysis of promotional program situation
    Internal analysis
        Promotional department organization
        Firm's ability to implement promotional program
        Agency evaluation and selection
        Review of previous program results

    External analysis
        Consumer behavior analysis
        Market segmentation and target marketing
        Market positioning

Analysis of communications process
    Analyze receiver's response processes
    Analyze source, message, channel factors
    Establish communications goals and objectives

Budget determination
    Set tentative marketing communications budget
    Allocate tentative budget

Develop integrated marketing communications program
    Advertising
        Set advertising objectives
        Determine advertising budget
        Develop message strategies
        Develop media strategies
    Direct marketing
        Set direct marketing objectives
        Determine direct marketing budget
        Develop direct marketing strategies

    Sales promotion
        Set sales promotion objectives
        Determine sales promotion budget
        Develop sales promotion strategies
    Public relations/publicity
        Set PR/publicity objectives
        Determine PR/publicity budget
        Develop PR/publicity functions
    Personal selling
        Set personal selling objectives
        Determine personal selling budget
        Develop selling roles and responsibilities

Integrate and implement marketing communications strategies
    Integrate promotional mix strategies
    Create and produce ads
    Purchase media time, space, etc.
    Design and implement direct marketing programs
    Design and distribute sales promotion materials
    Design and implement public relations/publicity programs

Monitor, evaluate, and control integrated marketing communications program
    Evaluate promotional program results/effectiveness
    Take measures to control and adjust promotional strategies

Internal analysis

The **internal analysis** assesses relevant areas involving the product/service offering and the firm itself. The capabilities of the firm and its ability to develop and implement a successful promotional program, the organization of the promotional department, and the successes and failures of past programs should be reviewed. The analysis should study the relative advantages and disadvantages of performing the promotional functions in-house as opposed to hiring an external agency (or agencies). For example, the internal analysis may indicate the firm is not capable of planning, implementing, and managing certain areas of the promotional program. If this is the case, it would be wise to look for assistance from an advertising agency or some other promotional facilitator. If the organization is already using an advertising agency, the focus will be on the quality of the agency's work and the results achieved by past and/or current campaigns.

This text will examine the functions advertising agencies perform for their clients, the agency selection process, compensation, and considerations in evaluating agency performance. We will also discuss the role and function of other promotional facilitators such as sales promotion firms, direct marketing companies, public relations agencies, and marketing and media research firms.

Another aspect of the internal analysis is assessing the strengths and weaknesses of the firm or the brand from an image perspective. Often, the image the firm brings to the market will have a significant impact on its promotional program. A firm with a strong corporate image, such as Rubbermaid, Citibank, Johnson & Johnson, or Sony, is already a step ahead when it comes to marketing its products or services. Companies or brands that are new to the market and those with a negative image may have to concentrate on their image as well as on the benefits or attributes of the specific product. For example, the Adolph Coors Co. is well known but not well liked by some groups, which have boycotted its products. So the company has spent a considerable amount of money on corporate image advertising in addition to its basic product-oriented ads (Exhibit 1–11).[21]

Another aspect of the internal analysis is assessment of the relative strengths and weaknesses of the product or service. Consider the relative advantages and disadvantages of the product/service; any unique selling points or benefits it may have; its packaging, price, and design; and so on. This information is particularly important to the creative personnel who must develop the advertising message for the brand.

Exhibit 1–12 is a checklist of some of the areas one might consider when performing an internal analysis for promotional planning purposes. Addressing these areas may require information the company does not have available internally and must gather as part of the external analysis.

External analysis

The **external analysis** focuses on factors such as characteristics of the firm's customers, market segments, positioning strategies, and competitors, as shown in Exhibit 1–12. An important part of the external analysis is a detailed consideration of customers in terms of their characteristics and buying patterns, their decision processes, and factors influencing their purchase decisions. Attention must also be given to consumers' perceptions and attitudes, lifestyles, and criteria used in making purchase decisions. Often, marketing research studies are necessary to answer some of these questions.

A key element of the external analysis is an assessment of the market. The attractiveness of various market segments must be evaluated and the decision made as to which segments to target. Once the target markets are chosen, the emphasis will be on determining how the product should be positioned. What image or place should it have in consumers' minds?

The external phase of the promotional program situation analysis also includes an in-depth examination of both direct and indirect competitors. While competitors were analyzed in the overall marketing situation analysis, even more attention is devoted to promotional aspects at this phase. Focus is on the firm's primary competitors: their specific strengths and weaknesses; their segmentation, targeting, and positioning strategies;

◉ **EXHIBIT 1–11**

This ad for Coors is designed to improve its image

and the promotional strategies they employ. The size and allocation of their promotional budgets, their media strategies, and the messages they are sending to the marketplace should all be considered.

Analysis of the Communications Process

At this stage of the promotional planning process, how the company can effectively communicate with consumers in its target markets is examined. The promotional planner must think about the process consumers will go through in responding to marketing communications. The response process for products or services where consumer decision making is characterized by a high level of interest is often different from that for low-involvement or routine purchase decisions. These differences will influence the promotional strategy.

Communication decisions regarding the use of various source, message, and channel factors must also be considered. The promotional planner should recognize the different effects various types of advertising messages might have on consumers and whether they are appropriate for the product or brand. Issues such as whether a celebrity spokesperson should be used and at what cost may also be studied. Preliminary discussion of various media mix options (print, TV, radio, newspaper, direct marketing) and their cost implications might also occur at this stage.

An important part of this stage of the promotional planning process is establishing communication goals and objectives. In this text, we stress the importance of distinguishing between communications and marketing objectives. **Marketing objectives** refer to what is to be accomplished by the overall marketing program. They are often stated in terms of sales, market share, or profitability.

Communication objectives refer to what the firm seeks to accomplish with its promotional program. They are often stated in terms of the nature of the message to be communicated or what specific communication effects are to be accomplished. Commu-

EXHIBIT   1–12   Areas covered in the situation analysis

Internal Factors	External Factors
Assessment of firm's promotional organization and capabilities Organization of promotional department Capability of firm to develop and execute promotional programs Determination of role and function of advertising agency and other promotional facilitators **Review of firm's previous promotional programs and results** Review previous promotional objectives Review previous promotional budgets and allocations Review previous promotional mix strategies and programs Review results of previous promotional programs **Assessment of firm or brand image and implications for promotion** **Assessment of relative strengths and weaknesses of product/service** What are the strengths and weaknesses of product or service? What are the product's/service's key benefits? Does the product/service have any unique selling points? Assessment of packaging/labeling/brand image How does our product/service compare with competition?	**Customer analysis** Who buys our product or service? Who makes the decision to buy the product? Who influences the decision to buy the product? How is the purchase decision made? Who assumes what role? What does the customer buy? What needs must be satisfied? Why do customers buy a particular brand? Where do they go or look to buy the product or service? When do they buy? Any seasonality factors? What are customers' attitudes toward our product/service? What social factors might influence the purchase decision? Do the customers' lifestyles influence their decisions? How is our product/service perceived by the customers? How do demographic factors influence the purchase decision? **Competitive analysis** Who are our direct and indirect competitors? What key benefits and positioning are used by our competitors? What is our position relative to the competition? How big are competitors' ad budgets? What message and media strategies are competitors using? **Environmental analysis** Are there any current trends or developments that might affect the promotional program?

nication objectives may include creating awareness or knowledge about a product and its attributes or benefits; creating an image; or developing favorable attitudes, preferences, or purchase intentions. Communication objectives should be the guiding force for development of the overall marketing communications strategy and of objectives for each promotional mix area.

Budget Determination

After the communications objectives are determined, attention turns to the promotional budget. Two basic questions are asked at this point: What will the promotional program cost? How will these monies be allocated? The amount a firm needs to spend on promotion should be determined by what must be done to accomplish its communications objectives. In reality, promotional budgets are often determined using a more simplistic approach, such as how much money is available or a percentage of a company's or brand's sales revenue. At this stage, the budget is often tentative. It may not be finalized until specific promotional mix strategies are developed.

Developing the Integrated Marketing Communications Program

Developing the IMC program is generally the most involved and detailed step of the promotional planning process. As discussed earlier, each promotional mix element has certain advantages and limitations. At this stage of the planning process, decisions have to be made regarding the role and importance of each element and their coordination with one another. As can be seen in Exhibit 1–10, each promotional mix element has its own set of objectives and a budget and strategy for meeting them. Decisions must be made and activities performed to implement the promotional programs. Procedures must be developed for evaluating performance and making any necessary changes.

For example, the advertising program will have its own set of objectives, usually involving the communication of some message or appeal to a target audience. A budget will be determined, providing the advertising manager and the agency with a sense of how much money is available for developing the ad campaign and purchasing media to disseminate the ad message.

Two important aspects of the advertising program are the development of the message and media strategy. Message development, often referred to as *creative strategy*, involves determining the basic appeal and message the advertiser wishes to convey to the target audience. This process, along with the advertisements that result, is to many students the most fascinating aspect of promotion. *Media strategy* involves determining which communications channels will be used to deliver the advertising message to the target audience. Decisions must be made regarding which types of media will be used (e.g., newspapers, magazines, radio, television, billboards) as well as specific media selections such as a particular magazine or TV program. This task requires careful evaluation of the media options' advantages and limitations, costs, and ability to deliver the message effectively to the target market.

Once the message and media strategies have been determined, steps must be taken to implement them. Most large companies hire advertising agencies to plan and produce their messages and to evaluate and purchase the media that will carry their ad. However, most agencies work very closely with their clients as they develop the ads and select media, because it is the advertiser that ultimately approves (and pays for) the creative work and media plan.

Monitoring, Evaluation, and Control

The final stage of the promotional planning process is monitoring, evaluating, and controlling the promotional program. It is important to determine how well the promotional program is meeting communications objectives and helping the firm accomplish its overall marketing goals and objectives. The promotional planner wants to know not only how well the promotional program is doing but also why. For example, problems with the advertising program may lie in the nature of the message or in a media plan that does not reach the target market effectively. The manager must know the reasons for the results in order to take the appropriate steps to correct the program.

This final stage of the process is designed to provide managers with continual feedback concerning the effectiveness of the promotional program, which in turn can be used as input into the planning process. As Exhibit 1–10 shows, information on the results achieved by the promotional program serves as an input to subsequent promotional planning and strategy development.

AN EXAMPLE OF AN INTEGRATED MARKETING COMMUNICATIONS PROGRAM

The promotional planning process describes the steps managers follow in planning, implementing, and evaluating the promotional program. To further explore the creation of a promotional strategy, we will examine the integrated marketing communications program used in marketing the San Diego Zoological Society and its two main attractions—the San Diego Zoo and Wild Animal Park.

Situation Analysis

Organizational background

One of the most popular tourist attractions in the United States is the world-famous San Diego Zoo. The zoo contains more than 800 species of animals from throughout the world living in enclosures as similar to their native habitat as possible. The zoo is owned by the San Diego Zoological Society, which also operates the San Diego Wild Animal Park. This is an 1,800-acre preserve where a 50-minute safari aboard a monorail allows visitors to view 2,500 animals living together in their recreated African and Asian habitats.

Competition

The southern California market is one of the most competitive entertainment attraction battlegrounds in the country. Obvious competitors include Sea World, which is also in San Diego; Disneyland and Knott's Berry Farm in nearby Orange County; and Universal Studios and Magic Mountain Amusement Park in the Los Angeles area. The zoo's marketing department also defines competition in a more generic sense as including any discretionary spending opportunity for a family entertainment or educational experience.

Customer analysis and target market

The San Diego Zoo defines its target audiences in geographic, demographic, and psychographic dimensions. In terms of geography, 40 percent of the visitors to the zoo and wild animal park come from San Diego County, 14 percent from other parts of southern California, 6 percent from other parts of California, 35 percent from the rest of the United

States, and 5 percent from foreign countries. The zoo also uses a variety of demographic variables to identify its target markets, including age, gender, education level, household income, occupation, and ethnicity. In terms of psychographics, research shows zoo visitors to be societally conscious and likely to be the traditional family-oriented type.

In addition to providing detailed demographic, geographic, and psychographic information on visitors and nonvisitors, marketing research is used to identify visitors' likes and dislikes, evaluations and ratings of various attractions, areas needing improvement, and new opportunities. Research information is gathered through telephone tracking surveys, exit gate intercept surveys, mail surveys, and focus group studies.

Communication Objectives

The marketing communications program for the San Diego Zoological Society has a number of objectives. First, it must provide funding for the society's programs and maintain a large and powerful base of supporters for financial and political strength. The communications program must educate the public about the society's various programs and maintain a favorable image on a local, regional, national, and even international level. A major objective of the IMC program is drawing visitors to the two attractions.

Integrated Marketing Communications

To achieve these objectives, the San Diego Zoological Society uses an integrated marketing communications program that employs a variety of promotional tools, including advertising, sales promotion, direct marketing, public relations, personal selling, and other methods (see Exhibit 1–13). An advertising agency assists in the marketing communications efforts. The agency's responsibilities include working with the zoo's marketing and sales department and planning and executing the advertising program. Examples of ads developed by the agency are shown in Exhibit 1–14 on page 28. The agency also works with the zoo's marketing department on public relations and publicity matters.

PERSPECTIVE AND ORGANIZATION OF THIS TEXT

Traditional approaches to teaching advertising, promotional strategy, or marketing communication courses have often treated the various elements of the promotional mix as separate communication functions. As a result, many of those who work in areas such as advertising, sales promotion, direct marketing, or public relations tend to approach marketing communication problems from the perspective of their particular specialty. For example, an advertising person may believe marketing communication objectives are best met through the use of media advertising; a promotional specialist argues for the use of a sales promotion program to motivate consumer response; a public relations person advocates the use of a PR campaign to tackle the problem. These orientations are not surprising, since each person has been trained to view marketing communications problems primarily from one perspective.

In the contemporary business world, however, individuals working in marketing, advertising, and other promotional areas are expected to understand and use a variety of marketing communications tools, not just the one in which they specialize. Advertising agencies no longer confine their services to the advertising area. Many are involved in sales promotion, public relations, direct marketing, event sponsorship, and other marketing communication areas. Individuals working on the client or advertiser side of the business, such as brand, product, or promotional managers, are developing marketing programs that use a variety of marketing communication methods.

This text views advertising and promotion from an integrated marketing communications perspective. We will examine all of the promotional mix elements and their role in an organization's integrated marketing communications efforts. Although media advertising may be the most visible part of the communications program, understanding its role in contemporary marketing requires attention to other promotional areas such as direct marketing, sales promotion, public relations, and personal selling. Not all the promotional mix areas are under the direct control of the advertising or marketing communications manager. For example, personal selling is typically a specialized marketing function outside the control of the advertising or promotional department. Likewise, publicity/public relations is often assigned to a separate department. There

EXHIBIT 1-13

The integrated marketing communications program for the San Diego Zoo

Advertising	
Objectives:	Drive attendance to Zoo and Wild Animal Park. Uphold image and educate target audience and inform them of new attractions and special events and promotions.
Audience:	Members and nonmembers of Zoological Society. Households in primary and secondary geographic markets consisting of San Diego County and 5 other counties in southern California. Tertiary markets of 7 western states. Tourist and group sales markets.
Timing:	As allowed and determined by budget. Mostly timed to coincide with promotional efforts.
Tools/media:	Television, radio, newspaper, magazines, direct mail, outdoor, tourist media (television and magazine).
Sales Promotions	
Objectives:	Use price, product, and other variables to drive attendance when it might not otherwise come.
Audience:	Targeted, depending on co-op partner, mostly to southern California market.
Timing:	To fit needs of Zoo and Wild Animal Park and cosponsoring partner.
Tools/media:	Coupons, sweepstakes, tours, broadcast tradeouts, direct mail: statement stuffers, fliers, postcards.
Public Relations	
Objectives:	Inform, educate, create, and maintain image for Zoological Society and major attractions, reinforce advertising message.
Audience:	From local to international, depending on subject, scope, and timing.
Timing:	Ongoing, although often timed to coincide with promotions and other special events. Spur-of-the moment animal news and information such as acquisitions, births, etc.
Tools/media:	Coverage by major news media, articles in local, regional, national and international newspapers, magazines and other publications such as visitors guides, tour books and guides, appearances by Zoo spokesperson Joanne Embery on talk shows (such as "The Tonight Show").

continued

should, however, be communication among all of these departments to coordinate all of the organization's marketing communication tools.

The purpose of this book is to provide you with a thorough understanding of the field of advertising and other elements of a firm's promotional mix and show how they are

Cause Marketing/Corporate Sponsorships/Events Underwriting

Objectives:	To provide funding for Zoological Society programs and promote special programs and events done in cooperation with corporate sponsor. Must be win-win business partnership for Society and partner.
Audience:	Supporters of both the Zoological Society and the corporate or product/service partner.
Timing:	Coincides with needs of both partners, and seasonal attendance generation needs of Zoo and Wild Animal Park.
Tools:	May involve advertising, publicity, discount co-op promotions, ticket trades, hospitality centers. Exposure is directly proportional to amount of underwriting by corporate sponsor, both in scope and duration.

Direct Marketing

Objectives:	Maintain large powerful base of supporters for financial and political strength.
Audience:	Local, regional, national and international. Includes children's program (Koala Club), seniors (60+), couples, single memberships, and incremental donor levels.
Timing:	On-going, year-round promotion of memberships.
Tools:	Direct mail and on-grounds visibility.

Group Sales

Objectives:	Maximize group traffic and revenue by selling group tours to Zoo and Wild Animal Park.
Audience:	Conventions, incentive groups, bus tours, associations, youth, scouts, schools, camps, seniors, clubs, military, organizations, domestic and foreign travel groups.
Timing:	Targeted to drive attendance in peak seasons or at most probable times such as convention season.
Tools:	Travel and tourism trade shows, telemarketing, direct mail, trade publication advertising.

combined to form an integrated marketing perspective program. To plan, develop, and implement an effective IMC program, those involved must understand marketing, consumer behavior, and the communications process. The first part of this book is designed to provide this foundation by examining the role of advertising and other forms of promotion in the marketing process and discussing how firms organize for IMC and make

@ **EXHIBIT 1-14**

Outdoor advertising is part of the marketing communications program for the San Diego Zoo

decisions regarding ad agencies and other firms that provide marketing and promotional services.

We then focus on consumer behavior and market segmentation and positioning for an understanding of these important areas can be helpful in developing promotional strategies and programs. We analyze the communications process and consider various models of value to promotional planners in developing strategies and establishing goals and objectives for advertising and other forms of promotion. We also consider how firms determine and allocate their marketing communications budget.

After laying the foundation for the development of a promotional program, this text will follow the integrated marketing communications planning model presented in Exhibit 1–10. We examine each of the promotional mix variables, beginning with advertising. Our detailed examination of advertising includes a discussion of creative strategy and the process of developing the advertising message, an overview of media strategy, and an evaluation of the various media (print, broadcast, and support media). The discussion then turns to the other areas of the promotional mix—direct marketing, sales promotion, public relations/publicity, and personal selling. Our examination of the IMC planning process concludes with a discussion of how the promotional program is monitored, evaluated, and controlled. Particular attention is given to measuring the effectiveness of advertising and other forms of promotion.

The final part of the text looks at special topic areas and perspectives that are becoming increasingly important in contemporary marketing, including business-to-business communications and international advertising and promotion. The text concludes with an examination of the environment in which advertising and promotion operates, including the regulatory, social, and economic factors that influence and are influenced by a firm's promotional program.

@ SUMMARY

Advertising and other forms of promotion are an integral part of the marketing process in most organizations. Over the past decade, the amount of money spent on advertising, sales promotion, direct marketing, and other forms of marketing communication has increased tremendously, both in the United States and in foreign markets. To understand the role of advertising and promotion in a marketing program, it is necessary to understand first what marketing's role and function are in an organization. The basic task of marketing is that of combining the four controllable elements, known as the marketing mix, into a comprehensive program that facilitates exchange with a target market. The elements of the marketing mix are the product or service, price, place or distribution, and promotion.

Many companies are recognizing the importance of integrated marketing communications, coordinating the various marketing and promotional elements to achieve more efficient and effective communication programs. A number of factors underlie the movement toward IMC by marketers as well as ad agencies and other promotional facilitators. The main reasons for the growing importance of the integrated marketing communications perspective are changes in the rules of marketing and the role of the traditional advertising agency.

Promotion is best viewed as the communication function of marketing. It is accomplished through a promotional mix that includes advertising, personal selling, publicity/public relations, sales promotion, and direct marketing. The inherent advantages and disadvantages of each of these promotional mix elements influence the role they play in the overall marketing program. In developing the promotional program, the marketer must consider which tools to use and how to combine them to achieve the organization's marketing and communication objectives.

Promotional management involves coordinating the promotional mix elements to develop an integrated program of effective marketing communication. The model of the integrated marketing communications planning process in Exhibit 1–10 contains a number of steps: a review of the marketing plan; promotional program situation analysis; analysis of the communications process; budget determination; development of an integrated marketing communications program; integration and implementation of marketing communication strategies; and monitoring, evaluating, and control of the promotional program.

KEY TERMS

marketing, p. 6
exchange, p. 6
marketing mix, p. 6
integrated marketing communications, p. 7
promotion, p. 9

promotional mix, p. 9
advertising, p. 11
direct marketing, p. 11
sales promotion, p. 12
publicity, p. 15
public relations, p. 16

personal selling, p. 16
promotional management, p. 16
promotional plan, p. 18
marketing plan, p. 18
internal analysis, p. 21

external analysis, p. 21
marketing objectives, p. 22
communication objectives, p. 22

DISCUSSION QUESTIONS

1. Analyze the Kellogg Co./NBC joint promotional program discussed at the beginning of the chapter from an integrated marketing communications perspective. How would this promotion be beneficial to each company?

2. Discuss the role advertising and promotion will play as companies continue to focus their attention on global markets. What are some of the challenges marketers will face in promoting their products to consumers in developing countries?

3. It has been argued that the way an organization communicates with its customers is not limited to promotion, as all marketing activities send a message. Discuss how an organization communicates with its customers through marketing activities other than promotion. Cite several examples.

4. What is meant by the concept of integrated marketing communications? How might a firm that is using IMC differ from one that looks at advertising and promotion in a more traditional way?

5. Discuss the reasons why the integrated marketing communications approach is becoming so popular among marketers. Do you think the growth of IMC will continue? Why or why not?

6. Find an example of a company that has recently adopted integrated marketing communications. What are some of the reasons why this company adopted an IMC approach? Analyze how this company is using the various marketing and promotional mix tools.

7. Analyze the five elements of the promotional mix and their role in an integrated marketing communications program for each of the following:
   a. A manufacturer of consumer products, such as Quaker Oats.
   b. A nonprofit organization, such as a symphony orchestra in a major city.
   c. A business-to-business marketer, such as Hewlett-Packard.

8. What are the advantages and disadvantages of the five elements of the promotional mix? Identify some situations where a firm might rely heavily on a particular element.

9. Discuss how publicity/public relations differs from other elements of the promotional mix. Identify a product, service, or cause that has been negatively or positively affected by publicity in recent years. Analyze any responses the company or organization took to deal with the problems or opportunities created by the publicity.

10. Why is it important for those who work in the field of promotion to appreciate and understand all elements of the promotional mix, not just the one in which they specialize?

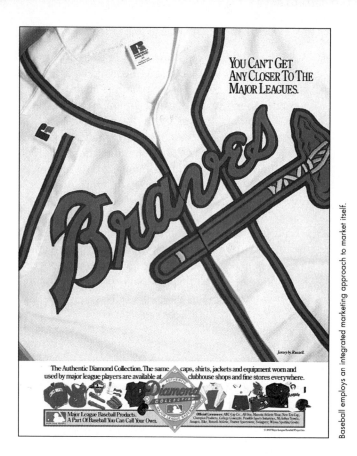

YOU CAN'T GET
ANY CLOSER TO THE
MAJOR LEAGUES.

Jersey by Russell.

The Authentic Diamond Collection. The same caps, shirts, jackets and equipment worn and used by major league players are available at clubhouse shops and fine stores everywhere.

Major League Baseball Products. A Part Of Baseball You Can Call Your Own.

Baseball employs an integrated marketing approach to market itself.

Chapter **2**

The Role of Advertising and Promotion in the Marketing Process

Chapter Objectives

● To examine the marketing process and the role of advertising and promotion in an organization's marketing program.

● To examine the various decision areas under each element of the marketing mix and how they influence and interact with advertising and promotional strategy.

● To understand classifications of various types of advertising targeted to both the consumer and business/professional markets.

● To examine the macroenvironment of marketing and the impact of various environmental influences on marketing and promotional strategy.

Major League Baseball Uses Integrated Marketing to Increase Attendance

In early 1993, it appeared as though "America's pastime" might be past its prime. Attendance was off 1.7 percent in 1992, TV ratings of regular season games continued to fall for the fifth straight year, and even the sport's popularity was declining according to a Harris poll, as only 18 percent of those surveyed named baseball as their favorite sport (down from 23 percent in 1985). The focus on labor–management relations, high salaries, slow games, and perceptions that the players themselves were distant from the fans had all contributed to the problem. Baseball owners realized that something had to be done.

What the Major League Baseball Association and individual teams did to turn around these trends was to discover marketing—more specifically, integrated marketing communications. A variety of programs were implemented by the league as well as individual teams.

This integrated marketing effort included the following:

- A promotional package offered by the Chicago White Sox called "Family Soxpack," with $12 covering a ticket, hot dog, Coke, potato chips, and a souvenir.
- "Autograph Mondays," a Philadelphia Phillies–sponsored event designed to "humanize" the players, in which the first 1,000 attendees were allowed access to players before the game to get autographs.
- Newspaper ads from the Boston Red Sox thanking their fans for sticking by them in a bad season.
- Featuring baseball's greatest stars in TV ads promoting the game (borrowing a strategy from the National Basketball Association).
- Integrated packages that include stadium signage, licensing, public relations, international advertising, print advertising, and increased TV and radio advertising.
- Tie-in promotions between baseball teams and corporate partners. For example, the St. Louis Cardinals and Ralston Purina cosponsored a promotion that offered fans the opportunity to win a trip to a baseball clinic.
- The promotion and sale of major league baseball apparel to increase team loyalties.

In addition, the league placed more emphasis on target marketing. The Hispanic market was approached with a new half-hour show on Telemundo, the Spanish-language network, and teams increased their advertising to kids.

Did the discovery of integrated marketing benefit baseball? The answer is a definite yes. The 1993 baseball season set an all-time attendance record, with approximately 70 million fans seeing a game—an increase of 13 million over 1992.

Sources: Erle Norton, "New Game Plan to Sell Baseball Is Pitching Stars," *The Wall Street Journal*, Oct. 25, 1993, p. B1; Joe Mandese, "Baseball Pact Pitches Integrated Marketing," *Advertising Age*, Oct. 17, 1993, p. 1; Michael J. McCarthy, "Sinking Attendance Leads Baseball Clubs to Come Up with a New Play: Marketing," *The Wall Street Journal*, Feb. 2, 1993, p. B1.

ajor league baseball's use of an integrated marketing communications approach demonstrates a number of points. First is the fact that such marketing efforts are not used only by product marketers. Second, it shows how effective an integrated marketing communications program can be. The 23 percent gain in attendance, while attributable in part to good pennant races, was largely the result of an effective marketing program. Third, it reflects the value that can accrue from mixing a variety of promotional tools, with each making its own contribution to the overall communications goals.

In this chapter, we take a closer look at how marketing influences the role of promotion and how promotional decisions must be coordinated with other areas of the marketing mix. We use the model in Exhibit 2–1 as a framework for analyzing how promotion fits into an organization's marketing strategy and programs.

This model consists of three major components: the organization's marketing strategy and plan, the marketing program development (which includes the promotional mix), and the target market. As the model shows, the marketing process begins with the development of a marketing strategy in which the company decides the product or service areas and particular markets where it wants to compete. The company must then coordinate the various elements of the marketing mix into a cohesive marketing program that will reach the target market effectively. Note in the exhibit that a firm's promotion program is directed not only to the final buyer but also to the channel or "trade" members that distribute its products to the ultimate consumer. These channel members must be convinced there is a demand for the company's products so they will carry them and will aggressively merchandise and promote them to the consumer. Thus, we will consider promotion's role in the marketing program for building and maintaining demand not only among final consumers but among the trade as well.

The second part of this chapter considers the environment in which marketing decisions are made, giving particular attention to the way they affect a company's promotional strategies and programs. Marketing is a dynamic field that must constantly

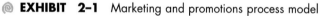

EXHIBIT 2–1   Marketing and promotions process model

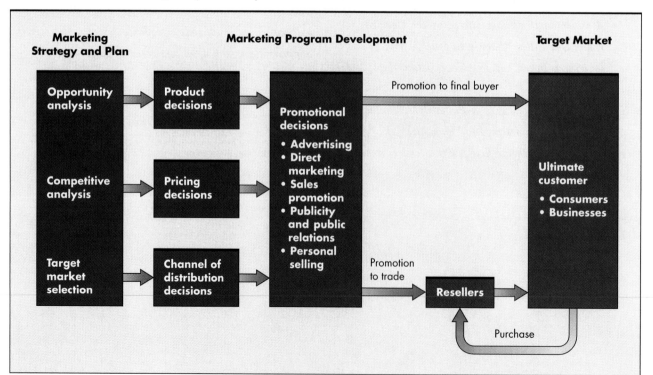

monitor and react to changing environmental conditions. These changes create marketing opportunities for some organizations but pose threats to others. They also have a direct influence on a firm's advertising and promotional strategy and programs.

MARKETING STRATEGY AND PLAN

Any organization that wants to exchange its products or services in the marketplace successfully should have a strategic marketing plan to guide the allocation of its resources. A **strategic marketing plan** usually evolves from an organization's overall corporate strategy and serves as a guide for specific marketing programs and policies. As we noted in the first chapter, marketing strategy is based on a situation analysis—a detailed assessment of the current marketing conditions facing the company, its product lines, or its individual brands. From this situation analysis, a firm develops an understanding of the market and the various opportunities it offers, the competition, and the market segments or target markets the company wishes to pursue. We examine each step of the marketing strategy phase in more detail.

Opportunity Analysis

A careful analysis of the marketplace should lead to alternative market opportunities for existing product lines in current or new markets, new products for current markets, or new products for new markets. **Market opportunities** represent areas where there are favorable demand trends, where the company believes customer needs and opportunities are not being satisfied, and where it can compete effectively. For example, the number of people who walk for exercise has increased tremendously in recent years, and the market for walking shoes has reached nearly $100 million. Athletic shoe companies such as Nike and Reebok see the walking shoe market as an opportunity to broaden their customer base to an older market. To capitalize on this opportunity, Nike brought out a line of walking shoes and Reebok acquired Rockport Co., one of the largest manufacturers of walking shoes. Road Runner Sports, a direct marketer of running shoes, opened a walking shoe division (Exhibit 2–2).

A company usually identifies market opportunities by carefully examining the marketplace and noting demand trends and competition in various **market segments**. A market can rarely be viewed as one large homogeneous group of customers; rather, it consists of many heterogeneous groups of segments. In recent years, many companies have recognized the importance of tailoring their marketing to meet the needs and demand trends of different market segments.[1]

For example, different market segments in the personal computer industry include the home, education, science, and business markets. These segments can be even further

EXHIBIT 2–2

Road Runner has taken advantage of a market opportunity created by an increased interest in walking

divided. The business market consists of both small companies and large corporations; the education market can range from elementary schools to colleges and universities. A company that is marketing its products in the personal computer industry must decide on the particular market segment or segments in which it wishes to compete. This decision will depend on the amount and nature of competition the brand will face in a particular market. For example, Apple Computer is very firmly entrenched in the education market but is also targeting the business segment, where IBM and Compaq are strong competitors. A competitive analysis is an important part of marketing strategy development and warrants further consideration.

Competitive Analysis

In developing the firm's marketing strategies and plans for its products, the manager must carefully analyze the competition the brand will face in the marketplace. This may range from direct brand competition (which can also include its own brands) to more indirect forms of competition, such as product substitutes. For example, General Foods markets Maxwell House coffee as its flagship brand in the regular ground-coffee segment of the market. Several years ago, the company introduced Master Blend, a high-yield brand that gives more cups per pound than regular coffee. The new product ended up taking away sales from Maxwell House. However, the combined sales of the two brands gave General Foods a net gain in its share of the ground market, as Master Blend helped slow the sales of competing brands such as Procter & Gamble's Folgers, Nestlé's Hills Brothers, and various regional brands.

In addition to these direct competitors, Maxwell House faces competition from other product forms such as instant and decaffeinated coffee. Also, many consumers have been switching to other beverages such as tea and soft drinks. Thus, competition is found not only in directly competing coffee brands but also in other products that satisfy consumers' needs for a beverage.

At a more general level, marketers must recognize they are competing for the consumer's discretionary income, so they must understand the various ways potential customers choose to spend their money. For example, sales of motorcycles in the United States declined from 1.3 million bikes in 1984 to under 500,000 in 1993. This decline in sales reflects shifting demographic patterns—aging baby boomers are less inclined to ride motorcycles, and the number of 18- to 34-year-old males has been declining. The drop in sales can also be attributed to the number of other options consumers can spend their discretionary income on, including Jet Skis, personal computers, home fitness equipment, Jacuzzis, and home entertainment systems such as large-screen TVs and stereos. Thus, motorcycle marketers such as Honda and Kawasaki must convince potential buyers that a motorcycle is worth a sizable portion of their disposable income in comparison to other purchase options.

An important aspect of marketing strategy development is the search for a **competitive advantage,** something special a firm does or possesses that gives it an edge over competitors. Ways to achieve a competitive advantage include having quality products that command a premium price, providing superior customer service, having the lowest production costs and lower prices, or dominating channels of distribution. Competitive advantage can also be achieved through advertising that creates and maintains product differentiation and brand equity. For example, the strong brand images of products such as Colgate toothpaste, Campbell's soup, Apple computers, and Budweiser beer give them a competitive advantage in their respective markets.

Recently, there has been concern that some marketers have not been spending enough money on advertising to allow leading brands to sustain their competitive edge.[2] Advertising proponents have been calling for companies to protect their brand equity and franchises by investing more money in advertising and less in costly trade promotions. Some companies, recognizing the important competitive advantage strong brands provide, have been increasing their advertising investment in them. For example, Campbell Soup Co. announced it would increase its advertising spending by 30 percent to "restore brand power."[3] Colgate-Palmolive also recently boosted its marketing and advertising spending to increase support for major brands.[4]

⊚ **EXHIBIT 2–3**

Advertising for Michelin tires stresses security as well as performance

Companies must be concerned with the ever-changing competitive environment. Competitors' marketing programs will have a major impact on the firm's marketing strategy and must be analyzed and monitored. The reactions of competitors to a company's marketing and promotional strategy are also very important. Competitors may cut price, increase promotional spending, develop new brands, or attack one another through comparative advertising. One of the more intense competitive rivalries is the battle between Coca-Cola and Pepsi-Cola. The latest round of the "cola wars" has been taken international, as discussed in Global Perspective 2–1.

A final aspect of competition is the growing number of foreign companies penetrating the U.S. market and taking business from domestic firms. In products ranging from electronics to automobiles to beer, imports are becoming an increasingly strong form of competition with which U.S. firms must contend. As we move from a national to a more global economy, U.S. companies must not only defend their domestic markets but also learn how to compete effectively in the international marketplace.

Target Market Selection

After evaluating the opportunities presented by various market segments, including a detailed competitive analysis, the company may select one or more as a target market. This target market becomes the focus of the firm's marketing effort, and goals and objectives are set according to where the company wants to be and what it hopes to accomplish in this market. As noted in Chapter 1, these goals and objectives are set in terms of specific performance variables such as sales, market share, and profitability. The selection of the target market (or markets) in which the firm will compete is an important part of its marketing strategy and has direct implications for its advertising and promotional efforts.

⊚ DEVELOPING THE MARKETING PROGRAM

The development of the marketing strategy and selection of a target market(s) tell the marketing department which customers to focus on and what needs to attempt to satisfy. The next stage of the marketing process involves combining the various elements of the marketing mix into a cohesive, effective marketing program. Each marketing mix element is multidimensional and includes a number of decision areas. We now examine these elements of the marketing mix and how each influences and interacts with promotion.

Product

An organization exists because it has some product, service, or idea to offer consumers, generally in exchange for money. This offering may come in the form of a physical product (such as a soft drink, pair of jeans, automobile), a service (banking, airlines, or legal assistance), a cause (United Way, March of Dimes), or even a person (a political

Global Perspective 2-1
The Cola Wars Go Global

For more than two decades, the Coca-Cola Co. and its arch-rival, Pepsi-Cola, have been battling for leadership of the U.S. soft-drink market. It is not hard to understand why the two superpowers spend hundreds of millions of dollars every year on advertising and promotion to remind consumers that it's "Always Coca-Cola" or they should "Think young" and drink Pepsi. Every percentage share point in the soft-drink market is worth approximately $460 million in sales!

While Coke and Pepsi have been competing against each other for decades, the battle intensified in 1975 when Pepsi launched its "Pepsi Challenge," which showed consumers preferring the taste of Pepsi over Coke in blind taste tests. The challenge campaign convinced many consumers that Pepsi had a superior taste and induced them to switch brands. By 1984, Pepsi had achieved a 2 percent market share lead over Coke in supermarket sales. Pepsi's success was a major factor in Coca-Cola's controversial decision to change the formula of its 99-year-old flagship brand and launch New Coke in 1985. Consumers loyal to the old formula protested, prompting the company to reintroduce original Coke as Coca-Cola Classic.

In the late 1980s, the battle shifted to the fast-growing sugar-free or diet segment, which represents nearly 25 percent of the soft-drink market. Both companies ran ads claiming superiority for their diet colas for several years before turning to celebrities to pitch both their diet and flagship brands. Coke used Elton John, Paula Abdul, Randy Travis, and others while Pepsi ads featured Michael J. Fox, Michael Jackson, Jimmy Connors, and supermodel Cindy Crawford. Diet Pepsi ads featuring Ray Charles singing "You've got the right one baby, uh huh," have been very profitable and seemed to give Pepsi the edge in advertising, for a while. However, recognizing that it was falling behind in the advertising war, Coca-Cola signed an

agreement with Hollywood superagent Michael Ovitz and the Creative Artists Agency (CAA) to develop the "Always Coca-Cola" campaign for Coca-Cola Classic.

While Coke and Pepsi continue to battle one another on the home front, the cola wars have also gone global in a big way. Coke generates 77 percent of its $8.9 billion annual revenue from and dominates most foreign markets. Pepsi is fighting back in Mexico, the Asian-Pacific region, and Eastern Europe. It invested over $500 million in Poland and took a 40 percent stake in Angkor Beverage Co. of Cambodia in an attempt to penetrate Indochina. Coke has countered with a $27 million prize promotion in Mexico and by investing $150 million to open 10 new bottling plants in China. Coke has also intensified its efforts in Japan and Eastern Europe.

Both companies are advertising heavily in foreign markets and using a variety of other promotional tools. Pepsi has sponsored several worldwide tours for singers such as Michael Jackson and Tina Turner while Coke has sponsored concerts throughout Europe as well. Coke has also spent heavily to be an official sponsor for the 1994 Winter Olympic games in Norway and the 1996 Summer games in its home city of Atlanta.

With the U.S. soft-drink market experiencing very slow growth Coke and Pepsi will continue to intensify their global battle. Soft drinks are experiencing tremendous growth in countries such as China, Indonesia, Mexico, and Brazil. You can be sure that Pepsi will want to be the "choice of a new generation" and Coke will want to be the "real thing" in these foreign markets as well as at home.

Sources: Sally D. Goll, "Pepsi Looks for Pop From Asian Market," *The Wall Street Journal*, June 25, 1993, p. B5; Seth Lubove, "We Have a Big Pond to Play In," *Forbes*, September 13, 1993, pp. 216–24; "Global Goliath: Coke Conquers the World," *U.S. News & World Report*, August 13, 1990, pp. 52–54; Alison Fahey, "Pepsi's Concerts versus Coke's Games," *Advertising Age*, February 10, 1992, p. 47.

candidate). In the broadest sense, the product consists of anything that can be marketed and that, when used or supported, gives satisfaction to the individual.

A product is not just a physical object; it is a bundle of benefits or values that satisfies the needs of consumers. The needs may be functional or they may include social and psychological benefits. For example, the ad for Michelin tires in Exhibit 2–3 on page 35 stresses the quality built into Michelin tires (value) as well as their performance and durability (function). The term **product symbolism** refers to what a product or brand means to consumers and what they experience in purchasing and using it.[5] For many products, strong symbolic features and social and psychological meaning may be more important than functional utility.[6] For example, designer clothing such as Guess?, Calvin Klein, and Jordache is often purchased on the basis of its symbolic meaning and image, particularly by teenagers and young adults. Advertising plays an important role in developing and maintaining the image of these brands (Exhibit 2–4 on page 38).

Product planning involves decisions not only about the item itself, such as design and quality, but also about aspects such as service and warranties as well as a brand name and package design. Branding and packaging decisions are particularly important as communication devices and warrant further discussion.

Global Perspective 2–1   Concluded

RAY: "Uh huh, you got the right
   one baby. You know I just love
   this new Diet Pepsi song, but
   do you think it's caught on yet?"
CROWD IN CHINA SINGS: "Uh huh. Uh
   huh, you got the right one baby!"
   "Uh huh. Uh huh. Diet Pepsi."
AFRICAN TRIBE SINGS: "Uh huh. Uh
   huh. Uh huh. Uh huh."
MAN FROM BANGLADESH SAYS: "If it's
   irresistably sippable . . . "

COWBOY SINGS: "Uncontestably
   tastable and eminently wonderful . . . "
ENGLISH WAITER: "You got the right one
   baby. Uh huh."
GOSPEL CHOIR SINGS: "You got the right
   one baby!"
GEISHA GIRLS SING: "Uh huh. Uh huh.
   You got the right one baby."

MONKS CHANT: "Uh huh. Uh huh. Uh
   huh. Uh huh."
UNITED NATIONS: "Uh huh. Uh huh . . . "
UNITED NATIONS: " . . . Diet Pepsi!"
RAY: "Do you think it's caught on yet? . . .
   Naaah!"
UH HUH GIRLS LAUGH.

Branding

Choosing a brand name for a product is important from a promotional perspective because brand names communicate attributes and meaning. Marketers search for brand names that can communicate product concepts and help position the product in the mind of the customer. Names such as Safeguard (soap), I Can't Believe It's Not Butter! (margarine), Easy-Off (oven cleaner), Arrid (antiperspirant deodorant), and Spic and Span (floor cleaner) all clearly communicate the benefits of using these products.

Many companies use individual brand names for each product because they want each brand to have a unique and distinct image and not be influenced by association to a company, family, or product line name. However, promotional costs for new products are generally higher when individual brand names are used, since the company must create awareness among both consumers and retailers without the benefit of prior associations.

In recent years, the high costs of introducing products and establishing an identity for a new brand have prompted many companies to use a **brand extension strategy** whereby a firm extends an existing brand name to a new product. There are two types

@ **EXHIBIT 2–4**

Advertising for designer
clothing helps create
symbolism and
image for consumers

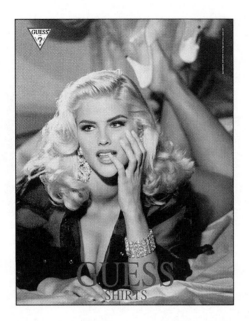

@ **EXHIBIT 2–5**

The Michelob brand name
has been extended to light,
dark, and dry versions of
beer

of brand extensions. A **line extension** applies an existing brand name to a product in one of the existing product categories. For example, the Coca-Cola brand name has been extended to a number of other soft drinks including Classic Coke, diet Coke, caffeine-free Coke, and Cherry Coke. Anheuser-Busch has also extended the Michelob name to several brands including Michelob Light, Michelob Dark, and its newest brand, Michelob Dry (Exhibit 2–5). A **category extension** applies an existing brand name to a new product category. Examples of category extensions include Jell-O pudding pops, Bic disposable lighters, Woolite rug cleaner, and Tropicana Twister Light fruit juices.

The use of brand extension strategies has almost become the norm among marketers introducing new package goods, as few new products carry new brand names. Marketers are relying on line extensions for several reasons. Many firms believe they can borrow on the equity in their established brand names and achieve immediate name recognition and some "affect transfer" whereby the positive feelings and benefits associated with a familiar brand are extended to the brand. Line extensions can also reduce the advertising and promotional expenditures required to introduce a new brand and make it easier to gain distribution and shelf space in stores.[7]

The use of brand line and category extensions has been criticized by some advertising experts on the grounds that excessive use of a brand name can erode brand image and create confusion among consumers.[8] Line extensions can weaken the core brand and may even hurt its sales. Brand extensions may also be risky if a new product does not live up to consumers' expectations, as this may hurt their perceptions of other products using the name.

The decision to use a brand extension strategy is a compromise between dilution of brand image and possible consumer confusion, on one hand, and advertising efficiency, on the other.[9] As media costs escalate and shelf space becomes increasingly scarce, companies with strong brand names are likely to continue to use brand extension strategies to reduce costs and increase awareness—and, they hope, acceptance—of their new products among both consumers and retailers.

One important role advertising plays in respect to branding strategies is creating and maintaining brand equity. *Brand equity* can be thought of as an intangible asset of added value or goodwill that results from the favorable image, impressions of differentiation, and/or the strength of consumer attachment to a company name, brand name, or trade-

⊚ **EXHIBIT 2–6**

What's in a name?
The value of the U.S.
top 25 brands

Financial World magazine estimates how much the USA's major consumer brands would be worth in cash.

Brand	Company	Value (billions)	Revenue (billions)
1. Marlboro cigarettes	Philip Morris	$31.2	$15.4
2. Coca-Cola soft drinks	Coca-Cola	24.4	9.4
3. Budweiser beer	Anheuser-Busch	10.2	6.2
4. Pepsi-Cola soft drinks	PepsiCo	9.6	5.5
5. Nescafe instant coffee	Nestlé	8.5	4.3
6. Kellogg cereals	Kellogg	8.4	4.7
7. Winston cigarettes	RJR Nabisco	6.1	3.6
8. Pampers disposable diapers	Procter & Gamble	6.1	4.0
9. Camel cigarettes	RJR Nabisco	4.4	2.3
10. Campbell soups	Campbell Soup	3.9	2.4
11. Nestlé sweets	Nestlé	3.7	6.0
12. Hennessy cognac	LVMH	3.0	0.9
13. Heineken beer	Heineken	2.7	3.5
14. Johnnie Walker Red scotch	Guinness	2.6	1.5
15. Louis Vuitton baggage	LVMH	2.6	0.9
16. Hershey sweets	Hershey	2.3	2.6
17. Guinness beer	Guinness	2.3	1.8
18. Barbie dolls, accessories	Mattel	2.2	0.8
19. Kraft cheese	Philip Morris	2.2	2.8
20. Smirnoff vodka	Grand Metropolitan	2.2	1.0
21. Del Monte fruits, vegetables	four owners[1]	1.6	2.3
22. Wrigley's chewing gum	Wm. Wrigley Jr.	1.5	1.0
23. Schweppes mixers	Cadbury-Schweppes	1.4	1.3
24. Tampax tampons	Tambrands	1.4	0.6
25. Heinz ketchup	HJ Heinz	1.3	0.8

[1] Del Monte Foods, Del Monte Foods International, Polly Peck International, Kikkoman
Sources: *Financial World* and *USA Today,* Aug. 12, 1992.

mark. Brand equity allows a brand to earn greater sales volume and/or higher margins than it could without the name, providing the company with a competitive advantage. The strong equity position a company and/or its brand enjoys is often reinforced through advertising. Exhibit 2–6 shows the value of the top 25 brands, while IMC Perspective 2–1 discusses some of the factors leading to the development of strong brands.

Packaging

Packaging is another aspect of product strategy that has become increasingly important. Traditionally, the package provided functional benefits such as economy, protection, and storage. However, the role and function of the package have changed because of the self-service emphasis of many stores and the fact that more and more purchase decisions are being made at the point of purchase. One study estimated that as many as two-thirds of all purchases made in the supermarket are unplanned.[10] The package is often the consumer's first exposure to the product, so it must make a favorable first impression.

A typical supermarket has more than 20,000 items competing for a consumer's attention. Not only must a package attract and hold the consumer's attention, but it must communicate information on how to use the product, divulge its composition and content, and satisfy any legal requirements regarding disclosure. Moreover, many firms design a package to carry a sales promotion message such as a contest, sweepstakes, or premium offer.

Many companies view the package as an important way to communicate with consumers and create an impression of the brand in their minds. Design factors such as size, shape, color, and lettering all contribute to the appeal of a package and can be as

IMC Perspective 2–1
Brand Names Fight Back

The past few years have proven to be quite difficult for many well-known brand names. The increasing popularity of private label brands coupled with consumers' search for value has resulted in intense competition for a number of well-known brands including Marlboro cigarettes, Pampers diapers, Heinz ketchup, and soft-drink market leaders, Coke and Pepsi. Many consumers are no longer loyal to any one brand nor are they willing to pay more for established brand names. A 1992 study by the Roper Organization found that only 37 percent of consumers felt that brands in premium categories are worth paying more for—down from 45 percent in 1988.

Many marketers contributed to the erosion in brand equity by decreasing their advertising budgets and allocating more monies to sales promotion. In 1982, 40 percent of the promotional budget of major packaged goods companies was allocated to advertising. By 1993, it was less than 30 percent as most of the promotional dollars were shifted into consumer and trade promotions. The increased use of sales promotion has led to increased price sensitivity among consumers, particularly during the recent recession. Many companies are struggling to hold on to consumers who are constantly looking for the best deal rather than a specific brand. As noted by the vice president for marketing at PepsiCo's Frito-Lay division, "Brand equity is being challenged like never before."

While major brands are having their problems, it may be premature to begin burying them as the financial numbers tell a different story. In 1992, 35 of the top 59 brands rated by *Financial World* rose in brand equity. Overall, brand values rose by 3.3 percent in an economy that grew by only 2.2 percent. The brands showing the strongest gains in value were market leaders such as Gillette razors, Mattel's Barbie line, Wrigley's gum, and Nike athletic shoes. The losers were primarily in commodity businesses such as cigarettes or those that have not kept pace with changing market trends—such as Green Giant canned and frozen vegetables.

Among the factors contributing to the increase in equity among brands are the following:

- The brands' ability to differentiate themselves from generics and private label competition.
- The successful use of line extension to leverage the value of the brand name.
- Larger advertising and promotional budgets along with more spending on research and development.
- The ability to control costs, cut prices, and increase advertising expenditures to ward off competition from private label brands.
- More power over distribution channels as a result of increased advertising and promotional funding.

Many companies are fighting back against private label products and are taking steps to preserve their brand equity or to try to rebuild brands that have lost some of their appeal to consumers. This will require that they convince increasingly skeptical consumers that their products are a good value worth the higher prices.

Sources: "Brands on the Run," *Business Week*, April 19, 1993, pp. 26–28; Alexandra Ourusoff, "Who Said Brands Are Dead?" *Brandweek*, August 9, 1993, pp. 21–23; Patricia Sellers, "Brands: It's Thrive or Die," *Fortune*, August 23, 1993, pp. 52–56.

important as a commercial in determining what goes from the store shelf to the consumer's shopping cart. Many products use packaging to create a distinctive brand image and identity. An example is Michelob beer, with its unusually shaped bottle and distinctive label (Exhibit 2–5). Packaging can also make a product more convenient to use. For example, Procter & Gamble introduced its Crest Neat Squeeze dispenser, which sucks the extra, unused toothpaste back into the container when you let go (Exhibit 2–7).

Price

The *price variable* refers to what the consumer must give up to purchase a product or service. While price is discussed in terms of the dollar amount exchanged for an item, the cost of a product to the consumer includes time, mental activity, and behavioral effort.[11] The marketing manager is usually concerned with establishing a price level, developing pricing policies, and monitoring competitors' and consumers' reactions to prices in the

EXHIBIT 2-7

Procter & Gamble introduces a neat way to squeeze its Crest toothpaste out of the container

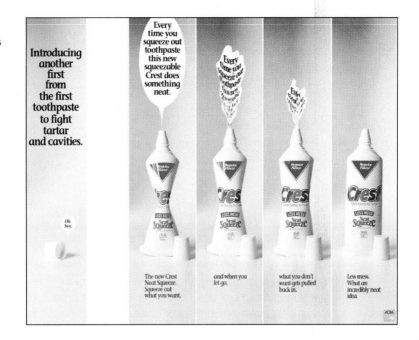

marketplace. A firm must consider a number of factors in determining the price it charges for its product or service, including costs, demand factors, competition, and perceived value.

Costs

Costs are a basic determinant of price. A firm will generally set a price that covers the costs of producing, distributing, and promoting its product or service and includes a profit figure that yields a certain return on its investment. While promotional expenses such as advertising, personal selling, and sales promotion must be covered in a firm's pricing structure, they also reduce costs by creating demand for the product that results in more sales and economies of scale in production and distribution.

Demand Factors

Another important consideration in setting price is the demand for the product or service that will be generated at various price levels. The relationship between price and demand is generally an inverse one: as price declines, demand will increase, and vice versa. However, in some situations, the relationship between price and demand may be positive if consumers perceive price as an indicator of quality.[12] Thus, a higher price may result in more sales for a product (up to a point).

Many firms try to increase demand through **nonprice competition** by using product differentiation, advertising, and other nonprice factors to influence demand. Under nonprice competition, the firm seeks to shift its demand curve upward and to the right, as shown in Exhibit 2–8, which makes demand more inelastic and less price sensitive and results in greater sales at a given price. Many premium products, such as Häagen-Dazs ice cream and Godiva chocolates, are made from more expensive ingredients and perceived by consumers as being of superior quality and value. This perception is reinforced through their advertising, which helps these brands command premium prices from consumers willing to pay more for the best quality (Exhibit 2–9 on page 43).

Competition

Another fundamental consideration in setting price is competition. Price is the one element of the marketing mix that is easiest to change, at least in the short run, and it is often used as a competitive tool. Many companies use **competition-oriented pricing,** basing prices primarily on what competitors are charging. Prices may be set to achieve

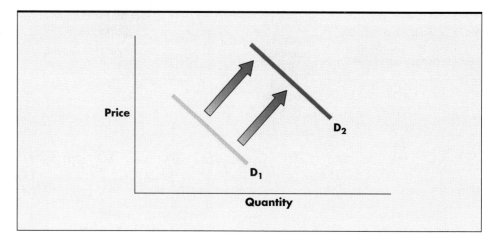

@ EXHIBIT 2–8

The goal of advertising under nonprice competition is to move the demand curve up and to the right

competitive parity, or a firm may seek to keep its prices lower or higher than the competition. When competition-oriented pricing is used, prices are subject to rapid change and are often lowered to meet competition in specific markets.

Competition-oriented pricing is common in the retailing area, particularly among grocery stores, and in the marketing of services, such as the airline industry. Intense competition can sometimes lead to price wars, as when airlines are forced to cut prices to remain competitive on certain routes.

Perceived value

Most marketers recognize that price levels for a product or service must be in line with its perceived value. Consumers often use price to determine a product's value, suggesting a relationship between price and perceived quality. For example, Curtis Mathes has used the advertising slogan "the most expensive television sets money can buy" for many years to promote its products as being of extremely high quality. Marketers often use nonprice variables such as superior product quality, service, warranties, and brand image to build perceived value in the consumer's mind and then price their products accordingly. In the ad shown in Exhibit 2–10, Yonex Corp. explains how the advanced technology behind its golf clubs leads to superior performance that is worth paying twice as much for.

Relating price to advertising

As we have seen, factors such as product quality, competition, and advertising all interact in determining what price a firm can and should charge. The relationship among price, product quality, and advertising was examined in one study using information on 227 consumer businesses from the PIMS (Profit Impact of Marketing Strategies) project of the Strategic Planning Institute.[13] Several interesting findings concerning the interaction of these variables emerged from this study:

- Brands with high relative advertising budgets were able to charge premium prices, whereas brands that spent less than their competitors on advertising charged lower prices.
- Companies with high-quality products charged high relative prices for the extra quality, but businesses with high quality *and* high advertising levels obtained the highest prices. Conversely, businesses with low quality and low advertising charged the lowest prices.
- The positive relationship between high relative advertising and price levels was stronger for products in the late stage of the product life cycle, for market leaders, and for low-cost products (under $10).
- Companies with relatively high prices and high advertising expenditures showed a higher return on investment than companies with relatively low prices and high advertising budgets.

◎ EXHIBIT 2–9

Some products compete on the basis of quality rather than price

◎ EXHIBIT 2–10

Yonex explains why its golf clubs cost much more than competitors' clubs

- Companies with high-quality products were hurt the most, in terms of return on investment, by inconsistent advertising and pricing strategies.

The study concluded that pricing and advertising strategies go together. High relative ad expenditures should accompany premium prices, and low relative ad expenditures should be tailored to low prices.

Channels of Distribution

As consumers, we generally take for granted the role of marketing intermediaries or channel members. If we want a six-pack of soda or a box of detergent, we can buy it at a supermarket, a convenience store, or even a drugstore. Manufacturers understand the value and importance of these intermediaries.

One of the most important marketing decisions a firm must make involves the way it makes its products and services available for purchase. A firm can have an excellent product at a great price, but it will be of little value unless it is available where the customer wants it, when the customer wants it, and with the proper support and service. **Marketing channels,** the place element of the marketing mix, are "sets of interdependent organizations involved in the process of making a product or service available for use or consumption."[14]

Channel decisions involve the selection, management, and motivation of intermediaries such as wholesalers, distributors, brokers, retailers, and other parties that help a firm make a product or service available to customers. These intermediaries, sometimes called **resellers,** are critical to the success of a company's marketing program.

EXHIBIT 2–11

Trade advertising is used to interest resellers in a manufacturer's product

A company can choose not to use any channel intermediaries and sell to its customers through **direct channels.** This type of channel arrangement is sometimes used in the consumer market by firms using direct-selling programs, such as Avon, Tupperware, or Fuller Brush, or firms that use direct-response advertising or telemarketing to sell their products. Direct channels are also frequently used by manufacturers of industrial products and services, which are often selling expensive and complex products that require extensive negotiations and sales efforts, as well as service and follow-up calls after the sale. Most consumer product companies distribute through **indirect channels,** usually using a network of wholesalers or institutions that sell to other resellers and/or retailers, which sell primarily to the final consumer.

Developing Promotional Strategies: Push versus Pull

Most of you are aware of advertising and other forms of promotion directed toward ultimate consumers or business customers. We see these ads in the media and are often part of the target audience for the promotions. In addition to developing a consumer marketing mix, a company must have a program to motivate the channel members as well. Programs designed to persuade the trade to stock, merchandise, and promote a manufacturer's products are part of a **promotional push strategy.** The goal of this strategy is to push the product through the channels of distribution by aggressively selling and promoting the item to the resellers or trade.

Promotion to the trade includes all the elements of the promotional mix. Company sales representatives call on resellers to explain the product, discuss the firm's plans for building demand among ultimate consumers, and describe special programs being offered to the trade, such as introductory discounts, promotional allowances, and cooperative ad programs. The company may use **trade advertising** to interest wholesalers and retailers and motivate them to purchase its products for resale to their customers. Trade advertising usually appears in publications that serve the particular industry. For example, buyers in the grocery industry read *Progressive Grocer;* drugstore managers and buyers read *Drug Store News.* An example of a trade ad for Ames Company, a manufacturer of garden tools, that appeared in a publication targeted to home improvement retailers is shown in Exhibit 2–11.

A push strategy tries to convince resellers they can make a profit on a manufacturer's product and encourage them to order the merchandise and push it through to their customers. Sometimes manufacturers face resistance from channel members who do not want to take on an additional product line or brand. In these instances, companies may turn to a **promotional pull strategy**, spending money on advertising and sales promotional efforts directed toward the ultimate consumer. The goal of a pull strategy is to create demand by consumers and encourage them to request the product from the retailer. Seeing the consumer demand, retailers will order the product from wholesalers (if they are used), which in turn will request it from the manufacturer. Thus, stimulating demand at the end-user level pulls the product through the channels of distribution.

Whether to emphasize a push or a pull strategy depends on a number of factors, including the company's relations with the trade, its promotional budget, and demand for the firm's products. Companies that have favorable channel relationships may prefer to use a push strategy and work closely with channel members to encourage them to stock and promote their products. A firm with a limited promotional budget may not have the funds for advertising and sales promotion that a pull strategy requires and may find it more cost effective to build distribution and demand by working closely with resellers. When the demand outlook for a product is favorable because it has unique benefits, is superior to competing brands, or is very popular among consumers, a pull strategy may be more appropriate. Companies often use a combination of push and pull strategies, with the emphasis often changing as the product moves through its life cycle.

Promotion to the Final Buyer

As is shown in the marketing model in Exhibit 2–1, the marketing program includes promotion both to the trade or channel members and to the company's ultimate customers. Marketers use the various promotional mix elements—advertising, sales promotion, direct marketing, publicity/public relations, and personal selling—to inform consumers about their products, prices, and places where they are available. Each promotional mix variable helps marketers achieve their promotional objectives. Advertising is generally relied on for communicating information about products and services to the consumer market and is becoming increasingly important in communicating with business customers as well. We will now examine the different forms of advertising used to communicate with the ultimate buyers of a product or service.

CLASSIFICATIONS OF ADVERTISING

The nature and purpose of advertising differ from one industry to another and/or across situations. The targets of an organization's advertising efforts often vary, as do its role and function in the marketing program. One advertiser may seek to generate immediate response or action from the customer: another may want to develop awareness or a positive image for its products over a longer period. Marketers advertise to the consumer market with national, retail/local, and direct-response advertising, which may involve stimulating primary or selective demand. For business/professional markets, they use industrial, professional, and trade advertising. To better understand the nature and purpose of advertising to the final buyer, it is useful to examine these classifications of the various types of advertising.

Advertising to the Consumer Market

National advertising

Advertising done by a company on a nationwide basis or in most regions of the country and targeted to the ultimate consumer market is known as **national advertising**. The companies that sponsor these ads are generally referred to as national advertisers. Most of the ads for well-known brands that we see on prime-time TV or in other major national or regional media are examples of national advertising. This form of advertising is usually very general; it rarely includes specific prices, directions for buying the product, or special services associated with the purchase. It informs or reminds consumers

@ **EXHIBIT 2-12**

This ad for Sheaffer is
an example of national
advertising

of the brand and its features, benefits, advantages, and uses or reinforces its image so
consumers will be predisposed to purchase it. The ad for Sheaffer pens in Exhibit 2–12
is an example of national advertising.

National advertising is the best known and most widely discussed form of promotion,
probably because of its pervasiveness. Exhibit 2–13 shows the advertising expenditures
of the 25 leading national advertisers for 1993. These figures reflect money spent in measured media as well as unmeasured media spending. Measured media include network
and spot (local) TV and radio, network cable TV, magazines, newspapers, and outdoor
advertising. Unmeasured media are support services such as direct mail, sales promotion, and co–op advertising programs.

@ **EXHIBIT 2-13**

25 leading advertisers in
1993

Rank	Advertiser	Ad spending
1	Procter & Gamble Co.	$2,397.5
2	Philip Morris Cos.	1,844.3
3	General Motors Corp.	1,539.2
4	Sears, Roebuck & Co.	1,310.7
5	PepsiCo	1,038.9
6	Ford Motor Co.	958.3
7	AT&T Co.	812.1
8	Nestlé SA	793.7
9	Johnson & Johnson	762.5
10	Chrysler Corp.	761.6
11	Warner-Lambert Co.	751.0
12	Unilever NV	738.2
13	McDonald's Corp.	736.6
14	Time Warner	695.1
15	Toyota Motor Corp.	690.4
16	Walt Disney Co.	675.7
17	Grand Metropolitan	652.9
18	Kellog Co.	627.1
19	Eastman Kodak Co.	624.7
20	Sony Corp.	589.0
21	J.C. Penney Co.	585.2
22	General Mills	569.2
23	Kmart Corp.	558.2
24	Anheuser-Busch Cos.	520.5
25	American Home Products Corp.	501.6

Figures in millions of dollars.
Source: *Advertising Age,* Sept. 28, 1994.

◉ EXHIBIT 2–14

Retail advertising often encourages consumers to take immediate action

◉ EXHIBIT 2–15

Retailers attempt to project certain images for their stores through advertising

Retail/local advertising

Another prevalent type of advertising directed at the consumer market is classified as **retail/local advertising.** This type of advertising is done by major retailers or smaller local merchants to encourage consumers to shop at a specific store or use a local service such as a bank, fitness club, or restaurant.

While the national advertisers sell their products at many locations, retail or local advertisers must give the consumer a reason to patronize their establishments. Retail advertising tends to emphasize specific customer benefits such as store hours, credit policies, service, atmosphere, merchandise assortments, or other distinguishing attributes. Product availability and price are important advertising themes, often used in conjunction with a sale or special event. Retailers are concerned with building store traffic, and often their promotions take the form of **direct-action advertising** designed to produce immediate store traffic or sales. A direct-action retail advertisement for Target is shown in Exhibit 2–14.

In addition to their product- and price-oriented advertising, many retailers use image advertising to influence consumers' perceptions of their stores.[15] Exhibit 2–15 shows an ad from the Broadway department store's life-style image advertising campaign.

Direct-response advertising

One of the fastest-growing sectors of the U.S. economy is direct marketing. **Direct-response advertising** is a method of direct marketing whereby a product is promoted through an ad that lets the customer purchase directly from the manufacturer. Traditionally, direct mail has been the primary medium for direct-response advertising, although television is becoming an increasingly important medium.

Direct-response advertising has become very popular in recent years owing primarily to changing lifestyles, particularly the increase in two-income households. This has meant more discretionary income but less time for in-store shopping. The convenience of shopping through the mail or by telephone has led to the tremendous increase in direct-response advertising. Credit cards and toll-free telephone numbers have also facilitated the purchase of products from direct-response advertisements.

EXHIBIT 2–16

This ad by market leader Campbell is designed to stimulate overall demand for soup

EXHIBIT 2–17

The pork industry positions pork as the other white meat

Primary and selective demand advertising

Another way of viewing advertising to the ultimate customer is in terms of whether the message is designed to stimulate either primary or selective demand. **Primary demand advertising** is designed to stimulate demand for the general product class or entire industry; **selective demand advertising** focuses on creating demand for a particular manufacturer's brands. Most advertising for various products and services is concerned with stimulating selective demand and emphasizes reasons for buying a particular brand. Advertisers generally assume there is a favorable level of primary demand for the product class and focus attention on increasing their market share. Thus, their advertising attempts to give consumers a reason to buy their brand.

Advertisers might concentrate on stimulating primary demand in several situations. When a company's brand dominates a market, it may focus on creating demand for the product class, since it will benefit the most from market growth. For example, Campbell has over 70 percent of the condensed soup market, and the company's advertising objective is to encourage consumers to eat more soup. Notice that the Campbell's "never underestimate the power of soup" slogan (Exhibit 2–16) emphasizes how soup can be used to prepare tasty meals.

Primary demand advertising is often used as part of a promotional strategy to help a new product gain acceptance among customers. Products in the introductory or growth stages of their life cycles often have primary demand stimulation as a promotional objective because the challenge is to sell customers on the product as much as it is to sell a particular brand.

Ethical Perspective 2-1
Keeping the Fur Selling—and Flying

Like many other luxury products, furs experienced strong sales growth during the free-spending decade of the 80s. Industry sales soared to $1.8 billion in 1987 but by 1991 had slipped to $1 billion. A number of factors contributed to the decline in retail fur sales including the recession, warm winter weather, a luxury tax, a glut of fur pelts on the international market that caused prices to decline, and an increasingly vocal animal rights movement. The decline in fur sales forced a number of fur retailers to close shop, and many department stores stopped carrying furs.

While some analysts predicted that demand for furs would continue to decline, the fur industry has actually made a strong comeback. Overall, industry sales increased 10 percent in 1991 while retail sales for 1993 increased another 9 percent, giving the industry a growth rate of nearly 20 percent in two years. To keep fur sales increasing, the Fur Information Council of America (FICA) began the largest advertising campaign in its history in late 1993. The $1 million campaign, which includes the group's first TV spot as well as print ads, is targeted to women 35 and older who are most likely to wear furs. Print ads were run in upscale fashion-oriented magazines such as *Vogue, Town & Country, Essence,* and *Harper's Bazaar.*

Unlike FICA's print campaign of a few years ago that defended wearing fur as a "matter of choice," the new ads focus on fashion and fur's image of luxury, beauty, and warmth. For example, print ads show women on the beach stylishly wrapped in sumptuous fur with tag lines such as, "The way it reveals, the way it embraces, the way it empowers. Fur, more than any other fabric."

While FICA wants to talk about the beauty and luxury of fur and how great it will make one feel when wearing it, not everyone likes the idea of encouraging consumers to buy furs. Animal rights activists such as People for the Ethical Treatment of Animals (PETA) contend that "fur doesn't empower—it symbolizes cruelty." PETA protested outside of *Vogue* immediately after the magazine carried the FICA print ad in October 1993 and has staged demonstrations at fashion shows where new fur lines were being shown. PETA also has run ads condemning the fur industry, some of which feature actresses Kim Bassinger and Sara Gilbert and singers k.d. Lang and Boy George.

The fur industry acknowledges that PETA and other groups have been successful in making an issue of the purchase and

Fur industry ads focus on the beauty and luxury of fur

wearing of fur. However, FICA feels that their impact has been overblown because of media sensationalism of PETA's campaign tactics. FICA's executive director notes that consumer research shows that the industry has not been affected by the animal activist campaigns. Of course, PETA has a different view of the controversy, arguing that its efforts have successfully impacted the sale of furs. PETA's international campaign manager argues that "for fur, there is no tomorrow." Ultimately, consumers will have to decide how they feel about wearing furs and whether to buy them.

Source: Bruce Horowitz, "Fur Industry Goes on the Offensive in Bid to Brighten Tarnished Image," *Los Angeles Times,* November 16, 1993, p. D6; Cyndee Miller, "Fur Industry Rebounds, Launches $1 Million Marketing Campaign," *Marketing News,* November 8, 1993, pp. 1–2.

Industry trade associations such as the American Dairy Association, the Florida Citrus Growers, and the Potato Board also seek to stimulate primary demand. These associations assess their members for funds to be used in promotional efforts to encourage the use of their product or services or to overcome declining primary demand trends, image problems, and the like. Ethical Perspective 2–1 describes how the fur industry is using advertising to successfully stimulate demand for furs—much to the chagrin of many animal rights activists. Major competitors may even work together to stimulate sluggish demand for their product class. For example, competitiors in the pork industry used primary demand advertising to stimulate consumption by positioning pork as "the other white meat" and stressing the fact that it is a healthful, versatile alternative appropriate for any meal (Exhibit 2–17).

@ **EXHIBIT   2-18**

Television commercials are being used more frequently to advertise business products

Advertising to the Business and Professional Markets

For many companies, the ultimate customer is not the mass consumer market but rather another business, industry, or profession. **Business-to-business advertising** is used by one business to advertise its products or services to another. The target for business advertising is individuals who either use a product or service or influence a firm's decision to purchase a product or service. Three basic categories of business-to-business advertising are industrial, professional, and trade advertising. (Trade advertising was discussed earlier in the chapter, under promotional push strategies.)

Industrial advertising

Advertising targeted at individuals who buy or influence the purchase of industrial goods or other services is known as **industrial advertising**. Industrial goods are those products that either become a physical part of another product (raw material, component parts), are used in manufacturing other goods (machinery, equipment), or are used to help the manufacturer conduct business (office supplies, computers, copy machines, etc.). Business services, such as insurance, financial services, and health care, are also included in this category.

Industrial advertising is usually found in general business publications (such as *Fortune*, *Business Week*, and *The Wall Street Journal*) or in trade publications targeted to the particular industry. In recent years, ads for industrial products and services have become more common in mass media such as television. Exhibit 2–18 shows a storyboard of a commercial for Xerox that stresses the company's Total Satisfaction Guarantee Program.

Industrial advertising is often not designed to sell a product or service directly, since the purchase of industrial goods is often a complex process involving a number of individuals. An industrial ad helps make the company and its product or service better known, assists in developing an image for the firm, and perhaps most important, opens doors for the company's sales reps when they call on industrial customers.

◎ **EXHIBIT 2–19**

Vipont uses ads targeted to
dentists to encourage them to
recommend Viadent products
to their patients

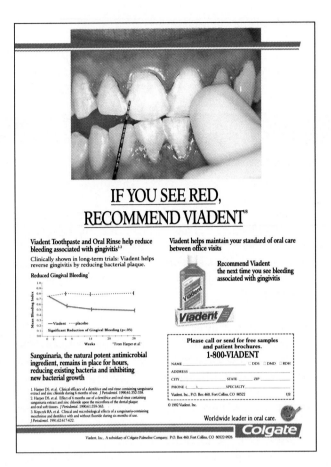

Professional advertising

Advertising that is targeted to professional groups—such as doctors, lawyers, dentists, engineers, or professors—to encourage them to use the advertiser's product or specify it for others' use is known as **professional advertising.** Professional groups are important because they constitute a market for products and services they use in their businesses. Also, their recommendation or specification of a product or service often influences many consumer purchase decisions. For example, Vipont Pharmaceutical initially targeted advertising for Viadent plaque-fighting toothpaste and oral rinse to dentists to encourage them to recommend these products to their patients (Exhibit 2–19).

Professional advertising should not be confused with advertising done by professionals. In recent years, advertising by professionals such as dentists, lawyers, and doctors has increased in popularity as legal restrictions were removed and competition increased.

These classifications of the various types of advertising demonstrate that this promotional element is used in a variety of ways and by a number of different organizations. Advertising is a very flexible promotional tool whose role in a marketing program will vary depending on the situation facing the organization and what information needs to be communicated.

◎ **ENVIRONMENTAL INFLUENCES ON MARKETING AND PROMOTION**

The three components of the marketing model we have just examined represent controllable factors that are determined by the organization. A firm's marketing strategy, selection of a target market, and development, implementation, and control of its marketing program are all directed by management. However, a number of factors cannot be controlled or directed by the firm or organization.

These uncontrollable forces constitute what is often referred to as the **macro-environment** of marketing. They include demographic, economic, technological,

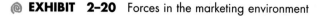

@ **EXHIBIT 2–20** Forces in the marketing environment

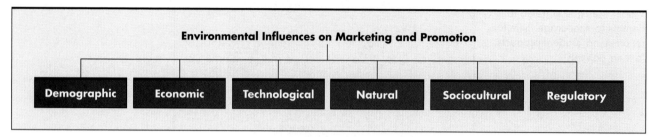

natural/physical, sociocultural, and regulatory factors (Exhibit 2–20). These environmental influences can have a significant impact on a firm's marketing strategy and programs in both the short and the long term, so they must be continually monitored and responded to. This section examines these environmental influences, giving particular attention to the impact of each on the promotional element of an organization's marketing program.

Demographic Environment

Demographics deals with the practice of analyzing and describing the distribution of the population according to selected characteristics such as age, sex, income, education, occupation, and geographic dispersion. Major demographic developments in the United States are affecting firms' marketing and promotional programs. These include the aging of the population, the increasing number of women in the labor force, and changing ethnic compositions. Some of their effects are discussed in the following pages.

Aging of the population

Perhaps one of the most notable characteristics of the U.S. population is the fact that it is aging as birth rates decline, life expectancies increase, and the baby boom generation gets older. A major reason for the graying of America is that the **baby boomers,** the 74 million Americans born between 1946 and 1964, are entering middle age. As this age cohort grows older, they represent a significant opportunity to marketers because of their size and purchasing power.

Baby boomers have a distinct profile compared with people of the same age in previous generations. They differ in terms of their values, lifestyles, education level, women's roles, tastes, buying habits, and affluence. For example, in the 1980s, many marketers focused attention on a segment of the baby boomers known as yuppies (young urban professionals). This segment represents the better-educated, more affluent, and according to many critics, more materialistic group of baby boomers.[16] Interest in yuppies has decreased somewhat in recent years as many baby boomers rebelled against the stereotypic lifestyle and values of this group, and many marketers became concerned about having their brands categorized as yuppie products. For example, BMW launched a new advertising campaign to position its cars as sensitive to concerns like safety and value and move away from the yuppie image.[17]

The aging of the population has also led marketers to put more emphasis on older consumers. In 1960, only 9 percent of the U.S. population was over 65 years of age, but by the year 2000, people over 65 are expected to be close to 22 percent of the population.[18] Older Americans, variously referred to as the "mature market," "welderly" (well-to-do elderly), and "gray powers," have become a prime target for marketers. Americans over age 50 constitute 25 percent of the population but have 50 percent of the nation's disposable income, buying $800 million worth of goods and services each year.[19] Exhibit 2–21 shows an advertisement for Choice Hotels International, which offers discounts to anyone over 60.

The aging of the population has also increased the demand for media that reach older consumers. For example, *Modern Maturity,* a magazine provided as part of the Amer-

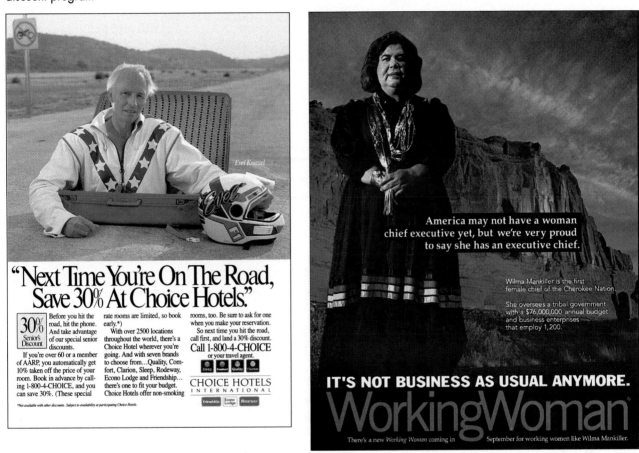

@ **EXHIBIT 2-21**

Choice Hotels International targets senior citizens with its discount program

@ **EXHIBIT 2-22**

Many magazines are targeted to women in the work force

ican Association of Retired Persons' (AARP) annual membership, has the largest paid circulation of any magazine in the United States, with over 22.5 million subscribers.[20] This magazine has become a popular media vehicle for reaching active senior citizens.

The changing role of women

One of the most significant changes in American society over the past two decades has been the increase in the number of working women. Adult women in the labor force increased from 36.7 percent in 1965 to 57.3 percent in 1993, and projections are that by the year 2000 nearly two-thirds of all women will be working outside the home.[21] This change has had a dramatic effect on the demand for a wide variety of products and services, among them child care services, microwave ovens, easy-to-prepare foods, restaurant meals, and women's clothing.

Another important effect of the increase in working women is the greater disposable income in the dual-earner household. This means families can purchase more products and services, take more trips and vacations, eat out more often, and basically enjoy a higher standard of living.

The increase in the number of working women has many implications for marketing and promotional strategy. Many marketers are directing more of their advertising to working women, as they not only constitute an important market segment but also are more likely to be involved in purchase decisions that were traditionally the domain of men. A study by the Young and Rubicam advertising agency found that working women

◉ EXHIBIT 2-23

Top 20 TV shows in Hispanic households

		Hispanic Rank	Total U.S. Rank
FOX	Simpsons	1	27
FOX	Martin**	2	T38
FOX	Beverly Hills 90210	3	45
ABC	Roseanne	4	2
FOX	In Living Color (1st season)	5	T74
NBC	Fresh Prince of Bel Air	6	15
FOX	Married . . . With Children	7	T41
ABC	NFL Monday Night Football	8	T11
FOX	In Living Color	9	T47
NBC	Blossom	10	24
ABC	Full House	11	T11
ABC	Step by Step**	12	T35
ABC	Dinosaurs	13	T59
ABC	Hangin' with Mr. Cooper**	14	T19
FOX	Melrose Place**	15	92
ABC	Family Matters	16	33
ABC	Sunday Movie	17	17
ABC	Home Improvement	18	3
ABC	Coach (Tue)	19	4
FOX	Cops 2	20	64

**New show. T=Tie.
Source: NHTI 1992–93, NTI 1992–1993/BBDO.

are more likely to be involved in decisions regarding financial services, travel, and the selection of an automobile than are women who don't work at paying jobs.[22]

Advertisers have also had to change their media strategies to reach working women, as they are less likely to be around the house watching television or reading traditional women's magazines such as *Good Housekeeping* and *Ladies Home Journal.* Over the past decade, a number of new magazines have been introduced to respond to the needs and interests of the working woman—for example, *Working Woman, Working Mother, Self,* and *New Woman* (Exhibit 2–22 on page 53).

Changing ethnic and racial profiles

The racial and ethnic profile of the U.S. population is changing rapidly. One in five Americans today is black, Hispanic, Asian, or a member of some other minority group. African-Americans are the largest minority group, numbering nearly 28 million and having an estimated purchasing power of nearly $600 billion—up 18 percent from 1990. The fastest-growing of all minority groups is the Hispanic, which comprises a number of different Spanish-speaking nationalities such as Mexican, Puerto Rican, and Cuban.

More than 20 million Hispanics account for 10 percent of the U.S. population and have an estimated purchasing power of over $170 billion. As a result of high immigration and birth rates, the Hispanic population is growing five times as fast as the general population and will soon constitute the country's largest minority group.[23] The increase in the Hispanic population has led to the introduction of Spanish television networks, numerous TV and radio stations, and a number of Hispanic-oriented newspapers and magazines. Over the past 10 years, nearly every segment of the Hispanic market has doubled its income, making this ethnic market very attractive to marketers.

The Asian population has also burgeoned as the number of Chinese, Japanese, Filipinos, Koreans, Asian Indians, and Vietnamese has increased over the past decade. In 1990, the Asian population in the United States was estimated at about 5.6 million.[24] This number is expected to increase to nearly 10 million by the end of the decade.

The sizes of these minority groups, as well as their diverse cultures, needs, and buying habits, make them important market segments for many companies. However, advertisers are finding that the Hispanic and Asian markets often cannot be reached effectively through the general media with traditional English-language appeals. As is demonstrated in Exhibit 2–23 these minorities may have different media habits as well. Thus, many companies are developing products and advertising appeals and making buys in media specifically for these markets.

It is important for marketers to monitor changes in the demographic environment and identify their implications for their industry and individual products and services. Fortunately, demographic changes are the most predictable of all the forces that constitute the macroenvironment. A wealth of demographic information is available from both government and commercial sources.[25]

Economic Environment

Marketing activity is influenced heavily by the state of the economy. Marketers must study economic conditions and trends and their potential impact on the demand for various products and services. They must pay attention to **macroeconomic conditions** that influence the state of the economy: changes in gross domestic product (GDP), whether the economy is in an inflationary or recessionary period, interest rates, and unemployment levels. **Microeconomic trends**—such as consumer income, savings, debt, and expenditure patterns—are also important. Consumers' ability to buy is a function of many factors, including changes in real income, disposable and discretionary income, savings, and debt levels.

Changes in economic conditions may have a significant impact on marketing and advertising strategies. During a recession, companies often cut back on marketing and advertising expenditures to meet budgets and/or profit plans. Advertising expenditures may be a prime candidate for cutbacks, since many executives question the need to spend large sums of money in this area. Unlike other areas such as interest expenses or capital costs, advertising is one of the easiest expenses to cut when profits (or profit projections) fall, because the savings go straight to the bottom line.

The recession of the 1990s has hit the advertising industry hard. As consumer spending slowed, many companies experienced declines in their sales and/or profits, which resulted in cuts in their advertising.

The recession also changed the way many companies promote their products and services. Many shifted spending away from advertising and into short-term promotions such as coupons, price deals, contests, and sweepstakes.[26] Many companies switched from image-oriented ads to appeals that focused on economy, value, and savings. The decline in advertising expenditures by many companies during the recession and shift in promotional strategies affects other participants in the advertising industry as well. Lower advertising budgets mean decreased billings for advertising agencies and less media spending.[27]

Technological Environment

Perhaps the most dramatic macroenvironmental force to affect marketing is technology. Changes in technology can affect an industry in several ways. Technology can result in the emergence of a new industry—for example, fax machines and personal computers.

Technology can also radically alter or even destroy an existing industry. Consider the growth of the VCR industry. Over 70 percent of U.S. households now own VCRs, creating tremendous opportunities for manufacturers of the players and tapes, the movie industry, and the video stores that rent tapes to consumers.[28] The growth of this industry, however, has posed a threat to other markets such as movie theaters and pay-TV companies. Attendance at movie theaters declined in the late 1980s and early 1990s as more people rented movies to watch at home. Likewise, fewer households subscribed to pay TV (such as HBO), since they could rent the movies before they were shown on the pay channels.

Technology can also stimulate new markets in related industries. For example, the penetration of the microwave oven into most of American homes has resulted in a resurgence of the frozen-dinner market. Products such as Le Menu, Stouffer's Entrees, and Lean Cuisine have enjoyed tremendous growth, partly due to the microwave convenience of preparing these dishes and partly due to improvements in product quality.

Natural Environment

The most difficult environmental influence to predict is change in the physical or natural environment. The natural environment includes the forces of nature as well as the availability of natural resources that influence a company's business and marketing strategy. Forces of nature such as weather patterns can influence demand for many products and services. For example, the severe weather in the Midwest and East during the winter of 1994 created high demand for products such as 4-wheel drive vehicles.

The natural environment also provides resources for producing goods and services. Changes in the availability and prices of raw materials have a significant impact on the companies that use them and on consumers. For example, the floods in the Midwest in the summer of 1993 resulted in millions of dollars of lost revenue due to damaged crops. Shortages in raw materials, increasing costs of energy, concern over increased levels of pollution, and increased intervention in resource management by governments and other agencies have also resulted in both threats and opportunities for many companies.

Sociocultural Environment

Marketing, and advertising in particular, is influenced by the basic beliefs, values, norms, customs, and lifestyle patterns of a society. Marketers must consider the core cultural beliefs and values of the countries that comprise their marketplace. Many U.S. firms are increasingly looking to international markets as the domestic market becomes saturated. While understanding the cultural values and customs of foreign markets is important to multinational companies, many marketers have their hands full tracking changes in the values, norms, and lifestyles of American consumers. Marketers must constantly monitor the sociocultural environment of the American public to spot new opportunities and new threats. They must monitor social trends and changes in consumer values and respond to them through their marketing and promotional programs.

In recent years, marketers have identified and responded to many changes in consumers' values and lifestyles. Consumers have become more concerned with physical fitness, health, and nutrition, which is reflected in the avalanche of new products and advertising that use health claims and appeals. Many consumers have become more socially conscious and less sensitive to status and image. Many companies have introduced new products or repositioned their brands to capitalize on these trends. For example, consumption of bottled water has experienced tremendous growth in the United States over the past few years. New clear products such as Crystal Pepsi and Zima (a clear malt beverage) (Exhibit 2–24) capitalize on consumer perceptions that clear may mean healthier.

@ **EXHIBIT 2–24**

More clear products have begun to enter the market

Regulatory Environment

The final, and in many ways most frustrating, component of the external environment is regulatory influences. Marketing decisions are constrained, directed, and influenced by the practices and policies of federal, state, and local governments. These policies are expressed through laws and regulations. Virtually every element of the marketing mix is influenced by some type of government regulation.

Of particular interest in this text are laws and regulations that affect advertising and promotion, which are closely monitored at both the state and federal levels. The Federal Trade Commission (FTC) and numerous other federal agencies scrutinize advertising to protect consumers from false or misleading ads and to prevent firms from gaining a competitive edge through unfair or deceptive advertising. The advertising industry is also policed by advertisers and the media through various self-regulatory programs.

SUMMARY

Promotion plays an important role in an organization's efforts to market its product, service, or ideas to its customers. Exhibit 2–1 shows a model for analyzing how promotion fits into a company's marketing program. The model includes marketing strategy and plan, marketing program development, and the target market. The marketing process begins with a marketing strategy that is based on a detailed situation analysis and guides for target market selection and development of the firm's marketing program.

The various elements of the marketing mix must be coordinated to develop a successful marketing program. Each marketing mix variable is multidimensional and includes a number of decision areas. Product planning involves decisions regarding the basic product as well as selection of a brand name and packaging, all of which are important from a communications perspective. Price levels and pricing policies must consider cost and demand factors as well as competition and the consumers' perceived value of the product or service.

One of a firm's most important decisions is the selection of marketing channels to make the product available to the customer. While some firms sell directly to the cus-

tomer, most use marketing intermediaries or resellers such as wholesalers and/or retailers. Marketing and promotional programs must be developed to encourage these intermediaries to stock, merchandise, and promote the manufacturer's product. Programs geared to the resellers or trade are part of a promotional push strategy; spending money on advertising and sales promotion to create demand among ultimate consumers constitutes a promotional pull strategy.

Promotion to the final buyer occurs through the various promotional mix elements, although advertising is the main element used to communicate information to both consumer and business markets. Classifications of advertising to final customers include national, retail/local, and business-to-business advertising, which covers industrial, trade, and professional advertising.

A number of factors that cannot be controlled or directed by the organization make up the macroenvironment of marketing. They include demographic, economic, technological, natural/physical, sociocultural, and regulatory influences. These uncontrollable forces can have a significant impact on a firm's marketing strategy and programs in both the short and the long term.

KEY TERMS

strategic marketing
 plan, p. 33
market opportunities,
 p. 33
market segments, p. 33
competitive advantage,
 p. 34
product symbolism,
 p. 36
brand extension
 strategy, p. 37
line extension, p. 38
category extension, p. 38
nonprice competition,
 p. 41

competition-oriented
 pricing, p. 41
marketing channels,
 p. 43
resellers, p. 43
direct channels, p. 44
indirect channels, p. 44
promotional push
 strategy, p. 44
trade advertising, p. 44
promotional pull
 strategy, p. 45
national advertising,
 p. 45

retail/local
 advertising, p. 47
direct-action
 advertising, p. 47
direct-response
 advertising, p. 47
primary demand
 advertising, p. 48
selective demand
 advertising, p. 48
business-to-business
 advertising, p. 50

industrial
 advertising, p. 50
professional
 advertising, p. 51
macroenvironment, p. 51
demographics, p. 52
baby boomers, p. 52
macroeconomic
 conditions, p. 55
microeconomic trends,
 p. 55

DISCUSSION QUESTIONS

1. Changes in the marketing environment often lead to market opportunities. Cite examples of recent market opportunities that have been created by changing environmental factors.
2. The text cites examples of brands that have increased and those that have decreased in value in recent years. Discuss some of the factors that lead to increases and/or decreases in brand value.

3. Find an example of a situation where a new product was recently introduced using a brand extension strategy. Discuss the advantages and disadvantages of this strategy. Do you think a brand extension was appropriate in this situation? Why or why not?
4. Describe the various classifications of advertising. Bring an example of each to class.

5. Discuss the differences between a promotional push strategy and a promotional pull strategy. What factors influence a firm's decision on which strategy to use?

6. What are the differences between primary and selective demand advertising? When would a company or organization use each?

7. Discuss the role of advertising in business-to-business firms that sell directly to other companies. Given that these companies rely heavily on personal selling, where do they need to advertise?

8. Discuss the implications of the aging of the U.S. population for marketers, giving particular attention to advertising and promotion.

9. How has the recession of the early 1990s affected advertising? Do you think it will be business as usual for advertisers when the recession ends, or have fundamental changes occurred in the way companies market their products and services?

10. Marketers have increased their efforts to reach ethnic markets. Explain why this may be occurring. Bring to class examples of ads targeted to various ethnic groups.

Chapter **3**

Organizing for Advertising and Promotion: The Role of Ad Agencies and Other Marketing Communication Organizations

Chapter Objectives

● *To understand how companies organize for advertising and other aspects of integrated marketing communications.*

● *To examine methods for selecting, compensating, and evaluating advertising agencies.*

● *To explain the role and functions of specialized marketing communication organizations.*

● *To examine various perspectives on the use of integrated services and responsibilities of advertisers versus agencies.*

Advertising Goes Hollywood

In 1989 the Coca-Cola Co. faced a serious problem: sales of its flagship brand, Coke Classic, were stagnant in the U.S. market, and archrival Pepsi's ads were consistently rating higher among consumers. The company began a secret and unorthodox study, called Project Balance, which tapped the talents of a number of unconventional thinkers for their views on how best to reach consumers in a media-saturated age. The first report from the group posed a provocative premise: "A brand advertised in a normal way, with normal media, is likely to develop a normal image, and not something special." The experts' advice: Don't be normal!

To help break away from normal advertising, Coca-Cola decided to have Hollywood talent agent Michael Ovitz's Creative Artists Agency (CAA) come up with some new creative ideas as well as McCann-Erickson Worldwide, its agency for the past 38 years. Several Coca-Cola top executives were reportedly intrigued by CAA's pipeline into pop culture and Hollywood's "raw creativity."

When presentation day came in October 1992, Mc-Cann proposed a half dozen platform ads positioning Coke as a ubiquitous product, for all people. However, the CAA presentation was a whirlwind 60 minutes in which 50 ideas were pitched in many styles for many audiences. One was the popular computer-generated polar bears spot. On seeing CAA's dazzling presentation, McCann-Erickson's former vice chairman reportedly slipped a note to an associate that read, "We are dead." Coke management selected 24 ideas from CAA's "Always Coca-Cola" campaign and only two from McCann.

Coca-Cola's decision to move much of its advertising to CAA sent shock waves through Madison Avenue. Many traditional advertising people have been critical of Coke's decision, and they argue that it is only a matter of time until Coke returns to a traditional full-service agency. However, just a week into his job, Coca-Cola's new director of worldwide marketing rejected McCann-Erickson's ideas for the company's global marketing campaign and announced that CAA would do Coke Classic's entire 1994 campaign. Many critics say the "Always" campaign is Coke's most successful advertising in over a decade. They argue that the days of "one sight, one sound, one sell," when Coke would run a handful of mass-market, big-budget commercials each year, appear to be over.

Coca-Cola is sending other signals that it will go anywhere for creative ideas. In October 1993 the company fired Lintas:New York, the ad agency that had handled Diet Coke since it was introduced 11 years earlier, and awarded the business to Lowe & Partners, a limber mid-size agency. The company has also moved some of its other brands (such as Cherry Coke and Mello Yello) to smaller, trendier agencies, including the Martin Agency, Chiat/Day, Wieden & Kennedy, and Fallon McElligott.

Coca-Cola is not the only company rethinking its advertising strategy. Nike recently hired CAA to help with sports marketing events for television and Apple Computer has retained CAA's services. Sony Corp. of America solicited ideas from its Columbia Pictures division on how to advertise its new point-and-shoot camcorder. Traditional ad agencies beware. Normal is out!

Sources: "How CAA Bottled Coca-Cola," Fortune, Nov. 15, 1993, p. 156; Mary Magiera and Melanie Wells, "Coke Thinks Bigger for Small Brands," Advertising Age, Nov. 15, 1993, pp. 3, 44; Melanie Wells, "Coke Welcomes Two More Agencies into Its Family," Advertising Age, Oct. 10, 1993, pp. 1, 46; Kevin Goldman, "Sony Unit Turns to Its Hollywood Sister," The Wall Street Journal, Dec. 7, 1993, p. 8.

eveloping and implementing an integrated marketing communications program is usually a complex and detailed process involving the efforts of many persons. As consumers, we generally give little thought to the individuals or organizations that create the clever advertisements that capture our attention or the contests or sweepstakes we hope to win. But for those involved in the marketing process, it is important to understand the nature of the industry and the structure and functions of the organizations involved. As you can see in the opening to this chapter, the advertising and promotions business is changing as marketers search for better ways to communicate with their customers.

This chapter examines the various organizations that participate in the integrated marketing communications process, their roles and responsibilities, and their relationship to one another. We discuss how companies organize internally for advertising and promotion. For most companies, advertising is planned and executed by an outside ad agency. Many large agencies offer a variety of other IMC capabilities, including public relations, sales promotion, and direct marketing. Thus, we will devote particular attention to the ad agency's role and the overall relationship between the company and agency.

Other participants in the promotional process, such as direct-response and sales promotion agencies and public relations firms, are becoming increasingly important as more companies take an integrated marketing communications approach to promotion. We examine the role of these specialized marketing communication organizations in the promotional process as well. The chapter concludes with a discussion of whether marketers are best served by using the integrated services of one large agency or a variety of communication specialists.

@ PARTICIPANTS IN THE INTEGRATED MARKETING COMMUNICATIONS PROCESS: AN OVERVIEW

Before discussing the specifics of the industry, we'll provide an overview of the entire system and identify some of the players. As shown in Exhibit 3–1, participants in the integrated marketing communications process can be broken into five major groups: the advertiser (or client), advertising agencies, media organizations, specialized communication services, and collateral services. Each group has specific roles in the promotional process.

The advertisers, or **clients,** are the key participants in the process. They have the products, services, or causes to be marketed, and they provide the funds that pay for advertising and promotions. The advertisers also assume major responsibility for developing the marketing program and making the final decisions regarding the advertising and promotional program to be employed. (In many cases, advertising agencies are assuming more of this responsibility, acting as partners with the advertisers in this process.) The organization itself may perform most of these efforts, either through its own advertising department or by setting up an in-house agency.

@ **EXHIBIT 3–1** Participants in the integrated marketing communications process

Participants in the Integrated Marketing Communications Process

Advertiser (client) · Advertising Agency · Marketing Communication Specialist Organizations · Direct Response Agencies · Sales Promotion Agencies · Public Relations Firms · Collateral Services

However, many organizations use an **advertising agency,** an outside firm that specializes in the creation, production, and/or placement of the communications message and that may provide other services to facilitate the marketing and promotions process. Many large advertisers retain the services of a number of agencies, particularly when they market a number of products. For example, Kraft/General Foods uses as many as 10 advertising agencies, while Procter & Gamble uses 10 promotional agencies for its Canadian business alone.[1]

Media organizations are another major participant in the advertising and promotions process. The primary function of most media is to provide information or entertainment to their subscribers, the viewers or readers. But from the perspective of the promotional planner, the purpose of media is to provide an environment for the firm's marketing communications message. The media must have editorial or program content that attracts consumers so advertisers and their agencies want to buy time or space with them. One publication's attempt to convince buyers of its value as a media vehicle is shown in Exhibit 3–2. While the media perform many other functions that help advertisers understand their markets and their customers, a medium's primary objective is to sell itself as a way for companies to reach their target markets with their messages effectively.

The next group of participants are organizations that provide **specialized marketing communications services.** They include direct marketing agencies, sales promotion agencies, and public relations firms. These organizations provide services in their areas of expertise. A direct-response agency develops and implements direct marketing programs, while sales promotion agencies are used to develop promotional programs such as contests and sweepstakes, premium offers, or sampling programs. Public relations firms are used to generate and manage publicity for a company and its products

@ **EXHIBIT   3–2**

L'Actualité advertises the value of its medium

and services as well as to focus on its relationships and communications with its relevant publics.

The final participants shown in the promotions process of Exhibit 3–1 are those that provide **collateral services,** the wide range of support functions used by advertisers, agencies, media organizations, and specialized marketing communications firms. These individuals and companies perform specialized functions the other participants use in planning and executing advertising and other promotional functions. We will now examine the role of each participant in more detail.

ORGANIZING FOR ADVERTISING AND PROMOTION IN THE FIRM: THE ROLE OF THE CLIENT

Virtually every business organization uses some form of marketing communications. However, the way the firm organizes for these efforts depends on several factors, including the size of the company, the number of products it markets, the role of advertising and promotion in the company's marketing mix, the advertising and promotion budget, and the marketing organization structure of the firm. Many individuals throughout the organization may be involved in the promotions decision-making process. Marketing personnel have the most direct relationship with advertising and are often involved in many aspects of the decision process, such as providing input to the campaign plan, agency selection, and evaluation of proposed programs. Top management is usually interested in how the advertising program represents the firm, which may also mean being involved in advertising decisions, even when these decisions are not included in their day-to-day responsibilities.

While many people both inside and outside the organization have some input into the advertising and promotion process, direct responsibility for administering the program must be assumed by someone within the firm. Many companies have an advertising department headed by an advertising or communications manager operating under a marketing director. An alternative used by many large multiproduct firms is a decentralized marketing or brand management system. A third option is to form a separate agency within the firm, an in-house agency. Each of these alternatives is examined in more detail in the following sections.

The Centralized System

In many organizations, marketing activities are divided along functional lines, with advertising placed alongside other marketing functions such as sales, marketing research, and product planning, as shown in Exhibit 3–3. The **advertising manager** is responsible for all promotions activities except sales. In the most common example of a **centralized system,** the advertising manager controls the entire promotions operation, including budgeting, coordinating creation and production of ads, planning media schedules, and monitoring and administering the sales promotions programs for all the company's products or services.

The specific duties of the advertising manager depend on the size of the firm and the importance placed on promotional programs. Basic functions the manager and staff perform include the following:

Planning and budgeting
The department is responsible for developing advertising and promotions plans that will be approved by management and recommending a promotions program based on the overall marketing plan, objectives, and budget. Formal plans are submitted annually or when a program is being changed significantly, as when a new campaign is developed. While the advertising department develops the promotional budget, the final decision on allocating funds is usually made by top management.

Administration and execution
The manager must organize the advertising department and supervise and control its activities. The manager also supervises the execution of the plan by subordinates and/or the advertising agency. This requires working with such departments as production, media, art, copy, and sales promotion. If an outside agency is used, the advertising depart-

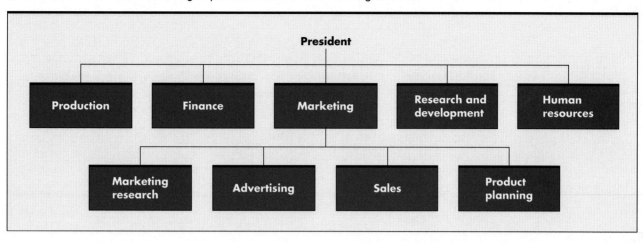

EXHIBIT 3–3 The advertising department under a functional organization

ment is relieved of much of the executional responsibility; however, it must review and approve the agency's plans.

Coordination with other departments

The manager must coordinate the advertising department's activities with those of other departments, particularly those involving other marketing functions. For example, the advertising department must communicate with marketing research and/or sales to determine which product features are important to customers and should be emphasized in the company's communications. Research may also provide profiles of product users and nonusers for the media department before it selects broadcast or print media. The advertising department may also be responsible for preparing material the sales force can use when calling on customers, such as sales promotions tools, advertising materials, and point-of-purchase displays.

Coordination with outside agencies and services

Many companies have an advertising department but still utilize many outside services. For example, companies may develop their advertising programs in-house while employing media buying services to place their ads and/or use collateral services agencies to develop brochures, point-of-purchase materials, and so on. The department serves as liaison between the company and any outside service providers and also determines which ones to use. Once outside services are retained, the manager will work with other marketing managers to coordinate their efforts and evaluate their performances.

Many companies prefer a centralized advertising department because developing and coordinating advertising programs from one central location facilitates communication regarding the promotions program, making it easier for top management to participate in decision making. A centralized system may also result in a more efficient operation because fewer people are involved in the program decisions, and as their experience in making such decisions increases, the process becomes easier.

At the same time, problems are inherent in a centralized operation. First, it is difficult for the advertising department to understand the overall marketing strategy for the brand. The department may also be slow in responding to specific needs and problems of a product or brand. As companies become larger and develop or acquire new products, brands, or even divisions, the centralized system may become impractical.

The Decentralized System

The centralized advertising department structure was the most commonly employed organization system for many years, but as companies grew, problems with coordination and responsibility arose. Marketing decisions were made by several functional managers and had to be coordinated by someone in the marketing department. No one department

EXHIBIT 3–4   The product manager organizational chart

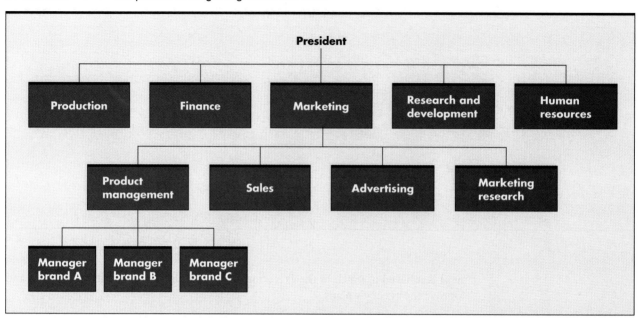

had specific responsibility for the welfare or problems of individual products or brands. Because of these problems, many companies developed **decentralized systems** such as the product or brand manager organization. (This organizational system is now the most dominant structure in large consumer and industrial products companies.)[2]

In this system, a **product manager** or management team is responsible for planning, implementing, and controlling the marketing program for an individual brand. The product manager is also responsible for sales projections and profit performance of the brand and must develop and coordinate the budget. Companies with this form of organization generally support product managers with a structure of marketing services including sales, marketing research, and advertising departments, as shown in Exhibit 3–4. The product manager uses these services in gathering information on customers, middlemen, competitors, product performance, and specific marketing problems and opportunities. (Both *brand manager* and *product manager* are used to describe this position.)

In a product management system, the responsibilities and functions associated with advertising and promotions are often transferred to the brand manager, who becomes the liaison with the outside service agencies as they develop the promotional program.

Some companies may have an additional layer of management above the brand managers to improve and coordinate efforts among groups of product categories. An example is the organizational structure of Procter & Gamble, shown in Exhibit 3–5. This system—generally referred to as a **category management** system—includes category managers as well as brand and advertising managers.

In a multiproduct firm, each brand may have its own advertising agency and, when positioned differently, may compete against other brands within the company as well as with outside competitors. For example, Exhibit 3–6 on page 68 shows ads for Cheer and Tide, which are both Procter & Gamble products that compete for a share of the market.

Under a product management organization, the advertising and sales promotion departments are part of marketing services and provide support for the brand manager. The role of marketing services is to assist the brand manager in planning and coordinating the integrated marketing communications program. The advertising manager may review and evaluate the various parts of the program and serve as consultant and

@ EXHIBIT 3–5

A Procter & Gamble division using the category management system of organization

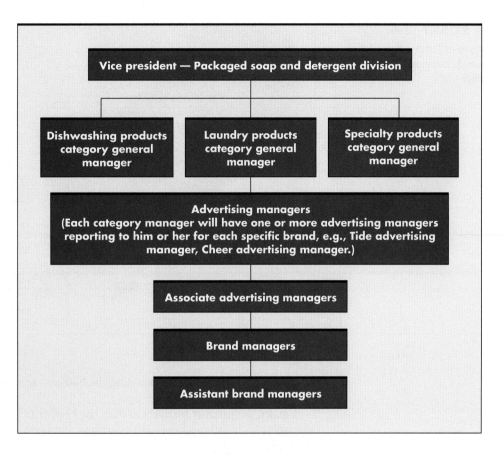

adviser. This person may have the authority to override the product manager's decisions on advertising. In some multiproduct firms that spend many dollars on advertising, the advertising manager may coordinate the work of the various agencies to obtain media discounts for the firm's large volume of media purchases. Recently many companies have been consolidating their media buying with one or two agencies to save money. For example, for many years Nestlé had as many as 11 agencies purchasing media time for its products. Then Nestlé consolidated its $250 to $300 million media buying into one agency, which gave the company more clout in the media buying market and saved a considerable amount of money.[3]

In some companies, the marketing services group may include a sales promotion department. The brand or category managers may work with sales promotion people to develop budgets, define strategies, and implement tactical executions for both trade and consumer promotions. Marketing services may also provide other types of support services, such as marketing research, package design, and merchandising assistance.

An advantage of the decentralized system is that each brand receives concentrated managerial attention, resulting in faster response to both problems and opportunities. The product manager system allows for increased flexibility in the advertising program, so the campaign may be adjusted more easily.

There are some drawbacks to the decentralized approach. Product managers often lack training and experience, particularly in advertising and promotion. The promotional strategy for a brand may be developed by a brand manager who does not really understand what advertising or sales promotion can and cannot do and how each should be used. Product managers may focus too much on short-run planning and administrative tasks, neglecting the development of long-term programs. Also, individual product managers often end up competing for resources, which can lead to unproductive rivalries and potential misallocation of funds. The persuasiveness of the manager may

⊚ EXHIBIT 3–6

Many of Procter & Gamble's brands compete against each other

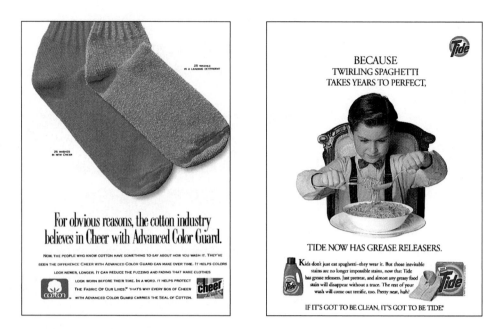

become a bigger factor in determining the budgets than the long-run profit potential of the brands.

Finally, the product manager system has been criticized for failing to provide brand managers with authority over the functions that are needed to implement and control the plans they develop.[4] Some companies have dealt with this problem by expanding the role and responsibility of the advertising and sales promotion managers and their staff of specialists. The staff specialists counsel the individual product managers, and advertising or sales promotion decision making involves the advertising and/or sales promotion manager, the product manager, and the marketing director.

In-House Agencies

Some companies, in an effort to reduce costs and maintain greater control over agency activities, have set up their own advertising agencies internally. An **in-house agency** is an advertising agency that is set up, owned, and operated by the advertiser. Some in-house agencies are little more than advertising departments, but in other companies they are given a separate identity and are responsible for the expenditure of large sums of advertising dollars. Large advertisers that use in-house agencies include Calvin Klein, Radio Shack, and Benetton (Exhibit 3–7). Many companies use in-house agencies exclusively; others may combine in-house efforts with those of outside agencies. (The specific roles performed by in-house agencies will become clearer when we discuss the functions of outside agencies.)

A major reason for using an in-house agency is to reduce advertising and promotion costs. Companies with very large advertising budgets pay a substantial amount to outside agencies in the form of media commissions. With an internal structure, these commissions go to the in-house agency. An in-house agency can also provide related work such as sales presentations and sales force materials, package design, and public relations at a lower cost than outside agencies. A study by M. Louise Ripley found that creative and media services were the most likely functions to be performed outside, while merchandising and sales promotion were the most likely to be performed in-house.[5]

Saving money is not the only reason companies use in-house agencies. Time savings, bad experiences with agencies, and the increased knowledge and understanding of the market that comes from working on advertising and promotion for the product or service

EXHIBIT 3–7

Benetton uses an in-house agency to create its advertising

day by day are also reasons. Companies also keep their advertising in-house to maintain tight control over the process and more easily coordinate promotions with the firm's overall marketing program. Some companies use an in-house agency simply because they believe they can do a better job than an outside agency could.[6]

Opponents of the in-house system say they cannot give the advertiser the experience and objectivity of an outside agency, nor the range of services. They argue that outside agencies have more highly skilled specialists and attract the best creative talent, and that using an external firm gives a company a more varied perspective on its advertising problems as well as greater flexibility. In-house personnel may become narrow or grow stale while working on the same product line, but outside agencies may have different people with a variety of backgrounds and ideas working on the account. Flexibility is greater because an outside agency can be more easily dismissed if the company is not satisfied, whereas changes in an in-house agency could be slower and more disruptive.

The cost savings of an in-house agency must be evaluated against these considerations. For many companies, high-quality advertising is critical to their marketing success and should be the major criterion in determining whether to use in-house services. Companies like L. A. Gear and Redken Laboratories have moved their in-house work to outside agencies in recent years. Redken cited the need for a "fresh look" and objectivity as the reasons, noting that management gets too close to the product to come up with different creative ideas.[7]

The ultimate decision as to which advertising organization to use depends on which arrangement works best for the company. The advantages and disadvantages of each system are summarized in Exhibit 3–8. We now turn our attention to the functions of outside agencies and their roles in the promotional process.

@ **EXHIBIT 3–8**

Comparison of advertising organization systems

Organizational System	Advantages	Disadvantages
Centralized	• Facilitated communications • Fewer personnel required • Continuity in staff • Allows for more top-management involvement	• Less involvement with and understanding of overall marketing goals • Longer response time • Inability to handle multiple product lines
Decentralized	• Concentrated managerial attention • Rapid response to problems and opportunities • Increased flexibility	• Ineffective decision making • Internal conflicts • Misallocation of funds • Lack of authority
In-house agencies	• Cost savings • More control • Increased coordination	• Less experience • Less objectivity • Less flexibility

@ **ADVERTISING AGENCIES**

Many major companies use an advertising agency to assist them in developing, preparing, and executing their promotional programs. An ad agency is a service organization that specializes in planning and executing advertising programs for its clients. Over 7,000 agencies are listed in the *Standard Directory of Advertising Agencies;* however, the majority of these companies are individually owned small businesses employing fewer than five people. The U.S. advertising agency business is highly concentrated. Nearly half of the domestic **billings** (the amount of client money agencies spend on media purchases and other equivalent activities) are handled by the top 500 agencies. In fact, just 10 U.S. agencies handle nearly one-third of the total volume of business done by the top 500 agencies in the United States. The top agencies also have foreign operations that generate substantial billings and income. The top 25 agencies, ranked by their U.S. gross income, are shown in Exhibit 3–9. The exhibit shows that the advertising business is also geographically concentrated, with 17 of the top 25 agencies headquartered in New York City.

During the latter half of the 1980s, the advertising industry became even more concentrated as large agencies merged with or acquired other agencies and support organizations to form large advertising organizations, or **superagencies.** These superagencies were formed so that agencies could provide clients with integrated marketing communication services worldwide. Exhibit 3–10 on page 72 lists the 10 top agencies worldwide. However, recently many advertisers have become disenchanted with the superagencies and moved to smaller agencies that are more flexible and responsive. IMC Perspective 3–1 on page 74 discusses how this trend is reshaping the advertising industry.

The Role of the Advertising Agency

The functions performed by advertising agencies might be conducted by the clients themselves through one of the designs discussed earlier in this chapter, but most large companies use outside firms. This section discusses some reasons advertisers use external agencies.

Reasons for using an agency

Probably the main reason outside agencies are used is that they provide the client with the services of highly skilled individuals who are specialists in their chosen fields. An advertising agency staff may include artists, writers, media analysts, researchers, and others with specific skills, knowledge, and experience who can help market the client's prod-

@ EXHIBIT 3–9

Top 25 agencies ranked by U.S. gross income (in millions)

Rank 1993	Agency, Headquarters	U.S. Gross Income 1993	U.S. Billings 1993
1	Leo Burnett Co., Chicago	$304.8	$2,106.4
2	J. Walter Thompson Co., New York	291.6	2,052.0
3	Grey Advertising, New York	282.7	1,885.7
4	McCann-Erickson Worldwide, New York	245.2	1,635.6
5	DDB Needham Worldwide, New York	231.4	1,909.7
6	BBDO Worldwide, New York	229.7	1,813.9
7	Saatchi & Saatchi Advertising, New York	227.3	1,818.0
8	Foote, Cone & Belding Communications, Chicago	221.8	2,611.2
9	D'Arcy Masius Benton & Bowles, New York	197.0	2,061.4
10	Young & Rubicam, New York	173.3	1,764.1
11	Lintas Worldwide, New York	166.3	1,109.1
12	Ogily & Mather Worldwide, New York	163.1	1,620.0
13	Bozell Worldwide, New York	123.9	1,070.0
14	Backer Spielvogel Bates Worldwide, New York	119.6	975.0
15	CME KHBB, Minneapolis	117.1	937.0
16	Chiat/Day, Venice, Calif.	102.5	788.5
17	Wells Rich Greene BDDP, New York	96.8	882.6
18	TMP Worldwide, New York	85.7	571.4
19	NW Ayer, New York	83.7	781.0
20	Ross Roy Communications, Bloomfield Hills, Mich.	81.0	540.0
21	Gage Marketing Group, Minneapolis	78.8	525.4
22	Ketchum Communications, Pittsburgh	75.6	629.7
23	Lowe & Partners/SMS, New York	70.0	500.2
24	Wunderman Cato Johnson Worldwide, New York	68.6	536.6
25	Hal Riney & Partners, San Francisco	53.125	425.0

Source: *Advertising Age*, April 13, 1994, p. 16.

ucts or services. Many agencies specialize in a particular type of business—for example, business-to-business advertising—and use their knowledge of the industry to assist their clients.

An outside agency can also provide an objective viewpoint of the market and its business that is not subject to internal company policies, biases, or other limitations. The agency can also draw on the broad range of experience it has gained while working on a diverse set of marketing problems for various clients. For example, an advertising agency that is handling a travel-related account may have individuals who have worked with airlines, cruise ship companies, travel agencies, hotels, and other travel-related industries, or the agency may have worked in this area. Sometimes the agency previously worked on the advertising account of the client's competitors. Thus, the agency can provide the client with insight into the industry (and in some cases, the competition).

Types of Advertising Agencies

Since ad agencies can range in size from a one- or two-person operation to large organizations with over 1,000 employees, the services offered and functions performed will vary. In this section, we examine the different types of agencies, the services they perform for their clients, and how they are organized.

Full-service agencies

Many companies employ what is known as a **full-service agency,** which offers its clients a full range of marketing, communications, and promotions services, including planning, creating, and producing the advertising, performing research, and selecting media. A full-service agency may also offer nonadvertising services such as strategic market planning; production of sales promotions, sales training, and trade show materials; package design; and public relations and publicity.

EXHIBIT 3-10 World's top 10 advertising organizations

Rank 1993	Advertising Organization, Headquarters	U.S.-Based Agencies Included	Worldwide Gross Income 1993 (in millions)
1	WPP Group, London	Ogilvy & Mather Worldwide; J. Walter Thompson Co.	$2,633.6
2	Interpublic Group of Cos., New York	Lintas Worldwide; Lowe Group; McCann-Erickson Worldwide	2,078.5
3	Omnicom Group, New York	BBDO Worldwide; DDB Needham Worldwide; other units: TBWA Advertising; Alcone Sims O'Brien; Atschiller Reitzfeld	1,876.0
4	Dentsu Inc., Tokyo	Dentsu Corp. of America	1,403.2
5	Saatchi & Saatchi Co., London/New York	Saatchi & Saatchi Advertising Backer Spielvogel Bates Worldwide; CME KHBB	1,355.1
6	Young & Rubicam, New York	Young & Rubicam; Chapman Direct; CMF&Z; Muldoon Agency; Sive/Young & Rubicam;	1,008.9
7	Euro RSCG Worldwide, Neuilly, France	Robert A. Becker Inc.; Cohn & Wells; Hadley Group; Messner Vetere Berger; McNamee Schmetterer; Tatham Euro RSCG	864.8
8	Grey Advertising, New York	Grey Advertising Beaumont Bennett Group, Font & Vaamonde, Grey Direct Marketing Group	765.7
9	Hakuhodo Inc., Tokyo	Hakuhodo Advertising America	667.8
10	Foote, Cone & Belding Communications, Chicago	Foote, Cone & Belding Communications; FCB Direct; Borders, Perrin & Norrander; IMPACT; Vicom/FCB	633.7

Source: *Advertising Age,* April 13, 1994, p. 12.

The full-service agency is made up of departments that provide the activities needed to perform the various advertising functions and serve the client, as shown in Exhibit 3–11.

Account services

Account services, or account management, is the link between the advertising agency and its clients. Depending on the size of the client and its advertising budget, one or more account executives serve as liaison. The **account executive** is responsible for understanding the advertiser's marketing and promotions needs and interpreting them to agency personnel. He or she coordinates agency efforts in planning, creating, and producing ads. The account executive also presents agency recommendations and obtains client approval.

As the focal point of agency–client relationships, the account executive must know a great deal about the client's business and be able to communicate this to specialists in the agency working on the account. The ideal account executive has a strong marketing background as well as a thorough understanding of all phases of the advertising process.

Marketing services

Over the past two decades, use of marketing services has increased dramatically. One service gaining increased attention is research, as agencies realize that to do an effective job of communicating with their clients' customers, they must have a good understanding of the target audience. As shown in Chapter 1, the advertising planning process begins with a thorough situation analysis, which is based on research and information about the target audience.

Most full-service agencies maintain a *research department* whose function is to gather, analyze, and interpret information that will be useful in developing advertising for their clients. This can be done through primary research—where a study is designed, executed, and interpreted by the research department—or through the use of secondary

@ **EXHIBIT 3–11** Full-service agency organizational chart

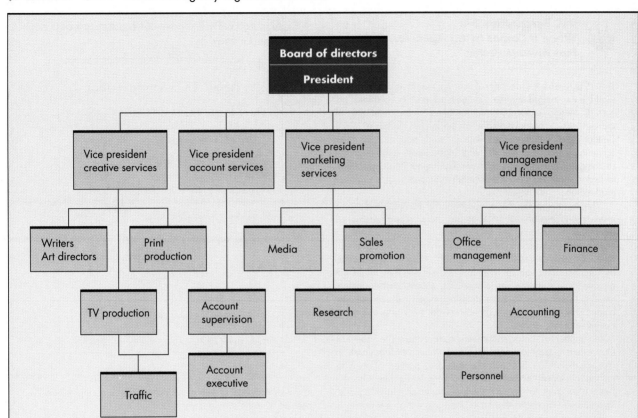

sources of information previously published. Sometimes the research department may acquire studies conducted by independent syndicated research firms or consultants. The research staff then interprets these reports and passes on the information to other agency personnel working on that account.

The research department may also design and conduct research to pretest the effectiveness of advertising the agency is considering. For example, copy testing is often conducted to determine how messages developed by the creative specialists are likely to be interpreted by the receiving audience.

The *media department* of an agency analyzes, selects, and contracts for space or time in the media that will be used to deliver the client's advertising message. The media department is expected to develop a media plan that will reach the target market and effectively communicate the message. Since most of the client's ad budget is spent on media time and/or space, this department must develop a plan that both communicates with the right audience and is cost effective.

Media specialists must know what audience the media reach, their rates, and how well they match the client's target market. Media departments review information on demographics, magazine and newspaper readership, radio listenership, and consumers' TV viewing patterns to develop an effective media plan. The media buyer implements the media plan by purchasing the actual time and space.

The media department is becoming an increasingly important part of the agency business as many large advertisers consolidate their media buying with one or a few agencies to save money and improve media efficiency. For example, General Motors recently consolidated its nearly $1 billion media buying assignment at two agencies.[8] An agency's strategic ability to negotiate prices and effectively use the vast array of media vehicles available is becoming as important as its ability to create ads.

IMC Perspective 3-1
When It Comes to Ad Agencies, Big Is Not Always Better

The 1980s was the decade of merger mania in the business world as a record number of mergers and acquisitions occurred. Merger mania was not confined to the client side of the advertising business; many of the largest agencies in the United States either merged with or were acquired by other agencies. The rule of the 80s was "consolidate and integrate" as mergers created mega-agencies that touted their capabilities to better serve the megacorporations competing in the global marketplace.

The creation of the large superagencies has received mixed reactions. Not everyone believes big companies need big ad agencies. In the past few years, more and more advertisers have seen little reason to one-stop shop. Many small to mid-size agencies have seized this opportunity to pursue large accounts by offering them special attention and service that might not be available from the mega-agencies. Many companies feel the big agencies have been devising expensive cookie-cutter campaigns that rely too much on network television and other commissionable media.

A number of major advertisers have done more than talk about their dissatisfaction with big, bureaucratic agencies. In the fall of 1993, IBM switched the U.S. portion of its $55 million personal computer account from Interpublic Group's Lintas:New York to the tiny Merkley Newman Harty agency. Two mid-size agencies that have been acquiring new accounts and expanding rapidly are Messner Vetere Berger McNamee Schmetterer/Euro RSCG and Ammirati & Puris. Besides having the most muddled name in the agency business, Messner Vetere is viewed as the model of the modern agency: lean and fast. Its clients include Volvo, Nasdaq, Stouffer's frozen foods and MCI—mostly scrappy underdogs in highly competitive markets.

Ammirati & Puris clients include Compaq Computer, RCA, and MasterCard. For its Aetna Life Insurance account, the agency took a somewhat radical approach. It advised its client *not* to spend more money. The agency eliminated the company's folksy slogan, "Aetna, I'm glad I met ya!" and added TV commercials with stark black-and-white messages and voice overs discussing issues like drunken driving, AIDS, and drug abuse. Aetna's consumer surveys show that awareness of its advertising is up 29 percent since the campaign began. The agency has positioned MasterCard with a new tag line: MasterCard. It's more than a credit card. It's smart money.™ This theme focuses on the credit card's extensive utility as a payment tool rather than on grand aspirations and acquisitions. Over the past year, MasterCard has been the fastest growing credit card

Ammirati & Puris repositions MasterCard as "smart money"

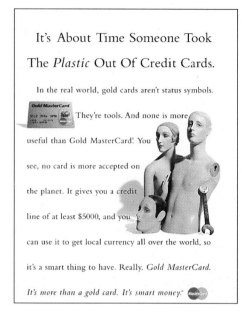

in the United States, with gross dollar volume up more than 23 percent over the previous year.

Large agencies are finding that they must delayer their management structure and unbundle their services to compete against the smaller agencies that cost less, work faster, and adapt to the broad needs of their clients. One example of this was DDB Needham's decision to spin off creative star Andy Berlin into his own agency to keep its $40 million Volkswagen of America's account from driving away.

Of course, not all large agencies are in trouble. BBDO, the world's fifth-largest agency, still delivers the most imaginative ads most consistently for clients such as Pepsi, Gillette, General Electric, DuPont, and Chrysler. Leo Burnett has a reputation for overservicing its accounts, which may be one reason half of its clients have stayed with the agency for at least 20 years. However, many large agencies lose sight of the fact that they operate primarily to serve their clients. When they do, there may be a smaller agency waiting to step in and take away the business.

Sources: Patricia Sellers, "Do You Need Your Ad Agency?" *Fortune,* Nov. 15, 1993, pp. 147–58; Kevin Goldman, "IBM Awards PC Account to Tiny Merkley," *The Wall Street Journal,* Oct. 22, 1993, p. B4.

The research and media departments perform most of the functions that full-service agencies need to plan and execute their client's advertising programs. Some agencies offer additional marketing services to their clients to assist in other promotional areas. An agency may have a sales promotion department, or merchandising department, that specializes in developing contests, premiums, promotions, point–of–sale materials, and other sales materials. It may have direct-marketing specialists and package designers, as well as a public relations/publicity department. The growing popularity of integrated

◉ EXHIBIT 3-12

CKS Partners offers its clients more than just advertising

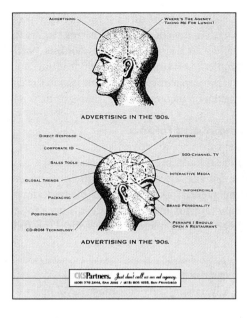

marketing communications has prompted many full-function agencies to develop capabilities and offer services in these other promotional areas. Exhibit 3–12 shows how CKS Partners promotes its ability to do more than just advertising.

Creative services

The creative services department is responsible for the creation and execution of the advertisements. The individuals who conceive the ideas for the ads and write the headlines, subheads, and body copy (the words constituting the message) are known as **copywriters.** Copywriters may also be involved in determining the basic appeal or theme of the ad campaign and often prepare a rough initial visual layout of the print ad or television commercial.

While copywriters are responsible for what the communication message says, the *art department* is responsible for how the ad looks. For print ads, the art director and graphics designers prepare *layouts*, which are drawings that show what the ad will look like and from which the final artwork will be produced. For TV commercials, the layout is known as a *storyboard*, a sequence of frames or panels that depict the commercial in still form.

Members of the creative department work together to develop ads that will communicate the key points determined to be the basis of the creative strategy for the client's product or service. Writers and artists generally work under the direction of the agency's creative director, who oversees all the advertising produced by the organization. The director sets the creative philosophy of the department and may even become directly involved in creating ads for the agency's largest clients.

Once the copy, layout, illustrations, and mechanical specifications of the advertisement have been completed and approved, the ad is turned over to the *production department*. Most agencies do not actually produce finished ads; they hire printers, engravers, photographers, typographers, and other suppliers to complete the finished product. For broadcast production, the approved storyboard must be turned into a finished commercial. The production department may supervise the casting of people to appear in the ad and the setting for the scenes as well as choosing an independent production studio. The department may hire an outside director to turn the creative idea or concept into a commercial. For example, Nike has used film director Spike Lee to direct a number of its commercials. Copywriters, art directors, account managers, people from research and planning, and representatives from the client side may all participate in production decisions, particularly when large sums of money are involved.

Creating an advertisement often involves many people and takes several months. In large agencies with many clients, coordinating the creative and production processes can be a major problem. A *traffic department* coordinates all phases of production to see that the ads are completed on time and that all deadlines for submitting the ads to the media are met. The traffic department may be located in the creative services area of the agency, or be part of media or account management, or be separate.

Management and finance

Like any other business, an advertising agency must be managed, and must perform basic operating and administrative functions such as accounting, finance, and human resources. It must also attempt to generate new business. A large agency employs administrative, managerial, and clerical people to perform these functions. The bulk of an agency's income (approximately 64 percent) goes to salary and benefits for its employees. Thus, an agency must manage its personnel carefully and get maximum productivity from them.

Agency organization and structure

Full-function advertising agencies must develop an organizational structure that will meet the needs of their clients and serve the agency's own internal requirements. Most medium-size and large agencies are structured under either a departmental or a group system. Under the **departmental system**, each of the agency functions shown in Exhibit 3–11 is set up as a separate department and is called on as needed to perform its specialty and serve all of the agency's clients. Ad layout, writing, and production are done by the creative department, while marketing services is responsible for any research or media selection and purchases, and the account services department handles the client contact. Some agencies prefer the departmental system because it gives employees the opportunity to become involved with, and develop expertise in servicing, a variety of accounts.

Many large agencies use the **group system,** in which individuals from each department work together in groups to service particular accounts. Each group is headed by an account executive or supervisor and has one or more media people, including media planners and buyers; a creative team, which includes copywriters, art directors, artists, and production personnel; and one or more account executives. The group may also include individuals from other departments such as marketing research, direct marketing, or sales promotion. The size and composition of the group varies depending on the client's billings and the importance of the account to the agency. For very important accounts, the group members may be assigned exclusively to one client. In some agencies, they may serve a number of smaller clients. Many agencies prefer the group system because employees become very knowledgeable about the client's business and it ensures continuity in servicing the account.

Other Types of Agencies and Services

Not every agency is a large full-service agency. Many smaller agencies expect their employees to handle a variety of jobs. For example, account executives may do their own research, work out their own media schedule, and coordinate the production of ads written and designed by the creative department.

Many advertisers, including some large companies, are not interested in paying for the services of a full-service agency but are interested in some of the specific services agencies have to offer. Over the past few decades, several alternatives to full-service agencies have evolved, including creative boutiques and media buying services.

Creative boutiques

A **creative boutique** is an agency that provides only creative services. These specialists have developed in response to some clients' desires to utilize only the creative talent of an outside provider while maintaining the other functions internally. The client may seek outside creative talent because it believes an extra creative effort is required or because its own employees do not have sufficient skills in this regard. Full-service agencies often

EXHIBIT   3-13

Western International Media is the leading independent media buying service

subcontract work to creative boutiques when they are very busy or want to avoid adding full-time employees to their payroll. Creative boutiques are usually founded by members of the creative departments of full-service agencies who leave the firm and take with them clients who want to retain their creative talents. These boutiques usually perform the creative function on a fee basis.

Media buying services

Media buying services are independent companies that specialize in the buying of media, particularly radio and television time. The task of purchasing advertising media has grown more complex, owing to the proliferation of specialized media, so media buying services have found a niche by specializing in the analysis and purchase of advertising time and space. Both agencies and clients utilize their services, usually developing their own media strategies and using the buying service to execute them. Some media buying services do help advertisers plan their media strategy. Because media buying services purchase such large amounts of time and space, they receive large discounts and can save the small agency or client money on media purchases. Media buying services are paid a fee or commission for their work.

Media buying services have been experiencing strong growth in recent years as clients seek alternatives to full-service agency relationships. Many companies have been unbundling agency services and consolidating media buying to get more clout from their advertising budgets. A number of companies, including Nike, Bugle Boy, and Pennzoil, have switched some or all of their media buying from full-service agencies to independent media buyers.[9] Exhibit 3–13 shows an ad promoting the services of Western International Media, the leading independent media buying company in the United States.

AGENCY COMPENSATION

As you have seen, the type and amount of services an agency performs vary from one client to another. As a result, agencies use a variety of methods to receive compensation for their services. Agencies are typically compensated in three ways: through commissions, through some type of fee arrangement, or through percentage charges.

Commissions from Media

The traditional method of compensating agencies is through a **commission system,** where the agency receives a specified commission (usually 15 percent) from the media on any advertising time or space it purchases for its client. (For outdoor advertising,

@ **EXHIBIT 3–14**

Example of commission system payment

Media Bills Agency		Agency Bills Advertiser	
Costs for magazine space	$100,000	Costs for magazine space	$100,000
Less 15% commission	−15,000	Less 2% cash discount	−1,700
Cost of media space	85,000	Advertiser pays agency	98,300
Less 2% cash discount	−1,700		
Agency pays media	$ 83,300	Agency income	$ 15,000

the commission is $16\frac{2}{3}$ percent.) This system provides a simple method of determining payments, as shown in the following example.

Assume an agency prepares a full-page magazine ad and arranges to place the ad on the back cover of a magazine at a cost of $100,000. The agency places the order for the space and delivers the ad to the magazine. Once the ad is run, the magazine will bill the agency for $100,000, less the 15 percent ($15,000) commission. The media will also offer a 2 percent cash discount for early payment, which the agency may pass along to the client. The agency will bill the client $100,000 less the 2 percent cash discount on the net amount, or a total of $98,300, as shown in Exhibit 3–14. The $15,000 commission represents the agency's compensation for its services.

Appraisal of the commission system

Use of the commission system to compensate agencies has been the target of considerable controversy for many years. A major problem centers on whether the 15 percent commission represents equitable compensation for services performed. Two agencies may require the same amount of effort to create and produce an ad. However, one client may spend $200,000 in commissionable media, which results in $30,000 in agency income, while the other spends $2 million, generating $300,000 in commissions. Critics argue that the commission system encourages agencies to recommend high media expenditures to increase their commission level.

Another criticism of the commission system is that it ties agency compensation to media costs. In periods of media cost inflation, the agency is (according to the client) disproportionately rewarded. The commission system has also been criticized for encouraging agencies to ignore cost accounting systems to justify the expenses attributable to work on a particular account. Still others charge that this system tempts the agency to avoid noncommissionable media such as direct mail, sales promotions, or advertising specialties, unless they are requested by the client.

Defenders of the commission system argue that it is easy to administer and it keeps the emphasis in agency competition on nonprice factors such as the quality of the advertising developed. Proponents argue that agency services are proportional to the size of the commission, since more time and effort are devoted to the large accounts that generate high revenue for the agency. They also say the system is more flexible than it appears because agencies often perform other services for large clients at no extra charge, justifying such actions through the large commission they receive.

The commission system has become a heated topic among advertisers. Opponents of the system have been called traitors by their colleagues, who argue that their lack of support costs everyone in the agency business money and that their opposition is nothing more than a competitive strategy designed to gain accounts.[10] However, those in support of an alternative system contend that the old system is outdated and must be changed. The chairman of the Leo Burnett agency has spoken out against the commission system: "It's incenting us to do the wrong thing, to recommend network TV and national magazines when other forms of communication like direct marketing or public relations might do the job better."[11]

Many advertisers have gone to a **negotiated commission**. This commission structure can take the form of reduced percentage rates, variable commission rates, and commissions with minimum and maximum profit rates. Negotiated commissions are designed to consider the needs of the client as well as the amount of time and effort exerted by the agency, avoiding some of the problems inherent in the traditional system. It is estimated that only 40 percent of advertising agencies' income now comes from the fixed commission, with the balance coming from a mix of fees and other charges.[12]

Fee, Cost, and Incentive-Based Systems

Since many believe the standard 15 percent commission system is not equitable to all parties, many agencies and their clients have developed some type of fee arrangement or cost-plus agreements for agency compensation. Some are using incentive-based compensation, which is a combination of a commission and a fee system.

Fee arrangement

There are two basic types of fee arrangement systems. In the straight- or **fixed-fee method,** the agency charges a basic monthly fee for all of its services and credits to the client any media commissions earned. Agency and client agree on the specific work to be done and the amount the agency will be paid for it. In some situations, agencies are compensated through a **fee-commission combination,** in which the media commissions received by the agency are credited against the fee. If the commissions are less than the agreed-on fee, the client must make up the difference. If the agency does much work for the client in noncommissionable media, the fee may be charged over and above the commissions received.

Both types of fee arrangements require the agency to carefully assess its costs of serving the client for the specified period, or for the project, plus a desired profit margin. To avoid any later disagreement, a fee arrangement should specify exactly what services the agency is expected to perform for the client.

Cost-plus agreement

Under a **cost-plus system,** the client agrees to pay the agency a fee based on the costs of its work plus some agreed-on profit margin (often a percentage of total costs). This system requires the agency to keep detailed records of the costs it incurs in working on the client's account. Direct costs (personnel time and out-of-pocket expenses) plus an allocation for overhead and a markup for profits determine the amount the agency bills the client.

Fee agreements and cost-plus systems are commonly used in conjunction with a commission system. The fee-based system can be advantageous to both the client and the agency, depending on the size of the client, advertising budget, media used, and services required. Many clients prefer fee or cost-plus systems because they receive a detailed breakdown of where and how their advertising and promotion dollars are being spent. However, these arrangements can be difficult for the agency, as they require careful cost accounting and may be difficult to estimate when bidding for an advertiser's business. Agencies are also reluctant to let clients see their internal cost figures.

Incentive-based compensation

Many clients these days are demanding more accountability from their agencies and tying agency compensation to performance through some type of **incentive-based system.** While there are many variations of this system, the basic idea is that the agency's ultimate compensation level will depend on how well it meets predetermined performance goals. These goals often include objective measures such as sales or market share as well as more subjective measures such as evaluations of the quality of the agency's creative work. Companies using incentive-based systems determine agency compensation through media commissions, fees, bonuses, or some combination of these methods. Some clients use a sliding scale whereby the agency's base compensation is less than the

EXHIBIT 3–15

The Calet, Hirsch & Ferrell Agency promotes its guaranteed idea program

There are 81 advertising agencies billing over $100,000,000. Only one of them is willing to guarantee its ideas.

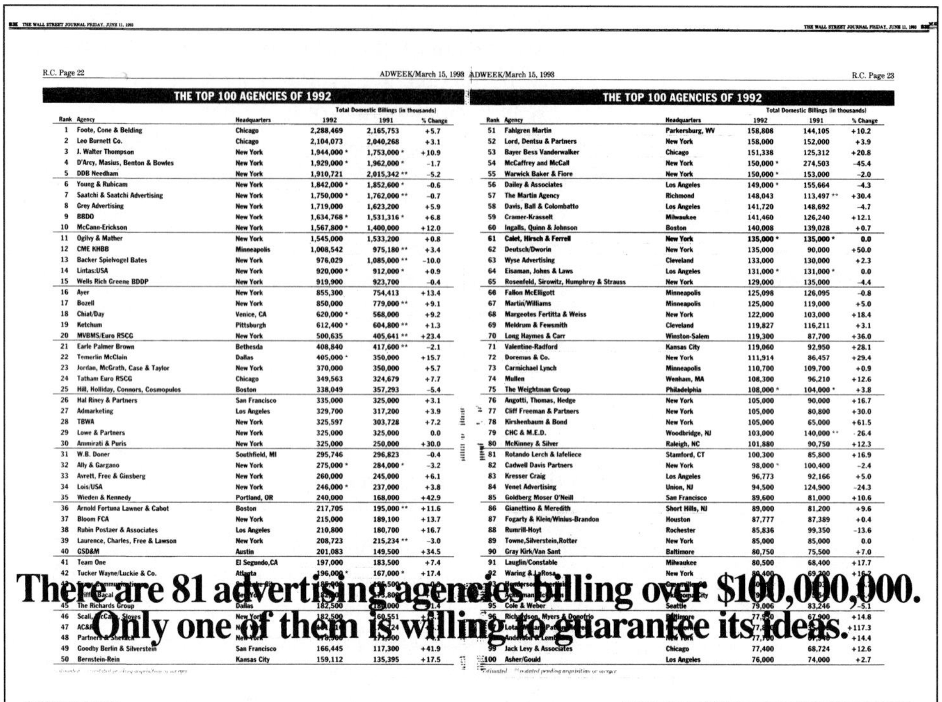

15 percent commission but it can earn extra commissions or bonuses depending on how it meets sales or other performance goals.

Recognizing the movement toward incentive-based systems, some agencies have offered to tie their compensation to performance. For example, in 1990 DDB Needham Worldwide announced a guaranteed results program: the agency receives a bonus in addition to the agreed-on compensation if its integrated marketing program improves the sales of the client's product. If sales do not improve, the agency rebates a substantial amount of its fee to the client.[13] Another agency that recently began tying agency compensation to a campaign's success is Calet, Hirsch & Ferrell.[14] Exhibit 3–15 shows an ad the agency ran promoting its guaranteed idea program.

Percentage Charges

Another way to compensate an agency is by adding a markup of **percentage charges** to various services the agency purchases from outside providers. These may include market research, artwork, printing, photography, and other services or materials. *Markup charges* usually range from 17.65 to 20 percent and are added to the client's overall bill. Since suppliers of these services do not allow the agency a commission, percentage charges cover administrative costs while allowing a reasonable profit for the agency's efforts. (A markup of 17.65 percent of costs added to the cost would yield a 15 percent commission. For example, research costs of $100,000 plus 17,650 times 17.65% equals $117,650. The $17,650 markup is approximately 15 percent of $117,650.)

The Future of Agency Compensation

As you can see, there is no one method of compensation to which everyone subscribes. Cost-conscious advertisers are rebelling against the traditional commission system. Less than a third of major advertisers pay full commission, and an increasing number prefer set fees or some type of incentive-based system.[15] As more companies adopt integrated marketing communications approaches, they are reducing their reliance on traditional media advertising and thus changing their compensation systems. Usually some combination of payment methods is agreed on.

Many companies are trying to reduce agency compensation, but most recognize that it is in their best interest that their account be profitable for the agency if they want quality work. Nestlé and Unilever, two of the world's largest consumer product marketers, recently revised their compensation policies to make sure that their agencies receive a reasonable profit and that they get the best results from their agencies.[16]

EVALUATING AGENCIES

Given the substantial amounts of monies being spent on advertising and promotion, demand for accountability of the expenditures has increased. Regular reviews of the agency's performance are necessary.

The agency evaluation process usually involves two types of assessments, one of which is financial and operational and the other more qualitative. The **financial audit** focuses on how the agency conducts its business. It is designed to verify costs and expenses, the number of personnel hours charged to an account, and payments to media and outside suppliers. The **qualitative audit** focuses on the agency's efforts in planning, developing, and implementing the client's advertising and promotions programs and considers the results achieved.

The agency evaluation is often done on a subjective, informal basis, particularly in smaller companies where ad budgets are low or advertising is not seen as the most critical factor in the firm's marketing performance. In some companies, formal systematic evaluation systems have been developed, particularly when budgets are large and the advertising function receives much emphasis. As advertising costs continue to rise, the top management of these companies wants to be sure money is being spent efficiently and effectively.

One example of a formal agency evaluation system is that used by Borden, Inc., which markets a variety of consumer products.[17] Borden's top executives meet twice a year with the company's various agencies to review their performances. Division presidents and other marketing executives complete the advertising agency performance evaluation, part of which is shown in Exhibit 3–16. These reports are compiled and reviewed with the agency at each semiannual meeting. Borden's evaluation process consists of three areas of performance. Agency performance in achieving market share goals accounts for 60 percent of the total score and creativity and cooperation each constitute 20 percent.

Borden has dropped agencies that have not scored well after two semiannual evaluations. Some companies doubt whether advertising effectiveness can be directly related to sales and have developed their own evaluation procedures. R. J. Reynolds emphasizes creative development and execution, marketing counsel and ideas, promotion support, and cost controls, without any mention of sales figures. Sears' approach focuses on the performance of the agency as a whole in an effort to establish a partnership between the agency and the client.

These and other evaluation methods are being used more regularly by advertisers. As fiscal controls tighten, clients will require more accountability from their provider and adopt formal evaluation procedures.

Gaining and Losing Clients

The evaluation process often results in outcomes that are not favorable to the agency. Although some companies keep the same agency for decades, long-term relationships are becoming less common. A 1992 study found that over a five-year period, the 50 largest agencies had lost 67 percent of their clients.[18] Exhibit 3–17 on page 83 shows some of the major account switching that has occurred recently.

There are a number of reasons clients switch agencies. Understanding these potential problems can help the agency avoid them.[19] In addition, it is important to understand the process agencies go through in trying to gain new clients.

Why agencies lose clients

Some of the more common reasons agencies lose clients follow:

- *Poor performance or service.*   The client becomes dissatisfied with the quality of the advertising and/or the service provided by the agency.

EXHIBIT 3-16 Borden's ad agency report card

	SECTION	PAGE
	12.00.0	15 of 22
	DATE ISSUED	DATE REVISED
	4/85	

Agency: _____
Product(s): _____

ACCOUNT REPRESENTATION AND SERVICE

	Excellent	Good	Average	Fair	Poor	Not Observed (Unknown)
1. Account Executives have *frequent personal contact* with product group.	( )	( )	( )	( )	( )	( )
2. Account persons act with *personal initiative*.	( )	( )	( )	( )	( )	( )
3. Account representatives *anticipate needs* in advance of direction by product group.	( )	( )	( )	( )	( )	( )
4. Account group *takes direction* well.	( )	( )	( )	( )	( )	( )
5. Agency readily *adapts to changes* in client's organization or needs.	( )	( )	( )	( )	( )	( )
6. Agency makes reasonable *recommendations* on allocation of budgets.	( )	( )	( )	( )	( )	( )
7. Account representatives function as *marketing advisors* rather than creative/media advisors only.	( )	( )	( )	( )	( )	( )
8. Account representatives *contribute effectively* to the development of new programs.	( )	( )	( )	( )	( )	( )
9. Account representatives respond to *client requests* in a timely fashion.	( )	( )	( )	( )	( )	( )
10. Agency recommendations are *founded on sound reasoning* and supported factually.	( )	( )	( )	( )	( )	( )
11. Account persons submit *alternative plans*, vs. a single plan/campaign/ad for brand review.	( )	( )	( )	( )	( )	( )
12. Account persons have a *firm point of view* and "sell" their recommendation.	( )	( )	( )	( )	( )	( )
13. Senior account management *is involved*, where appropriate.	( )	( )	( )	( )	( )	( )
14. Other areas not mentioned: _____	( )	( )	( )	( )	( )	( )
_____	( )	( )	( )	( )	( )	( )
_____	( )	( )	( )	( )	( )	( )

	Excellent	Good	Average	Fair	Poor
Overall evaluation of Account Representation and Service	( )	( )	( )	( )	( )

General Comments on Account Representation and Service: _____

	SECTION	PAGE
	12.00.0	16 of 22
	DATE ISSUED	DATE REVISED
	4/85	

Agency: _____
Product(s): _____

CREATIVE SERVICES

	Excellent	Good	Average	Fair	Poor	Not Observed (Unknown)
1. Agency produces *fresh ideas* and original approaches.	( )	( )	( )	( )	( )	( )
2. Agency *accurately interprets* facts, strategies and objectives into usable advertisements and plans.	( )	( )	( )	( )	( )	( )
3. Creative group is *knowledgeable* about Consumer Products Division's products, markets and strategies.	( )	( )	( )	( )	( )	( )
4. Creative personnel are concerned with *good advertising communications* and develops campaigns/ads that exhibit this concern.	( )	( )	( )	( )	( )	( )
5. Creative group *produces on time*.	( )	( )	( )	( )	( )	( )
6. Creative team *performs well under pressure*.	( )	( )	( )	( )	( )	( )
7. Agency presentations are well organized with sufficient *examples of proposed executions*.	( )	( )	( )	( )	( )	( )
8. Creative team *participates* in major campaign presentations.	( )	( )	( )	( )	( )	( )
9. Agency presents *ideas and executions* not requested but felt to be good *opportunities*.	( )	( )	( )	( )	( )	( )
10. Overall *quality of agency's television* creative ideas and executions.	( )	( )	( )	( )	( )	( )
11. Overall *quality of agency's radio* creative ideas and executions.	( )	( )	( )	( )	( )	( )
12. Overall *quality of agency's print* creative ideas and executions.	( )	( )	( )	( )	( )	( )
13. Other ares not mentioned: _____	( )	( )	( )	( )	( )	( )
_____	( )	( )	( )	( )	( )	( )
_____	( )	( )	( )	( )	( )	( )

	Excellent	Good	Average	Fair	Poor
Overall evaluation of Creative Services:	( )	( )	( )	( )	( )

General Comments on Creative Services: _____

- *Poor communication.* The client and agency personnel fail to develop or maintain the level of communication necessary to sustain a favorable working relationship.
- *Unrealistic demands by the client.* The client places demands on the agency that exceed the amount of compensation received and reduce the account's profitability.
- *Personality conflicts.* Personnel working on the account on the client and agency sides do not have enough rapport to work well together.
- *Personnel changes.* A change in personnel at either the agency or the advertiser can create problems. New managers may wish to use an agency with whom they have established ties. Agency personnel often take accounts with them when they switch agencies or start their own.
- *Changes in size of the client or agency.* The client may outgrow the agency or decide it needs a larger agency to handle its business. If the agency gets too large, the client may represent too small a percentage of its business to command attention.
- *Conflicts of interest.* A conflict may develop when an agency merges with another agency or when a client is part of an acquisition or merger. In the United States, an agency cannot handle two accounts that are in direct competition with each other. In some cases, even indirect competition will not be tolerated. For example, Lintas lost its $60 million Noxell assignment when Procter & Gamble bought Noxell, because of Lintas's extensive work for P&G archrival Haileve.[20]

⊚ EXHIBIT 3-17 A rash of advertisers switch agencies

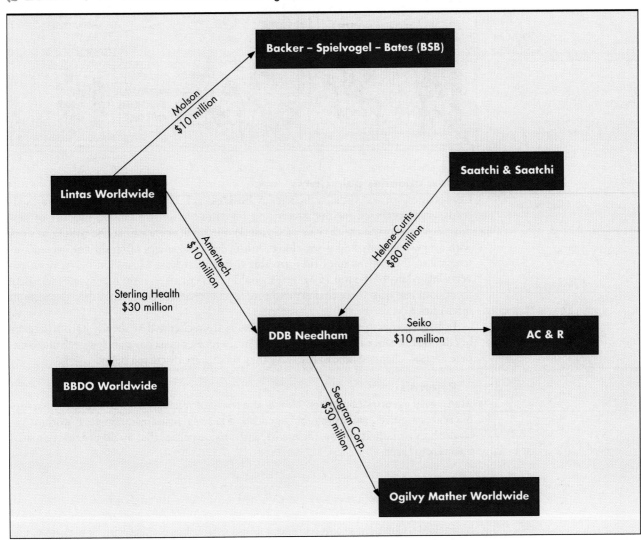

- *Changes in the client's marketing strategy.* A client may change its marketing strategy and think a new agency is needed to carry out the new program.
- *Declining sales.* When sales of the client's product or service are stagnant or declining, advertising may be seen as contributing to the problem. A new agency may be sought for a new approach.
- *Conflicting compensation philosophies.* Disagreement may develop over the level or method of compensation.
- *Changes in policies.* Policy changes may result when either party reevaluates the importance of the relationship, the agency acquires a new (and larger) client, or either side undergoes a merger or acquisition.

If the agency recognizes these warning signs, it can try to adapt its programs and policies to make sure the client is satisfied. Some of the situations discussed here are unavoidable, and others may be beyond the control of the agency. But to ensure maintenance of the account, those within the agency's control must be addressed.

The time may come when the agency decides it is no longer in its best interest to continue to work with the client. Personnel conflicts, changes in management philosophy, and/or insufficient financial incentives are just a few of the reasons for such a decision. Then the agency may terminate the account relationship.

How agencies gain clients

Competition for accounts in the agency business is intense, since most companies already have organized for the advertising function and only a limited number of new businesses require such services each year. While small agencies may be willing to work with a new company and grow along with it, larger agencies often do not become interested in these firms until they are able to spend at least $1 million per year on advertising. Many of the top 15 agencies wouldn't accept an account that spends less than $5 million per year. Once that expenditure level is reached, competition for the account intensifies.

In large agencies, most new business results from clients that already have an agency but decide to change their relationships. Thus, agencies must constantly search and compete for new clients. Some of the ways they do this are discussed below.

Referrals

Many good agencies obtain new clients as a result of referrals from existing clients, media representatives, and even other agencies. These agencies maintain good working relationships with their clients, the media, and outside parties that might provide potential business to them.

Solicitations

One of the more common ways to gain new business is through direct solicitation. In smaller agencies, the president may solicit new accounts. In most large agencies, a new business development group searches for and establishes contact with new clients. The group is responsible for writing solicitation letters, making cold calls, and following up on leads.

Presentations

A basic goal of the new business development group is to receive an invitation from a company to make a presentation. This gives the agency the opportunity to present information about itself, including its experience, personnel, capabilities, and operating procedures, as well as to demonstrate its previous work.

The agency may be asked to make a speculative presentation, in which it examines the client's marketing situation and proposes a tentative communications campaign. Because presentations require a great deal of time and preparation and may cost the agency a considerable amount of money without a guarantee of gaining the business, many firms refuse to participate in "creative shootouts." They argue that agencies should be selected based on their experience and the services and programs they have provided for previous clients.[21] Nevertheless, most agencies do participate in this form of solicitation, either by choice or because they must do so to gain accounts.

Due in part to the emphasis placed on speculative presentations, a very important role has developed for *presentation consultants*, who specialize in helping clients choose ad agencies. Because their opinions are respected by clients, the entire agency review process may be structured according to their guidelines. As you might imagine, these consultants wield a great deal of power and are respected by both clients and agencies.

@ **EXHIBIT 3–18**

Agencies often advertise themselves to gain new business

SOME HOME RUNS CLEAR THE BENCHES, OURS CLEAR THE SHELVES. From a pin drop heard round the world for Sprint® to six words that taught consumers to butter their bread with Philly® instead. From the Few, the Proud, the Marines to a question asked by our consumer research that helped make Ford Escort the best-selling small car and Ford Taurus the best-selling wagon in the U.S.A. From candid testimonials that helped Jenny Craig® grow from 200,000 clients to over a million to a slogan that became a battle cry, "Nupe It.™" We hit home runs-we're J.Walter Thompson. Winning 50 EFFIES for effective advertising, 1987-1991. More EFFIES, for more clients, than any other agency. Need a home run? Call Ron Burns or Jim Patterson at (212) 210-7000. Give us the chance to go to bat for you.

JWT
NORTH AMERICA

Public relations

Agencies also seek business through publicity/public relations efforts. They often participate in civic and social groups and work with charitable organizations pro bono (at cost, without pay) to earn respect in the community. Participation in professional associations such as the American Association of Advertising Agencies, and the Advertising Research Foundation can also lead to new contacts. Successful agencies often receive free publicity throughout the industry as well as in the mass media.

Image and reputation

Perhaps the most effective way an agency can gain new business is through its reputation. Agencies that consistently develop excellent campaigns acquire favorable reputations and are often approached by clients. Agencies may enter their work in award competitions or advertise themselves to enhance their image in the marketing community (see Exhibit 3–18).

Global Perspective 3–1
Integrated Marketing Communications North of the Border

If you ask most people who the United States' largest trading partner is, they are likely to name a European country or Japan. But Canada has been our largest trading partner for years, and the Canadian market takes on even more importance with the passage of the North American Free Trade Agreement (NAFTA), which eliminates many of the trade barriers among the United States, Canada, and Mexico. More and more U.S. companies are adopting the concept of integrated marketing communications, and many want to approach the Canadian market the same way.

Companies hoping to use IMC in Canada will find that our northern neighbor has all of the services, technologies, and message delivery systems needed to fully utilize this approach. Virtually every major U.S. ad agency has offices or affiliations in Canada. There are a number of excellent Canadian agencies throughout the country, which are particularly important in adapting IMC to the specialized needs of French Canada.

Direct marketing is becoming an integral part of successful IMC programs in Canada. Some direct marketers knowledgeable about trends on both sides of the border claim Canadians are not bombarded with as much direct mail as Americans. With less clutter in their mailboxes, Canadians respond better to mail solicitations. A number of companies, among them CMAC, R. L. Polk, Compusearch, and Tetrad, provide special software and databases to target those of the Canada Post Corp.'s 25,000-plus mail walks that match a marketer's customer profile. There are also plenty of good mailing lists available. Much of the software used in the United States to support marketing databases can be used in Canada. Several U.S.-based database marketing companies have established a strong presence in Canada, and there are numerous Canadian direct marketing agencies.

A trend that is sweeping the Canadian market is the unbundling of media buying services; 60 percent of media planning and buying is assigned to an agency other than the one handling the creative end. Independent media buying services hold only about 6 percent of the U.S. media marketplace. Canada offers broadcast and print media measurement services that closely resemble those used in the United States. For example, A. C. Nielsen and the Bureau of Broadcast Measurement in Toronto provide meter and diary results to subscribers for most broadcast programming, including U.S. stations that reach Canadians.

For companies seeking information on the Canadian market, there are a number of professional survey research companies throughout Canada. Larger companies like Gallup of Canada and Market Facts of Canada offer syndicated tracking surveys

HOW TO SAY
CLOUT
IN FRENCH

PNMD/PUBLITEL, Québec partners of BBDO Worldwide, in a market that's distinctly different from any other in North America. From banking to beer, our passion for advertising and powerful regional expertise, coupled with an international outlook, creates breakthrough campaigns that ultimately change behavior, not just perceptions. In Québec, that's French for clout.

PNMD/PUBLITEL
A member of BBDO Worldwide

For information, please call Raymond Boucher, President, at (514) 939-4100
Fax: (514) 939-4006

similar to their U.S. counterparts. Canada's census bureau is also an excellent source of information. The bureau's Statistics Canada's *Survey of Family Expenditures* provides a wealth of detail on virtually all classes of consumer purchases across 17 metropolitan areas in Canada.

Canada has many demographic, cultural, and lifestyle diversities that must be recognized. Its 27.3 million people live in about 10 million households, and nearly 70 percent are within a two-hour drive to the U.S. border. About 40 percent of the Canadian population doesn't use English as its preferred language. Of the non-English speakers, about 60 percent are French Canadians, with the balance spread among a dozen or so other languages. Like the United States, Canada has seen the ethnic composition of its immigrants change over the past decade. More than half of the country's immigrants come from Asia and only about one-quarter from Europe. Many of the country's Asian immigrants are quite wealthy and are settling in either Vancouver or Toronto.

U.S. marketers cannot simply transplant their IMC strategy north of the border. However, companies doing business in Canada will find all the resources and services they need for customer-focused IMC.

Sources: Dan Huck and Martin Dunphy, "Adapting IMC to Canada Requires a Custom Fit," *Marketing News*, Aug. 16, 1993, p. 2; Laurie Freeman, "Media Unbundling Gains Big Momentum in Canada Market; U.S. Is on Notice," *Advertising Age*, Aug. 23, 1993, p. 8.

SPECIALIZED SERVICES

Many companies assign the development and implementation of their promotional programs to an advertising agency. But several other types of organizations provide specialized services that complement the efforts of ad agencies. Direct-response agencies, sales promotion agencies, and public relations firms are important to marketers in developing and executing integrated marketing communications programs in the United States as well as international markets. Global Perspective 3–1 discusses specialized services for companies that want to adapt their integrated marketing communications to the Canadian marketplace. Let us examine the functions these organizations perform.

EXHIBIT 3–19

Top 10 direct-response
agencies by U.S. volume

Rank 1992	Rank 1991	Agency, Headquarters	U.S. Direct Response 1992
1	1	Ogilvy & Mather Direct, New York	$390.0
2	3	Wunderman Cato Johnson, New York	330.8
3	4	Bronner Slosberg Humphrey, Boston	301.0
4	2	Rapp Collins Marcoa, New York	297.2
5	6	Lintas: Marketing Communications, Warren, Mich.	266.5
6	5	FCB Direct/U.S., Chicago	198.8
7	7	Kobs & Draft Worldwide, Chicago	174.2
8	8	DIMACDirect, Bridgeton, Mo.	163.5
9	13	Chapman Direct Advertising, New York	153.3
10	10	Barry Blau & Partners, Fairfield, Conn.	151.4

Source: *Advertising Age*, July 12, 1993, p. S-1.

**Direct-Response
Agencies**

One of the fastest-growing areas in IMC promotions is direct marketing, where companies communicate with consumers through telemarketing, direct mail, and other forms of direct-response advertising. As this industry has grown, numerous direct-response agencies have evolved that offer companies their specialized skills in both the consumer and business markets. Exhibit 3–19 shows the top 10 direct-response agencies (several of which, including Ogilvy & Mather Direct, Lintas: Marketing Communications, and FCB Direct, are divisions or subsidiaries of large ad agencies).

Direct response agencies provide a variety of services, including database management, direct mail, research, media services, and creative and production capabilities. While direct mail is their primary weapon, many direct-response agencies are expanding their services to include such areas as production of infomercials and database management. Database development and management is becoming one of the most important services provided by direct-response agencies. Many companies are using database marketing to pinpoint new customers and build relationships and loyalty among existing customers.[22]

A typical direct-response agency is divided into three main departments: account management, creative, and media. Some agencies also have a department whose function is to develop and manage databases for their clients. The account managers work with their clients to plan direct marketing programs and determine their role in the overall integrated marketing communications process. The creative department consists of copywriters, artists, and producers. Creative is responsible for developing the direct-response message, while the media department is concerned with its placement.

Like advertising agencies, direct-response agencies must solicit new business and have their performance reviewed by their existing clients, often through formal assessment programs. Most direct-response agencies are compensated on a fee basis, although some large advertisers still prefer the commission system.

**Sales Promotion
Agencies**

Developing and managing sales promotion programs such as contests, sweepstakes, refunds and rebates, premium and incentive offers, and sampling programs is a very complex task. Most companies use a **sales promotion agency** to develop and administer these programs. Some large ad agencies have created their own sales promotion department or acquired a sales promotion firm. However, most sales promotion agencies are independent companies that specialize in providing the services needed to plan, develop, and execute a variety of sales promotion programs (Exhibit 3–20).

Sales promotion agencies often work in conjunction with the client's advertising and/or direct-response agencies to coordinate their efforts with the advertising and direct marketing programs. Services provided by large sales promotion agencies include promotional planning, creative, research, tie-in coordination, fulfillment, premium design and manufacturing, catalog production, and contest/sweepstakes management. Many sales promotion agencies are also developing direct/database marketing and

 **EXHIBIT 3–20**

Advertising promoting a sales promotion agency

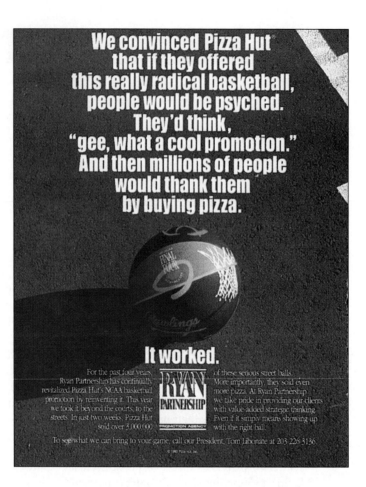

telemarketing to expand their integrated marketing services capabilities. Sales promotion agencies are generally compensated under a fee arrangement.

Public Relations Firms

Many large companies use both an advertising agency and a PR firm. The **public relations firm** develops and implements programs to manage the organization's publicity, image, and affairs with consumers and other relevant publics, including employees, suppliers, stockholders, government, labor groups, citizen action groups, and the general public. The job of the public relations firm is to analyze the relationships between the client and these various publics, determine how the client's policies and actions relate to and affect these publics, develop PR strategies and programs, implement these programs using various public relations tools, and evaluate their effectiveness.

The activities of a public relations firm include planning the PR strategy and program, generating publicity, conducting lobbying and public affairs efforts, becoming involved in community activities and events, preparing news releases and other communication materials, conducting research, promoting and managing special events, and crisis management and communication. As companies adopt an integrated marketing communications approach to promotional planning, they are coordinating their public relations activities with advertising and other promotional areas. Many companies are integrating public relations and publicity into the marketing communications mix to increase message credibility and save media costs.[23] Public relations firms are generally compensated under some type of retainer arrangement. We will examine the role of PR firms in more detail in Chapter 19.

COLLATERAL SERVICES

The final participants in the promotional process are those that provide various collateral services. They include marketing research companies, package design firms, consultants, media buying services, photographers, printers, and video production houses.

Marketing Research Companies

One of the more widely used collateral service organizations is the marketing research firm. Companies are increasingly turning to marketing research to help them understand their target audiences and to gather information that will be of value in designing their advertising and promotions programs and evaluating these programs. While some advertisers have their own marketing research departments, many do not. Even companies with marketing research departments often hire outside research agencies to perform some services. Many research companies are used because they offer specialized services and can gather objective information that is valuable to the advertiser's promotional programs. They conduct *qualitative* research such as in-depth interviews and focus groups, as well as *quantitative* studies such as market surveys.

INTEGRATED MARKETING COMMUNICATION SERVICES

You have seen that marketers can choose from a variety of specialized organizations to assist them in planning, developing, and implementing an integrated marketing communications program. But companies must decide whether to use a different organization for each marketing communications function or consolidate them with a large advertising agency that offers all of these services under one roof.

As noted in Chapter 1, during the 1980s many of the large agencies realized that their clients were shifting their promotional dollars away from traditional advertising to other forms of promotion and began developing integrated marketing communication capabilities.[24] Some did this through mergers and acquisitions and became superagencies consisting of advertising, public relations, sales promotion, and direct-response agencies. Other agencies expanded their IMC capabilities. For example, Lintas:USA, in conjunction with the University of Chicago, developed an intensive training program to teach its employees how to handle communication tools ranging from Yellow Pages to telemarketing.[25] IMC Perspective 3–2 discusses how the Leo Burnett Agency became one of the leaders in integrated marketing communications without making any outside acquisitions.

Pros and Cons of Integrated Services

It has been argued that the concept of integrated marketing is nothing new, particularly in smaller companies and communication agencies that have been coordinating a variety of promotional tools for years. And larger advertising agencies have been trying to gain more of their clients' promotional business for over 20 years. However, in the past, the various services were run as separate profit centers. Each was motivated to push its own expertise and pursue its own goals rather than develop truly integrated marketing programs. Moreover, the creative specialists in many agencies resisted becoming involved in sales promotion or direct marketing. They preferred to concentrate on developing magazine ads or television commercials rather than designing coupons or direct mail pieces.

Proponents of the integrated marketing, or one-stop shop, services agency contend that past problems are being solved and the various individuals in the agencies and subsidiaries are learning to work together to deliver a consistent message to the client's customers. They argue that maintaining control of the entire promotional process achieves greater synergy among each of the communication program elements. They also note that it is more convenient for the client to coordinate all of its marketing efforts—media advertising, direct mail, special events, sales promotion, and public relations—through one agency. An agency with integrated marketing capabilities can create a single image for the product or service and address everyone, from the wholesaler to the consumer, with one voice.

Not everyone agrees with the idea of turning the entire integrated marketing communications program over to one agency, however. Opponents say the providers become involved in political wrangling over budgets, do not communicate with each other as well and as often as they should, and do not achieve synergy. They also claim that efforts by agencies to control all aspects of the promotional program are nothing more than an attempt to hold on to business that might otherwise be lost to independent providers. They note that synergy and economies of scale, while nice in theory, have been difficult to achieve, and competition and conflict among agency subsidiaries have been a major problem.[26]

Many companies, such as Miller Brewing and Reebok, use a variety of vendors for communication functions, choosing the specialist they believe is best suited for each

IMC Perspective 3–2
Integrated Marketing Communications the Leo Burnett Way

During the 1980s, many of the world's largest advertising agencies recognized that their clients were shifting more and more of their promotional budgets away from traditional media advertising to areas such as direct marketing, sales promotion, and event sponsorships. In response to this trend, big agencies such as Saatchi & Saatchi and Ogilvy & Mather began acquiring companies that were specialists in these areas rather than teaching their own people different skills. Many agencies turned the specialized firms they acquired into profit-centered departments or revenue-producing subsidiaries that often ended up battling one another for a piece of their client's promotional dollars. And while the agencies point to these specialists when touting their integrated marketing capabilities, there really is little emphasis on integrating the various communication functions.

One agency that has taken a different approach to IMC is the Chicago-based Leo Burnett agency. Like many of its competitors, the agency offers a variety of communication services including sales promotion, direct marketing, event marketing, public relations, and package design. But unlike most agencies, the agency does not have a division, a subsidiary, a group, or a compensation plan dedicated to generating revenue from these nonadvertising areas.

Leo Burnett first began developing integrated communication services in 1986 by hiring senior-level marketing specialists in a variety of disciplines whose job was to develop integrated strategic thinking and execution for the agency's clients in the U.S. and abroad. The push began when the agency hired Jerry Reitman, executive vice president of Ogilvy & Mather Direct, who immediately developed a direct mail capability, not for generating new business but to service existing accounts. After direct marketing came the development of sales promotion and event marketing services.

Over the past seven years, Leo Burnett has brought in nearly 100 direct marketing, sales promotion, event marketing, and public relations professionals and dispersed them throughout the agency (rather than isolating them in one group) to teach their disciplines and to learn about advertising. They are fully integrated with the agency's client services, creative, media, research, database, and production departments and have taught more than 700 staffers how to use the various promotional tools in their clients' campaigns.

The Leo Burnett philosophy is that no component of a campaign is more or less important than the others in terms of brand image. The agency's CEO, Richard Fizdale, says, "Every piece of communication that reaches a consumer has some image quotient. . . . Our mission is to put together marketing programs coordinated so that the brands they represent show exactly the same face to consumers in every form of media." Burnetters the world over are expected to interact with clients not as advertising specialists who happen to know about sales promotion, direct marketing, or public relations, but as strategic generalists able to work in a variety of disciplines and media without favoritism.

Leo Burnett has applied this philosophy successfully for 162 clients worldwide including United Airlines, Keebler's, McDonald's, Kellogg's, Marlboro, Miller beer, and Hallmark. Recently the agency added Reebok to its list of clients with ideas on how to blare its advertising messages through a variety of media formats.

When Leo Burnett first announced its plans to integrate, CEO Fizdale was asked by a senior manager how long it would take for everyone to "get it." His response was an advertising generation, which he views as about 10 years. While Leo Burnett may still have a few years to go before its integrated communication philosophy is fully understood, it is far ahead of agencies that haven't even begun the process.

Sources: "It's All Advertising," *PROMO* magazine, Oct. 1991, pp. 6, 7, 32, 50; Leo Burnett Integrated Marketing Communications fact sheet.

---

promotional task, such as advertising, sales promotion, or public relations. Many marketers agree with the vice president of advertising at Reebok, who noted, "Why should I limit myself to one resource when there is a tremendous pool of fresh ideas available?"[27]

Responsibility for IMC: Agency versus Client

Many advertisers prefer to orchestrate their own coordinated communication programs. Several surveys of leading advertisers found that while most companies support the concept of integrated marketing, company executives believe they are better suited than agencies to coordinate diversified communication programs. A 1993 survey of advertisers and agency executives conducted by *Advertising Age* found that both groups believe integrated marketing is important to their organization's success and that its importance will be even greater in five years.[28] However, marketers and agency executives have very different opinions regarding who should be in charge of the integrated marketing communications process.

As can be seen in Exhibit 3–21 on page 92, while most marketers believe it is their responsibility to set strategy for and coordinate integrated campaigns, the majority of agency executives see this as their domain. Moreover, while the agency executives consider themselves the architects of integrated marketing programs, the marketers see them as teammates or partners.

Two-thirds of the agency respondents thought their shops were structured to handle the various elements an integrated campaign requires, but less than half of the marketers,

IMC Perspective 3–2 concluded

The Leo Burnett Agency developed an integrated campaign for United Airlines lines that included print, direct mail, mail and television

and only 39 percent of large marketers, agreed. Exhibit 3–21 also shows factors that are perceived as barriers to successful integrated marketing campaigns. Marketing and agency executives agreed that the biggest obstacle to implementing IMC is the lack of people with the broad perspective and skills to make it work. Agencies are felt to lack expertise in database marketing, marketing research, and information technology. A study by Thomas Duncan and Stephen Everett agreed that marketers perceive agencies' lack of knowledge about more than one area as a barrier to integrated marketing communications. Internal turf battles, agency egos, and fear of budget reductions were also seen as major barriers.[29]

@ **EXHIBIT 3–21**

Client versus agency perceptions of involvement in integrated marketing communications

Domain Disputes			
Who set the strategy in most recent integrated campaign?			
	Marketer	**Agency**	**Both**
Marketer	82.9%	6.1%	9.8%
Agency	14.7%	65.3%	16.8%
Who was most responsible for coordinating and implementing the strategy?			
	Marketer	**Agency**	**Both**
Marketer	76.8%	19.5%	3.7%
Agency	11.6%	80.0%	7.4%
Which best describes the agency's role?			
	Partner	**Creative Leader**	**Architect**
Marketer	28.0%	22.0%	4.9%
Agency	24.2%	21.1%	29.5%
	Teammate	**Specialist**	**Integrator**
Marketer	23.2%	14.6%	2.4%
Agency	10.5%	4.2%	8.4%

Roadblocks						
Barriers to successful integrated marketing campaigns						
	Broad Perspective	**Money/ Budgets**	**Cooperation/Client Organization**	**Focused Message**	**Customer Insight**	**Money/Agency Compensation**	**Cooperation/Agency Organization**
Marketer	61.0%	52.0%	43.0%	42.0%	33.0%	22.0%	18.0%
Agency	55.0%	52.0%	44.0%	26.0%	29.0%	33.0%	30.0%

Source: OmniTech Consulting Group, in *Advertising Age*, Nov. 8, 1993, pp. S-1, 2. Graph by Kim Rome.

While ad agencies are adding more resources to offer their clients a full line of services, it appears that many marketers are not yet interested in having all of their integrated marketing communication functions performed by one agency. Many marketers still want to set the strategy for their IMC campaigns and seek specialized expertise, more quality and creativity, and greater control and cost efficiency by using multiple providers.

The *Advertising Age* survey found clients overwhelmingly disagreed with the idea that "advertising agencies should stick primarily to advertising and not try to offer integrated marketing communications." Thus, there is an opportunity for agencies to broaden their services beyond advertising—but they will have to develop true expertise in a variety of integrated marketing communications areas. One thing is certain: as companies continue to shift their promotional dollars away from media advertising to sales promotion, direct marketing, and other nonmedia forms of promotion, agencies will continue to explore ways to keep these monies under their roofs.

@ *SUMMARY*

The development, execution, and administration of an advertising and promotions program involve the efforts of many individuals, both within the company and outside it. Participants in the integrated marketing communications process include the advertiser or client, advertising agencies, media organizations, special marketing communication firms, and providers of collateral services.

Companies use three basic systems to organize internally for advertising and promotion. Centralized systems offer the advantages of facilitated communications, lower personnel requirements, continuity in staff, and more top management involvement. Disadvantages include a lower involvement with overall marketing goals, longer response

times, and difficulties in handling multiple product lines. Decentralized systems offer the advantages of concentrated managerial attention, more rapid responses to problems, and increased flexibility, though they may be limited by ineffective decision making, internal conflicts, misallocation of funds, and a lack of authority. In-house agencies, while offering the advantages of cost savings, control, and increased coordination, also have the disadvantage of less experience, objectivity, and flexibility.

Many firms use advertising agencies to help develop and execute their programs. These agencies may take on a variety of forms, including full-service agencies, creative boutiques, and media buying services. The first offers the client a full range of services including creative, account, marketing, and financial and management services, while the other two specialize in creative services and media buying, respectively. Agencies are compensated through commission systems, percentage charges, and fee- and cost-based systems. Recently, the emphasis on agency accountability has increased. Agencies are being evaluated on both financial and qualitative aspects, and some clients are using incentive-based compensation systems that tie agency compensations to performance measures such as sales and market share.

In addition to advertising agencies, marketers also utilize the services of other marketing communication spe-

cialists including direct marketing agencies, sales promotion agencies, and public relation firms. A marketer must decide whether to use a different specialist for each promotional function or have all of its integrated marketing communication done by an advertising agency that offers all of these services under one roof.

Recent studies have found that most marketers believe it is their responsibility, not the ad agency's, to set strategy for and coordinate integrated marketing communication campaigns. The lack of a broad perspective and specialized skills in nonadvertising areas is seen as the major barrier to agencies' increased involvement in integrated marketing communications.

⊚ KEY TERMS

clients, p. 62
advertising agency, p. 63
media organizations,
  p. 63
specialized marketing
  communications
  services, p. 63
collateral services, p. 64
advertising manager,
  p. 64
centralized system, p. 64
decentralized system,
  p. 66

product manager, p. 66
category management,
  p. 66
in-house agency, p. 68
billings, p. 70
superagencies, p. 70
full-service agency, p. 71
account executive, p. 72
copywriters, p. 75
departmental system,
  p. 76
group system, p. 76
creative boutique, p. 76

media buying services,
  p. 77
commission system,
  p. 77
negotiated commission,
  p. 78
fixed-fee method, p. 79
fee-commission
  combination, p. 79
cost-plus system, p. 79
incentive-based system,
  p. 79
percentage charges, p. 80

financial audit, p. 81
qualitative audit, p. 81
direct response agency,
  p. 87
sales promotion agency,
  p. 87
public relations firm,
  p. 88

⊚ DISCUSSION QUESTIONS

1. Analyze the decision by the Coca-Cola Co. to switch its creative assignment from McCann-Erickson to Creative Artists Agency, which really is not a traditional advertising agency. Do you think more companies will use the services of nontraditional agencies in the future?

2. Who are the five major participants in the integrated marketing communications process? Briefly discuss the roles and responsibilities of each.

3. What are some of the specific responsibilities and duties of the advertising manager under a centralized advertising department structure? Is an advertising manager needed if a company uses an outside agency?

4. What are the advantages of using a decentralized system? Discuss the responsibilities of a product manager with respect to advertising and promotions.

5. Discuss the pros and cons of using an in-house agency. Why do companies such as Benetton and Calvin Klein use in-house agencies?

6. Discuss the reasons companies use outside agencies. Analyze the importance of the various services provided by a full-service agency.

7. What are some of the reasons companies are switching from large to mid-size agencies? What do large agencies have to do to retain these clients?

8. What are the pros and cons of the commission method of agency compensation? Do you think the commission system is outdated and needs to be replaced? Defend your position.

9. A number of companies have implemented incentive-based compensation systems whereby agencies are paid based on performance measures such as sales or market share. Do you believe this system is fair? Would you accept it if you were an agency?

10. Who should have responsibility for development of the integrated marketing communications strategy—the agency or the client? Why?

11. What are some of the barriers agencies and clients encounter when trying to implement integrated marketing communications? How might these obstacles be overcome?

"WHEN I WAS 25, I HAD ONE REASON TO BUY A BMW. NOW I HAVE THREE MORE."

THE NEW V8 530i TOURING.

V8 luxury means many things to many people. But what does it mean to people who fell in love with the BMW legend years ago and now have new reasons to buy a car?

Reasons that revolve around the well-being of one's family, the shuttling of offspring, the transportation of gear for sporting activities and the faithful scheduling of quality carpooling.

With this in mind, BMW introduces responsive

© 1993 BMW of North America, Inc. The BMW trademark and logo are registered.

luxury in a car that gives you all you ever wanted, and all you've grown to need. A versatile V8, the new 530i Touring.

A car whose combination of power, deft handling, extra cargo space and over 50 active and passive safety features, including all-weather traction control, has a wondrous effect on long distances.

Long as they are, those distances become miraculously short.

Test drive the new 530i Touring. When you

do, watch how quickly its styling, versatility and spirited performance make you feel 25 again.

For the dealer near you, call 1-800-334-4BMW.

THE ULTIMATE DRIVING MACHINE.

Chapter **4**

Perspectives on Consumer Behavior

Chapter Objectives

● *To examine the role consumer behavior plays in the development and implementation of advertising and promotional programs.*

● *To examine the consumer decision-making process and how it varies for different types of purchases.*

● *To understand various internal psychological processes, their influence on consumer decision making, and implications for advertising and promotion.*

● *To examine various approaches to studying the consumer learning process and their implications for advertising and promotion.*

● *To examine external factors such as culture, social class, group influences, and situational determinants and how they affect consumer behavior.*

and here is the best reason to test drive a BMW

BMW invites MARTHA STEWART LIVING readers to experience the quality and performance of a BMW. And receive a COMPLIMENTARY GIFT.

(see back for details)

TEST DRIVE CERTIFICATE

Test drive any BMW model and we'll send you an elegant Martha Stewart book of your choice – compliments of BMW. Just bring this card to your nearest BMW dealer and take a test drive by October 31, 1993. For the BMW dealer nearest you, call 1-800-334-4BMW. You'll also receive a complimentary video on the benefits of BMW ownership.

NAME

ADDRESS

CITY/STATE/ZIP

TELEPHONE

PLEASE SELECT ONE:
☐ ENTERTAINING   ☐ GARDENING   ☐ NEW OLD HOUSE
☑ COMPLIMENTARY BMW VIDEO

I currently drive a   Year   Make   Model

Please estimate the time until your next automotive purchase/lease:
☐ 0-3 months ☐ 4-6 months ☐ 7-11 months ☐ 12+ months

To be validated by your BMW dealer

BMW Model Driven   Date

Authorized Dealer Signature   Dealer Code

The test driver must be at least 21 years old and a licensed driver. This card must be validated by an authorized BMW dealer. Test drive must be taken by October 31, 1993. Offer limited to one gift per card. No reproductions or facsimiles accepted. Your gift will arrive in 4-6 weeks after receipt of the validated card.

Auto Makers Study the New Professional Woman

In a landmark research study conducted in 1974, Harry Davis and Benny Rigaux provided marketers with great insights into the relative influence that husbands and wives had in the purchase decisions of a variety of products and services. The study determined that for the purchase of automobiles, the husband was much more likely to dominate the selection. Well, things have changed!

Due to a number of factors—including the fact that more women are in the work force, women's roles are changing, and gender differences have dwindled— women are not likely to just sit back and be content while their husbands make the major decisions on the auto purchase. Whether they are buying the car for themselves or as a family car, women are now much more involved.

One of the many auto companies that has realized this change in roles is BMW. In fact, the affluent, upwardly mobile woman has become a prime target market for the sporty BMW 318i sedan. Cadillac and Chevrolet have also made serious attempts to understand and reach women. Such marketers have conducted focus group research studies and seminars for women, sponsored athletic events and professional gatherings, created women's advisory councils, and hired women as managers. Scantily clad models in auto ads have been replaced by women in design and marketing positions as well as female engineers. Companies now know that simply putting a woman in an ad will not sell a car to one.

In addition to conducting research to learn more about women's behaviors as consumers, the auto companies have increased their marketing efforts by using integrated marketing communications programs. Ford and Chrysler have had women's councils since the '80s. BMW offers a women drivers' school, sponsors women's triathlons, and sends direct mailers to women aged 35–50. Cadillac reaches female executives through conventions, and Acura lets women take its cars for two- to three-day test drives. All of these companies want their share of the more than $70 million women will spend on cars in 1995.

Sources: Fara Warner, "In the Fast Lane," *Brandweek*, July 5, 1993, pp. 21–24; Harry L. Davis and Benny P. Rigaux, "Perception of Marital Roles in Decision Processes," *Journal of Consumer Research* 1 (June 1974), pp. 5–14.

The development of successful marketing communication programs begins with understanding why consumers behave as they do. Those who develop advertising and other promotional strategies begin by identifying relevant markets and then analyzing the relationship between target consumers and the product/service or brand. As discussed in the opening vignette, the decision process for women in the purchase of automobiles has changed in recent years. It has become obvious that marketers cannot compete successfully in the women's market with auto programs targeted to men. The attitudes, roles, and lifestyles of these women have led to significant differences in the way they think. These are just a few of the aspects of consumer behavior promotional planners must consider in developing integrated marketing communication programs. Consumer choice is influenced by a variety of factors.

It is beyond the scope of this text to examine consumer behavior in depth. However, promotional planners need a basic understanding of consumer decision making, factors that influence this process, and how this knowledge can be used in developing promotional strategies and programs. We begin with an overview of consumer behavior.

OVERVIEW OF CONSUMER BEHAVIOR

A common challenge faced by all marketers is their desire to influence the purchase behavior of consumers in favor of the product or service they offer. For companies such as American Express, this means getting consumers to charge more purchases on their American Express cards. For BMW, it means getting them to purchase or lease an automobile; for business-to-business marketers such as Canon or Ricoh, it means getting organizational buyers to purchase more of their copiers or fax machines. While the ultimate goal of marketers is to influence purchase behavior of customers, most marketers understand that the actual purchase is only part of an overall process.

Consumer behavior can be defined as the process and activities people engage in when searching for, selecting, purchasing, using, evaluating, and disposing of products and services so as to satisfy their needs and desires. For many products and services, purchase decisions are the result of a long, detailed process that may include an extensive information search, brand comparisons and evaluations, and other activities. Other purchase decisions are more incidental and may result from little more than seeing a product prominently displayed at a discount price in a store. Think of how many times you have made impulse purchases in stores.

Marketers' success in influencing purchase behavior depends in large part on how well they understand consumer behavior. Marketers need to know the specific needs customers are attempting to satisfy and how they translate into purchase criteria. They

EXHIBIT 4-1

This Jeep ad stresses lifestyles

need to understand how consumers gather information regarding various alternatives and use this information to select from alternative brands. They need to understand how customers make purchase decisions. Where do they prefer to buy a product? How are they influenced by marketing stimuli at the point of purchase? Marketers also need to understand how the consumer decision process and reasons for purchase vary among different types of customers. For example, purchase decisions may be influenced by the personality or lifestyle characteristics of the consumer.[1] Notice how the ad shown in Exhibit 4–1 suggests that Jeep owners are unique and enjoy their lifestyle.

The conceptual model in Exhibit 4–2 will be used as a framework for analyzing the consumer decision process. We will discuss what occurs at the various stages of this model and how advertising and promotion can be used to influence decision making. We will also examine the influence of various psychological concepts, such as motivation, perception, attitudes, and integration processes. Variations in the consumer decision-making process will be examined, as will alternative perspectives regarding consumer learning. The chapter concludes with a consideration of external influences on the consumer decision process.

THE CONSUMER DECISION-MAKING PROCESS

As shown in Exhibit 4–2, the consumer's purchase decision process is generally viewed as consisting of steps through which the buyer passes in purchasing a product or service. This model shows that decision making involves a number of internal psychological processes. Motivation, perception, attitude formation, integration, and learning are important to promotional planners, since they influence the general decision-making process of the consumer. We will examine each stage of the purchase decision model and discuss how the various subprocesses influence what occurs at this step of the consumer behavior process. We will also discuss how promotional planners can influence this process.

Problem Recognition

Exhibit 4–2 shows that the first stage in the consumer decision-making process is **problem recognition,** when the consumer perceives a need and becomes motivated to solve the problem. The problem recognition stage initiates the subsequent decision processes.

Problem recognition is caused by a difference between the consumer's *ideal state* and *actual state.* A discrepancy exists between what the consumer wants the situation to be like and what the situation is really like. (Note that *problem* does not always imply a negative state. A goal exists for the consumer, and this goal may be the attainment of a more positive situation.)

EXHIBIT 4–2   A basic model of consumer decision making

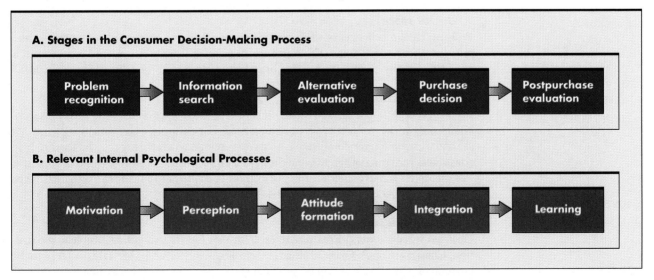

⦿ EXHIBIT 4–3

The new Oral-B toothbrush helps consumers recognize when they need to replace it

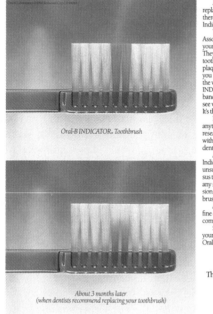

Your dentist can't remind you when to replace your toothbrush. That's our job.

Although dentists advise you to replace your brush, they really can't be there to tell you when. But the Oral-B Indicator can.

You see, the American Dental Association recommends you replace your toothbrush every three months. They believe strongly that a worn toothbrush is less effective at removing plaque. That's why most dentists tell you to change your toothbrush. And the very reason Oral-B developed the INDICATOR₊Toothbrush. The blue band fades with brushing, so you can see when it's time for a new Indicator. It's that simple.

But developing the Indicator was anything but. It's been thoroughly researched over an extensive period with more than 1,500 patients and 300 dentists and hygienists.

Also, like all Oral-B brushes, the Indicator was clinically shown to be unsurpassed at removing plaque versus the other leading brands. Without any sign of gingival irritation or abrasion. No wonder Oral-B is the toothbrush more dentists use.

All in all, the Indicator is another fine example of Oral-B's ongoing commitment to serious dental care.

So listen to your dentist. Replace your brush with the Indicator from Oral-B. It's the ultimate gentle reminder.

Oral-B INDICATOR₊ Toothbrush

About 3 months later (when dentists recommend replacing your toothbrush)

Oral-B

The Brand More Dentists Use.

⦿ EXHIBIT 4–4

Innovative products such as fax machines are being purchased for the home as well as the office

Panasonic introduces a complete communications center for the home office.

Every time you miss a call, miss a fax or miss a message, you may be missing an opportunity. That's why Panasonic introduces an automated communications center specially designed for home offices and small businesses. The new Panasonic KX-F90. This sophisticated system knows when an incoming call is a phone call or a fax and automatically switches to the proper function. Which means it can handle all your calls, messages or faxes with just one phone line.

With its automatic paper cutter and a 10-page document feeder, you don't have to stay in the room to send or receive faxes. And since it can produce 16 shades of grey, your faxes will have excellent reproduction of charts, graphs and photographs.

And its phone system and built-in answering machine has what every business person needs—Privacy Ring. It lets you know if a call is important before you answer it.

Today opportunity doesn't knock. And it can slip through your fingers if you don't get the new Panasonic KX-F90 communications center. ■

TODAY OPPORTUNITY DOESN'T KNOCK. IT CALLS, IT FAXES AND IT LEAVES MESSAGES.

Panasonic
just slightly ahead of our time.

Sources of problem recognition

The causes of problem recognition may range from very simple to very complex and may result from changes in the consumer's current and/or desired state. These causes may be influenced by internal as well as external factors.

Out of stock

Problem recognition occurs when consumers use their existing supply of a product and must replenish their stock. The purchase decision is usually simple and routine and is often resolved by choosing a familiar brand or one to which the consumer may be loyal.

Dissatisfaction

Problem recognition is created by the consumer's dissatisfaction with the current state of affairs and/or the product or service being used. For example, a consumer may think her ski boots are no longer comfortable or stylish enough. Advertising may be used to help consumers recognize when they might have a problem and/or need to make a purchase. For example, Oral-B added a feature to its toothbrush to help consumers recognize when it is time to buy a new brush (Exhibit 4–3).

New needs/wants

Changes in consumers' lives often result in new needs, triggering problem recognition. Changes in one's financial situation, employment status, or lifestyle may lead to the creation of new needs and trigger problem recognition. For example, when you graduate from college and begin your professional career, your new job may necessitate a change in your wardrobe. (Good-bye blue jeans and T-shirts, hello suits and ties.)

Not all product purchases are based on needs. Some products or services sought by consumers are not essential but nevertheless are desired. A **want** has been defined as a felt need that is shaped by a person's knowledge, culture, and personality.[2] Many products sold to consumers satisfy their wants rather than basic needs.

Related products/purchases

Problem recognition can also be stimulated by the purchase of a product. For example, the purchase of a new camera may lead to the recognition of a need for accessories such as additional lenses or a carrying case. The purchase of a personal computer may prompt the need for software programs or upgrades.

Marketer-induced problem recognition

Another source of problem recognition comes from marketers' actions that encourage consumers not to be content with their current state or situation. Ads for personal hygiene products such as mouthwash, deodorant, and foot sprays may be designed to create insecurities among consumers that can be resolved through the use of these products. Marketers change fashions and clothing designs and create perceptions among consumers that their wardrobes are out of style.

Marketers also take advantage of consumers' tendency toward *novelty-seeking behavior,* which leads them to try different brands. Consumers often try new products or brands even though they are basically satisfied with their regular brand. Marketers encourage brand switching by introducing new brands into markets that are already saturated and by using advertising and sales promotion techniques such as free samples, introductory price offers, and coupons.

New products

Problem recognition can also occur when innovative products are introduced and brought to the attention of consumers. Marketers are constantly introducing innovative products and services and telling consumers about the types of problems they solve. For example, marketers of cellular phones tell us why we need telephones in our cars and stress the time savings and convenience they offer. Communicating by fax is becoming so prevalent that nearly every business recognizes the need for a fax machine. Even consumers who work at home are finding fax capabilities necessary in their home offices (Exhibit 4–4).

Marketers' attempts to create problem recognition among consumers are not always successful. Consumers may not see a problem or need for the product the marketer is selling. A main reason many consumers have been reluctant to purchase personal computers is that they fail to see what problems owning one will solve. One way PC manufacturers have attempted to activate problem recognition is by stressing how a computer helps children improve their academic skills and do better in school.

In most instances, the marketer is trying to respond to consumers' attempts to solve problems. Global Perspective 4–1 discusses some of the demands consumers are making and marketers' methods of responding to them.

Examining Consumer Motivations

Marketers recognize that while problem recognition is often a basic, simple process, the way a consumer perceives a problem and becomes motivated to solve it will influence the remainder of the decision process. For example, one consumer may perceive the need to purchase a new watch from a functional perspective and focus on reliable, low-priced alternatives. Another consumer may see the purchase of a watch as more of a fashion statement and focus on the design and image of various brands. To better understand the reasons underlying consumer purchases, marketers devote considerable attention to examining **motives**—that is, those factors that compel a consumer to take a particular action.

Global Perspective 4–1
Consumer Decision Makers Keep Marketers on their Toes

Consumers around the world are becoming more sophisticated and more complex when it comes to making purchase decisions. As a result, marketers have had to change the way they think and do business as well. As consumers' decision processes evolve, smart companies' communications programs are evolving as well.

The company that hopes to compete internationally must constantly monitor the consumer and understand the factors involved in the purchase decision. Consider the following:

- Germans are considered the toughest customers to sell athletic footwear, avidly perusing the specifications and expecting proof that the materials deliver the promised shoe. They are obsessed with the automobile. They prefer hot cereals to cold.

- Japanese are considered the toughest customers when it comes to selling automobiles, disposable diapers, irons, and refrigerators. In the purchase of a car, appearance is critical. They are similar to the Germans in making shoe decisions, buy only Japanese-made cosmetics, and will not eat cold cereals.

- Americans are brand conscious and demand comfort in athletic shoes. But they are much more forgiving when it comes to automobiles. They are increasingly concerned with nutrition in breakfast cereals and demand value for their money when purchasing cosmetics. They are considered the toughest customers for VCRs.

In addition to changing the choice criteria, consumers are becoming smarter and making more demands. They complain more, bombarding companies with letters, griping in focus groups, and even organizing boycotts. They are not as loyal as in the past.

Many manufacturers view the smarter shopper as an opportunity. In both the consumer and business-to-business markets, these companies have redesigned their programs to satisfy customer needs. Improved quality at lower costs, everyday low price strategies, and improved customer service are just some of the ways these companies are adapting. Toll-free phone numbers provide more information and service to customers, and customer relations reps are more sophisticated. Smart companies, like smart consumers, are changing how the game is played.

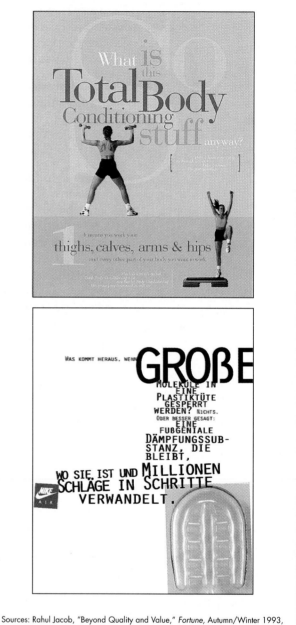

Sources: Rahul Jacob, "Beyond Quality and Value," *Fortune*, Autumn/Winter 1993, pp. 8–11; Faye Rice, "How to Deal with Tougher Customers," *Fortune*, Dec. 3, 1990, pp. 38–40.

Hierarchy of needs

One of the most popular approaches to understanding consumer motivations is based on the classic theory of human motivation popularized many years ago by psychologist Abraham Maslow.[3] His **hierarchy of needs** theory postulates five basic levels of human needs, arranged in a hierarchy based on their importance. As shown in Exhibit 4–5, the five needs are: (1) *physiological needs*—the basic level of primary needs for things required to sustain life, such as food, shelter, clothing, and sex; (2) *safety needs*—the need for security and safety from physical harm; (3) *social/love and belonging needs*—the desire to have satisfying relationships with others and feel a sense of love, affection, belonging, and acceptance; (4) *esteem needs*—the need to feel

◎ EXHIBIT 4–5

Maslow's hierarchy of needs

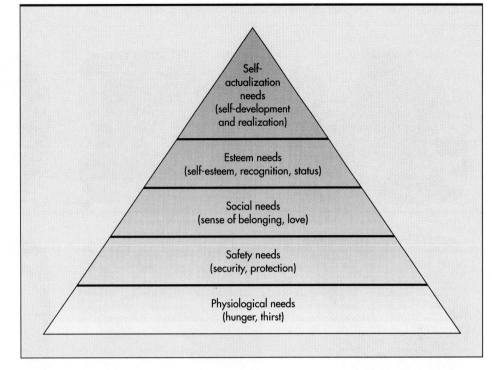

Self-
actualization
needs
(self-development
and realization)

Esteem needs
(self-esteem, recognition, status)

Social needs
(sense of belonging, love)

Safety needs
(security, protection)

Physiological needs
(hunger, thirst)

a sense of accomplishment and gain a sense of recognition, status, and respect from others; and (5) *self-actualization needs*—the need for self-fulfillment and a desire to realize one's own potential.

According to Maslow's theory, the lower-level physiological and safety needs have to be satisfied before the higher-order needs become meaningful. Once these basic needs are satisfied, the individual moves on to attempting to satisfy higher-order needs such as self-esteem and self-actualization. In reality, it is unlikely that individuals move through the need hierarchy in a stairstep manner. Lower-level needs are an ongoing source of motivation for consumer purchase behavior. However, since basic physiological needs are met in most developed countries, marketers often sell products that fill basic physiological needs by appealing to consumers' higher-level needs. For example, in marketing its condensed soups, Campbell Soup Co. focuses on the love between a parent and child (social needs) in addition to the nutritional value of the product (Exhibit 4–6).

While problems have been noted with Maslow's need hierarchy, it offers a framework for marketers to use in determining what needs they want to show their products and services as satisfying. Advertising campaigns can then be designed to show how a brand can fulfill these needs. Marketers also recognize that different market segments emphasize different need levels. For example, a young single person may be attempting to satisfy social or self-esteem needs in purchasing a car, while a family with children will focus more on safety needs. Volvo has used ads like the one in Exhibit 4–7 on page 103 to position its cars as meeting the safety needs of consumers with children.

Psychoanalytic theory

A somewhat more controversial approach to the study of consumer motives is the **psychoanalytic theory** pioneered by Sigmund Freud.[4] Although Freud's work dealt with the structure and development of personality, he also studied the underlying motivations for human behavior. Psychoanalytic theory had a strong influence on the development of modern psychology and on explanations of motivation and personality. It has also been applied to the study of consumer behavior by marketers interested in probing deeply rooted motives that may underlie purchase decisions.

EXHIBIT 4–6   Campbell appeals to love and belonging needs in this ad

BOY SINGS: (VO) There's nothing
    like getting
to the bottom of a bowl of soup.
Puts me in a real good mood.
There's nothing like getting

to the bottom of a bowl of soup.
ANNCR: (VO) Campbell's Chicken
    Noodle Soup.
So good, and like most of Campbell's
    soups

so low in cholesterol
BOY SINGS: (VO) Cause at the
    bottom of it all
soup is good food.
BOY: (VO) Campbell's!

Those who attempt to relate psychoanalytic theory to consumer behavior believe consumers' motivations for purchasing are often very complex and unclear to the casual observer—and to the consumers themselves. Many motives for purchase and/or consumption may be driven by deeply rooted motives one can determine only by probing the subconscious.

Among the first to conduct this type of research in marketing, Ernest Dichter and James Vicary were employed by a number of major corporations to use psychoanalytic techniques to determine consumers' purchase motivations. The work of these researchers and others who continue to use this approach assumed the title of **motivation research.**

Motivation research in marketing

Motivation researchers use a variety of methodologies to gain insight into the underlying causes of consumer behavior. Methods employed include in-depth interviews, projective techniques, association tests, and focus groups in which consumers are encouraged to bring out associations related to products and brands (see Exhibit 4–8 on page 104). As one might expect, such associations often lead to interesting insights as to why people purchase. For example:

- A man buys a convertible as a substitute mistress.
- Women like to bake cakes because they feel like they are giving birth to a baby.
- Women wear perfume to "attract a man" and "glorify their existence."

EXHIBIT 4–7

Volvo appeals to consumers'
safety needs

- Men like frankfurters better than women because cooking them (frankfurters, not men!) makes women feel guilty. It's an admission of laziness.
- When people shower, their sins go down the drain with the soap as they rinse.[5]

As you can see from these examples, motivation research has led to some very interesting, albeit controversial, findings and to much skepticism from marketing managers. However, major corporations and advertising agencies continue to use motivation research to help them market their products.

Problems and contributions of psychoanalytic theory and motivation research

Psychoanalytic theory has been criticized as being too vague, unresponsive to the external environment, and too reliant on the early development of the individual. It also uses a small sample for drawing conclusions. Because of the emphasis on the unconscious, results are difficult if not impossible to verify, leading motivation research to be criticized for both the conclusions drawn and its lack of experimental validation. Since motivation research studies typically employ so few participants, there is also concern that it really discovers the idiosyncrasies of a few individuals and its findings are not generalizable to the whole population.

Still, it is difficult to ignore the psychoanalytic approach in furthering our understanding of consumer behavior. These insights can often be used as a basis for advertising messages aimed at buyers' deeply rooted feelings, hopes, aspirations, and fears. These strategies are often more effective than rationally based appeals.

Some advertising agencies have used motivation research to gain further insights into how consumers think. Examples include the following:[6]

- McCann-Erickson asked women to draw and describe how they felt about roaches. The agency concluded that many women associated roaches with men who had abandoned them. The agency concluded that was why women preferred roach killers that let them see the roaches die.
- Saatchi & Saatchi Advertising used psychological probes to conclude that Ronald McDonald created a more nurturing mood than did the Burger King (who was perceived as more aggressive and distant).

@ EXHIBIT 4–8

Some of the marketing
research methods employed
to probe the mind of the
consumer

In-depth interviews

Face-to-face situations in which an interviewer asks a consumer to talk freely in an unstructured interview using specific questions designed to obtain insights into his or her motives, ideas, or opinions.

Projective techniques

Efforts designed to gain insights into consumers' values, motives, attitudes, or needs that are difficult to express or identify by having them project these internal states upon some external object.

Association tests

A technique in which an individual is asked to respond as to the first thing that comes to mind when he or she is presented with a stimulus; the stimulus may be a word, picture, ad, and so on.

Focus groups

A small number of people with similar backgrounds and/or interests are brought together to discuss a particular product, idea, or issue.

- Foote, Cone & Belding gave consumers stacks of photographs of faces and asked them to associate the faces with the kind of person who might use particular products.

While often criticized, motivation research has also contributed to the marketing discipline. The qualitative nature of the research is considered important in assessing how and why consumers buy. Focus groups and in-depth interviews are valuable methods for gaining insights into consumers' feelings, and projective techniques are often the only means of getting around stereotypical or socially desirable responses. In addition, motivation research is the forerunner of psychographics, or lifestyle research, a popular basis for segmenting markets and developing consumer profiles that will be discussed in Chapter 5.

Finally, we know that buyers are sometimes motivated by symbolic as well as functional drives in their purchase decisions. (Thus, we see the use of sexual appeals and symbols in ads like Exhibit 4–9.)

Information Search

The second step in the consumer decision-making process is *information search*. Once consumers perceive a problem or need that can be satisfied by the purchase of a product or service, they begin to search for information needed to make a purchase decision. The initial search effort often consists of an attempt to scan information stored in memory to recall past experiences and/or knowledge regarding various purchase alternatives.[7] This information retrieval is referred to as **internal search**. For many routine, repetitive purchases, previously acquired information that is stored in memory (such as past performance or outcomes from using a brand) is sufficient for comparing alternatives and making a choice.

If the internal search does not yield enough information, the consumer will seek additional information by engaging in **external search**. External sources of information include:

@ **EXHIBIT 4–9**

This Guess? ad uses a sexual appeal

- *Personal sources,* such as friends, relatives, or co-workers.
- Commercial or *marketer controlled* sources, such as information from advertising, salespeople, or point-of-purchase displays and materials.
- *Public sources,* including articles in magazines or newspapers and reports on television programs.
- *Personal experience,* such as actually handling, examining, or testing the product.

Determining how much and which sources of external information to use involves several factors, including the importance of the purchase decision, the effort needed to acquire information, the amount of past experience relevant, the degree of perceived risk associated with the purchase, and the time available. For example, the selection of a movie to see on a Friday night might entail simply talking to a friend or checking the movie guide in the daily newspaper. A more complex purchase, such as a new car, might use a number of information sources—perhaps a review of *Road & Track, Motortrend,* or *Consumer Reports;* discussion with family members and friends; and test driving of cars. At this point in the purchase decision, the information-providing aspects of advertising are extremely important.

Perception

Knowledge of how consumers acquire and use information from external sources is important to marketers in formulating communication strategies. Marketers are particularly interested in (1) how consumers sense external information, (2) how they select and attend to various sources of information, and (3) how this information is interpreted and given meaning. These processes are all part of **perception,** the process by which an individual receives, selects, organizes, and interprets information to create a meaningful picture of the world.[8] Perception is an individual process; it depends on internal factors such as a person's beliefs, experiences, needs, moods, and expectations. The perceptual process is also influenced by the characteristics of a stimulus such as its size, color, and intensity, and the context in which it is seen or heard.

⊚ **EXHIBIT 4–10**

This ad reminds consumers of how advertising responds to their needs

Sensation

Perception involves three distinct processes. **Sensation** is the immediate, direct response of the senses (taste, smell, sight, touch, and hearing) to a stimulus such as an ad, package, brand name, or point-of-purchase display. Perception uses these senses to create a representation of the stimulus. Marketers recognize that it is important to understand consumers' physiological reactions to marketing stimuli. For example, the visual elements of an ad or package design must attract consumers' favorable attention.

Marketers sometimes try to increase the level of sensory input so that their advertising messages will get noticed. For example, marketers of colognes and perfumes often use strong visuals as well as scent strips to appeal to multiple senses and attract the attention of magazine readers. Some advertisers have even inserted microcomputer chips into their print ads to play a song or deliver a message.

Selecting information

Sensory inputs are important but are only one part of the perceptual process. Other determinants of whether marketing stimuli will be attended to and how they will be interpreted include internal psychological factors such as the consumer's personality, needs, motives, expectations, and experiences. These psychological inputs explain why people focus attention on some things and ignore others. Two people may perceive the same stimuli in very different ways because they select, attend, and comprehend differently. An individual's perceptual processes usually focus on elements of the environment that are relevant to their needs and tune out irrelevant stimuli. Think about how much more attentive you are to advertising for personal computers, tires, or stereos when you are

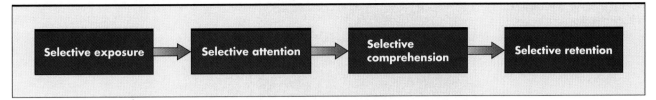

◉ EXHIBIT 4–11 The selective perception process

in the market for one of these products (a point that is made by the message from the American Association of Advertising Agencies in Exhibit 4–10).

Interpreting the information

Once a consumer selects and attends to a stimulus, the perceptual process focuses on organizing, categorizing, and interpreting the incoming information. This stage of the perceptual process is very individualized and is influenced by internal psychological factors. The interpretation and meaning an individual assigns to an incoming stimulus is also a function of the nature of the stimulus. For example, many advertisements are objective, and their message is clear and straightforward. Other ads are more ambiguous, and their meaning is strongly influenced by the consumer's individual interpretation.

Selectivity occurs throughout the various stages of the consumer's perceptual process. Perception may be viewed as a filtering process in which internal and external factors influence what is received and how it is processed and interpreted. The sheer number and complexity of the marketing stimuli a person is exposed to in any given day require that this filtering occur. **Selective perception** may occur at the exposure, attention, comprehension, or retention stage of perception, as shown in Exhibit 4–11.

Selective perception

Selective exposure occurs as consumers choose whether or not to make themselves available to information. For example, a viewer of a television show may change channels or leave the room during commercial breaks.

Selective attention occurs when the consumer chooses to focus attention on certain stimuli while excluding others. One study of selective attention estimates the typical consumer is exposed to nearly 1,500 ads per day yet perceives only 76 of these messages.[9] This means advertisers must make considerable effort to get their messages noticed. Advertisers often use the creative aspects of their ads to gain the consumer's attention. For example, some advertisers set their ads off from others by showing their products in color against a black-and-white background (Exhibit 4–12). This creative tactic has been used in advertising for many products, among them Cherry 7-Up, Nuprin, and Pepto-Bismol.[10]

Even if the consumer does notice the advertiser's message, there is no guarantee it will be interpreted in the intended manner. Consumers may engage in **selective comprehension,** interpreting information based on their own attitudes, beliefs, motives, and experiences. Consumers often interpret information in a manner that supports their own position. For example, an ad that disparages a consumer's favorite brand may be seen as biased or untruthful, and its claims may not be accepted.

The final screening process shown in Exhibit 4–12 is **selective retention,** which means consumers do not remember all the information they see, hear, or read even after attending to and comprehending it. Advertisers attempt to make sure information will be retained in the consumer's memory so as to be available when it is time to make a purchase. **Mnemonics** such as symbols, rhymes, associations, and images that assist in

@ **EXHIBIT 4–12**

Splash of color ads help attract attention

the learning and memory process are helpful. Many advertisers use telephone numbers that spell out the company name and are easy to remember. Eveready put pictures of its pink bunny on packages to remind consumers at the point of purchase of its creative advertising.

Subliminal perception

Advertisers know consumers use selective perception to filter out irrelevant or unwanted advertising messages, so they employ various creative tactics to get their messages noticed. One controversial tactic advertisers have been accused of using is appealing to consumers' subconscious. **Subliminal perception** refers to the ability to perceive a stimulus that is below the level of conscious awareness. Psychologists generally agree it is possible to perceive things without being consciously aware of them.

As you might imagine, the possibility of using hidden persuaders such as subliminal audio messages or visual cues to influence consumers might be intriguing to advertisers but would not be welcome by consumers. The idea of marketers influencing consumers at a subconscious level has strong ethical implications. As discussed in Ethical Perspective 4–1, researchers believe subliminal messages are not likely to be effective in influencing consumer behavior. The use of subliminal techniques is not a creative tactic we would recommend to advertisers!

Alternative Evaluation

The evoked set

After acquiring information during the information search stage of the decision process, the consumer moves to alternative evaluation. In this stage, the consumer compares the various brands or products and services he or she has identified as being capable of solving the consumption problem and satisfying the needs or motives that initiated the decision process. The various brands identified as purchase options to be considered during the alternative evaluation process are referred to as the consumer's *evoked set*.

The evoked set is generally only a subset of all the brands of which the consumer is aware. The consumer reduces the number of brands to be reviewed during the alternative evaluation stage to a manageable level. The exact size of the evoked set varies from one consumer to another and depends on such factors as the importance of the purchase and the amount of time and energy the consumer wants to devote to comparing alternatives.

≋ Ethical Perspective 4–1
Subliminal Perception: Fact or Fiction?

The advertising industry states its position on subliminal messages

One of the most controversial topics in all of advertising is subliminal advertising. Rooted in psychoanalytic theory, subliminal advertising supposedly influences consumer behaviors by subconsciously altering perceptions or attitudes toward products without the knowledge—or consent—of the consumer. Marketers have promoted subliminal self-help audiotapes, weight-loss videos, and improved golf games. The majority of American consumers believe that advertisers sometimes use subliminal advertising.

The concept of subliminal advertising was introduced in 1957 when a marketing research group reported it increased the sales of popcorn and Coke by subliminally flashing "Eat popcorn" and "Drink Coca-Cola" across the screen during a movie in New Jersey. Since then, numerous books and research studies have been published regarding the effectiveness of this advertising form. In 1982, Timothy Moore, in the *Journal of Marketing,* reviewed the vast literature on subliminal perception. He wrote, "While subliminal perception is a bona fide phenomenon, the effects obtained are subtle and obtaining them typically requires a carefully structured context. Subliminal stimuli are usually so weak that the recipient is not just unaware of the stimulus but is also oblivious to the fact that he/she is being stimulated . . . These factors pose serious difficulties for any marketing application."

Subliminal directives have not been shown to be effective. The literature on subliminal perception shows that the most clearly documented effects are obtained only in highly artificial situations. Any effects are brief and of small magnitude. Moore concluded, "These processes have no apparent relevance to the goals of advertising."

In 1988, after additional research in this area, Moore said, "There continues to be no evidence that subliminal messages can influence motivation or complex behavior." Joel Saegart and Jack Haberstroh have also supported Moore's conclusions. When Haberstroh asked advertising agency executives if they had ever deliberately used subliminal advertising, 96 percent said no, 94 percent said they had never supervised the use of implants, and 91 percent denied knowing anyone who had ever used this technique. It seems few people in the advertising world think subliminal advertising works and even fewer claim to use it. Now if they could only convince consumers!

PEOPLE HAVE BEEN TRYING TO FIND THE BREASTS IN THESE ICE CUBES SINCE 1957.

The advertising industry is sometimes charged with sneaking seductive little pictures into ads.
Supposedly, these pictures can get you to buy a product without your even seeing them.
Consider the photograph above. According to some people, there's a pair of female breasts

hidden in the patterns of light refracted by the ice cubes.
Well, if you really searched you probably *could* see the breasts. For that matter, you could also see Millard Fillmore, a stuffed pork chop and a 1946 Dodge.
The point is that so-called "subliminal advertising" simply

doesn't exist. Overactive imaginations, however, most certainly do.
So if anyone claims to see breasts in that drink up there, they aren't in the ice cubes.
They're in the eye of the beholder.

ADVERTISING
ANOTHER WORD FOR FREEDOM OF CHOICE.
American Association of Advertising Agencies

Sources: Martha Rogers and Kirk H. Smith, "Public Perceptions of Subliminal Advertising," *Journal of Advertising Research,* March/April 1993, pp. 10–17; Jack Haberstroh, "Can't Ignore Subliminal Ad Charges,"*Advertising Age,* Sept. 17, 1984, pp. 3, 42–44; Timothy Moore, "Subliminal Advertising: What You See Is What You Get,"*Journal of Marketing* 46, no. 2 (Spring 1982), pp. 38–47; Timothy Moore, "The Case against Subliminal Manipulation," *Psychology and Marketing* 5, no. 4 (Winter 1988), pp. 297–316; and Joel Saegert, "Why Marketing Should Quit Giving Subliminal Advertising the Benefit of the Doubt," *Psychology and Marketing* 4, pp. 107–120.

The goal of most advertising and promotional strategies is to increase the likelihood that a brand will be included in the consumer's evoked set and considered during alternative evaluation. Marketers use advertising to create *top-of-mind awareness* among consumers so their brands are part of the evoked set of their target audiences. Popular brands with large advertising budgets use *reminder advertising* to maintain high awareness levels and increase the likelihood they will be considered by consumers in the market for the product. Marketers of new brands or those with a low market share need to gain awareness among consumers and break into their evoked sets. They can do this through methods such as comparative advertising, where a brand is compared to market leaders. The Elantra ad (Exhibit 4–13) is an example of this strategy. This ad encourages prospective car buyers thinking of purchasing a Japanese car to consider the Korean-made Hyundai as well, including it in their evoked sets.

@ **EXHIBIT 4–13**

This Hyundai ad is designed to get the car in the consumers' evoked set

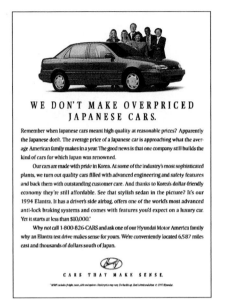

@ **EXHIBIT 4–14**

This ad emphasizes the positive consequences of using the Top-Flite XL golf ball

Advertising is a valuable promotional tool for creating and maintaining brand awareness and making sure a brand is included in the evoked set. However, marketers also work to promote their brands in the actual environment where purchase decisions are made. Point-of-purchase materials and promotional techniques such as in-store sampling, end-aisle displays, or shelf tags touting special prices encourage consumers to consider brands that may not have initially been in their evoked set.

Evaluative criteria and consequences

Once consumers have identified an evoked set and have a list of alternatives, they must evaluate the various brands. This involves comparing of the choice alternatives on specific criteria important to the consumer. **Evaluative criteria** are the dimensions or attributes of a product or service that are used to compare different alternatives. Evaluative criteria can be objective or subjective. For example, in buying an automobile, consumers use objective attributes such as price, warranty, and fuel economy ratings as well as subjective factors such as image, styling, quality, and performance.

Evaluative criteria are usually viewed as product or service attributes. Many marketers view their products or services as *bundles of attributes,* but consumers tend to think about products or services in terms of their *consequences* instead. J. Paul Peter and Jerry Olson refer to consequences as specific events or outcomes that consumers experience when they purchase and/or consume a product or service.[11] They distinguish between two broad types of consequences. **Functional consequences** are concrete outcomes of product or service usage that are tangible and directly experienced by consumers. The taste of a soft drink or potato chip, the acceleration of a car, and the clarity of a fax transmission are examples of functional consequences. **Psychosocial consequences** refer to abstract outcomes that are more intangible, subjective, and personal, such as how a product makes you feel or how you think others will view you for purchasing or using it.

Marketers should distinguish between product/service attributes and consequences, because the importance and meaning consumers assign to an attribute is usually determined by its consequences for them. Moreover, advertisers must be sure consumers understand the linkage between a particular attribute and a consequence. For example, the Top-Flite ad in Exhibit 4–14 focuses on the consequences of using the new Top-Flite XL golfball, such as more distance and lower scores. Note how the highlighted scorecard is used to reinforce the point that the Top-Flite XL can help golfers achieve better scores.

Product/service attributes and the consequences or outcomes consumers think they will experience from a particular brand are very important, for they are often the basis on which consumers form attitudes and purchase intentions and decide among various choice alternatives. Two subprocesses are very important during the alternative evaluation stage: (1) the process by which consumer attitudes are created, reinforced, and changed and (2) the consumer decision rules or integration strategies consumers use to compare brands and make purchase decisions. We will examine each of these processes in more detail.

Attitudes

Attitudes are one of the most heavily studied concepts in consumer behavior. According to Gordon Allport's classic definition, "attitudes are learned predispositions to respond to an object."[12] More recent perspectives view attitudes as a summary construct that represents an individual's overall feelings toward or evaluation of an object.[13] Consumers hold attitudes toward a variety of objects that are important to marketers, including individuals (celebrity endorsers such as Joe Montana or Michael Jordan), brands (Cheerios, Kix), companies (Exxon, IBM), product categories (beef, pork, tuna), retail stores (Kmart, Sears), or even advertisements (the Energizer bunny ads).

Attitudes are important to marketers because they theoretically summarize a consumer's evaluation of an object (brand, company) and represent positive or negative feelings and behavioral tendencies. Marketers' keen interest in attitudes is based on the assumption that they are related to consumers' purchase behavior. Considerable evidence supports the basic assumption of a relationship between attitudes and behavior.[14] The attitude–behavior link does not always hold; many other factors can affect behavior.[15] But attitudes are very important to marketers. Advertising and promotion are used to create favorable attitudes toward new products/services or brands, reinforce existing favorable attitudes, and/or change negative attitudes. An approach to studying and measuring attitudes that is particularly relevant to advertising is multiattribute attitude models.

Multiattribute attitude models

Consumer researchers, as well as marketing practitioners, have been using multiattribute attitude models to study consumer attitudes over the past two decades.[16] A **multiattribute attitude model** views an attitude object, such as a product or brand, as possessing a number of attributes that provide the basis on which consumers form their attitudes. According to this model, consumers have beliefs about specific brand attributes and attach different levels of importance to these attributes. Using this approach, an attitude toward a particular brand can be represented as

$$A_B = \sum_{i=1}^{n} B_i \times E_i$$

where A_B = attitude toward a brand
   B_i = beliefs about the brand's performance on attribute i
   E_i = importance attached to attribute i
   n = number of attributes considered

For example, a consumer may have beliefs (B_i) about various brands of toothpaste on certain attributes. One brand may be perceived as having fluoride and thus preventing cavities, tasting good, and helping control tartar buildup. Another brand may not be perceived as having these attributes, but consumers may believe it performs well on other attributes such as freshening breath and whitening teeth.

@ **EXHIBIT 4-15**

IBM adds a new attribute for consumers to consider

To predict attitudes, one must know how much importance consumers attach to each of these attributes (E_i). For example, parents purchasing toothpaste for their children may prefer a brand that performs well on cavity prevention, which leads to a more favorable attitude toward the first brand. Teenagers and young adults may prefer a brand that freshens their breath and makes their teeth white and thus prefer the second brand.

Consumers may hold a number of different beliefs about brands in any product or service category. However, not all of these beliefs are activated in forming an attitude. Beliefs concerning specific attributes or consequences that are activated and form the basis of an attitude are referred to as **salient beliefs.** Marketers should identify and understand these salient beliefs. They must also recognize that the saliency of beliefs varies among different market segments, over time, and across different consumption situations.

Attitude change strategies

Multiattribute models help marketers understand and diagnose the underlying basis of consumers' attitudes. By understanding the beliefs that underlie consumers' evaluations of a brand and the importance of various attributes or consequences, the marketer is better able to develop communication strategies for creating, changing, or reinforcing brand attitudes. The multiattribute model provides insight into several ways marketers can influence consumer attitudes, including:

- Increasing or changing the strength or belief rating of a brand on an important attribute.
- Changing consumers' perceptions of the importance or value of an attribute.
- Adding a new attribute to the attitude formation process.
- Changing perceptions of belief ratings for a competing brand.

The first strategy is commonly used by advertisers. They identify an attribute or consequence that is important and remind consumers how well their brand performs on this attribute. In situations where consumers do not perceive the marketer's brand as possessing an important attribute or the belief strength is low, advertising strategies may be targeted at changing the belief rating. Even when belief strength is high, advertising may be used to increase the rating of a brand on an important attribute. United Airlines' Fly

@ **EXHIBIT 4–16**

Geze compares its ski
bindings to competing brands
on specific attributes

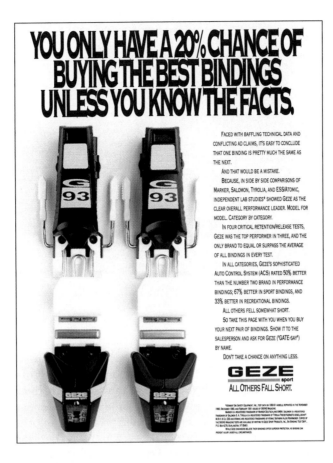

the Friendly Skies campaign is a good example of a strategy designed to create a belief
and reinforce it through advertising.

Marketers often attempt to influence consumer attitudes by changing the relative importance of a particular attribute. This second strategy involves getting consumers to
attach more importance to the attribute in forming their attitude toward the brand. Marketers using this strategy want to increase the importance of an attribute their particular
brand has.

The third strategy for influencing consumer attitudes is to add or emphasize a new
attribute that consumers can use in evaluating a brand. Marketers often do this by improving their products or focusing on additional benefits or consequences associated with
using the brand. Exhibit 4–15 shows how IBM is helping Windows users by adding a new
application called Rapid Resume. The objective of this ad is to persuade consumers to
consider this attribute in forming attitudes toward computers.

A final strategy marketers use is changing consumer beliefs about the attributes of
competitive brands or product categories. This strategy has become much more common
with the increase in comparative advertising where marketers compare their brands to
competitors' on specific product attributes. An example of this is the Geze ad shown in
Exhibit 4–16, where the company compares a number of important attributes of its ski
bindings to those of competitors.

**Integration Processes
and Decision Rules**

Another important aspect of the alternative evaluation stage is the way consumers combine information about the characteristics of brands to arrive at a purchase decision.
Integration processes are the way product knowledge, meanings, and beliefs are combined to evaluate two or more alternatives.[17] Analysis of the integration process focuses
on the different types of *decision rules* or strategies consumers use to decide among purchase alternatives.

Market leaders such as Budweiser often appeal to consumer affect

Consumers often make purchase selections by using formal integration strategies or decision rules that require examination and comparison of alternatives on specific attributes. This process involves a very deliberate evaluation of the alternatives, attribute by attribute. When consumers apply such formal decision rules, marketers need to know which attributes are being considered so as to provide the information the consumers require.

Sometimes consumers make their purchase decision using more simplified decision rules known as **heuristics**. Peter and Olson note that heuristics are easy to use and are highly adaptive to specific environmental situations (such as a retail store).[18] For familiar products that are purchased frequently, consumers may use heuristics such as price-based decision rules (buy the least expensive brand) or promotion-based heuristics (choose the brand for which I can get a price reduction through a coupon, rebate, or special deal).

One type of heuristic is the **affect referral decision rule**,[19] in which consumers make a selection on the basis of an overall impression or summary evaluation of the various alternatives under consideration. This decision rule suggests that consumers have affective impressions of brands stored in memory that can be accessed at the time of purchase. How many times have you gone into a store and made purchases based on your overall impressions of the brands rather than going through detailed comparisons of the alternatives' specific attributes?

Marketers selling familiar and popular brands may appeal to an affect referral rule by stressing overall affective feelings or impressions about their products. Market leaders, whose products enjoy strong overall brand images, often use ads that promote the brand as the best overall. Coke's campaign "Always Coca-Cola," Diet Pepsi's "You've Got the Right One Baby, Uh Huh!" and Budweiser's "The King of Beers" (Exhibit 4–17), are all examples of this strategy.

Purchase Decision

At some point in the buying process, the consumer must stop searching for and evaluating information about alternative brands in the evoked set and make a *purchase decision*. As an outcome of the alternative evaluation stage, the consumer may develop a **purchase intention** or predisposition to buy a certain brand. Purchase intentions are generally based on a matching of purchase motives with attributes or characteristics of brands under consideration. Their formation involves many of the personal subprocesses discussed in this chapter, including motivation, perception, attitude formation, and integration.

A purchase decision is not the same as an actual purchase. Once a consumer chooses which brand to buy, he or she must still implement the decision and make the actual purchase. Additional decisions may be needed, such as when to buy, where to buy, and how much money to spend. Often, there is a time delay between the formation of a purchase intention or decision and the actual purchase, particularly for highly involved and complex purchases such as automobiles, personal computers, and consumer durables.

For nondurable products, which include many low-involvement items such as consumer package goods, the time between the decision and the actual purchase may be short. Before leaving home, the consumer may make a shopping list that includes specific brand names because the consumer has developed **brand loyalty**—a preference for a particular brand that results in its repeated purchase. Marketers strive to develop and maintain brand loyalty among consumers. They use reminder advertising to keep their brand names in front of consumers, maintain prominent shelf positions and displays in stores, and run periodic promotions to deter consumers from switching brands.

Maintaining consumers' brand loyalty is not easy. Competitors use many techniques to encourage consumers to try their brands, such as new product introductions, free samples, and other promotional offers. As can be seen from Exhibit 4–18, for many products less than 50 percent of consumers are loyal to one brand. Marketers must continually battle to maintain their loyal consumers, while at the same time replacing those who switch brands.

Purchase decisions for nondurable, convenience items sometimes take place in the store, almost simultaneous with the purchase. Marketers must ensure that consumers have top-of-mind awareness of their brands so they are quickly recognized and considered. These types of decisions are influenced at the actual point of purchase. Packaging, shelf displays, point-of-purchase materials, and promotional tools such as on-package coupons or premium offers can influence decisions made through constructive processes at the time of purchase.

Postpurchase Evaluation

The consumer decision process does not end with the purchase. After using the product or service, the consumer compares the level of performance with expectations and is either satisfied or dissatisfied. *Satisfaction* occurs when the consumer's expectations are either met or exceeded; *dissatisfaction* results when performance is below expectations. The postpurchase evaluation process is important because the feedback acquired from actual use of a product will influence the likelihood of future purchases. Positive performance means the brand is retained in the evoked set and increases the likelihood it will be purchased again. Unfavorable outcomes may lead the consumer to form negative attitudes toward the brand, lessening the likelihood it will be purchased again or even eliminating it from the consumer's evoked set.

Another possible outcome of purchase is **cognitive dissonance**, a feeling of psychological tension or postpurchase doubt that a consumer experiences after making a difficult purchase choice. Dissonance is more likely to occur in important decisions where the consumer must choose among close alternatives (especially if the unchosen alternative has unique or desirable features that the selected alternative does not have).

Consumers experiencing cognitive dissonance may use a number of strategies to attempt to reduce it. They may seek out reassurance and opinions from others to confirm the wisdom of their purchase decision; they may lower their attitudes or opinions of the unchosen alternative; they may deny or distort any information that does not support the choice they made; or they may look for information that does support their choice. An important source of this supportive information is advertising; consumers tend to be more attentive to advertising for the brand they have chosen.[20] Thus, it may be important for companies to advertise to reinforce consumer decisions to purchase their brands.

EXHIBIT 4–18   Percentage of users of these products who are loyal to one brand

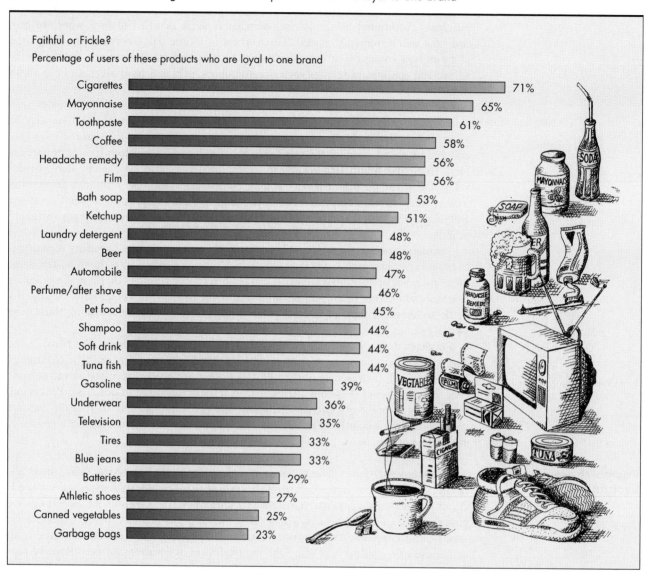

Faithful or Fickle?
Percentage of users of these products who are loyal to one brand

Product	Percentage
Cigarettes	71%
Mayonnaise	65%
Toothpaste	61%
Coffee	58%
Headache remedy	56%
Film	56%
Bath soap	53%
Ketchup	51%
Laundry detergent	48%
Beer	48%
Automobile	47%
Perfume/after shave	46%
Pet food	45%
Shampoo	44%
Soft drink	44%
Tuna fish	44%
Gasoline	39%
Underwear	36%
Television	35%
Tires	33%
Blue jeans	33%
Batteries	29%
Athletic shoes	27%
Canned vegetables	25%
Garbage bags	23%

Marketers must recognize the importance of the postpurchase evaluation stage. Dissatisfied consumers who experience dissonance are not only unlikely to repurchase the marketer's product, but they may also spread negative word-of-mouth information that deters others from purchasing the product or service. The best guarantee of favorable postpurchase evaluations is to provide consumers with a quality product or service that always meets their expectations. Marketers must be sure their advertising and other forms of promotion do not create unreasonable expectations their products cannot meet.

Marketers are recognizing that postpurchase communication is also important. Some companies send follow-up letters and brochures to reassure buyers and reinforce the wisdom of their decision. Many companies have set up toll-free numbers for consumers to call if they need information or have a question or complaint regarding a product. Marketers also offer liberalized return and refund policies and extended warranties and guarantees to ensure customer satisfaction. For example, the ad in Exhibit 4–19 promotes Ford Motor Co.'s commitment to customer service.

@ **EXHIBIT 4–19**

Ford's commitment to
customer service helps
ensure postpurchase
satisfaction

**Variations in
Consumer
Decision Making**

The preceding pages describe a general model of consumer decision making. But consumers do not always engage in all five steps of the purchase decision process or proceed in the sequence presented. They may minimize or even skip one or more stages if they have previous experience in purchasing the product or service or if the decision is of low personal, social, or economic significance. To develop effective promotional strategies and programs, marketers need some understanding of the problem-solving processes their target consumers use to make purchase decisions.[21]

Many of the purchase decisions we make as consumers are based on a habitual or routine choice process. For many low-priced, frequently purchased products, the decision process consists of little more than recognizing the problem, engaging in a quick internal search, and making the purchase. The consumer spends little or no effort engaging in external search or alternative evaluation.

Marketers of products characterized by a routine response purchase process should attempt to get and/or keep their brands in the consumer's evoked set and to avoid anything that may result in their removal from consideration. Established brands that have strong market share position are likely to be in the evoked set of most consumers. Marketers of these brands want consumers to follow a routine choice process and continue to purchase their products. This means maintaining high levels of brand awareness through reminder advertising, periodic promotions, and prominent shelf positions in retail stores.

Marketers of new brands or those with a low market share face a different challenge. They must find ways to disrupt consumers' routine choice process and get them to consider different alternatives. High levels of advertising may be used to encourage trial or brand switching, along with sales promotion efforts in the form of free samples, special price offers, high-value coupons, and the like.

A more complicated decision-making process may occur when the consumer has a limited amount of experience in purchasing a particular product or service and little or no knowledge of the brands available and/or the criteria to use in making a purchase decision. They may have to learn what attributes or criteria should be used in making a purchase decision and how the various alternatives perform on these dimensions. For products or services characterized by limited or extensive problem solving marketers should make information available that will help consumers make their decision. Advertising that provides consumers with detailed information about a brand and how it can

EXHIBIT 4–20

This ad for Epson laser printer shows how marketers can appeal to consumers engaging in extended problem solving

satisfy their purchase motives and goals is important. Marketers may also want to give consumers information at the point of purchase, through either displays or brochures. Distribution channels should have knowledgeable sales personnel available to explain the features and benefits of the company's product or service and why it is superior to competing products.

The Epson ad in Exhibit 4–20 is a good example of how advertising can appeal to consumers who may be engaging in extended problem solving when purchasing a laser printer. Notice how the ad communicates with consumers who know little about how to purchase this product. The ad also makes more detailed information available by offering a free booklet designed to help first-time buyers.

Alternative Perspectives on Consumer Behavior

The discussion of the decision process shows that the way consumers make a purchase varies depending on a number of factors, including the nature of the product or service, the amount of experience the consumer has with the product, and the importance of the purchase. One factor in the level of problem solving to be employed is the consumer's *involvement* with the product or brand. Chapter 6 examines the meaning of involvement, the difference between low- and high-involvement decision making, and the implications of involvement for developing advertising and promotional strategies.

Our examination of consumer behavior thus far has looked at the decision-making process from a *cognitive orientation*. The five-stage decision process model views the consumer as a problem solver and information processor who engages in a variety of mental processes to evaluate various alternatives and determine the degree to which they might satisfy needs or purchase motives. There are, however, alternative perspectives regarding how consumers acquire the knowledge and experience they use in making purchase decisions. To understand these alternative perspectives, we examine various approaches to learning and their implications for advertising and promotion.

THE CONSUMER LEARNING PROCESS

Consumer learning has been defined as "the process by which individuals acquire the purchase and consumption knowledge and experience they apply to future related behavior."[22] Two basic approaches to learning are the behavioral approach and cognitive learning theory.

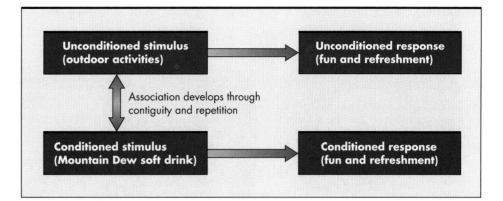

◉ EXHIBIT 4–21

The classical conditioning process

Behavioral Learning Theory

Behavioral learning theories emphasize the role of external, environmental stimuli in causing behavior while minimizing the significance of internal psychological processes. Behavioral learning theories are characterized by the or *stimulus–response orientation* (S–R) because they are based on the premise that learning occurs as the result of responses to external stimuli in the environment. Behavioral learning theorists believe learning occurs through the connection between a stimulus and a response. We will examine the basic principles of two behavioral learning theory approaches: classical conditioning and operant conditioning.

Classical conditioning

Classical conditioning assumes that learning is an *associative process* with an already existing relationship between a stimulus and a response. Probably the best-known example of this type of learning comes from the studies done with animals by the Russian psychologist Pavlov.[23] Pavlov noticed that at feeding times, his dogs would salivate at the sight of food. The connection between food and salivation is not taught; it is an innate reflex reaction. Because this relationship exists before the conditioning process, the food is referred to as an *unconditioned stimulus* and salivation is an *unconditioned response.* To see if salivation could be conditioned to occur in response to another neutral stimulus, Pavlov paired the ringing of a bell with the presentation of the food. After a number of trials, the dogs learned to salivate at the sound of the bell alone. Thus, the bell became a **conditioned stimulus** that elicited a **conditioned response** resembling the original unconditioned reaction.

Two factors are important for learning to occur through the associative process. The first is *contiguity*, which means the unconditioned stimulus and conditioned stimulus must be close in time and space. In Pavlov's experiment, the dog learns to associate the ringing of the bell with food because of the contiguous presentation of the two stimuli. The other important principle is *repetition*, or the frequency of the association. The more often the unconditioned and conditioned stimuli occur together, the stronger the association between them will be.

Applying classical conditioning

Learning through classical conditioning plays an important role in marketing. Buyers can be conditioned to form favorable impressions and images of various brands through the associative process. Advertisers strive to associate their products and services with perceptions, images, and emotions known to evoke positive reactions from consumers. Many products are promoted through image advertising in which the brand is shown with an unconditioned stimulus that elicits pleasant feelings. When the brand is presented simultaneously with this unconditioned stimulus, the brand itself becomes a conditioned stimulus that elicits the same favorable response. Exhibit 4–21 provides a diagram of this process, and the ad for Mountain Dew in Exhibit 4–22 shows an application of this

EXHIBIT 4–22 This commercial uses classical conditioning by associating Mountain Dew with summertime fun and refreshment

(MUSIC STARTS)
BEING COOL YOU'LL FIND
IS A STATE OF MIND, A REFRESHING
  ATTITUDE
WHEN THINGS GET HOT

COOL IS ALL YOU GOT
DOING IT COUNTRY COOL
MOUNTAIN DEW
SO CHILL ON OUT WHEN THE
  HEAT COMES ON

WITH THE COOL SMOOTH
MOUNTAIN DEW
DOING IT COUNTRY COOL.
MOUNTAIN DEW, DOING IT
  COUNTRY COOL, (FADING
  OUT) MOUNTAIN DEW.

strategy. Notice how this commercial associates Mountain Dew with fun and refreshment by showing people drinking it at a summertime party.

Classical conditioning can also associate a product or service with a favorable emotional state. A study by Gerald Gorn used this approach to examine how background music in advertisements influenced product choice.[24] He found that subjects were more likely to choose a product when it was presented against a background of music they liked rather than music they disliked. These results suggest the emotions generated by a commercial are important because they may become associated with the advertised product through classical conditioning. Advertisers often attempt to pair a neutral product or service stimulus with an event or situation that arouses positive feelings, such as humor, an exciting sports event, or popular music.

Operant conditioning

Classical conditioning views the individual as a passive participant in the learning process who simply receives stimuli. Conditioning occurs as a result of exposure to a stimulus that occurs before the response. In the **operant conditioning** approach, the individual must actively *operate* or act on some aspect of the environment for learning to occur. Operant conditioning is sometimes referred to as *instrumental conditioning* because the individual's response is instrumental in getting a positive reinforcement (reward) or negative reinforcement (punishment).

@ **EXHIBIT 4–23**

Instrumental conditioning
in marketing

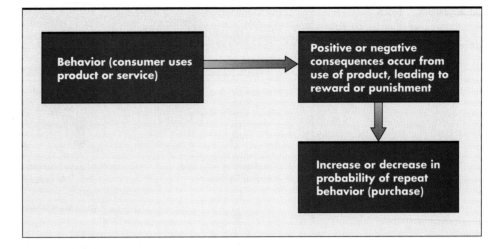

Reinforcement, the reward or favorable consequences associated with a particular response, is an important element of instrumental conditioning. Behavior that is reinforced strengthens the bond between a stimulus and a response. Thus, if a consumer buys a product in response to an ad and experiences a positive outcome, the likelihood of the consumer using this product again increases. If the outcome is not favorable, the likelihood of buying the product again decreases.

The principles of operant conditioning can be applied to marketing, as shown by Exhibit 4–23. Companies attempt to provide their customers with products and services

@ **EXHIBIT 4–24**

This ad shows how Dixie bathroom cups can help consumers avoid negative consequences

@ **EXHIBIT 4–25**

Application of shaping procedures in marketing

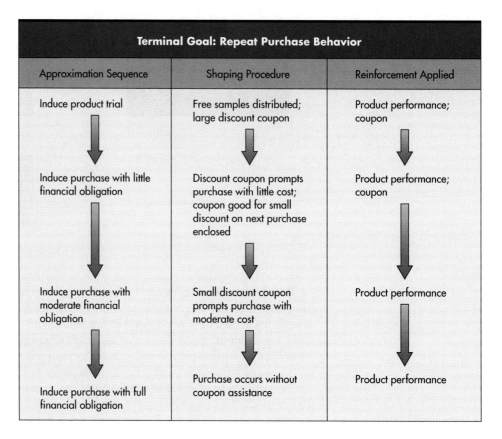

Terminal Goal: Repeat Purchase Behavior		
Approximation Sequence	Shaping Procedure	Reinforcement Applied
Induce product trial	Free samples distributed; large discount coupon	Product performance; coupon
Induce purchase with little financial obligation	Discount coupon prompts purchase with little cost; coupon good for small discount on next purchase enclosed	Product performance; coupon
Induce purchase with moderate financial obligation	Small discount coupon prompts purchase with moderate cost	Product performance
Induce purchase with full financial obligation	Purchase occurs without coupon assistance	Product performance

that satisfy their needs and reward them to reinforce the probability of repeat purchase. Reinforcement can also be implied in advertising; many ads emphasize the benefits or rewards a consumer will receive from using a product or service. Reinforcement also occurs when an ad encourages consumers to use a particular product or brand to avoid unpleasant consequences. For example, the ad for Dixie bathroom cups shown in Exhibit 4–24 on page 121 shows that using this product will help avoid negative consequences.

Two concepts that are particularly relevant to marketers in their use of reinforcement through promotional strategies are schedules of reinforcement and shaping. Different **schedules of reinforcement** result in varying patterns of learning and behavior. Learning occurs most rapidly under a *continuous* reinforcement schedule in which every response is rewarded, but the behavior is likely to cease when the reinforcement stops. Marketers must provide continuous reinforcement to consumers or risk their switching to brands that do.

Learning occurs more slowly but lasts longer when a *partial* or *intermittent* reinforcement schedule is used and only some of the individual's responses are rewarded. Promotional programs are an example of partial reinforcement schedules. A firm may offer consumers an incentive to use the company's product. The firm does not want to offer the incentive every time (continuous reinforcement), because consumers might become dependent on it and stop buying the brand when the incentive is withdrawn. A study that examined the use of a continuous versus partial reinforcement on bus ridership found that discount coupons given as rewards for riding the bus were as effective when given on a partial schedule as on a continuous schedule.[25] The cost of giving the discount coupons under the partial schedule, however, was considerably less.

Reinforcement schedules can also be used to influence consumer learning and behavior through a process known as **shaping,** the reinforcement of successive acts that lead to a desired behavior pattern or response. Rothschild and Gaidis argue that shaping is a very useful concept for marketers:

> Shaping is an essential process in deriving new and complex behavior because a behavior cannot be rewarded unless it first occurs; a stimulus can only reinforce acts that already occur. New, complex behaviors rarely occur by chance in nature. If the only behavior to be rewarded were the final complex sought behavior, one would probably have to wait a long time for this to occur by chance. Instead, one can reward simpler existing behaviors; over time, more complex patterns evolve and these are rewarded. Thus the shaping process occurs by a method of successive approximations.[26]

In a promotional context, shaping procedures are used as part of the introductory program for new products. Exhibit 4–25 provides an example of how samples and discount coupons can be used to introduce a new product and take a consumer from trial to repeat purchase. Marketers must be careful in their use of shaping procedures: dropping the incentives too soon may result in the consumer failing to establish the desired behavior, while overusing them may result in the consumer's purchase becoming contingent on the incentive rather than the product or service.

Cognitive Learning

Behavioral learning theories have been criticized for assuming a mechanistic view of the consumer that puts too much emphasis on external stimulus factors. They ignore internal psychological processes such as motivation, thinking, and perception, assuming that the external stimulus environment will elicit fairly predictable responses. Many consumer researchers and marketers disagree with the simplified explanations of behavioral learning theories and are more interested in examining the complex mental processes that underlie consumer decision making. The cognitive approach to studying learning and decision making has dominated the field of consumer behavior in recent years. Exhibit 4–26 shows how cognitive theorists view the learning process.

As consumer behavior typically involves choices and decision making, the cognitive perspective has particular appeal to those who study it. Cognitive learning theory is particularly relevant for important and involved purchase decisions. Cognitive processes such as perception, formation of beliefs about brands, attitude development and change, and integration processes are important to understanding the decision-making process for many types of purchases. The subprocesses examined during our discussion of the five-stage decision process model are all relevant to a cognitive learning approach to consumer behavior.

⊚ ENVIRONMENTAL INFLUENCES ON CONSUMER BEHAVIOR

The consumer does not make purchase decisions in isolation. A number of external factors have been identified that may influence consumer decision making, and are shown in Exhibit 4–27. The remainder of this chapter examines some of these factors.

Culture

The broadest and most abstract of the external factors that influence consumer behavior is culture. **Culture** refers to the complexity of learned meanings, values, norms, and customs shared by members of a society. Cultural norms and values offer direction and guidance to members of a society in all aspects of their lives, including their consumption behavior. It is becoming increasingly important to understand the impact of culture on consumer behavior as marketers expand their international marketing efforts. Each country has certain cultural traditions, customs, and values that marketers must understand as they develop marketing programs.

Marketers must also be aware of changes that may be occurring in a particular culture and the implications of these changes on their advertising and promotional strategies and programs. American culture continually goes through many changes that have direct implications for advertising. Marketing researchers continually monitor these changes and their impact on the ways companies market their products and services.

◎ EXHIBIT 4–26

The cognitive learning process

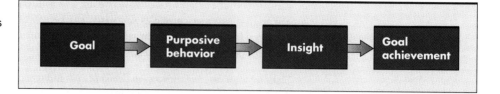

While marketers recognize that culture exerts a demonstrable influence on consumers, they often find it difficult to respond to cultural differences in various markets. The subtleties of various cultures are often difficult to understand and appreciate. Marketers must understand the cultural context in which consumer purchase decisions are made and adapt their advertising and promotional programs accordingly.

Subcultures

Within a given culture are generally found smaller groups or segments whose beliefs, values, norms, and patterns of behavior set them apart from the larger cultural mainstream. These **subcultures** may be based on age, geography, religious, racial, and/or ethnic differences. A number of subcultures exist within the United States. The three largest racial/ethnic subcultures are African-Americans, Hispanics, and various Asian groups. As noted in Chapter 2, these racial/ethnic subcultures are important because of their size, growth, purchasing power, and distinct purchasing patterns. IMC Perspecive 4–1 discusses how marketers recognize the importance of these subcultures as target markets for various products and services.

Social Class

Virtually all societies exhibit some form of social stratification whereby individuals can be assigned to a specific social category based on criteria important to members of that society. **Social class** refers to relatively homogeneous divisions in a society into which people sharing similar lifestyles, values, norms, interests, and behaviors can be grouped. While a number of methods for determining social class exist, class structures in the United States are generally based on occupational status, educational attainment, and source of income. Sociologists generally agree there are three broad levels of social classes in the United States: the upper (14 percent), middle (70 percent), and lower (16 percent) classes.[27]

◎ EXHIBIT 4–27

External influences on consumer behavior

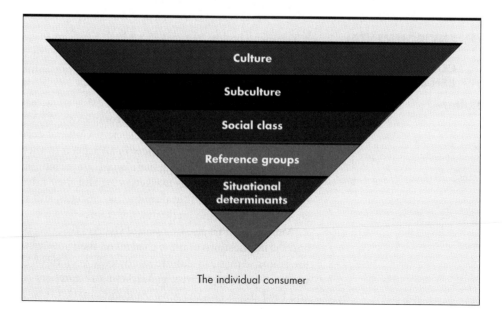

The individual consumer

IMC Perspective 4–1
The Mass Market No Longer Exists

Advertisers have come to the realization that the mass market no longer exists. The increasing ethnic diversity of the United States has forced marketers to become subcultural experts.

Ethnic minority shoppers spent over $600 billion on consumer products in 1993. By the year 2000, they will account for approximately 30 percent of the U.S. economy. African-

Kenya, the doll that's just like her. Remember when you used to play with your dolls? You had to make believe they were just like you.

Well, now you can give your little girl what you never had. A doll she'll love because it really is just like her. Kenya, with hair she can braid and bead. Hair she can straighten or leave curly and natural.

Kenya will give your daughter hours and hours of fun while she's helping your child see the beauty that lies within herself. And her own family.

Kenya and Baby Kenya (in her fancy dress and kente bag) come in three natural skintones. One is just like hers. Aren't you glad you can give your daughter Kenya?

KENYA Just like her. TYCO

Americans alone now number over 31 million, spending more than $223 billion a year.

Of major importance to marketers is the fact that these ethnic groups make consumer choices in a way all their own. Hispanics have been shown to have different media choices from whites. Blacks have stated that one of the most important criteria in their store selection is whether or not blacks are treated the same as others, and Asians make three times as many phone calls overseas as the average American.

To keep abreast of these niche markets, marketers have engaged in a number of activities. Yankelovich Partners has teamed up with the black-owned agency Burrell Communications to produce an exhaustive study on African-American lifestyles. P&G spends 5 percent ($250 million) of its advertising budget on ethnic ads, while more and more companies—including AT&T, McDonald's, and Coca-Cola—are using agencies that specialize in ethnic marketing. In 1992, companies spent $500 million on advertising to reach minorities, including bilingual billboards, sweepstakes, parades, and sponsorships. This number is expected to exceed $900 million by the year 2000.

These efforts are apparently paying off. By relying less on mass media like network TV and general circulation magazines and more on specialized media like cable TV and ethnic-oriented magazines, advertisers have achieved success. This success comes as a result of better addressing the needs of ethnic groups as well as avoiding ethnic faux pas. With so much money at stake, the niches are becoming as valuable as the mass markets themselves.

Sources: Thomas McCarroll, "It's a Mass Market No More," *Time,* Fall 1993, pp. 80–81; Bruce Horowitz, "Blacks Flex Buying Power," *Los Angeles Times,* May 17, 1993, pp. D6–7.

Social class is an important concept to marketers, since consumers within each social stratum often exhibit similar values, lifestyles, and buying behavior. Thus, the various social class groups provide a natural basis for market segmentation. Consumers in the various social classes differ in the degree to which they use various products and services and in their leisure activities, shopping patterns, and media habits. Marketers respond to these differences through the positioning of their products and services, the media strategies they use to reach different social classes, and the types of advertising appeals they develop. The ad for Concord's Saratoga watch in Exhibit 4–28 shows how a product targeted to the upper classes attempts to appeal to this group in both copy and illustration.

Reference Groups

Think about the last time you attended a party. As you dressed for the party, you probably asked yourself (or someone else) what others would be wearing. Your selection of attire may have been influenced by those likely to be present. This simple example reflects one form of impact that groups may exert on your behavior.

A *group* has been defined as "two or more individuals who share a set of norms, values, or beliefs and have certain implicitly or explicitly defined relationships to one another such that their behavior is interdependent."[28] Groups are one of the primary factors influencing learning and socialization, and group situations constitute many of our purchase decisions.

@ **EXHIBIT 4–28**

Concord targets the upper class

A **reference group** is "a group whose presumed perspectives or values are being used by an individual as the basis for his or her judgments, opinions, and actions." Consumers use reference groups as a guide to specific behaviors, even when they are not present.[29] In the party example, your peers—although not present—provided a standard of dress that you referred to in your clothing selection. Likewise, your college classmates, family, co-workers, or even a group to which you aspire may serve as referents, and your consumption patterns will typically conform to the expectations of these groups.

Marketers utilize reference group influences in developing advertisements and promotional strategies. The ads in Exhibit 4–29 are examples of *aspirational* reference groups (to which we might like to belong) and *disassociative* groups (to which we do not wish to belong), respectively.

Family decision making: an example of group influences

In some instances, the group may be involved more directly than just as a referent. Family members may serve as referents to each other, or they may actually be involved in the purchase decision process—acting as an individual buying unit. As shown in Exhibit 4–30, family members may assume a variety of roles in the decision-making process.[30] Each role has implications for marketers.[31]

First, the advertiser must determine who is responsible for the various roles in the decision-making process, so messages can be targeted at that person (or those people). These roles will also dictate media strategies, since the appropriate magazines, newspapers, or television or radio stations must be used. Second, understanding the decision-making process and the use of information by individual family members is critical to the design of messages and choice of promotional program elements. In sum, an overall understanding of how the decision process works and the role that each family member plays is necessary to an effective promotional program.

Situational Determinants

The final external factor is the purchase and usage situation. The specific situation in which consumers plan to use the product or brand directly affects their perceptions, preferences, and purchasing behaviors.[32] Three types of **situational determinants** may have an effect—the specific usage situation, the purchase situation, and the communications situation.

@ **EXHIBIT 4-29** An example of an ad showing an aspirational reference group (left) This ad stresses a disassociative reference group (right)

Usage refers to the circumstance in which the product will be used. For example, purchases made for private consumption may be thought of differently from those in which the purchase will be obvious to the public. The *purchase* situation more directly involves the environment operating at the time of the purchase. Time constraints, store

@ **EXHIBIT 4-30**

Roles in the family decision-making process

> **The initiator.** The person responsible for initiating the purchase decision process; for example, the mother who determines she needs a new car.
>
> **The information provider.** The individual responsible for gathering information to be used in making the decision; the teenage car buff who knows where to find product information in specific magazines or collects it from dealers; and so on.
>
> **The influencer.** The person who exerts influence as to what criteria will be used in the selection process. All members of the family may be involved. The mother may have her criteria, whereas others may each have their own input.
>
> **The decision maker(s).** That person(s) who actually makes the decision. In our example, it may be the mother alone or in combination with another family member.
>
> **The purchasing agent.** That individual who performs the physical act of making the purchase. In the case of an auto, husband and wife may decide to pick a car together and sign the purchase agreement.
>
> **The consumer.** The actual user of the product. In the case of a family car, all family members are consumers. For a private car, only the wife might be the consumer.

environments, and other factors may all have an impact. The *communications* situation is the condition in which an advertising exposure occurs (in a car listening to the radio, with friends, etc.). This may be most relevant to the development of promotional strategies because the impact on the consumer will vary according to the particular situation. For example, a consumer may pay more attention to a commercial that is heard alone while driving in a car than in the presence of friends, at work, or anywhere a number of distractions may be present. If advertisers can isolate a particular time when the listener is likely to be attentive, they will probably earn his or her undivided attention.

In sum, situational determinants may either enhance or detract from the potential success of a message. To the degree that advertisers can assess situational influences that may be operating, they will increase the likelihood of successfully communicating with their target audiences.

SUMMARY

This chapter introduced you to the field of consumer behavior and examined its relevance to promotional strategy. Consumer behavior is best viewed as the process and activities that people engage in when searching for, selecting, purchasing, using, evaluating, and disposing of products and services to satisfy their needs and desires. A five-stage model of the consumer decision-making process consists of problem recognition, search, alternative evaluation, purchase, and postpurchase evaluation. Internal psychological processes that influence the consumer decision-making process include motivation, perception, attitude formation and change, and integration processes.

Three variations in the consumer decision-making process are routine response behavior, limited problem solving, and extended problem solving. The decision process model views consumer behavior primarily from a cognitive orientation. The chapter considered alternative perspectives by examining various approaches to consumer learning and their implications for advertising and promotion. Behavioral learning theories such as classical conditioning and operant (instrumental) conditioning were discussed. Problems with behavioral learning theories were noted, and the alternative perspective of cognitive learning was discussed.

The chapter concluded with an examination of relevant external factors that influence consumer decision making. Culture, subculture, social class, reference groups, and situational determinants were discussed, along with their implications for the development of promotional strategies and programs.

KEY TERMS

consumer behavior, p. 96
problem recognition, p. 97
want, p. 99
motives, p. 99
hierarchy of needs, p. 100
psychoanalytic theory, p. 101
motivation research, p. 102
internal search, p. 104
external search, p. 104
perception, p. 105
sensation, p. 106
selective perception, p. 107

selective exposure, p. 107
selective attention, p. 107
selective comprehension, p. 107
selective retention, p. 107
mnemonics, p. 107
subliminal perception, p. 108
evaluative criteria, p. 110
functional consequences, p. 110
psychosocial consequences, p. 110

multiattribute attitude model, p. 111
salient beliefs, p. 112
integration processes, p. 113
heuristics, p. 114
affect referral decision rule, p. 114
purchase intention, p. 114
brand loyalty, p. 115
cognitive dissonance, p. 115
classical conditioning, p. 119
conditioned stimulus, p. 119

conditioned response, p. 119
operant conditioning, p. 120
reinforcement, p. 121
schedules of reinforcement, p. 122
shaping, p. 123
culture, p. 123
subcultures, p. 124
social class, p. 124
reference group, p. 126
situational determinants, p. 126

DISCUSSION QUESTIONS

1. Why is it important for promotional planners to understand consumer behavior? What are some aspects of consumer behavior they need to understand?

2. Discuss some of the problems associated with the application of psychoanalytic theory to consumer behavior.

3. What is subliminal perception? Describe how marketers are attempting to use this concept in the marketing of goods and services.

4. Discuss the three variations of the consumer decision-making process. What is the importance of communications in each type?

5. Discuss how psychoanalytic theory can be applied to marketing and advertising. Find three ads that apply psychoanalytic theory techniques and explain why.

6. Explain the process of shaping. Give an example of a marketing communications strategy that employs this technique.

7. What problems does the selective perception process create for advertisers? How might they overcome some of these problems?

8. Discuss the various attitude change strategies recognized by the multiattribute model. How could an airline use some of these attitude change strategies in its marketing and advertising programs?

9. Discuss how promotional planners can use the principles of various behavioral learning theories, such as classical and operant conditioning and modeling, in the design of advertising and promotional strategies.

10. Describe the five different environmental influences on consumer behavior. Find advertisements that reflect each of these.

Chapter 5

Market Segmentation and Positioning

Chapter Objectives

- To review the strategies available to the marketer for selecting and entering a market.
- To examine the concept of target marketing and its use in advertising and promotion.
- To explain market segmentation and its use in advertising and promotion.

- To understand the use of positioning and repositioning strategies in advertising and promotion.
- To examine the factors to consider in developing a positioning strategy.

Generation X: The New Target Market

The boomers are gone. So are the yuppies. At least this is the attitude shared by many marketers who have now focused their attentions on consumers under 35 years old. This new market segment—given a variety of titles, but most commonly known as Generation X—constitutes a $125 billion market, and everyone wants a part of it. For example, Pepsi has doubled Mountain Dew's ad budget to about $40 million and will push the brand through advertising and promotions, much of it targeted to Generation X. The ads for Mountain Dew and Diet Mountain Dew focus on high adventure sports like air-biking, cliff-kayaking, and sky diving. The Diet Mountain Dew ads carry the tagline "Do Diet Dew" while the Mountain Dew ads use "Get Vertical" in an attempt to appeal to the Generation Xers' lifestyles. The company also plans to use a "Vertical Bucks" promotion in which consumers can win such items as pogo sticks, T-shirts, and ice coolers.

Unfortunately for marketers, the battle cry of Generation X is "I am not a target market." What this means is that unlike their baby-boomer counterparts, Generation Xers are not a consumption oriented group. In fact, they have disavowed virtually everything their predecessors adopted. They have been characterized as hostile, alienated, cynical, and completely uninterested in marketing appeals targeted specifically to them.

Nevertheless, marketers have not given up. Auto companies such as Geo, Acura, and Hyundai have developed integrated marketing communications specifically for this age group. Acura estimates that Generation X may represent as many as 50 percent of its prospective Integra buyers, and has developed campaigns using custom animation and a spokes-dog called Leonard to reach them. The dog never talks, but the audience is able to hear his thoughts as spoken by comic Dennis Miller.

Many media have also changed their focus to be more appealing (Generation Xers have abandoned the three major networks, and they prefer magazines such as Details, Spin, Vibe, and The Source over Time, Newsweek, and Rolling Stone), and have attempted to integrate Xers values into their ad campaigns. Nintendo, Bamboo Lingerie, and Chrysler (among others) have all created specific campaigns focusing on the untraditional generation. New England Ford dealers successfully implemented a promotional program proclaiming, "The New Fords. They're not most cars." Saturn found that no-haggle pricing and low-pressure sales tactics work best with this group.

Of course, not everyone believes that Generation X is worth pursuing—or, for that matter, that it even exists. Jon Van Meter, editor of Vibe magazine, says Generation X is a mythical generation. Still others think the appeals targeting Xers may alienate other segments who cannot relate to the out-of-the-mainstream ads. Only time will tell who is right.

Sources: John Leo, "Madison Avenue's Gender War," U.S. News & World Report, Oct. 25, 1993, p. 25; Scott Donaton, "The Media Wakes Up to Generation X," Advertising Age, Jan. 1, 1993, pp. 16–17; Raymond Serafin and Cleveland Horton, "X Marks the Spot for Car Marketing," Advertising Age, Aug. 9,1993, p. 8; Cara Appelbaum, "As Cola Sales Dip, Pepsi Turns on Mountain Dew," Adweek's Marketing Week, Feb. 24, 1992, p. 6.

s the Generation X story demonstrates, companies often target a specific market. In the case of Generation X, the task appears to be a monumental one. Because of the diversity of consumers' needs and wants and the increase in competitive offerings in the past few decades, marketers have segmented their markets and concentrated on marketing their products to specific groups rather than to the whole market. This means they develop specific integrated marketing communications strategies for each of these markets. In this chapter, we examine the concepts of market segmentation, target marketing, and market positioning and their relevance to the promotional planning process.

Recall from our discussion of the integrated marketing communications planning program that the situation analysis is conducted at the beginning of the promotional planning process. Specific objectives—both marketing and communication—are derived from the situation analysis, and the promotional mix strategies are developed to achieve these objectives. Marketers rarely go after the entire market with one product, brand, or service offering. Rather, they pursue a number of different strategies, breaking the market into *segments*, and targeting one or more of these segments for marketing and promotional efforts. This means different objectives may be established, different budgets may be used, and the promotional mix strategies may vary, depending on the market approach used.

Because few, if any, products can satisfy the needs of all consumers, companies often develop different marketing strategies to satisfy different consumer needs. The process by which marketers do this (presented in Exhibit 5–1) is referred to as **target marketing** and involves four basic steps: identifying markets with unfulfilled needs, segmenting the market, targeting specific segments, and positioning one's product or service through marketing strategies.

@ IDENTIFYING MARKETS

Besides target marketing, marketers attempt to satisfy the needs of consumers through **product differentiation**, whereby the manufacturer produces a variety of products from which the consumer can choose, as demonstrated by the Anheuser Busch product line shown in Exhibit 5–2. A second approach is target marketing, in which the marketer identifies the specific needs of groups of people (or segments), selects one or more of these segments as a target, and develops marketing programs directed to each. This latter approach has found increased applicability in marketing for a number of reasons, including changes in the market (consumers are becoming much more diverse in their needs, attitudes, and lifestyles); increased use of segmentation by competitors; and more managers being trained in segmentation, realizing the advantages associated with this strategy. Perhaps the best explanation, however, comes back to the basic premise that you must understand as much as possible about consumers to design marketing programs to meet their needs most effectively.

Segmenting isolates consumers with similar lifestyles, needs, and the like, and increases our knowledge of their specific requirements. The more marketers can establish this common ground with consumers, the more effective they will be in addressing these requirements in their communications programs and informing and/or persuading potential consumers that the product or service offering will meet their needs.

Let's use the beer industry as an example. Years ago, beer was just beer, with little differentiation, many local distributors, and few truly national brands. The industry began consolidating; many brands were assumed by the larger brewers or ceased to exist. As

@ **EXHIBIT   5–1**   The target marketing process

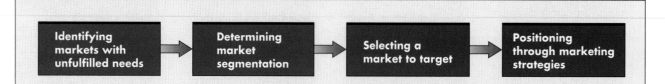

| Identifying markets with unfulfilled needs | → | Determining market segmentation | → | Selecting a market to target | → | Positioning through marketing strategies |

@ **EXHIBIT 5–2**

Anheuser Busch's approach
to product differentiation

the number of competitors decreased, competition among the major brewers increased. To compete more effectively, brewers began to look at different tastes, lifestyles, and so on of beer drinkers and used this information in their marketing strategies. This process segmented the marketplace.

As you can see in Exhibit 5–3, the beer market has become quite segmented, offering super premiums, premiums, populars (low price), imports, lights (low calorie), and malts. Low-alcohol and nonalcoholic brands have also been introduced, as has draft beer in bottles and cans. And there are now imported lights, super premium drafts, dry beers, and on and on. Given that most of these product groups are thriving, each must satisfy its own set of needs. While taste is certainly one factor, others include image, costs, and the size of one's waistline. A variety of reasons for purchasing are also operating, including social class, lifestyle, and economic considerations, any of which may be reflected in the brand's image.

The market has been segmented into a number of individual markets, each with its own specific characteristics and each requiring a separate marketing and promotions effort. The remainder of this chapter discusses ways to approach this task.

@ **SEGMENTING MARKETS**

It is not possible to develop marketing strategies for every consumer. Rather, the marketer attempts to identify broad classes of buyers who have the same needs and will respond similarly to marketing actions. As noted by Eric N. Berkowitz, Roger A. Kerin, and William Rudelius, **market segmentation** is "dividing up a market into distinct groups that (1) have common needs and (2) will respond similarly to a marketing action."[1] The segmentation process involves five distinct steps:

1. Finding ways to group consumers according to their needs.
2. Finding ways to group the marketing actions—usually the products offered—available to the organization.
3. Developing a market–product grid to relate the market segments to the firm's products or actions.
4. Selecting the target segments toward which the firm directs its marketing actions.
5. Taking marketing actions to reach target segments.

The more marketers segment the market, the more precise is their understanding of it. But the more the market becomes divided, the fewer consumers are in each segment. Thus, a key decision is, how far should one go in the segmentation process? Where does the process stop? As you can see by the strategy taken in the beer industry, it can go far!

In planning the promotional effort, managers consider whether the target segment will support individualized strategies. More specifically, they consider whether this

@ **EXHIBIT 5–3**

Beer market breakdown by
product (percent share)

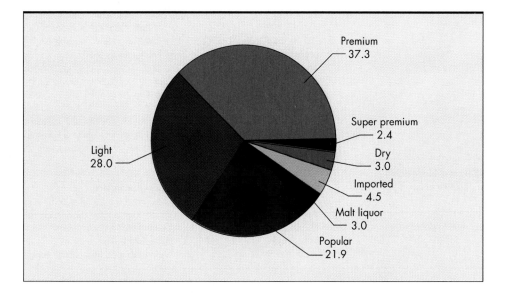

◉ EXHIBIT 5–4 Bases for market segmentation

A. Segmentation variables and breakdowns for consumer markets

Main Dimension	Segmentation Variables	Typical Breakdowns
Customer Characteristics		
Geographic	Region	Pacific; Mountain; West North Central; West South Central; East North Central; East South Central; South Atlantic; Middle Atlantic; New England
	City or metropolitan statistical area (MSA) size	Under 5,000; 5,000 to 19,999; 20,000 to 49,999; 50,000 to 99,999; 100,000 to 249,999; 250,000 to 499,999; 500,000 to 999,999; 1,000,000 to 3,999,999; 4,000,000 or over
	Density	Urban; suburban; rural
	Climate	Northern; southern
Demographic	Age	Infant, under 6; 6 to 11; 12 to 17; 18 to 24; 25 to 34; 35 to 49; 50 to 64; 65 or over
	Sex	Male; female
	Family size	1 to 2; 3 to 4; 5 or over
	Stage of family life cycle	Young single; young married, no children; young married, youngest child under 6; young married, youngest child 6 or older; older married, with children; older married, no children under 18; older single; other older married, no children under 18
	Ages of children	No child under 18; youngest child 6 to 17; youngest child under 6
	Children under 18	0; 1; more than 1
	Income	Under $5,000; $5,000 to $14,999; $15,000 to $24,999; $25,000 to $34,999; $35,000 to $49,999; $50,000 or over
	Education	Grade school or less; some high school; high school graduate; some college; college graduate
	Race	Asian; black; Hispanic; white; other
	Home ownership	Own home; rent home
Psychographic	Personality	Gregarious; compulsive; extroverted; aggressive; ambitious
	Lifestyle	Use of one's time; values and importance; beliefs
Buying Situations		
Benefits sought	Product features	Situation specific; general
	Needs	Quality; service; economy
Usage	Rate of use	Light user; medium user; heavy user
	User states	Nonuser; ex-user; prospect; first-time user; regular user
Awareness and intentions	Readiness to buy	Unaware; aware; informed; interested; intending to buy
	Brand familiarity	Insistence; preference; recognition; nonrecognition; rejection
Buying condition	Type of buying activity	Minimum effort buying; comparison buying; special effort buying
	Kind of store	Convenience; wide breadth; specialty

B. Segmentation variables and breakdowns for industrial markets

Customer Characteristics		
Geographic	Region	Pacific; Mountain; West North Central; West South Central; East North Central; East South Central; South Atlantic; Middle Atlantic; New England
	Location	In MSA; not in MSA
Demographic	SIC code	2-digit; 3-digit; 4-digit categories
	Number of employees	1 to 19; 20 to 99; 100 to 249; 250 or over
	Number of production workers	1 to 19; 20 to 99; 100 to 249; 250 or over
	Annual sales volume	Less than $1 million; $1 million to $10 million; $10 million to $100 million; over $100 million
	Number of establishments	With 1 to 19 employees; with 20 or more employees
Buying Situations		
Nature of good	Kind	Product or service
	Where used	Installation; component of final product; supplies
	Application	Office use; limited production use; heavy production use
Buying condition	Purchase location	Centralized; decentralized
	Who buys	Individual buyer; group
	Type of buy	New buy; modified rebuy; straight rebuy

@ **EXHIBIT 5–5**

Road Runner Sports employs
geographic segmentation

group is *accessible*. Can it be reached with a communications program? For example, you will see in Chapter 12 that in some instances there are no media that can be used to reach some targeted groups. Or the promotions manager may identify a number of segments but be unable to develop the required programs to reach them. The firm may have insufficient funds to develop the required advertising campaign, inadequate sales staff to cover all areas, or other promotional deficiencies. Having determined that a segmentation strategy is in order, the marketer must then establish the *basis* on which it will address the market. The following section discusses some of the bases for segmenting markets and demonstrates advertising and promotions applications.

Bases for Segmentation

As shown in Exhibit 5–4, a variety of methods are available for segmenting markets. Marketers may use one of the segmentation variables or a combination of approaches. Consider the market segmentation strategy that might be employed to market snow skis. The consumer's lifestyle—active, fun-loving, enjoys outdoor sports—is certainly important. But so are other factors, such as age (Participation in downhill skiing drops off significantly at about age 30) and income (Have you seen the price of a lift ticket lately?). Let us review the bases for segmentation and examine some promotional strategies employed in each.

Geographic segmentation

In the **geographic segmentation** approach, markets are divided into different geographic units. These units may include nations, states, counties, or even neighborhoods. Consumers often have different buying habits depending on where they reside. For example, General Foods has identified regional differences in coffee tastes and developed various package sizes accordingly. Other companies have developed programs targeted at specific states. Exhibit 5–5 demonstrates how Road Runner Sports used geographic segmentation by including different cities on the covers of its direct mail pieces. This strategy proved to be much more successful than sending the same cover to all cities. Still other companies have developed alternative strategies for areas as small as neighborhoods due to differences in these areas.

Demographic segmentation

Dividing the market on the basis of demographic variables such as age, sex, family size, education, income, and social class is called **demographic segmentation**. Secret deodorant is an example of a product that has met with a great deal of success by

EXHIBIT 5–6

Lange USA initiated an advertising campaign to increase sales of its ski boots to women

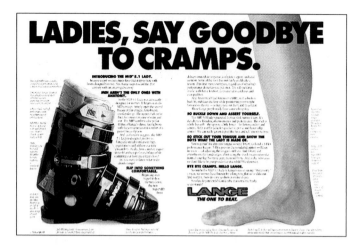

using the demographic variable of sex as a basis for segmentation effectively targeting women.

Although market segmentation on the basis of demographics may seem obvious, companies sometimes discover that they need to focus more attention on a specific demographic group. For example, Lange USA has targeted women in an advertising campaign stressing the fact that its ski boots are comfortable for women (Exhibit 5–6). The goal of the campaign was to grab a larger share of the ski boot market, of which 45 percent is in women's boots. In 1991, Lange sold 7,000 pairs of mid-entry boots. In 1992, it sold 60,000 pairs.[2]

Other products that have successfully employed demographic segmentation include Virginia Slims cigarettes (sex), Affinity shampoo (age), cars (income), and prepackaged dinners (family size).

While demographics may still be the most commonly used method of segmenting markets, it is important to recognize that other factors may be the underlying basis for homogeneity and/or consumer behaviors. For example, as noted by Robert Rueff, "Consumer attitudes and behaviors are not demographically driven and, in many cases, are not even demographically related."[3] In addition, broad demographic segments (such as the commonly used age breakdowns 18–34 and 35–49) may include consumers who behave very differently. Eighteen-year-olds have very different lifestyles from 34-year-olds and may have different needs and wants as well. The astute marketer will identify additional bases for segmenting and will recognize the limitations of demographics.

Psychographic segmentation

Dividing the market on the basis of personality and/or lifestyles is referred to as **psychographic segmentation**. While there is some disagreement as to whether personality is useful as a basis for segmentation, lifestyle factors have been used effectively. Many consider lifestyles the most effective criterion for segmentation.

The determination of lifestyles is usually based on an analysis of the activities, interests, and opinions (AIOs) of consumers. These lifestyles are then correlated with the consumers' product, brand, and/or media usage. For many products and/or services, lifestyles may be the best discriminator between use and nonuse, accounting for differences in food consumption, clothing apparel, and automobile selections, among numerous other consumer behaviors.[4]

Psychographic segmentation has been increasingly accepted with the advent of the **values and lifestyles program (VALS)** (although marketers employed lifestyle segmentation long before VALS). Developed by the Stanford Research Institute (SRI), VALS has become one of the more popular methods for applying lifestyle segmentation. VALS 2 divides Americans into eight lifestyle segments that exhibit distinctive attitudes, behaviors, and decision-making patterns.[5] When combined with an estimate of the resources the consumer can draw on (education, income, health, energy level, self-confidence, and degree of consumerism), SRI believes the VALS 2 system is an excellent predictor of consumer behaviors. A variety of companies, including Chevron, Mercedes-Benz, and Eastman Kodak, have employed the VALS 2 program.

VALS 2 is not the only lifestyle system available to marketers. While it is not possible here to detail all the alternatives, we will mention a few:

- **ClusterPlus.** This market segmentation system uses as its basis 47 lifestyle clusters. The Donnelley Marketing Information Services assigns each neighborhood in the country to one of the lifestyle clusters, representing groups of people with similar demographic characteristics and consumer behavior patterns.
- **Prism.** Claritas' system classifies 540,000 neighborhoods by demographic characteristics, consumer behavior patterns, and 40 basic lifestyle clusters.
- **MicroVision.** Equifax/National Decision Systems classifies all U.S. consumer households into 50 distinctive lifestyle segments at the Zip+4 level of geography, providing insight into purchase behavior, media habits, attitudes, and lifestyle activities.

Behavioristic segmentation

Dividing consumers into groups according to their usage, loyalties, or buying responses to a product is **behavioristic segmentation.** For example, segmentation may be based on product or brand usage, degree of use (heavy versus light), and/or brand loyalty. These characteristics are then combined with demographic and/or psychographic criteria to develop profiles of market segments. In the case of usage, the marketer assumes that nonpurchasers of a brand or product who have the same characteristics as purchasers hold greater potential for adoption than those with different characteristics. A profile (demographic or psychographic) of the user is developed, which serves as the basis for promotional strategies designed to attract new users. For example, teenagers—who share certain similarities in their consumption behaviors—who do not currently own a Sony Discman might be more likely to be potential buyers than those in other age groups.

Degree of use relates to the fact that a few consumers may account for a disproportionate amount of the share of purchase for many products or brands. In industrial markets, many marketers refer to the **80–20 rule,** meaning 20 percent of their buyers account for 80 percent of their sales volume. Again, when the characteristics of these users are identified, targeting them allows for a much greater concentration of efforts and less wasted time and monies. The same heavy-half strategy is possible in the consumer market as well. The majority of purchases of many products (for example, soaps and detergents, shampoos, cake mixes, beer, dog food, colas, bourbon, and toilet tissue—yes, toilet tissue!) is accounted for by a small proportion of the population (Exhibit 5–7).[6] Perhaps you can think of some additional examples.

Benefit segmentation

In purchasing products, consumers are generally trying to satisfy specific needs and/or wants. These consumers are looking for specific benefits that products might provide in satisfying these needs. The grouping of consumers on the basis of attributes sought in a product is known as **benefit segmentation,** a widely utilized basis for many firms.

Consider the purchase of a wristwatch. While you might buy a watch for particular benefits such as accuracy, water resistance, or stylishness, others may seek a different set of benefits. Watches are commonly given as gifts for birthdays, Christmas, and graduation. Certainly some of the same benefits are considered in the purchase of a gift, but the benefits the purchaser derives are different from those the user will obtain. Advertisements that portray watches as good gifts stress a different set of criteria to consider in the purchase decision. The next time you see an ad or commercial for a watch, think about the basic appeal and the benefits it offers.

EXHIBIT 5–7

Heavy and light users of consumer products

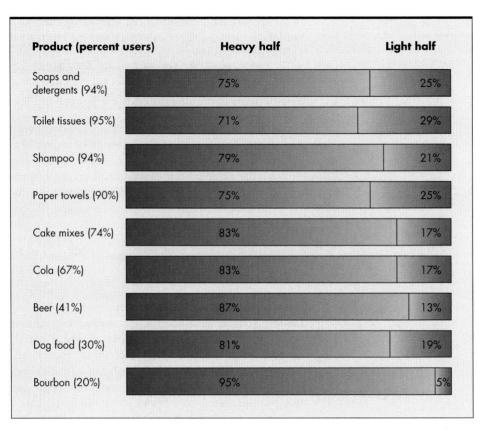

Product (percent users)	Heavy half	Light half
Soaps and detergents (94%)	75%	25%
Toilet tissues (95%)	71%	29%
Shampoo (94%)	79%	21%
Paper towels (90%)	75%	25%
Cake mixes (74%)	83%	17%
Cola (67%)	83%	17%
Beer (41%)	87%	13%
Dog food (30%)	81%	19%
Bourbon (20%)	95%	5%

Another example of benefit segmentation can be seen in the toothpaste market. Some consumers want a product with fluoride (Crest, Colgate); others prefer one that freshens their breath (Close-Up, Aqua-Fresh). More recent benefit segments are those offering tartar control (Crest) and plaque reduction (Viadent). The Den-Mat Corp. introduced Rembrandt whitening toothpaste for consumers who want whiter teeth (Exhibit 5–8).

The Process of Segmenting a Market

The segmentation process develops over time and is an integral part of the situation analysis. It is in this stage that marketers attempt to determine as much as they can about the market: what needs are not being fulfilled, what benefits are being sought, and what characteristics distinguish between the various groups in seeking these products and services. A number of alternative segmentation strategies may be considered and employed. Each time a specific segment is identified, additional information is gathered to assist in the understanding of this group.

For example, once a specific segment is identified based on benefits sought, lifestyle characteristics and demographics will be examined to help characterize this group and to further the marketer's understanding of this market. Behavioristic segmentation criteria will also be examined. In the ski boot example, specific benefits may be sought—flexibility or stiffness, for example—depending on the type of skiing the buyer does. All this information will be combined to provide a complete profile of the skier.

A number of companies now offer research services to help marketing managers define their markets and develop strategies targeted to these groups. The VALS, MicroVision, and ClusterPlus systems discussed earlier are just a few of the services offered. As you can see by examining the clusters shown in Exhibit 5–9, MicroVision uses demographic, socioeconomic, and geographic data to cluster consumer households into 50 distinctive, "micro-geographic," segments. These are built at the Zip+4 level of geography for precision market analysis and targeting.

Whether these microunits meet the criteria considered necessary for useful segmentation will be determined by the user of the system. A national company might not attempt

⊚ **EXHIBIT 5–8**

Rembrandt toothpaste stresses the benefit
of its superior whitening ability

⊚ **EXHIBIT 5–9**

The 50 market segments of MicroVision are organized into nine groups.*
Since each group comprises segments that have similar characteristics or
habits, you can easily target several market segments that share common
lifestyles and purchasing behaviors

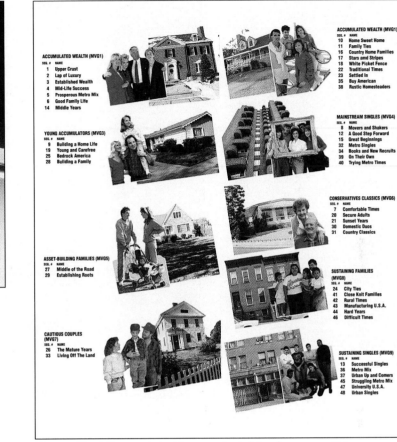

*Segments 49 and 50 were not placed in a group due to their nonhomogeneous nature

to define such small segments, but it might be useful for companies operating within one
city or geographical area.

Having completed the segmentation analysis, the marketer now moves to the third
phase shown in Exhibit 5–1: targeting a specific market.

⊚ **SELECTING A
TARGET MARKET**

The outcome of the segmentation analysis will reveal the market opportunities available. The next phase in the target marketing process involves two steps: (1) determining how many segments to enter and (2) determining which segments offer the most
potential.

**Determining How
Many Segments
to Enter**

Three market coverage alternatives are available to the firm. **Undifferentiated marketing** involves ignoring segment differences and offering just one product or service
to the entire market. For example, when Henry Ford brought out the first assembly-line
automobile, all potential consumers were offered the same basic product—a black Ford.
For many years, Coca-Cola offered only one product version. While this standardized
strategy saves the company money, it does not allow the opportunity to offer different
versions of the product.

Differentiated marketing involves marketing in a number of segments, developing separate marketing strategies for each. The Dewar's ads in Exhibit 5–10 reflect
this strategy. The profile ad appears to target a specific group (perhaps upwardly mobile,

EXHIBIT 5-10 Dewar's uses different appeals for the same product

young to middle-aged?); the second example might appeal more to older (perhaps more traditional) individuals.

While an undifferentiated strategy offers the opportunity to reduce costs through increased production, it does not allow for variety or tailoring to specific needs. Through differentiation, products—or advertising appeals—may be developed for the various segments, increasing the opportunity to satisfy the needs and wants of various groups.

The third alternative, **concentrated marketing,** is used when the firm selects one segment and attempts to capture a large share of this market. Volkswagen used this strategy in the 1950s when it was the only major automobile company competing in the economy car segment in the United States. While Volkswagen has now assumed a more differentiated strategy, other companies have found the concentrated strategy to be effective. For example, Above the Rim markets only basketball clothing and accessories. The company has built a loyal following among young consumers who like its functional features (Exhibit 5–11 on page 142).

Determining Which Segments Offer Potential

The second step in selecting a market involves determining the most attractive segment. The firm must examine the sales potential of the segment, the opportunities for growth, the competition, and its ability to compete.

The firm must then decide whether it can market to this group. Stories abound of companies that have entered new markets only to find their lack of resources or expertise would not allow them to compete successfully. For example, Royal Crown (RC) Cola has often been quite successful in identifying new segment opportunities but because of limited resources has been less able to capitalize on them than Coke and Pepsi. RC was the first to bring to market diet colas and caffeine-free colas, but it has not been able to establish itself as a market leader in either market.

Ethical Perspective 5–1
Segmentation and Target
Marketing on Trial

Ever hear of the brands Uptown, Dakota, and Powermaster? If you haven't already, you probably never will. Each was withdrawn from the market before national distribution because of public outcry over the segmentation and targeting strategies to be employed.

Uptown, an R. J. Reynolds Tobacco Co. cigarette, and Powermaster, a G. Heileman Brewing Co. malt liquor, were both targeted to blacks. Dakota, another Reynolds cigarette, was targeted to young, poorly educated white women whose favorite pastimes include cruising, partying, and attending hot rod shows and tractor pulls.

Public interest groups, consumer organizations, and government agencies all joined in the protest against the companies' new product introductions. Some question the ethics of the basic premise of segmenting and targeting markets, particularly when the segments targeted are minorities. Both sides are armed with reasons these strategies should or should not be permitted. Pros:

1. All marketing is targeted. Different people have very different needs and wants, and marketers cannot attempt to sell their products to everyone.
2. By definition, all target markets are minorities. Market segmentation requires the determination of smaller niches of society with similar needs and wants. Any such small group could be called a minority of the population.
3. Targeting leads to better products and services. The strategy requires a better understanding of the segments sought, so the marketer can develop better products and services to satisfy these consumers.

4. Targeting leads to more efficient and effective marketing programs. By appealing only to those groups with an interest, marketers develop more effective strategies, eliminate waste, and are more efficient. The cost savings are passed on to the consumer in the form of lower prices, better information, and so on.

Cons:

1. Minorities are often the target for detrimental products. Because of their lower educational and socioeconomic status, minorities are often selected as target markets for harmful products. They are considered easy game for more sophisticated marketers.
2. Targeting exacerbates social problems. Because of its effectiveness, targeting can lead to increased consumption of harmful products like cigarettes and alcohol.
3. Targeting leads to control. Because large marketers are so powerful, they can control certain segments of the population, leading them to desire products they do not need.
4. Target marketing is greedy. The purpose of targeting is to maximize profits and capitalize on the marketplace.

You can see how controversial targeting has become. On the one hand, marketers consider targeting a necessary strategy for successful marketing. On the other, opponents consider it exploitative and unfair to those being targeted. The battle may have ended, but the war has not.

Source: John E. Calfee, "Targeting the Problem," *Advertising Age*, July 22, 1991, p. 16; "Target: Minorities," *Marketing & Media Decisions*, Oct. 1990, pp. 70–71.

Target marketing has recently come under fire from a variety of nonmarketing groups. Ethical Perspective 5–1 examines some reasons for the controversy and arguments on both sides of the issue.

After selecting the segments to target and determining that it can compete, the firm proceeds to the final step in Exhibit 5–1, the market positioning phase.

MARKET POSITIONING

Positioning has been defined as "the art and science of fitting the product or service to one or more segments of the broad market in such a way as to set it meaningfully apart from competition."[7] As you can see, the position of the product, service, or even store is the image that comes to mind and the attributes consumers perceive as related to it. This communication occurs through the message itself—which explains these benefits—as well as the media strategy employed to reach the target group. Take a few moments to think about how some products are positioned and how their position is conveyed to you. For example, what comes to mind when your hear Mercedes, Dr Pepper, or United Airlines? What about department stores such as Neiman–Marcus, Sears, and JC Penney? Now think of the ads for each of these products and companies. Are their approaches different from their competitors'? When and where are these ads shown?

Approaches to Positioning

Positioning strategies generally assume one of two approaches—one focusing on the consumer, the other on the competition. While both approaches involve the association of product benefits with consumer needs, the former does so by linking the product with the benefits the consumer will derive or creating a favorable brand image, as shown in

@ **EXHIBIT 5-11**

Above the Rim pursues a
concentrated marketing
strategy

Exhibit 5–12. The latter approach positions the product by comparing it, and the benefit
it offers, to the competition, as shown in Exhibit 5–13. Products such as Scope mouthwash (positioning itself as better tasting than Listerine) and Now cigarettes (comparing
the amount of nicotine in it versus several other brands) have also employed this strategy
successfully.

Many advertising practitioners consider market positioning the most important factor in establishing a brand in the marketplace. David Aaker and John Myers note that
the term *position* has recently been used to indicate the brand's or product's image in
the marketplace.[8] Jack Trout and Al Ries suggest that this brand image must contrast
with competitors'. They say, "In today's marketplace, the competitors' image is just as
important as your own. Sometimes more important."[9] Thus, *positioning*, as used in this
text, relates to the image of the product and or brand relative to competitive products or
brands. The position of the product or brand is the key factor in communicating the benefits it offers and differentiating it from the competition. Let us now turn to strategies
marketers use to position a product.

@ **EXHIBIT 5-12**

Positioning that focuses on the
consumer (left) Timex stresses
benefits to position its product
(right) Gucci effectively
creates a brand image

@ **EXHIBIT 5–13**

Almay positions itself relative to the competition

Developing a Positioning Strategy

To create a position for a product or service, Trout and Ries suggest that managers ask themselves six basic questions:[10]

1. What position, if any, do we already have in the prospect's mind? (This information must come from the marketplace, not the managers' perceptions.)
2. What position do we want to own?
3. What companies must be outgunned if we are to establish that position?
4. Do we have enough marketing money to occupy and hold the position?
5. Do we have the guts to stick with one consistent positioning strategy?
6. Does our creative approach match our positioning strategy?

A number of positioning strategies might be employed in developing a promotional program. David Aaker and J. Gary Shansby discuss six such strategies: positioning by product attributes, price/quality, use, product class, users, and competitor.[11] Aaker and Myers add one more approach, positioning by cultural symbols.[12]

Using product attributes

A common approach to positioning is setting the brand apart from competitors based on specific characteristics or benefits offered. Sometimes a product may be positioned on more than one product benefit.

Positioning by price/quality

Marketers often use price/quality characteristics to position their brands. One way of using this positioning approach is to use ads that reflect the image of a high quality brand where cost, while not irrelevant, is considered secondary to the quality benefits derived from using the brand. Premium brands positioned at the high end of the market use this approach to positioning.

Another way to use price/quality characteristics for positioning is to focus on the quality or value offered by the brand at a very competitive price. For example, the Oneida ad shown in Exhibit 5–14 uses this strategy by suggesting that quality need not be unaffordable. An important factor to remember in this approach is that although price is an important consideration, the product quality must be comparable to, or even better than, competing brands if the positioning strategy is to be effective.

◉ **EXHIBIT 5–14**

Oneida positions its brand on
quality for the right price

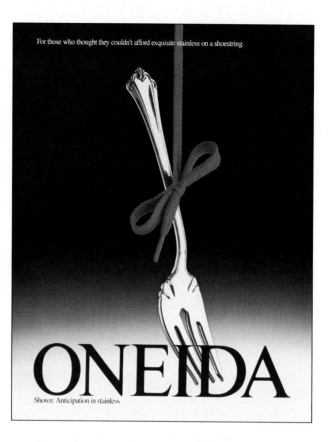

Positioning by use or application

Another way to communicate a specific image or position for a brand is to associate it with a specific *use* or *application*. For example, in Exhibit 5–15, Avia positions its FT5100 model as an all-around fitness training shoe.

While this strategy is often used to enter a market based on a particular use or application, it is also an effective way to expand the usage of a product. For example, Arm & Hammer baking soda has been promoted for everything from baking to relieving heartburn to eliminating odors in carpets and refrigerators (Exhibit 5–16).

◉ **EXHIBIT 5–15**

Avia positions its FT5100
model as an all-around fitness
shoe

⊚ **EXHIBIT 5–16**

Arm & Hammer baking
soda demonstrates numerous
product uses

Positioning by product class

Often the competition for a product comes from outside the product class. For example, those involved in the airline industry know that while they compete with other airlines, trains and buses are also viable alternatives. Amtrak has positioned itself as an alternative to airplanes, citing cost savings, enjoyment, and other advantages. Manufacturers of music CDs must compete with those in the cassette industry; many margarines position themselves against butter. Rather than positioning against another brand, an alternative strategy is to position oneself against another product category, as shown in Exhibit 5–17.

⊚ **EXHIBIT 5–17**

An example of positioning by
product class

@ **EXHIBIT 5–18**

Brands that have become
cultural symbols

Positioning by product user

Positioning a product by associating it with a particular user or group of users is yet another approach utilized by marketers. An example of this approach would be the Dewar's ads shown earlier in Exhibit 5–10. Both of these campaigns emphasize identification or association with a specific group, such as the young upwardly mobile or older, more sopisticated consumer.

Positioning by competitor

Competitors may be as important to positioning strategy as a firm's own product or services. As Trout and Ries observe, the old strategy of ignoring one's competition no longer works in today's marketplace.[13] (Advertisers used to think it was a cardinal sin to mention a competitor in their advertising.) In today's market, an effective positioning strategy for a product or brand may focus on specific competitors. This approach is similar to positioning by product class, although in this case the competition is within the same product category. Perhaps the best-known example of this strategy was Avis, which positioned itself against the car-rental leader, Hertz, by stating, "We're number two, so we try harder." The Almay ad shown earlier (Exhibit 5–13) is an example of positioning a brand against the competition. It emphasizes that while Almay is as good as Clinique, it costs only half as much. When positioning by competitor, a marketer must often employ another positioning strategy as well to differentiate the brand.

Positioning by cultural symbols

Aaker and Myers include an additional positioning strategy in which *cultural symbols* are used to differentiate brands. Examples are the Jolly Green Giant, the Keebler elves, Speedy Alka-Seltzer, Bud Man, Buster Brown, Ronald McDonald, Chiquita Banana, and Mr. Peanut. Each of these companies has successfully differentiated its product from competitors' by creating symbols that represent it (Exhibit 5–18).

The use of cultural symbols has become so common in our society that psychologists and sociologists have examined the mythological foundations underlying many characters and dissected the inherent meanings consumers ascribe to them. A museum of modern mythology that features 20th-century cultural symbols of advertising has been started in San Francisco. Part of the museum's attraction is that it traces the evolution of the characters over time, considering the changing culture of the United States and its impact on such symbols.

Repositioning

One final positioning strategy involves altering or changing a product's or brand's position. **Repositioning** a product usually occurs because of declining or stagnant sales or because of anticipated opportunities in other market positions. Repositioning is often difficult to accomplish because of entrenched perceptions about and attitudes toward

@ **EXHIBIT 5-19**

This ad is one of a series used in the campaign to reposition *Rolling Stone* magazine

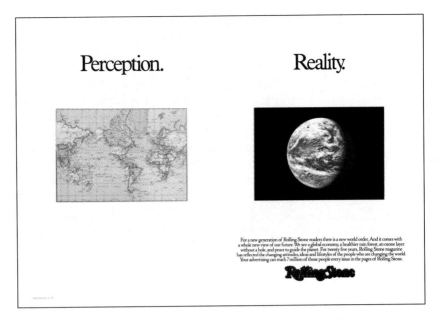

the product or brand. Many companies' attempts to change their positions have met with little or no success. For example, Sears attempted to reposition itself as a store of higher quality, appealing to more well-to-do customers. The strategy was unsuccessful and subsequently abandoned. Later, Sears again attempted a repositioning strategy, this time to a lower-priced store, again with limited success.

One extremely successful effort at repositioning was employed by *Rolling Stone* magazine. In an attempt to change the image advertisers held of the type of person who reads *Rolling Stone,* the company embarked on an extensive advertising campaign directed at potential advertisers. The ad shown in Exhibit 5–19 is just one example of how this strategy was successfully implemented.

Other companies have also been successful in attempts to reposition. For example, Pontiac effectively repositioned its product as a sportier car that adds excitement. Dutch Boy paints changed its image to reach upscale, fashion-oriented consumers, and JC Penney successfully targeted the middle class. IMC Perspective 5–1 describes how other companies were successful in their repositioning efforts.

Determining the Positioning Strategy

Having explored the alternative positioning strategies available, the marketer must determine which strategy is best suited for the firm or product and begin developing the positioning platform. As you remember from the promotional planning process in Chapter 1, the input into this stage will be derived from the situation analysis—specifically, the marketing research conducted therein. Essentially, the development of a positioning platform can be broken into a six-step process:[14]

1. **Identification of competitors.** This process requires broad thinking. Competitors may not be just those products and/or brands that fall into your product class or with which you compete directly. For example, a red wine competes with other red wines of various positions. At the same time, competition may include white wines, champagnes, and nonalcoholic wines. Wine coolers provide an alternative, as do beer and other alcoholic drinks. Other nonalcoholic drinks may come into consideration at various times and/or situations. The marketer must consider all likely competitors, as well as the various effects of use and situations on the consumer.

2. **Assessing consumers' perceptions of competitors.** Once we define the competition, we must determine how they are perceived by consumers. Which attributes are important to consumers in evaluating a product and/or brand? As you might expect, for many products, a wide variety of attributes or product

benefits may be considered—most if not all of which are important. Much of marketing firms' research is directed at making such determinations. Consumers are asked to take part in focus groups and/or complete surveys indicating which attributes are important to them in their purchase decisions. For example, attributes considered important in the selection of a bank may include convenience, teller friendliness, financial security, and a host of other factors. This process establishes the basis for the determination of competitive positions.

3. **Determining competitors' positions.** Having determined the relevant attributes and their relative importance to consumers, we must determine how each competitor (including our own entry) is positioned with respect to each attribute. This will also show how the competitors are positioned relative to each other. Consumer research is required to make this assessment.

4. **Analyzing the consumers' preferences.** Our discussion of segmentation noted various factors that may distinguish among groups of consumers, including lifestyles, purchase motivations, demographic differences, and so on. Each of these segments may have different purchase motivations and different attribute importance ratings. One way to determine these differences is to consider the *ideal* brand or product, defined as the object the consumer would prefer over all others, including objects that can be imagined but do not exist. Identifying the ideal product can help you identify different ideals among segments or identify segments with similar or the same ideal points.

5. **Making the positioning decision.** Going through the first four steps should let you decide which position to assume in the marketplace. Such a decision is not always clear and well defined, however, and conducting research may provide only limited input. In that case, the marketing manager or groups of managers must make some subjective judgments. These judgments raise a number of questions:

   - **Is the segmentation strategy appropriate?** Positioning usually entails a decision to segment the market. Consider whether the market segment sought will support an entry and whether it is in the best interests of the company to deemphasize the remaining market. When a specific position is chosen, consumers may believe this is what the product is for. Those not looking for that specific benefit may not consider the brand. If the marketer decides on an undifferentiated strategy, it may be possible to be general in the positioning platform. For example, Toyota's slogan, "I love what you do for me—Toyota" allows consumers to assume they will get what they are looking for in the brand—whatever that may be.

   - **Are there sufficient resources available to communicate the position effectively?** It is very expensive to establish a position. One ad, or even a series of ads, is not likely to be enough to engrain the position. The marketer must commit to a long-range effort in all aspects of the marketing campaign to make sure the objectives sought are obtained. Too often, the firm abandons a position and/or advertising campaign long before it can establish a position successfully. The *Rolling Stone* repositioning discussed earlier is an excellent example of sticking with a campaign: The basic theme has been running for a number of years. In contrast, both Wendy's and Burger King have switched agencies and/or campaigns so often in the past few years it has been impossible for them to establish a distinct position in the consumer's mind. Further, once a successful position is attained, it is likely to attract competitors. It may become expensive to ward off me-too brands—brands that attempt to assume the same position as the leader—and continue to hold on to the brand distinction.

   - **How strong is the competition?** The marketing manager must ask whether a position sought is likely to be maintained, given the strengths of the competition. For example, General Foods often makes it a practice not to be the first entry into a market. When competitors develop new markets with their entries, General Foods simply improves on the product and captures a large

IMC Perspective 5–1
Repositioning Success Stories

While positioning a brand may require a significant effort, attempts to reposition may be even harder. Often it is easier to create an image for a product or brand than it is to change one already held in the minds of consumers. Companies like Dutch Boy Paints, the Florida Orange Juice Commission, and Pontiac have all employed repositioning strategies. General Mills and Kellogg have repositioned cereals as "eat from the box" finger foods that could be consumed all day long by those "too busy to sit down and eat cereal." Oldsmobile was much less sucessful in repositioning its cars to younger buyers through the campaign, "This is not your father's Oldsmobile!"

The strategy of repositioning has been attempted by numerous firms, sometimes successfully, sometimes not. Following are some of the winners.

- *Iron City Beer.* Showing sales declines, Iron City repositioned by using local Pittsburgh talent in ads touting the beer as the "hometown team." Taking advantage of consumers' strong loyalty to their city, the ideas for many of the ads were actually developed by consumers submitting beer commercial fantasies. The 'Burgh thing campaign has led to a 400 percent increase in brand awareness and a 2 percent share increase.
- *Geritol.* This product had been positioned as a cure for iron-poor blood for over two decades. Sales languished in the 1980s until it was purchased by SmithKline Beecham, which implemented a new campaign targeted to middle-aged consumers with a more lively lifestyle. Geritol brands notched a 19 percent increase within the year.
- *Carnival Cruise Lines.* Long thought of as a vacation alternative for old people, cruise vacations had little appeal to younger adults and families. Repositioned as fun for all via the "Fun Ships" concept which includes new ships, singles cocktail parties, Las Vegas-style shows, Camp Carnival, and

Nautica Spa programs, Carnival has become the largest and most successful company in the cruise industry.
- *Jell-O.* Stressing public relations activities, recipes, and a new advertising campaign targeted to parents, Jell-O was born again. While always a successful and durable brand, the brand experienced sales declines in the 1970s. By tying into family values and recipes that stress nutrition and fun for kids, Jell-O is on the rise again.

Sources: Judith D. Schwartz, "New Recipes, Repositioning Put the Jiggle Back in Jell-O," *Brandweek*, May 10, 1993, pp. 26–27; "Cruise Control," *Mediaweek*, Oct. 11, 1993, pp. 24–25; Alison Fahey, "Iron City Beer: It's a 'Burgh Thing," *Brandweek*, Jan. 25, 1993, pp. 14–19; "Geritol Overcomes Its 'Iron-Poor' Image," *Adweek's Marketing Week*, Nov. 12, 1990, pp. 32–36.

percentage of the market share. This leads to two basic questions: First, if our firm is first into the market, will we be able to maintain the position (in terms of quality, price, etc.)? Second, if positioned as finest quality, it must be. If it is positioned as lowest cost, it has to be. Otherwise, the position claimed is sure to be lost.

- **Is the current positioning strategy working?** There is an old saying, "If it ain't broke, don't fix it." If your current efforts are not working, then it may be time to consider an alternative positioning strategy. But if they are working, a change is usually unwise. Sometimes executives become bored with a theme and decide it is time for a change. Often this change causes confusion in the marketplace and weakens a brand's position. Unless there is strong reason to believe a change in positioning is necessary, stick with the current strategy.

6. **Can we monitor the position?** Once a position has been established, it is necessary to monitor how well this position is being maintained in the marketplace. Tracking studies measure the image of the product or firm over time. Changes in consumers' perceptions can be determined, with any slippage immediately noted and reacted to. At the same time, the impact of competitors can be determined.

Before leaving this chapter, you might stop to think for a moment about the positioning (and repositioning) strategies pursued by different companies. Any successful product that comes to mind probably occupies a distinct market position.

SUMMARY

In the planning process, the situation analysis requires determining the marketing strategy to be assumed. The promotional program is developed with this strategy as a guide. One of the key decisions to be made regards target marketing, a process that involves identifying, segmenting, targeting, and positioning the markets.

Market segmentation—dividing the market into smaller groups—allows for the development of specifically targeted marketing strategies. Bases for segmentation include geographic, demographic, psychographic, behavioristic, and benefit segmentation. More than one basis for segmentation may be employed at a time. For example, a market may be segmented based on the lifestyles of consumers and their income levels.

Targeting the market involves determining the number of markets to enter and the most attractive segment—that is, the one with the greatest potential. The next step is positioning, or creating an image of the product in consumers' minds. Positioning strategies include positioning by product attributes, price/quality, use or application, product class, product user, competitor, and cultural symbol.

Sometimes it is necessary to reposition, or change the positioning of a product or brand. Sears, *Rolling Stone*, and JC Penney, among many others, have at one time or another pursued a repositioning strategy.

Finally, it is important to remember that the process of target marketing is indeed that—a process. Market segmentation and target marketing and positioning do not just happen; rather, a series of steps are required, ultimately leading to a strategy. After going through this process in the situation analysis, the manager is ready to establish specific objectives to be sought.

KEY TERMS

target marketing, p. 132
product differentiation, p. 132
market segmentation, p. 133
geographic segmentation, p. 135

demographic segmentation, p. 135
psychographic segmentation, p. 136
values and lifestyles program (VALS), p. 136

behavioristic segmentation, p. 137
80–20 rule, p. 137
benefit segmentation, p. 137
undifferentiated marketing, p. 139

differentiated marketing, p. 139
concentrated marketing, p. 140
positioning, p. 141
positioning strategies, p. 141
repositioning, p. 146

DISCUSSION QUESTIONS

1. Discuss the concept of target marketing. Why is it so important to marketers?
2. Cite examples of companies that have engaged in product differentiation strategies to compete in a given market.
3. Discuss the process involved in segmenting a market. What are some factors one must consider in determining how to segment the market?
4. Analyze the automobile industry from a market segmentation perspective. Discuss the various market segments and how competitors position themselves to compete in these markets.
5. What is meant by benefit segmentation? Find three ads that are designed to appeal to specific benefits segments.
6. Discuss how marketers can use consumer lifestyles as a basis for segmenting markets. Provide examples of a company that uses lifestyle segmentation.

7. What is meant by positioning? Discuss the various approaches to positioning and give examples of companies or brands that use each approach.
8. What factors would lead a marketer to the use of a repositioning strategy? Find a product or service that has been repositioned recently and analyze the strategy.
9. Six positioning strategies are discussed in the text. Collect and discuss advertisements that exemplify each.
10. Ethical Perspective 5–1 discusses how several tobacco and liquor companies have been criticized recently for targeting specific market segments. Evaluate the arguments for and against each company's rights to target such market segments as minorities, young people, or those with little education.

If you think there are only two choices for business systems,

think again.

© 1992 Hewlett-Packard Company NSG0201 5091-3637E

Selecting the best computer system for your business is never an easy task. Because, quite often, the right answers lie beyond the obvious choices.

Case-in-point: Hewlett-Packard Business Computer Systems.

While HP may not be the first name that comes to mind in business systems, we've been a leading innovator in the category for twenty years. Our systems

interconnect well in multivendor environments. They run all the leading business applications. And they do so while delivering far better price/performance than the industry leader in mid-range systems.

Some people still believe that the best way to keep up with the competition is to go with the system everyone else has. Others think that just keeping up isn't enough.

They're looking for ways to get ahead. That means rethinking the conventional ways of doing business. And looking for new choices.

Call **1-800-637-7740, Ext. 2959** for more information.

Think again.

(hp) **HEWLETT PACKARD**

Chapter **6**

The Communications Process

Chapter Objectives

- To understand the basic elements of the communications process and the role of communications in marketing.
- To examine various models of the communications process.

- To analyze the response processes of receivers of marketing communications, including alternative response hierarchies and their implications for promotional planning and strategy.
- To examine the nature of consumers' cognitive processing of marketing communications.

Two Different Products, Two Different Approaches

If you were asked to name two products that are at opposite ends of the spectrum in terms of the consumer decision-making process, computers and candy bars would be good answers. Computers and related products like printers represent a major investment for the individuals or organizations that buy them and are usually purchased after detailed decision making. On the other hand, candy bars are usually an impulse purchase characterized by minimal evaluation or decision making. However, these products do have one thing in common; creative advertising and promotion can play an important role in the marketing of each, as Hewlett-Packard Co. and Nestlé have shown. Both companies won Sales & Marketing Management magazine's 1993 marketing achievement awards, which recognize marketing excellence in various product and service categories.

Hewlett-Packard (H-P) is the world's second-largest computer systems company, trailing only perennial leader IBM. H-P often deals with customers who are very knowledgeable—and very demanding. To compete in this market, H-P has reorganized its whole sales and marketing effort around listening to customers and understanding their needs. The company reorganized its sales force so that sales reps are assigned to industries, not geographic territories. The company wants its reps to become experts in the industry they cover. All of the information gathered from customers through meetings, on-site visits, and sales calls is used to design products with customer needs in mind.

To help capture new customers, H-P used bold advertising featuring Rodin's The Thinker as the central image in a TV and print campaign challenging rivals IBM and Digital Equipment Corporation (DEC). The ads twitted IBM's longtime motto, "Think", and targeted Fortune 500 executives with the cheeky tagline: "If you think there are only two choices for business systems, think again."

Nestlé has shown how marketing and advertising prowess can bring new life to an old product. The 65-year-old Butterfinger candy bar is enjoying a second childhood thanks to the "Nobody better lay a finger on my Butterfinger" campaign featuring smart aleck Bart Simpson. Nestlé has owned Butterfinger only since 1990, when it purchased the brand from RJR/Nabisco. As part of the deal, Nestlé inherited an agreement with the Fox network to use the Simpson characters. Nestle's brand managers teamed up with its ad agency to create spots in which various Simpson characters—including Lisa, Homer, and the school bully—plot to steal Bart's Butterfinger. As The Simpsons on Fox took off, Butterfinger became the fastest-growing established candy, outpacing category growth by 300 percent. The brand's fiscal 1993 sales were up nearly 10 percent from a year earlier.

Nestlé recognizes that advertising and promotion are key to the success of a candy bar. Since candy is generally purchased on impulse and consumed before the buyer returns home, the challenge is to keep Butterfingers at candy cravers' fingertips. The Simpson tie-in has been a tremendous success, and Nestlé continues to play off the theme. However, Chris Simonds, the promotion manager for Butterfinger, recognizes that the brand's visibility could easily fade as the show becomes more mainstream. Thus, Simonds loses no opportunity to help bolster Butterfinger's irreverent image and, as he describes it, "keep the brand out on the fringe and appealing to the left-wing candy eater." Nestlé has used promotional tie-ins with movies such as Dennis the Menace, sponsored screenings of Fear of a Planet (a feature-length film on snowboarding), and teamed up with Paramount Pictures on advertising and merchandise offers when the movie Wayne's World was released on video. Nestlé's research has shown that chocolate lovers are fickle. They have four to eight favorite brands but aren't loyal to any one. Nestlé has found a way to make Butterfinger one of their choices.

Source: "Playing to Win," Sales & Marketing Management, Aug. 1993, pp. 37–41.

he function of all elements of the promotional mix is to communicate. An organization's advertising and promotional strategy is implemented through the communications it sends to current or prospective customers. Thus, advertising and promotional planners need to understand the communications process. As you can see from the opening vignette, the way marketers communicate with their customers varies depending on the type of product or service they are selling and the process the customer goes through in making a purchase decision. Creating an effective marketing communications program is far more complicated than just choosing a product feature or attribute to emphasize. Marketers must understand how consumers will perceive and interpret their messages and how these reactions will shape their responses toward the product or service.

This chapter reviews the fundamentals of communications and examines various perspectives regarding how consumers respond to promotional messages. Our goal is to demonstrate how valuable an understanding of the communications process can be in planning, implementing, and evaluating the marketing communications program.

THE NATURE OF COMMUNICATION

Communication has been variously defined as "the passing of information," "the exchange of ideas," or the process of establishing a commonness or oneness of thought between a sender and a receiver.[1] These definitions suggest that for communication to occur, there must be some common thinking between two parties and information must be passed from one person to another (or from one group to another). As you will see in this chapter, establishing this commonality in thinking is not always as easy as it might seem; many attempts to communicate are unsuccessful.

The communications process is often very complex, with success depending on such factors as the nature of the message, the audience's interpretation of it, and the environment in which it is received. The receiver's perception of the source and the medium used to transmit the message may also affect the ability to communicate, as do many other factors. Words, pictures, sounds, and colors may have different meanings to different audiences, and people's perceptions and interpretations of them vary. For example, if you ask for a soda on the East Coast or West Coast, you'll receive a soft drink such as

EXHIBIT 6–1

A model of the communications process

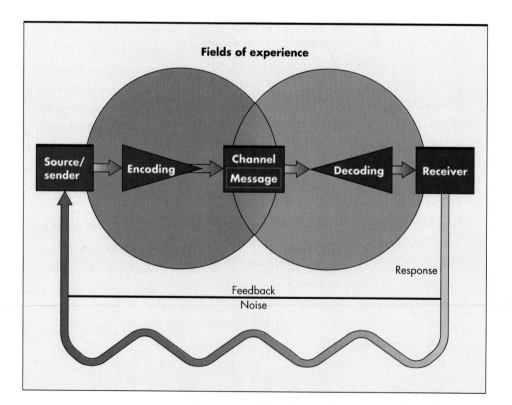

Global Perspective 6–1
***Communication Problems in
International Marketing***

Communication is a major problem facing U.S. companies that market their products in foreign countries. International marketers must be aware of the connotation of the words, signs, symbols, and expressions they use as brand names or logos or in various forms of promotion. Advertising copy and slogans as well as certain symbols do not always transfer well into other languages. This not only creates communication problems but also sometimes results in embarrassing blunders that can damage a company's or brand's credibility or image and cost it customers.

Mistranslations and faulty word choices have often created problems for firms engaging in international marketing. For example, the slogan "Come alive with Pepsi" translated too literally in some countries. The German translation became "come out of the grave," while in Chinese it read, "Pepsi brings your ancestors back from the dead." An American airline competing in Brazil advertised "rendezvous lounges" in its jets—until it discovered that in the Brazilian dialect of Portuguese this meant a place to make love.

International marketers can also have linguistic problems with brand names and their meaning or pronunciation, as when Coca-Cola introduced its product to China. The Chinese translated the name into Chinese characters that sounded like Coca-Cola but meant "bite the wax tadpole." With the help of a language specialist, the company substituted four Mandarin characters that sound like Coca-Cola but mean "Can happy, mouth happy."

Honda Motor Co. also faced a communications dilemma when choosing a name for its Acura automobile a few years ago. The brand-naming firm that created the name noted it would be better to spell it with two Cs because more people would make the connection to "accurate" and pronounce it correctly. However, Honda wanted a name it could use around the world, and a double C is difficult to pronounce in some languages.

International marketers may also encounter problems with the way certain cultures interpret certain visual signs and symbols. For example, AT&T found that the thumbs up sign used in its "I plan" campaign presented a problem when translated into other languages. Thumbs up signifies affirmation to most Americans, but to Russians and Poles, the fact that the person's palm was visible gave the ad an offensive meaning. AT&T hired YAR Communications, a company that specializes in translations, to

reshoot the graphic element in the ad so that only the back of the person's hand showed, conveying the intended meaning to Russian and Polish consumers.

Merrill Lynch & Co. also encountered problems when it tried to use its trademark bull symbol in advertising for the Russian market. YAR placed ads in Russian newspapers and magazines describing the company's services and explaining that the trademark bull stands for strength and is not, as some Russian consumers thought, a source of meat. The ads used a stylized image of a bull and a new Merrill Lynch logo.

Many multinational companies are trying to develop world brands that can be marketed internationally using the same brand name and advertising. However, marketers must be careful that brand names, advertising slogans, and other forms of marketing communication translate properly into foreign languages.

Source: Ron Alsop, "Firms Create Unique Names, but Are They Pronounceable?" *The Wall Street Journal*, April 2, 1987, p. 29; "We Are the World," *Adweek's Marketing Week*, Sept. 1990, pp. 61–68; Riccardo A. Davis, "Many Languages—One Ad Message," *Advertising Age*, Sept. 20, 1993, p. 50.

Coke or Pepsi. However, in parts of the Midwest and South, a soft drink is referred to as *pop*. If you ask for a soda, you may get a glass of pop with ice cream in it. Marketers must understand the meanings that words and symbols take on and how they influence consumers' interpretation of products and messages. This can be particularly challenging to companies marketing their products in foreign countries, as discussed in Global Perspective 6–1.

A BASIC MODEL OF COMMUNICATIONS

Over the years, a basic model of communications has evolved of the various elements of the communications process, as shown in Exhibit 6–1.[2] Two elements represent the major participants in the communications process, the sender and the receiver. Another two are the major communications tools, message and channel. Four others are the major

⊚ EXHIBIT 6–2

The source of this ad is Motorola, Inc.

communications functions and processes: encoding, decoding, response, and feedback. The last element, noise, refers to any extraneous factors in the system that can interfere with the process and work against effective communication.

Source Encoding

The sender, or **source**, of a communication is the person or organization who has information to share with another person or group of people. The source may be an individual (for example, a salesperson or hired spokesperson, such as a celebrity, who appears in a company's advertisements) or a nonpersonal entity (such as the corporation or organization itself). For example, the source of the ad shown in Exhibit 6–2 is Motorola, Inc., as no specific spokesperson or source is shown. But in Exhibit 6–3, the source is golfer Lee Trevino, as Motorola's advertising spokesperson.

Because the receiver's perceptions of the source influence how the communication is received, marketers must be careful to select a communicator the receiver believes is knowledgeable and trustworthy or with whom the receiver can identify or relate in some manner. (How these characteristics influence the receiver's responses is discussed further in Chapter 7.)

The communications process begins when the source selects words, symbols, pictures, and the like to represent the message that will be delivered to the receiver(s). The process known as **encoding** refers to putting thoughts, ideas, or information into a symbolic form. The sender's goal is to encode the message in such a way that it will be understood by the receiver. This means using words, signs, or symbols that are familiar to the target audience. Many symbols have universal meaning, such as the familiar circle with a line through it to denote no parking, no smoking, and so forth. Many companies also have highly recognizable symbols, such as McDonald's golden arches or the Coca-Cola trademark.

Message

The encoding process leads to development of a **message** that contains the information or meaning the source hopes to convey. The message may be verbal or nonverbal, oral or written, or symbolic. Messages must be put into a transmittable form that is appropriate for the channel of communication being used. In advertising, this may range from simply writing some words or copy that will be read as a radio message to producing an expensive television commercial. For many products, it is not the actual words of the message that determine its communication effectiveness but rather the impression or image the advertisement creates. Notice how Spellbound perfume in Exhibit 6–4 uses only a picture to deliver its message. However, the product name and picture help communicate a feeling of entrancement and fascination between the couple shown in the ad.

@ **EXHIBIT 6–3**

Motorola uses Lee Trevino as
a spokesperson.

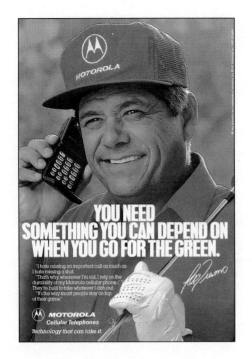

To better understand the symbolic meaning that might be conveyed in a communication, advertising and marketing researchers have begun focusing attention on **semiotics**,
which involves the study of the nature of meaning and asks how our reality—words,
gestures, myths, products/services, theories—acquires meaning.[3] Marketers are using
individuals trained in semiotics to better understand the conscious and subconscious
meaning the nonverbal signs and symbols in their ads transmit to consumers.

Look at the ad for Snuggle fabric softener shown in Exhibit 6–5 and think about
what the teddy bear might symbolize. Lever Brothers Co. conducted a semiotic analysis
to help understand the meaning of the huggable teddy bear (Snuggle) that has become
such a successful advertising symbol. The semiologist concluded Snuggle is a "symbol of
tamed aggression," a perfect symbol for a fabric softener that "tames" the rough texture
of clothing.[4]

Some advertising and marketing people are skeptical about the value of semiotics.
They question whether social scientists read too much into advertising messages and are

@ **EXHIBIT 6–4**

The image projected by an
ad often communicates more
than words

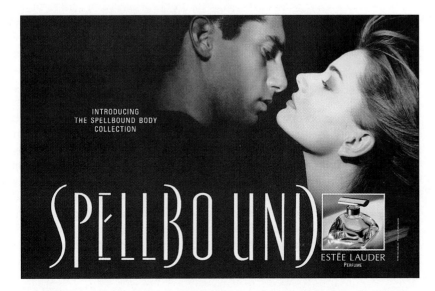

@ **EXHIBIT 6–5**

Semiotic research suggests
that the Snuggle Bear
symbolizes tamed
aggression

overly intellectual in interpreting them. However, the meaning of an advertising message or other form of marketing communication lies not in the message, but with the people who see and interpret it. Moreover, consumers behave based on the meanings they ascribe to marketplace stimuli. Thus, marketers must consider the meanings consumers attach to the various signs and symbols. Semiotics may be helpful in analyzing how various aspects of the marketing program—such as advertising messages, packaging, brand names, and even the nonverbal communications of salespeople (gestures, mode of dress)—are interpreted by receivers.[5]

Channel

The **channel** is the method by which the communication travels from the source or sender to the receiver. At the broadest level, channels of communication are of two types, personal and nonpersonal. *Personal channels* of communication are direct interpersonal (face-to-face) contact with target individuals or groups. Salespeople serve as personal channels of communication when they deliver their sales message to a buyer or potential customer. Social channels of communication such as friends, neighbors, associates, coworkers, or family members are also examples. The latter often represent *word-of-mouth communications*, a powerful source of information for consumers.[6]

Nonpersonal channels of communication are those that carry a message without interpersonal contact between sender and receiver. Nonpersonal channels are generally referred to as the **mass media** or mass communications, as the message is sent to many individuals at one time. For example, a television commercial broadcast on a prime-time show may be seen by 20 million households in a given evening. Nonpersonal channels of communication consist of two major types, print and broadcast, with several subtypes within each category. Print media include newspapers, magazines, direct mail, and billboards; broadcast media include radio and television.

Receiver/Decoding

The **receiver** is the person or persons with whom the sender shares thoughts or information. Generally, receivers are the consumers in the audience or market targeted by a company who read, hear, and/or see the marketer's message and decode it. **Decoding** is the process of transforming the sender's message back into thought. This process is heavily influenced by the receiver's frame of reference or **field of experience**, which refers to the experiences, perceptions, attitudes, and values he or she brings to the communications situation.

For effective communication to occur, the message decoding process of the receiver must match the encoding of the sender. Simply put, this means the receiver understands and correctly interprets what the source is trying to communicate. As can be seen in Exhibit 6–1, the source and the receiver each have a frame of reference they bring to the communications situation. Effective communication is more likely when there is some *common ground* between the two parties. (This is represented by the overlapping of the two circles, representing the fields of experience.) The more knowledge the sender has about the receivers, the greater the likelihood of understanding their needs, empathizing with them, and communicating effectively.

While this notion of common ground between sender and receiver may sound basic, it often causes great difficulty in the advertising communications process. Marketing and advertising people often have a very different field of experience from the consumers who constitute the mass markets with whom they must communicate. For example, most advertising and marketing people are college educated and work and/or reside in large urban areas such as New York, Chicago, or Los Angeles. Yet they are attempting to develop commercials that will effectively communicate with millions of consumers who have never attended college, work in blue-collar occupations, and live in rural areas or small towns. The executive creative director of a large advertising agency described how advertising executives become isolated from the cultural mainstream: "We pull them in and work them to death. And then they begin moving in sushi circles and lose touch with Velveeta and the people who eat it."[7]

IMC Perspective 6–1 discusses some interesting findings from a study comparing individuals who work in advertising agencies with the general public.

Advertisers spend millions of dollars every year to understand the frame of reference of the target markets who receive their messages. They also spend much time and money pretesting messages to ensure they are understood by consumers and decoded in the manner the advertiser intended.

Noise

Throughout the communications process, the message is subject to extraneous factors that can distort or interfere with its reception. This unplanned distortion or interference in the communications process is known as **noise**. Errors or problems that occur in the encoding of the message, distortion in a radio or television signal, or distractions at the point of reception are examples of noise. When you are watching your favorite commercial on television and a problem occurs in the signal transmission, this will obviously interfere with your reception, lessening the impact of the commercial.

Noise may also occur because the fields of experience of the sender and receiver don't overlap. Lack of common ground may result in improper encoding of the message—using a sign, symbol, or words that are unfamiliar or have different meaning to the receiver. The more common ground there is between the sender and the receiver, the less likely it is this type of noise will occur.

Response/Feedback

The receiver's set of reactions after seeing, hearing, or reading the message is known as a **response**. Receivers' responses can range from nonobservable actions such as storing information in memory to immediate action such as dialing an 800 number to order a product advertised on television. Marketers are very interested in **feedback**, that part of the receiver's response that is communicated back to the sender. Feedback, which may take a variety of forms, closes the loop in the communications flow and lets the sender monitor how the intended message is being decoded and received.

IMC Perspective 6–1
Are Advertising People Different?

It has often been argued that people who work in advertising are different from the typical consumers who represent the target market for their clients' products and services. A study conducted by the DDB Needham Worldwide advertising agency suggests there are some significant differences between advertising people and consumers. The agency's Chicago office ran an abridged version of its annual lifestyle study questionnaire in an in-house publication and received about 200 responses from its employees. Martin Horn, the agency vice president who presides over the lifestyle study, compared the responses of agency personnel with the sample of average Americans who participated in the full study and found big differences between the two groups.

The sample of DDB Needham agency personnel is not representative of all people working in ad agencies. There were, however, some major differences between agency people and the general public in their level of agreement with various statements regarding activities, interests, and opinions. From these findings, Horn concluded: "Assuming the target customer to be just like us, we may end up with advertising that talks to no one other than ourselves." Horn titled the article in which he summarized the results of this study "I Have Met the Customer, and He Ain't Me."

Percentage of respondents agreeing with statement.

	Agency	Public
I want to look different from others.	82%	62%
There's too much sex on prime-time TV.	50	78
TV is my primary form of entertainment.	28	53
I went to a bar or tavern in the past year.	91	50
I like the feeling of speed.	66	35
There should be a gun in every home.	9	32
I hate to lose even friendly competition.	58	44
My favorite music is classic rock.	64	35
My favorite music is easy listening.	27	51
Couples should live together before getting married.	50	33
My greatest achievements are still ahead of me.	89	65
Job security is more important than money.	52	75
I bought a lottery ticket in the previous year.	75	61

Source: Joseph M. Winski, "Study: 'The Customer Ain't Me,'" *Advertising Age*, Jan. 20, 1992, p. 18.

For example, in a personal selling situation, customers may pose questions, comments, or objections or indicate their reactions through nonverbal responses such as gestures and frowns.[8] The salesperson has the advantage of receiving instantaneous feedback through the customer's reactions. But this is generally not the case when mass media are used. Because advertisers are not in direct contact with the customers, they must use other means to determine how their messages have been received. While the ultimate form of feedback occurs through sales, there are often problems in attempting to show a direct relationship between advertising and purchase behavior. So marketers use other methods to obtain feedback, among them customer inquiries, store visits, coupon redemptions, and reply cards. Research-based feedback analyzes readership and recall of ads, message comprehension, attitude change, and other forms of response. With this information, the advertiser can analyze reasons for success or failure in the communications process and make adjustments.

Successful communications are accomplished when the marketer selects an appropriate source, develops an effective message or appeal that is encoded properly, and then selects the channels or media that will best reach the target audience so that the message can be effectively decoded and delivered. In Chapter 7, we will examine the source, message, and channel decisions and see how promotional planners work with these controllable variables to develop communications strategies. Since these decisions must consider how the target audience will respond to the promotional message, the remainder of this chapter examines the receiver and the process by which consumers respond to advertising and other forms of marketing communications.

ANALYZING THE RECEIVER

To communicate effectively with their customers, marketers must understand who the target audience is, what (if anything) the market knows or feels about the company's product or service, and how to communicate with the audience to influence its decision-

@ EXHIBIT 6–6

Levels of audience
aggregation

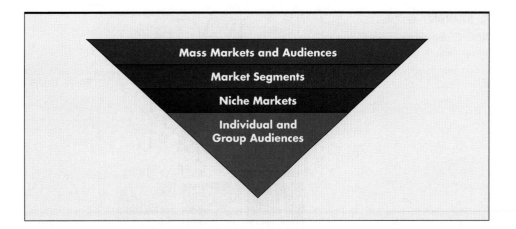

making process. In addition, marketers need to know how the market is more likely to respond to various sources of communications or different types of messages. Before they make decisions regarding source, message, and channel variables, promotional planners must understand the potential effects associated with each of these factors. In this section, we focus on the receiver of the marketing communication and examine how the audience is identified and the process it may go through in responding to a promotional message. This information serves as a foundation for evaluating the controllable communications variable decisions in the next chapter.

Identifying the Target Audience

The marketing communications process really begins with identifying the audience that will be the focus of the firm's advertising and promotions efforts. The target audience may consist of individuals, groups, market segments, or a general public or mass audience (Exhibit 6–6). Marketers approach each of these audiences differently.

Individual and group audiences

The target market may consist of individuals who have specific needs and for whom the communication must be specifically tailored. This often requires person-to-person communication and is generally accomplished through personal selling. Other forms of communication such as advertising may be used to attract the audience's attention to the firm, but the detailed message is carried by a salesperson who can respond to the specific needs of the individual customer. Life insurance, financial services, and real estate are examples of products and services promoted this way.

A second level of audience aggregation is represented by the group. Marketers often must communicate with a group of people who influence or make the purchase decision. For example, organizational purchasing often involves buying centers or committees that vary in size and composition. Companies marketing their products and services to other businesses or organizations must understand who is on the purchase committee, what aspect of the decision each individual influences, and the criteria each member uses to evaluate a product. Advertising might be directed to each member of the buying center, and multilevel personal selling may be necessary to reach those individuals who influence or actually make decisions. Exhibit 6–7 shows different ads IVAC Corp., a company that sells vital signs measurement systems and intravenous infusion instruments to hospitals, uses to target hospital administrators and nurses.

As you may recall from Chapter 4, decision making in the consumer market can include a group when family members become involved in the purchase of, say, a car, furniture, or the family vacation. To develop an effective communications program in either of these markets, advertisers need to know who is involved in the decision-making process, what role they play, and how best to reach them.

@ **EXHIBIT 6–7A**

IVAC Corporation targets
nurses with this ad

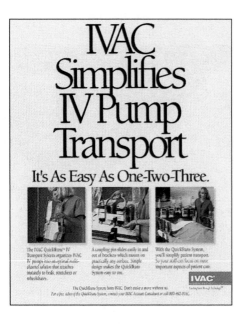

Market segments and mass audiences

Marketers look for customers who have similar needs and wants and thus represent some type of market segment that can be reached with the same basic communication strategy. Very small, well-defined groups of customers are often referred to as *market niches*. They can usually be reached through personal selling efforts or highly targeted media such as direct mail. The next level of audience aggregation is market segments, broader classes of buyers who have similar needs and can be communicated to with similar messages. As we saw in Chapter 5, there are various ways of segmenting markets and reaching the customers in these segments. As market segments get larger, marketers usually turn to broader-based media such as newspapers, magazines, and television to reach them.

Many advertisers communicate with very large numbers of consumers—mass markets. Marketers of most consumer products attempt to attract the attention of large numbers of present or potential customers through mass communications. Mass communications are a one-way flow of information. The message flows from the marketer to the consumer, and feedback on the audience's reactions to the message is generally indirect and difficult to measure.

To communicate with large market segments or mass audiences, the marketer uses some form of mass communication, such as advertising or publicity. TV advertising, for example, lets the marketer send a message to millions of consumers at the same time. However, this does not mean effective communication has occurred. This may be only one of several hundred messages the consumer is exposed to that day. There is no guarantee the information will be attended to, processed, comprehended, or stored in memory for later retrieval. Even if the advertising message is processed, it may be misinterpreted by consumers or may not interest them. Studies by Jacob Jacoby and Wayne D. Hoyer have shown that nearly 20 percent of all print ads and even more TV commercials are miscomprehended by readers.[9]

Unlike the personal or face-to-face communication situation, mass communication offers the marketer no opportunity to explain or clarify the message to make it more effective. The marketer must enter the communication situation with knowledge of the target audience and how it is likely to react to the message. This means the receiver's response process must be understood, along with its implications for promotional planning and strategy.

EXHIBIT 6–7B IVAC uses a different ad for hospital administrators

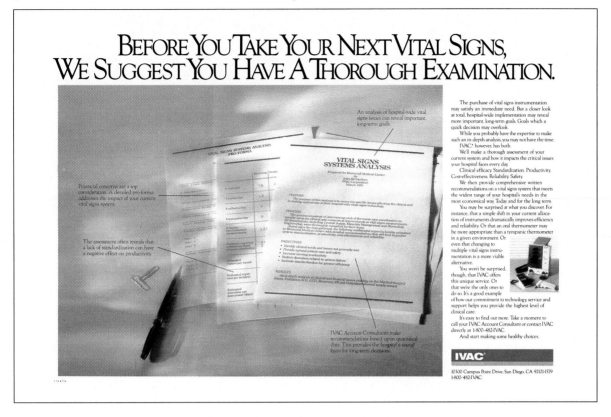

THE RESPONSE PROCESS

Perhaps the most important aspect of developing effective communications programs involves understanding the *response process* the receiver may go through in moving toward a specific behavior (like purchasing a product) and how the promotional efforts of the marketer influence these responses. In many instances, the marketer's only objective may be to create awareness of the company or brand name, which may trigger interest in the product. In other situations, the marketer may want to convey detailed information to change consumers' knowledge of and attitudes toward the brand and ultimately change their behavior.

Traditional Response Hierarchy Models

A number of models have been developed to depict the stages a consumer might pass through in moving from a state of not being aware of a company, product, or brand to actual purchase behavior. Exhibit 6–8 shows four of the best-known response hierarchy models. While these response models may appear similar, they were developed for different reasons.

The **AIDA model** was developed to represent the stages a salesperson must take a customer through in the personal selling process.[10] This model depicts the buyer as passing successively through attention, interest, desire, and action. The salesperson must first get the attention of the customer and then arouse some interest in the company's product or service. Strong levels of interest should create desire to own or use the product. The action stage in the AIDA model involves getting the customer to make a purchase commitment and closing the sale. To the marketer, this is the most important stage in the selling process, but it can also be the most difficult. Companies train their sales representatives in closing techniques to help them complete the selling process.

◉ EXHIBIT   6–8   Models of the response process

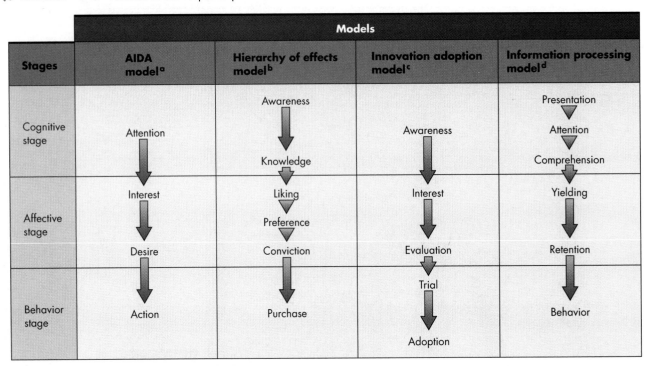

Stages	AIDA model[a]	Hierarchy of effects model[b]	Innovation adoption model[c]	Information processing model[d]
Cognitive stage	Attention	Awareness ↓ Knowledge	Awareness	Presentation ↓ Attention ↓ Comprehension
Affective stage	Interest ↓ Desire	Liking ↓ Preference ↓ Conviction	Interest ↓ Evaluation	Yielding ↓ Retention
Behavior stage	Action	Purchase	Trial ↓ Adoption	Behavior

Perhaps the best known of these response hierarchies is the model developed by Robert Lavidge and Gary Steiner as a paradigm for setting and measuring advertising objectives.[11] Their **hierarchy of effects model** shows the process by which advertising works and assumes a consumer passes through a series of steps in sequential order from initial awareness of a product or service to actual purchase. A basic premise of this model is that advertising effects occur over a period of time. Advertising communication may not lead to immediate behavioral response or purchase; rather, a series of effects must occur, with each step fulfilled before the consumer can move to the next stage in the hierarchy. As we will see in Chapter 8, the hierarchy of effects model has become the foundation for objective setting and measurement of advertising effects in many companies.

The **innovation-adoption model** evolved from work on the diffusion of innovations.[12] This model represents the stages a consumer passes through in adopting an inno-

◉ EXHIBIT   6–9

Sampling or demonstration programs are used to encourage trial of new products such as disposable contact lenses

◎ EXHIBIT 6–10

Methods of obtaining feedback in the response hierarchy

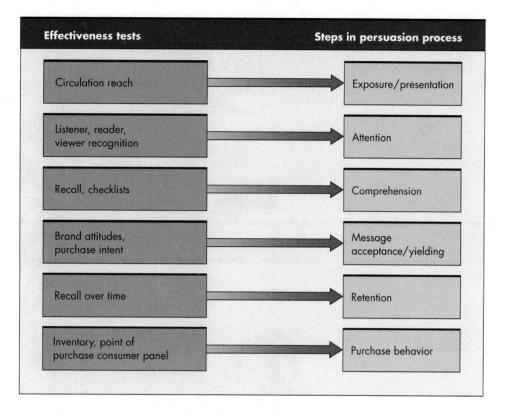

vation such as a new product. Like the other models, this model says potential adopters must be moved through a series of steps before taking some action (in this case deciding to adopt a new product). The steps preceding adoption include awareness, interest, evaluation, and trial. The challenge facing companies introducing new products is to create awareness and interest among consumers and then get them to evaluate the product favorably. The best way to evaluate a new product is through actual use so that performance can be judged. Marketers often encourage trial by using demonstration or sampling programs or allowing consumers to use a product with minimal commitment (Exhibit 6–9). After trial, consumers either adopt the product or reject it.

The final hierarchy model shown in Exhibit 6–8 is the **information-processing model** of advertising effects, developed by William McGuire.[13] This model assumes the receiver in a persuasive communication situation like advertising is an information processor or problem solver. He suggests the series of steps a receiver goes through in being persuaded constitutes a response hierarchy. The stages of this model are similar to the hierarchy of effects sequence; attention and comprehension are similar to awareness and knowledge, and yielding is synonymous with liking. McGuire's model includes a stage not found in the other models: retention, or the receiver's ability to retain that portion of the comprehended information that he or she accepts as valid or relevant. This stage is important since most promotional campaigns are designed not to motivate consumers to take immediate action but rather to provide information that will be used later when a purchase decision is made.

Each stage of the response hierarchy is a dependent variable that must be attained and that may serve as an objective of the communications process. As shown in Exhibit 6–10, each stage can be measured, providing the advertiser with feedback regarding the effectiveness of various strategies designed to move the consumer to purchase. The information-processing model may serve as an effective framework for planning and evaluating the effects of a promotional campaign.

@ **EXHIBIT 6–11**

Advertising for Philips DCC system promotes the benefits of this new product

Implications of the traditional hierarchy models

The hierarchy models of communication response are useful to promotional planners from several perspectives. First, they delineate the series of steps potential purchasers must be taken through to move them from a state where they are unaware of a product or service to the point where they are ready to purchase it. Second, potential buyers may be at different stages in the hierarchy, so the advertiser will face different sets of communication problems. For example, a company introducing an innovative product like Philips' digital compact cassette system may need to devote considerable effort to making people aware of the product, how it works, and what its benefits are (Exhibit 6–11). Marketers of a mature brand that enjoys customer loyalty may need only supportive or reminder advertising to reinforce positive perceptions and maintain the awareness level for the brand.

The hierarchy models can also be useful as intermediate measures of communication effectiveness. The marketer needs to know where audience members are on the response hierarchy. For example, research may reveal that one target segment has low awareness of the advertiser's brand, whereas another is aware of the brand and its various attributes but has a low level of liking or brand preference.

For the first segment of the market, the communications task would involve increasing the awareness level for the brand. The number of ads might be increased or a product sampling program could be used. For the second segment, where awareness is already high but liking and preference are low, the advertiser must determine the reason for the negative feelings and then attempt to address this problem in future advertising.

Global Perspective 6–2
Changing the Image of Air Canada

Before reading this vignette, answer the following questions: What is the name of Canada's government-owned airline? What markings do its planes carry? Most Americans and nearly 8 out of 10 Canadians will answer Air Canada in response to the first question. Moreover, most people even remotely familiar with Canada know that the airline has white planes with bright-red lettering and a big red maple leaf on the tail—symbols that are synonymous with Canada itself.

While most airlines would love to have this kind of instant brand recognition, the strong image is a real problem for Air Canada. Why? According to Air Canada's chief operating officer, "Canadians think of their government as stodgy, bureaucratic, and dull." A recent poll of citizens found that 49 percent of Canadians were "very dissatisfied" with their government—the highest dissatisfaction rating of the 16 developed nations surveyed. Moreover, the negative association with the Canadian government would be bad enough if Air Canada really were state-owned, but it is not. The airline was privatized in 1988 and today is as private as American Airlines, United, or Delta.

To better compete against its chief rival, Canadian Airlines International, in 1992 Air Canada hired the U.S. design firm of Diefenbach Elkins to develop a corporate identity that would sever its perceived ties to government. While Air Canada still wants to be perceived as the country's flag carrier, it does not want its image to be tarred by association with the government bureaucracy.

Before Diefenbach Elkins could begin revamping the image of the airline, it had to figure out how Canadians really felt about Canada. Nearly $120,000 was spent on marketing research to discover that Canadians adore Canada but dislike its politicians. Canadians attribute a variety of values to themselves and their country, including compassion, friendliness, a progressive outlook, and a law-abiding nature. The design firm concluded that it should play up the Canadianness of Air Canada while scotching any association with the government. It also decided to ignore altogether the deep rift between English- and French-speaking Canadians. The firm recommended that Air Canada portray the country it serves as a modern melting pot—a kind

of innocent America, untainted by ethnic tensions and urban blight.

To help execute this strategy, Air Canada's ad agency produced a TV commercial depicting Canada as a diverse nation of Indians, Greeks, Chinese, and other immigrant groups, all of whom happily coexist. The image portrayed in the ad seems appropriate, since Canadians of non-European descent have risen from 2 percent of the population 20 years ago to nearly 40 percent today.

As part of the image makeover, Diefenbach Elkins came up with a new design for Air Canada's fleet of 103 planes. After much debate, the design firm decided to keep the ubiquitous maple leaf (which adorns nearly everything in Canada) but to render it in a more natural earthy red on a new evergreen tail. The logic was that the old, stark red-on-white design smacked more of the big government bureaucracy. While the new paint job retains the vibrant red lettering, the firm believes the overall effect makes the planes look a lot less like flying Mounties.

It will take time to determine whether the makeover of Air Canada will help. But the carrier does feel that the new identity will help get the government moose off its back once and for all.

Source: Joshua Levine, "Ah, Canada," *Forbes*, Jan. 3, 1994, p. 74.

When research or other evidence reveals a company is perceived favorably on a particular attribute or performance criterion, the company may want to take advantage of this in its advertising. Global Perspective 6–2 discusses how Air Canada addressed a problem of high brand recognition but a negative image resulting from misperceptions of being a government–owned airline.

Evaluating traditional response hierarchy models

As you saw in Exhibit 6–8, the four models presented all view the response process as consisting of movement through a sequence of three basic stages. The *cognitive stage* represents what the receiver knows or perceives about the particular product or brand. This state includes awareness that the brand exists and knowledge, information, or comprehension about its attributes, characteristics, or benefits. The *affective stage* refers to the receiver's feelings or affect level (like or dislike) for the particular brand. This stage also

@ **EXHIBIT 6–12**

Alternative response hierarchies: the three-orders model of information processing

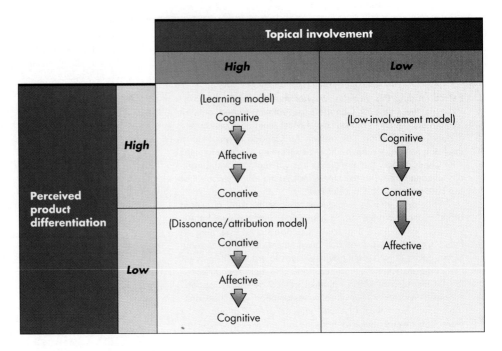

includes stronger levels of affect such as desire, preference, or conviction. The *behavioral stage* refers to the consumer's action toward the brand: trial, purchase, adoption, or rejection.

These models also assume a similar ordering of these three stages. Cognitive development precedes affective reactions, which in turn precede behavior. One might assume that consumers become aware of and knowledgeable about a brand, develop feelings toward it, form a desire or preference, and then make a purchase. While this logical progression is accurate in many situations, the response sequence does not always operate this way.

Over the past two decades, considerable research in marketing, social psychology, and communications has led to questioning the traditional notion of a cognitive → affective → behavioral sequence of response. Several other configurations of the response hierarchy have been theorized. Michael Ray has developed a model of information processing that identifies three alternative orderings of the three stages based on perceived product differentiation and product involvement level.[14]

Alternative Response Hierarchies

Three alternative response hierarchies are the standard learning, dissonance/attribution, and low-involvement models (Exhibit 6–12).

The standard learning hierarchy

In many purchase situations, the consumer will go through the response process in the sequence depicted by the traditional communications models. Ray terms this a **standard learning model**, which consists of a learn → feel → do sequence. Information and knowledge acquired or *learned* about the various brands become the basis for developing affect or *feelings* that guide what the consumer will *do* (e.g., actual trial or purchase). In this hierarchy, the consumer is viewed as an active participant in the communications process who seeks or gathers information through active learning.

Ray suggests the standard learning hierarchy is likely when the consumer is highly involved in the purchase process and there is much differentiation among competing brands. High-involvement purchase decisions such as those for industrial products and services and consumer durables like personal computers, VCRs, and cars are areas where a standard learning hierarchy response process is likely. Ads for products and services in these areas are usually very detailed and attempt to give consumers a great deal of information about the brand.

The dissonance/attribution hierarchy

A second response hierarchy proposed by Ray involves situations where consumers first behave, then develop attitudes or feelings as a result of that behavior, and then learn or process information that supports the earlier behavior. This **dissonance/attribution model**, or do → feel → learn, occurs in situations where consumers must choose between two alternatives that are similar in quality but are complex and may have hidden or unknown attributes. The consumer may purchase the product based on the recommendation of some nonmedia source and then attempt to support the decision by developing a positive attitude toward the brand and perhaps even developing negative feelings toward the rejected alternative(s). This reduces any *postpurchase dissonance* or anxiety the consumer may experience resulting from doubt over the purchase (as discussed in Chapter 4). Dissonance reduction involves *selective learning,* whereby the consumer seeks information that supports the choice made and avoids information that questions the wisdom of the decision.

According to this model, marketers need to recognize that in some situations, attitudes develop *after* purchase, as does learning from the mass media. Ray suggests that in these situations the main effect of the mass media is not so much to promote original choice behavior and attitude change but rather to reduce dissonance by reinforcing the wisdom of the purchase or providing supportive information.

As with the standard learning model, this response hierarchy is likely to occur when the consumer is involved in the purchase situation; it is particularly relevant for postpurchase situations. For example, a consumer may purchase a life insurance policy through the recommendation of a general agent and then develop a favorable attitude toward the company and pay close attention to its ads to reduce dissonance.

Perhaps the major problem with this view of the response hierarchy is accepting the notion that the mass media have no effect on the consumer's initial purchase decision. But it doesn't claim the mass media have no effect, just that their major impact occurs after the purchase has been made. Marketing communications planners must be aware of the need for advertising and promotion efforts both to encourage brand selection and to reinforce choices and ensure that a purchase pattern will continue.

The low-involvement hierarchy

Perhaps the most intriguing of the three response hierarchies proposed by Ray is the **low-involvement hierarchy**, in which the receiver is viewed as passing from cognition to behavior to attitude change. This learn → do → feel sequence is thought to characterize situations of low consumer involvement in the purchase process. Ray suggests this hierarchy tends to occur when involvement in the purchase decision is low, there are minimal differences among brand alternatives, and mass media (especially broadcast) advertising is important.

The notion of a low-involvement hierarchy is based in large part on Herbert Krugman's theory explaining the effects of television advertising.[15] Krugman wanted to find out why TV advertising produced a strong effect on brand awareness and recall but little change in consumers' attitudes toward the product. He hypothesized that TV is basically a low-involvement medium and the viewer's perceptual defenses are reduced or even absent during commercials. In a low-involvement situation, the consumer does not compare the message with previously acquired beliefs, needs, or past experiences. The commercial results in subtle changes in the consumer's knowledge structure, particularly with repeated exposure. This change in the consumer's knowledge does not result in attitude change but is related to learning something about the advertised brand,

@ **EXHIBIT 6–13**

Advertising promoting
consistent quality has helped
Heinz dominate the ketchup
market

such as a brand name, ad theme, or slogan. According to Krugman, when the consumer enters a purchase situation, this information may be sufficient to trigger a purchase. The consumer will then form an attitude toward the purchased brand as a result of experience with it. Thus, in the low-involvement situation the response sequence is as follows:

Message exposure under low involvement →
Shift in cognitive structure → Purchase →
Positive or negative experience → Attitude formation

In the low-involvement hierarchy, the consumer engages in passive learning and random information catching rather than active information seeking. The advertiser must recognize that a passive, uninterested consumer may focus more on nonmessage elements such as music, characters, symbols, and slogans or jingles than actual message content. The advertiser might capitalize on this situation by developing a catchy jingle that is stored in the consumer's mind without any active cognitive processing and becomes salient when he or she enters the actual purchase situation.

Advertisers of low-involvement products also repeat simple product claims such as a key copy point or distinctive product benefit. A recent study by Scott Hawkins and Stephen Hoch found that under low-involvement conditions, repetition of simple product claims increased consumers' memory of and belief in that claim.[16] They noted advertisers of low-involvement products might find it more profitable to pursue a heavy repetition strategy than to reach larger audiences with lengthy, more detailed messages. For example, Heinz has dominated the ketchup market for over 20 years by repeatedly telling consumers that its brand is the thickest and richest. Heinz has used a variety of advertising campaigns over the years, but they all repeat the same same basic theme and focus on the consistent quality of the brand (Exhibit 6–13).

Low-involvement advertising appeals prevail in much of the advertising we see for frequently purchased consumer products: Ads for Charmin toilet paper implore buyers, "Please, don't squeeze the Charmin!" Wrigley's Doublemint gum invites consumers to "Double your pleasure." Bounty paper towels claim to be the "quicker picker upper." Oscar Meyer uses the catchy jingle, "I wish I were an Oscar Meyer wiener." Each of these appeals is designed to help consumers make an association without really attempting to formulate or change an attitude.

@ **EXHIBIT 6–14**

Morris the cat has
been a very effective
VIP for 9-Lives cat food

@ **EXHIBIT 6–15**
Integrated Information
Response Model

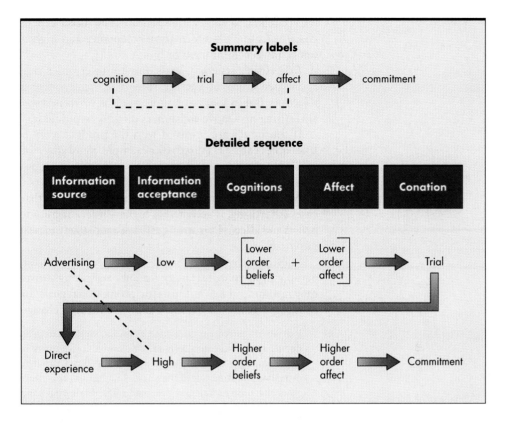

Another popular creative strategy used by advertisers of low-involvement products is
what advertising analyst Harry McMahan calls VIP, or visual image personality.[17] Advertisers often use symbols like the Pillsbury doughboy, Morris the cat, Tony the tiger,
Speedy Alka-Seltzer, and Mr. Clean to develop visual images that will lead consumers to
identify and retain ads. The campaign featuring Morris the cat has helped make 9-Lives
a leading brand of cat food, and the feline has become so popular that he even has his
own fan club (Exhibit 6–14).

**The Integrated
Information
Response Model**

Advertising and consumer researchers recognize that not all response sequences and
behaviors are explained adequately by either the traditional or alternative response hierarchies. Advertising is just one source of information consumers use in forming attitudes
and/or making purchase decisions. Moreover, for many consumers, purchase does not
reflect commitment to a brand but is merely a way to obtain first-hand information from
trial use of a product.

Robert Smith and William Swinyard developed a revised interpretation of the advertising response sequence.[18] Their **integrated information response model**, shown
in Exhibit 6–15, integrates concepts from both the traditional and low-involvement response hierarchy perspectives. It also accounts for the effects of direct experience and
recognizes that different levels of belief strength result from advertising versus personal
experience with a product.

The integrated information response model suggests several different response patterns that can result from advertising. For low-involvement purchases, a cognition →
trial → affect → commitment response sequence may be operating. This can be seen
in the top line of Exhibit 6–15. According to this sequence, advertising generally leads
to low information acceptance, lower-order beliefs, and low-order affect. However, as
repetitive advertising builds awareness, consumers become more likely to engage in a

trial purchase to gather information. The direct experience that results from trial purchase leads to high information acceptance and higher-order beliefs and affect, which can result in commitment or brand loyalty.

Advertising generally leads only to lower-order beliefs and affect because it is seen as a biased source of interest, subject to much source and message discounting and/or rejection. But in some situations, such as when perceived risk and involvement are low, advertising may move consumers directly to purchase.

If consumers are involved with the product, they may seek additional information from other external sources (for example, more advertising, word of mouth, salespeople) and/or from direct experience. This means the response sequence is similar to the traditional hierarchy of effect model (cognition → affect → commitment). The higher-order response path (bottom line of Exhibit 6–15) shows that direct experience, and in some cases advertising, is accepted at higher-order magnitudes, which results in higher-order beliefs and affect. This strong affect is more likely to result in preferences and committed purchases.

Smith and Swinyard discuss the implications of the integrated response model regarding promotional strategy for low- versus high-involvement products. For example, they recommend less enthusiastic promotional goals for low-involvement products, because advertising has a limited ability to form or change higher-order beliefs and affect:

> Low-involvement products, for example, could benefit from advertisements oriented to inducing trial by creating generally favorable lower order beliefs. This could be accomplished with campaigns designed to reduce perceived risk through repetition and familiarity, or those directly advocating a trial purchase. In addition, the integrated response model suggests that other marketing strategies designed to facilitate trial should be coupled with the advertising campaign. Free samples, coupons, price-cuts, or effective point-of-purchase displays could all be integrated with media advertising to produce an environment highly conducive to trial. So too, because low-involvement products are frequently homogeneous, subsequent advertisements might be designed to reaffirm the positive aspects of trial. If successful, these efforts might generate brand loyalty based upon higher order beliefs and affect. This could be a major advantage for advertisers of low-involvement products where frequent brand switching may be based on the absence of antecedents for commitment (i.e., higher order beliefs and affect).[19]

For high-involvement products, more basic attitude change strategies are warranted. However, Smith and Swinyard note that the higher-order response sequence focuses attention on message acceptance as a prerequisite for affective development:

> In this instance, the advertising manager should attempt to isolate the conditions facilitating the formation of higher order beliefs. Factors influential in this process could include whether the message claims are easily verifiable/(e.g., price) and/or demonstrable (e.g., styling), whether the individual knows the sponsoring company and its reputation/credibility, selection of a credible spokesperson to deliver the message, whether the message is consistent with already established beliefs, etc. It also is likely that interactions could exist between acceptance factors, and that certain message configurations would be much more successful than others.[20]

Smith and Swinyard point out that communication strategies for high-involvement products may be difficult to implement since media advertising often has little effect on higher-order attitude formation or change. Thus, they suggest that marketing communication focus on facilitating a product demonstration rather than a direct urge to purchase. Product demonstrations and information received from compelling personal communication sources, such as knowledgeable and well-trained in-store sales personnel, are more likely to change higher-order beliefs and affect and lead to purchase.

An important implication of the integrated information response model is that consumers are likely to take information from advertising, as well as other sources, and integrate it with direct experience in forming judgments about a brand. For example, in a recent study Robert Smith found that advertising can lessen the negative effects of an unfavorable trial experience on brand evaluations when the ad is processed prior to trial. However, when a negative trial experience precedes exposure to an ad, cognitive evaluations of the ad are more negative.[21] Thus it is important to consider how consumers integrate advertising with other brand information sources, both before and after trial or purchase.

Implications of the alternative response models

The various response models offer an interesting perspective on the ways consumers respond to advertising and other forms of marketing communication. They also provide insight into promotional strategies marketers might pursue in different situations. A review of these alternative models of the response process shows that the traditional standard learning model of the response sequence does not always apply. The notion of a highly involved consumer who engages in active information processing and learning and acts on the basis of higher-order beliefs and a well-formed attitude may be inappropriate for some types of purchases. Sometimes, consumers make a purchase decision based on a general awareness resulting from repetitive exposure to advertising, and attitude development occurs after the purchase, if at all. The integrated information response model suggests that the role of advertising and other forms of promotion may be to induce trial, so consumers can develop brand preferences primarily on the basis of their direct experience with the product.

From a promotional planning perspective, it is important that marketers examine the communications situation for their product or service and determine which type of response process is most likely to occur. They should analyze involvement levels and product/service differentiation as well as consumers' use of various information sources and their levels of experience with the product or service. Once the manager has determined which response sequence is most likely to operate, the integrated marketing communications program can be designed to influence the response process in favor of the company's product or service. However, all of this requires that marketers determine the involvement level of consumers in their target markets, so we examine the concept of involvement in more detail.

UNDERSTANDING INVOLVEMENT

Over the past two decades, consumer behavior and advertising researchers have extensively studied the concept of involvement.[22] Involvement is viewed as a variable that can help explain how consumers process advertising information and how this information might affect message recipients. One problem that has plagued the study of involvement has been agreeing on how to define and measure it. Advertising managers must be able to determine targeted consumers' involvement levels with their products.

Some of the problems in conceptualizing and measuring involvement have been addressed in research by Judith Zaichkowsky. Based on an extensive review, she has noted that although there is no single precise definition of involvement, there is an underlying theme focusing on *personal relevance*.[23] Zaichkowsky developed an involvement construct (shown in Exhibit 6–16) that includes three antecedents, or variables proposed to precede involvement. The first is characteristics of the person (value system, unique experiences, needs). The second factor is characteristics of the stimulus, or differences in type of media (TV, radio, or print), content of the communication, or product class variations. The third antecedent factor is situational factors such as whether one is or is not in the market for a particular product.

The various antecedent factors can influence the consumer's level of involvement in several ways, including the way the consumer responds to the advertising, the products being advertised, and the actual purchase decision. This involvement theory shows that a variety of outcomes or behaviors can result from involvement with advertising, products, or purchase decisions.

@ **EXHIBIT 6–16**   Involvement concept

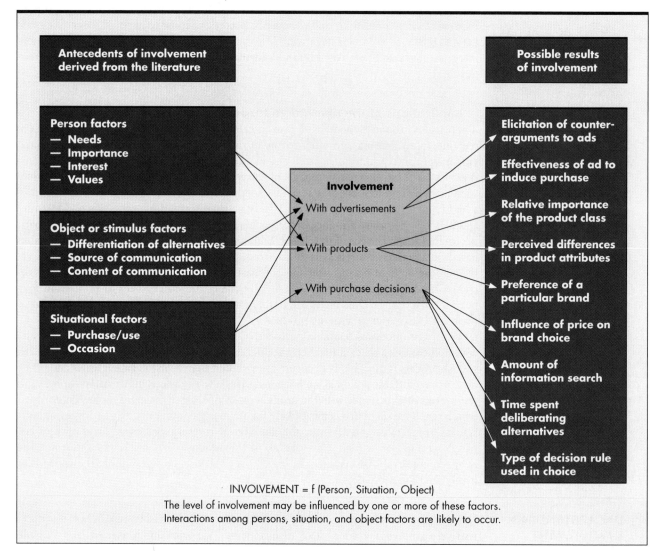

Person factors
— Needs
— Importance
— Interest
— Values

Object or stimulus factors
— Differentiation of alternatives
— Source of communication
— Content of communication

Situational factors
— Purchase/use
— Occasion

Antecedents of involvement derived from the literature

Involvement
With advertisements
With products
With purchase decisions

Possible results of involvement

Elicitation of counter-arguments to ads

Effectiveness of ad to induce purchase

Relative importance of the product class

Perceived differences in product attributes

Preference of a particular brand

Influence of price on brand choice

Amount of information search

Time spent deliberating alternatives

Type of decision rule used in choice

INVOLVEMENT = f (Person, Situation, Object)
The level of involvement may be influenced by one or more of these factors.
Interactions among persons, situation, and object factors are likely to occur.

In recent years, several advertising planning grids have been developed that consider involvement levels as well as several other factors, including response processes and motives that underlie attitude formation and subsequent brand choice.

The FCB Planning Model

An interesting approach to analyzing the communications situation comes from the work of Richard Vaughn of the Foote, Cone & Belding advertising agency. Vaughn and his associates developed an advertising planning model by building on traditional response theories such as the hierarchy of effects model and its variants and research on high and low involvement.[24] They added the dimension of thinking versus feeling processing at each involvement level by bringing in theories regarding brain specialization. The right/left brain theory suggests the left side of the brain is more capable of rational, cognitive thinking, while the right side is more visual and emotional and engages more in the affective or feeling functions. Their model, which became known as the FCB grid, delineates four primary advertising planning strategies—informative, affective, habitual, and satisfaction—along with the most appropriate variant of the alternative response hierarchies (Exhibit 6–17).

⊚ **EXHIBIT 6–17**

The Foote, Cone & Belding
(FCB) grid

	Thinking	Feeling
High involvement	**1. Informative (thinker)** Car–house–furnishings– new products model: Learn–feel–do (economic?) **Possible implications** Test: Recall Diagnostics Media: Long copy format Reflective vehicles Creative: Specific information Demonstration	**2. Affective (feeler)** Jewelry–cosmetics– fashion apparel–motorcycles model: Feel–learn–do (psychological?) **Possible implications** Test: Attitude change Emotional arousal Media: Large space Image specials Creative: Executional Impact
Low involvement	**3. Habit formation (doer)** Food–household items model: Do–learn–feel (responsive?) **Possible implications** Test: Sales Media: Small space ads 10 second I.D.'s Radio; POS Creative: Reminder	**4. Self-satisfaction (reactor)** Cigarettes–liquor–candy model: Do–feel–learn (social?) **Possible implications** Test: Sales Media: Billboards Newspapers POS Creative: Attention

Vaughn suggests that the *informative strategy* is for highly involving products and services where rational thinking and economic considerations prevail, and the standard learning hierarchy is the appropriate response model. The *affective strategy* is for highly involving/feeling purchases. For these types of products, advertising should stress psychological and emotional motives such as fulfilling self-esteem or enhancing one's ego or self-image.

The *habitual strategy* is for low-involvement/thinking products with such routinized behavior patterns that learning occurs most often after a trial purchase. The response process for these products is consistent with a behavioristic learning-by-doing model (remember our discussion of operant conditioning in Chapter 4?). The *self-satisfaction strategy* is for low-involvement/feeling products where appeals to sensory pleasures and social motives are important. Again, the do → feel or do → learn hierarchy is operating, since product experience is an important part of the learning process. Vaughn acknowledges that some minimal level of awareness (passive learning) may precede purchase of both types of low-involvement products, although deeper, active learning is not necessary. This suggests that the low-involvement hierarchy discussed earlier (learn → do → feel) is consistent with the FCB grid.

The FCB grid provides a useful way for those involved in the advertising planning process, such as creative specialists, to analyze consumer/product relationships and develop appropriate promotional strategies. Consumer research can be used to determine how consumers perceive products or brands on the involvement and thinking/feeling dimensions.[25] This information can then be used to develop effective creative options such as using rational versus emotional appeals, increasing involvement levels, or even getting consumers to evaluate a think-type product on the basis of feelings. The ad for the KitchenAid refrigerator in Exhibit 6–18 is an example of this latter strategy. Notice how it uses beautiful imagery to appeal to emotional concerns such as style and appearance. Appliances are traditionally sold on the basis of more rational, functional motives.

◎ EXHIBIT 6–18

A think-type product is advertised by an appeal to feelings

◎ COGNITIVE PROCESSING OF COMMUNICATIONS

The hierarchical response models were for many years the primary focus of approaches to study the receivers' responses to marketing communications. Attention centered on identifying relationships between specific controllable variables (such as source and message factors) and outcome or response variables (such as attention, comprehension, attitudes, and purchase intentions). This approach has been criticized on a number of fronts, including its black box nature, since it can't explain what might be causing these reactions.[26] In response to these concerns, researchers began trying to understand the nature of cognitive reactions to persuasive messages. Several approaches have been developed to examine the nature of consumers' cognitive processing of advertising messages.

The Cognitive Response Approach

One of the most widely used methods for examining consumers' cognitive processing of advertising messages is assessment of their **cognitive responses**, the thoughts that occur to them while reading, viewing, and/or hearing a communication.[27] These thoughts are generally measured by having consumers write down or verbally report their reactions to a message. The assumption is that these thoughts reflect the recipient's cognitive processes or reactions and help shape ultimate acceptance or rejection of the message.

The cognitive response approach has been widely used in advertising research by both academicians and advertising practitioners. Its focus has been to determine the types of responses evoked by an advertising message and how these responses relate to attitudes toward the ad, brand attitudes, and purchase intentions. Exhibit 6–19 depicts the three basic categories of cognitive responses researchers have identified—product/message, source-oriented, and ad execution thoughts—and how they may relate to attitudes and intentions.

Product/message thoughts

The first category of thoughts is those directed at the product or service and/or the claims being made in the communication. Much attention has focused on two particular types of responses, counterarguments and support arguments.

Counterarguments are thoughts the recipient has that are opposed to the position taken in the message. For example, consider the ad for Ultra Tide shown in Exhibit 6–20. A consumer may express disbelief or disapproval of a claim made in an ad. ("I don't believe that any detergent could get that stain out!") Other consumers who see

@ **EXHIBIT 6–19** A model of cognitive response

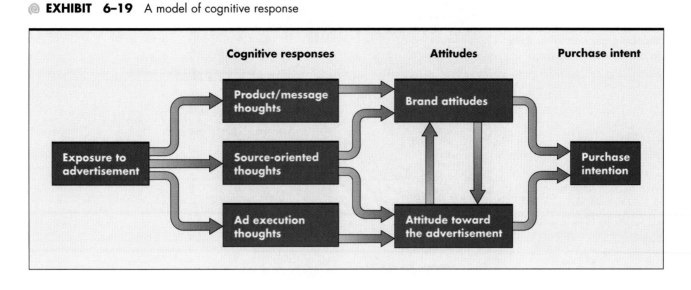

this ad may generate **support arguments**, or thoughts that affirm the claims made in the message. ("Ultra Tide looks like a really good product—I think I'll try it.")

The likelihood of counterarguing is greater when the message makes claims that oppose the beliefs held by the receiver. For example, a consumer viewing a commercial that attacks a favorite brand is likely to engage in counterarguing. Counterarguments relate negatively to message acceptance; the more the receiver counterargues, the less likely he or she is to accept the position advocated in the message.[28] Support arguments, on the other hand, relate positively to message acceptance. Thus, the marketer should develop ads or other promotional messages that minimize counterarguing and encourage support arguments.

Source-oriented thoughts

A second category of cognitive responses is directed at the source of the communication. One of the most important responses in this category is **source derogations**, or negative thoughts about the spokesperson or organization making the claims. Such thoughts generally lead to a reduction in message acceptance. If consumers find a particular spokesperson annoying or distrustful, they are less likely to accept what these sources have to say.

Of course, source-related thoughts are not always negative. Receivers who react favorably to the source generate favorable thoughts, or **source bolsters**. As you would expect, most advertisers attempt to hire spokespeople their target audience likes so as to carry this effect over to the message. However, a recent trend among some advertisers has been to use antihero role models, as discussed in Ethical Perspective 6–1.

Ad execution thoughts

The third category of cognitive responses shown in Exhibit 6–19 is the individual's thoughts about the ad itself. Many of the thoughts receivers have when reading or viewing an ad do not concern the product and/or message claims directly. Rather, they are affective reactions representing the consumer's feelings toward the ad. These thoughts may include reactions to ad execution factors such as the creativity of the ad, the quality of the visual effects, colors, and voice tones. Ad execution–related thoughts can be either favorable or unfavorable. They are important because of their effect on attitudes toward the advertisement as well as the brand.

In recent years, much attention has focused on consumers' affective reactions to ads, especially TV commercials.[29] **Attitude toward the ad** (A→ad) represents the receivers' feelings of favorability or unfavorability toward the ad. Advertisers are interested in con-

EXHIBIT 6–20

Consumers often generate support arguments in response to ads for quality products

sumers' reactions to the ad because they know that affective reactions are an important determinant of advertising effectiveness, since these reactions may be transformed to the brand itself or directly influence purchase intentions. One study found that people who enjoy a commercial are twice as likely as those who are neutral toward the ad to be convinced that the brand is the best.[30]

Consumers' feelings about the ad may be just as important as their attitudes toward the brand (if not more so) in determining an advertisement's effectiveness.[31] The importance of affective reactions and feelings generated by the ad depend on several factors, among them the nature of the ad and the type of processing engaged in by the receiver.[32] Many advertisers have begun to use emotional ads designed to evoke feelings and affective reactions as the basis of their creative strategy. The success of this strategy depends in part on the consumers' involvement with the brand and their likelihood of attending to and processing the message. We end our analysis of the receiver by examining a model that integrates some of the factors that may account for different types and levels of cognitive processing of a message.

The Elaboration Likelihood Model (ELM)

Differences in the ways consumers process and respond to persuasive messages are addressed in the **elaboration likelihood model (ELM)** of persuasion, shown in Exhibit 6–21 on page 180.[33] The ELM was devised by Richard Petty and John Cacioppo to explain the process by which persuasive communications (such as ads) lead to persuasion by influencing *attitudes*. According to this model, the attitude formation or change process depends on the amount and nature of *elaboration*, or processing, of relevant information that occurs in response to a persuasive message. High elaboration means the receiver engages in careful consideration, thinking, and evaluation of the information or arguments contained in the message. Low elaboration occurs when the receiver does not engage in

Ethical Perspective 6–1
Changing the Way Athletes Are Portrayed

The use of popular athletes to endorse companies and their products and services has become commonplace in advertising. Corporations look for athletes whose presence in their ads will attract the attention of viewers or readers and enhance the image of the company or brand they are endorsing. Superstar athletes such as Joe Montana, Michael Jordan, Arnold Palmer, and Chris Evert have traditionally been portrayed as positive role models—superachieving, larger-than-life figures worthy of admiration, emulation, and respect.

Occasionally an athlete who did not have a favorable image might get an endorsement. For example, in the early 1980s Bic used tennis star John MacEnroe in commercials for its disposable razors by having him poke fun at his reputation as the bad boy of tennis.

In the 1990s, however, many marketers are changing the traditional role of the athlete as hero in their ads. A marketing consultant notes that the intense media scrutiny of athletes is demystifying their image and hero worship is declining. Incidents such as the arrest of O. J. Simpson, baseball's all-time hit leader Pete Rose being banned from the game for gambling, boxer Mike Tyson's rape conviction, Earvin ("Magic") Johnson's HIV diagnosis, and Michael Jordan's golf bets have contributed to consumers' growing skepticism about athletes. Moreover, reports of athletes' exorbitant salaries and lucrative endorsement contracts have tarnished their credibility as spokespeople. Many consumers discount athlete endorsers' opinions because they know they are being paid huge sums of money to promote a brand.

Motivated by these changing consumer attitudes toward athletes, some marketers are replacing mythmaking hero worship with gritty, realistic ads featuring edgy antiheroes who tell it like it is. For example, in 1993 Nike ran its "NBA unplugged" campaign, featuring Michael Jordan and other basketball superstars pondering the cost of celebrity and what it takes to play the game. One of the most controversial spots features Phoenix Suns star Charles Barkley glowering at the camera and declaring, "I am not a role model." Nike has noted that the ads are not designed to repudiate its past ads, which have depicted athletes such as Jordan and Bo Jackson as heroes, but rather are part of a continuing effort to capture the essence of sports.

British Knights took the changing portrayal of athletes a step further in commercials featuring Lloyd Daniels, a guard for the San Antonio Spurs. In the documentary-style spots Daniels, a former drug user, is shown revisiting his old haunts in New York City, where he suffered gunshot wounds outside a crack house before attracting the attention of NBA scouts. As the commercial follows Daniels through the city streets wearing his British Knights athletic shoes, he comments: "There are a lot of stories about me growing up in Brooklyn—and they're all true." Of course, some people question the logic of linking a brand to an endorser with such a troubled past.

Other marketers have developed ads that strip away the hype of athlete as hero and focus on the basics of sport itself. Reebok's spots feature realistic footage of football star Emmitt Smith of the Dallas Cowboys crashing head-on into opponents, complete with sounds of grunting linemen and the crunching of shoulder pads. Another spot featured figure skater Nancy Kerrigan talking about all the obstacles she had to overcome to make it to the Olympics. A Reebok spokesperson said, "We don't want to put the athletes on a pedestal but to present them as human beings and not necessarily superstars." However, he also noted, "We select athletes who view themselves as role models, who feel a responsibility that they have to give something back to the community."

While some advertisers are turning the role of athlete as hero in advertising upside down, they still may want consumers to be able to turn it right side up.

Sources: Jeff Jensen, "Bad Role Model Can Make Good Ad," *Advertising Age*, Sept. 27, 1993, p. 10; Jeff Jensen, "Barkley Salts Away More Endorsements," *Advertising Age*, Jan. 24, 1994, p. 14.

active information processing or thinking but rather makes inferences about the position being advocated in the message based on simple positive or negative cues.

The ELM shows that elaboration likelihood is a function of two elements, motivation and ability to process the message. *Motivation* to process the message depends on such factors as involvement, personal relevance, and individuals' needs and arousal levels. *Ability* to process depends on whether the individual has the knowledge, intellectual capacity, and opportunity to process the message. For example, an individual viewing a humorous commercial or one containing an attractive model may be distracted from processing the information about the product.

According to the ELM, there are two basic routes to persuasion or attitude change. Under the **central route to persuasion**, the receiver is viewed as a very active, involved participant in the communications process whose ability and motivation to attend, comprehend, and evaluate messages are high. When central processing of an advertising message occurs, the consumer pays close attention to message content and scrutinizes the message arguments. A high level of cognitive response activity or processing occurs, and the ad's ability to persuade the receiver depends primarily on the receiver's evaluation

EXHIBIT 6–21

The elaboration likelihood model of persuasion

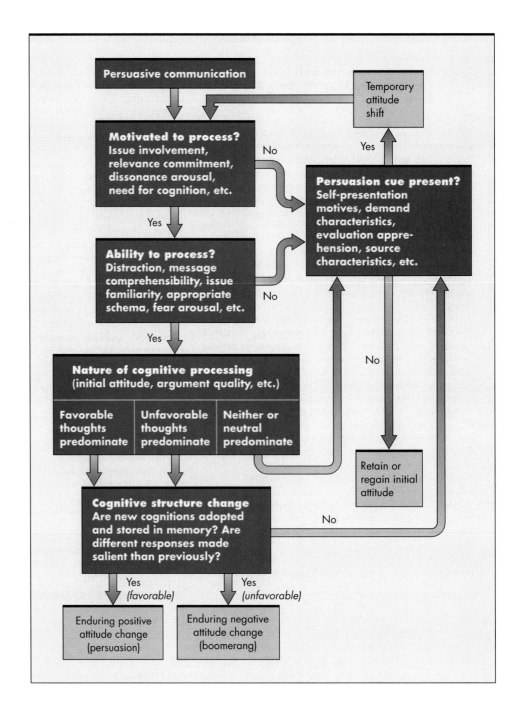

of the quality of the arguments presented. Predominantly favorable cognitive responses (support arguments and source bolsters) lead to favorable changes in cognitive structure, which lead to positive attitude change or persuasion.

Conversely, if the cognitive processing is predominantly unfavorable and results in counterarguments and/or source derogations, the changes in cognitive structure are unfavorable and *boomerang*, or result in negative attitude change. Attitude change that occurs through central processing is relatively enduring and should resist subsequent efforts to change it.

Under the **peripheral route to persuasion**, shown on the right side of Exhibit 6–21, the receiver is viewed as lacking the motivation or ability to process information and is not likely to engage in detailed cognitive processing. Rather than evaluating the information presented in the message, the receiver relies on peripheral cues that may

@ **EXHIBIT 6–22**

This ad contains peripheral
cues such as a celebrity
endorser

be incidental to the main arguments. The receiver's reaction to the message depends on how he or she evaluates these peripheral cues.

The consumer may use several types of peripheral cues or cognitive shortcuts rather than carefully evaluating the message arguments presented in an advertisement.[34] Favorable attitudes may be formed if the endorser in the ad is viewed as an expert or is attractive and/or likable, or if the consumer likes certain executional aspects of the ad such as the way it is made, the music, or the imagery. Notice how the ad in Exhibit 6–22 for Right Guard pure power deodorant and antiperspirant contains several positive peripheral cues including a popular celebrity endorser (basketball star Charles Barkley) and excellent visual imagery. These cues might help consumers form a positive attitude toward the brand even if they do not process the message portion of the ad.

Peripheral cues can also lead to rejection of a message. For example, ads that advocate extreme positions, use endorsers who are not well liked or have credibility problems, or are not executed well (such as low-budget ads for local retailers) may be rejected without any consideration of their information or message arguments. As shown in Exhibit 6–21, the ELM views attitudes resulting from peripheral processing as temporary. So continual exposure to the peripheral cues, such as through repetitive advertising, is needed to maintain these favorable attitudes.

Implications of the ELM

The elaboration likelihood model has important implications for marketing communication, particularly with respect to involvement. For example, if the involvement level of consumers in the target audience is high, an ad or sales presentation should contain strong arguments that are difficult for the message recipient to refute or counterargue. If the involvement level of the target audience is low, peripheral cues may be more important than detailed message arguments.

An interesting test of the ELM showed that the effectiveness of a celebrity endorser in an ad depends on the receiver's involvement level.[35] When involvement was low, a celebrity endorser had a significant effect on attitudes. When the receiver's involvement level was high, however, the use of a celebrity had no effect on brand attitudes; the quality of the arguments used in the ad was more important.

The explanation given for these findings was that a celebrity may serve as a peripheral cue in the low-involvement situation, allowing the receiver to develop favorable attitudes based on feelings toward the source rather than engaging in extensive processing of the message. A highly involved consumer, however, engages in more detailed central processing of the message content. The quality of the message claims becomes more important than the celebrity status of the endorser.

The ELM suggests that the most effective type of message depends on the route to persuasion the consumer follows. Many marketers recognize that involvement levels are low for their product categories and consumers are not motivated to process advertising messages in any detail. That's why marketers of low-involvement products often rely on creative tactics that emphasize peripheral cues and use repetitive advertising to create and maintain favorable attitudes toward their brand.

A FINAL WORD ON THE RESPONSE PROCESS

As you have seen from our analysis of the receiver, the process consumers go through in responding to marketing communications can be viewed from a number of perspectives. We hope the various communication models presented in this chapter give you a better understanding of how consumers process persuasive messages. The promotional planner needs to learn as much as possible about the company's target market and how it may respond to the firm's marketing communication efforts. Marketers who understand the process by which their target audience responds to persuasive communications will be able to make better decisions regarding the promotional program.

SUMMARY

The function of all elements of the promotional mix is to communicate, so promotional planners must understand the communications process. This process can be very complex; successful marketing communication depends on a number of factors, including the nature of the message, the audience's interpretation of it, and the environment in which it is received. A basic model shows the key elements of the communications process. For effective communication to occur, the sender must encode a message in such a way that it will be decoded by the receiver in the intended manner. Feedback from the receiver helps the sender determine whether proper decoding has occurred or whether noise has interfered with the communications process.

Promotional planning begins with the receiver or target audience, as marketers must understand how the audience is likely to respond to various sources of communication or types of messages. For promotional planning, the receiver can be analyzed both with respect to its composition (i.e., individual, group, or mass audiences) and the response process it goes through. Different orderings of the traditional response hierarchy include the standard learning, dissonance, and low-involvement models. The information response model integrates concepts from both the high- and low-involvement response hierarchy perspectives and recognizes the effects of direct experience with a product.

The cognitive response approach examines the thoughts evoked by a message and how they shape the receiver's ultimate acceptance or rejection of the communication. The elaboration likelihood model of attitude formation and change recognizes two forms of message processing, the central and peripheral routes to persuasion, which are a function of the receiver's motivation and ability to process a message.

KEY TERMS

communication, p. 154
source, p. 156
encoding, p. 156
message, p. 156
semiotics, p. 157
channel, p. 158

mass media, p. 158
receiver, p. 159
decoding, p. 159
field of experience, p. 159
noise, p. 159

response, p. 159
feedback, p. 159
AIDA model, p. 163
hierarchy of effects model, p. 164

innovation-adoption model, p. 164
information-processing model, p. 165
standard learning model, p. 168

dissonance/attribution
   model, p. 169
low-involvement
   hierarchy, p. 169
integrated information
   response model, p. 171

cognitive responses,
   p. 176
counterarguments,
   p. 176
support arguments,
   p. 177

source derogations,
   p. 177
source bolsters, p. 177
attitude toward the ad,
   p. 177

elaboration likelihood
   model (ELM), p. 178
central route to
   persuasion, p. 179
peripheral route to
   persuasion, p. 180

DISCUSSION QUESTIONS

1. What is meant by encoding? Discuss how the encoding process differs for radio versus television commercials.

2. Discuss how the science of semiotics can be of value to the field of integrated marketing communications. Select a specific stimulus such as an advertisement, package, or other relevant marketing symbol and conduct a semiotic analysis of it.

3. Those responsible for most of the advertising and promotion decisions for consumer products are brand managers (client side) and account executives (agency side). These individuals are usually well-paid, well-educated marketing professionals living in urban areas. Consider the typical consumer for a brand such as Budweiser beer or Pringles potato chips. What differences might there be between the marketing professionals and the consumers who are the primary users of these brands? What problems could these differences present in developing an IMC program for these brands? How might these problems be overcome?

4. Why are personal channels of communication often more effective than nonpersonal channels?

5. Discuss the various forms feedback might take in the following situations:
   - An office copier salesperson has just made a sales presentation to a potential account.
   - A consumer has just seen a direct-response ad for an exercise machine on late-night TV.
   - Millions of consumers are exposed to an ad for a sports car during a Sunday afternoon football game.

6. Explain how a company like Hewlett-Packard might use the four models of the response process shown in Exhibit 6–8 to develop promotional strategies for its various products.

7. An implication of the integrated information response model is that consumers are likely to take information from advertising and integrate it with direct experience to form judgments about a product. Explain how advertising might lessen the negative outcomes a consumer experiences when trying a brand.

8. Analyze the success of the Simpsons campaign for the Butterfinger candy bar (discussed at the beginning of the chapter) using the low-involvement response hierarchy.

9. Find examples of ads for a product or service that fit into particular cells of the FCB model. Discuss whether and how the ads fit the creative recommendations of these planning models.

10. Analyze the decision by advertisers such as Nike and British Knights to portray star athletes as anti-heroes rather than role models. Do you view this as socially responsible advertising? Why or why not?

11. Compare the central and peripheral routes to persuasion. Provide examples of an ad you think would be processed by a central route and one where you think peripheral processing would occur.

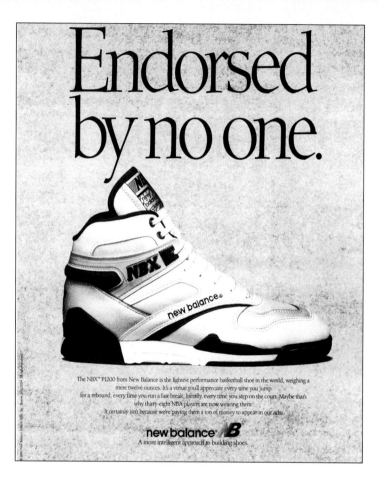

The NBX™ P1200 from New Balance is the lightest performance basketball shoe in the world, weighing a mere twelve ounces. It's a virtue you'll appreciate every time you jump for a rebound, every time you run a fast break, literally, every time you step on the court. Maybe that's why thirty-eight NBA players are now wearing them. It certainly isn't because we're paying them a ton of money to appear in our ads.

new balance *B*

A more intelligent approach to building shoes.

Chapter **7**

Source, Message, and Channel Factors

Chapter Objectives

- To study the major variables in the communications system and how they influence consumers' processing of promotional messages.

- To examine the considerations involved in selecting a source or communicator of a promotional message.

- To examine different types of message structures and appeals that can be used to develop a promotional message.

- To consider how the channel or medium used to deliver a promotional message influences the communications process.

Rethinking Celebrity Endorsers

For many years, marketers held an unwavering belief that celebrity endorsers are a great way to sell a product. The use of celebrities in advertising began half a century ago, when Bob Hope first pinned the Texaco star to his chest and Ronald Reagan hawked Chesterfield cigarettes. Since then, numerous companies have paid large sums of money to align themselves and their products with big-name celebrities in hopes that their popularity and fame might entice consumers to buy. However, many marketers are re-evaluating the value of celebrity endorsements.

Critics argue that the use of celebrities has become too risky and they rarely do much to help business. A number of celebrities have been involved in major controversies that some feel have detracted from their value as endorsers. In 1991, basketball star Earvin (Magic) Johnson was a highly paid spokesman for several companies including Converse, Pepsi, and Target when he announced he was retiring from basketball because he had contracted the HIV virus. Some argue that basketball superstar Michael Jordan's endorsement value declined when he was linked to sizable gambling debts. The Florida Citrus Commission paid actor Burt Reynolds more than $500,000 to be its spokesperson but decided to drop him when his nasty divorce from actress Loni Anderson became the talk of the tabloids.

And then there is singer Michael Jackson, who has received endorsement fees of $20 million from Pepsi over the past decade. Jackson was on an international tour sponsored by Pepsi during the summer of 1993 when the father of a 13-year-old boy accused Jackson of molesting his son. Jackson denied the allegations but ended up paying the boy millions of dollars in an out-of-court settlement. Pepsi terminated its relationship with him.

Critics also argue that celebrity endorsers do little to help sales. L. A. Gear paid millions to Michael Jackson a few years ago to design and promote a line of offbeat sneakers, which were a total flop. Executives close to Frito-Lay concede that the multimillion-dollar signing of Chevy Chase as a pitchman failed to boost Doritos sales. Some ad experts argue that consumers have become too skeptical about celebrity endorsements and many are losing their trust in the celebrities themselves.

Not everyone agrees with the negative assessment of celebrity endorsements, however. Pepsi officials note that while the company was sponsoring three Michael Jackson tours and featuring him in its advertising, it picked up two market share points on archrival Coca-Cola, each point worth an estimated $500 million in annual sales. Executives at Sprint claim that "Murphy Brown" star Candice Bergen has helped the company develop an image that separates it from AT&T and MCI and its market share has climbed nearly two points since it began using her as a spokesperson.

Some advertising people think the marketers who want to use celebrities have Hollywood tinsel in their eyes and a desire to rub elbows with the stars. But if marketing executives can't prove that the use of a celebrity makes sense, their company may join the ranks of those such as New Balance Athletic Shoe Inc., which has an across-the-board policy against hiring celebrities. The president of the company says, "If you want the best shoe for yourself, you don't really give a hoot if Michael Jordan wears it. . . . We'd rather put the money into our factories than into the hands of celebrities."

Sources: Bruce Horowitz, "Wishing on a Star," Los Angeles Times, Nov. 7, 1993, pp. D1, 7; Bruce Horowitz, "Sneaker Firms, Pitchmen Not Always in Step," Los Angeles Times, Nov. 7, 1993, pp. D1,8.

n this chapter, we analyze the major variables in the communications system: the source, the message, and the channel. We examine the characteristics of sources, how they influence reactions to promotional messages, and why one type of communicator is more effective than another. We then focus on the message itself and how structure and type of appeal influence its effectiveness. Finally, we consider how factors related to the channel or medium affect the communications process.

◎ PROMOTIONAL PLANNING THROUGH THE PERSUASION MATRIX

To develop an effective advertising and promotional campaign, a firm must select the right spokesperson to deliver a compelling message through appropriate channels or media. Source, message, and channel factors are controllable elements in the communications model. The **persuasion matrix** (Exhibit 7–1) helps marketers see how each controllable element interacts with the consumer's response process.[1] The matrix has two sets of variables. Independent variables represent the controllable components of the communications process, outlined in Chapter 6; dependent variables represent the steps a receiver goes through in being persuaded. Marketers can choose the person or source who delivers the message, the type of message appeal used, and the channel or medium. And although they can't control the receiver, they can select their target audience. The destination variable is included because the initial message recipient may pass on information to others, such as friends or associates, through word of mouth.

Promotional planners need to know how decisions about each independent variable influence the stages of the response hierarchy so they don't enhance one stage at the expense of another. A humorous message may gain attention but result in decreased comprehension if consumers fail to process its content. Many ads that use humor, sexual appeals, or celebrities capture consumers' attention but result in poor recall of the brand name or message. The following examples, which correspond to the numbers in Exhibit 7–1, illustrate decisions that can be evaluated with the persuasion matrix.

1. **Receiver/comprehension: Can the receiver comprehend the ad?** Marketers must know their target market to make their messages clear and understandable. A less educated person may have more difficulty interpreting a compli-

◎ EXHIBIT 7–1

The persuasion matrix

Dependent variables: Steps in being persuaded	Independent variables: The communication components				
	Source	Message	Channel	Receiver	Destination
Message presentation			(2)		
Attention	(4)				
Comprehension				(1)	
Yielding		(3)			
Retention					
Behavior					

cated message. Jargon may be unfamiliar to some receivers. The more marketers know about the target market, the more they understand which words, symbols, and expressions their customers understand.

2. **Channel/presentation: Which media will increase presentation?** A top-rated, prime-time TV program will be seen by nearly 30 million households each week. *TV Guide* and *Reader's Digest* reach nearly 16 million homes with each issue. But the important issue is how well they reach the marketer's target audience. CNN's "Moneyline" reaches only around a million viewers each weekday evening, but its audience consists mostly of upscale businesspeople who are prime prospects for expensive cars, financial services, and business-related products.

3. **Message/yielding: What type of message will create favorable attitudes or feelings?** Marketers generally try to create agreeable messages that lead to positive feelings toward the product or service. Humorous messages often put consumers in a good mood and evoke positive feelings that may become associated with the brand being advertised. Music adds emotion that makes consumers more receptive to the message. Many advertisers use explicit sexual appeals designed to arouse consumers or suggest they can enhance their appeal to the opposite sex. Some marketers compare their brand to the competition.

4. **Source/attention: Who will be effective in getting consumers' attention?** The large number of ads we are bombarded with every day makes it difficult for advertisers to break through the clutter. Marketers deal with this problem by using sources who will attract the target audience's attention—actors, athletes, rock stars, or attractive models. Each year, *Advertising Age* gives a star presenter award to the individual it believes has been the most effective advertising spokesperson. The winners for the past 17 years are shown in Exhibit 7–2. These star presenters don't just attract attention. They successfully influence other steps in the response hierarchy behavior, as measured by increased sales.

⊚ SOURCE FACTORS

The source component is a multifaceted concept. When Michael Jordan appears in a commercial for Wheaties, is the source Jordan himself, the company (General Mills), or some combination of the two? And, of course, consumers get information from friends, relatives, and neighbors; in fact, personal sources may be the most influential factor in a purchase decision. MCI has taken advantage of personal sources' ability to influence one another with its highly successful Friends & Family program (Exhibit 7–3).

⊚ **EXHIBIT 7–2**

Advertising Age star presenters

1993	Michael Jordan
1992	Candice Bergen
1991	John Cleese
1990	Ray Charles
1989	Bo Jackson
1988	Wilford Brimley
1987	Michael J. Fox
1986	Paul Hogan
1985	William Perry
1984	Cliff Robertson
1983	John Cleese
1982	Rodney Dangerfield
1981	John Houseman
1980	Brooke Shields
1979	Robert Morley
1978	James Garner/Mariette Hartley
1977	Bill Cosby
1976	O.J. Simpson
1975	Karl Malden

◉ **EXHIBIT 7–3**

MCI's Friends & Family
program relies on inter-
personal influence

We use the term **source** to mean the person involved in communicating a market-ing message, either directly or indirectly. A direct source is a spokesperson or endorser who delivers a message and/or demonstrates a product or service, like football coach Bill Walsh (Exhibit 7–4). An indirect source, say, a model, doesn't actually deliver a message but draws attention to and/or enhances the appearance of the ad. Some ads use neither a direct or indirect source; the source is the organization with the message to communi-cate. Since most research focuses on individuals as a message source, our examination of source factors follows this approach.

Companies are very careful when selecting individuals to deliver their selling mes-sages. Many firms spend huge sums of money for a specific person to endorse their prod-uct or company. They also spend millions recruiting, selecting, and training salespeople to represent the company and deliver sales presentations. Marketers recognize that the characteristics of the source affect the sales and advertising message.

Marketers try to select individuals whose characteristics will maximize message in-fluence. The source may be knowledgeable, popular, and/or physically attractive; typify

◉ **EXHIBIT 7–4**

Football coach Bill Walsh
serves as a spokesperson for
Sharp copiers

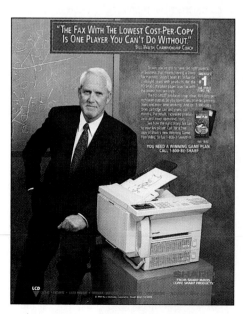

@ **EXHIBIT 7–5**

Source attributes and receiver
processing modes

Source attribute	Process
Credibility ⟶	Internalization
Attractiveness ⟶	Identification
Power ⟶	Compliance

the target audience; or have the power to reward or punish the receiver in some manner. Herbert Kelman developed three basic categories of source attributes: credibility, attractiveness, and power.[2] Each influences the recipient's attitude or behavior through a different process (see Exhibit 7–5).

Source Credibility

Credibility is the extent to which the recipient sees the source as having relevant knowledge, skill, or experience and trusts the source to give unbiased, objective information. There are two important dimensions to credibility, expertise and trustworthiness.

A communicator seen as knowledgeable—someone with *expertise*—is more persuasive than one with less expertise. But the source also has to be *trustworthy*—honest, ethical, and believable. The influence of a knowledgeable source will be lessened if audience members think he or she is biased or has underlying personal motives for advocating a position (such as being paid to endorse a product).

One of the most reliable effects found in communications research is that expert and/or trustworthy sources are more persuasive than sources who are less expert or trustworthy.[3] Information from a credible source influences beliefs, opinions, attitudes, and/or behavior through a process known as **internalization**, which occurs when the receiver adopts the opinion of the credible communicator since he or she believes information from this source is accurate. Once the receiver internalizes an opinion or attitude, it becomes integrated into his or her belief system and may be maintained even after the source of the message is forgotten.

A highly credible communicator is particularly important when message recipients have a negative position toward the product, service, company, or issue being promoted, because the credible source is likely to inhibit counterarguments. As discussed in Chapter 6, reduced counterarguing should result in greater message acceptance and persuasion.

Applying expertise

Because attitudes and opinions developed through an internalization process become part of the individual's belief system, marketers want to use communicators with high credibility. Companies use a variety of techniques to convey source expertise. Sales personnel are trained in the product line, which increases customers' perceptions of their expertise. Marketers of highly technical products recruit sales reps with specialized technical backgrounds in engineering, computer science, and other areas to ensure their expertise.

Spokespeople are often chosen because of their knowledge, experience, and expertise in a particular product or service area. Endorsements from individuals or groups recognized as experts, such as doctors or dentists, are also common in advertising (Exhibit 7–6). The importance of using expert sources was shown in a study by Roobina Ohanian, who found that the perceived expertise of celebrity endorsers was more important in explaining purchase intentions than their attractiveness or trustworthiness. She suggests that celebrity spokespeople are most effective when they are knowledgeable, experienced, and qualified to talk about the product they are endorsing.[4]

@ **EXHIBIT 7–6**

Dove promotes the fact that
it is recommended by an
experts in skin care

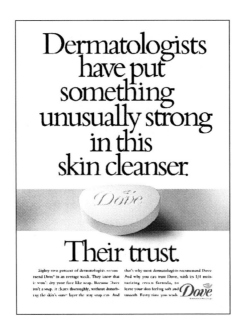

Applying trustworthiness

While expertise is important, the target audience must also find the source believable. Finding celebrities or other figures with a trustworthy image is often difficult. Many trustworthy public figures hesitate to endorse products because of the potential impact on their reputation and image. It has been suggested that former CBS news anchor Walter Cronkite, who has repeatedly been rated one of the most trusted people in America, could command millions of dollars as a product spokesperson. Global Perspective 7–1 discusses how some American celebrities protect their image by endorsing products abroad rather than in the United States.

Advertisers use various techniques to increase the perception that their sources are trustworthy. Hidden camera techniques are used to show that the consumer is not a paid spokesperson and is making an objective evaluation of the product. Disguised brands are compared. (Of course, the sponsor's brand *always* performs better than the consumer's regular brand, and he or she is always surprised.) Most consumers are skeptical of these techniques, so they may have limited value in enhancing perceptions of credibility.

Using corporate leaders as spokespeople

Another way of enhancing source credibility is to use the company president or chief executive officer as a spokesperson in the firm's advertising. Many companies believe the use of a president or CEO is the ultimate expression of the company's commitment to quality and customer service. In some cases, these ads have not only been successful but also helped turn the company leaders into celebrities.[5] Lee Iacocca appeared in more than 60 commercials for Chrysler Corp. and became a national business hero for guiding the successful turnaround of the company. Another popular corporate spokesperson is Dave Thomas, the founder of Wendy's fast food restaurants (Exhibit 7–7 on page 192).

Some research suggests the use of a company president or CEO can improve attitudes and increase the likelihood consumers will inquire about the company's product or service.[6] It is becoming common to see local retailers use the owner or president in their ads. Companies are likely to continue using their top executives in their advertising, particularly when they have celebrity value that helps enhance the firms' image. However, there can be problems with this strategy. CEO spokespeople who become very popular may get more attention than their company's product/service or advertising message. If a firm's image becomes too closely tied to a popular leader, there can be problems if that person leaves the company.

Global Perspective 7-1
Selling Out, but Only Abroad

Many American celebrities make huge sums of money endorsing products and serving as advertising spokespeople. Some big stars won't do endorsements because they don't want fans to think they've sold out. But many stars who resist the temptation to cash in on their fame in the United States are only too happy to appear in ads in foreign countries.

Actress Kim Bassinger models hosiery in Italy; Woody Allen wrote and directed a series of commercials for the country's largest grocery chain, Co-op Italia, for several million dollars. Sharon Stone, who became a superstar with her sexy roles in movies like *Basic Instinct* and *Sliver*, received between $1 million and $2 million to star in a racy ad for Pirelli Tires in Europe. An executive for the agency that did the ads noted that "Pirelli's brand image is very Italian, quite sexy....We chose Sharon Stone because of who she is—very sexy, grown up, in control."

Nowhere are ads starring American celebrities more prevalent than in Japan. While the Japanese flood the United States with cars, TVs, and VCRs, the trade in celebrity endorsers flows the other way. Arnold Schwarzenegger pitches Nissin Cup Noodle and Chi Chin vitamin drink and can be seen straddling a rocket that blasts off and shoots him out of the frame in a commercial for Takeda Chemical Industries. Gene Hackman and Sylvester Stallone each received $1 million to represent Kirin beer. Bruce Willis appears on Japanese television selling Subarus and Post Water, while his wife, actress Demi Moore, pushes cosmetics. Japan's two major airlines have used Frank

Sinatra and Richard Gere to fill seats. Actress Jodi Foster flirts with a group of men to the tune of the Fine Young Cannibals' "She Drives Me Crazy" in a Honda ad.

Western celebrities are used to promote products in Japan for a number of reasons. Many Japanese identify with the Western style of life, and the celebrity endorsements give brands a certain international cachet. Also, Japanese advertising emphasizes style and mood rather than substance; consumers expect to be entertained by ads rather than bored by product testimonials. And many celebrities have fun doing the ads. In a spot for Post Water, Bruce Willis spoofs his action movie image by crashing through a window, rolling on the floor, and swinging from a chandelier onto a food-laden table before quenching his thirst with a bottle of the mineral water. Another reason is that Japanese commercials commonly last only 15 seconds, so advertisers find an instantly recognizable Western celebrity who can capture viewers' attention is well worth the money.

Many celebrities cashing in on foreign commercials try to protect their image at home. The stars commonly have nondisclosure clauses in their contracts, specifying that the ads cannot be shown—or sometimes even discussed (oops!)—outside the country for which they were intended. The worldwide head of commercials at the William Morris talent agency says that actors "believe that knowledge of that endorsement should stay within that country." Sorry about that.

Sources: Lauren David Peden, "Seen the One Where Arnold Sells Noodles?" *The New York Times*, June 20, 1993, p. 28; David Kilburn, "Japanese Airlines Tap U.S. Stars," *Advertising Age*, April 8, 1991; "The Celebrity Is the Message," *Forbes*, July 14, 1986, pp. 88–89.

Limitations of credible sources

Several studies have shown that a high-credibility source is not always an asset, nor is a low-credibility source always a liability. High- and low-credibility sources are equally effective when they are arguing for a position opposing their own best interest.[7] A high-credibility source is more effective when message recipients are not in favor of the position advocated in the message.[8] However, a high-credibility source is less important when the audience has a neutral position and may even be less effective than a moderately credible source when the receiver's initial attitude is favorable.[9]

Another reason a low-credibility source may be as effective as a high-credibility source is the **sleeper effect**, whereby the persuasiveness of a message increases with the passage of time. The immediate impact of a persuasive message may be inhibited because of its association with a low-credibility source. But with time, the association of the message with the low-credibility source diminishes, and the receiver's attention focuses more on favorable information in the message, which results in more support arguing. However, many studies have failed to demonstrate the presence of a sleeper effect.[10] Many advertisers question the strategy of relying on the sleeper effect, since exposure to a credible source is a more reliable strategy.[11]

Source Attractiveness

A source characteristic frequently used by advertisers is **attractiveness**, which encompasses similarity, familiarity, and likability.[12] *Similarity* is a supposed resemblance between the source and the receiver of the message, while *familiarity* refers to knowledge of the source through exposure. *Likability* is an affection for the source as a result of physical appearance, behavior, or other personal characteristics. Even when these sources are not athletes or movie stars, consumers often admire their physical appearance, talent, and/or personality.

⊚ EXHIBIT 7–7

Dave Thomas is a very effective spokesperson for Wendy's

Source attractiveness leads to persuasion through a process of **identification**, whereby the receiver is motivated to seek some type of relationship with the source and thus adopts a similar position in terms of beliefs, attitudes, preferences, or behavior. Maintaining this position depends on the source's continued support for the position as well as the receiver's continued identification with the source. If the source changes position, the receiver may also change. Unlike internalization, information from an attractive source does not usually become integrated into the receiver's belief system. Thus, the receiver may maintain the attitudinal position or behavior only as long as it is supported by the source or the source remains attractive.

Marketers recognize that receivers of persuasive communications are more likely to attend to and identify with people they find likable or similar to themselves. Similarity and likability are the two source characteristics marketers seek when choosing a communicator.

Applying similarity

Marketers recognize that people are more likely to be influenced by a message coming from someone with whom they feel a sense of similarity.[13] If the communicator and receiver have similar needs, goals, interests, and lifestyles, the position advocated by the source is better understood and received. Similarity is used in various ways in marketing communications. Companies select salespeople who have characteristics that match well with their customers. A sales position for a particular region may be staffed by someone local who has background and interests in common with the customers. Global marketers often hire foreign nationals as salespeople so customers can relate more easily to them.

Companies may also try to recruit former athletes to sell sporting goods or beer, since their customers usually have a strong interest in sports. Several studies have shown that customers who perceive a salesperson as similar to themselves are more likely to be influenced by his or her message.[14]

Similarity is also used to create a situation where the consumer feels empathy for the person shown in the commercial. In a slice-of-life commercial, the advertiser usually starts by presenting a predicament with the hope of getting the consumer to think, "I can see myself in that situation." This can help establish a bond of similarity between the communicator and the receiver, increasing the source's level of persuasiveness.

Applying likability: Using celebrities

Advertisers recognize the value of using spokespeople who are admired: TV and movie stars, athletes, musicians, and other popular public figures. More than 20 percent of all TV commercials feature celebrities, and advertisers pay hundreds of mil-

@ **EXHIBIT 7-8**
Michael Jordan's many endorsements include Gatorade

lions of dollars for their services. Recently retired basketball superstar Michael Jordan makes an estimated $36 million a year in endorsement fees from companies such as McDonald's, Nike, General Mills, Hanes, and Quaker Oats (makers of Gatorade) (Exhibit 7–8).[15]

Why do companies spend huge sums to have celebrities appear in their ads and endorse their products? They think celebrities have stopping power. That is, they draw attention to advertising messages in a very cluttered media environment. Marketers think a popular, admired celebrity will favorably influence consumers' feelings, attitudes, and purchase behavior. And they believe celebrities can enhance the target audience's perceptions of the product in terms of image and/or performance. For example, a well-known athlete may convince potential buyers that the product will enhance their own performance (Exhibit 7–9).

A number of factors must be considered when a company decides to use a celebrity spokesperson.

Overshadowing the product
How will the celebrity affect the target audience's processing of the advertising message? Consumers may focus their attention on the celebrity and fail to note the brand. Mazda dropped actor James Garner as its spokesperson to focus exclusively on its cars. Said Mazda's vice president of advertising, "We want the cars to be the stars."[16]

Overexposure
Consumers are often skeptical of endorsements because they know the celebrities are being paid.[17] This problem is particularly pronounced when a celebrity endorses too many products or companies and becomes overexposed. For example, a few years ago actor Bill Cosby appeared in ads for Jell-O, Coca-Cola, Kodak, Texas Instruments, and E. F. Hutton.[18] Advertisers can protect themselves against overexposure with an exclusivity clause limiting the number of products a celebrity can endorse. However, such clauses are usually expensive and most celebrities agree not to endorse similar products anyway. Many celebrities, knowing their fame is fleeting, try to earn as much endorsement money as possible, yet they must be careful not to damage their credibility by endorsing too many products.

Target audiences
Consumers who are particularly knowledgeable about a product or service or have strongly established attitudes may be less influenced by a celebrity than those with little knowledge or neutral attitudes. For example, one study found that college-age students were more likely to have a positive attitude toward a product endorsed by a celebrity than were older consumers.[19] The teenage market segment is generally very receptive to

@ **EXHIBIT 7–9**

Lee Trevino attracts attention
and delivers a convincing
message about the product

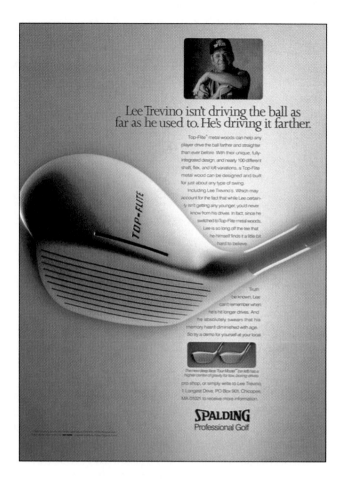

celebrity endorsers, as evidenced by the frequent use of entertainers and athletes in ads targeted to this group for products such as soft drinks, apparel, and cosmetics.

Some studies suggest that celebrity endorsements are becoming less important in influencing purchase decisions for a broad range of consumers.[20] In a survey conducted by the Athletic Footwear Association, consumers cited celebrity endorsements as the least important factor for buying a particular brand of shoe (Exhibit 7–10).

Risk to the advertiser

A celebrity's behavior may pose a risk to a company. As noted in the opening vignette, a number of entertainers and athletes have been involved in activities that could embarrass the companies whose products they endorsed. Pepsi dropped a TV ad featuring pop singer Madonna when some religious groups and consumers objected to her "Like a Prayer" video and threatened to boycott Pepsi products.[21] The Beef Industry Council suffered embarrassment when spokesperson Cybil Shepherd was quoted as saying that she didn't eat red meat.[22] To avoid these problems, companies often research a celebrity's personal life and background. Many contracts include a morals clause allowing the company to terminate the contract if a controversy arises.

Understanding the meaning of celebrity endorsers

Advertisers must try to match the product or company's image, the characteristics of the target market, and the personality of the celebrity.[23] The image celebrities project to consumers can be just as important as their ability to attract attention. A new perspective on celebrity endorsement has been developed recently by Grant McCracken.[24] He argues that credibility and attractiveness don't sufficiently explain how and why celebrity endorsements work and offers a model based on *meaning transfer* (Exhibit 7–11 on page 196).

@ **EXHIBIT 7–10**

Importance of various
information sources in the
purchase of athletic shoes

Selling Sneakers

When 30,000 consumers nationwide were asked what they considered the most important source of information for buying sneakers, celebrity endorsements finished dead last. Here is how customers, ages 13 to 75, ranked the factors that swayed them to buy one brand over another.

Information Source	Percent Who Consider It Important
All advertising	69
Store displays	57
TV commercials	53
Friends	48
Observing others	41
Magazine articles	19
Salespeople	19
Newspaper articles	13
Mail-order catalogs	11
Celebrity endorsements	10

Source: Athletic Footwear Assn.

According to this model, a celebrity's effectiveness as an endorser depends on the culturally acquired meanings he or she brings to the endorsement process. Each celebrity contains many meanings, including status, class, gender, and age as well as personality and lifestyle. In explaining stage 1 of the meaning transfer process, McCracken notes:

> Celebrities draw these powerful meanings from the roles they assume in their television, movie, military, athletic, and other careers . . . Each new dramatic role brings the celebrity into contact with a range of objects, persons, and contexts. Out of these objects, persons, and contexts are transferred meanings that then reside in the celebrity.[25]

Examples of meanings that have been acquired by celebrities include actor Bill Cosby as the perfect father (from his role on "The Cosby Show") and Bo Jackson as the ultimate athlete (based on his excelling in both pro football and baseball).

McCracken suggests celebrity endorsers bring their meanings into the advertisement and transfer them to the products they are endorsing (stage 2 of the model in Exhibit 7–11). For example, long-distance carrier Sprint's use of Candice Bergen as its spokesperson takes advantage of the glib, caustic journalist she plays on her popular television show. Murphy Brown's character embodies the irreverent, alternative image Sprint wants to project in competing as the underdog, and it comes across in the ads when Bergen delivers sarcastic little zingers at industry leader AT&T.

Marketers using a celebrity endorser try to capture the exact set of meanings being sought from the celebrity in the ad campaign and not to transfer unwanted meaning. For example, Bristol-Myers does an excellent job of using Jimmy Connors in ads for Nuprin by focusing on his appeal as an aging yet defiant tennis star who can still compete against younger players but "hurts all over" when he is done playing (Exhibit 7–12 on page 197).

In the final stage of McCracken's model, the meanings the celebrity has given to the product are transferred to the consumer. Jimmy Connors's endorsement helps position Nuprin as the body pain medicine and encourages consumers to use the product to relieve their own aches and pains. McCracken notes that this final stage is complicated and difficult to achieve. The way consumers take possession of the meaning the celebrity has transferred to a product is probably the least understood part of this process.

The meaning transfer model has some important implications for companies using celebrity endorsers. Marketers must first decide on the image or symbolic meanings

EXHIBIT 7–11   Meaning movement and the endorsement process

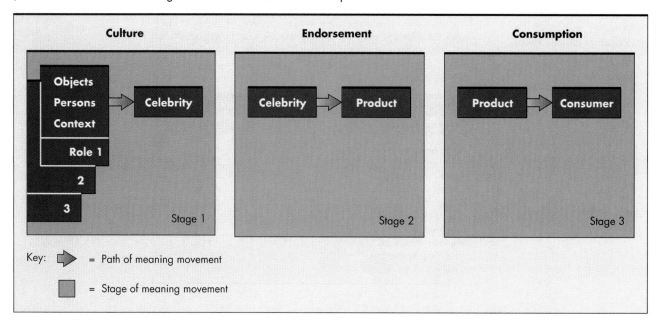

important to their target audience for this particular product or company. They must then determine which celebrity best represents the meaning or image to be projected. An advertising campaign must be designed that captures the meaning of the celebrity in the product and moves this meaning from the product to the consumer. Marketing and advertising personnel often rely on intuition in choosing celebrity endorsers for their companies or products, but some companies conduct research studies to determine consumers' perceptions of celebrities' meaning.

Marketers may also pretest ads to determine whether they transfer the proper meaning to the product. When celebrity endorsers are used, the marketer should track the campaign's effectiveness. Does the celebrity continue to be effective in communicating the proper meaning to the target audience? Celebrities who are no longer in the limelight may lose their ability to transfer any significant meanings to the product.

As we have seen, marketers must consider many factors when choosing a celebrity to serve as an advertising spokesperson for the company or a particular brand. IMC Perspective 7–1 on page 198 discusses some interesting issues regarding the choice of celebrity endorsers.

Applying likability: decorative models

Advertisers often draw attention to their ads by featuring a physically attractive person who serves as a passive or decorative model rather than as an active communicator. Research suggests that physically attractive communicators generally have a positive impact and generate more favorable evaluations of both ads and products than less attractive models.[26] The gender appropriateness of the model for the product being advertised and his or her relevance to the product are also important considerations.[27] Products such as cosmetics or fashionable clothing are likely to benefit from the use of an attractive model, since physical appearance is very relevant in marketing these items.

Some models draw attention to the ad but not to the product or message. Studies show that an attractive model facilitates recognition of the ad but does not enhance copy readership or message recall.[28] Thus, advertisers must ensure that the consumer's attention will go beyond the model to the product and advertising message.

EXHIBIT 7–12

The use of Jimmy Connors as an endorser helps position Nuprin as the body pain medicine

Source Power

EXHIBIT 7–13

Actor Charles Bronson's authoritative image makes him an effective source

The final characteristic in Kelman's classification scheme is **source power**. A source has power when he or she can actually administer rewards and punishments to the receiver. As a result of this power, the source may be able to induce another person(s) to respond to the request or position he or she is advocating. The power of the source depends on several factors. The source must be perceived as being able to administer positive or negative sanctions to the receiver (*perceived control*) and the receiver must think the source cares about whether or not the receiver conforms (*perceived concern*). The receiver's estimate of the source's ability to observe conformity is also important (*perceived scrutiny*).

When a receiver perceives a source as having power, the influence process occurs through a process known as **compliance**. The receiver accepts the persuasive influence of the source and acquiesces to his or her position in hopes of obtaining favorable reaction or avoiding punishment. The receiver may show a public agreement with the source's position but not have an internal or private commitment to this position. Thus, persuasion induced through compliance may be superficial and last only as long as the receiver perceives that the source can administer some reward or punishment.

Power as a source characteristic is very difficult to apply in a nonpersonal influence situation such as advertising. A communicator in an ad generally cannot apply any sanctions to the receiver or determine whether compliance actually occurs. An indirect way of using power is by using an individual with an authoritative personality as a spokesperson. Actor Charles Bronson, who typifies this image, has appeared in public service campaigns commanding people not to pollute or damage our natural parks (Exhibit 7–13).

The use of source power applies more in situations involving personal communication and influence. For example, in a personal selling situation, the sales rep may have some power over a buyer if the latter anticipates receiving special rewards or favors for complying with the salesperson. Some companies provide their sales reps with large expense accounts to spend on customers for this very purpose. Representatives of companies whose product demand exceeds supply are often in a position of power; buyers may comply with their requests to ensure an adequate supply of the product. Sales reps must be very careful in their use of a power position, since abusing a power base to maximize short-term gains can damage long-term relationships with a customer.

IMC Perspective 7–1
Choosing a Celebrity Endorser

Obviously many marketers believe strongly in the value of celebrity spokespeople, as the amount of money paid to them has soared to record levels. Marketers look for a celebrity who will attract viewers' or readers' attention and enhance the image of their company or brand. But how do they choose the right one? While some executives rely on their own gut feeling, many turn to research that measures a celebrity's appeal to help them choose an endorser.

Marketing Evaluations Inc.'s TVQ Services surveys more than 7,000 people each year to come up with recognizability scores and its well-known Q rating for TV and movie actors, athletes, authors, businesspeople, and other personalities. The recognizability score indicates what percentage of people recognize the celebrity. The Q score tells the percentages of people recognizing the celebrity who rate him or her as one of their favorite performers. For example, Bill Cosby set a record a few years ago when 96 percent of those surveyed recognized him and he had a Q score of 71 (i.e., 71 percent of those who recognized him said he was one of their favorite performers). The average Q score for performers is 18. Marketing Evaluations' celebrity ratings are also broken down by various demographic groups such as age, income, occupation, education, and race. Thus, marketers have some idea of how a celebrity's popularity varies among different groups of consumers.

Video Storyboard Tests, Inc., conducts an annual survey of more than 3,000 adult TV viewers to measure attitudes toward celebrities as endorsers, their persuasiveness, and credibility. The table here shows consumers' ratings of the most popular entertainer and athlete endorsers for TV in 1993. The list is carefully scrutinized by ad executives and talent agencies to determine the most effective spokespeople for various companies.

Marketers also consider the celebrities' visibility and personalities. Among athletes, basketball players, tennis players, and golfers are popular spokespeople, since the public buys the footwear, clubs, balls, rackets, and clothing these highly visible athletes use. It also helps to be perceived as a winner. Most of the top athlete endorsers are current or former stars in their sports and have led their teams to championships. And, of course, physical attractiveness is always an asset, particularly for celebrities endorsing health and beauty products, such as Cher, Cindy Crawford, and Kathie Lee Gifford.

Athletes also find that good looks increase their value as endorsers. An ad executive noted that Troy Aikman, who has led the Dallas Cowboys to two consecutive Super Bowl victories, has "the looks, the talent, and the dominant team to become the next Joe Montana of endorsements." Aikman already appears in ads for Nike, Lay's potato chips, and Wheaties.

Athletes

Rank 1993	Rank 1992	Endorser	Endorsements
1	1	Michael Jordan	Nike, McDonald's, Hanes, Gatorade, Ball Park Franks
2	5	Joe Namath	FlexAll
3	9	Larry Bird	McDonald's, Converse
4	3	Bo Jackson	Nike, Lipton Tea, Pepsi
5	2	Magic Johnson	Pepsi, Upper Deck, Nintendo, Target, Tiger Electronics
6	–	Joe Montana	L.A. Gear, Hanes
7	–	Chris Evert	Nuprin
8	10	Charles Barkley	Nike
9	–	Shaquille O'Neal	Reebok, Pepsi
10	7	Jimmy Connors	Nuprin

Entertainers

Rank 1993	Rank 1992	Endorser	Endorsements
1	3	Candice Bergen	Sprint
2	2	Bill Cosby	Jell-O, Coke
3	–	Cher	Equal
4	3	Cindy Crawford	Pepsi, Revlon
5	–	Burt Reynolds	Florida orange juice
6	–	Regis Philbin	Ultra Slim-Fast
7	–	Susan Lucci	Ford
8	–	Sally Struthers	Christian Children's Fund
9	1	Ray Charles	Diet Pepsi
10	8	Kathie Lee Gifford	Carnival Cruise Lines, Ultra Slim-Fast

Source: Video Storyboard Tests.

Sources: Kevin Goldman, "Candice Bergen Leads the List of Top Celebrity Endorsers," *The Wall Street Journal*, Sept. 17, 1993, pp. B1, 10; Kevin Goldman, "Athletes Find Endorsements Hard to Win," *The Wall Street Journal*, Jan. 27, 1994, p. B10.

MESSAGE FACTORS

The way marketing communications are presented is very important in determining their effectiveness. Promotional managers must consider not only the content of their persuasive messages but also how this information will be structured for presentation and what type of message appeal will be used. Advertising, in all media except radio, relies heavily on visual as well as verbal information. Many options are available

@ **EXHIBIT 7–14**

Ad message recalls a
function of order of
presentation

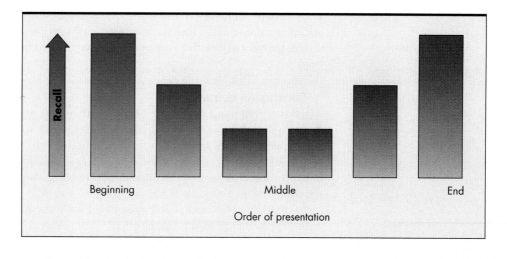

@ **EXHIBIT 7–14**

Ad message recalls a
function of order of
presentation

with respect to the design and presentation of a message. This section examines the structure of a message and considers the effects of different types of appeals used in advertising.

Message Structure

Marketing communications usually consist of a number of message points that the communicator wants to get across. An important aspect of message strategy is knowing the best way to communicate these points and overcome any opposing viewpoints audience members may hold. Extensive research has been conducted on how the structure of a persuasive message can influence its effectiveness, including order of presentation, conclusion drawing, message sidedness, refutation, and verbal versus nonverbal message characteristics.

Order of presentation

A basic consideration in the design of a persuasive message concerns the order of presentation of the arguments. Should the most important message points be placed at the beginning of the message, in the middle, or at the end? Research on learning and memory generally indicates that items presented first and last are remembered better than those presented in the middle (see Exhibit 7–14).[29] This suggests that a communicator's strongest arguments should be presented early or late in the message but never in the middle.

Presenting the strongest arguments at the beginning of the message assumes a **primacy effect** is operating, whereby information presented first is most effective. Putting the strong points at the end assumes a **recency effect**, whereby the last arguments presented are most persuasive.

Whether to place the strongest selling points at the beginning or the end of the message depends on several factors. If the target audience is opposed to the communicator's position, presenting strong points first can reduce the level of counterarguing. Putting weak arguments first might lead to such a high level of counterarguing that strong arguments would not be believed. Putting strong arguments at the beginning of the message may also be necessary if the audience is not interested in the topic, so the arguments can arouse interest in the message. When the target audience is predisposed toward the communicator's position or is highly interested in the issue or product, strong arguments can be saved for the end of the message. This may result in a more favorable opinion as well as better retention of the information.

The order of presentation can be critical when a long, detailed message with many arguments is being presented. Most effective sales presentations open and close with strong selling points and bury weaker arguments in the middle. For short communications, such as a 15- or 30-second TV or radio commercial, the order may be less critical. However, many product and service messages are received by consumers with low involvement and minimal interest. Thus, an advertiser may want to present the brand name and key selling points early in the message as well as at the end to enhance recall and retention.

Conclusion drawing

Marketing communicators must decide whether their messages should explicitly draw a firm conclusion or allow the audience to draw their own conclusions. Research suggests that, in general, messages with explicit conclusions are more easily understood and effective in influencing attitudes. However, other studies have shown that the effectiveness of conclusion drawing may depend on the target audience, the type of issue or topic, and the nature of the situation.[30]

More highly educated people prefer to draw their own conclusions and may be annoyed at an attempt to explain the obvious or to draw an inference for them. But stating the conclusion may be necessary for a less educated audience, who may never draw a conclusion or may make an incorrect inference from the message. Marketers must also consider the audience's level of involvement in the topic. For highly personal or ego-involving issues, message recipients may want to make up their own minds and resent any attempts by the communicator to draw a conclusion. A recent study found that open-ended ads without explicit conclusions were more effective than closed-ended arguments that did include a specific conclusion—but only for involved audiences.[31]

Whether to draw a conclusion for the audience also depends on the complexity of the topic. Even a highly educated audience may need assistance if its knowledge level in a particular area is low. Does the marketer want the message to trigger immediate action or a more long-term effect? If immediate action is an objective, the message should draw a definite conclusion. This is a common strategy in political advertising, particularly for ads run close to election day. When immediate impact is not the objective and repeated exposure will give the audience opportunities to draw a conclusion, an open-ended message may be used.

Drawing a conclusion in a message may make sure the target audience gets the point the marketer intended. But many advertisers believe that letting customers draw their own conclusions reinforces the points being made in the message. For example, a health services agency in Kentucky found that open-ended ads were more memorable and more effective in getting consumers to use health services than ads stating a conclusion. Ads that posed questions about alcohol and drug abuse and left them unanswered resulted in more calls by teenagers to a help line for information than did a message offering a resolution to the problem.[32]

Message sidedness

Another message structure decision facing the marketer involves message sidedness. A **one-sided message** mentions only positive attributes or benefits. A **two-sided message** presents both good and bad points. One-sided messages are most effective when the target audience already holds a favorable opinion about the topic. They also work better with a less educated audience.[33]

Two-sided messages are more effective when the target audience holds an opposing opinion or is highly educated. Two-sided messages may enhance the credibility of the source.[34] A better-educated audience usually knows there are opposing arguments, so by presenting both sides of an issue, the communicator is likely to be seen as less biased and more objective.

Most advertisers use one-sided messages. They are concerned about the negative effects of acknowledging a weakness in their brand or don't want to say anything positive about their competitors. There are exceptions, however. Sometimes advertisers compare brands on several attributes and do not show their product as being the best on every one.

@ **EXHIBIT 7–15**

A refutational appeal is used to counter claims that rice cakes are bland and boring

Refutation

In a special type of two-sided message known as a **refutational appeal**, the communicator presents both sides of an issue and then refutes the opposing viewpoint. Since refutational appeals tend to "inoculate" the target audience against a competitor's counterclaims, they are more effective than one-sided messages in making consumers resistant to an opposing message.[35]

Refutational messages may be useful when marketers wish to build attitudes that resist change and must defend against attacks or criticism of their products. In Exhibit 7–15, Quaker Oats refutes arguments that rice cakes taste bland. Market leaders, who are often the target of comparative messages, may find it advantageous to acknowledge competitors' claims and then refute them to help build resistant attitudes and customer loyalty.

Verbal versus nonverbal messages

Thus far our discussion has focused on the information, or verbal, portion of the message. However, the nonverbal, visual elements of an ad are also very important. Many ads provide minimal amounts of information and rely on visual elements to communicate. Pictures are commonly used in advertising to convey information or reinforce copy or message claims.

Both the verbal and visual portions of an ad influence the way the advertising message is processed.[36] Consumers may develop images or impressions based on the visual elements such as an illustration in an ad or the scenes in a television commercial. In some cases, the visual portion of an ad may reduce its persuasiveness, since the processing stimulated by the picture may be less controlled and consequently less favorable than that stimulated by words.[37]

◉ **EXHIBIT 7–16**

Visual images are often designed to support verbal
appeals

**THIS IS HOW BIG OTHER SKI AREAS WILL
FEEL AFTER YOU SKI MAMMOTH.**

We have no apologies for the fact that our 11,053 foot peak with 3,100 foot vertical will take
your breath away. Nor are we at all concerned that you'll find our 150 trails, 30 lifts and 3,500
skiable acres almost too much variety to withstand. We don't even feel guilty about the notion that our
24-page Travel Planner will have you overly euphoric with anticipation (Get it by calling 1-800-832-7320).
Our only regret is that after you've skied Mammoth, it'll spoil your memories of having skied anywhere else.
Don't worry, we think you'll get over it. **MAMMOTH** No other mountain lives up to its name.

Mammoth recycles aluminum and glass. Please join us in preserving our environment for future generations.

Pictures affect the way consumers process accompanying copy. A recent study showed
that when verbal information was low in imagery value, the use of pictures providing
examples increased both immediate and delayed recall of product attributes.[38] However,
when the verbal information was already high in imagery value, the addition of pictures
did not increase recall. Advertisers often design ads where the visual image supports the
verbal appeal to create a compelling impression in the consumer's mind. Notice how the
ad for Mammoth Mountain ski resort uses visual elements to support the claims made
in the copy regarding the size of Mammoth versus other ski areas (Exhibit 7–16).

Message Appeals

One of the advertiser's most important creative strategy decisions involves the choice of
an appropriate appeal. Some ads are designed to appeal to the rational, logical aspect of
the consumer's decision-making process; others appeal to feelings in an attempt to evoke
some emotional reaction. Many believe that effective advertising combines the practical
reasons for purchasing a product with emotional values. In this section we will examine
several common types of message appeals, including comparative advertising, fear, and
humor.

Comparative advertising

Comparative advertising refers to the practice of either directly or indirectly naming
competitors in an ad and comparing one or more specific attributes.[39] This form of advertising became popular after the Federal Trade Commission (FTC) began advocating its
use in 1972. The FTC reasoned that direct comparison of brands would provide better
product information, giving consumers a more rational basis for making purchase decisions. Television networks cooperated with the FTC by lifting their ban on comparative
ads, and the result was a flurry of comparative commercials.

@ **EXHIBIT 7-17**

California Slim uses a comparative message to position itself against Ultra Slim-Fast

EXHIBIT 7-17

California Slim uses a comparative message to position itself against Ultra Slim-Fast

Initially, the novelty of comparative ads resulted in greater attention. But since they have become so common, their attention-getting value has probably declined. Some studies show that recall is higher for comparative than noncomparative messages, but comparative ads are generally not more effective for other response variables, such as brand attitudes or purchase intentions.[40] Advertisers must also consider how comparative messages affect credibility. Users of the brand being attacked in a comparative message may be particularly skeptical about the advertiser's claims.

Comparative advertising may be particularly useful for new brands, since it allows a new market entrant to position itself directly against the more established brands and to promote its distinctive advantages. Direct comparisons can help position a new brand in the evoked, or choice, set of brands the customer may be considering. In the comparative ad shown in Exhibit 7–17, California Slim compares its brand to Ultra Slim-Fast, the leading brand in the meal replacement drink market.

Comparative advertising is often used for brands with a small market share. They compare themselves to an established market leader in hopes of creating an association and tapping into the leader's market. Market leaders, on the other hand, often hesitate to use comparison ads, as most believe they have little to gain by featuring competitors' products in their ads. There are exceptions, of course; Coca-Cola resorted to comparative advertising in response to challenges made by Pepsi that were reducing Coke's market share.

Fear appeals

Fear is an emotional response to a threat that expresses, or at least implies, some sort of danger. Ads sometimes use **fear appeals** to evoke this emotional response and arouse individuals to take steps to remove the threat. Some, like the antidrug ads used by the Partnership for a Drug-Free America, stress physical danger that can occur if behaviors are not altered (Exhibit 7–18). Others—like those for deodorant, mouthwash, or dandruff shampoos—threaten disapproval or social rejection.

EXHIBIT 7-18

Fear appeals are used to show the dangers of using drugs

SFX: (MUSIC TO "HAPPY BIRTHDAY TO YOU" BEGINS A HAUNTING LYRIC)
SFX: ("HOW OLD ARE YOU NOW? DA-DE-DA-DA-DA-DA...")
(VO) If you don't tell your children about the danger of drugs.

(VO) You may find a problem staring you right in the face.
(VO) A problem that won't go away.
(VO) Or even worse, one that does.
SUPER: Partnership for a Drug-Free America.

How fear operates

Before deciding to use a fear appeal–based message strategy, the advertiser should consider how fear operates, what level to use, and how different target audiences may respond. One theory suggests that the relationship between the level of fear in a message and acceptance or persuasion is *curvilinear*, as shown in Exhibit 7–19.[41] This means that message acceptance increases as the amount of fear used rises. This increase in message acceptance does not continue, however. Beyond a certain point, acceptance decreases as the level of fear rises.

This relationship between fear and persuasion can be explained by the fact that fear appeals have both facilitating and inhibiting effects.[42] A low level of fear can have *facilitating effects*; it attracts attention and interest in the message and may motivate the receiver to act to resolve a threat. Thus, increasing the level of fear in a message from low to moderate can result in increased persuasion. High levels of fear, however, can produce *inhibiting effects*; the receiver may emotionally block the message by tuning it out, perceiving it selectively, or denying its arguments outright. Exhibit 7–19 illustrates how these two countereffects operate to produce the curvilinear relationship between fear and persuasion.

Recently an alternative approach to the curvilinear explanation of fear has been offered—the *protection motivation model*.[43] According to this theory, four cognitive appraisal processes mediate the individual's response to the threat: appraising 1) the information available regarding the severity of the perceived threat, 2) the perceived probability the threat will occur, 3) the perceived ability of a coping behavior to remove the threat, and 4) the individual's perceived ability to carry out the coping behavior. This model suggests that both the cognitive appraisal of the information in a fear appeal

@ **EXHIBIT 7–19**

Relationship between fear
levels and message accep-
tance

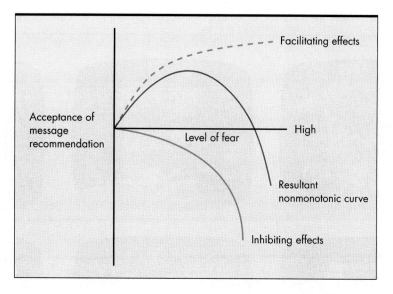

message and the emotional response mediate persuasion. An audience is more likely
to continue processing threat-related information, which increases the likelihood that
a coping behavior will occur.

The protection motivation model suggests that ads using fear appeals should give a
target audience information about the severity of the threat, the probability of its occur-
rence, the effectiveness of a coping response, and the ease with which the response can
be implemented.[44] For example, ads for American Express travelers' checks show how
easily a vacation can be ruined if you lose all your cash. Then they reduce the anxiety by
offering a solution to the problem—using the company's travelers' checks and getting
an immediate refund if they are lost or stolen.

It is also important to consider how the target audience may respond to fear appeals.
Fear appeals are more effective when the message recipient is self-confident and prefers
to cope with dangers rather than avoid them.[45] They are also more effective among
nonusers of a product than among users. Thus, a fear appeal may be more useful in
keeping nonsmokers from starting than persuading smokers to stop.

Humor appeals

Humorous ads are often the best known and best remembered of all advertising messages. The humorous commercials for Miller Lite beer featuring ex-athletes and other
celebrities were the basis of one of the most effective, longest-running ad campaigns
ever developed (Exhibit 7–20). Many other advertisers, among them Federal Express
and Little Caesar's pizza, have also used humor appeals effectively.

Advertisers use humor for many reasons. Humorous messages attract and hold consumers' attention. They enhance effectiveness by putting consumers in a positive mood,
increasing their liking of the ad itself and their feeling toward the product or service. And
humor can act as a distraction, reducing the likelihood that the receiver will counterargue
against the message.[46]

Critics argue that funny ads draw people to the humorous situation but distract them
from the brand and its attributes. Also, effective humor can be difficult to produce and
some attempts are too subtle for mass audiences. And, as discussed in IMC Perspective
7–2 on page 207, there is concern that humorous ads may wear out faster than serious
appeals.

Clearly, there are valid reasons both for and against the use of humor in advertising.
Not every product or service lends itself to a humorous approach. An interesting study
surveyed the research and creative directors of the top 150 advertising agencies.[47] They

EXHIBIT 7–20 Miller Lite used humorous ads in a campaign that lasted over 20 years

BOOG: For years now we've been kidding Jim here about his eyesight.
The fact is that Jim has the eyes of an eagle.
JIM: Thanks, Boog.
BOOG: Why, he was one of the first guys to spot Lite Beer from Miller.

He saw right away that Lite tastes great . . . and is less filling.
JIM: Sure, all you have to do is read the label.
JIM: It says Lite has 1/3 less calories than their regular beer.
BOOG: I think you want this, Jim.

JIM: As I was saying, it's as plain as the nose on your face.
ANNCR: (VO) Lite Beer from Miller. Everything you always wanted in a beer. And less.
BOOG: I don't believe this!

were asked questions regarding which communications objectives are facilitated through the use of humor and the appropriate situational use of humor in terms of media, product, and audience factors. The general conclusions of this study are shown in Exhibit 7–21.

CHANNEL FACTORS

The final controllable variable of the communications process is the channel, or medium, used to deliver the message to the target audience. While a variety of methods are available to transmit marketing communications, as noted in Chapter 6 they can be classified into two broad categories, personal and nonpersonal media.

Personal versus Nonpersonal Channels

There are a number of basic differences between personal and nonpersonal communications channels. Information received from personal influence channels is generally more persuasive than information received via the mass media. Reasons for the differences are summarized in the following comparison of advertising versus personal selling:

> From the standpoint of persuasion, a sales message is far more flexible, personal, and powerful than an advertisement. An advertisement is normally prepared by persons having minimal personal contact with customers. The message is designed to appeal to a large number of persons. By contrast, the message in a good sales presentation is not determined in advance. The salesman has a tremendous store of knowledge about his product or service and selects appropriate items as the interview progresses. Thus, the salesman can adapt this to the thinking and needs of the customer or prospect at the time of the sales call. Furthermore, as objections arise and

IMC Perspective 7-2
Do Humorous Ads Wear Out Too Fast?

An issue of much concern to advertisers is the problem of commercial wearout, or the tendency of a message to lose its effectiveness when it is seen repeatedly. Wearout may occur for several reasons. One is inattention; consumers may no longer attend to an ad after several exposures, so the message loses its effectiveness. Another reason is that consumers may become annoyed at seeing an ad many times.

While wearout is a problem for any type of commercial, some advertising experts argue that humorous ads wear out much sooner than other formats because once the viewer gets the joke, the ad becomes boring. However, advocates of humor argue that ads filled with yuks are effective longer because consumers can tolerate a well-executed humorous commercial again and again.

So who is right? Well, a study conducted by Research Systems Corp. concludes that neither view is correct. Humorous ads wear out at the same rate as other types of ads, whether the commercials include comparative messages, celebrity spokespeople, or other approaches. According to the study, the average ad's effectiveness wears out within eight weeks.

Not everyone agrees with this study. Another research firm, Video Storyboard Tests, Inc., claims that humorous ads lose their effectiveness faster than other ads. Notes the company's president, "The first time the ad is funny, the second time the ad is acceptable, and the third time it is a bore."

While individual humorous ads may get old fast, advertisers often get around this problem by using humorous campaigns consisting of many different commercials. For example, the Little Caesar's pizza chain has run more than 35 humorous ads in the past five years. Federal Express, Energizer batteries, and Miller Lite beer have also made effective use of humor by constantly developing new commercials and working them into the ad rotation.

Some individual humorous commercials seem to have been immune to wearout. "Where's the beef?" which was used heavily by Wendy's in the mid-1980s, is a classic example of how to use humor to sell a product and not get in the way of the message.

One media consultant argues that it's quite simple to determine if a humorous spot or campaign is wearing out. "If the viewers laugh with you, you can be in it for the long haul. It's when they laugh at you that you're in trouble."

Sources: Kevin Goldman, "Ever Hear the One about the Funny Ad?" *The Wall Street Journal*, Nov. 2, 1993, p. B11; George E. Belch and Michael A. Belch, "An Investigation of the Effects of Repetition on Cognitive and Affective Reactions to Humorous and Serious Television Commercials," in *Advances in Consumer Research*, Volume 11, Association for Consumer Research, 1984, pp. 4–10.

are voiced by the buyer, the salesman can treat the objections in an appropriate manner. This is not possible in advertising.[48]

Effects of Alternative Mass Media

The various mass media that advertisers use to transmit their messages differ in many ways, including the number and type of people they reach, costs, information processing requirements, and qualitative factors. The mass media's costs and how efficiently they expose a target audience to a communication will be evaluated in the media chapters. However, we should recognize differences in how information is processed and how communications are influenced by context or environment.

@ EXHIBIT 7-21

Summary of top advertising agency research and creative directors' opinions regarding use of humor

Humor does aid awareness and attention, which are the objectives best achieved by its use.
Humor may harm recall and comprehension in general.
  Humor may aid name and simple copy registration.
  Humor may harm complex copy registration.
  Humor may aid retention.
Persuasion in general is not aided by humor.
  Humor may aid persuasion to switch brands.
  Humor creates a positive mood that enhances persuasion.
Source credibility is not aided by humor.
Humor is generally not very effective in bringing about action/sales.
Creatives are more positive on the use of humor to fulfill all the above objectives than the research director.
Radio and TV are the best media in which to use humor, whereas direct mail and newspaper are least suited
Consumer nondurables and business services are best suited to humor, whereas corporate advertising and industrial products are least suited.
Humor should be related to the product.
Humor should not be used with sensitive goods or services.
Audiences that are younger, better educated, upscale, male, and professional are best suited to humor; older, less educated, and downscale groups are least suited to humor appeals.

@ **EXHIBIT 7–22**

Travel & Leisure magazine creates an excellent reception environment for travel-related ads

Differences in information processing

There are basic differences in the manner and rate at which information from various forms of media is transmitted and can be processed. Information from ads in print media, such as newspapers, magazines, or direct mail, is *self-paced*; readers process the ad at their own rate and can study it as long as they desire. In contrast, information from the broadcast media of radio and television is *externally paced*; the transmission rate is controlled by the medium.

The difference in the processing rate for print and broadcast media has some obvious implications for advertisers. Self-paced print media make it easier for the message recipient to process a long, complex message. Advertisers often use print ads when they want to present a detailed message with a lot of information. Broadcast media are more effective for transmitting shorter messages or, in the case of TV, presenting pictorial information along with a verbal message.

While there are limits to the length and complexity of broadcast messages, advertisers can deal with this problem. One strategy is to use a radio or television ad to get consumers' attention and direct them to specific print media for a more detailed message. For example, home builders use radio ads to draw attention to new developments and direct listeners to the real estate section of the newspaper for more details. Some advertisers develop a broadcast and print version of the same message. The copy portion of the message is similar in both media, but the print ad can be processed at a rate comfortable to the receiver.

Effects of Context and Environment

Interpretation of an advertising message can be influenced by the context or environment in which the ad appears. Communication theorist Marshall McLuhan's thesis, "The medium is the message," implies that the medium communicates an image that is independent of any message it contains.[49] A **qualitative media effect** is the influence the medium has on a message. The image of the media vehicle can affect reactions to the message. For example, an ad for a high-quality men's clothing line might have more of an impact in a fashion magazine like *GQ* than in *Sports Afield*. Airlines, destination resorts, and travel-related services advertise in publications such as *Travel & Leisure* partly because the articles, pictures, and other ads help to excite readers about travel (Exhibit 7–22).

Media environments can also be created by the nature of the program in which a commercial appears. One study found that consumers reacted more positively to commercials seen during a happy TV program than a sad one.[50] Advertisers pay premium dollars to advertise on popular programs that create positive moods, like the Olympic Games and Christmas specials. Conversely, advertisers tend to avoid programs that create a negative mood among viewers or may be detrimental to the company or its products. Many companies won't advertise on programs with excessive violence or sexual content. As a corporate policy, Coca-Cola never advertises on TV news programs because it thinks bad news is inconsistent with Coke's image as an upbeat, fun product.

Clutter

Another aspect of the media environment is the problem of **clutter**, which refers to all the nonprogram material that appears in the broadcast environment—commercials, promotional messages for shows, public service announcements (PSAs), and the like. Clutter has become an increasing concern to advertisers since there are so many messages competing for the consumer's attention. This annoys consumers and makes it difficult for ads to communicate effectively.[51] The problem has become compounded in television advertising by increases in nonprogram time and the trend toward shorter commercials. While the 30-second commercial replaced 60-second spots as the industry standard in the 1970s, many advertisers are now using 15-second spots.

The advertising industry continues to express concern over the highly cluttered commercial viewing environment. An industry-sponsored study found that the amount of clutter had increased as much as 14 percent over the past 10 years and averaged around 11 minutes per prime time hour on the major networks.[52] The problem is even greater during popular shows, to which the networks add more commercials because they can charge more. And, of course, advertisers and their agencies perpetuate the problem by pressuring the networks to squeeze their ads into top-rated shows with the largest audiences.

Advertisers and agencies want the networks to commit to a minimum amount of program time and then manage the nonprogram portion however they see fit. If the networks want to add more commercials, it would come out of their promos, PSAs, or program credit time. The problem is not likely to go away, however, and advertisers will continue to search for ways to break through the clutter such as using humor, celebrity spokespersons, or novel, creative approaches.

◉ SUMMARY

This chapter focused on the controllable variables that are part of the communications process, including source, message, and channel factors. Decisions regarding each of these variables should consider the impact on the various steps of the response hierarchy the message receiver passes through. The persuasion matrix helps assess the effect of controllable communication decisions on the response process.

Selection of the appropriate source or communicator to deliver a message is an important aspect of communication strategy. Three important attributes are source credibility, attractiveness, and power. Marketers use source characteristics to enhance message effectiveness by hiring communicators who are experts in a particular area and/or have a trustworthy image. The use of celebrities to deliver advertising messages has become very popular; advertisers hope they will catch the receivers' attention and influence their attitudes or behavior through an identification process. The chapter discusses the meaning a celebrity brings to the endorsement process and the importance of matching the image of the celebrity with that of the company or brand.

The design of the advertising message is a critical part of the communications process. There are various options regarding message structure, including order of presentation of message arguments, conclusion drawing, message sidedness, refutation, and verbal versus nonverbal traits. The advantages and disadvantages of different message appeal strategies were considered, including comparative messages and emotional appeals such as fear and humor.

Finally, the channel or medium used to deliver the message was considered. Differences in personal and nonpersonal channels of communication were discussed. Alternative mass media can have an effect on the communications process as a result of information processing and qualitative factors. The context in which an ad appears and the reception environment are important factors to consider in the selection of mass media. Clutter has become a serious problem for advertisers, particularly on TV, where commercials have become shorter and more numerous.

◎ *KEY TERMS*

persuasion matrix, p. 186

source, p. 188

credibility, p. 189

internalization, p. 189

sleeper effect, p. 191

attractiveness, p. 191

identification, p. 192

source power, p. 197

compliance, p. 197

primacy effect, p. 199

recency effect, p. 199

one-sided message, p. 200

two-sided message, p. 200

refutational appeal, p. 201

comparative advertising, p. 202

fear appeals, p. 203

qualitative media effect, p. 208

clutter, p. 209

◎ *DISCUSSION QUESTIONS*

1. Choose a current print ad or television commercial and use the persuasion matrix to analyze how it might influence consumers' response process.

2. What are the differences between the source credibility components of expertise and trustworthiness? Provide an example of an ad or other form of marketing communication that uses these source characteristics.

3. Most marketers choose message sources with high credibility. Discuss some reasons why it may be unnecessary or even detrimental to use a source who is high in credibility.

4. Discuss the ethics of celebrities endorsing products in foreign countries but not in the United States to protect their image. Do you think celebrities hurt their reputations by doing endorsements? Why or why not?

5. Choose three celebrities currently being used as advertising spokespeople and analyze their endorsements, using the meaning transfer model presented in Exhibit 7–11.

6. Discuss the pros and cons of using celebrities as advertising spokespeople. Provide examples of two celebrities you believe are very appropriate (or inappropriate) for the brands they are endorsing and explain why.

7. Discuss the pros and cons of using a two- versus one-sided advertising message. Why do marketers rarely use two-sided advertising messages?

8. Evaluate the argument that humorous messages may wear out faster than other types of advertising appeals. Do you agree or disagree with this position?

9. Assume that you have been asked to consult for a government agency that wants to use a fear appeal message to encourage college students not to drink and drive. Explain how fear appeals might affect persuasion and what factors should be taken into consideration in developing the ads.

10. What is meant by a qualitative media effect? Choose several media and analyze their qualitative factors.

Chapter **8**

Determining Advertising and Promotional Objectives

Chapter Objectives

- To analyze the importance and value of setting specific objectives for advertising and promotion.

- To examine the role objectives play in the IMC planning process and the relationship of promotional objectives to marketing objectives.

- To consider the differences between sales and communications objectives and issues regarding the use of each.

- To examine the value and limitations of the DAGMAR approach to setting advertising objectives.

- To examine some problems marketers encounter in setting objectives for their IMC programs.

Reengineering Compaq

Companies often find that in order to survive and prosper they must change their entire marketing strategy. In recent years, few companies have been as successful at this as Compaq Computer. A few years ago Compaq seemed to be coming apart at the seams. After a decade of explosive growth, it posted its first quarterly loss in October 1991 and had to lay off 1,700 employees. For years Compaq had competed by offering highly engineered products for which customers would willingly pay a premium price. But now Compaq, like IBM, was facing increased competition from fast-growing upstarts such as Dell Computer, AST Research, Zeos, and Gateway, who were flooding the market with low-priced machines.

To deal with the changing market, Compaq made sweeping changes in its marketing strategy. Compaq's new strategy involves transforming itself from a supplier of PCs to corporations to a manufacturer of machines for every market, from pocket communicators to home computers, at a very competitive price. Compaq's new CEO, Eckhard Pfeiffer, planted the idea of engineering to cost, rather than engineering at any cost, throughout the company.

Compaq has stung the competition by rushing dozens of new products to market and cutting prices as much as a third. The new products include the Presario (a line of home computers that is Compaq's most successful new PC ever) and the Contura Aero subnotebook (a line of highly portable PCs that weigh less than four pounds and cost $500 less than their IBM counterpart, the popular Thinkpad 500). Marketing surveys revealed that consumers had trouble finding Compaq products, so the company abandoned its dealers-only distribution strategy and quintupled the number of retailers from 2,000 to more than 10,000 in just two years.

The new strategy is also resulting in changes on the marketing communications front. Compaq hired a new ad agency, Ammirati & Puris/New York, and began spending heavily to deliver the key brand messages to support the change in strategy. An agency executive described the advertising challenge as follows: "We had to clearly communicate that Compaq had changed, but in introducing lower-priced products also communicate that we were not compromising on the things that made a Compaq a Compaq." The new advertising thrust began with a 12-page insert in major news and business publications that asked readers, "People in the computer business have been trying to improve on Compaq for years. Guess who finally did it?" After three years of no TV advertising, Compaq launched a $12 million campaign that included a Presario ad in which a training class was forced to parrot computer terms like gigabyte and WYSIWYG. The closing line was, "Instead of sounding smart about computers, you can be smart about computers."

Compaq also found other ways to reach consumers. For example, it spent $240,000 to put eye-catching cardboard strips around Compaq's monitors at store displays. The glossy, multicolored monitor hood, which is printed with information about the computer's features, helped increase sales of those models by 11 percent. The company also launched DirectPlus, a catalog operation, to compete in the lucrative direct mail market and help Compaq penetrate the small office/home office market segment. To signal its new vitality, Compaq developed a cleaner, bright-red corporate logo and began working with Interbrand Corp. to devise more meaningful names for future products.

Since changing its strategy, Compaq has increased its share of the $35 billion-a-year PC and workstation market from 3.8 percent to 10 percent. The company appears to be well on its way to achieving its goal of becoming the number one computer maker by 1996.

Sources: Stephanie Losee, "How Compaq Keeps the Magic Going," Fortune, Feb. 21, 1994, pp. 90–92; Gerry Khermooch, "A Role Model for Big Blue," BrandWeek, April 5, 1993, pp. 16–18.

T he saga of Compaq Computer illustrates how goals and objectives for integrated marketing communications follow from a company's overall marketing strategy. Although Compaq was making sweeping changes in the way it operated, the new ad agency felt that it was important to preserve the brand equity built up during the company's highly successful first decade. And with its products rolling through an unprecedented array of marketing channels, almost like a packaged good, maintaining a strong identity became more critical than ever.

For years Compaq's advertising was driven by its engineering-oriented heritage. The product was hero and the company allowed itself to be positioned by the sum of all of its product messages. The new strategy places the highest priority on the Compaq brand rather than product features and attributes. Compaq's director of marketing communications has noted that rather than starting the advertising planning process with a briefing on the product, marketing and agency personnel ask, "What message do we want to get across? What technology will be forthcoming over the next year or two, and how do we translate that into marketing messages that will position the company?"[1]

Unfortunately, many companies have difficulty with the most critical step in the promotional planning process—setting realistic objectives that will guide the development of the integrated marketing communications program. Complex marketing situations, conflicting perspectives regarding what advertising and other promotional mix elements are expected to accomplish, and uncertainty over resources make the setting of marketing communication objectives "a job of creating order out of chaos."[2] While the task of setting objectives can be complex and difficult, it must be done properly, because specific goals and objectives are the foundation on which all other promotional decisions are made. Budgeting for advertising and other promotional areas, as well as creative and media strategies and tactics, evolve from these objectives. They also provide a standard against which performance can be measured.

Setting specific objectives should be an integral part of the planning process. However, many companies either fail to use specific marketing communication objectives or set ones that are inadequate for guiding the development of the promotional plan or measuring its effectiveness. Many marketers are uncertain as to what integrated marketing communications should be expected to contribute to the marketing program. The goal of their company's advertising and promotional program is simple: to generate sales. They fail to recognize the specific tasks that advertising and other promotional mix variables must perform in preparing customers to buy a particular product or service.

@ **EXHIBIT   8–1**

The objective of this ad is to promote Dow's concern for the environment

As we know, advertising and promotion are not the only marketing activities involved in generating sales. Moreover, it is not always possible to measure the effects of advertising in terms of sales. For example, the Dow Chemical ad in Exhibit 8–1 is designed to promote the company's concern for the environment. Consider the Toyota ad shown in Exhibit 8–2. What objectives (other than generating sales) might the company have for this ad? How might its effectiveness be measured?

This chapter examines the nature and purpose of objectives and the role they play in guiding the development, implementation, and evaluation of an integrated marketing communications program. Attention is given to the various types of objectives appropriate for different situations. We also examine a model that has been used effectively for many years to set advertising objectives.

THE VALUE OF OBJECTIVES

Perhaps one reason many companies fail to set specific objectives for their integrated marketing communications programs is that they don't recognize the value of doing so. Advertising and promotional objectives are needed for several reasons, including the functions they serve in communication, planning and decision making, and measurement and evaluation.

Communications

Specific objectives for the promotional program facilitate coordination of the various groups working on the campaign. Many people are involved in the planning and development of an integrated marketing communications program on the client side as well as in the various promotional agencies. The advertising and promotional program must be coordinated within both the company and the advertising agency, as well as between the two. Any other parties involved in the promotional campaign, such as public relations and/or sales promotion firms, research specialists, or media buying services, must also

EXHIBIT 8-2

What might the objectives of this Toyota ad be?

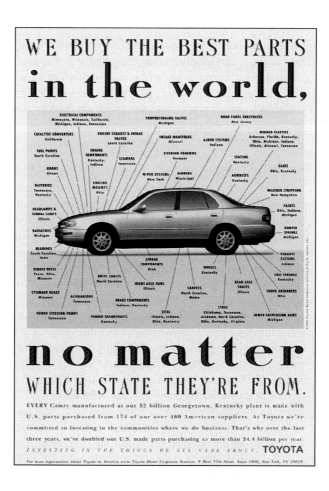

know what the company hopes to accomplish through its marketing communications program. Many problems can be avoided if all parties have written, approved objectives to guide their actions and serve as a common base for discussing issues related to the promotional program.

Planning and Decision Making

Specific promotional objectives also guide development of the integrated marketing communications plan. All phases of a firm's promotional strategy should be based on the established objectives, including budgeting, creative, and media decisions as well as supportive programs such as direct marketing, public relations/publicity, sales promotion, and/or reseller support.

Specific, meaningful objectives can also be useful as a guide for decision making. Promotional planners are often faced with a number of strategic and tactical options in terms of choosing creative options, selecting media, and allocating the budget among various elements of the promotional mix. Choices should be made based on how well a particular strategy matches the firm's promotional objectives.

Measurement and Evaluation of Results

An important reason for setting specific objectives is that they provide a benchmark against which the success or failure of the promotional campaign can be measured. Without specific objectives, it is extremely difficult to determine what the firm's advertising and promotion efforts accomplished. As we will see later in this chapter, one characteristic of good objectives is that they are *measurable;* they specify a method and criteria for determining how well the promotional program is working. By setting specific and meaningful objectives, the promotional planner provides a measure(s) that can be used to evaluate the effectiveness of the marketing communications program. Most organizations are concerned about the return on their promotional investment, and comparing actual performance against measurable objectives is the best way to determine if the return justifies the expense.

DETERMINING PROMOTIONAL OBJECTIVES

Integrated marketing communication objectives should be based on a thorough situation analysis that identifies the marketing and promotional issues facing the company or a brand. The situation analysis is the foundation on which marketing objectives are determined and the marketing plan is developed. Promotional objectives evolve from the company's overall marketing plan and are rooted in its marketing objectives. Advertising and promotion objectives are not the same as marketing objectives (although many firms tend to treat them as synonymous).

Marketing versus Communications Objectives

Marketing objectives are generally stated in the firm's marketing plan and are statements of what is to be accomplished by the overall marketing program within a given time period. Marketing objectives are usually defined in terms of specific, measurable outcomes such as sales volume, market share, profits, or return on investment. Good marketing objectives are quantified and include a delineation of the target market, and note the time frame for accomplishing the goal (often one year). For example, a personal computer company may have as its marketing objective "to increase sales by 10 percent in the small business segment of the market during the next 12 months."

A company with a very high market share may seek to increase its sales volume by stimulating growth in the product category. It might accomplish this by increasing consumption by current users or encouraging nonusers to use the product. Some firms have as their marketing objectives expanding distribution and sales of their product in certain market areas. Companies often have secondary marketing objectives that are related to actions they must take to solve specific problems and thus achieve their primary objectives. For example, 10 years ago San Antonio–based Pace Foods, Inc., began a promotional campaign to expand its business beyond its traditional Texas base. To achieve this objective its agency set out to establish a position of authenticity and make Mexican food seem fun. An advertising campaign for Pace picante sauce pokes fun of the New York City origins of a fictitious rival brand. Pace's vice president of sales and marketing says the idea behind the campaign was that Pace's sauce is created by people who live "where

@ **EXHIBIT 8-3**

Pace Foods' New York
City campaign has helped
expand sales beyond the
Texas market

folks know what salsa should be." Pace also uses various sales promotion tools such as
coupons, promotional tie-ins, and point-of-purchase displays to generate sales (Exhibit
8–3). In the past five years, sales of Pace picante sauce have tripled and its 28 percent
brand share makes it the market leader in a category that has surpassed ketchup.[3]

Once the marketing communications manager has reviewed the marketing plan, he
or she should understand where the company hopes to go with its marketing program,
how it intends to get there, and the role advertising and promotion will play. Marketing
goals defined in terms of sales, profit, or market share increases are usually not appropriate as promotional objectives. They are objectives for the entire marketing program,
and achieving them depends on the proper coordination and execution of all the marketing mix elements, including not just promotion but product planning and production,
pricing, and distribution.

Integrated marketing communications objectives are statements of what various aspects of the IMC program will accomplish. They should be based on the particular
communications tasks required to deliver the appropriate messages to the target audience. Managers must be able to translate general marketing goals into communications
goals and specific promotional objectives. Some guidance in doing this may be available
from the marketing plan, as the situation analysis should provide important information on

- The market segments the firm wants to target and the target audience (demographics, psychographics, and purchase motives).
- The product and its main features, advantages, benefits, uses, and applications.
- The company's and competitors' brands (sales and market share in various segments, positioning, competitive strategies, promotional expenditures, creative and
  media strategies, and tactics).
- Ideas on how the brand should be positioned and specific behavioral responses being sought (trial, repurchase, brand switching, and increased usage).

For example, the ads for Del Monte stewed tomatoes and Snack Cups in Exhibit
8–4 were part of the company's marketing strategy to increase sales and market share
for its various food products by targeting existing or lapsed users as well as new, younger
customers. The 12-month, $20 million advertising campaign used a series of four-color

◎ EXHIBIT 8–4

These ads for Del Monte food products were part of a marketing strategy designed to increase sales and market share

ads featuring new recipe ideas and serving suggestions. All of the ads used the same graphic format to help build the overall franchise for Del Monte brands while promoting individual products. The campaign resulted in increased market share for all four of the advertised categories.

Sometimes companies do not have a formal marketing plan, and the information needed may not be readily available. In this case, the promotional planner must attempt to gather as much information as possible about the product and its markets from sources both inside and outside the company.

After reviewing all the information, the promotional planner should see how integrated marketing communication fits into the marketing program and what the firm hopes to achieve through advertising and other promotional elements. The next step is to set objectives in terms of specific communications goals or tasks.

Many promotional planners approach promotion from a communications perspective and believe the objective of advertising and other promotional mix elements is usually to communicate information or a selling message about a product or service. Other managers argue that sales or some related measure, such as market share, is the only meaningful goal for advertising and promotion and should be the basis for setting objectives. These two perspectives have been the topic of considerable debate and are worth examining further.

◎ SALES VERSUS COMMUNICATIONS OBJECTIVES

Sales-Oriented Objectives

To many managers, the only meaningful objective for their promotional program is sales. They take the position that the basic reason a firm spends money on advertising and promotion is to sell its product or service. Promotional spending represents an investment of a firm's scarce resources that requires an economic justification. Rational managers generally compare investment options on a common financial basis, such as return on investment (ROI). As will be discussed in Chapter 9, determining the specific return on advertising and promotional dollars is often quite difficult. However, many managers believe that monies spent on advertising and other forms of promotion should produce measurable results, such as increasing sales volume by a certain percentage or dollar amount or increasing the brand's market share. They believe objectives (as well as the success or failure of the campaign) should be based on the achievement of sales results.

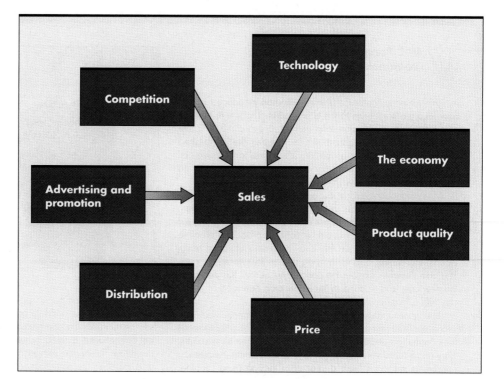

EXHIBIT 8–5

Factors influencing sales

Some managers prefer sales-oriented objectives to make the individuals involved in advertising and promotion think in terms of how the promotional program will influence sales. Or they may confuse marketing objectives with advertising and promotional objectives. For example, a firm's marketing goal may be to increase a brand's sales level to $200 million. This goal not only becomes the basis of the marketing plan but carries over as the primary objective of the promotional program. The success of the advertising and promotional campaign is judged only by attainment of this target.

Problems with sales objectives

If the company just described failed to achieve its target sales level of $200 million, does this mean the advertising and promotional program was ineffective? It might help to compare this situation to a football game and think of the role of advertising as a quarterback. The quarterback is one of the most important players on the team but can be effective only with support from the other players. If the team loses, is it fair to blame the loss entirely on the quarterback? Of course not. Just as the quarterback is but one of the players on the football team, promotion is but one element of the marketing program, and there are many other reasons why the targeted sales level was not reached. The quarterback can lead his team to victory only if the linemen block, the receivers catch the quarterback's passes, and the running backs help the offense establish a balanced attack of running and passing. The quarterback can play an outstanding game but the team can still lose if the defense gives up too many points.

In the business world, poor sales results could be due to any of the other marketing mix variables, including product design or quality, packaging, distribution, or pricing. Advertising can make consumers aware of and interested in the brand, but this does not mean they will buy it, particularly if it is not readily available or is priced higher than a competing brand. As shown in Exhibit 8–5, sales are a function of many factors, not just advertising and promotion. IMC Perspective 8–1 discusses Nissan Motor Co.'s search for an advertising campaign that will help increase sales of its Infiniti automobiles in the highly competitive luxury segment of the U.S. market.

IMC Perspective 8–1
Relaunching Infiniti

In 1989, Nissan Motor Co.'s Infiniti division introduced its two new luxury automobiles to the U.S. market. The Infiniti division was formed to manufacture and market cars to compete in the luxury sports sedan segment, which includes the established European imports such as BMW, Mercedes, and Volvo, as well as two Japanese luxury cars—Acura (a division of Honda Motors) and Lexus (a division of Toyota).

Many ad agencies introduce new automobiles by immediately focusing on the cars and saying great things about them. But Hill, Holliday, Connors, Cosmopulos, the original agency for Infiniti, decided to take an unconventional approach by creating commercials and print ads that showed scenes of rocks, trees, clouds, the ocean, and even flying geese—but never the cars. The ads aimed to explain the philosophy behind the design of the new cars and to position the Infiniti as a new kind of luxury car with a "Japanese sense of luxury."

The teaser campaign used to launch the Infiniti was very successful from several perspectives. The ads generated requests for information about the cars and visits to dealer showrooms. They also scored very high in surveys of advertising awareness; consumers still cited them a year after they stopped running. Yet initial sales of the Infiniti were well below forecast, so the company responded to dealer demands for more product-oriented advertising.

Ensuing campaigns focused on the cars and hammered home the performance theme, but by March of 1993 Infiniti had only a 3.9 percent share of the U.S. luxury market, compared with Lexus' 7.7 percent and Mercedes' 4.5 percent. The company aims to change this with its 1994 Q45, which has been redesigned to move Infiniti into the mainstream of the market, with more than 70 enhancements intended to push the traditional luxury car buyer's hot button. Infiniti has also embarked on a new advertising approach that represents a sharp change from earlier campaigns.

A new agency, Chiat/Day Advertising, Inc., has been hired, and the company is spending as much money on the new campaign as it did to launch the Infiniti. The new strategy involves presenting the car, and the company, in a series of individual ads that each highlight a single Infiniti feature. The

look of the campaign is sparse: a dramatically lit car on a sweeping expanse of white background. Chiat/Day wanted to use an actor in the commercials to explain the car's features, but did not want a celebrity who would steal the limelight. Most important, it needed someone who would sound sophisticated and intelligent yet could interject warmth and even a little humor into the ads. After more than a month of searching, the agency came up with actor Jonathan Pryce, who played the male lead in the musical *Miss Saigon* and leveraged buyout king Henry Kravis in the HBO movie *Barbarians at the Gate.*

Some critics say the original campaign and subsequent advertising for the Infiniti did not send the right message to the luxury car buyer. Others say Infiniti's problems have been due to a declining market for luxury cars and intense competition in this market segment. It will be interesting to see if the new advertising campaign can help increase sales. Infiniti's vice president and general manager says, "It's more than a launch of a new car. In a sense, because the Q is our flagship, it's the relaunch of Infiniti."

Sources: Bradley A. Stertz, "Nissan's Infiniti Gets Off to Slow Start," *The Wall Street Journal,* Jan. 8, 1990, p. B6; "Infiniti Ads Trigger Auto Debate," *Advertising Age,* Jan. 22, 1990, p. 49; and Larry Armstrong, "Infiniti: If at First You Don't Succeed . . . ," *Business Week,* May 3, 1993, pp. 126–27.

Another problem with sales objectives is that the effects of advertising often occur over an extended period. Many experts recognize that advertising has a lagged or **carryover effect;** monies spent on advertising do not necessarily have an immediate impact on sales.[4] Advertising may create awareness, interest, and/or favorable attitudes toward a brand, but these feelings will not result in an actual purchase until the consumer enters the market for the product, which may occur later. A review of econometric studies that examined the duration of cumulative advertising effects found that for mature, frequently purchased, low-priced products, advertising's effect on sales lasts up to nine months.[5] Models have been developed to account for the carryover effect of advertising and to help determine the long-term effect of advertising on sales.[6] The carryover effect adds to the difficulty of determining the precise relationship between advertising and sales.

Another problem with sales objectives is that they offer little guidance to those responsible for planning and developing the promotional program. The creative and media

@ **EXHIBIT   8–6**

The effectiveness of sales promotion programs is often measured in terms of sales

people working on the account need some direction as to the nature of the advertising message the company hopes to communicate, the intended audience, and the particular effect or response sought. As you will see later in this chapter, communications objectives are recommended because they provide operational guidelines for those involved in planning, developing, and executing the advertising and promotional program.

Where sales objectives are appropriate

While there can be many problems in attempting to use sales as objectives for a promotional campaign, there are situations where sales objectives are appropriate. Certain types of promotion efforts are direct action in nature; they attempt to induce an immediate behavioral response from the prospective customer. A major objective of most sales promotion programs is to generate short-term increases in sales. The Alka-Seltzer "Feel better fast fest" shown in Exhibit 8–6 was a six-week promotion that tied in with summer activities through local event sponsorships, a sweepstakes, couponing, and sampling to generate sales. While increasing brand awareness was an objective of the promotion, Miles Laboratories can evaluate its success by measuring the increase in Alka-Seltzer sales during the promotional period.

Direct-response advertising is one type of advertising that evaluates its effectiveness on the basis of sales. Merchandise is advertised in material mailed to customers, in newspapers and magazines, or on television. The consumer purchases the merchandise by mail or by calling a toll-free number. The direct-response advertiser generally sets objectives and measures success in terms of the sales response generated by the ad. For example, objectives for and the evaluation of a direct-response ad on TV are based on the number of orders received each time a station broadcasts the commercial. Because

◉ **EXHIBIT 8–7**

Sales results are an appropriate objective for direct response advertising

advertising is really the only form of communication and promotion used in this situation and response is generally immediate, setting objectives in terms of sales is appropriate. The ad for the Escort radar detector shown in Exhibit 8–7 is an example of a product sold through direct-response advertising.

Retail advertising, which accounts for a significant percentage of all advertising expenditures, is another area where the advertiser often seeks a direct response, particularly when sales or special events are being promoted. The ad for the Broadway two-day sale shown in Exhibit 8–8 is designed to attract consumers to stores during the sales

◉ **EXHIBIT 8–8**

Retail advertising often has an objective of generating immediate sales

period (and to generate sales volume). Broadway management can determine the effectiveness of its promotional effort by analyzing store traffic and sales volume during sale days and comparing them to figures for nonsale days. But retailers may also allocate advertising and promotional dollars to image-building campaigns designed to create and enhance favorable perceptions of their stores. In this case, sales-oriented objectives would not be appropriate because the effectiveness of the campaign would be based on its ability to create or change consumers' image of the store.

Sales-oriented objectives are also used when advertising plays a dominant role in a firm's marketing program and other factors are relatively stable. For example, many package-goods products compete in mature markets with established channels of distribution, stable competitive prices and promotional budgets, and products of similar quality. They view advertising and sales promotion as the key determinants of a brand's sales or market share, so it may be possible to isolate the effects of these promotional mix variables.[7] Many companies have accumulated enough market knowledge with their advertising, sales promotion, and direct marketing programs to have considerable insight into the sales levels that should result from their promotional efforts. Thus, they believe it is reasonable to set objectives and evaluate the success of their promotional efforts in terms of sales results. Established brands are often repositioned (as discussed in Chapter 5) with the goal of improving their sales or relative market share.

Advertising and promotional programs tend to be evaluated in terms of sales, particularly when expectations are not being met. Marketing and brand managers under pressure to show sales results often take a short-term perspective in evaluating advertising and sales promotion programs. They are often looking for a quick fix for declining sales or loss of market share. The pitfalls of making direct links between advertising and sales are ignored, and campaigns, as well as ad agencies, may be changed if sales expectations are not being met. As discussed in Chapter 3, many companies want their agencies to accept incentive-based compensation systems tied to sales performance. Thus, while sales may not be an appropriate objective in many advertising and promotional situations, managers are inclined to keep a close eye on sales and market share figures and make changes in the promotional program when these numbers become stagnant.

Communications Objectives

Many marketers do recognize the problems associated with sales-oriented objectives. They recognize that the primary role of promotional mix elements such as advertising is to communicate and that planning should be based on communications objectives. Advertising and other promotional efforts are designed to achieve such communications as brand knowledge and interest, favorable attitudes and image, and purchase intentions. Consumers are not expected to respond immediately; rather, advertisers realize they must provide relevant information and create favorable predispositions toward the brand before purchase behavior will occur.

For example, the ad for the new Panasonic SuperFlat System TV in Exhibit 8–9 is designed to inform consumers of the product's sophisticated features and technological superiority. While there is no call for immediate action, the ad creates favorable impressions about the product so that consumers will consider it when they enter the market for video equipment.

Advocates of communications-based objectives generally use some form of the hierarchical models discussed in Chapter 6 when setting advertising and promotion objectives. In all these models, consumers pass through three successive stages—cognitive, affective, and conative. As consumers proceed through the three stages, they move closer to making a purchase. Exhibit 8–10 shows the various steps in the Lavidge and Steiner hierarchy-of-effects model as the consumer moves from awareness to purchase, along with examples of types of advertising or promotion relevant to each step.

Communications effects pyramid

Advertising and promotion perform communications tasks as a pyramid is built, by first accomplishing lower-level objectives such as awareness and knowledge or comprehension.[8] Subsequent tasks involve moving consumers who are aware of or knowledge-

EXHIBIT 8-9

Some ads have an objective of creating favorable attitudes

able about the product or service to higher levels in the pyramid. The initial stages, at the base of the pyramid, are easier to accomplish than those toward the top, such as trial and repurchase or regular use. Thus, the percentage of prospective customers will decline as they move up the pyramid. We use the communications effects pyramid in Exhibit 8–11 on page 226 to show how a company introducing a new brand of shampoo targeted at 18- to 34-year-old females might set its advertising and promotion objectives.

The first task of the promotional program for a new product is to create a broad level of awareness among the target audience. This can be done through repetitive advertising in magazines, TV, and radio programs that reach 18- to 34-year-old females. The specific objective is

> To create a 90 percent awareness of Backstage shampoo among 18- to 34-year-old females during the first six weeks of the campaign.

The next step in the pyramid is to communicate information so a certain percentage of the target audience will not only be aware of the new product but also understand its features and benefits. Let us assume the new Backstage brand is being positioned as a milder shampoo that contains no soap and improves the texture and shine of hair. The specific objective for the second stage is

> To communicate the specific benefits of Backstage shampoo—that it contains no soap and improves the texture and shine of the hair—to 70 percent of the target audience to interest them in the brand.

At the next level, the promotional campaign is designed to create positive feelings toward Backstage. A certain percentage of the consumers who have been made aware of the new brand must be moved to the affective stages of liking and preference. The advertising must effectively communicate the benefits to create favorable attitudes toward the product. Only a certain percentage of the target audience will develop a liking for the brand, and even fewer will move to the preference block. The specific objective at this stage is

> To create positive feelings toward Backstage shampoo among 40 percent of the target audience and a preference for the brand among 25 percent.

Once these steps are accomplished, a certain percentage of the target audience will move to the action stage at the top of the pyramid. The promotional plan may be designed

EXHIBIT 8–10

Effect of advertising on
consumers: movement from
awareness to action

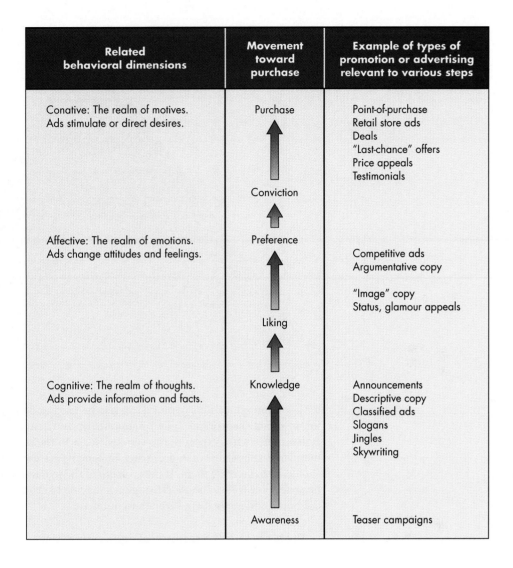

to create trial among consumers who will be influenced not only by advertising but also by sales promotion techniques such as couponing and sampling. The objective at this stage might be

> To use sampling and cents-off coupons, along with advertising, to elicit trial of Backstage shampoo among 20 percent of 18- to 34-year-old females during the first three months.

The ultimate goal of the promotional program is to make consumers loyal to the new brand so they will repurchase it. Repurchase and regular use of Backstage shampoo will depend on the consumers' evaluations after using it. The promotional program may call for continued advertising and periodic sales promotions not only to retain those consumers who have tried Backstage shampoo but also to take new consumers through the pyramid and get them to try the brand. The shampoo market is extremely competitive; only a few brands have more than a 10 percent market share. Thus, the ultimate goal may be to get a percentage of women who try the brand to become regular users and to continue to attract new customers. Keeping in mind the problems of using sales objectives for advertising and promotion, the final objective would be

> To develop and maintain regular use of Backstage shampoo among 5 percent of the 18- to 34-year-old females.

EXHIBIT 8–11

Communication effects pyramid

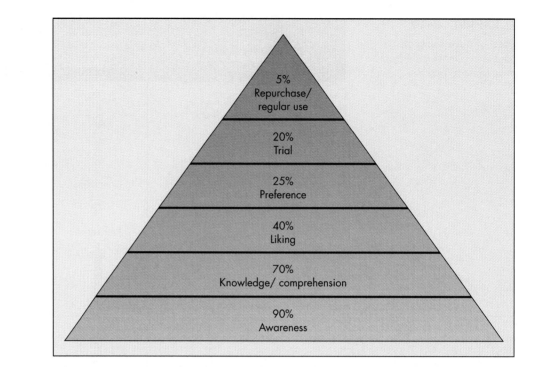

The communications pyramid can also be used to determine promotional objectives for an established brand. The promotional planner must determine where the target audience lies with respect to the various blocks in the pyramid. If awareness levels for a brand and knowledge of its features and benefits are low, the communications objective should be to increase them. If these blocks of the pyramid are already in place, but liking or preference is low, the advertising goal may be to change the target markets' image of the brand and move them through to purchase.

Problems with communications objectives

Not all marketing and advertising managers accept communications objectives because they say it is too difficult to translate a sales goal into a specific communications objective. But at some point a sales goal must be transformed into a communications objective. If the marketing plan for an established brand has as an objective increasing sales by 10 percent, the promotional planner will eventually have to think in terms of the message that will be communicated to the target audience to achieve this. Possible objectives include the following:

- Increasing the percentage of consumers in the target market who associate specific features, benefits, or advantages with our brand.
- Increasing the number of consumers in the target audience who prefer our product over the competition's.
- Encouraging current users of the product to use it more frequently or in more situations.
- Encouraging consumers who have never used our brand to try it.

In some situations, promotional planners may gain insight into communication objectives' relationship to sales from industry research. Evalucom, Inc., conducted a study of commercials for new products that were either successful or unsuccessful in stimulating anticipated levels of sales. Exhibit 8–12 shows four factors the study identified that affect whether a commercial for a new product is successful in generating sales.

In attempting to translate sales goals into specific communications objectives, promotional planners often are not sure what constitutes adequate levels of awareness, knowl-

@ **EXHIBIT 8-12**

Factors related to success of
advertising for new products

> • **Communicating that something is different about the product.** Successful
> introductory commercials communicated some point of difference for the new
> product.
> • **Positioning the brand difference in relation to the product category.**
> Successful commercials positioned their brand's difference within a specific product
> category. For example, a new breakfast product was positioned as the "crispiest
> cereal" or a new beverage as the "smoothest soft drink."
> • **Communicating that the product difference is beneficial to consumers.**
> Nearly all of the successful commercials linked a benefit directly to the new
> product's difference.
> • **Supporting the idea that something about the product is different
> and/or beneficial to consumers.** All the successful commercials communicated
> support for the product's difference claim or its relevance to consumers. Support
> took the form of demonstrations of performance, information supporting a uniqueness
> claim, endorsements, or testimonials.

Source: Kirby Andrews, "Communications Imperatives for New Products," *Journal of Advertising Research* 26, no. 5
(Oct.–Nov. 1986), pp. 29–32.

edge, liking, preference, or conviction. There are no formulas to provide this information. The promotional manager will have to use his or her personal experience and that of the brand or product managers, as well as the marketing history of this and similar brands. Average scores on various communications measures for this and similar products should be considered, along with the levels achieved by competitors' products. This information can be related to the amount of money and time spent building these levels as well as the resulting sales or market share figures.

At some point, sales-oriented objectives must be translated into what the company hopes to communicate and to whom they hope to communicate it. For example, Milwaukee-based Midwest Express Airlines recently found itself in a situation where business travelers, its primary market, assumed that the airline's high level of service meant premium prices. To combat this perception, the "Best care. Same fare" campaign was developed. In the commercials, a man claimed Midwest's fares were higher, only to be told flatly by a female colleague that he was wrong. The conversations occurred in humorous settings, such as one where a man scrambles up a down escalator to keep up with a woman (Exhibit 8–13). Midwest was able to communicate its competitive fares and achieve its sales objective. The number of people who thought Midwest cost more than competitors declined by 17 percent within six months, while the airline's market share grew from 19 percent to 25 percent.[9]

Many marketing and promotional managers recognize the value of setting specific communications objectives and their important role as operational guidelines to the planning, execution, and evaluation of the promotional program. Communications objectives are the criteria used in the DAGMAR approach to setting advertising goals and objectives, which has become one of the most influential approaches to the advertising planning process.

@ DAGMAR: AN APPROACH TO SETTING OBJECTIVES

In 1961, Russell Colley prepared a report for the Association of National Advertisers titled *Defining Advertising Goals for Measured Advertising Results* (DAGMAR).[10] In it, Colley developed a model for setting advertising objectives and measuring the results of an advertising campaign. The major thesis of the **DAGMAR** model is that communications effects are the logical basis for advertising goals and objectives against which success or failure should be measured. Colley's rationale for communications-based objectives was as follows:

> Advertising's job, purely and simply, is to communicate to a defined audience information and a frame of mind that stimulates action. Advertising succeeds or fails depending on how well it communicates the desired information and attitudes to the right people at the right time and at the right cost.[11]

@ **EXHIBIT 8-13**

Midwest Express increased its market share by advertising its competitive fares

Under the DAGMAR approach, an advertising goal involves a communications task that is specific and measurable. A **communications task**, as opposed to a marketing task, can be performed by, and attributed to, advertising rather than to a combination of several marketing factors. Colley proposed that the communications task be based on a hierarchical model of the communications process with four stages:

- *Awareness*—making the consumer aware of the existence of the brand or company.
- *Comprehension*—developing an understanding of what the product is and what it will do for the consumer.
- *Conviction*—developing a mental disposition in the consumer to buy the product.
- *Action*—getting the consumer to purchase the product.

As discussed earlier, other hierarchical models of advertising effects can be used as a basis for analyzing the communications response process. Some advertising theorists prefer the Lavidge and Steiner hierarchy-of-effects model, since it is more specific and provides a better way to establish and measure results.[12]

While the hierarchical model of advertising effects was the basic model of the communications response process used in DAGMAR, Colley also studied other specific tasks that advertising might be expected to perform in leading to the ultimate objective of a sale. He developed an advertising task checklist consisting of 52 tasks to characterize the contribution of advertising and use as a starting point for establishing objectives.

Characteristics of Objectives

A second major contribution of DAGMAR to the advertising planning process was its definition of what constitutes a good objective. Colley argued that advertising objectives should be stated in terms of concrete and measurable communications tasks, specify a

@ **EXHIBIT 8–14**

Sonance's target audience is
the upscale audio enthusiast
and design trendsetter

target audience, indicate a benchmark starting point and the degree of change sought, and specify a time period for accomplishing the objective(s).

Concrete, measurable tasks

The communications task specified in the objective should be a precise statement of what appeal or message the advertiser wants to communicate to the target audience. Advertisers generally use a copy platform to describe their basic message. The objective or copy platform statement should be specific and clear enough to guide the creative specialists who develop the advertising message. For example, in the Midwest Express example, the objective was to combat the perception that its fares were higher than competitors'.

According to DAGMAR, the objective must also be measurable. There must be a way to determine whether the intended message has been communicated properly. Midwest Express measured its communication objective by asking airline travelers whether they thought Midwest's air fares were higher than those of competing airlines.

Target audience

Another important characteristic of good objectives is a well-defined target audience. Generally, the primary target audience for a company's product or service is described in the situation analysis. It may be based on descriptive variables such as geography, demographics, and psychographics (on which advertising media selection decisions are based) as well as on behavioral variables such as usage rate or benefits sought. For example, Sonance, a company that makes architectural audio systems that include in-wall speakers and controls, defines its target audience as "affluent audio enthusiasts who are also design trendsetters." To reach this target market and communicate its message of "total audio ambiance," Sonance advertises in upscale, design-oriented magazines such as *Architectural Digest* (Exhibit 8–14).

Benchmark and degree of change sought

To set objectives, you must know the target audience's present status concerning response hierarchy variables such as awareness, knowledge, image, attitudes, and intentions, and then determine the degree to which consumers must be changed by the advertising campaign. Determining the target market's present position regarding the various response stages requires **benchmark measures**. Often a marketing research study must be conducted to determine prevailing levels of the response hierarchy. In the case

IMC Perspective 8–2
Selling Hush Puppies to a New Generation

For more than 30 years the cuddly, rumpled, droopy-eyed Hush Puppies hound has been an advertising icon familiar to most consumers. But the brand has suffered from image problems for nearly as long. To many consumers, Hush Puppies are old-fashioned, conservative, fuzzy pigskin loafers. The last time Hush Puppies were considered hip, John F. Kennedy was president. Now Wolverine Worldwide, Inc., the maker of Hush Puppies, is out to change this.

Wolverine's CEO, Geoff Bloom, says, "We want to see those nifty, natural, contemporary younger people wearing our shoes." To achieve this goal, the company developed a new mix of products and recently launched a $5 million print ad campaign aimed at casting aside Hush Puppies' loafer image and appealing to Americans who are more familiar with MTV than Ed Sullivan. Advertising spending was increased fourfold; ads in magazines such as *GQ, Details,* and *Glamour* show Hush Puppies on the feet of youthful models whom Wolverine calls "aspirational" people who will inspire readers to welcome Hush Puppies into their 1990s lifestyle. Previous advertising focused on the company's shoes. But there are no close-ups of the product in the new campaign, only copy explaining how Hush Puppies can fit not only one's feet but also one's psyche.

Wolverine believes the Hush Puppies brand name still has the power to attract younger consumers. Actually, Hush Puppies has had more luck recently with younger buyers outside the United States. Young people in 60 countries buy Hush Puppies for their American cachet. Foreign sales of Hush Puppies totaled 7 million pairs in 1992, 40 percent more than the 5 million pairs sold in the U.S. Now Wolverine hopes to reverse its declining domestic sales.

Hush Puppies faces strong competition from competitors such as G. H. Bass; Reebok's casual-shoe division, Rockport;

and Dexter Shoe Co. These competitors have capitalized on a back-to-basics trend that has made casual shoes the rage over the past several years. Wolverine hopes its new mix of products and ad campaign will help change its image among younger consumers and also win over retailers who have become bored with Hush Puppies' bland image. Even the Hush Puppies hound is getting hip. He kicked off the youth movement by appearing on the cover of Wolverine's annual report with his typical pout, but this time in the arms of a beaming, jeans-clad young couple.

Source: Oscar Suris, "Ads Aim to Sell Hush Puppies to New Yuppies," *The Wall Street Journal,* July 28, 1993, pp. B1, 6.

of a new product or service, the starting conditions are generally at or near zero for all the variables, so no initial research is needed.

Establishing benchmark measures gives the promotional planner a basis for determining what communications tasks need to be accomplished and for specifying particular objectives. For example, a preliminary study for a brand may reveal that awareness is high but consumer perceptions and attitudes are negative. The objective for the advertising campaign would be to change the target audience's perceptions of and attitudes toward the brand. IMC Perspective 8–2 discusses how Hush Puppies shoes developed a new advertising campaign in response to this situation.

Quantitative benchmarks are not only valuable in establishing communications goals and objectives but essential to determining whether the campaign was successful. Objectives provide the standard against which the success or failure of a campaign is measured. An ad campaign that results in a 90 percent awareness level for a brand among its target audience cannot really be judged effective unless one knows what percentage of the consumers were aware of the brand before the campaign began. A 70 percent precampaign awareness level would lead to a different interpretation of the campaign's success than would a 30 percent level.

Specified time period

A final consideration in setting advertising objectives is specifying the time period in which they must be accomplished. Appropriate time periods can range from a few days to a year or more. Most ad campaigns specify time periods from a few months to a year, depending on the situation facing the advertiser and the type of response being sought. For example, awareness levels for a brand can be created or increased fairly quickly through an intensive media schedule of widespread, repetitive advertising to the target audience. Repositioning of a product requires a change in consumers' perceptions and takes much more time. For example, the repositioning of Marlboro cigarettes from a feminine brand to one with a masculine image took several years.

Assessment of DAGMAR

The DAGMAR approach to setting objectives has had considerable influence on the advertising planning process. Many promotional planners use this model as a basis for setting objectives and assessing the effectiveness of their promotional campaigns. DAGMAR also focused advertisers' attention on the value of using communications-based rather than sales-based objectives to measure advertising effectiveness and encouraged the measurement of stages in the response hierarchy to assess a campaign's impact. Colley's work has led to improvements in the advertising and promotional planning process by providing a better understanding of the goals and objectives toward which planners' efforts should be directed. This usually results in less subjectivity and also leads to better communication and relationships between the client and its agency.

Criticisms of DAGMAR

While DAGMAR has contributed to the advertising planning process, it has not been totally accepted by everyone in the advertising field. A number of problems have led to questions regarding its value as an advertising planning tool.[13]

Problems with the response hierarchy

A major criticism of the DAGMAR approach is its reliance on the hierarchy-of-effects model. The fact that consumers do not always go through this sequence of communications effects before making a purchase has been recognized, and alternative response models have been developed.[14] DAGMAR MOD II recognizes that the appropriate response model will depend on the situation and emphasizes identifying the sequence of decision-making steps that apply in a buying situation.[15]

Promotional managers must determine which response sequence is relevant in the purchase process for the product or service being advertised and what role advertising and other promotional mix elements play in moving consumers through the applicable hierarchy. Appropriate objectives can then be set to guide the promotional program.

Sales objectives

Another objection to DAGMAR comes from those who argue that the only relevant measure of advertising objectives is sales. They have little tolerance for ad campaigns that achieve communications objectives but fail to increase sales. Advertising is seen as effective only if it induces consumers to make a purchase.[16] The problems with this logic were addressed in our discussion of communications objectives.

Practicality and costs

Another criticism of DAGMAR concerns the difficulties involved in implementing it. A manager attempting to use DAGMAR has to determine what constructs or variables are relevant and how they should be measured. Money must be spent on research to establish quantitative benchmarks and measure communications results. This is costly and time consuming and can lead to considerable disagreement over method, criteria, measures, and so forth.

Many critics argue that DAGMAR is practical only for large companies with big advertising and research budgets and the capabilities to conduct the research needed to establish benchmarks and measure changes in the response hierarchy. Many firms do not want to spend the money on research that is needed to use DAGMAR effectively.

Inhibition of creativity

A final criticism of DAGMAR is that it inhibits advertising creativity by imposing too much structure on the people responsible for developing the advertising. Creative people in advertising are often searching for the great idea that will result in a unique, effective campaign. Many creative personnel feel that the DAGMAR approach is too concerned with quantitative assessment of a campaign's impact on awareness, brand name recall, or specific persuasion measures. The emphasis is on passing the numbers test rather than developing a message that is truly creative and contributes to brand equity.

There is little question that DAGMAR makes the creative personnel more accountable and may inhibit their freedom to search for the great creative idea. On the other hand, spectacular advertising ideas are not easy to come by, and many advertisers are more concerned with avoiding ineffective advertising. Well-planned campaigns using DAGMAR are viewed by many advertising and marketing managers as a way to avoid ads with no specific direction or purpose, even if the result is some restriction on the creative department.

PROBLEMS IN SETTING OBJECTIVES

Although the DAGMAR model suggests a logical process for advertising and promotion planning, most advertisers and their agencies fail to follow these basic principles. They fail to set specific objectives for their campaigns and/or do not have the proper evidence to determine the success of their promotional programs. A classic study conducted by Stewart H. Britt examined problems with how advertisers set objectives and measure their accomplishment.[17] The study showed that most advertising agencies did not state appropriate objectives for determining success and thus could not demonstrate whether a supposedly successful campaign was really a success. Even though these campaigns may have been doing something right, they generally did not know what it was.

Although this study was conducted in 1969, the same problems exist in advertising today. A more recent study examined the advertising practices of business-to-business marketers to determine whether their ads used advertising objectives that met Colley's four DAGMAR criteria.[18] Entries from the annual Business/Professional Advertising Association Gold Key Awards competition, which solicits the best marketing communications efforts from business-to-business advertisers, were evaluated with respect to their campaigns' objectives and summaries of results. Most of these advertisers did not have concrete advertising objectives, specify objective tasks, measure results in terms of stages of a hierarchy of effects, or match objectives to evaluation measures. The authors concluded: "Advertising practitioners have only partially adopted the concepts and standards of objective setting and evaluation set forth 25 years ago."[19]

Improving Promotional Planners' Use of Objectives

As we have seen, it is important that advertisers and their agencies pay close attention to the objectives they set for their campaigns. They should strive to set specific and measurable objectives that not only guide promotional planning and decision making but also can be used as a standard for evaluating performance. Unfortunately, many companies do not set appropriate objectives for their integrated marketing communications programs.

Many companies fail to set appropriate objectives because top management has only an abstract idea of what the firm's IMC program is supposed to be doing. A study by the American Business Press that measured the attitudes of chairmen, presidents, and other senior managers of business-to-business advertising companies found that more than 50 percent of the 427 respondents said they did not know whether their advertising was working, and less than 10 percent thought it was working well.[20] This study showed overwhelmingly that top management did not even know what their company's advertising was supposed to do, much less how to measure it.

© **EXHIBIT 8–15**

Traditional view of marketing
communications

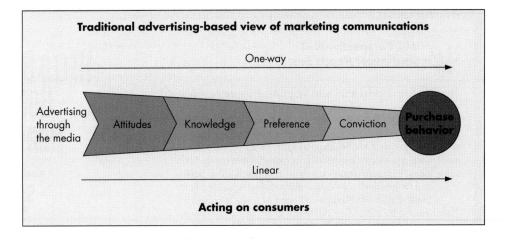

It is unlikely that most firms will set objectives that meet all the criteria set forth in DAGMAR. However, promotional planners should set objectives that are specific and measurable and go beyond basic sales goals. Even if specific communications response elements are not always measured, meeting the other criteria will sharpen the focus and improve the quality of the integrated marketing communications planning process.

Setting Objectives for the IMC Program

One reason so much attention is given to advertising objectives is that for many companies advertising has traditionally been the major way of communicating with target audiences. Other promotional mix elements such as sales promotion, direct marketing, and publicity are used intermittently to support and complement the advertising program.

Another reason is that traditional advertising-based views of marketing communications planning, such as DAGMAR, have dominated the field for so long. These approaches are based on a hierarchical response model and consider how marketers can develop and disseminate advertising messages to move consumers along an effects path. This approach, shown in Exhibit 8–15, is what professor Don Schultz calls *inside out* planning. He says, "It focuses on what the marketer wants to say, when the marketer wants to say it, about things the marketer believes are important about his or her brand, and in the media forms the marketer wants to use.[21]

Schultz advocates the use of an *outside in* planning process to IMC that starts with the customer and builds backwards to the brand. This means that promotional planners study the various media customers and prospects use, when the marketer's messages might be most relevant to customers, and when they are likely to be most receptive to the message.

A similar approach is suggested by professor Tom Duncan, who argues that IMC should use **zero-based communications planning,** which involves determining what tasks need to be done and which marketing communications functions should be used and to what extent.[22] This approach focuses on the task to be done and searches for the best ideas and media to accomplish it. He notes that as with a traditional advertising campaign, the basis of an IMC campaign is a big idea. However, in IMC the big idea can be public relations, direct response, packaging, or sales promotion. Duncan suggests that an effective IMC program should lead with the marketing communication function that most effectively addresses the company's main problem or opportunity and should use a promotional mix that draws on the strengths of whichever communications functions relate best to the particular situation. IMC Perspective 8–3 discusses how Southwest Airlines used public relations to lead its entry into the East Coast market.

Many of the considerations for determining advertising objectives are relevant to setting goals for other elements of the integrated marketing communications program. The

IMC Perspective 8–3
Southwest Heads East

The past several years have been very difficult for the airline industry. While others suffer record earnings declines, one carrier stands alone as the nation's only profitable airline: Dallas-based Southwest Airlines. Southwest's lower costs and more productive work force permit it to offer fares as much as 25 percent below its competitors. Major carriers such as United, Delta, and USAir have been trying to figure out how to operate like Southwest, and for good reason—because *Southwest is headed East.*

In September 1993, Southwest began its foray into the East Coast market by expanding its service to Baltimore which was dominated by USAir. The airline knew service to this city would be a milestone in its 23-year history. The company's whole corporate philosophy had to be communicated to a region that had little or no knowledge of Southwest and the low-fare, no-frills, high-frequency services approach that makes it successful. To enter the Baltimore market, Southwest employed its time-tested start-up formula by dispatching the "diamond team"— a half-dozen planners from marketing and sales, promotion, advertising, and public relations areas.

Southwest's low-cost philosophy means it needs cost-effective ways to communicate with consumers, so the airline always starts with a public relations push to announce inaugural service to a city. The goal is to already be considered a part of the community by the time it begins service. The diamond team analyzed demographic data and quietly fanned out in search of events, sports teams, or cultural institutions to sponsor. The team looks for key areas that are important to the community, and in Baltimore's case it was baseball. Southwest signed up with the Orioles for advertising and joint marketing promotions, including ticket contests.

Five weeks before the first flight, a news conference was held to announce the airline's entry into Baltimore. Southwest chairman Herb Kelleher presented the governor of Maryland with a flotation device, calling it a lifesaver from high airfares for the people of Baltimore. Following the conference, Southwest linked its PR efforts to the baseball theme. To launch its $49 fare to Cleveland, Southwest treated 49 elementary schoolchildren to a day at the Cleveland Metroparks Zoo. Before the flight, Boog Powell (the former Orioles player and Hall of Famer) gave the kids hitting lessons.

Although Southwest's media budget is not large, advertising was integrated into the mix to support the PR effort. To ensure that the locals did not mistake Southwest for some fly-by-night operator, the airline used newspaper and TV advertising, stressing

its modern jet fleet and industry-beating profitability record. The TV commercials used the established "Just Plane Smart" theme and credited the city and its residents for being smart to allow Southwest to come to the city. A direct mailing to frequent short-haul travelers in the Baltimore area offered a special promotion to join Southwest's frequent-flier program. Print ads were run in the *Washington Post* to encourage people from the nearby Washington, D.C., area to drive to the Baltimore airport and try Southwest. To reinforce the PR and advertising messages, employees took to the streets, handing out fliers promoting the "Just Plane Smart" theme and peanuts (all Southwest serves on its low-cost flights).

Baltimore responded quite well to Southwest's integrated marketing communications program. In the fourth quarter, passenger boardings at the airport increased more than 30 percent and USAir's market share dropped four percentage points. Southwest now says that Baltimore is one of its most successful new cities and plans to add more flights as soon as it gets the needed planes and six new gates.

Sources: Michael J. McCarthy and Bridget O'Brian, "Lean, Nimble Airlines Head East, Targeting Region's Plump Prices," *The Wall Street Journal*, Feb. 28, 1994, pp. A1, 6; Jennifer Lawrence, "Integrated Mix Makes Expansion Fly," *Advertising Age*, Nov. 8, 1993, pp. S10, 12.

promotional planner should determine what role various sales promotion techniques, publicity and public relations, direct marketing, and personal selling will play in the overall marketing program and how they will interact with advertising as well as with one another. When setting objectives for these promotional elements, planners must consider what the firm hopes to communicate through the use of this element, among what target audience, and during what time period. As with advertising, results should be measured and evaluated against the original objectives, and attempts should be made to isolate the effects of each promotional element. Objectives for marketing communication elements other than advertising are discussed more thoroughly in Part V of the text.

SUMMARY

This chapter has examined the role of objectives in the planning and evaluation of the integrated marketing communications program. Specific objectives are needed to guide the development of the promotional program as well as to provide a benchmark against which performance can be measured and evaluated. Objectives serve important functions as communications devices, as a guide to planning the IMC program and deciding on various alternatives, and for measurement and evaluation.

Objectives for IMC evolve from the organization's overall marketing plan and are based on the roles various promotional mix elements play in the marketing program. Promotional objectives are determined after a thorough situation analysis has been conducted and the marketing and promotional issues have been identified. Many managers use sales or a related measure such as market share as the basis for setting objectives. However, because of the various problems associated with sales-based objectives, many promotional planners believe the role of advertising and other promotional mix elements is to communicate. They use communications-based objectives like those in

the response hierarchy as the basis for setting goals. The communication effects pyramid illustrated possible objectives for the various stages in the hierarchy.

The DAGMAR approach to setting objectives was examined in detail. Good advertising objectives meet four basic criteria: They are set in concrete, measurable communications terms; they specify a target audience; they contain a benchmark and indicate the degree of change being sought; and they specify a time period for accomplishing the objectives. Many companies fail to meet these criteria in setting objectives for their advertising and promotional programs.

Much of the emphasis in setting objectives has been on traditional advertising-based views of marketing communications. However, many companies are moving toward zero-based communications planning, which focuses on what tasks need to be done, which marketing communication functions should be used, and to what extent. Many of the principles used in setting advertising objectives can be applied to other elements in the promotional mix.

KEY TERMS

marketing objectives, p. 216

integrated marketing communications objectives, p. 217

carryover effect, p. 220

DAGMAR, p. 227

communications task, p. 228

benchmark measures, p. 229

zero-based communications planning, p. 233

DISCUSSION QUESTIONS

1. Discuss the role of integrated marketing communications in the new marketing strategy being pursued by Compaq Computer. How is the marketing strategy influencing Compaq's advertising and promotional strategy?

2. Discuss the value of setting objectives for the integrated marketing communications program. What important functions do objectives serve?

3. What are the differences between marketing objectives and communications objectives? Why do so many managers confuse the two?

4. You are in a meeting to discuss plans for a new advertising and promotional program for your company. The vice president of marketing opens the meeting by stating that there is only one objective for the new campaign—to increase sales. How do you respond to this statement?

5. What is meant by an advertising carryover effect? Discuss the problems carryover creates for managers who are trying to determine the impact of their advertising on sales.

6. Discuss three situations where sales are an appropriate measure of the effects of advertising or some other marketing communications element.

7. The advertising launch campaign for the Infiniti automobile (discussed in IMC Perspective 8–1) was very successful in creating awareness as well as getting consumers to request information about the cars and visit dealer showrooms. However, many critics argue the campaign was unsuccessful because sales projections were not met. Discuss the role advertising plays in marketing cars. Is it appropriate to measure the success or failure of a campaign based on sales?

8. What are the four characteristics of good objectives suggested by DAGMAR? Do you think these requirements place too much of a constraint on promotional planners? Why or why not?

9. What is the difference between outside in planning for IMC versus inside out planning?

10. What is meant by zero-based communications planning for IMC?

Chapter *9*

The Advertising and Promotions Budget

Chapter Objectives

- *To understand the process of advertising and promotions budget setting.*
- *To understand theoretical issues involved in budget setting.*

- *To examine the various methods for establishing an advertising budget.*
- *To examine factors influencing the size and process of allocating the advertising and promotions budget.*

Where Do Car Product Advertisers Spend Their Money?

A lot of money is being spent to advertise automobile products in this country. The average advertising budget for auto and truck manufacturers totaled $74.93 million in 1993. When all automotive category advertisers—manufacturers, parts makers, tire companies, and oil and gas retailers—are thrown in, the total spending on advertising and promotion hit approximately $3.93 billion in 1994. This is a lot of money to spread around, and of course every medium wants its share. So who is going to get it? MediaWeek magazine surveyed advertisers to see how these monies would be allocated.

National television gets the bulk of the spending (approximately 38 percent), followed by consumer events and cable TV (13 percent and 11 percent respectively). Syndicated TV receives the lowest allocation—only about 3 percent. The budget allocations changed from 1992, with some promotional tools gaining at the others' expense. Publications and magazines (a 23 percent increase) and consumer events seemed to be the winners, while co-op advertising and retailer allowances took the biggest hit. Specific media also gained or lost in this battle for the bucks. US News & World Report, considered by auto advertisers the best advertising value, was expected to gain advertising clients and expenditures; Car & Driver was mentioned as a medium likely to lose clients. Motor Trend was expected to gain three new clients and have six increase their ad budgets, but at the same time lose two and have four likely to reduce their expenditures. ABC was considered the best TV advertising value, followed by CBS and Fox.

The allocations also differed by size of the company. Companies with less than $1 million in advertising spend about 69 percent on advertising and 31 percent on promotion, while companies with more than $100 million spend about 92 percent on advertising and 8 percent on promotion. As you can see, allocating the budget is not a cut-and-dried decision, and different companies spend their money in different places.

Source: "The Road to Upfront," Automotive MediaWeek, May 31, 1993, pp. 21–28.

ften when we think of promotional expenditures of firms, we think only about the huge amounts being spent. We don't usually take the time to think about how these monies are being allocated and about the recipients of these dollars. As shown in the lead-in to this chapter, the budgeting decisions of advertisers have a significant impact not only on the firm itself but also on numerous others involved either directly or indirectly. This chapter provides insight into some underlying theory with respect to budget setting, discusses how companies budget for promotional efforts, and demonstrates the inherent strengths and weaknesses associated with these approaches. Essentially, we focus on two primary budgeting decisions—establishment of a budget amount and the budget allocation decision.

ESTABLISHING THE BUDGET

The size of a firm's advertising and promotions budget can vary from a few thousand dollars to more than a billion. When companies like Procter & Gamble and General Motors spend over a billion dollars per year to promote their products, they expect such expenditures to accomplish their stated objectives. The budget decision is no less critical to a firm spending only a few thousand dollars; its ultimate success or failure may depend on the monies spent. One of the most critical decisions facing the marketing manager is how much to spend on the promotional effort.

EXHIBIT 9–1

The AAAA promotes the continued use of advertising in a recession

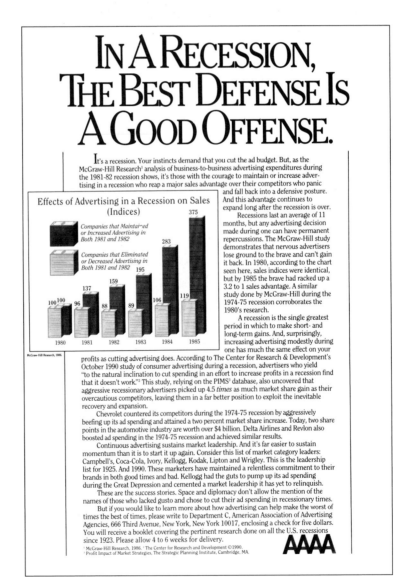

Unfortunately, many managers fail to realize the value of advertising and promotion. They treat the communications budget as an expense rather than an investment. Instead of viewing the dollars spent as contributing to additional sales and market share, they focus on the impact of budget expenses against profits. As a result, when times get tough, the advertising and promotional budget is the first to be cut—even though there is strong evidence that exactly the opposite should occur, as demonstrated by Exhibit 9–1. Moreover, the decision is not a one-time responsibility. A new budget is formulated every year, each time a new product is introduced, or when either internal or external factors necessitate a change to maintain competitiveness.

While it is one of the most critical decisions, budgeting has perhaps been the most resistant to change. A comparison of advertising and promotional texts over the past 10 years would reveal the same methods for establishing budgets. The theoretical basis for this process remains rooted in economic theory and marginal analysis. (Advertisers also use an approach based on **contribution margin**—the difference between the total revenue generated by a brand and its total variable costs. But, as noted by Robert Steiner, marginal analysis and contribution margin are essentially synonymous terms.)[1] We begin our discussion of budgeting with an examination of these theoretical approaches.

Theoretical Issues in Budget Setting

Most of the models used to establish advertising budgets can be categorized as taking an economic or a sales response perspective.

Marginal analysis

Exhibit 9-2 graphically represents the concept of **marginal analysis**. As advertising/promotional expenditures increase, sales and gross margins also increase to a point, but then they level off. Profits are shown to be a result of the gross margin minus advertising expenditures. Using this theory to establish its budget, a firm would continue to spend advertising/promotional dollars as long as the marginal revenues created by these expenditures exceeded the incremental advertising/promotional costs. As shown on the graph, the optimal expenditure level is the point where marginal costs equal the marginal revenues they generate (Point *A*). If the sum of the advertising/promotional expenditures exceeded the revenues these efforts generated, one would conclude the appropriations were too high and scale down the budget. If revenues were higher, a higher budget might be in order. (We will see later in this chapter that this approach can also be applied to the allocation decision.)

EXHIBIT 9–2

Marginal analysis

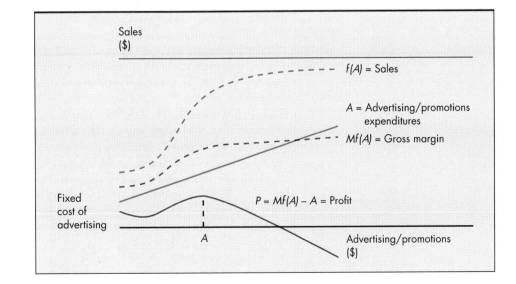

⊚ EXHIBIT 9–3

Leadership and responsiveness to a growing market contribute to Lockheed's corporate growth

This new business lineup includes an F-28, Boeing 757, DC-10, and Boeing 747.

Look who's coming to Lockheed.

Leveraging skills proven on more than 200,000 aircraft, Lockheed is now the most experienced and fastest-growing aircraft maintenance and modification company in the world. New airline customers come to Lockheed centers every day.

Forecasts say the world's commercial fleet will grow by as much as 50%, and existing commercial and military fleets will be used longer. That means a bigger market, and the opportunity for Lockheed to grow stronger in this thriving service industry. One example: a new partnership agreement with Japan Airlines will help fill the bays with 747s at our newest center in San Bernardino, California.

Establishing leadership positions on existing capabilities is a cornerstone of Lockheed's plan to build shareholder value and create the premier aerospace company in the world.

Lockheed leads.

Watch NOVA on PBS, Tuesdays at 8 p.m.

While marginal analysis seems logical intuitively, certain weaknesses limit its usefulness. These weaknesses include the assumptions that 1) sales are a direct result of advertising and promotional expenditures and this effect can be measured and 2) advertising and promotion are solely responsible for sales. Let us examine each of these assumptions in more detail.

1. *Assumption that sales are a direct measure of advertising and promotions efforts.* In Chapter 8, we discussed the fact that the advertiser needs to set communications objectives that contribute to accomplishing overall marketing objectives but at the same time are separate. One reason for this strategy is that it is often difficult, if not impossible, to demonstrate the effects of advertising and promotions on sales. In studies using sales as a direct measure, it has been almost impossible to establish the contribution of advertising and promotion. As noted by Frank Bass, "There is no more difficult, complex, or controversial problem in marketing than measuring the influence of advertising on sales."[2] In the words of David Aaker and James Carman, "Looking for the relationship between advertising and sales is somewhat worse than looking for a needle in a haystack."[3] Thus, to try to show that the size of the budget will directly affect sales of the product is misleading. A more logical approach would be to examine the impact of various budgets on the attainment of communications objectives.

   As we saw in the discussion of communications objectives, sales are not the only goal of the promotional effort. Awareness, interest, attitude change, and other communications objectives are often sought, and while the bottom line may be to sell the product, these objectives may serve as the basis on which the promotional program is developed.

2. *Assumption that sales are determined solely by advertising and promotion.* This assumption ignores the remaining elements of the marketing mix—price,

@ **EXHIBIT 9–4**   Advertising sales/response functions

A. The concave-downward response curve

B. The S-shaped response function

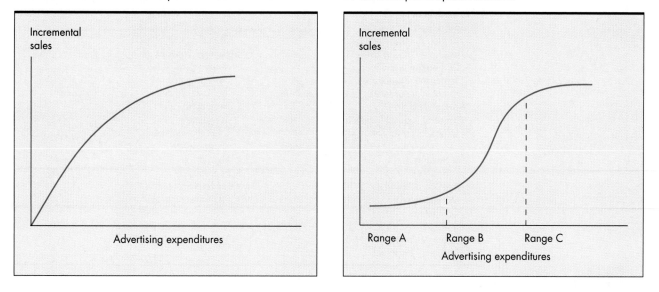

product, and distribution—which do contribute to a company's success. Environmental factors may also affect the promotional program, leading the marketing manager to assume the advertising was or was not effective when some other factor may have helped or hindered the accomplishment of the desired objectives (see Exhibit 9–3).

Overall, you can see that while the economic approach to the budgeting process is a logical one, the difficulties associated with determining the effects of the promotional effort on sales and revenues limit its applicability. Marginal analysis is seldom used as a basis for budgeting (except for direct-response advertising).

Sales response models

You may have wondered why the sales curve in Exhibit 9–2 shows sales leveling off even though advertising and promotions efforts continue to increase. The relationship between advertising and sales has been the topic of much research and discussion designed to determine the shape of the response curve.

Almost all advertisers subscribe to one of two models of the advertising/sales response function: the concave-downward function and the S-shaped response curve.

The concave-downward function

After reviewing over 100 studies of the effects of advertising on sales, Julian Simon and Johan Arndt concluded that the effects of advertising budgets follow the microeconomic law of diminishing returns.[4] That is, as the amount of advertising increases, its incremental value decreases. The logic is that those with the greatest potential to buy will likely act on the first (or earliest) exposures, while those less likely to buy are not likely to change as a result of the advertising. For those who may be potential buyers, each additional ad will supply little or no new information that will affect their decision. Thus, according to the **concave-downward function** model, the effects of advertising quickly begin to diminish, as shown in Exhibit 9-4a. Budgeting under this model suggests that fewer advertising dollars may be necessary to create the optimal influence on sales.

The S-shaped response function

Many advertising managers assume the **S-shaped response curve** (Exhibit 9-4b), which projects an S-shaped response function to the budget outlay, with the response again measured in sales. Initial outlays of the advertising budget have little impact (as

@ **EXHIBIT 9–5**

Factors influencing
advertising budgets

Factor	Relationship of Advertising/Sales	Factor	Relationship of Advertising/Sales
Product factors		**Customer factors**	
Basis for differentiation	+	Industrial products users	–
Hidden product qualities	+	Concentration of users	+
Emotional buying motives	+	**Strategy factors**	
Durability	–	Regional markets	–
Large dollar purchase	–	Early stage of	+
Purchase frequency	Curvilinear	brand life cycle	
Market factors		High margins in	–
Stage of product life cycle		channels	
Introductory	+	Long channels of	+
Growth	+	distribution	
Maturity	–	High prices	+
Decline	–	High quality	+
Inelastic demand		**Cost factors**	
Market share	–	High profit margins	+
Competition			
Active	+		
Concentrated	+		
"Pioneer" in market	–		

Note: + relationship means the factor leads to a positive effect of advertising on sales; – relationship indicates little or no effect of advertising on sales.

indicated by the essentially flat sales curve in range A). After a certain budget level has been reached (the beginning of range B), advertising and promotional efforts begin to have an effect, as additional increments of expenditures result in increased sales. This incremental gain continues only to a point, however, because at the beginning of range C additional expenditures begin to return little or nothing in the way of sales. This model suggests a small advertising budget is likely to have no impact beyond the sales that may have been generated through other means (for example, word of mouth). At the other extreme, more does not necessarily mean better: additional dollars spent beyond range B have no additional impact on sales and for the most part can be considered wasted. As with marginal analysis, one would attempt to operate at that point on the curve in area B where the maximum return for the money is attained.

Weaknesses in these sales response models render them of limited use to practitioners for direct applications. Many of the problems seen earlier—the use of sales as a dependent variable, measurement problems, and so on—limit the usefulness of these models. At the same time, you should keep in mind the purpose of discussing such models. Even though marginal analysis and the sales response curves may not apply directly, they give managers some insight into a theoretical basis of how the budgeting process should work. Some empirical evidence indicates the models may have validity. One study, based on industry experience, has provided support for the S-shaped response curve; the results indicate that a minimum amount of advertising dollars must be spent before there is a noticeable effect on sales.[5] The studies discussed in earlier chapters on learning and the hierarchy of effects also demonstrate the importance of repetition on gaining awareness and on subsequent higher-order objectives such as adoption. Thus, while these models may not provide a tool for setting the advertising and promotional budget directly, we can use them to guide our appropriations strategy from a theoretical basis. As you will see later in this chapter, such a theoretical basis offers an advantage over many of the methods currently being utilized for budget setting and allocation.

Additional Factors in Budget Setting

While the theoretical bases just discussed should be considered in establishing the budget appropriation, a number of other issues must also be considered. A weakness in attempting to use sales as a *direct* measure of response to advertising is that various situational fac-

@ **EXHIBIT 9-6**

A strong basis for differentiation could show a noticeable effect of advertising on sales

tors may have an effect. In one comprehensive study, 24 variables were shown to affect the advertising/sales ratio. Exhibit 9–5 lists these factors and their relationships.[6] For a product characterized by emotional buying motives, hidden product qualities, and/or a strong basis for differentiation, advertising would have a noticeable impact on sales (see Exhibit 9–6). Products characterized as large dollar purchases and those in the maturity or decline stages of the product would be less likely to benefit. The study showed that other factors involving the market, customer, costs, and strategies employed have different effects.

The results of this study are interesting but limited, since they relate primarily to the percentage of sales dollars allocated to advertising and the factors influencing these ratios. As we will see later in this chapter, the percentage of sales method of budgeting has inherent weaknesses in that the advertising and sales effects may be reversed. So we cannot be sure whether the situation actually led to the advertising/sales relationship or vice versa. Thus, while these factors should be considered in the budget appropriation decision, they should not be the sole determinants of where and when to increase or decrease expenditures.

The *Advertising Age* Editorial Sounding Board consists of 92 executives of the top 200 advertising companies in the United States (representing the client side) and 130 executives of the 200 largest advertising agencies and 11 advertising consultants (representing the agency side). A survey of the board yielded the factors shown in Exhibit 9–7 that are gaining and losing in importance in budget setting. Clearly, there is little consensus as to what is becoming more or less important in determining the size of the budget. While clients most commonly cite intended changes in advertising strategy and/or creative approaches as important in setting the ad budget, those on the agency side are more likely to cite *profit contribution goals* or other financial targets of the client as growing in

@ **EXHIBIT 9–7**

Importance of factors in
budget setting

Advertisers—Referring to Own Companies	
Increasing in Importance	
Intended changes in advertising strategy and/or creative approach	51%
Competitive activity and/or spending levels	47
Profit contribution goal or other financial target	43
Decreasing in Importance	
Level of previous year's spending, with adjustment	17
Senior management dollar allocation or set limit	11
Volume share projections	8

Agencies—Referring to Client Companies	
Increasing in Importance	
Profit contribution goal or other financial target	56%
Competitive activity and/or spending levels	43
Intended changes in advertising strategy and/or creative approach	37
Decreasing in Importance	
Projections/assumptions on media cost increases	25
Level of previous year's spending, with adjustment	24
Modifications in media strategy and/or buying techniques	17

importance. In respect to which factors are decreasing in importance, only the level of the previous year's spending is a key factor to both groups.

Overall, the responses of these two groups reflect in part their perceptions as to how budgets are set. To understand the differences in the relative importance of these factors, it is important to understand the approaches currently employed in budget setting. The next section of this chapter examines these.

@ **BUDGETING APPROACHES**

The theoretical approaches to establishing the promotional budget are seldom employed. In smaller firms, they may never be used. Instead, a number of methods developed through practice and experience are implemented. This section reviews some of the more traditional methods of setting budgets and the relative advantages and disadvantages of each. First, you must understand two things: 1) Many firms employ more than one method, and 2) budgeting approaches vary according to the size and sophistication of the firm.

Top-Down Approaches

The approaches discussed in this section may be referred to as **top-down approaches** because a budgetary amount is established (usually at an executive level) and then the monies are passed down to the various departments (as shown in Exhibit 9–8). These budgets are essentially predetermined and have no true theoretical basis. Top-down methods include the affordable method, arbitrary allocation, percentage of sales, competitive parity, and return on investment (ROI).

The affordable method

In the **affordable method** (often referred to as the all-you-can-afford method), the firm determines the amount to be spent in various areas such as production and operations. Then it allocates remaining dollars to advertising and promotion, considering this to be the amount it can afford. The task to be performed by the advertising/promotions function is not considered, and the likelihood of under- or overspending is high, as no guidelines for measuring the effects of various budgets are established.

Strange as it may seem, this approach is common among small firms. Unfortunately, it is also used in large firms, particularly those that are not marketing driven and do not understand the role of advertising and promotion. For example, many high-tech firms focus on new product development and engineering, assuming the product, if good enough, will sell itself. In many of these companies, little money is left for performing the advertising and promotions tasks.

◎ **EXHIBIT   9–8**

Top-down versus bottom-up
approaches to budget setting

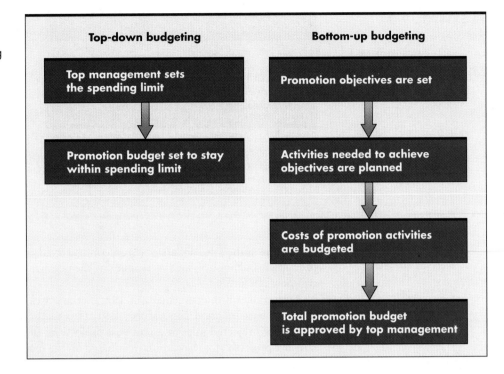

Top-down budgeting	Bottom-up budgeting
Top management sets the spending limit	Promotion objectives are set
Promotion budget set to stay within spending limit	Activities needed to achieve objectives are planned
	Costs of promotion activities are budgeted
	Total promotion budget is approved by top management

The logic for this approach stems from "We can't be hurt with this method" thinking. That is, if we know what we can afford and we do not exceed it, we will not get into financial problems. While this may be true in a strictly accounting sense, it does not reflect sound managerial decision making from a marketing perspective. Often this method does not allocate enough money to get the product off the ground and into the market. In terms of the S-shaped sales response model, the firm is operating in range A. Or the firm could be spending more than necessary, operating in range C. In other instances, once the market gets tough and sales and/or profits begin to fall, this method would likely lead to budget cuts at a time when the budget should be increased.

Arbitrary allocation

Perhaps an even weaker method than the affordable method for establishing a budget is **arbitrary allocation**, in which virtually no theoretical basis is considered and the budgetary amount is often set by fiat. That is, the budget is determined by management solely on the basis of what is felt to be necessary. In a discussion of how managers set advertising budgets, Melvin Salveson reported that these decisions may reflect "as much upon the managers' psychological profile as they do economic criteria."[7] While Salveson was referring to larger corporations, the approach is no less common in small firms and nonprofit organizations.

The arbitrary allocation approach has no obvious advantages. No systematic thinking has occurred, no objectives have been budgeted for, and the concept and purpose of advertising and promotion have been largely ignored. Other than the fact that the manager believes some monies must be spent on advertising and promotion and then picks a number, there is no good explanation why this approach continues to be used. Yet budgets continue to be set this way, and our purpose in discussing it is to point out that this method is used—not recommended.

Percentage of sales

Perhaps the most commonly used method for budget setting (particularly in large firms) is the **percentage of sales method**, in which the advertising and promotions budget is based on sales of the product. Management determines the amount by either (1) taking a

@ **EXHIBIT 9-9**

Alternative methods for computing percentage of sales for Entree Cologne

Method 1: Straight Percentage of Sales		
1993	Total dollar sales	$1,000,000
	Straight % of sales at 10%	$100,000
1994	Advertising budget	$100,000

Method 2: Percentage of Unit Cost		
1993	Cost per bottle to manufacturer	$4.00
	Unit cost allocated to advertising	1.00
1994	Forecasted sales, 100,000 units	
1994	Advertising budget (100,000 × $1.00)	$100,000

percentage of the sales dollars or (2) assigning a fixed amount of the unit product cost to promotion and multiplying this amount by the number of units sold. These two methods are shown in Exhibit 9–9.

A variation on the percentage of sales method uses a percentage of projected future sales as a base (method 2 in Exhibit 9–9). This method also uses either a straight percentage of projected sales or a unit cost projection. In the straight percentage method, sales are projected for the coming year based on the marketing manager's estimates. The budget is a percentage of these sales, often an industry standard percentage like those presented in Exhibit 9–10.

One advantage of using future sales as a base is that the budget is not based on last year's sales. As the market changes, management must factor the effect of these changes on sales into the next year's forecast rather than relying on past data. The resulting budget is more likely to reflect current conditions and be more appropriate.

Exhibit 9-10 reveals that the percentage allocated varies from one industry to the next. Some firms budget a very small percentage (for example, 0.3 percent in construction machinery), and others spend a much higher proportional amount (8.2 percent in the beverage industry). Actual dollar amounts spent vary markedly according to the company's total sales figure. Thus, a smaller percentage of sales in the construction machinery industry may actually result in significantly more advertising dollars being spent.

Proponents of the percentage of sales method cite a number of advantages. It is financially safe and keeps ad spending within reasonable limits, as it bases spending on the past year's sales or what the firm expects to sell in the upcoming year. Thus, there will be sufficient monies to cover this budget, with increases in sales leading to budget increases and sales decreases resulting in advertising decreases. The percentage of sales method is simple, straightforward, and easy to implement. Regardless of which basis—past or future sales—is employed, the calculations used to arrive at a budget are not difficult. Finally, this budgeting approach is generally stable. While the budget may vary with increases and decreases in sales, as long as these changes are not drastic the manager will have a reasonable idea of the parameters of the budget.

At the same time, the percentage of sales method has some serious disadvantages, including the basic premise on which the budget is established: *sales.* Using sales as the basis for setting the advertising appropriation puts the cart before the horse. Letting the level of sales determine the amount of advertising and promotions dollars to be spent reverses the cause-and-effect relationship between advertising and sales. Advertising is considered an expense associated with making a sale rather than an investment. As discussed in IMC Perspective 9–1 on page 248, companies that consider promotional expenditures an investment reap the rewards.

A second problem with this approach was actually cited as an advantage earlier: stability. Proponents say that if all firms use a similar percentage, that will bring stability to the marketplace. But what happens if someone varies from this standard percentage? The problem is that this method does not allow for changes in strategy either internally or

@ **EXHIBIT   9–10** Advertising-to-sales ratios (by industry), 1993

Industry	Ad Dollars as Percentage of Sales	Ad Dollars as Percentage of Margin	Industry	Ad Dollars as Percentage of Sales	Ad Dollars as Percentage of Margin
Abrasive, asbestos, misc minerals	1.1	3.9	Computer communication equipment	1.9	4.0
Adhesives and sealants	2.7	5.9	Computer peripheral equip, NEC	1.9	4.1
Agriculture chemicals	0.7	3.1	Computer storage devices	1.4	4.8
Agriculture production—crops	2.2	7.1	Computers and software—wholesale	0.6	5.2
Air cond, heating, refrig equip	1.7	6.5	Construction, mining, matl handle equip	4.4	12.9
Air courier services	1.2	9.9	Convert paper, paprbd, except boxes	2.3	5.2
Air transport, scheduled	1.9	65.5	Dairy products	4.1	11.2
Aircraft and parts	0.6	3.1	Drug and proprietary stores	1.6	5.6
Aircraft parts, aux equip, NEC	0.8	3.1	Durable goods—wholesale, NEC	3.6	7.6
Auto and home supply stores	2.2	8.9	Educational services	6.9	15.7
Auto rent and lease, no drivers	2.4	3.6	Electrical indl apparatus	2.0	6.2
Automatic regulating controls	3.3	11.5	Electrical measure and test instruments	2.6	5.4
Bakery products	8.0	47.6	Electr, other elec equip, except computers	2.2	5.6
Beverages	8.6	14.6	Electric lighting, wiring equip	2.5	8.5
Books: publishing and printing	2.9	6.0	Electromedical apparatus	1.3	2.2
Broadwoven fabric mill, cotton	4.3	21.7	Electronic comp, accessories	0.7	2.3
Business services, NEC	2.7	6.5	Electronic components, NEC	1.0	3.4
Cable and other pay TV services	2.9	6.0	Electronic computers	3.6	7.2
Calculate, acct mach, except computers	1.7	4.4	Electronic connectors	1.0	4.2
Catalog, mail-order houses	6.9	17.7	Electronic parts, equip—whsl, NEC	2.0	7.5
Chemicals and allied prods-whsl	4.2	18.0	Engineering services	0.4	1.9
Chemicals and allied products	2.3	6.1	Engines and turbines	1.3	6.6
Cmp programming, data process	0.2	0.6	Engr, acc, resrch, mgmt, rel svcs	1.4	6.7
Computer and comp software stores	0.6	3.1	Equip rental and leasing, NEC	0.7	2.4
Computer integrated system design	1.5	4.1	Fabricated plate work	1.0	3.7
Computer processing, data prep svc	1.5	2.9			
Computer programming SVC	1.7	8.9			
Commercial printing	2.7	10.4			
Communications equipment, NEC	2.1	4.9			
Communications services, NEC	1.3	3.2			
Computer and office equipment	1.6	3.3			

IMC Perspective 9–1
Investing in Advertising and Promotions

To many marketers, advertising and promotions are thought of as an expense of making a sale. When it comes time to cut costs, the promotional budget often takes the big hit. More astute companies take a different perspective. They consider advertising and promotion an investment that will pay off in the long run—sometimes years later (see chart). Consider the following examples:

- **Zantac.** This ulcer medication introduced by Glaxo was predicted to gain no more than a 10 percent share against the incumbent Tagamet. As a result of an aggressive, investment-driven campaign, Zantac achieved a 50 percent share, replacing Tagamet as the leading brand.
- **Hawaiian Punch.** After spending $10 to $20 million a year on promotions throughout the 1980s, Del Monte cut expenditures to less than $2 million. Even though sales eroded as a result, they remained above $100 million a year. In addition, consumers remembered the character Punchy three years after the ads ran, reflecting carryover from the larger budget.

- **Philip Morris.** Introduced in the 1920s, Marlboro cigarettes had only a 1 percent brand share 30 years later. In 1954, the company invested in a distinctive brand image (the cowboy) it has maintained into the present. Marlboro now holds a 60 percent to 70 percent brand share among young smokers in the United States, and the cowboy image is recognized around the world.

Derrith Lambka, corporate advertising manager for Hewlett-Packard Co., notes that there is more and more pressure on marketing departments to prove that advertising and promotions are a good investment. He says managers are looking at spending to receive the "greatest return possible." If they are patient and look at the investment strategies of Ivory soap, Ritz crackers, and Heinz ketchup as well as those mentioned above, they just may find that advertising and promotions fit the bill.

Sources: Adrian J. Slywotzky and Benson P. Shapiro, "Leveraging to Beat the Odds: The New Marketing Mind-Set," *Harvard Business Review,* Sept./Oct. 1993, pp. 97–107; Mary Welch, "Upbeat Marketers Wield Bigger Budgets, Shift Marketing Mix," *Business Marketing,* Feb. 1993, p. 23.

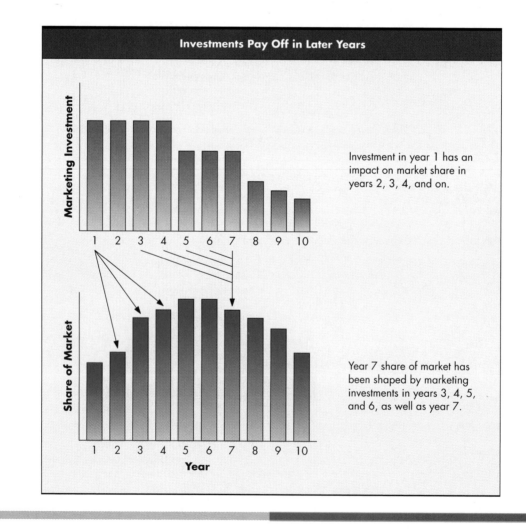

Investments Pay Off in Later Years

Investment in year 1 has an impact on market share in years 2, 3, 4, and on.

Year 7 share of market has been shaped by marketing investments in years 3, 4, 5, and 6, as well as year 7.

from competitors. An aggressive firm may wish to allocate more monies to the advertising and promotions budget—a strategy that is not possible with a percentage of sales method unless the manager is willing to deviate from industry standards.

The percentage of sales method of budgeting may result in severe misappropriation of funds. If advertising and promotion have a role to perform in marketing a product, then allocating more monies to advertising will, as shown in the S-shaped curve, generate incremental sales (to a point). If products with low sales have smaller promotion budgets, this will hinder sales progress. At the other extreme, very successful products may have an excess budget, some of which may be better appropriated elsewhere.

The percentage of sales method is also difficult to employ for new product introductions (see Exhibit 9–11 on page 250). If no sales histories are available, there is no basis for establishing the budget. Projections of future sales may be difficult, particularly if the product is highly innovative and/or has fluctuating sales patterns.

Finally, if the budget is contingent on sales, decreases in sales will lead to decreases in budgets when they most need to be increased. Continuing to cut the advertising and promotion budgets may just add impetus to the downward sales trend. On the other hand, some of the more successful companies have allocated additional funds during hard times or downturns in the cycle of sales. Companies that maintain or increase their ad expenditures during recessions achieve increased visibility and higher growth in both sales and market share (compared to those that reduce advertising outlays). For example, Sunkist can attribute at least some of its success in establishing and maintaining its strong image to the fact that it has maintained consistent levels of advertising expenditures over 80 years, despite recessions.[8]

While the percentage of future sales method has been proposed as a remedy for some of the problems discussed here, the reality is that problems with forecasting, cyclical growth, and uncontrollable factors limit its effectiveness.

Competitive parity

If you asked marketing managers if they ever set their advertising and promotions budgets based on what their competitors allocated, they probably would deny it. Yet if you examined the advertising expenditures of these companies, both as a percentage of sales and in respect to the media where they are allocated, you would see little variation in the percentage of sales figures for firms within a given industry. Such results do not happen by chance alone. Companies that provide competitive advertising information, trade associations, and other advertising industry periodicals are sources for competitors' expenditures. Larger corporations often subscribe to services such as LNA/Arbitron (Exhibit 9–12), which estimates the top 1,000 companies' advertising in 10 media and in total. Smaller companies often use a **clipping service**, which clips competitors' ads from local print media, allowing the company to work backwards to determine the cumulative costs of the ads placed.

In the **competitive parity method**, managers establish budget amounts by matching the percentage sales expenditures of the competition. The argument is that setting budgets in this fashion takes advantage of the collective wisdom of the industry. It also takes the competition into consideration, which leads to stability in the marketplace by minimizing marketing warfare. If companies know that competitors are unlikely to match their increases in promotional spending, they are less likely to take an aggressive posture to attempt to gain market share. This minimizes unusual or unrealistic ad expenditures.

The competitive parity method has a number of disadvantages, however. For one, it ignores the fact that advertising and promotions are designed to accomplish specific objectives by addressing certain problems and opportunities. Second, it assumes that because firms have similar expenditures, their programs will be equally effective. This assumption ignores the contributions of creative executions and/or media allocations, as well as the success or failure of various promotions. Further, it ignores possible advantages of the firm itself; some firms simply make better products than others.

Percentage of sales budgeting is difficult to use for new product introductions

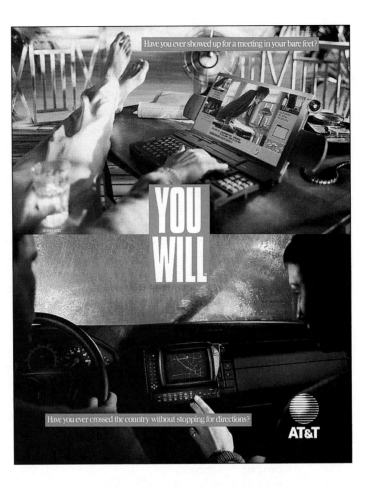

Also, there is no guarantee the competition will continue to pursue their existing strategies. Since competitive parity figures are determined by examination of competitors' previous years' promotional expenditures (short of corporate espionage), changes in market emphasis and/or spending may not be recognized until the competition has already established an advantage. Further, there is no guarantee the competition will not increase or decrease its own expenditures, regardless of what other companies do. Finally, promotional wars may not be avoided. Coke versus Pepsi and Anheuser-Busch versus Miller have been notorious for their spending wars, each responding to the others' increased outlays.

In summary, few firms employ the competitive parity method as a sole means of establishing the promotional budget. This method is typically used in conjunction with the percentage of sales or other methods. It is never wise to ignore the competition. Managers must always be aware of what competitors are doing, but they should not just emulate them in setting goals and developing strategies.

Return on investment (ROI)

In the percentage of sales method, sales dictate the level of advertising appropriations. But advertising causes sales. In the marginal analysis and S-shaped curve approaches, incremental investments in advertising and promotions lead to increases in sales. The key word here is *investment*. In the **ROI budgeting method**, advertising and promotions are considered investments, like plant and equipment. Thus, the budgetary appropriation (investment) leads to certain returns. Like other aspects of the firm's efforts, advertising and promotion are expected to earn a certain return.

While the ROI method looks good on paper, the reality is that it is rarely possible to assess the returns provided by the promotional effort—at least as long as sales continue to

@ **EXHIBIT 9–12** The leading national advertisers 1989–1993 ranked by 1993 advertising expenditures in magazines, Sunday magazines, newspapers, outdoor, network TV, spot TV, syndicated TV, cable TV, network radio, and national spot radio

Company	1993	1992	1991	1990	1989
1. Procter & Gamble Co.	1,299,926,200	1,174,705,700	1,166,454,500	1,224,263,600	869,429,300
2. General Motors Corp.	1,099,349,100	947,877,100	1,056,501,200	1,100,929,200	959,639,500
3. Philip Morris Companies Inc.	999,744,900	1,090,793,700	1,110,355,700	1,199,799,400	1,081,920,300
4. Ford Motor Co.	722,759,500	601,780,900	517,700,200	471,335,200	447,266,000
5. Pepsico Inc.	633,091,900	555,651,800	542,040,400	546,964,400	473,042,300
6. Sears Roebuck & Co.	594,671,400	545,991,400	462,340,000	590,765,500	525,336,500
7. Chrysler Corp.	585,343,700	567,330,700	414,781,100	412,717,300	375,638,300
8. American Telephone & Telegraph Co.	481,443,400	378,901,900	391,693,500	505,433,300	353,963,200
9. Toyota Motor Corp.	469,516,800	440,091,200	442,511,900	406,538,300	277,146,300
10. Unilever NV	461,033,800	420,937,600	371,396,500	355,852,800	376,462,300

be the basis for evaluation. Thus, while managers are certain to ask how much return they are getting for such expenditures, the question remains unanswered, and ROI remains a virtually unused method of budgeting.

Summary of top-down budgeting methods

You are probably asking yourself why we even discussed these budgeting methods if they are not recommended for use or have severe disadvantages that limit their effectiveness. But you must understand the various methods used in order to recognize their limitations, especially since these flawed methods are commonly employed by marketers, as demonstrated in Exhibit 9-13. Tradition and top management's desire for control are probably the major reasons why top-down methods continue to be popular.

As shown in Exhibit 9–13, the use of percentage of sales methods remains high, particularly that based on anticipated sales. Fortunately, both the affordable and arbitrary methods appear to be on the decrease, as do quantitative methods. On the increase is a method not yet discussed, the objective and task method. Let us now turn our discussion to this method, reserving quantitative models for later.

Build-Up Approaches

The major flaw associated with the top-down methods is that these judgmental approaches lead to predetermined budget appropriations often not linked to objectives and the strategies designed to accomplish them. A more effective budgeting strategy would be to consider the firm's communications objectives and budget what is deemed necessary to attain these goals. The promotional planning model in Chapter 1 shows the budget decision as an interactive process, with the communications objectives on one hand and the promotional mix alternatives on the other. The idea is to budget so these promotional mix strategies can be implemented to achieve the stated objectives.

Objective and task method

It is important that objective setting and budgeting go hand in hand rather than sequentially. It is difficult to establish a budget without specific objectives in mind, and setting objectives without regard to how much money is available makes no sense. For example, a company may wish to create awareness among X percent of its target market. A minimal budget amount will be required to accomplish this goal, and the firm must be willing to spend this amount.

The **objective and task method** of budget setting uses a **build-up approach** consisting of three steps: 1) defining the communications objectives to be accomplished, 2) determining the specific strategies and tasks needed to attain these objectives, and 3) estimating the costs associated with performance of these strategies and tasks. The total budget is based on the accumulation of these costs.

@ **EXHIBIT 9–13**

Comparison of general methods used by consumer advertisers to set advertising budgets

Method	Percentage of Respondents Using Each Method		
	San Augustine and Foley (1975)	**Patti and Blasko (1981)**	**Lancaster and Stern (1983)**
Quantitative methods	4	51	20
Objective and task	12	63	80
Percentage anticipated sales	52	53	53
Unit anticipated sales	12	22	28
Percentage past sales	16	20	20
Unit past sales	12	n.a.	15
Affordable	28	20	13
Arbitrary	16	4	n.a.
Match competitors	n.a.	24	25
Outspend competitors	n.a.	n.a.	8
Share of voice/market	n.a.	n.a.	5
Previous budget	n.a.	n.a.	3
Others	20	n.a.	12

n.a. = not applicable
Note: Totals exceed 100% due to multiple responses and rounding.

Implementing the objective and task approach is somewhat more involved. The manager must monitor this process throughout and change strategies depending on how well objectives are attained. As shown in Exhibit 9–14, this process involves several steps.

1. *Isolate objectives.* When the promotional planning model is presented, a company will have two sets of objectives to accomplish—the marketing objectives for the product and the communications objectives. After the former are established, the task involves determining what specific communications objectives will be designed to accomplish these goals. Communications objectives must be specific, attainable, and measurable, as well as time limited.

2. *Determine tasks required.* A number of elements are involved in the strategic plan designed to attain the objectives established. (These strategies constitute the remaining chapters in this text.) These tasks may include advertising in various media, sales promotions, and/or other elements of the promotional mix, each with its own role to perform.

3. *Estimate required expenditures.* Build-up analysis requires determining the estimated costs associated with the tasks developed in the previous step. For example, it involves costs for developing awareness through advertising, trial through sampling, and so forth.

4. *Monitor.* As you will see in Chapter 20 on measuring effectiveness, there are ways to determine how well one is attaining established objectives. Performance should be monitored and evaluated in light of the budget appropriated.

5. *Reevaluate objectives.* Once specific objectives have been attained, monies may be better spent on new goals. Thus, if one has achieved the level of consumer awareness sought, the budget should be altered to stress a higher-order objective such as evaluation or trial.

The major advantage of the objective and task method is that the budget is driven by the objectives to be attained. The managers closest to the marketing effort will have input and specific strategies that will be considered in the budget-setting process.

The major disadvantage of this method is the difficulty of determining which tasks will be required and the costs associated with each. For example, specifically what tasks are needed to attain awareness among 50 percent of the target market? How much will it cost to perform these tasks? While these decisions are easier to determine for certain objectives—for example, estimating the costs of sampling required to stimulate trial in a

@ **EXHIBIT 9–14**

The objective and task
method

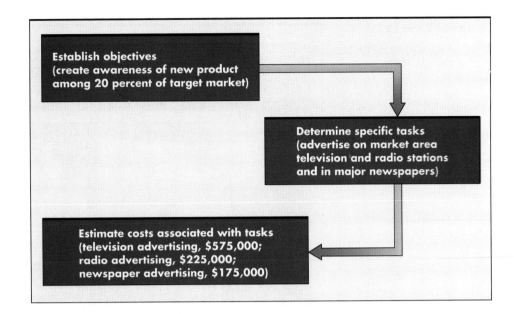

defined market area—it is not always possible to know exactly what is required and/or
how much it will cost to complete the job. This process is easier if there is past experience
to use as a guide, with either the existing product or a similar one in the same product
category. But it is especially difficult for new product introductions. As a result, budget
setting using this method is not as easy to perform or as stable as some of the methods
discussed earlier. Given this disadvantage, many marketing managers have stayed with
those top-down approaches for setting the total expenditure amount.

The objective and task method offers advantages over methods discussed earlier, but is
more difficult to implement when there is no track record for the product. The following
section addresses the problem of budgeting for new product introductions.

Payout planning

The first months of a new product's introduction typically require heavier than normal
advertising and promotion appropriations to stimulate higher levels of awareness and
subsequent trial. After studying more than 40 years of Nielsen figures, James O. Peckham
estimated that the average share of advertising to sales ratio necessary to launch a new
product successfully is approximately 1.5:2.0.[9] This means that a new entry should be
spending at approximately twice the desired market share, as shown in the two examples
in Exhibit 9–15. For example, in the food industry, brand 101 gained a 12.6 percent
market share by spending 34 percent of the total advertising dollars in this category.
Likewise, brand 401 in the toiletry industry had a 30 percent share of advertising dollars
to gain 19.5 percent of sales.

To determine how much to spend, marketers often develop a **payout plan** that determines the investment value of the advertising and promotion appropriation. The basic
idea is to project the revenues the product will generate over two to three years, as well
as the costs it will incur. Based on an expected rate of return, the payout plan will assist
in determining how much advertising and promotions expenditures will be necessary
when the return might be expected. A three-year payout plan is shown in Exhibit 9–16.
The product would lose money in year 1, almost break even in year 2, and finally begin
to show substantial profits by the end of year 3.

The advertising and promotion figures are highest in year 1 and decline in years 2
and 3. This appropriation is consistent with Peckham's findings and reflects the additional outlays needed to make as rapid an impact as possible. (Keep in mind that shelf

@ **EXHIBIT 9–15**

Share of advertising/sales relationship (two-year summary)

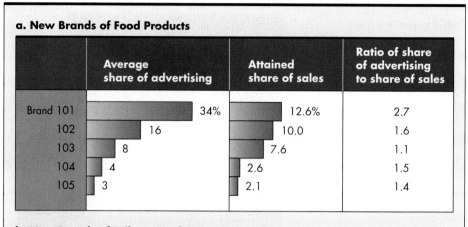

a. New Brands of Food Products

	Average share of advertising	Attained share of sales	Ratio of share of advertising to share of sales
Brand 101	34%	12.6%	2.7
102	16	10.0	1.6
103	8	7.6	1.1
104	4	2.6	1.5
105	3	2.1	1.4

b. New Brands of Toiletry Products

	Average share of advertising	Attained share of sales	Ratio of share of advertising to share of sales
Brand 401	30%	19.5%	1.5
402	25	16.5	1.5
403	20	16.2	1.2
404	12	9.4	1.3
405	16	8.7	1.8
406	19	7.3	2.6
407	14	7.2	1.9
408	10	6.0	1.7
409	7	6.0	1.2
410	6	5.9	1.0
411	10	5.9	1.7
412	6	5.2	1.2

space is limited, and store owners are not likely to wait around for a product to become successful.) The budget also reflects the firm's guidelines for new product expenditures, since companies generally have established deadlines by which the product must begin to show a profit. Finally, keep in mind that building market share may be more difficult than maintaining it—thus the substantial dropoff in expenditures in later years.

In summary, while the payout plan is not always perfect, it does guide the manager in establishing the budget. When used in conjunction with the objective and task method, it provides a much more logical approach to budget setting than the top-down approaches previously discussed.

Quantitative models

Attempts to apply *quantitative models* to budgeting have met with limited success. For the most part, these methods employ **computer simulation models** involving statistical techniques such as multiple regression analysis to determine the relative contribution of the advertising budget to sales. Because of problems associated with these methods, their acceptance has been limited, as demonstrated in the figures reported earlier in Exhibit 9–13. Quantitative models have yet to reach their potential. As computers continue to

@ **EXHIBIT 9–16**

Example of three-year payout plan ($ millions)

	Year 1	Year 2	Year 3
Product sales	15.0	35.50	60.75
Profit contribution (@ $0.50/case)	7.5	17.75	30.38
Advertising/promotions	15.0	10.50	8.50
Profit (loss)	(7.5)	7.25	21.88
Cumulative profit (loss)	(7.5)	(0.25)	21.63

find their way into the advertising domain, better models may be forthcoming. Specific discussion of these models is beyond the scope of this text, however. Such methods do have merit but may need more refinement before achieving widespread success.

Summary of Budgeting Methods

There is no universally accepted method of setting a budget figure. Weaknesses in each method may make them unfeasible or inappropriate. As Exhibit 9–13 shows, the use of the objective and task method continues to increase, whereas less sophisticated methods are declining in favor. More advertisers are also employing the payout planning approach. By using these approaches in combination with the percentage of sales methods, these advertisers are likely to arrive at a more useful, accurate budget. For example, many firms now start the budgeting process by establishing the objectives they need to accomplish and then limit the budget by applying a percentage of sales or other method to decide whether or not it is affordable. Competitors' budgets may also influence this decision.

@ **ALLOCATING THE BUDGET**

Once the budget has been appropriated, the next step is to allocate it. The allocation decision involves determining which markets, products, and/or promotional elements will receive which amounts of the funds appropriated.

Allocating to Advertising and Promotion Elements

As noted earlier, advertisers have begun to shift some of their budget dollars away from traditional advertising media and into sales promotions targeted at both the consumer and the trade. Direct marketing and other promotional tools are also receiving increased attention and competing for more of the promotional budget (see Exhibit 9–17). The advantage of more target selectivity has led to an increased emphasis on direct marketing, while a variety of new media (which will be discussed in Chapter 15) have given marketers new ways to reach prospective customers. Rapidly rising media costs, the ability of sales promotions to motivate trial, maturing of the product and/or brand, and the need for more aggressive promotional tools have also led to shifts in strategy.[10] (We will discuss consumer and trade promotions and the reasons for some of these changes in Chapter 17.)

Some marketers have also used the allocation decision to stretch the advertising dollar and get more impact from the same amount of money. For example, General Motors recently reevaluated its advertising and promotional expenditures and made significant shifts in allocations by both media and product.[11] Other companies have reevaluated as well, as demonstrated in IMC Perspective 9–2.

Client/Agency Policies

Another factor that may influence budget allocation is the individual policy of the company or the advertising agency. The agency may discourage the allocation of monies to sales promotion, preferring to spend them on the advertising area. The agency position is that promotional monies are harder to track in terms of effectiveness and may be used improperly if not under its control. (In many cases commissions are not made on this area, and this fact may contribute to the agency's reluctance.)[12]

The orientation of the agency or the firm may also directly influence where monies are spent. Many ad agencies are managed by officers who have ascended through the creative ranks and are inclined to emphasize the creative budget. Others may have preferences for

@ **EXHIBIT 9–17**

Companies like Edible
Advertising offer a novel
way to promote a product
or company

specific media. For example, BBDO Worldwide, one of the largest advertising agencies in the United States, has positioned itself as an expert in cable television programming and often spends more client money in this medium. Both the agency and the client may favor certain aspects of the promotional program, perhaps based on past successes, that will influence to a large degree where dollars are spent.

Market Size

While the budget should be allocated according to the specific promotional tools necessary to accomplish the stated objectives, the *size* of the market will affect the decision. In smaller markets, it is often easier and less expensive to reach the target market. Too much of an expenditure in these markets will lead to saturation and a lack of effective spending. In larger markets, the target group may be more dispersed and thus more expensive to reach. Think about the cost of purchasing media in Chicago or New York City versus a smaller market like Columbus, Ohio, or Birmingham, Alabama. The former would be much more costly and would require a higher budget appropriation.

Market Potential

For a variety of reasons, some markets hold more potential than others. Marketers of snow skis would find greater returns on their expenditures in Denver, Colorado, than in Fort Lauderdale, Florida. Imported Mexican beers sell better in the border states (Texas, Arizona, California) than in the Midwest. A disproportionate number of imported cars are sold in California and New England. When particular markets hold higher potential, the marketing manager may decide to allocate additional monies to them. (Keep in mind that just because a market does not have high sales does not mean it should be ignored. The key is *potential*—and a market with low sales but high potential may be a candidate for additional appropriations.)

There are several methods for estimating marketing potential. Many marketers conduct research studies to forecast demand and/or use secondary sources of information such as those provided by government agencies or syndicated services like Dun & Bradstreet, A. C. Nielsen, and Audits and Surveys. One source for consumer goods information is the *Survey of Buying Power*, published annually by *Sales & Marketing Management* magazine. The survey contains population, income, and retail sales data for states, counties,

IMC Perspective 9-2
Sometimes It Doesn't Pay to Advertise

The 1980s trend of selling health care in the same way as consumer products has come to an abrupt end. After reaching its peak of $2.1 billion in 1991, promotional spending by hospitals dropped by 24 percent in 1992, as budgets were severely slashed or completely abandoned.

Why the switch? Many hospital marketing managers have concluded that hospitals just can't be sold like other consumer services. For one thing, it is estimated that in as many as 70 percent of hospital admissions, the hospital choice is made by the doctor, not the patient. Affiliation with a health care plan and convenience account for much of the choice in the remaining decisions. Advertising, it seems, just doesn't have an impact—at least, not all advertising.

There are some exceptions:

* Doctors Hospital in Columbus, Georgia, ran a TV and radio ad campaign that included a wind-up toy to promote its inpatient mental health program. Psychiatric admissions rose by 27 percent.
* Denton Medical Center in Denton, Texas, promoted Club Mom to attract maternity patients for two years. The promotion included giveaways like calendars, baby bottle holders, and discount coupons, and was considered quite a success.
* Sacramento's Sutter Health Group and Sentara Health Systems of Norfolk, Virginia, have found success by investing in sophisticated databases, while the University of Chicago has improved its success rate by more effective ad scheduling.

So maybe the real answer is that advertising and promotions can work for health care providers. They may just have to employ more integrated strategies!

Source: Christopher Palmeri and Terzah Ewing, "When It Doesn't Pay to Advertise," *Forbes*, Dec. 20, 1993, pp. 234–36.

metropolitan statistical areas, and cities in the United States and Canada with populations of 40,000 or more.

Market Share Goals

Two recent studies in the *Harvard Business Review* discussed advertising spending with the goal of maintaining and increasing market share.[13] John Jones compared the brand's share of market with its share of advertising voice (the total value of the main media exposure in the product category). Jones classified the brands as "profit taking brands, or underspenders" and "investment brands, those whose share of voice is clearly above their share of market." His study indicated that for those brands with small market shares, profit takers are in the minority; however, as the brands increase their market share, nearly three out of five have a proportionately smaller share of voice.

Jones notes that three factors can be cited to explain this change. First, new brands generally receive higher than average advertising support. Second, older, more mature brands are often "milked"—that is, when they reach the maturity stage, advertising support is reduced. Third, there's an advertising economy of scale whereby advertising works harder for well-established brands, so a lower expenditure is required. Jones concludes that for larger brands, it may be possible to reduce advertising expenditures and still maintain market share. Smaller brands, on the other hand, have to continue to maintain a large share of voice.

James Schroer addressed the advertising budget in a situation where the marketer wishes to increase market share. His analysis suggests that marketers should:

* Segment markets, focusing on those markets where competition is weak and/or underspending instead of on a national advertising effort.

@ **EXHIBIT 9–18**

The share of voice (SOV) effect and ad spending: priorities in individual markets

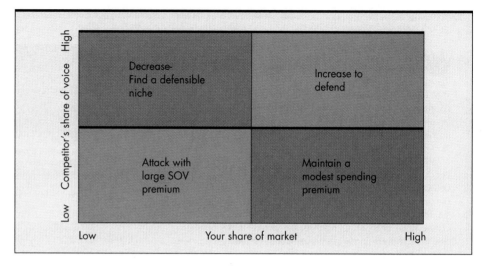

- Determine their competitors' cost positions—how long the competition can continue to spend at the current or increased rate.
- Resist the lure of short-term profits that result from ad budget cuts.
- Consider niching strategies as opposed to long-term wars.

Exhibit 9–18 shows Schroer's suggestions for spending priorities in various markets.

Economies of Scale in Advertising

Some studies have presented evidence that firms and/or brands maintaining a large share of the market have an advantage over smaller competitors and thus can spend less money on advertising and realize a better return.[14] Larger advertisers can maintain advertising shares that are smaller than their market shares because they get better advertising rates, have declining average costs of production, and accrue the advantages of advertising several products jointly. In addition, more favorable time and space positions, cooperation of middle people, and favorable publicity are more likely to accrue. These advantages are known as **economies of scale**.

Reviewing the studies in support of this position and then conducting research over a variety of small-package products, Kent Lancaster found that this situation did not hold true and that in fact larger brand share products might actually be at a disadvantage.[15] His results indicated that leading brands spend an average of 2.5 percentage points *more* than their brand share on advertising. More specifically, his study concluded:

1. There is no evidence that larger firms can support their brands with lower relative advertising costs than smaller firms.
2. There is no evidence that the leading brand in a product group enjoys lower advertising costs per sales dollar than do other brands.
3. There is no evidence of a static relationship between advertising costs per dollar of sales and the size of the advertiser.

The results of this and other studies suggest there are really no **economies of scale** to be accrued from the size of the firm or the market share of the brand.[16]

Organizational Characteristics

In a review of the literature on how allocation decisions are made between advertising and sales promotion, George Low and Jakki Mohr concluded that organizational factors play an important role in determining how communications dollars are spent.[17] The authors note that the following factors influence the allocation decision. These factors vary from one organization to another, and each influences the relative amounts assigned to advertising and promotion.

- The organization's structure—centralized versus decentralized, formalization, and complexity.
- Power and politics in the organizational hierarchy.
- The use of expert opinions (for example, consultants).
- Characteristics of the decision maker (preferences and experience).
- Approval and negotiation channels.
- Pressure on senior managers to arrive at the optimal budget.

One example of how these factors might influence allocations relates to the level of interaction between marketing and other functional departments, such as accounting and operations. The authors note that the relative importance of advertising versus sales promotion might vary from department to department. Accountants, being dollars-and-cents minded, would argue for the sales impact of promotions, while operations would argue against sales promotions because the sudden surges in demand that might result would throw off production schedules. The marketing department might be influenced by the thinking of either of these groups in making its decision.

The use of outside consultants to provide expert opinions might also affect the allocation decision. Trade journals, academic journals, and even books might also be valuable inputs into the decision maker's thinking. In sum, it seems obvious that many factors must be taken into account in the budget allocation decision. Market size and potential, specific objectives sought, and previous company and/or agency policies and preferences all influence this decision.

@ SUMMARY

As you have probably concluded, the budget decision is not typically based on supporting experiences or strong theoretical foundations. Nor is it one of the more soundly established elements of the promotional program. The major problem with the budgeting methods used now is that they are not based on a sound theoretical approach. Economic models are limited, they often try to demonstrate the effects on sales directly, and they ignore other elements of the marketing mix. Some of the methods discussed have no theoretical basis and ignore the roles advertising and promotion are meant to perform.

One possible way to improve the budget appropriation is to tie the measures of effectiveness to communications objectives rather than to the broader-based marketing objectives. Using the objective and task approach with com-

munications objectives may not be the ultimate solution to the budgeting problem, but it is an improvement over the top-down methods.

Marketers often find it advantageous to employ a combination of methods. Some companies establish the dollar amount of the budget by using a percentage of sales method, then allocate these monies by employing an objective and task approach. Others combine payout planning and objective and task approaches.

As with budget determination, managers must consider a number of factors when allocating advertising and promotions dollars. Market size and potential, agency policies, and the preferences of management itself may influence the allocation decision.

@ KEY TERMS

@ DISCUSSION QUESTIONS

1. Explain the difference between investing in advertising and spending. Cite examples of companies that have successfully invested.

2. Compare the S-shaped response curve and the concave-downward sales response models. What types of products and/or services are most likely to be characterized by each?

3. Discuss how you would explain to a small business owner why he or she needs to budget a larger amount to advertising and promotion. Base your argument on the S-shaped response function.

4. Explain the difference between top-down and bottom-up approaches to budget setting. Which is likely to be more effective?

5. Discuss the major strengths of the percentage-of-sales budgeting method.

6. Describe the five steps involved in the objective and task method of budget setting.

7. Discuss the strategies recommended by Schroer for brands pursuing a growing market share.

8. What factors may influence the budget allocation decision? Give an example of each.

9. Some advertisers believe economies of scale are accrued in the advertising process. Discuss their reasons for taking this position. Does research evidence support it?

10. What are some possible reasons why the use of quantitative models in the budgeting process is declining?

The Subaru Legacy

Weld a peace sign to the hood and make believe you're driving a Mercedes that gets really great gas mileage.

THE BRAZEN audacity. To compare a Subaru® Legacy™ to one of Germany's finest and most-revered automobiles.

Hey, why not. They both are designed to do the same thing. Transport people and their stuff from point A to point B. And they both perform that basic automotive function effectively and comfortably.

For example, the Legacy LSi Sedan, which costs many thousands less than the cheapest Mercedes, offers most of the amenities you'd only expect from a fine, absurdly priced luxury car:

Soft grain leather seats. All-Wheel Drive. Compact disc player. Moonroof. Driver's-side air bag. The 4-Channel Anti-Lock Braking System which monitors each wheel to help prevent the car from locking up during emergency stops. And the Legacy is also blessed

Subaru Legacy LSi

with numerous other engineering features which translate into the type of durability Subaru is famous for.

(Important selling point — 93% of all Subaru cars registered in the last 10 years are still on the road and running today.¹)

Now, if you've read this far, you'd probably like a second opinion about the Legacy. Alright, here's one from *Car and Driver:* "The Subaru Legacy is the nicest driving, least expensive, and best equipped 4-wheel drive sedan on the market."²

We repeat — nicest driving, least expensive, best equipped.

So if you're into haughty status symbols, go into the closet and grab that medallion off that ancient Nehru jacket and affix it to the hood. Or, then again, with all the money you'll be saving on your new Legacy you could just imagine you're driving the world's peppiest, most elegantly styled Brink's truck.

Subaru. What to drive.™

¹ Based on R.L. Polk & Co., registration statistics. ² May, 1990. For additional information, 1-800-284-8584. © Subaru of America, 1991.

Chapter **10**

Creative Strategy: Planning and Development

Chapter Objectives

● To discuss what is meant by advertising creativity and examine the role of creative strategy in advertising.

● To examine creative strategy development and the roles of various client and agency personnel involved in it.

● To examine the process that guides the creation of advertising messages and the various research inputs into the stages of the creative process.

● To examine various approaches used for determining major selling ideas that form the basis of an advertising campaign.

Making the Message Clear

With heightened competition in nearly every market, finding a clear advertising message is more important than ever for marketers. Recently, however, many advertisers appear to be having difficulty coming up with ad campaigns that communicate clearly with consumers and can move the sales needle. There were more than the usual number of failed campaigns in 1993, leading many advertisers to change ad agencies in desperate pursuit of effective advertising.

Subaru of America put the brakes on the two-year-old "what to drive" campaign developed by the Wieden & Kennedy agency, which is known for its outstanding creative work for companies such as Nike. The campaign tried to attract a broader audience, including women, by focusing on the utilitarian features of a Subaru while poking fun at those who view a car as a status symbol. Critics argued that Subaru strayed too far from its once successful message, "Inexpensive. And built to stay that way."

Coca-Cola scrapped its "taste it all" and the corollary, "one awesome calorie" campaign after just seven months. It was hoped that the "taste it all" slogan, which served as the main lyric in a new Diet Coke jingle and was prominently shown on cans and bottles, would become the basis for a global campaign for the brand. Some marketing experts argue that Coca-Cola made the classic mistake of going after change for change's sake. Diet Coke had used "just for the taste of it" since the brand was introduced in 1982 but the company and its agency, Lintas: New York, got restless with the same message. Coca-Cola also got restless with Lintas; the agency lost the U.S. portion of the account to Lowe & Partners, who have come up with a new campaign theme, "this is refreshment!"

Critics say that the message was also not coming through clearly in campaigns for American Express Co. and American Telephone & Telegraph (AT&T). The American Express ads feature smart-aleck comedian Jerry Seinfeld using his cutting-edge humor in ads that talk about the nerve of a salesman choosing a customer's tie or show him designing zany membership applications. While he does tick off the advantages of an American Express card in the ads, some feel the message is lost in lame attempts at humor. American Express defends the ads, noting that Seinfeld appeals to the younger audience the company is trying to target with the campaign.

In early 1993, AT&T began advertising its long distance consumer discount program called the "i plan" in response to competition from MCI's "friends & family" and Sprint's "be there" campaigns. The commercials, which relied on a number of high-tech gimmicks and featured the voice of actor Tom Selleck, were criticized for not explaining the program clearly. AT&T scrapped the campaign in December 1993—along with McCann-Erickson, the agency that created it—in favor of new sentimental ads using "the real you coming through" slogan.

Why are so many campaigns running into problems? The president of Mapes & Ross, a communications research firm, notes, "We're in a bad situation where clients want their ad agencies to be different just to be different without answering a fundamental question for advertising: Is the message clear?" The president of Creative Focus, an advertising consulting firm, faults agencies for focusing too much on the artistic quality of their work: "There is so much emphasis on the creative aspect of the ads, sort of 'Aren't we clever?' that the message is lost."

Many advertisers will continue to ask their agencies for clever ads that can break through the clutter and grab consumers' attention, However, Lee Weinblatt, chair of the Pretesting Co., argues that advertisers will be well served if they follow a simple rule: Speak to the real needs of the people. "Please, don't tell me about middle-aged lawyers who can climb mountains."

Source: Kevin Goldman, "The Lead Balloon Campaigns of 1993," *The Wall Street Journal*, Dec. 28, 1993, pp. B1, 8; Kevin Goldman, "The Message, Clever as It May Be, Is Lost in a Number of High-Profile Campaigns," *The Wall Street Journal*, July 27, 1993, pp. B1, 8.

As the opening vignette shows, one of the most important components of an integrated marketing communications program is the advertising message. While the fundamental role of an advertising message is to communicate information, it does much more. The commercials we watch on TV or hear on radio and the print ads we see in magazines and newspapers are a source of entertainment, motivation, fascination, fantasy, and sometimes irritation as well as information. Ads and commercials appeal to, and often create or shape, consumers' problems, desires, and goals. From the marketer's perspective, the advertising message is a way to tell consumers how the product or service can solve a problem or help satisfy desires or achieve goals. Advertising can also be used to create images or associations and position a brand in the consumer's mind as well as transform the experience of buying and/or using a product or service. Many consumers who have never driven or even ridden in a BMW perceive it as "the ultimate driving machine." Many people feel good about sending Hallmark greeting cards because they have internalized the company's advertising theme, "when you care enough to send the very best" (Exhibit 10–1).

One need only watch an evening of commercials or peruse a few magazines to realize there are myriad ways to convey an advertising message. Underlying all of these messages, however, are a **creative strategy** that involves determining what the advertising message will say or communicate and **creative tactics** dealing with how the message strategy will be executed. In this chapter, we focus on advertising creative strategy. We consider what is meant by creativity, particularly as it relates to advertising, and examine a well-known approach to creativity in advertising.

We also examine the creative strategy development process and various approaches to determining the *big idea* that will be used as the central theme of the advertising campaign and translated into attention-getting, distinctive, and memorable messages. Creative specialists are finding it more and more difficult to come up with big ideas that will break through the clutter and still satisfy the concerns of their risk-averse clients. Yet their clients are continually challenging them to find the creative message that will strike a responsive chord with their target audience.

@ **EXHIBIT 10–1**

Excellent advertising helps make consumers feel good about sending Hallmark cards

Some of you may not be directly involved in the design and creation of advertisements; you may choose to work in another agency department or on the client side of the business. However, because creative strategy is often so crucial to the success of the firm's promotional effort, everyone involved in the promotional process should understand the creative strategy and tactics that underlie the development of advertising campaigns and messages, as well as the creative options available to the advertiser. Also, individuals on the client side as well as agency people outside the creative department must work with the creative specialists in developing the advertising campaign, implementing it, and evaluating its effectiveness. Thus, marketing and product managers, account representatives, researchers, and media personnel must appreciate the creative process and develop a productive relationship with creative personnel.

THE IMPORTANCE OF CREATIVITY IN ADVERTISING

For many students, as well as many advertising and marketing practitioners, the most interesting aspect of advertising is the creative side. We have all at one time or another been intrigued by an ad and admired the creative insight that went into it. A great ad is a joy to behold and often an epic to create, as the cost of producing television commercials often can exceed $1 million. Many companies see this as money well spent. They realize the manner in which the advertising message is developed and executed is often critical to the success of the promotional program, which in turn can influence the effectiveness of the entire marketing program. Procter & Gamble, Anheuser-Busch, Coca-Cola, Pepsi-Cola, Nike, McDonald's, and many other companies spend millions of dollars each year to produce advertising messages and hundreds of millions more to purchase media time and space to run these ads. While these companies make excellent products, they realize creative advertising is also an important part of their marketing success.

Good creative strategy and execution can often be central to determining the success of a product or service or reversing the fortunes of a struggling brand. Conversely, an advertising campaign that is poorly conceived or executed can be a liability. Many companies have solid marketing and promotional plans and spend substantial amounts of money on advertising, yet have difficulty coming up with a creative campaign that will differentiate them from their competitors. For example, Burger King changed its advertising campaign theme 16 times in the past 18 years and changed agencies 5 times in search of an advertising approach that would give the chain a strong identity in the fast-food market (Exhibit 10–2). The chain has seen its market share drop over the past several years and its franchisees have been unhappy with the company's inability to come up with an effective campaign.[1]

Just because an ad or commercial is creative or popular does not mean it will increase sales or revive a declining brand. Many ads have won awards for creativity but failed to

EXHIBIT 10–2   Hungry for a winning campaign

Burger King's ad path, from "Have it your way" to "BK Tee Vee"

- Burger King dismisses BBDO, creator of its most famous slogan, "Have it your way," and hires J. Walter Thompson, New York (Aug. 1976)
- "America loves burgers, and we're America's Burger King" (Nov. 1977–Feb. 1978)
- "Who's got the best darn burger?" (Feb. 1978–Jan. 1980)
- "Make it special. Make it Burger King." (Jan. 1980–Jan. 1982)
- "Aren't you hungry for Burger King now?" (Jan. 1982–Sept. 1982)
- "Battle of the burgers" (Sept. 1982–March 1983)
- "Broiling vs. frying" campaign tied to "Aren't you hungry?" (March 1983–Sept. 1983)
- "The big switch" campaign (Sept. 1983–Nov. 1985)
- "Search for Herb" campaign (Nov. 1985–June 1986)
- "This is a Burger King town" (June 1986–Jan. 1987)
- "The best food for fast times" (Jan. 1987–Oct. 1987)
- BK hires NW Ayer, New York, and fires JWT (Oct. 1987)
- "We do it like you'd do it" (April 1988–May 1989)
- BK hires D'Arcy Masius Benton & Bowles, and Saatchi & Saatchi, New York, firing Ayer (May 1989)
- "Sometimes you gotta break the rules" (Oct. 1989–April 1991)
- "Your way. Right away."(April 1991–Oct. 1992)
- "BK Tee Vee: I love this place!" (Oct. 1992–present)

Source: Jeanne Whalen, "BK Caters to Franchisees with New Review," *Advertising Age*, Oct. 25,1993, p. 3.

 **EXHIBIT   10–3**   Alka Seltzer's creative advertising was not effective in reversing the brand's sales decline

increase sales. In some instances, the failures to generate sales has cost the agency the account. For example, many advertising people believe some of the best ads of all time were those done for Alka-Seltzer a number of years ago, including the classic "Mama Mia! That's a spicy meatball!" and "I can't believe I ate the whole thing" (Exhibit 10–3). While the commercials won numerous creative awards, Alka-Seltzer sales still declined and the agencies lost the account.[2]

Many advertising and marketing people have become ambivalent toward, and in some cases even critical of, advertising awards.[3] They argue that agency creative people are often more concerned with creating ads that win awards than ones that sell their clients' products. Other advertising people believe awards are an appropriate way of recognizing creativity that often does result in effective advertising. Global Perspective 10–1 discussed how the emphasis on creative awards has shifted to the international arena with awards like the Cannes Gold Lion Trophies.

As we saw in Chapter 8, the success of an ad campaign cannot always be judged in terms of sales. However, many advertising and marketing personnel, particularly those on the client side, believe advertising must ultimately lead the consumer to purchase the product or service. Finding a balance between creative advertising and effective advertising is difficult. To better understand this dilemma, we turn to the issue of creativity and its role in advertising.

ADVERTISING CREATIVITY

What Is Creativity?

Creativity is probably one of the most commonly used terms in advertising. Ads are often called creative. The people who develop ads and commercials are known as creative types. And advertising agencies develop reputations for their creativity. Perhaps so much attention is focused on the concept of creativity because many people view the specific challenge given to those who develop an advertising message as being creative. It is their

Global Perspective 10–1
Cannes Lions Become Advertising's New Status Symbol

For many years the most coveted prize for creativity in advertising was a Clio award. But in recent years the Clios have lost much of their prestige, particularly after financial problems resulted in cancellation of the 1992 awards ceremony. The Cannes International Advertising Film Festival is now widely considered the most prestigious advertising award competition. And judging by the results of the 1993 competition, U.S. agencies appear to be falling behind their foreign counterparts when it comes to creativity.

Most of the Lion awards were won by agencies and production companies from Britain and Spain, with U.S. shops placing third. British agencies won a total of 20 gold, silver, and bronze Lions. Spanish shops pulled in 19, including five Gold Lions—the most of any country. Three of the five Gold Lions were won by Spain's hottest agency, Casadevall Pedreno of Barcelona. U.S. agencies took away 17 Lions, but they submitted a massive 802 entries (more than the Spanish and British agencies combined). The Grand Prix winner of the festival was produced by a Japanese agency, Hakuhodo Tokyo, for Nissin Food Products of Japan. It featured an animated army of cavemen chasing a gigantic moa, an extinct ostrich-like bird that looks much like a dinosaur, for their dinner. At the edge of a cliff, the bird jumps into the air; the people run underneath it and fall off. A deep voiceover then resonates: "Hungry? Cup Noodles!"

The commercial that received the highest marks from the Cannes jury was produced by little-known Streetsmart Advertising of New York for the Coalition for the Homeless. The spot showed a sobering series of homeless people singing the classic Frank Sinatra song, "New York, New York." However,

since it was for a charity it was ineligible for the Grand Prix award. Other commercials from U.S. agencies that won Gold Lions included a Nike spot by Wieden & Kennedy called "Don Quincy," which featured the Olympic runner performing in a mock opera, and a Lee jeans spot from Fallon McElligott in which an opera-singing man emerges from the shower and begins to sing soprano after zipping up too-tight jeans.

The creative star in Cannes was Tarsem (no last name), a young Indian who directs ads for Spots Films Services International in London. He collected two Gold Lions for a classy Smirnoff vodka ad called "message in a bottle," which shows a ship's waiter negotiating his way through a group of partying passengers while balancing a Smirnoff bottle on a tray. Viewed through the bottle, the scene is transformed into surrealistic images: a woman's hair turns into an octopus's tentacles and a chain around another woman's neck becomes a snake.

One of the most popular entries in the Cannes competition was a humorous spot for Braathens Safe airlines promoting senior citizen discounts and done by the Leo Burnett office in Oslo, Norway. In the "naked lunch" spot, a husband, revved up for a romantic evening with his wife, returns home, undresses, puts a rose in his teeth and bursts into the living room. To his surprise, she is having tea with her parents. The tagline: "Warning: We're flying your in-laws for half price."

While many advertising people are critical of creative awards, the Cannes festival attracted 3,822 entries, so someone must think they are important. One fan is Streetsmart Advertising. For little-known agencies struggling for recognition, the prestige of a Cannes Gold Lion award can attract new business and put them on the map.

Sources: Karoline Durr, "Recession-Scarred Industry Finds Less Glamour, Glitz at Cannes," *The Wall Street Journal*, July 1, 1993, p. B3; Laurel Wentz, "Hakuhodo's Animals Score Cannes Surprise," *Advertising Age*, June 28, 1993, pp. 1, 50.

job to turn all of the information regarding product features and benefits, marketing plans, consumer research, and communication objectives into a creative concept that will bring the advertising message to life. This begs the question: What is meant by *creativity* in advertising?

Different Perspectives on Advertising Creativity

Perspectives on what constitutes creativity in advertising vary. At one extreme are those who argue that advertising is creative only if it sells the product. An advertising message or campaign's impact on sales counts more than whether it is innovative or wins awards. At the other end of the continuum are those who judge the creativity of an ad in terms of its artistic or aesthetic value and originality. They contend creative ads can break through the competitive clutter, grab the consumer's attention, and have some impact.

As you might expect, perspectives on advertising creativity often depend on one's role. A study by Elizabeth Hirschman examined the perceptions of various individuals involved in the creation and production of TV commercials, including management types (product managers and account executives) and creatives (art director, copy writer, commercial director, and producer).[4] She found that product managers and account executives view ads as promotional tools whose primary purpose is to communicate favorable impressions to the marketplace. They believe a commercial should be evaluated in terms of its fulfillment of the client's marketing and communicative objectives. The perspective of those on the creative side was much more self-serving, as Hirschman noted:

> In direct contrast to this client orientation, the art director, copywriter, and commercial director viewed the advertisement as a communication vehicle for promoting their own aesthetic viewpoints and personal career objectives. Both the copywriter and art director made this point explicitly, noting that a desirable commercial from their standpoint was one which communicated their unique creative talents and thereby permitted them to obtain "better" jobs at an increased salary.[5]

In her interviews, Hirschman also found that the product manager was much more risk averse and wanted a more conservative commercial than the creative people, who wanted to maximize the impact of the message.

What constitutes creativity in advertising is probably somewhere between the two extremes. To break through the clutter and make an impression on the target audience, an ad often must be unique and entertaining. As noted in Chapter 6, research has shown that a major determinant of whether a commercial will be successful in changing brand preferences is its "likability," or the viewer's overall reaction.[6] Television commercials and print ads that are well designed and executed and generate emotional responses can create positive feelings that are transferred to the product or service being advertised. Many creative people believe this type of advertising can come about only if they are given considerable latitude in developing advertising messages. But ads that are creative only for the sake of being creative often fail to communicate a relevant or meaningful message that will lead consumers to purchase a product or service.

Everyone involved in planning and developing an advertising campaign must understand the importance of balancing the "it's not creative unless it sells" perspective with the novelty/uniqueness and impact position. Marketing and product managers or account executives must recognize that imposing too many sales- and marketing-oriented communication objectives on the creative team can result in mediocre advertising, which is often ineffective in today's competitive, cluttered media environment. At the same time, the creative specialists must recognize that the goal of advertising is to assist in selling the product or service and good advertising must communicate in a manner that helps the client achieve this goal.

Advertising creativity is the ability to generate fresh, unique, and appropriate ideas that can be used as solutions to communication problems. To be *appropriate* and effective, a creative idea must be relevant to the target audience. Many ad agencies recognize the importance of developing advertising that is creative and different yet communicates relevant information to the target audience. Exhibit 10–4 shows the D'Arcy Masius Benton

@ **EXHIBIT   10–4**   D'Arcy Masius Benton & Bowles' universal advertising standards

---

1. *Does this advertising position the product simply and with un-mistakable clarity?*

    The target audience for the advertised product or service must be able to see and sense in a flash *what* the product is for, *whom* it is for, and *why* they should be interested in it.

    Creating this clear vision of how the product or service fits into their lives is the first job of advertising. Without a simple, clear, focused positioning, no creative work can begin.

2. *Does this advertising bolt the brand to a clinching benefit?*

    Our advertising should be built on the *most compelling and persuasive* consumer benefit—not some unique-but-insignificant peripheral feature.

    Before you worry about how to say it, you must be sure you are saying *the right thing*. If you don't know what the most compelling benefit is, you've got to find out before you do anything else.

3. *Does this advertising contain a Power Idea?*

    The Power Idea is the vehicle that transforms the strategy into a dynamic, creative communications concept. It is the core creative idea that sets the stage for brilliant executions to come. The ideal Power Idea should:

    • Be describable in a simple word, phrase, or sentence without reference to any final execution.
    • Be likely to attract the prospect's attention.
    • Revolve around the clinching benefit.
    • Allow you to brand the advertising.
    • Make it easy for the prospect to vividly experience our client's product or service.

4. *Does this advertising design in Brand Personality?*

    The great brands tend to have something in common: the extra edge of having a Brand Personality. This is something beyond merely identifying what the brand *does* for the consumer; all brands *do* something, but the great brands also *are* something.

    A brand can be whatever its designers want it to be—and it can be so from day one.

5. *Is this advertising unexpected?*

    Why should our clients pay good money to wind up with advertising that looks and sounds like everybody else's in the category? They shouldn't.

We must dare to be different, because sameness is suicide. We can't be outstanding unless we first stand out.

The thing is not to *emulate* the competition but to *annihilate* them.

6. *Is this advertising single-minded?*

    If you have determined the right thing to say and have created a way to say it uncommonly well, why waste time saying anything else?

    If we want people to remember one big thing from a given piece of advertising, let's not make it more difficult than it already is in an overcommunicated world.

    The advertising should be all about that *one big thing*.

7. *Does this advertising reward the prospect?*

    Let's give our audience something that makes it easy—even pleasurable—for our message to penetrate: a tear, a smile, a laugh. An emotional stimulus is that special something that makes them want to see the advertising again and again.

8. *Is this advertising visually arresting?*

    Great advertising you remember—and can play back in your mind—is unusual to look at: compelling, riveting, a nourishing feast for the eyes. If you need a reason to strive for *arresting* work, go no further than Webster: "Catching or holding the attention, thought, or feelings. Gripping. Striking. Interesting."

9. *Does this advertising exhibit painstaking craftsmanship?*

    You want writing that is really *written*. Visuals that are *designed*. Music that is *composed*.

    Lighting, casting, wardrobe, direction—all the components of the *art* of advertising are every bit as important as the *science* of it. It is a sin to nickel-and-dime a great advertising idea to death.

    Why settle for good, when there's great? We should go for the absolute best in concept, design, and execution.

    This is our craft—the work should sparkle.

    "Our creative standards are not a gimmick," Steve emphasizes. "They're not even revolutionary. Instead, they are an explicit articulation of a fundamental refocusing on our company's only reason for being.

    "DMB&B's Universal Advertising Standards are the operating link between our vision today—and its coming reality."

& Bowles agency's universal advertising standards, nine principles that were developed by the agency to guide its creative efforts and help achieve superior creativity consistently. The agency views a creative advertising message as one built around a creative core or power idea and using excellent design and execution to communicate information that interests the target audience.

Advertising creativity is not the exclusive domain of those who work on the creative side of advertising. The nature of the business requires creative thinking from everyone involved in the promotional planning process. Individuals in the agency, such as account executives, media planners, researchers, and attorneys, as well as those on the client side, such as marketing and brand managers, must all seek creative solutions to problems encountered in planning, developing, and executing an advertising campaign. IMC Perspective 10–1 discusses how creative synergy between the media and creative departments as well as with the client is becoming more commonplace.

IMC Perspective 10-1
Media-Driven Creative Strategies

In most companies and ad agencies, the usual approach is to create print ads and TV commercials and then determine the media in which to place them. The task of deciding which ads will run in which media is often assigned to junior media planners and buyers who have little if any input into the planning and execution of creative strategy. But now many agencies and their clients are realizing that synergy between the media and creative departments as well as creative thinking by clients themselves are important in developing a successful ad campaign. A number of advertisers, including Absolut vodka and Coca-Cola, recognize the value of using media-driven creative strategies.

TBWA, the agency for Absolut, developed an advertising campaign that plays off the distinctive shape of the bottle and makes it the hero of the ads by depicting it with visual puns and witty headlines. The campaign's objective has been to build awareness of the brand and make Absolut a "fashionable symbol of smartness and sophistication that consumers would want to be associated with." This goal has been accomplished through outstanding creative execution. Underlying this creativity are a spirit of cooperation between the media and creative departments of TBWA and a unique creative alliance between the agency and Michael Roux, the chair of Carillon Importers (which was the importer of the brand until Sweden's state liquor company sold the marketing rights for Absolut to Seagram Co. in late 1993).

Roux recognized early that the advertising campaign could be carried further by playing on the name Absolut, highlighting the distinctive shape of the bottle, and tailoring the print ads for the magazines or regions where they appear. For example, for New York media, the agency created "Absolut Manhattan," showing Central Park in the shape of a vodka bottle. "Absolut L.A." ads featured a swimming pool shaped like an Absolut bottle. Ads appearing in *Ski* and *Skiing* magazines show ski slopes curving around pine trees formed in the shape of the bottle, with the tagline "Absolut Peak."

Absolut's annual media schedule covers up to 100 magazines, including various consumer and business publications. The creative and media departments work together selecting magazines and deciding on ads that will appeal to the readers of each publication. The creative department is often asked to create media-specific ads to run in a particular publication. The media-driven creative strategy for Absolut has paid off; the brand is the number one imported vodka and ninth most popular liquor brand in the United States.

ABSOLUT PEAK.

Coca-Cola is also finding that the message is the media. Coke, its agency, McCann-Erickson Worldwide, and Hollywood talent shop Creative Artists Agency (CAA) collaborated on a worldwide campaign for the flagship Coke Classic brand that was conceived for and driven by the media in which it runs. CAA developed the overall strategy of tailoring the message to the medium, while McCann is executing the media strategy. The strategy for the campaign is to take advantage of certain types of media programming and create a diverse array of executions different in tone and in demographic and seasonal appeal.

CAA produced more than two dozen ads in many moods and styles for 20 different TV networks. The ads include quick-cutting commercials that air on MTV, wholesome heart-tuggers for adult shows such as "Murder She Wrote," and a spot called Spaceship that imitates "Star Trek: The Next Generation," which is a hit among teenage boys. The new campaign is being used globally. Spots air on MTV Europe, MTV Asia, and CNN in Europe, Asia, and Latin America. The campaign began in early 1993 and has been hailed as Coke's most successful in over a decade.

Sources: Laureen Miles, "Coke's New Campaign: Message Is the Media," *Mediaweek*, Feb. 15, 1993, pp. 1, 3; Valerie H. Free, "Absolut Original," *Marketing Insights*, Summer 1991, pp. 64–72; and Gary Levin, " 'Meddling' in Creative More Welcome," *Advertising Age*, April 9, 1990, pp. S-4, S-8.

PLANNING CREATIVE STRATEGY

The Creative Challenge

Those who work on the creative side of advertising often face a real challenge. They must take all the research, creative briefs, strategy statements, communication objectives, and other input and transform them into an advertising message. Their job is to write copy, design layouts and illustrations, or produce commercials that effectively communicate the central theme on which the campaign is based. Rather than simply stating the features or benefits of a product or service, they must put the advertising message into a form that will engage the audience's interest and make the ads memorable.[7]

The job of the creative team is challenging because every marketing situation is different and each campaign or advertisement may require a different creative approach. Numerous guidelines have been developed for creating effective advertising,[8] but there

@ **EXHIBIT 10–5**

Wieden & Kennedy's belief in taking risks has resulted in creative advertising for clients like Nike

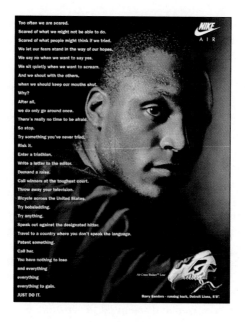

is no magic formula for developing effective advertising. As advertising copywriter Hank Sneiden notes in his book, *Advertising Pure and Simple:*

> Rules lead to dull stereotyped advertising, and they stifle creativity, inspiration, initiative, and progress. The only hard and fast rule that I know of in advertising is that there are no rules. No formulas. No right way. Given the same problem, a dozen creative talents would solve it a dozen different ways. If there were a sure-fire formula for successful advertising, everyone would use it. Then there'd be no need for creative people. We would simply program robots to create our ads and commercials and they'd sell loads of product—to other robots.[9]

Taking a Creative Risk

Many creative people follow proven formulas when creating ads because they are safe. Clients are often *risk averse* and feel uncomfortable with advertising that is too different. Bill Tragos, chair of TBWA, the advertising agency noted for its excellent creative work for Absolut vodka, Evian, and many other clients said, "Very few clients realize that the reason that their work is so bad is that they are the ones who commandeered it and directed it to be that way. I think that at least 50 percent of an agency's successful work resides in the client."[10]

Many creative people say it is important for clients to take some risks if they want breakthrough advertising that gets noticed. One of the fastest-growing agencies is Wieden & Kennedy, best known for its excellent creative work for Nike (Exhibit 10–5). The agency's founders believe a key element to their success has been a steadfast belief in taking risks when most agencies and their clients have been retrenching and becoming more conservative.[11] The agency can develop great advertising partly because clients like Nike are willing to take risks and go along with the agency's priority system, which places the creative work first and the client/agency relationship second. The agency has even terminated relationships with such large clients as Gallo when they interfered too much with the creative process.

Not all companies or agencies agree that advertising has to be risky to be effective, however. Many marketing managers are more comfortable with advertising that simply communicates product or service features and benefits and gives the consumer a reason to buy. They see their advertising campaigns as multimillion-dollar investments whose goal is to sell the product rather than finance the whims of their agency's creative staff. They argue that some creative people have lost sight of advertising's bottom line: Does it sell?

The issue of how much latitude creative people should be given and how much risk the client should be willing to take is ongoing and open to considerable debate.

However, clients and agency personnel generally agree that the ability to develop novel yet appropriate approaches to communicating with the customer makes the creative specialist valuable—and often hard to find.

Creative Personnel

The image of the creative advertising person perpetuated in novels, movies, and TV shows is often one of a freewheeling, free-thinking, eccentric personality. The educational background of creative personnel is often in nonbusiness areas such as art, literature, music, humanities, or journalism, so their interests and perspectives tend to differ from those of managers with a business education or background. Creative personnel tend to be more abstract and less structured, organized, or conventional in their approach to a problem, relying on intuition more often than logic.

Advertising creatives are sometimes stereotyped as odd nonconformists, perhaps because they dress differently and do not always work the conventional 9-to-5 schedule. Of course, from the perspective of the creatives, it is the marketing or brand managers and account executives who are strange. (Many creatives refer to account executives and product managers as "suits" because they often wear coats and ties every day.) In many agencies, you can't tell the creative personnel from the executives by their dress or demeanor. Yet the differences between creative and managerial personalities and perspectives must be recognized and tolerated for creative people to do their best work and to ensure cooperation among all those involved in the advertising process.

Most agencies thrive on creativity, for it is the major component in the product they produce. Thus, they must create an environment that fosters the development of creative thinking and creative advertising. Clients must also understand the differences between the perspectives of the creative personnel and marketing and product managers. While the client has ultimate approval of the advertising, the opinions of creative specialists must be respected when advertising ideas and content are evaluated. (Evaluation of the creative's ideas and work is discussed in more detail in Chapter 11.)

THE CREATIVE PROCESS

Some advertising people say creativity in advertising is best viewed as a process and creative success is most likely when some organized approach is followed. This does not mean there is an infallible blueprint to follow to create effective advertising; as we saw earlier, many advertising people reject attempts to standardize creativity or develop rules. However, most do follow a process when developing an advertisement.

One of the most popular approaches to creativity in advertising was developed by James Webb Young, a former creative vice president at the J. Walter Thompson agency. Young said that "the production of ideas is just as definite a process as the production of Fords; that the production of ideas, too, runs an assembly line; that in this production the mind follows an operative technique which can be learned and controlled; and that its effective use is just as much a matter of practice in the technique as in the effective use of any tool."[12] Young's model of the creative process contains five steps:

1. **Immersion**   Gathering raw material and information through background research and immersing yourself in the problem.
2. **Digestion**   Taking the information, working it over, and wrestling with it in the mind.
3. **Incubation**   Putting the problems out of your conscious mind and turning the information over to the subconscious to do the work.
4. **Illumination**   The birth of an idea—the "Eureka! I have it!" phenomenon.
5. **Reality or verification**   Studying the idea to see if it still looks good or solves the problem, then shaping the idea to practical usefulness.

Young's process of creativity is similar to a four-step approach outlined much earlier by English sociologist Graham Wallas:

1. **Preparation**   Gathering background information needed to solve the problem through research and study.

2. **Incubation**   Getting away and letting ideas develop.
3. **Illumination**   Seeing the light or solution.
4. **Verification**   Refining and polishing the idea and seeing if it is an appropriate solution.

Models of the creative process are valuable to those working in the creative area of advertising, since they offer an organized way to approach an advertising problem. Preparation or gathering of background information is the first step in the creative process. As we saw in earlier chapters, the advertiser and agency start by developing a thorough understanding of the product or service, the target market, and the competition. Attention is also focused on the role of advertising in the marketing and promotional program.

These models do not say much about how this information will be synthesized and used by the creative specialist because this part of the process is unique to the individual. In many ways, it's what sets apart the great creative minds and strategists in advertising. The following section examines how various types of research and information can provide input to the creative process of advertising.

Inputs to the Creative Process: Preparation/ Incubation/Illumination	### Background research Only the most foolish creative person or team would approach an assignment without first learning as much as possible about the client's product or service, the target market, the competition, and any other relevant background information. The creative specialist should also be knowledgeable about general trends, conditions, and developments in the marketplace, as well as research on specific advertising approaches or techniques that might be effective. The creative specialist can acquire background information in numerous ways. Some informal fact-finding techniques have been noted by Sandra Moriarty:

- Reading anything related to the product or market—books, trade publications, general interest articles, research reports, and the like.
- Asking everyone involved with the product for information—designers, engineers, sale personnel, and consumers.
- Listening to what people are talking about. Visits to stores, malls, restaurants, and even the agency cafeteria can be informative. Listening to the client can be particularly valuable, since he or she often knows the product and market best.
- Using the product or service and becoming familiar with it. The more you use a product, the more you know and can say about it.
- Working in and learning about the client's business to understand better the person you're trying to reach.[13]

To assist in the preparation, incubation, and illumination stages, many agencies provide creative people with both general and product-specific preplanning input. **General preplanning input** can include books, periodicals, trade publications, scholarly journals, pictures, and clipping services, which gather and organize magazine and newspaper articles on the product, the market, and the competition, including the latter's ads. This input can also come from research studies conducted by the client, agency, media, or other sources.

Another useful general preplanning input concerns trends, developments, and happenings in the marketplace. Information is available from a variety of sources, including local, state, and federal government organizations, secondary research suppliers, and research reports from various industry trade associations as well as advertising and media organizations. For example, advertising industry groups like the American Association of Advertising Agencies and media organizations like the National Association of Broadcasters (NAB) and Magazine Publishers Association of America (MPA) publish reports and newsletters that provide information on market trends and developments and how they might affect consumers. Those involved in developing creative strategy can also gather relevant and timely information by reading such industry and business publications as *Advertising Age, Brand Week,* and *The Wall Street Journal* (Exhibit 10–6).

◎ EXHIBIT 10–6

Industry publications such as *Advertising Age* are excellent sources of information on market trends

Product/service-specific research

In addition to general background research and preplanning input, creative people also receive **product/service-specific preplanning input**. This information generally comes in the form of specific studies conducted on the product or service, the target audience, or a combination of the two. Quantitative and qualitative consumer research such as attitude studies; market structure and positioning studies such as perceptual mapping and lifestyle research; focus group interviews; demographic and psychographic profiles of users of a particular product, service, or brand are examples of product-specific preplanning input.

Many product- or service-specific studies helpful to the creative team are conducted by the client or the agency. For example, a number of years ago, the BBDO ad agency developed an approach for finding ideas around which creative strategies could be based called **problem detection**.[14] This research technique involves asking consumers familiar with a product (or service) to generate an exhaustive list of things that bother them or problems they encounter when using it. The consumers rate these problems in order of importance and evaluate various brands in terms of their association with each problem. A problem detection study can provide valuable input for product improvements, reformulations, or new products. It can also give the creative people ideas regarding attributes or features to emphasize and guidelines for positioning new or existing brands.

Some agencies conduct psychographic studies annually and construct detailed psychographic or lifestyle profiles of product or service users. DDB Needham Worldwide conducts a large-scale psychographic study each year using a sample of 4,000 U.S. adults. The agency's Life Style Study provides its creative teams with a better understanding of the target audience for whom they are developing ads.

Qualitative research input

Many agencies, particularly larger ones with strong research departments, have their own research programs and specific techniques they use to assist in the development of creative strategy and provide input to the creative process. In addition to the various quantitative research studies, qualitative research techniques such as in-depth interviews or focus groups can provide the creative team with valuable insight at the early stages of the creative process. **Focus groups** are a research method whereby consumers (usually 10 to 12) from the target market are led through a discussion regarding a particular topic. Focus groups give insight as to why and how consumers use a product or service, what is important to them in choosing a particular brand, what they like and don't like about various products or services, and any special needs they might have that aren't being satisfied. A focus group session might also include a discussion of types of ad appeals to use or evaluations of the advertising of various companies.

Focus group interviews bring the creative people and others involved in creative strategy development into contact with the customer. Listening to a focus group gives copywriters, art directors, and other creative specialists a better sense of who the target audience is, what the audience is like, and who the creatives need to write, design, or direct to in creating an advertising message. Focus groups can also be used to evaluate the viability of different creative approaches under consideration and provide insight as to the best direction to pursue.[15] Generally, creative personnel are open to any research or information that will help them understand the client's target market better and assist in generating creative ideas. IMC Perspective 10–2 discusses how the Rubin Postaer & Associates ad agency used focus groups in developing the "A Car Ahead" theme used to launch the redesigned 1994 Honda Accord.

Inputs to the Creative Process: Verification/Revision

The verification/revision stage of the creative process evaluates ideas generated during the illumination stage, rejects inappropriate ones, refines and polishes those that remain, and gives them final expression. Techniques used at this stage include directed focus groups to evaluate creative concepts, ideas, or themes; message communication studies; portfolio tests; and evaluation measures such as viewer reaction profiles.[16]

At this stage of the creative process, members of the target audience may be asked to evaluate rough creative layouts and to indicate what meaning they get from the ad, what they think of its execution, or how they react to a slogan or theme. The creative team can gain insight into how a TV commercial might communicate its message by having members of the target market evaluate the ad in storyboard form. A **storyboard** is a series of drawings used to present the visual plan or layout of a proposed commercial. It contains a series of sketches of key frames or scenes along with a description of the copy or audio portion for each scene (Exhibit 10–7 on page 277).

Testing a commercial in storyboard form can be difficult because storyboards are often too abstract for most consumers to understand. To make the creative layout more realistic and easier to evaluate, the agency may produce an **aniamatic**, a videotape of the storyboard along with an audio soundtrack. Storyboards and aniamatics are useful for research purposes as well as for presenting the creative idea to other agency personnel or to the client for discussion and approval.

At this stage of the process, the creative team is attempting to find the best creative approach or execution style before moving ahead with the campaign themes and going into actual production of the ad. The verification/revision process may include more formal, extensive pretesting of the ad before a final decision is made. Pretesting and other related procedures are examined in detail in Chapter 20.

CREATIVE STRATEGY DEVELOPMENT

Like any other area of the marketing and promotional process, the creative aspect of advertising is guided by specific goals and objectives. A creative strategy that focuses on what must be communicated will guide the development of all messages used in the ad campaign. Creative strategy is based on several factors, including an identification of the target audience; the basic problem, issue, or opportunity the advertising must address; the major selling idea or key benefit the message needs to communicate; and any supportive information that needs to be included in the advertisement. Once these factors are determined, a creative strategy statement should describe the message appeal and execution style that will be used in the ad. Many advertising agencies outline these elements in a document known as the copy or creative platform.

Copy Platform

The written **copy platform** specifies the basic elements of the creative strategy. Different agencies may call this document a creative platform or work plan, creative blueprint, or a creative contract. The account representatives or manager assigned to the account usually prepare the copy platform. In larger agencies, an individual from research or the strategic planning department may write the copy platform. Individuals from the agency

Probably the most coveted segment of the U.S. automobile market is in the mid-size sedan segment, which represents about 37 percent of all cars sold. For years American Honda Motor Co. dominated this segment with its popular Accord model, which was America's best-selling car from 1989 to 1991 and accounts for more than 50 percent of the company's $14 billion in U.S. sales. But for the past few years the Accord has been facing intense competition from the Toyota Camry, Nissan Altima, Mazda 626, Chrysler's LH sedans, and the Ford Taurus—which was, fleet sales included, the 1992 best-selling car. While Accord remained the best-selling retail car in the U.S. in 1993, Honda introduced a new, redesigned 1994 model it hopes will help the company regain its leadership position. Honda and its agency, Rubin Postaer & Associates, knew that advertising would play a critical role in launching the new Accord.

Honda's last redesign of the Accord was for its 1990 model, and although this model was the country's best-selling car for three years, some at Honda thought its styling was too conservative. The average age of Accord buyers climbed to 44.5 years for the '90 model from 40 for the '86; their average income jumped from $47,000 to $55,000. Honda was concerned that if this trend continued it would be making family cars for people who no longer needed them. With strong Honda product loyalty established among the oldest of the baby boomers, the company decided to target the 1994 model at a younger market, around 40 years old for the sedan and 35 for the coupe. It also identified several other specific goals that would be important to the new Accord's marketing and advertising strategy: differentiating, improving the price/value relationship, and leveraging Honda loyalty.

Even with these objectives in mind, the agency needed more insight into how to motivate car buyers before developing the advertising campaign that would relaunch the Accord. So nearly a year before the first ad came out, the agency began the most extensive research project it had ever undertaken as 44 focus groups were held around the country. The agency decided to use qualitative research through focus groups since it was more interested in hearing how people talk about the process of buying a new car than in limited responses to survey questions. It also wanted to gather information that went beyond the syndicated research studies available to all companies.

The research showed that while in the 1980s consumers sought to empower themselves through acquisition, today they seek power from control. This translates into a concern over how much money the dealer will make rather than negotiating how much they can save. Brand heritage was another important factor derived from the research. Consumers had witnessed Honda's growth from a marketer of small economy cars to a major company with two divisions. As more companies reached the acceptable level of quality, Honda could differentiate itself by drawing on its heritage in the United States. Durability was also found to be important. Consumers replacing their cars with new cars in the same class are facing sticker shock, so they plan to keep their cars longer.

Honda and its agency have always been praised for outstanding advertising. For years, the cerebral "We Make It Simple" theme was its slogan. For the past eight years Honda thrived without a tagline, even though every major competitor uses one. The research convinced Rubin Postaer that a slogan was needed and sold Honda on the tagline "A Car Ahead." According to Larry Postaer, the agency's creative director, the line just wrote itself. "It's a way to differentiate us from the pack." The agency believes the new slogan is in keeping with the traditionally understated tone of Honda's advertising yet carries a harder edge, reflecting the heightened competition Honda faces and the insights gained from the focus groups. According to Postaer, "For the consumer, buying a car is a game you win or you lose. You win by not hearing from your neighbor that you didn't get the best deal. And the real win is when the car lasts seven or eight years."

Honda hopes to convince consumers that they can win by buying the new Accord and be "A Car Ahead."

Sources: Cleveland Horton, "Moving Honda 'Ahead'," *Advertising Age*, Oct. 11, 1993, p. 26; Cleveland Horton, "Honda Revs for Crucial Relaunch of Its Accord," *Advertising Age*, Aug. 23, 1993, pp. 1, 30; "A Car Is Born," *Business Week*, Sept. 13, 1993, pp. 64–72.

@ **EXHIBIT   10–7**   Insight can be gained into consumers' reactions to a commercial by showing them a storyboard layout

SFX: CAR AND FOOT TRAFFIC AMBIENCE
VO: Why did the chicken cross the road?
To open a 7/24 Savings Plan at San
   Diego Trust.
Because with $500 in savings...

... he can avoid getting henpecked by
monthly charges on a checking account.
What's more, he can access his nest egg
   through our huge ATM network...
SFX: BANK AMBIENCE
   ... and round-the-clock phone service.

VO: And of course, the interest he'll earn on
   savings isn't just chicken feed.
So open a 7/24 Savings Plan at San Diego
   Trust.
And give yourself a good reason to...
SFX: COCKA DOODLE DOO

@ **EXHIBIT 10–8**
Copy platform outline

1. Basic problem or issue the advertising must address
2. Advertising and communication objectives
3. Target audience
4. Major selling idea or key benefits to communicate
5. Creative strategy statement (campaign theme, appeal, and execution technique to be used)
6. Supportive information and requirements

team or group assigned to the account, including creative personnel as well as representatives from media and research, have input into this document. The advertising manager and/or the marketing and product managers from the client side ultimately approve the copy platform. Exhibit 10–8 is a sample copy platform outline that can be used to guide the creative process. Just as there are different names for the copy platform, there are variations in the outline and format used and in the level of detail included.

Several components of the copy platform were discussed in previous chapters. For example, Chapter 8 examined the DAGMAR model and showed how the setting of advertising objectives requires specifying a well-defined target audience and developing a communications task statement that spells out what message needs to be communicated to this audience. Determining what problem the product or service will solve or what issue must be addressed in the ad helps in establishing communication objectives for the message to accomplish. Many copy platforms also include supportive information and requirements (brand identifications, disclaimers, and the like). The final two components of the copy platform, the development of the major selling idea and creative strategy development, are often the responsibility of the creative team or specialist and form the basis of the advertising campaign.

Advertising Campaigns

Most ads are part of a series of messages that make up an **advertising campaign**, which often consists of multiple messages in a variety of media that center on a single theme or idea. Determining the central theme, idea, position, or image is a critical part of the creative process, as it sets the tone for the individual ads that make up the campaign. Some campaigns last only a short time, usually because they are ineffective or market conditions change. A successful campaign theme and creative strategy may last for years. Philip Morris has been using the "Marlboro country" campaign for over 25 years, while Campbell Soup Co. first began airing radio spots using the familiar "M'm! M'm! Good!" theme in radio spots in the 1930s.[17] Recruitment advertising for the United States Army has used the "Be all you can be" campaign theme for many years (Exhibit 10–9). Exhibit 10–10 lists some of the more enduring advertising campaign themes.

Once the creative theme is established and approved, attention turns to what type of appeal and creative execution approach to use. Before considering these parts of creative strategy, we examine how major selling ideas are determined.

@ **EXHIBIT 10–9**

The U.S. Army has used the "Be all you can be" campaign theme for many years

@ **EXHIBIT 10–10**

Examples of successful
long-running advertising
campaigns

Company or Brand	Campaign Theme
Marlboro cigarettes	"Marlboro country"
Hathaway shirts	"The man in the Hathaway shirt"
Allstate Insurance	"You're in good hands with Allstate."
Hallmark cards	"When you care enough to send the very best"
United Airlines	"Fly the friendly skies."
BMW automobiles	"The ultimate driving machine"
State Farm Insurance	"Like a good neighbor, State Farm is there."
Timex watches	"It takes a licking and keeps on ticking."
Dial soap	"Aren't you glad you use Dial?"
U.S. Army	"Be all you can be."

The Search for the Major Selling Idea

An important part of creative strategy is determining the central theme that will become the **major selling idea** of the ad campaign. As A. Jerome Jeweler states in his book *Creative Strategy in Advertising*:

> The major selling idea should emerge as the strongest singular thing you can say about your product or service. This should be the claim with the broadest and most meaningful appeal to your target audience. Once you determine this message, be certain you can live with it; be sure it stands strong enough to remain the central issue in every ad and commercial in the campaign.[18]

Some advertising experts argue that for an ad campaign to be effective it must contain a big idea that attracts the consumer's attention, gets a reaction, and sets the advertiser's product or service apart from the competition's. Well-known ad man John O'Toole describes the *big idea* as "that flash of insight that synthesizes the purpose of the strategy, joins the product benefit with consumer desire in a fresh, involving way, brings the subject to life, and makes the reader or audience stop, look, and listen."[19]

Of course, the real challenge to the creative team is coming up with the big idea to use in the ad. Many products and services offer virtually nothing unique, and it can be difficult to find something interesting to say about them. David Ogilvy, generally considered one of the most creative advertising copywriters ever to work in the business, has stated:

> I doubt if more than one campaign in a hundred contains a big idea. I am supposed to be one of the more fertile inventors of big ideas, but in my long career as a copywriter I have not had more than 20, if that.[20]

While really great ideas in advertising are difficult to come by, there are many examples of big ideas that became the basis of very creative, successful advertising campaigns. Classic examples include "we try harder," which positioned Avis as the underdog rental car company that provided better service than Hertz; "tastes great, less filling," used for over 20 years for Miller Lite beer; the "Pepsi generation" theme and subsequent variations like "the taste of a new generation"; and AT&T's "reach out and touch someone" emotional ads for its long-distance service. More recent big ideas that have resulted in effective advertising include the "perception/reality" campaign for *Rolling Stone* magazine and Nike's "just do it."

Big ideas are important in business-to-business advertising as well. For example, Beacon Manufacturing Co. was unimpressed with the way blankets were advertised and wanted to do something different to get the attention of retail stores buyers and merchandise managers. Beacon and its agency, Easterby & Associates, leveraged the popularity of the company's vice president of sales, Ted Smith, into an advertising campaign. "Adventures of Teddy" elevated Smith into an Everyman willing to go the extra mile to prove his product's superiority. The ads have shown Smith being tossed in the air by a Beacon blanket, wrapped in a Beacon blanket and dangled from a helicopter, using one as a parachute, and keeping sharks at bay with a blanket (Exhibit 10–11). The idea resulted in great advertising that has helped Beacon increase sales three times the industry average.

@ **EXHIBIT 10–11**

The "Adventures of Teddy" campaign for Beacon blankets is an excellent example of a big idea in business-to-business advertising

It is difficult to pinpoint the inspiration for a big idea or to teach advertising people how to find them. However, several approaches can guide the creative team's search for a major selling idea and offer solutions for developing effective advertising. Some of the best-known approaches follow:

- Using a unique selling proposition.
- Creating a brand image.
- Finding the inherent drama.
- Positioning.

Unique selling proposition

The concept of the **unique selling proposition (USP)** was developed by Rosser Reeves, former chair of the Ted Bates agency, and is described in his influential book *Reality in Advertising*. Reeves noted three characteristics of unique selling propositions:

1. Each advertisement must make a proposition to the consumer. Not just words, not just product puffery, not just show window advertising. Each advertisement must say to each reader: "Buy this product and you will get this benefit."
2. The proposition must be one that the competition either cannot or does not offer. It must be unique either in the brand or in the claim.
3. The proposition must be strong enough to move the mass millions, that is, pull over new customers to your brand.[21]

Reeves said the attribute claim or benefit that formed the basis of the USP should dominate the ad and be emphasized through repetitive advertising. An example of advertising based on a USP is the campaign for Castrol Syntec synthetic motor oil. Other companies had marketed synthetic oils with little success. However, a unique feature of Castrol Syntec is its ability to offer superior protection because it bonds to the engine. A TV commercial was created showing dozens of revving engines running on conventional motor oil and one on Syntec. The oil was drained from the engines and they were restarted. While the conventional ones ground to a halt, the engine using Syntec kept going thanks to its unique bonding properties (Exhibit 10–12).

For Reeves' approach to work, there must be a truly unique product or service attribute, benefit, or inherent advantage that can be used in the claim. This may require considerable research on the product and consumers not only to determine the USP but also to document the claim. As we shall see in Chapter 23, the Federal Trade Commission objects to advertisers making claims of superiority or uniqueness without support-

ⓐ **EXHIBIT   10–12**

Advertising for Castrol
Syntec motor oil uses a
unique selling proposition

ing data. Also, some companies have sued their competitors for making unsubstantiated uniqueness claims.[22]

Advertisers must also consider whether the unique selling proposition affords them a *sustainable competitive advantage* that cannot easily be copied by competitors. In the package-goods field in particular, companies quickly match a brand feature for feature, which means advertising based on USPs becomes obsolete. For example, a few years ago, Procter & Gamble invented a combination shampoo and conditioner to rejuvenate its struggling Pert brand. The reformulated brand was called Pert Plus and its market share rose from 2 percent to 12 percent, making it the leading shampoo. But then competing brands such as Revlon and Suave quickly launched their own two-in-one formula products.[23]

Creating a brand image

In many product and service categories, competing brands are so similar it is very difficult to find or create a unique attribute or benefit to use as the major selling idea. Many of the package-goods products that account for many of the advertising dollars spent in the United States are difficult to differentiate on a functional or performance basis. The creative strategy used to sell these products is based on the development of a strong, memorable identity for the brand through **image advertising**.

David Ogilvy popularized the idea of brand image in his famous book *Confessions of an Advertising Man*. Ogilvy noted that with image advertising, "Every advertisement should be thought of as a contribution to the complex symbol which is the brand image." He

ⓐ **EXHIBIT   10–13**

Ads such as this help create a
unique image for No Fear

◎ **EXHIBIT** **10–14** This Kellogg's Raisin Bran commercial uses an inherent drama approach

(SFX: RING)
SAM: Patrino.
(AVO): The news spread throughout the raisin business.
SAM: (ON PHONE) More raisins?
(AVO): Now Kellogg's puts two bigger scoops in Kellogg's Raisin Bran for even more raisins.

SAM: (GIVING ORDERS TO LOADERS) More raisins!
(AVO): Raisin brokers, raisin shippers and raisin raisers worked furiously to meet the Kellogg's demand.
SAM: (TO PICKERS) More raisins, more raisins!

(AVO): It's been tough on some of us . . .
SAM: (IN BED) More raisins.
(AVO): . . . but it's been worth it. 'Cause now two scoops in Kellogg's Raisin Bran . . . means even more raisins than ever before.
SAM: Mmmm—more raisins.

argued that the image or personality of the brand is particularly important when brands are similar:

> The greater the similarity between brands, the less part reason plays in brand selection. There isn't any significant difference between the various brands of whiskey, or cigarettes, or beer. They are all about the same. And so are the cake mixes and the detergents and the margarines. The manufacturer who dedicates his advertising to building the most sharply defined personality for his brand will get the largest share of the market at the highest profit. By the same token, the manufacturers who will find themselves up the creek are those shortsighted opportunists who siphon off their advertising funds for promotions.[24]

Image advertising has been used as the main selling idea for a variety of products and services, including soft drinks, liquor, cigarettes, automobiles, airlines, financial services, perfume/colognes, and clothing. Many consumers wear designer jeans or Ralph Lauren polo shirts or drink certain brands of beer or soft drinks because of the image of these brands. The key to successful image advertising is developing an image that will appeal to product users. For example, No Fear uses ads such as the one shown in Exhibit 10–13 on page 281 to create a unique image for its line of clothing.

Finding the inherent drama

Another approach to determining the major selling idea is finding the **inherent drama** or characteristic of the product that makes the consumer purchase it. The inherent drama approach expresses the advertising philosophy of Leo Burnett, founder of the Leo Burnett agency in Chicago. Burnett said inherent drama "is often hard to find but it is always

@ **EXHIBIT 10-15**

A P&G detergent for every washday need

Brand	Positioning	Share
TIDE	Tough, powerful cleaning	31.1%
CHEER	Tough cleaning and color protection	8.2
BOLD	Detergent plus fabric softener	2.9
GAIN	Sunshine scent and odor-removing formula	2.6
ERA	Stain pre-treated and stain removal	2.2
DASH	Value brand	1.8
OXYDOL	Bleach-boosted formula, whitening	1.4
SOLO	Detergent and fabric softener in liquid form	1.2
DREFT	Outstanding cleaning for baby clothes, safe for tender skin	1.0
IVORY SNOW	Fabric and skin safety on baby clothes and fine washables	0.7
ARIEL	Tough cleaner, aimed at Hispanics	0.1

Source: Jennifer Lawrence, "Don't Look for P&G to Pare Detergents," *Advertising Age*, May 31, 1993, p. 3.

there, and once found it is the most interesting and believable of all advertising appeals."[25] He believed advertising should be based on a foundation of consumer benefits with an emphasis on the dramatic element in expressing these benefits.

Burnett advocated a down-home type of advertising that presents the message in a warm and realistic way. Some of the more famous ads developed by the Leo Burnett agency using the inherent drama approach include those for Maytag appliances and Kellogg's cereals. Notice how the commercial shown in Exhibit 10–14 dramatizes the fact that Kellogg's Raisin Bran contains more raisins than ever before.

Positioning

The concept of *positioning* as a basis for advertising strategy was introduced by Jack Trout and Al Ries in the early 1970s and has become a popular basis of creative development.[26] The basic idea is that advertising is used to establish or "position" the product or service in a particular place in the mind of the consumer.

Trout and Ries originally described positioning as the image consumers had of the brand in relation to competing brands in the product or service category, but the concept has been expanded beyond direct competitive positioning. As discussed in Chapter 5, products can be positioned on the basis of product attributes, price/quality, usage or application, product users, or product class. Any of these can spark a major selling idea that becomes the basis of the creative strategy and results in the brand occupying a particular place in the minds of the target audience. Since positioning can be done on the basis of a distinctive attribute, the positioning and unique selling proposition approaches can overlap. Positioning approaches have been used as the foundation for a number of successful creative strategies.

Positioning is often the basis of a firm's creative strategy when it has multiple brands competing in the same market. For example, Procter & Gamble markets more than 10 brands of laundry detergents—and positions each one differently, as shown in Exhibit 10–15.

The USP, brand image, inherent drama, and positioning approaches are often used as the basis of the creative strategy for ad campaigns. These creative styles have become associated with some of the most successful advertising creative minds and their agencies.[27] However, many other creative approaches are available.

Specific agencies are by no means limited to any one creative approach. For example, the famous Marlboro country campaign, a classic example of image advertising, was

Ethical Perspective 10–1
Using Advertising to Appeal to Social Consciousness

In recent years, many creative people complain, advertising has become bland and boring because advertisers are too concerned about offending someone and restrict themselves to ads that are politically correct. However, not all advertisers are worried about their ads offending; some are even deliberately creating controversial ads. Critics call this new genre *shock advertising* and claim that its intent is to elicit attention for a brand name by jolting consumers. However, Benetton, the Italian-based clothing manufacturer whose ads are well known worldwide for their shock value, says it has a different reason for using this type of advertising. Benetton's creative director, Oliviero Toscani, says the controversial images are designed to raise public awareness of social issues and position the company as a cutting-edge, socially conscious marketer.

Benetton has been regarded as a renegade of the advertising world since 1989, when it ran a print ad featuring a black woman nursing a white baby. Other shock ads have featured such images as a black man's hand handcuffed to a white man's, a priest kissing a nun, an AIDS patient and his family moments before his death, a boatload of refugees, an automobile ablaze after a car bomb, and naked adults with naked children.

One of the latest images is a symbolic picture from the war in Bosnia. The idea for the ad came when a young woman who fled Sarajevo after her family was killed in the war wrote Toscani and asked, "Why don't you do something about what's going on in my country?" Toscani had a Benetton representative visit a morgue in the war-torn country and contact families of slain soldiers, seeking permission to photograph their possessions left behind as a reminder of the war's horrors. Toscani selected a slain soldier whose father attached a note to his uniform that read: "I, Gojko Gagro, father of the deceased Marinko Gagro, born in 1963 at Blizanci in the province of Citluk, would like my son's name and all that remains of him be used in the name of peace and against war." The ad, which was photographed by Toscani, shows a single arresting image of a bloody camouflage uniform. The copy, in its author's native Serbo-Croatian, is Mr. Gagro's letter. Toscani has stated, "The language in the ad belongs to a dictionary the Western world doesn't want to open."

Benetton's shock ads often ignite criticism and stir up industry debate over their purpose. Peter Fressola, a Benetton North America spokesman, said, "Yes, we mean to shock some people with our ads. But people who are shocked by this have been living in a cocoon. They need to be shocked into seeing what's really going on in the world. We believe that when that many

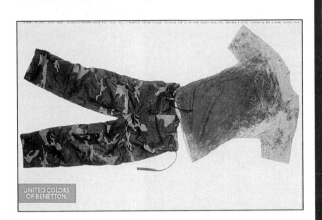

UNITED COLORS OF BENETTON.

people see an image this powerful, it can raise their collective consciousness. And that can result in action."

Critics argue that the real goal of the Benetton ads is to generate publicity. Some accuse Benetton of exploiting human suffering to sell its products. The Benetton ads are controversial even in more liberal European countries. Advertising self-regulatory bodies in Britain, France, and Spain have condemned the ads and urged magazines in these countries to reject many of them. The Vatican newspaper, *L'Osservatore Ramon*, ran an editorial denouncing the Bosnian image ad as "advertising terrorism." However, Amnesty International applauded the ad for drawing attention to the war and Sarajevo's daily newspaper asked Benetton for posters of the ad to plaster across the city.

Toscani sees the negative reactions to the Benetton ads as nothing less than a debate between advertising and art. He argues that in the art world, debatably offensive images are accepted, while in other realms such as advertising they are not. A Benetton spokesperson said Toscani wants to explore the limits of art and advertising—where one begins and the other ends and how tolerance shifts from one realm to the next. However, an attorney for France's self-regulating advertising body replied, "Advertising versus art or whatever, Benetton always has an explanation. That's not the point. The point is they've broken the rules." It is likely that Benetton will continue breaking the rules and shocking people. Of course, it may also get them to think about some of the world's problems in the process.

Sources: Gary Levin, "Benetton Ad Lays Bare the Bloody Toll of War," *Advertising Age*, Feb. 21, 1994, p. 38; Lisa Bannon and Margaret Studer, "Two Ads Show Benefits of Overexposure," *The Wall Street Journal*, June 17, 1993, p. B6; Bruce Horowitz, "Shock Ads: New Rage That Spawns Rage," *Los Angeles Times*, March 22, 1992, pp. D1, 7.

developed by the Leo Burnett agency, which is known more for the inherent drama approach. Many different agencies have followed the unique selling proposition approach advocated by Rosser Reeves and the former Ted Bates agency. The challenge to the creative specialist or team is to find a major selling idea, whether it be based on a unique selling proposition, brand image, inherent drama, position in the market, or some other approach, and use it as a guide in developing an effective creative strategy.

In their search for a big idea, advertisers consider many different creative options that might grab consumers' attention. However, as discussed in Ethical Perspective 10–1, many people believe some advertisers are going too far in their efforts to break through the advertising clutter and have an impact on consumers.

SUMMARY

The creative development and execution of the advertising message are a crucial part of a firm's integrated marketing communications program and are often the key to the success of a marketing campaign. Marketers generally turn to advertising agencies to develop, prepare, and implement their creative strategy since they are specialists in the creative function of advertising. The creative specialist or team is responsible for developing an effective way of communicating the marketer's message to the customer. Other individuals on both the client and agency sides work with the creative specialists to develop the creative strategy, implement it, and evaluate its effectiveness.

The challenge facing the writers, artists, and others who develop ads is to be creative and come up with fresh, unique, and appropriate ideas that can be used as solutions to communications problems. Creativity in advertising is a process of several stages, including preparation,

incubation, illumination, and verification. Various sources of information are available to help the creative specialists determine the best campaign theme, appeal, or execution style.

Creative strategy development is guided by specific goals and objectives and is based on a number of factors, including the target audience, the basic problem the advertising must address, the objectives the message seeks to accomplish, and the major selling idea or key benefit the advertiser wants to communicate. These factors are generally stated in a copy platform, which is a work plan used to guide development of the advertising campaign. An important part of creative strategy is determining the major selling idea that will become the central theme of the campaign. There are several approaches to doing this, including using a unique selling proposition, creating a brand image, looking for inherent drama in the brand, and positioning.

KEY TERMS

creative strategy, p. 264
creative tactics, p. 264
advertising creativity, p. 268
general preplanning input, p. 273

product/service-specific preplanning input, p. 274
problem detection, p. 274
focus groups, p. 274
storyboard, p. 275

aniamatic, p. 275
copy platform, p. 275
advertising campaign, p. 278
major selling idea, p. 279

unique selling proposition (USP), p. 280
image advertising, p. 281
inherent drama, p. 282

DISCUSSION QUESTIONS

1. The chapter opening discusses problems Subaru, AT&T, and Diet Coke have had with recent ad campaigns. Analyze the current campaigns being used for these companies or brands. Do you think they are more effective than the previous ad campaigns? Why or why not?

2. How should advertising creativity be judged? Who should be responsible for judging it—clients or agency creative specialists?

3. What is your opinion of advertising awards, such as the Cannes Lions, that are based solely on creativity? Should agencies pride themselves on their creative awards? Why or why not?

4. Why do you think Burger King is having such a difficult time finding an effective advertising campaign? What problems might it be creating by changing campaign themes so often?

5. What is meant by a media-driven creative strategy? What are the advantages of taking this approach to creative strategy development?

6. Assume you have been assigned to work on the development of an advertising campaign for a new brand of cereal. Describe the various types of general and product-specific preplanning input you might provide for the creative team.

7. Find an example of an ad campaign theme that has been around for a very long time. Why do you think the advertiser has been able to use this theme for so long?

8. What is meant by a unique selling proposition? Find an example of an ad that uses a USP as its major selling idea. Evaluate this ad against the three characteristics of USPs discussed in the chapter.

9. Discuss the role brand image plays in the advertising of a particular product or service category such as soft drinks, cologne, or airlines. What are the images used by various companies competing in this market?

10. Evaluate the position taken by Oliviero Toscani, creative director of Benetton, that debatably offensive images are acceptable in the art world and thus should also be acceptable for advertising. Do you think companies like Benetton are using shock advertising to make social statements or merely to get publicity that will help sell their products? Defend your position.

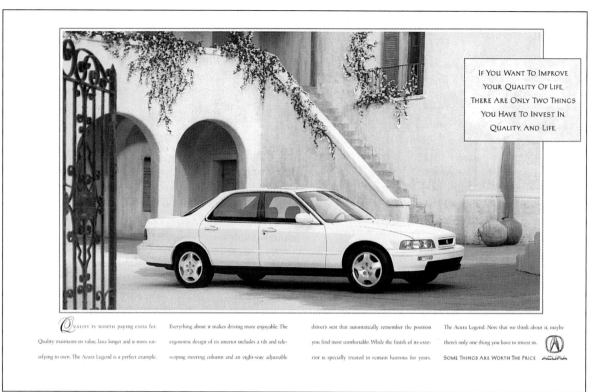

IF YOU WANT TO IMPROVE
YOUR QUALITY OF LIFE,
THERE ARE ONLY TWO THINGS
YOU HAVE TO INVEST IN.
QUALITY. AND LIFE.

Chapter **11**

Creative Strategy: Implementation and Evaluation

Chapter Objectives

- To analyze various types of appeals that can be used in the development and implementation of an advertising message.
- To analyze the various creative execution styles that can be used by advertisers and the advertising situations where they are most appropriate.

- To analyze various tactical issues involved in the creation of print advertising and television commercials.
- To consider how clients evaluate the creative work of their agencies and discuss guidelines for the evaluation and approval process.

Convincing Car Buyers That "Some Things Are Worth the Price"

How do you convince car buyers to spend upwards of $40,000 on a car? Some automotive marketing experts suggest telling them about the quality, reliability, state-of-the-art technology, durability, and other features that make the car a great value, even at a high price. But what do you do if consumers already see your car as having all of these positive attributes? This was the problem facing American Honda Co.'s Acura division when it set out to develop the 1994 advertising strategy for its flagship models, the Legend sedan and coupe.

The Acura Legend had an excellent reputation for quality and durability. It ranked number one on these attributes for three years running in the influential J. D. Power & Associates performance index surveys. The Legend also was perceived as offering very good value for the money. While Acura and its agency, Ketchum Advertising, knew the Legend had everything the upscale car buyer wanted in a luxury car, there was one important feature missing—a prestige image. They felt the Legend needed to be perceived as more prestigious, particularly if it wanted to compete against Lexus, Infiniti, Mercedes, and BMW in the luxury car market.

Focus groups and one-on-one interviews with upscale car buyers revealed that while luxury is important to them, it is really not a differentiating factor. All luxury cars had safety features such as antilock brakes and dual airbags, as well as leather interiors, power seats, high-quality sound systems, and other amenities. The research revealed these car buyers also want to feel a sense of prestige from owning and driving a luxury car. Prestige was expressed as an emotion with both internal and external aspects. Luxury car buyers wanted a sense of internal validation, a "yes, I deserve it and I'm worth it" feeling. They also wanted external recognition—for others to recognize their success and good taste.

Acura recognized that creating a prestigious image for the Legend would involve all aspects of buying and owning a luxury car, including the product, showroom experience, customer service, and all marketing communications. Acura had traditionally focused on the "gearhead" segment of the upscale car market, which was primarily concerned with performance. However, the largest segment of the market was defined as "epicures"—those with fine, discriminating tastes. To attract these buyers, Acura would need to create more of a prestige image for the Legend and move it into the same perceptual category as Lexus, Infiniti, BMW, and Mercedes.

Key to creating a prestige image for the Legend is advertising. The agency's creative strategy is to create beautiful images and prestigious symbols the upscale buyer can relate to. While the ads have to be visually striking, they must communicate two other important messages. They must convince luxury car buyers that paying a premium for Acura's quality is well worth the price over time and that they will be comfortable with their decision for a long time to come. The theme for Acura's 1994 ad campaign is, "Some things are worth the price." The various TV and print executions, as well as all other sales and marketing communications, use the theme to attract new customers and reinforce the purchase decisions of Acura owners.

The major goal of the campaign is to move the Legend sedan and coupe upscale to compete more directly with the competition. Acura knows that advertising execution will play an important role in convincing the discriminating car buyer that the Legend is indeed worth the price.

Sources: Ketchum Advertising, Los Angeles; American Honda Motor Co., Acura Division.

n Chapter 10, we discussed the importance of advertising creativity and examined the various steps in the creative process. We focused on determining *what* the advertising message will communicate. This chapter focuses on *how* the message will be executed. We examine various appeals and execution styles that can be used to develop the ad and tactical issues involved in the design and production of effective advertising messages. We conclude by presenting some guidelines clients can use to evaluate the creative work of their agencies.

APPEALS AND EXECUTION STYLES

The **advertising appeal** refers to the approach used to attract the attention of consumers and/or to influence their feelings toward the product, service, or cause. An advertising appeal can also be viewed as "something that moves people, speaks to their wants or needs, and excites their interest."[1] The **creative execution style** refers to the way a particular appeal is turned into an advertising message presented to the consumer. According to William Weilbacher:

> The appeal can be said to form the underlying content of the advertisement, and the execution the way in which that content is presented. Advertising appeals and executions are usually independent of each other; that is, a particular appeal can be executed in a variety of ways and a particular means of execution can be applied to a variety of advertising appeals. Advertising appeals tend to adapt themselves to all media, whereas some kinds of executional devices are more adaptable to some media than others.[2]

Advertising Appeals

Hundreds of different appeals can be used as the basis for advertising messages. At the broadest level, these approaches are generally broken into two categories: informational/rational appeals and emotional appeals. In this section, we focus on ways to use rational and emotional appeals as part of creative strategy. We also consider how rational and emotional appeals can be combined in developing the advertising message.

Informational/rational appeals

Informational/rational appeals focus on the consumer's practical, functional, or utilitarian need for the product or service and emphasize features of a product or service and/or the benefits or reasons for owning or using a particular brand. The content of these messages emphasizes facts, learning, and the logic of persuasion.[3] Rational-based appeals tend to be informative, and advertisers using them generally attempt to convince

EXHIBIT   11–1

Rayovac uses a rational appeal to introduce its Renewal battery

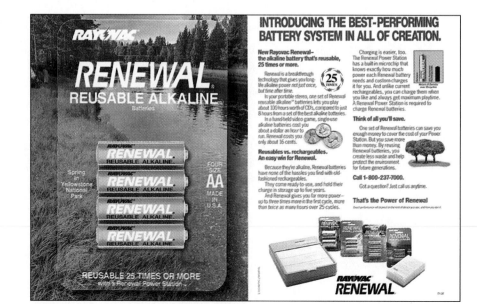

consumers that their product or service has a particular attribute(s) or provides a specific benefit that satisfies their needs. Their objective is to persuade the target audience to buy the brand because it is the best available or does a better job of meeting consumers' needs. For example, Rayovac uses a rational appeal to explain why its new Renewal battery represents a technological breakthrough and is a superior product (Exhibit 11–1).

Many rational motives can be used as the basis for advertising appeals, including comfort, convenience, economy, and health and sensory benefits such as touch, taste, and smell. Other rational motives or purchase criteria commonly used in advertising include quality, dependability, durability, efficiency, efficacy, and performance. The particular features, benefits, or evaluative criteria that are important to consumers and can serve as the basis of an informational/rational appeal vary from one product or service category to another as well as among various market segments.

Weilbacher identified several types of advertising appeals that fall under the category of rational approaches, among them feature, competitive advantage, favorable price, news, and product/service popularity appeals.

Ads that use a *feature appeal* focus on the dominant characteristics of the product or service. These ads tend to be highly informative and present the customer with a number of important product attributes or features that will lead to favorable attitudes and can be used as the basis for a rational purchase decision. Technical and high-involvement products often use this advertising approach. However, this type of appeal can also be used for a service. Notice how the Continental Airlines ad in Exhibit 11–2 focuses on the various features of its BusinessFirst class of service.

When a *competitive advantage appeal* is used, the advertiser makes either a direct or an indirect comparison to another brand (or brands) and usually claims superiority on one or more attributes. This type of appeal was discussed in Chapter 7 under comparative advertising.

A *favorable price appeal* makes the price offer the dominant point of the message. Price appeal advertising is used most often by retailers to announce sales, special offers, or low everyday prices. Price appeal ads have become more popular with national advertisers during the recession. Many fast-food chains have made price an important part of their marketing strategy through promotional deals and "value menus" or lower overall prices, and their advertising strategy is designed to communicate this. Many other types of

◎ EXHIBIT 11–2

Continental uses a feature appeal ad to promote its BusinessFirst class of service

@ **EXHIBIT 11–3**

A price appeal is used to promote Swiss Miss Gels

advertisers use price appeals as well. In Exhibit 11–3, Hunt-Wesson, Inc. uses a price appeal to promote the cost savings of its Swiss Miss Gels.

News appeals are those where some type of news or announcement about the product, service, or company dominates the advertisement. This type of appeal can be used for a new product or service or to inform consumers of significant modifications or improvements in the product/service. This appeal works best when a company has important news it wants to communicate to its target market. The ad shown in Exhibit 11–1, which was used to introduce the Rayovac Renewal battery, is a good example of a news appeal ad.

Product/service popularity appeals stress the popularity of a product or service by pointing out the number of consumers who use the brand or have switched to it or its leadership position in the market. The main point of this advertising appeal is that the wide use of the brand is evidence of the product/service's quality or value and other customers should consider using it. The Ford ad in Exhibit 11–4 shows this type of advertising appeal.

@ **EXHIBIT 11–4**

This Ford ad promotes the popularity of the company's cars and trucks

@ EXHIBIT 11–5

Bases for emotional appeals

Personal States or Feelings	Social-Based Feelings
Safety	Recognition
Security	Status
Love	Respect
Affection	Involvement
Happiness	Embarrassment
Joy	Affiliation/belonging
Nostalgia	Rejection
Sentiment	Acceptance
Excitement	Approval
Arousal/stimulation	
Sorrow/grief	
Pride	
Achievement/ accomplishment	
Self-esteem	
Actualization	
Pleasure	
Ambition	
Comfort	

Emotional appeals

Emotional appeals relate to the customers' social and/or psychological needs for purchasing a product or service. Many of consumers' motives for their purchase decisions are emotional, and their feelings about a brand can be more important than knowledge of its features or attributes. Rational, information-based appeals are viewed by advertisers for many products and services as dull. Many advertisers believe appeals to consumers' emotions work better at selling brands that do not differ markedly from competing brands, since rational differentiation is difficult.

Many feelings or needs can serve as the basis for advertising appeals designed to influence consumers on an emotional level, as shown in Exhibit 11–5. These appeals are based on the psychological states or feelings directed to the self (such as pleasure or excitement) as well as those with a more social orientation (such as status or recognition). The advertising campaign for the Acura Legend discussed at the beginning of this chapter is an emotional appeal; a goal of these ads is to appeal to luxury car buyers' needs for prestige and recognition.

Advertisers can use emotional appeals in many ways in their creative strategy. Ads using humor, sex, and other appeals that are very entertaining, arousing, upbeat, and/or exciting can affect the emotions of consumers and/or put them in a favorable frame of mind. Many TV advertisers use poignant ads that create a lump in the throats of viewers. Hallmark, AT&T, Kodak, and McDonald's often create commercials that evoke feelings of warmth, nostalgia, and/or sentiment. Marketers use emotional appeals in hopes that the positive feelings they evoke will transfer to the brand. Research shows that positive mood states created by advertising can have a favorable effect on consumers' evaluation of a product.[4] Research has also shown that emotional advertising is better remembered than nonemotional messages.[5]

Another reason for using emotional appeals is to influence consumers' interpretations of their product usage experience. One way of doing this is through what is known as transformational advertising. A **transformational ad** is defined as "one which associates the experience of using (consuming) the advertised brand with a unique set of psychological characteristics which would not typically be associated with the brand experience to the same degree without exposure to the advertisement."[6]

Transformational ads create feelings, images, meanings, and beliefs about the product or service that may be activated when consumers use it, transforming their interpretation

⊚ EXHIBIT 11–6

Lexus addresses both rational and emotional appeals in this clever ad

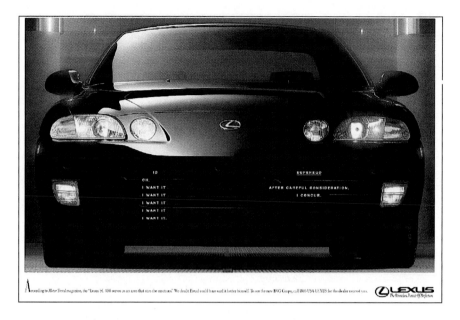

of the usage experience. Christopher Puto and William Wells note that a transformational ad has two characteristics:

1. It must make the experience of using the product richer, warmer, more exciting, and/or more enjoyable than that obtained solely from an objective description of the advertised brand.
2. It must connect the experience of the advertisement so tightly with the experience of using the brand that consumers cannot remember the brand without recalling the experience generated by the advertisement.[7]

The "reach out and touch someone" campaign used by AT&T over the past decade to encourage consumers to keep in touch with family and friends via the telephone is a successful use of transformational advertising. McDonald's has also used transformational advertising very effectively to position itself as the fast-food chain where parents (or grandparents) can enjoy a warm, happy experience with their children.

Combining rational and emotional appeals

In many advertising situations, the decision facing the creative specialist is not choosing between an emotional versus a rational appeal but rather determining how to combine the two approaches. As noted copywriters David Ogilvy and Joel Raphaelson have stated:

> Few purchases of any kind are made for entirely rational reasons. Even a purely functional product such as laundry detergent may offer what is now called an emotional benefit—say, the satisfaction of seeing one's children in bright clean clothes. In some product categories the rational element is small. These include soft drinks, beer, cosmetics, certain personal care products, and most old-fashioned products. And who hasn't experienced the surge of joy that accompanies the purchase of a new car?[8]

Consumer purchase decisions are often made on the basis of both emotional and rational motives, and attention must be given to both elements in developing effective advertising. Exhibit 11–6 shows a very clever ad that uses the Freudian concepts of id and superego to suggest that there are both emotional and rational reasons for purchasing the Lexus SC 400 Coupe.

Advertising researchers and agencies have been giving considerable attention to the relationship between rational and emotional motives in consumer decision making and how advertising influences both. The McCann-Erickson Worldwide agency, in conjunction with advertising professor Michael Ray, developed a proprietary research technique

@ **EXHIBIT 11–7**

Levels of relationships with brands

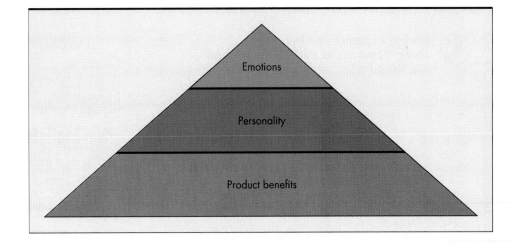

@ **EXHIBIT 11–8**

This ad serves as a reminder for Hershey's Kisses chocolates during the holiday season

known as *emotional bonding*. This technique evaluates how consumers feel about brands and the nature of any emotional rapport they have with a brand compared to the ideal emotional state they associate with the product category.[9]

The basic concept of emotional bonding is that consumers develop three levels of relationships with brands, as shown in Exhibit 11–7. The most basic relationship indicates how consumers *think* about brands in respect to product benefits. This occurs, for the most part, through a rational learning process and can be measured by how well advertising communicates product information. Consumers at this stage are not very brand loyal, and brand switching is common.

At the next stage, the consumer assigns a *personality* to a brand. For example, a brand may be thought of as self-assured, aggressive, and adventurous as opposed to compliant and timid. The consumer's judgment of the brand has moved beyond its attributes or delivery of product/service benefits. In most instances, consumers judge the personality of a brand based on an assessment of overt or covert cues found in its advertising.

McCann-Erickson researchers believe the strongest relationship that develops between a brand and the consumer is based on feelings or emotional attachments to the brand. Consumers develop *emotional bonds* with certain brands, which result in positive psychological movement toward them. The marketer's goal is to develop the greatest emotional linkage between its brand and the consumer. McCann-Erickson believes advertising can develop and enrich emotional bonding between consumers and brands. McCann and its subsidiary agencies use emotional bonding research to provide strategic input into the creative process and determine how well advertising is communicating with the consumer. Global Perspective 11–1 discusses how McCann-Erickson used this approach in developing a popular advertising campaign for Taster's Choice instant coffee, the idea for which was borrowed from the agency's London office.

Additional types of appeals

Not every ad fits neatly into the categories of rational or emotional appeals. For example, the ad for Hershey's Kisses in Exhibit 11–8 can be classified as **reminder advertising**. This ad does not rely on any specific type of appeal; its only objective is to keep the brand name in the mind of the consumer. Well-known brands and market leaders often use reminder advertising.

Advertisers introducing a new product often use **teaser advertising**, which is designed to build curiosity and excitement about a product or brand by talking about it but not showing it. Teaser ads are often used for new movies and are particularly popular among automotive advertisers when they introduce a new model or make significant changes in a car. The nature campaign used to introduce the Infiniti, discussed in Chapter 8, is an example of teaser advertising. Chrysler also used a teaser campaign before

Global Perspective 11–1
Using Romance to Sell Coffee around the World

In 1990, Nestlé Corp. and its agency, McCann-Erickson, were looking for a new advertising approach for Taster's Choice instant coffee. For more than 20 years advertising for the brand had focused primarily on the product, positioning Taster's Choice as "tasting closest to fresh brewed." But there was concern that U.S. consumers were beginning to perceive coffee as a commodity and becoming highly responsive to price and sales promotion. The agency recommended abandoning the product-oriented advertising and developing a more emotionally driven campaign.

McCann-Erickson conducted emotional bonding research among instant-coffee drinkers and found that typical users of Taster's Choice were discriminating, self-assured, and sophisticated. These personality traits matched well with the premium image of Taster's Choice. The agency recommended a campaign that would involve consumers emotionally in the advertising and in the brand. Some competitors, such as General Foods International Coffees, were already using emotional appeals. But one emotional dimension that was absent in coffee advertising was romance. Thus, the client and agency decided the new campaign for Taster's Choice would add a touch of romance to the brand's sophisticated image.

Generally, at this point, an ad agency would have to begin thinking about how to execute the creative strategy. However, McCann-Erickson's London office had created a campaign for Nestlé U.K.'s Gold Blend instant coffee brand that fit very well with the creative strategy chosen for Taster's Choice in the United States. The campaign was based on soap opera–style commercials featuring two flirtatious neighbors, Tony and Sharon, whose relationship develops in each episode. The coffee plays a background role to the evolving romantic tension between the couple.

The "brewing romance" campaign was introduced in the United Kingdom in 1987 and quickly developed an avid following. British tabloids chronicled the series and viewers wrote in for autographs of the actors who played the couple and even sent in script suggestions. Nestlé had the whole country anticipating the couple's wedding. The campaign lasted for six years and 12 episodes and as the romance heated up so did Gold Blend's sales, which soared by 40 percent and helped the brand become the U.K.'s number two instant coffee.

The U.K. campaign finally ended in 1993 with the couple driving happily off into the sunset in a Mercedes as Sharon reveals that she has left the new tenant of her apartment a little present—a jar of Gold Blend and two cups. Tony asks, "Why two cups?" and she responds, "You never know." Well, the agency knows; it is extending the U.K. campaign in a direction suggesting a love triangle may be brewing among the new characters. In initial spots in the new campaign, the girlfriend of the young man who has taken over Sharon's apartment seems tempted to add a young artiste to her straitlaced boyfriend.

The campaign's success in the U.K. inspired Nestlé and McCann-Erickson Worldwide to take the ads to the United States, Canada, Chile, Australia, and New Zealand. A Japanese version is also being considered. Nestlé began using the Tony and Sharon campaign in the United States in 1991, and initial consumer reactions were nearly as feverish as in the United Kingdom. The first two commercials generated more positive mail and phone calls than any other campaign in Nestlé's history. The debut of each new "episode" became a major media event, often premiering on network shows such as ABC's "Good Morning America." In a 1993 episode Tony invites Sharon to Paris, where he is on a business trip, and they finally kiss; 1994 episodes introduce a new twist as Sharon's grown son appears on the scene.

Many people in the United States, as well as many other countries, are anxiously waiting for Tony and Sharon to tie the knot. However, as long as the campaign is capturing consumer interest and anticipation *and* selling coffee, Nestlé will keep it moving slowly. In its first two years, the campaign helped Taster's Choice gain several market share points in the U.S. market. It was chosen as one of the 10 most popular TV campaigns of 1993 in a survey conducted by Video Storyboard Tests Inc. If the campaign is as successful in other countries as it has been in the United Kingdom and the United States, Nestlé is likely to keep the romance brewing around the world for a quite a long time.

Sources: Judann Dagnoli and Elena Bowes, "A Brewing Romance," *Advertising Age*, April 8, 1991, p. 22; Bradley Johnson, "Romance Warms," *Advertising Age*, Feb. 24, 1992, p. 4; Bradley Johnson and Joe Mandes, "Nestlé, ABC Strike Taster's Choice Deal," *Advertising Age*, Feb. 3, 1992, p. 3; Laurel Wentz, "New Coffee Romance: Same Old Problem," *Advertising Age*, Nov. 29, 1993, p. 3; and Kevin Goldman, "Year's Top Commercials Propelled by Star Power," *The Wall Street Journal*, March 16, 1994, pp. B1, 5.

@ **EXHIBIT 11–9**

Chrysler used teaser ads before introducing the new Neon

PEOPLE DON'T
REALLY UNDERSTAND
THE IDEA THAT SHAPED IT.

IT CONTAINS PLATINUM.
RHODIUM.
AND NEWLY FORMED
MATERIALS.

IT'S SHIELDED WITH A
DRY POWDER THAT WAS
MELTED TO A VIRTUALLY
IMPERMEABLE FINISH.

IT'S DEEPLY CONCERNED WITH
OUR PLANET'S ENVIRONMENT.

AND NO ONE HAS EVER SEEN
ANYTHING QUITE LIKE IT.

neon

SEE IT ON THE SUPER BOWL.
JANUARY 30, 1994.

@ **EXHIBIT 11–10**

Valvoline uses a straight sell execution style in this ad

IT OUTPERFORMS
CONVENTIONAL
MOTOR OILS.
IT COSTS LESS THAN
OTHER SYNTHETICS.
IT'S NEW VALVOLINE®
DURABLEND.™
AND IT'S ABOUT TIME.

PEOPLE WHO KNOW USE VALVOLINE®

introducing its new Jeep Grand Cherokee and more recently in launching the ad campaign for the new Neon subcompact (Exhibit 11–9). Teaser campaigns can generate interest in a new product, but advertisers must be careful not to extend them too long or they will lose their effectiveness.[10]

Many ads are not designed to sell a product or service but rather to enhance the image of the company or meet other corporate goals such as soliciting investment or recruiting employees. These are generally referred to as corporate image advertising and are discussed in detail in Chapter 18.

Advertising Execution

Once the specific advertising appeal that will be used as the basis for the advertising message has been determined, the creative specialist or team begins its execution. *Creative execution* refers to the way an advertising appeal is presented. While it is obviously important for an ad to have a meaningful appeal or message to communicate to the consumer, the manner in which the ad is executed is also important.

One of the best-known advocates of the importance of creative execution in advertising was William Bernbach, founder of the Doyle Dane Bernbach agency. In his famous book on the advertising industry, *Madison Avenue*, Martin Mayer notes Bernbach's reply to David Ogilvy's Rule 2 for copywriters that "what you say in advertising is more important than how you say it."

Bernbach replied, "Execution can become content, it can be just as important as what you say. . . . A sick guy can utter some words and nothing happens; a healthy vital guy says them and they rock the world."[11]

An advertising message can be presented in numerous ways:

- Straight sell or factual message
- Scientific/technical evidence
- Demonstration
- Comparison
- Testimonial
- Slice of life
- Animation
- Personality symbol
- Fantasy
- Dramatization
- Humor
- Combinations

We now examine some of these formats and considerations involved in their use.

@ **EXHIBIT 11–11**

This Dermasil ad cites a scientific study

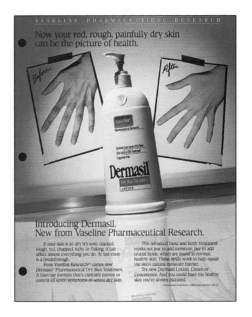

Straight sell or factual message

One of the most basic types of creative executions is the straight sell or factual message. This type of ad relies on a straightforward presentation of information concerning the product or service. This execution is often used with informational/rational appeals, where the focus of the message is the product or service and its specific attributes and/or benefits. It is commonly used in print ads. A picture of the product or service occupies part of the ad and the factual copy takes up the remainder of the ad space. (See the ad for Valvoline motor oil in Exhibit 11–10.) Straight sell executions are also used in TV advertising, with an announcer generally delivering the sales message while the product/service is shown on the screen. Ads for high-involvement consumer products as well as industrial and other business-to-business products generally use this format.

Scientific/technical evidence

In a variation of the straight sell, scientific or technical evidence is presented in the ad. Advertisers often cite technical information, results of scientific or laboratory studies, or endorsements by scientific bodies or agencies to support their advertising claims. For example, Procter & Gamble used an endorsement from the American Council on Dental Therapeutics concerning the value of fluoride in helping prevent cavities as the basis of the campaign that made Crest the leading brand on the market. The ad for Dermasil Pharmaceutical Dry Skin Treatment shown in Exhibit 11–11 uses this execution style to emphasize the breakthrough from Vaseline Research.

Demonstration

Demonstration advertising is designed to illustrate the key advantages of the product/service by showing it in actual use or in some contrived or staged situation. Demonstration executions can be very effective in convincing consumers of a product's utility or quality and of the benefits of owning or using the brand. TV is particularly well suited for demonstrating executions, since the benefits or advantages of the product can be shown right on the screen. Although perhaps a little less dramatic than TV, demonstration ads can also work in print, as shown in the ad for IVAC's Controlled Release Infusion System (CRIS) (Exhibit 11–12).

Comparison

Brand comparisons can also be the basis for the advertising execution. The comparison execution approach has become increasingly popular among advertisers, since it offers a direct way of communicating a brand's particular advantage over its competitors or

@ **EXHIBIT   11-12**   This ad demonstrates the ease of use of a drug delivery system

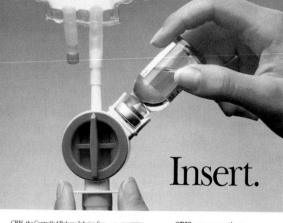
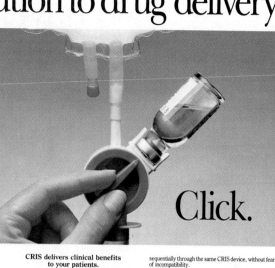

CRIS. The simple solution to drug delivery.

Insert.

Click.

CRIS, the Controlled Release Infusion System from IVAC, simplifies drug delivery. The CRIS system adapts to your existing IV administration sets and uses the primary IV solution to deliver secondary medications.

And the CRIS system delivers directly from previously reconstituted single-dose drug vials. So minibags and secondary sets are eliminated.

Designed for ease of use.

With the CRIS dial in the upright 12 o'clock position, the primary solution alone is infusing.

Administering a secondary drug is an easy two-step process. Simply insert a reconstituted single-dose vial onto the CRIS spike. Then click the dial clockwise into the 2 o'clock position.

The primary solution now flows through the vial and delivers the drug.

CRIS saves you time.

When administering medications, the CRIS system can save time.* Because you do not hang a minibag, prime a secondary set, or connect and disconnect additional tubing. And, with fewer connects and disconnects, the potential for needle sticks is greatly reduced.

For hospitals where nurses are responsible for admixing medications, the CRIS system can also significantly reduce preparation time.

After the drug has been delivered using 60 ml of primary IV solution, the vial remains in place until the next dose is required. This ensures the sterility of the spike. And the primary IV solution continues to flow uninterrupted through the vial, eliminating the need to flush the line and reducing the potential for clotted lines and unscheduled restarts.

With the CRIS dial in the 2 o'clock position, the primary IV solution flows uninterrupted through the reconstituted vial and delivers the secondary medication to the patient.

CRIS delivers clinical benefits to your patients.

By using the primary IV solution for delivery, the CRIS system minimizes the total fluid volume to the patient.

Plus, the CRIS device administers 100% of the labeled dose while some "piggyback" systems may leave from 7% to 16% undelivered in the secondary set and container.**

CRIS fits into your system.

The CRIS system works with the IV solution containers, administration sets and instruments you're now using.

The CRIS device remains as a part of the primary set, so you replace it only as frequently as you change the set.

And, because the primary solution continuously flushes the line, different medications can be administered

*Mangino P.: ASHP Annual Meeting, Washington, D.C. 1987.
Smith C.: Ames R: ASHP Annual Meeting, Washington, D.C 1987
Smith T.: Kitzenos J: American Journal of Hospital Pharmacy 1986; 43: 1830–35.
**Documentation available upon request.

sequentially through the same CRIS device, without fear of incompatibility.

What's more, the CRIS system can be used with a roller clamp or electronic rate control, and heparin locks.

CRIS is easy to implement.

For years, IVAC's District Managers and Clinical Consultants have helped implement systems in hospitals throughout the country. Their experience will help to ensure a smooth and easy implementation of the CRIS system in your hospital.

IVAC also provides in-service instructional videos, educational literature, or on-site training.

To find out more about the CRIS system, call your IVAC District Manager. Or call us direct at 1-800-482-IVAC.

IVAC CORPORATION

Touching Lives Through Technology™
10300 Campus Point Drive, San Diego, CA 92121-1579

---

positioning a new or lesser-known brand with industry leaders. Comparison executions are often used to execute competitive advantage appeals, as discussed earlier.

Testimonial

Many advertisers prefer to have their messages presented by way of a testimonial, where a person praises the product or service based on his or her personal experience with it (Exhibit 11–13). Testimonial executions can have ordinary satisfied customers discuss their own experiences with the brand and the benefits of using it. This approach can be very effective when the person delivering the testimonial is someone with whom the target audience can identify or has a particularly interesting story to tell. The testimonial must be based on actual use of the product or service to avoid legal problems, and the spokesperson must be credible.

Testimonials can be particularly effective when they come from a recognizable or popular source. Ultra Slim-Fast has used a variety of celebrities, including Los Angeles Dodgers manager Tommy Lasorda, talk-show host Kathie Lee Gifford, and her husband, sportscaster Frank Gifford, to deliver testimonials on its effectiveness in weight loss. The company is currently using actress Brooke Shields to reach a younger market.[12]

A related execution technique is the endorsement, where a well-known or respected individual such as a celebrity or expert in the product or service area speaks on behalf of the company or the brand. When endorsers promote a company or its products or services, the message is not necessarily based on their personal experiences.

@ **EXHIBIT 11–13**

This ad effectively uses a testimonial execution

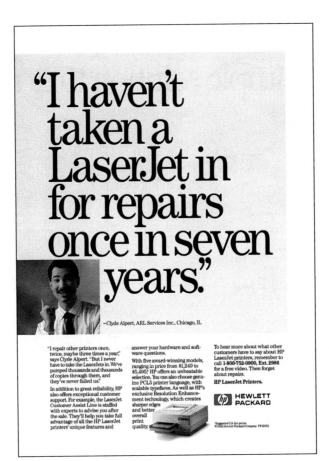

Slice of life

A widely used advertising format, particularly for package-goods products, is the slice-of-life execution, which is generally based on a problem/solution approach. This type of ad portrays a real-life situation involving a problem or conflict that consumers might face in their daily lives. The ad then shows how the advertiser's product or service can resolve the problem.

Slice-of-life executions are often criticized for being unrealistic and irritating to watch because they are often used to remind consumers of problems of a personal nature, such as dandruff, bad breath, body odor, and laundry problems. Often these ads come across as contrived, silly, phony, or even offensive to consumers. However, many advertisers still prefer this style because they believe it is effective at presenting a situation to which most consumers can relate and at registering the product feature or benefit that helps sell the brand.

For many years, Procter & Gamble was known for its reliance on slice-of-life advertising executions. In 1980, two-thirds of the company's commercials used either the slice-of-life or testimonial format. However, P&G has begun breaking away from slice-of-life commercials and using humor, animation, and other less traditional execution styles. Now only one in four of the company's ads relies on slice-of-life or testimonials.[13]

Slice-of-life or problem/solution execution approaches are not limited to consumer product advertising. A number of business-to-business marketers use a variation of this style to demonstrate how their products and services can be used as solutions to business problems. In the late 1980s and early 90s, a new advertising genre that some advertising people refer to as *slice-of-death* became popular. One well-known example was the "busi-

EXHIBIT   11–14   Slice-of-death ads remind executives of the consequences of making bad business decisions

"Whose bright idea was it to buy a phone system that was obsolete six months after we got it? I thought we were in business to make money, not throw it away."

Planned obsolescence is an unfortunate reality with many of today's business phone systems. Some manufacturers won't let you upgrade to a better system without first replacing most of your equipment.

And they make new technology available only in their latest systems.

AT&T is different. We respect your investment. Our systems are designed to be flexible. To adapt. To grow as you grow.

For example, AT&T Systems 85 & 75 allow you to add messaging, networking and other features as needed.

And we can incorporate new technology

as it becomes available. We're the first vendor to support the ISDN Primary Rate Interface, a standard that will allow today's customers an easy transition to the integrated networks of the future.

And our upgrade policies mean there are no unexpected costs or capability surprises.

AT&T protects your investment. Because we

believe the products and services you use today shouldn't be useless tomorrow.

From equipment to networking, from computers to communications, AT&T is the right choice. Call 1 800 247-1212.

AT&T
The right choice.

ness realities" campaign used by AT&T Business Systems. The campaign was targeted toward businesspeople purchasing a phone system for their company (Exhibit 11–14). The director of advertising at AT&T noted, "Businesspeople are not always nice and polite to one another. They operate under a great deal of confusion and decisions are critical to their careers. What we're saying is don't make a mistake."[14] Slice-of-death ads have also been used by other business-to-business advertisers such as Apple and Wang.

Animation

An advertising execution approach that has increased in popularity in recent years is animation. With this technique, animated scenes are drawn by artists or created on the computer, and cartoons, puppets, or other types of fictional characters may be used in the ad. Cartoon animation is especially popular for creating commercials targeted at children.

Animated cartoon characters have also been used successfully by the Leo Burnett agency in campaigns for Green Giant vegetables (valley of the Jolly Green Giant) and Keebler cookies (the Keebler elves). Another successful example of animation execution was the ad campaign developed for the California Raisin Advisory Board. A technique called Claymation was used to create the dancing raisin characters used in these ads.

The use of animation as an execution style may increase as creative specialists discover the advanced animation techniques available with computer-generated graphics and other technological innovations. Will Vinton, the developer of Claymation, developed a new technique called dimensional animation that combines three forms of production: Claymation, stop-motion animation, and computer animation. The technique was used for the first time in early 1994 in a commercial for Nabisco Chips Ahoy! cookies (Exhibit 11–15).[15]

◎ EXHIBIT 11–15

This Chips Ahoy! commercial uses a new technique known as dimensional animation

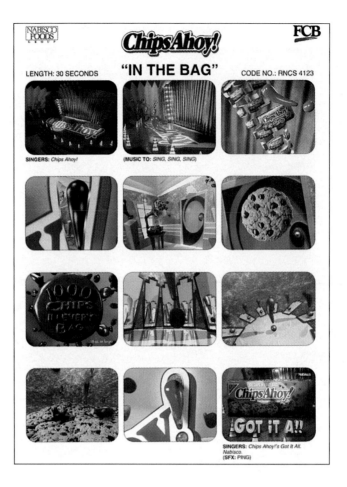

Some advertisers have begun using Roger Rabbit–style ads that mix animation with real people. Nike has used this technique to develop several creative, entertaining commercials; one featured Michael Jordan and Bugs Bunny trouncing a foursome of bullies on the basketball court.

Personality symbol

Another type of advertising execution involves developing a central character or personality symbol that can deliver the advertising message and with which the product or service can be identified. This character can be a person, like Mr. Whipple, who would request shoppers, "Please don't squeeze the Charmin," or the Maytag repairman, who sits anxiously by the phone but is never needed because the company's appliances are so reliable (Exhibit 11–16).

◎ EXHIBIT 11–16

The Maytag repairman is an example of an advertising personality symbol

Personality symbols can also be based on fantasy characters or animals. As discussed in Chapter 6, the use of visual image personalities (VIPs) is a popular way to create interest for low-involvement products. Morris, the finicky feline, has been promoting 9-Lives catfood since 1969, Charlie the Tuna first started tricking fishermen into catching him in Starkist tuna commercials in 1961, and Tony the Tiger has been touting Kellogg's Frosted Flakes as Grrreat for over three decades.

One of the most popular advertising personality symbols in recent years was Spuds MacKenzie, the bull terrier who was used to promote Bud Light beer for several years. However, Anheuser-Busch had to deal with complaints from some groups that it was using Spuds to appeal to minors—a charge the company strongly denied. Actually, the controversy over Spuds MacKenzie was mild compared to the furor over the use of Old Joe, the cartoon camel who appears in ads for Camel cigarettes. Ethical Perspective 11–1 discusses the continuing controversy surrounding the "smooth character" campaign for Camels.

≈≈≈ **Ethical Perspective 11-1**
The Controversy over Joe Camel
Continues

In late 1987, RJR Nabisco launched the "smooth character" advertising campaign featuring Old Joe, a cartoon camel. The campaign was soon criticized as an effort by RJR to reposition Camels to appeal to young people. Critics argued that ads showing Old Joe accompanied by beautiful women, racecars, jet airplanes, and other appealing images are particularly intriguing to children. They also suggested the campaign was another example of the tobacco industry's efforts to sustain sales by attracting teenagers, since 90 percent of people who smoke start before they reach the age of 21.

The controversy surrounding the campaign heated up in 1991, when three studies published in the *Journal of the American Medical Association* concluded the smooth character ads were more successful at marketing Camels to children than to adults. One of the studies concluded the ad campaign boosted RJR's share of the children's cigarette market from less than 1 percent to 32.8 percent. Another found that 91.6 percent of six-year-olds associated Old Joe with cigarettes, a level nearly equal to the association of Mickey Mouse with the Disney Channel.

These findings led a powerful coalition of health groups—formed by the American Medical Association, the American Cancer Society, and the American Lung Association—to petition the Federal Trade Commission to take immediate action against RJR's use of the smooth character ads. In 1992, Antoine Novella, the U.S. Surgeon General at the time, urged RJR to voluntarily stop using the Joe Camel ads because of their appeal to children. She also asked billboard companies and magazines and newspaper publishers to stop running the ads. In August 1993, Federal Trade Commission staff recommended the FTC seek an outright ban of the campaign on the grounds that it entices minors to smoke. In June 1994, the FTC voted 3-2 not to ban the Joe Camel ads. However, the issue may be raised again in the future and put to another vote.

Despite all the criticism, RJR says it has no intention of stopping the campaign, arguing that its responsibility is to its shareholders and it would be wrong to interrupt it solely because of criticism from antismokers. RJR officials have characterized some of the conclusions of the *JAMA* studies as absurd. The company says the campaign is targeted at adults and any appeal to children is unintentional. An RJR spokeswoman noted that the company has studies showing that despite a high awareness of Joe Camel among children, kids still don't like smoking, and that the company does not want them to smoke.

In February 1994, RJR released the results of a survey of young people aged 10 to 17 conducted by the research firm of Roper Starch; only 3 percent of the youths who recognized Joe Camel said they had a positive attitude toward smoking, and those respondents were all 16- to 17-year-olds. The study also found that while 73 percent of the youths surveyed recognized Joe Camel, he was actually among the least recognized of nine major advertising symbols. More recognized symbols included the Energizer bunny, Ronald McDonald, and Tony the Tiger.

RJR also says it adheres to guidelines of the Tobacco Institute, the industry trade association, that are designed to shield children from advertising and promotion. Under the self-imposed measures, cigarette companies cannot advertise in publications read primarily by young people. Company officials argue that young people's decision to smoke is primarily a result of peer-group pressure and lifestyle rather than tobacco advertising.

Critics still contend the Joe Camel ads are an example of the subtle ways tobacco companies appeal to children and that young people are the real target audience for the campaign. In early 1994 RJR provided antismoking advocates with a new target when it introduced Josephine Camel into the campaign. Critics say this is a blatant attempt to broaden the traditionally male brand's appeal to female smokers. Moreover, they argue the only way the problem can be resolved is by banning all forms of tobacco advertising and promotion. It will be interesting to see how long Old Joe and his friends keep smoking those Camels.

Sources: Bruce Horowitz, "Cigarette Ads under Fire," *Los Angeles Times*, March 10, 1992, pp. D1, 6; Eben Shapiro, "FTC Staff Recommends Ban of Joe Camel Campaign," *The Wall Street Journal*, Aug. 11, 1993, p. B1; Kevin Goldman, "A Stable of Females Has Joined Joe Camel in Controversial Cigarette Ad Campaign," *The Wall Street Journal*, Feb. 18, 1994, pp. B1, 8; Ira Teinowitz, "Joe Camel Is No Tony Tiger to Kids," *Advertising Age*, Feb. 21, 1994, p. 36; Steven W. Calford and Ira Teinowitz, "Joe Camel Gets Reprieve, for Now," *Advertising Age*, June 6, 1994, p. 52.

Fantasy

An execution technique that is popular for emotional types of appeals such as image advertising is fantasy. Fantasy executions are particularly well suited for television, as the commercial can become a 30-second escape for the viewer into another lifestyle. The product or service becomes a central part of the situation created by the advertiser. Cosmetics ads often use fantasy appeals to create images and symbols that become associated with the brand.

Dramatization

Another execution technique particularly well suited to television is dramatization, where the focus is on telling a short story with the product or service as the star. Dramatization is somewhat akin to slice-of-life execution in that it often relies on the problem/solution approach, but it uses more excitement and suspense in telling the story. The purpose of using drama is to draw the viewer into the action it portrays. Advocates of drama note that when it is successful, the audience becomes lost in the story and

EXHIBIT 11-17

This Zerex ad uses a dramatization execution

experiences the concerns and feelings of the characters.[16] According to Sandra Moriarty, there are five basic steps to a dramatic commercial:

> First is exposition, where the stage is set for the upcoming action. Next comes conflict, which is a technique for identifying the problem. The middle of the dramatic form is a period of rising action where the story builds, the conflict intensifies, the suspense thickens. The fourth step is the climax, where the problem is solved. The last part of a drama is the resolution, where the wrapup is presented. In advertising that includes product identification and call to action.[17]

The real challenge facing the creative team is how to encompass all these elements into a 30-second commercial. A good example of the dramatization execution technique is the ad for Zerex antifreeze in Exhibit 11–17, which shows a woman's sense of relief when her car starts at the airport on a cold winter night. The ad concludes with a strong identification slogan, "The temperature never drops below Zerex," that connects the brand name to its product benefit.

Humor

Like comparisons, humor was discussed in Chapter 7 as a type of advertising appeal, but this technique can also be used as a way of presenting other advertising appeals. Humorous executions are particularly well suited to television or radio, although some print ads attempt to use this style. The pros and cons of using humor as an executional technique are similar to those associated with its use as an advertising appeal.

Combinations

Many of the execution techniques can be combined to present the advertising message. For example, animation is often used to create personality symbols or present a fantasy. Slice-of-life ads are often used to demonstrate a product or service, whereas comparisons are sometimes made using a humorous approach. It is the responsibility of the creative specialist(s) to determine whether more than one execution style can or should be used in creating the ad.

CREATIVE TACTICS

Our discussion thus far has focused on the development of creative strategy and various appeals and execution styles that can be used for the advertising message. Once the creative approach, type of appeal, and execution style have been determined, attention turns to creating the actual advertisement. The design and production of advertising messages involve a number of activities, among them writing copy, developing illustrations and other visual elements of the ad, and bringing all of the pieces together to create an effective message. In this section, we examine the verbal and visual elements of an ad and discuss tactical considerations in creating print ads and TV commercials.

Creative Tactics for Print Advertising

The three basic components of a print ad are the headline, the body copy, and the visual or illustrations. The headline and body copy portions of the ad are the responsibility of the copywriters; artists, often working under the direction of an art director, are responsible for the visual presentation. Art directors also work with the copywriters to develop a layout, or arrangement of the various components of the ad—headlines, subheads, body copy, illustrations, captions, logos, and the like. We briefly examine the three components of a print ad and how they are coordinated.

Headlines

The **headline** refers to the words in the leading position of the ad—the words that will be read first or are positioned to draw the most attention.[18] Headlines are usually set in larger type and are often set apart from the body copy or text portion of the ad to give them prominence. Most advertising people consider the headline the most important part of a print ad.

The most important function of a headline is attracting readers' attention and making them interested in the rest of the message. While the visual portion of an ad is obviously important, the headline often shoulders most of the responsibility of attracting the readers' attention. Research has shown the headline is generally the first thing people look at in a print ad, followed by the illustration. Only 20 percent of readers go beyond the headline and read the body copy.[19] So in addition to attracting attention, the headline must give the reader sufficient reason to read the copy portion of the ad, which contains more detailed and persuasive information about the product or service. To do this, the headline must put forth the main theme, appeal, or proposition of the advertisement in a few words. Some print ads contain little if any body copy, so the headline must work with the illustration to communicate the entire advertising message.

Headlines also preform a segmentation function by engaging the attention and interest of consumers who are most likely to buy a particular product or service. Advertisers begin the segmentation process by choosing to advertise in certain types of publications (e.g., a travel, general interest, or fashion magazine). An effective headline goes even further in selecting good prospects for the product by addressing their specific needs, wants, or interests. For example, the headline in the Audemars Piguet ad shown in Exhibit 11–18 suggests this unique watch is for a very elite target market.

Types of headlines

There are numerous headline possibilities. The type used depends on several factors, including the creative strategy, the particular advertising situation (e.g., product type, media vehicle(s) being used, timeliness), and its relationship to other components of the ad, such as the illustration or body copy. Headlines can be categorized as direct and indirect. **Direct headlines** are straightforward and informative in terms of the message they are presenting and the target audience it is directed toward. Common types of direct headlines include those offering a specific benefit, making a promise, or announcing a reason the reader should be interested in the product or service.

◉ **EXHIBIT 11–18**

The headline of this ad is likely to engage the attention of a very elite target audience

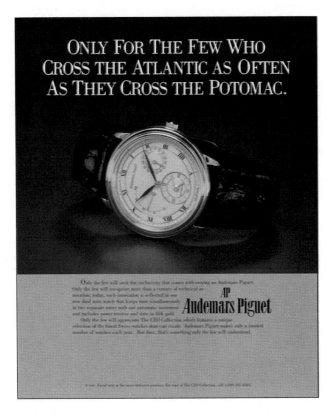

Indirect headlines are not straightforward about identifying the product or service or getting to the point. But they are often more effective at attracting readers' attention and/or interest because they provoke curiosity and lure the reader into the body copy to learn an answer or get an explanation. Techniques for writing indirect headlines include the use of questions, provocations, how-to statements, and challenges.

Indirect headlines rely on their ability to generate curiosity or intrigue so as to motivate the reader to become involved with the ad and read the body copy to find out the point of the message. This can be risky if the headline is not provocative enough to get the readers' interest. Advertisers deal with this problem by using a visual appeal that helps attract attention and offers another reason for reading more of the message. For example, in Exhibit 11–19, the question headline is accompanied by an amusing illustration that entices travelers to read the message to learn more about Delta's new Los Angeles to San Francisco shuttle and Person to Person service. Do you think this ad would have been as effective with a more traditional illustration such as a harried business traveler?

Subheads

While many ads have only one headline, it is also common to see print ads containing the main headline and one or more secondary headlines or **subheads**. Subheads usually appear in a type size smaller than the main headline but larger than the body copy. Subheads are usually found above or below the main headline, although they may also appear within the body copy. The Delta ad in Exhibit 11–19 uses subheads in the latter two positions.

Subheads are often used to enhance the readability of the message by breaking up large amounts of body copy and highlighting key sales points. Their content reinforces the headline and advertising slogan or theme.

Body copy

The main text portion of a print ad is referred to as the **body copy** (or sometimes as copy). While the body copy is usually the heart of the advertising message, getting the target audience to read it is often difficult. The copywriter faces a dilemma: the body

@ EXHIBIT 11–19

This ad combines a question headline with an amusing illustration to attract readers' attention

copy must be long enough to communicate the advertiser's message yet short enough to hold readers' interest.

Body copy content often flows from the points made in the headline or various subheads, but the specific content depends on the type of advertising appeal and/or execution style being used. For example, straight-sell copy that presents relevant information, product features and benefits, or competitive advantages is often used with the various types of rational appeals discussed earlier in the chapter. Emotional appeals often use narrative copy that tells a story or provides an interesting account of a problem or situation involving the product.

Advertising body copy can be written to go along with various types of creative appeals and executions—comparisons, price appeals, demonstrations, humor, dramatizations, and the like. Copywriters choose a copy style that is appropriate for the type of appeal being used and effective for executing the creative strategy and communicating the advertiser's message to the target audience.

Visual elements

The third major component of a print ad is the visual element. The illustration is often a dominant part of a print ad and plays an important role in determining its effectiveness. The visual portion of an ad must attract attention, communicate an idea or image, and work in a synergetic fashion with the headline and body copy to produce an effective message. Notice how the visual portion of the British Airways ad in Exhibit 11–20 helps reinforce the message announcing the airline's new arrival facilities for passengers at the two London airports.

A number of decisions have to be made regarding the visual portion of the ad: what identification marks should be included in the ad (brand name, company or trade name, trademarks, logos); whether to use photos or hand-drawn or painted illustrations; what colors to use (or even perhaps black and white or just a splash of color); and what the focus of the visual should be.

EXHIBIT 11–20

The visual portion of this ad interacts very well with the message

Nonstop to London.
Showers expected upon arrival.

British Airways' new arrival facilities at London's Heathrow and Gatwick airports are making quite a splash. Now, ClubWorld™ and First Class passengers can enjoy a hot shower and breakfast or even catch up on business in our private lounge. You'll be off to a flying start. *It's the way we make you feel* that makes us the world's favourite airline.

BRITISH AIRWAYS
The world's favourite airline™

Layout

While each individual component of a print ad is important, the key factor is how these elements are blended into a finished advertisement. A **layout** is the physical arrangement of the various parts of the ad, including the headline, subheads, illustrations, body copy, and any identifying marks. The layout shows where each part of the ad will be placed and gives guidelines to the people working on the ad. For example, the layout helps the copywriter determine how much space he or she has to work with and how much copy should be written. The layout can also guide the art director in determining the size and type of photos. Layouts are often done in rough form and presented to the client so the advertiser can visualize what the ad will look like before giving preliminary approval. The agency should get client approval of the layout before moving to the more costly stages of print production.

Creative Tactics for Television

As consumers, we see so many TV commercials that it's easy to take for granted the amount of time, effort, and money that goes into making them. Creating and producing commercials that break through the high level of clutter on TV and communicate effectively is a detailed, expensive process. On a cost-per-minute basis, commercials are the most expensive productions seen on television.[20]

TV is a unique and powerful advertising medium because it contains the elements of sight, sound, and motion, which can be combined to create a variety of advertising appeals and executions. Unlike print, the viewer does not control the rate at which the message is presented, so there is no opportunity to review points of interest or reread things that are not communicated clearly. As with any form of advertising, one of the first goals in creating TV commercials is to get the viewers' attention and then maintain it. This can be particularly challenging because of the clutter, and people often view TV commercials while doing other things (reading a book or magazine, talking).

Like print ads, TV commercials have several components. The video and audio must work together to create the right impact and communicate the advertiser's message.

Video

The video elements of a commercial are what is seen on the TV screen. The visual portion generally dominates the commercial, so it must attract viewers' attention and communicate an idea, message, and/or image. A number of visual elements may have to be coordinated to produce a successful ad. Decisions have to be made regarding the product, the presenter, action sequences, demonstrations, and the like, as well as the setting(s), the talent or characters who will appear in the commercial, and such other factors as lighting, graphics, color, and identifying symbols.

Audio

The audio portion of a commercial includes voices, music, and sound effects. Voices are used in different ways in commercials. They may be heard through the direct presentation of a spokesperson or as a conversation among various people appearing in the commercial. A common method for presenting the audio portion of a commercial is through a **voiceover**, where the message is delivered or action on the screen is narrated or described by an announcer who is not visible. A recent trend among major advertisers is to have distinctive celebrities do voiceovers for their commercials. Actor Gene Hackman does many of the voiceovers for United Airlines spots, Jack Lemmon does Honda commercials, Joanne Woodward is the voice on many AT&T ads, and Rob Morrow does MasterCard. Music is also an important part of many TV commercials and can play a variety of roles.[21] In many commercials, the music provides a pleasant background or helps create the appropriate mood. Advertisers often use *needledrop*, which Linda Scott describes as follows:

> Needledrop is an occupational term common to advertising agencies and the music industry. It refers to music that is prefabricated, multipurpose, and highly conventional. It is, in that sense, the musical equivalent of stock photos, clip art, or canned copy. Needledrop is an inexpensive substitute for original music; paid for on a one-time basis, it is dropped into a commercial or film when a particular normative effect is desired.[22]

In other commercials, music is much more central to the advertising message. It can be used to get attention, break through the advertising clutter, communicate a key selling point, help establish an image or position, or add feeling. For example, music can work through a classical conditioning process to create positive emotions that become associated with the advertised product or service.[23] Music can also create a positive mood that makes the consumer more receptive toward the advertising message.[24]

Because music can play such an important role in the creative strategy, many companies have paid large sums of money for the rights to use popular songs in their commercials. Recently advertisers have been developing commercials around classic songs from the 1960s and 70s. Exhibit 11–21 lists some of the advertisers and the songs they have used.

Another important musical element in both TV and radio commercials is **jingles**, catchy songs about a product or service that usually carry the advertising theme and a simple message. For example, Doublemint gum has used the well-known "Double your pleasure, double your fun with Doublemint, Doublemint gum" for years. The jingle is very memorable and serves as a good reminder of the mint flavor of the product. Jingles can be used by themselves as the basis for a musical commercial. For example, commercials for Diet Pepsi are built around Ray Charles singing the jingle for the brand, which incorporates the "You've got the right one, baby! Uh huh!" slogan. In some commercials, jingles are used more as a form of product identification and appear at the end of the message. Jingles are often composed by companies that specialize in writing commercial music for advertising. These jingle houses work with the creative team to determine the role music will play in the commercial and the message that needs to be communicated.

@ **EXHIBIT 11–21**

Classic songs that have been used in commercials

If finally happened—Bob Dylan has allowed *The Times They Are A-Changin'* to be used in an advertisement on television. The ad went on the air this month, but it is not the first—only the most amazing—example of the commercial use of a rebellious classic.

- Song: *The Times They Are A-Changin'*, **Bob Dylan**
- Product: **Coopers & Lybrand,** accountants

For an undisclosed sum, Dylan permitted the Big Six firm to use folkie Richie Havens' rendition of his protest anthem. The company cannot use Dylan's name, even when discussing the spot.

- Song: *Teach Your Children*, **Crosby, Stills, Nash & Young**
- Product: **Fruit of the Loom** underwear

For $1.5 million, Fruit of the Loom used 30 seconds of the song, with writer Nash himself rerecording it. "I'm not that precious about my music. We're not talking Mozart here," he said.

- Song: *Revolution*, **the Beatles**
- Product: **Nike** athletic shoes

Michael Jackson owned the rights to the Lennon and McCartney composition, Capitol Records owned the original masters, and so for $500,000 Nike was allowed to use the actual voices of the Beatles.

- Song: *Born to Be Wild*, **Steppenwolf**
- Product: The **Ford Mercury Cougar**

With a yuppie, his leather jacket, and his cougar, the ad was part of a campaign that also used *Proud Mary* and the Beatles' *Help*. In three years the average age of Cougar buyers fell from 44 to 35.

- Song: *Satisfaction*, **the Rolling Stones**
- Product: **Snickers** candy bars

Mick Jagger and Keith Richards, the songwriters, and ABKCO, the owner of the rights to the song, were made an irresistible offer in 1991: $4 million, with $2.8 million going to the composers.

- Song: *Turn! Turn! Turn!*, **the Byrds**
- Product: **Time** the weekly newsmagazine

Folk legend Pete Seeger set words from the *Book of Ecclesiastes* to music, and the Byrds' version became a huge early hippie hit. In the ad it segued into "Hi, I'm Nancy, an operator here at TIME."

Source: *Time*, January 31, 1994, p. 23.

Planning and production of TV commercials

One of the first decisions that has to be made in planning a TV commercial is the type of appeal and execution style that will be used. Television is well suited to both rational and emotional advertising appeals or combinations of both. Various execution styles used with rational appeals, such as a straight sell or announcement, demonstration, testimonial, or comparison, work well on TV.

Advertisers recognize that they need to do more than talk about, demonstrate, or compare their products or services. Their commercials must break through the clutter and grab the attention of viewers. An example of this is the commercial for the Acura Integra shown in Exhibit 11–22, which is targeted at young baby boomers and recalls the days of playing with Hot Wheels, the toy cars marketed by Mattel. To convey how much fun the Integra is to drive, the agency went to great pains to show it negotiating a giant Hot Wheels track in the desert. The spot has been very effective in enhancing perceptions of the sportiness of the Integra and making it the best-selling import in the sportscar category.

Advertisers must often appeal to emotional, as well as rational, buying motives. Television is essentially an entertainment medium, and many advertisers recognize that their commercials are successful because they entertain as well as inform. Exhibit 11–23 shows the 10 most popular television campaigns of 1993. Many of these campaigns are characterized by commercials with strong entertainment value, such as Coca-Cola ads and the McDonald's spots featuring former basketball stars Larry Bird and Michael Jordan trying to outdo one another in a shooting contest with seemingly impossible "nothing but net" shots. TV is particularly well suited to drama and emotion; no other advertising medium can touch the emotions of consumers as well. Various emotional appeals

◎ **EXHIBIT 11-22**

The creative "Hot Wheels" commercial has helped make the Acura Integra a leading import sportscar

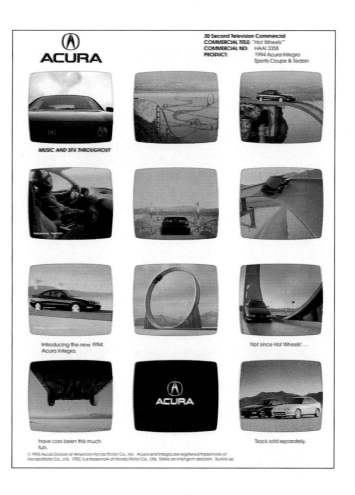

◎ **EXHIBIT 11-22**

The creative "Hot Wheels" commercial has helped make the Acura Integra a leading import sportscar

such as humor, fear, and fantasy work well on TV, as do dramatizations and slice-of-life executions.

Planning the commercial

The various elements of a TV commercial are brought together in a **script**, a written version of a commercial that provides a detailed description of its video and audio content. The script shows the various audio components of the commercial—the copy to be spoken by voices, music, and sound effects. The video portion of the script provides the visual plan of the commercial—camera actions and angles, scenes, transitions, and other important descriptions. Scripts also show how the video corresponds to the audio portion of the commercial.

◎ **EXHIBIT 11-23**

Top 10 television campaigns of 1993

1993 Rank	1992 Rank	Brand	Ad Agency
1	5	McDonald's	Leo Burnett
2	2	Pepsi	BBDO
3	9	Coca-Cola	Creative Artists Agency
4	3	Nike	Wieden & Kennedy
5	1	Little Caesars	Cliff Freeman & Partners
6	7	Budweiser	DMB & B
7	—	Taco Bell	Foote, Cone & Belding
8	10	Taster's Choice	McCann-Erickson
9	4	DuPont Stainmaster	BDDO
10	16	Lexus	Team One

Source: Video Storyboard Tests Inc.; Kevin Goldman, "Year's Top Commercials Propelled by Star Power," *The Wall Street Journal*, March 16, 1994, pp. B1, 5.

EXHIBIT 11-24 Three phases of production for electronic media

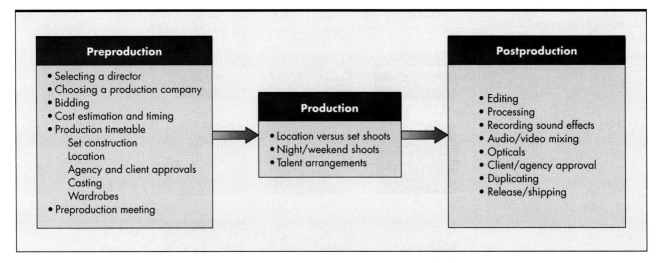

Once the basic script has been conceived, the writer and art director get together to produce a storyboard, a series of drawings used to present the visual plan or layout of a proposed commercial. The storyboard contains still drawings of the video scenes and descriptions of the audio that accompanies each scene. Like layouts for print ads, storyboards provide those involved in the production and approval of the commercial with a good approximation of what the final commercial will look like. In some cases an aniamatic, a videotape of the storyboard along with the soundtrack, may be produced if a more finished form of the commercial is needed for client presentations or pretesting.

Production

Once the storyboard or aniamatic of the commercial is approved, it is ready to move to the production phase, which involves three stages:

1. **Preproduction**—all the work and activities that occur before the actual shooting/recording of the commercial.
2. **Production**—the period during which the commercial is filmed or videotaped and recorded.
3. **Postproduction**—activities and work that occur after the commercial has been filmed and recorded.

The various activities of each phase are shown in Exhibit 11–24. Before the final production process begins, however, the client must usually review and approve the creative strategy and the various tactics that will be used in creating the advertising message.

CLIENT EVALUATION AND APPROVAL OF CREATIVE WORK

While the creative specialists have much responsibility for determining the advertising appeal and execution style to be used in a campaign, the client must evaluate and approve the creative approach before any ads are produced. A number of people on the client side may be involved in evaluating the creative work of the agency, including the advertising or communications manager, product or brand managers, marketing director or vice president, representatives from the legal department, and sometimes even the president or chief executive officer (CEO) of the company or the board of directors.

The amount of input each of these individuals has in the creative evaluation and approval process varies depending on the company's policies, the importance of the product to the company, the role of advertising in the marketing program, and the advertising approach being recommended. IMC Perspective 11–1 discusses how the Chiat/Day agency had to convince Apple's board of directors to air the "1984" commercial used to introduce the Macintosh personal computer.

IMC Perspective 11-1
The Commercial That Changed Advertising—and Why We Almost Didn't See It

In 1983, Apple Computer was planning the introduction of its line of Macintosh personal computers, which was designed to take on its main competitor, corporate giant IBM. Apple had just lost its lead in the PC market to IBM and its previous product introduction, the $10,000 Lisa, had not been very successful. Some analysts suggested that the survival of Apple might depend on the market's response to the Mac.

Apple's marketing strategy called for the introduction of the Macintosh to be a major event that would generate immediate support for the new product. The advertising agency, Chiat/Day, was given the creative challenge of coming up with a blockbuster idea that would result in a dramatic commercial to introduce the Mac. Chiat/Day's creative team developed a commercial based on the concept of Big Brother (purportedly symbolizing IBM) from George Orwell's classic novel *1984*. The ad used stark images of Orwell's vision of Big Brother and a dramatic scene of a young woman throwing a mallet through a movie screen to destroy the controlling force. More than $500,000 was spent to produce the "1984" commercial, which was filmed in London by well-known film director Ridley Scott and contained a cast of more than 200.

When the commercial was first shown at Apple's annual sales meeting in October 1983, there was stunned silence followed by a 15-minute standing ovation. Apple was ready to showcase the 60-second commercial in two spots during the 1984 Super Bowl that would cost $500,000 each. However, there was still one problem—getting approval from Apple's board of directors for the avant-garde ad and the million-dollar media purchase.

The board thought the commercial was too controversial and might be detrimental to Apple's image, particularly in the business market. The cost-conscious board also thought the Super Bowl rates were too expensive and directed the agency to sell off the two spots. The agency began working to sell off the media time while simultaneously lobbying Apple not to cancel

the ad. The agency did manage to sell one of the 60-second spots but could not attract a reasonable offer for the other. Two days before the game, the Apple board reluctantly approved airing the commercial.

The Super Bowl showing of "1984" was the only time it ever appeared as a commercial spot on network TV. The impact of the ad was tremendous. It was the focus of attention in the media and the talk of the advertising and marketing industries. Perhaps most important, the ad helped Apple achieve a very ambitious sales goal. Apple projected sales of 50,000 Macs the first 100 days; actual sales surpassed 72,000 units.

Over time the "1984" spot became one of the most talked-about commercials ever. In 1990, *Advertising Age*, the ad industry's leading trade publication, chose it as the commercial of the decade and Chiat/Day was named agency of the decade. Ten years after the commercial first ran, it still receives numerous accolades. In January 1994, *Advertising Age* published a feature story that said the "1984" spot had changed the nature of advertising forever. It helped turn the Super Bowl from a football game into advertising's super event of the year. And it ushered in the era of advertising as news: the three major TV networks replayed parts or all of the spot as a story on nightly news programs. John O'Toole, president of the American Association of Advertising Agencies, noted that "1984" was the beginning of a new era of integrated marketing communications as event marketing, with sales promotion and PR built in.

Many view the Macintosh PC as one of the most significant new products ever introduced, since it revolutionized personal computing and transformed the production of graphics around the world. The "computer for the rest of us" is also credited with helping to bring computing power to the people. As *Advertising Age* critic Bob Garfield said, "This is what happens when breakthrough technology is given the benefit of the greatest TV commercial ever made."

Sources: Bradley Johnson, "10 Years after '1984': The Commercial, and the Product That Changed Advertising," *Advertising Age*, June 1994, pp. 1, 12–14; Bob Garfield, "Breakthrough Product Gets Greatest TV Spot," *Advertising Age*, Jan. 10, 1994, p. 14; Cleveland Horton, "Apple's Bold '1984' Scores on All Fronts," *Advertising Age*, Jan. 1, 1990, p. 12.

Earlier in the chapter, we noted that Procter & Gamble has been moving away from testimonials and slice-of-life advertising executions to somewhat riskier and more lively forms of advertising. But the company remains very conservative and has been slow to adopt the avant-garde ads used by many of its competitors. Agencies that do the advertising for various P&G brands recognize that quirky executions that challenge the company's subdued corporate culture are not likely to be approved.[25]

In many cases, top management is involved in selecting an ad agency and must approve the theme and creative strategy for the campaign. Evaluation and approval of the individual ads proposed by the agency often rest with the advertising and product managers who are primarily responsible for the brand. The account executive and a member of the creative team present the creative concept to the client's advertising and product and/or marketing mangers for their approval before beginning production. A careful evaluation should be made before the ad actually enters production, since this stage requires considerable time and money as suppliers are hired to perform the various functions required to produce the actual ad. The client's evaluation of the print layout or commercial storyboard can be difficult, since the advertising or product manager is generally not a creative expert and must be careful not to reject viable creative approaches or accept ideas that will result in inferior advertising. However, personnel on the client side can use certain guidelines to judge the efficacy of creative approaches suggested by the agency.

Guidelines for Evaluating Creative Output

Advertisers use numerous criteria to evaluate the creative approach suggested by the agency. In some instances, the client may want to have the rough layout or storyboard pretested to get quantitative information to assist in the evaluation. However, the evaluation process is usually more subjective; the advertising or product manager relies on qualitative considerations. Basic criteria for evaluating creative approaches are discussed below.

- **Is the creative approach consistent with the brand's marketing and advertising objectives?** One of the most important factors the client must consider is whether the creative appeal and execution style recommended by the agency are consistent with the marketing strategy for the brand and the role advertising and promotion have been assigned in the overall marketing program. This means the creative approach must be compatible with the image of the brand and the way it is positioned in the marketplace and should contribute to the marketing and advertising objectives.

- **Is the creative approach consistent with the creative strategy and objectives? Does it communicate what it is supposed to?** The advertising appeal and execution must meet the communications objectives laid out in the copy platform, and the ad must say what the advertising strategy calls for it to say. Creative specialists can lose sight of what the advertising message is supposed to be and come up with an approach that fails to execute the advertising strategy. Individuals responsible for approving the ad should ask the creative specialists to explain how the appeal or execution style adheres to the creative strategy and helps meet communication objectives.

- **Is the creative approach appropriate for the target audience?** Generally, much time has been spent defining, locating, and attempting to understand the target audience for the advertiser's product or service. Careful consideration should be given to whether the ad appeal or execution recommended will appeal to, be understood by, and communicate effectively with the target audience. This involves a careful consideration of all elements of the ad and how the audience will respond to them. Advertisers do not want to approve advertising that they believe will receive a negative reaction from the target audience. For example, it has been suggested that advertising targeted to older consumers should use models that are 10 years younger than the average age of the target audience, since most people feel younger than their chronological age.[26] Advertisers also face a considerable challenge developing ads for the teen market because of the rapidly changing styles, fashions, language, and values of this age group. They may find they are using an advertising approach, a spokesperson, or even an expression that is no longer popular among teens.

- **Does the creative approach communicate a clear and convincing message to the customer?** Most ads are supposed to communicate a message that will help sell the brand. However, as noted in the opening vignette to Chapter 10, many ads fail to communicate a clear and convincing message that motivates consumers to use a brand. While creativity is important in advertising, it is also important that the advertising communicate information attributes, features and benefits, and/or images that give consumers a reason to buy the brand.

- **Does the creative execution overwhelm the message?** A common criticism of advertising, and TV commercials in particular, is that so much emphasis is placed on creative execution that the advertiser's message gets overshadowed. Many creative, entertaining commercials have failed to register the brand name and/or selling points effectively.

  For example, a few years ago the agency for North American Philips Lighting Corp. developed an award-winning campaign that focused on the humorous results when lightbulbs fail at just the wrong time. The spots included a woman who appears to accidentally vacuum up her screeching cat after a lightbulb blows out and an elderly couple using Philips Pastel bulbs to create a romantic mood (Exhibit 11–25). While the purpose of the campaign was to help Philips make inroads into General Electric's dominance in the lightbulb market, many consumers did not notice the Philips brand name. A Video Storyboard survey showed that many viewers thought the ads were for GE lightbulbs rather than for Philips. Surveys taken a year later by the agency that created the campaign showed that brand awareness and sales had increased considerably, but some advertising people still think the ad was too creative and entertaining and overwhelmed the message.[27]

  With the increasing amount of clutter in most advertising media, it may be necessary to use a novel creative approach to gain the viewer's or reader's attention. However, the creative execution cannot overwhelm the message. Clients must walk a fine line to make sure the sales message is not lost and be careful not to stifle the efforts of the creative specialists and force them into producing dull, boring advertising.

- **Is the creative approach appropriate for the media environment in which it is likely to be seen?** Each media vehicle has its own particular climate that results from the nature of its editorial content, the type of reader or viewer it attracts, and the nature of the ads it contains. Consideration should be given to how well the ad fits into the media environment in which it will be shown. For example, the Super Bowl has become a showcase for commercials. People who care very little about advertising know how much a 30-second commercial costs and pay as much attention to the ads as to the game itself. So many advertisers feel compelled to develop new ads for the Super Bowl or to save new commercials for the game.

- **Is the advertisement truthful and tasteful?** The ultimate responsibility for determining whether an ad deceives or offends the target audience lies with the client. It is the job of the advertising or product manager to evaluate the approach suggested by the creative specialists against company standards. The firm's legal department may be asked to review the ad to determine whether the creative appeal, message content, or execution could cause any problems for the company. It is much better to catch any potential legal problems before the ad is shown to the public.

These factors are basic guidelines the advertising manager, product manager, or other personnel on the client side can use in reviewing, evaluating, and approving the ideas offered by the creative specialists. There may be other factors specific to the firm's ad-

@ **EXHIBIT 11–25** Some advertising experts think these Philips Lighting commercials may have been too creative and overwhelmed the message

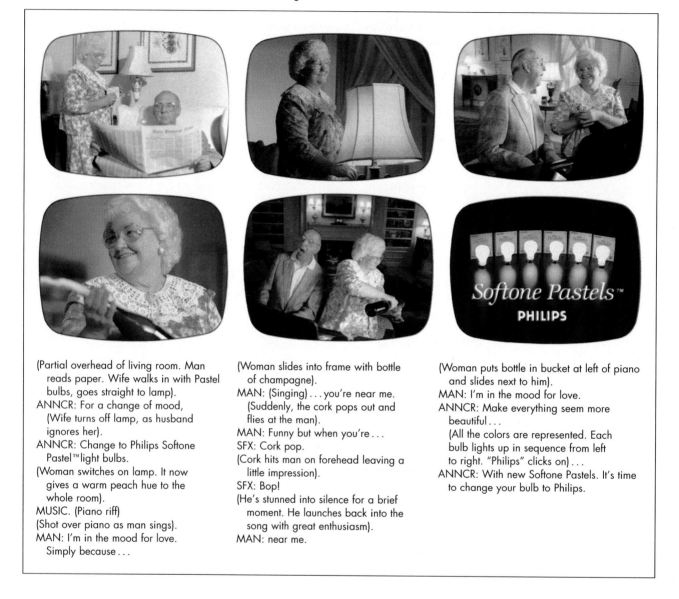

(Partial overhead of living room. Man reads paper. Wife walks in with Pastel bulbs, goes straight to lamp).
ANNCR: For a change of mood,
(Wife turns off lamp, as husband ignores her).
ANNCR: Change to Philips Softone Pastel™ light bulbs.
(Woman switches on lamp. It now gives a warm peach hue to the whole room).
MUSIC. (Piano riff)
(Shot over piano as man sings).
MAN: I'm in the mood for love. Simply because . . .

(Woman slides into frame with bottle of champagne).
MAN: (Singing) . . . you're near me.
(Suddenly, the cork pops out and flies at the man).
MAN: Funny but when you're . . .
SFX: Cork pop.
(Cork hits man on forehead leaving a little impression).
SFX: Bop!
(He's stunned into silence for a brief moment. He launches back into the song with great enthusiasm).
MAN: near me.

(Woman puts bottle in bucket at left of piano and slides next to him).
MAN: I'm in the mood for love.
ANNCR: Make everything seem more beautiful . . .
(All the colors are represented. Each bulb lights up in sequence from left to right. "Philips" clicks on) . . .
ANNCR: With new Softone Pastels. It's time to change your bulb to Philips.

vertising and marketing situation. Also, there may be situations where it is acceptable to deviate from the standards the firm usually uses in judging creative output. As we shall see in Chapter 20, the client may want to move beyond these subjective criteria and use more sophisticated pretesting methods to determine the value of a particular approach suggested by the creative specialist or team.

@ *SUMMARY*

In this chapter, we examined how the advertising message will be implemented and executed. Once the creative strategy that will guide the advertising campaign has been determined, attention turns to the specific type of advertising appeal and execution format to carry out the creative plan. The appeal is the central message used in the ad to elicit some response from consumers or influ-

ence their feelings. Appeals can be broken into two broad categories, rational and emotional. Rational appeals focus on consumers' practical, functional, or utilitarian need for the product or service; emotional appeals relate to social and/or psychological reasons for purchasing a product or service. Numerous types of appeals are available to advertisers within each category.

The creative execution style is the way the advertising appeal is presented in the message. A number of common execution techniques were examined in the chapter, along with considerations for their use. Attention was also given to tactical issues involved in creating print and TV advertising. The components of a print ad include headlines, body copy, illustrations, and layout. We also examined the video and audio components of TV commercials and various considerations involved in the planning and production of commercials.

Creative specialists are responsible for determining the advertising appeal and execution style as well as the tactical aspects of creating advertisements. However, the client must review, evaluate, and approve the creative approach before any ads are produced or run. A number of criteria can be used by advertising, product, or brand managers and others involved in the promotional process to evaluate the advertising messages before approving final production.

KEY TERMS

advertising appeal, p. 288

creative execution style, p. 288

informational/rational appeals, p. 288

emotional appeals, p. 291

transformational ad, p. 291

reminder advertising, p. 293

teaser advertising, p. 293

headline, p. 303

direct headlines, p. 303

indirect headlines, p. 304

subheads, p. 304

body copy, p. 304

layout, p. 306

voiceover, p. 307

jingles, p. 307

script, p. 309

DISCUSSION QUESTIONS

1. Analyze the strategy of Acura, discussed in the opening vignette, to reposition its Legend model as a prestigious car that is worth a premium price. Do you think this strategy will be successful? Why or why not?

2. Discuss the differences between an advertising appeal and a creative execution style. Choose several ads and analyze the particular appeal and execution style used in each.

3. For what type of products or services would an advertiser be likely to use a feature appeal? Find an example of this type of advertising appeal and describe why it is appropriate.

4. Emotional appeals have become very common in advertising over the past decade. Find an example of an advertising campaign that uses an emotional appeal effectively and one that you think does not use emotions very well. Analyze the use of emotion in each campaign.

5. What is meant by transformational advertising? For what types of products or services would a transformational ad be most suitable?

6. Some people claim the distinction between rational and emotional advertising appeals is irrelevant because all advertising includes aspects of both. Do you agree or disagree with this statement?

7. Some advertising critics believe the Taster's Choice "brewing romance" campaign is no longer effective, since it is difficult to keep a serial theme going for several years. Do you think this campaign is still effective? Why or why not?

8. Discuss the ethical implications of using personality symbols who might appeal to young people for advertising alcohol or tobacco. Do you agree or disagree with the advertisers who say they do not intentionally try to reach young people with ads using these personality symbols?

9. R. J. Reynolds released the results of a study conducted by the Roper Starch research firm showing that more teenagers who were aware of cigarette advertising remembered the Philip Morris Marlboro man than remembered the Joe Camel character (47 percent to 26 percent). How would you interpret this finding? Can RJR use it as part of its defense in the controversy involving the Joe Camel ad campaign?

10. What are the various roles of the headline in a print ad? Find examples of print ads that use direct and indirect headlines.

11. Discuss the role of music in TV commercials. Evaluate the strategy of advertisers to pay large sums of money to use some of the classic songs of the 60s and 70s in their commercials.

12. Choose a current advertising campaign and analyze it with respect to the creative criteria discussed in the last section of the chapter. Do you think the advertising meets all of the guidelines?

Chapter **12**

Media Planning and Strategy

Chapter Objectives

- To introduce the key terminology necessary to understand media planning.
- To provide an understanding of the development of a media plan.

- To provide an understanding of the process of developing and implementing media strategies.
- To introduce sources of media information and characteristics of media.

New Media Require Marketers to Rethink Their Strategies

As soon as advertisers think they have a grip on the variety of media available to them, some change makes it even more obvious that they don't. New media seem to be added almost daily, the existing media are constantly being transformed, and consumers' response to both new and existing vehicles isn't constant either. The media planner's job—never an easy one—is becoming even more complicated.

Consider just a few of the changes that are taking place:

- Television will soon offer up to as many as 500 channels on an interactive basis (see insert), allowing consumers to control their own times of exposure and perhaps offering them the option to pay to view commercial-free programming.
- There may be ads in space—literally. Advertisers are exploring the possibility of lighting up the night sky with ads placed in the stars.
- Consumers may soon be able to order through interactive Yellow pages without ever talking to a live person.
- Advertising on Internet, a computer network with 35 million users worldwide, is on the rise. Actions have already been taken to limit the amount of junk E-mail.

Compounding this problem is the fact that consumers are unaware, excited, apprehensive, and even afraid of the many new options available to them. Consumers say that they welcome the wealth of information that will be available to them but worry about becoming couch potatoes addicted to their TV sets. Many feel overwhelmed already. As you can imagine, media buyers are constantly having to learn about new vehicles, reevaluate their existing strategies, and explore new options. According to James Cantalupo, CEO of McDonald's International, "Understanding the new media is the single largest business challenge that marketers have faced since the creation of TV." So what is the best way to reach one's audience? According to Patricia Sellers, writing in Fortune magazine, marketers must be willing to embrace change. Sellers suggests four ways to reach consumers in the changing media environment:

1. De-mass the marketing program. In other words, fine tune advertising to reach specific audiences.
2. Take advantage of captive consumers at live events. Increase public relations and advertising at stadiums, bingo halls, and other venues.
3. Be selective in unconventional media buys such as in-store advertising, and be creative with more conventional media such as newspapers, magazines, and radio.
4. Use the new media to sell directly to consumers. That is, make advertising a selling tool.

The new media require new thinking by marketers. The changes are not likely to stop soon!

Sources: Patricia Sellers, "The Best Way to Reach Your Buyers," *Fortune*, Autumn/Winter 1993, pp. 14–17; Max Robbins, "Internet Advertising Must Reflect Network 'Culture,'" *Business Marketing*, Jan. 1994, pp. 70–72. Alison Brower, "The Unconvinced Majority," *Mediaweek*, Sept. 13, 1993, p. 10.

he introduction of new and evolution of existing media contribute to the already difficult task of media planning. Planning when, where, and how the message is to be delivered is a complex and involved process. The primary objective of the media plan is to develop a framework that will deliver the message to the target audience in the most efficient, cost-effective manner possible—that will communicate what the product and/or brand can do.

This chapter presents the various methods of message delivery available to the marketer, examines some key considerations in making media decisions, and discusses the development of media strategy and plans. Later chapters will explore the relative advantages and disadvantages of the various media and examine each in more detail.

AN OVERVIEW OF MEDIA PLANNING

The media planning process is not an easy one. Options include mass media such as television, newspapers, radio, and magazines (and the choices available within each of these categories) as well as out-of-the-home media such as outdoor advertising, transit advertising, and electronic billboards. A variety of support media such as direct marketing, specialty advertising, and in-store point-of-purchase options must also be considered.

While at first glance the choice among these alternatives might seem relatively straightforward, this is rarely the case. Part of the reason media selection becomes so involved is due to the nature of the media themselves. TV combines both sight and sound, an advantage not offered by other media. Magazines can convey more information and may keep the message available to the potential buyer for a much longer time. Newspapers also offer their own advantages, as do outdoor, direct media, and each of the others. The characteristics of each alternative must be considered, along with many other factors. This process becomes even more complicated when the manager has to choose between alternatives within the same medium—for example, between *Time* and *Newsweek* or between "Roseanne" and "Murphy Brown."

The potential for achieving effective communications through a well-designed media strategy warrants the added attention. The power of an effective media strategy was demonstrated by a flower company called PC Flowers. In 1990, PC Flowers was the smallest of the 25,000 members in the Florists' Transworld Delivery Association. The company then started to advertise its services on Prodigy, a computer service with 2 million subscribers. PC Flowers moved into the top 10 within four months and now consistently ranks as one of the top two FTD members in the world.[1] Likewise, MCI, the number two long-distance company, was losing market share to AT&T until it began blitzing the market with promotions and other ad messages. In 1993, MCI ran more than 50 different TV commercials in addition to specialized spots on Chinese, Hispanic, and Russian television. The company effectively stemmed the market share erosion.[2]

The product and/or service being advertised affects the media planning process. As demonstrated in Exhibit 12–1, firms have found some media more useful than others in conveying their messages to specific target audiences. For example, Procter & Gamble tends to rely more heavily on TV advertising, whereas General Motors prefers print media. The result is placement of advertising dollars in these preferred media—and significantly different media strategies.

Some Basic Terms and Concepts

Before beginning our discussion of media planning, we review some basic terms and concepts used in the media planning and strategy process.

Media planning is the series of decisions involved in delivering the promotional message to the prospective purchasers and/or users of the product or brand. Media planning is a process, which means a number of decisions are made, each of which may be altered or abandoned as the plan develops.

The media plan is the guide for media selection. It requires development of specific **media objectives** and specific **media strategies**—plans of action—designed to attain these objectives. Once the decisions have been made and the objectives and strategies formulated, this information is organized into the media plan.

◉ **EXHIBIT** **12–1** Expenditures of top advertisers in various media

		Top 1000 Companies Ranked By 10 Media Dollars (000)										
Rank	Company	18-Media Total	Magazines	Sunday magazines	Newspapers	Outdoor	Network television	Spot television	Syndicated television	Cable TV networks	Network radio	National spot radio
1.	Proctor & Gamble Co.	1,299,926.2	197,282.8	4,648.8	2,205.6	73.4	633,967.1	172,390.6	132,834.7	136,955.4	16,907.2	2,640.6
2.	General Motors Corp.	1,899,349.1	299,659.8	14,981.0	55,637.2	1,169.7	454,224.7	164,468.2	61,066.6	15,434.4	4,422,1	
3.	Philip Morris Cos. Inc.	999,744.9	195,023.7	18,056.6	9,531.8	47,289.8	368,547.1	179,129.9	116,190.0	46,763.0	5,610.3	12,095.2
4.	Ford Motor Co.	322,759.5	220,456.7	2,456.7	35,924.2	294.5	281,970.8	145,521.3	7,608.3	24,061.1	2,670.8	1,354.5
5.	Pepsico Inc.	633,091.9	7,903.8	117.8	5,684.1	7,893.1	310,129.3	254,145.5	10,886.4	24,480.8		11,855.1
6.	Sears Roebuck & Co	594,671.4	36,660.6	6,173.7	177,434.4	38.7	177,755.2	54,246.2	23,509.9	33,673.6	69,188.1	15,940.9
7.	Chysler Corp.	585,343.7	144,440.2	3,856.2	29,128.5	656.2	158,395.0	217,832.0	2,749.7	29,633.2	4,723.6	929.7
8.	American Telephone & Telegraph Co	481,443.4	43,899.0	2,326.8	27,234.7	1,654.3	288,675.6	103,655.5	18,848.1	42,256.6	22,797.6	10,794.2
9.	Toyota Motor Corp	463,516.8	108,440.3	5,511.4	27,301.1	166.7	166,627.5	136,100.0	4,256.4	14,759.6		353.8
10.	Unlever Plc	461,033.8	99,142.2	9,239.5	4,733.9	179.4	245,737.8	61,686.3	55,697.3	17,556.7	4,199.5	3,467.2

©Copyright 1994 by Competitive Media Reporting, and Publishers Information Bureau, Inc.

The **medium** is the general category of available delivery systems, which includes broadcast media such as TV and radio, print media such as newspapers and magazines, direct mail, outdoor advertising, and other support media. The **media vehicle** is the specific carrier within a medium category. For example, *Time* and *Newsweek* are print vehicles; "Beverly Hills 90210" and "60 Minutes" are broadcast vehicles. As you will see in succeeding chapters, each vehicle has its own characteristics as well as its own relative advantages and disadvantages. Specific decisions must be made as to the value of each in delivering the message.

Reach is a measure of the number of different audience members exposed at least once to a media vehicle in a given period of time. *Coverage* refers to the potential audience that might receive the message through a vehicle. (It is important to distinguish between coverage and reach, as the former relates to potential audience and the latter to the actual audience delivered. The importance of this distinction will become more obvious later in this chapter.) Finally, *frequency* refers to the number of times the receiver is exposed to the media vehicle in a specified period.

The Media Plan

The media plan determines the best way to get the advertiser's message to the market. In a basic sense, the goal of the media plan is to find that combination of media that enables the marketer to communicate the message in the most effective manner to the largest number of potential customers at the lowest cost.

The activities involved in developing the media plan and the purposes of each are presented in Exhibit 12–2. As you can see, a number of decisions must be made throughout this process. As the plan evolves, events may occur that necessitate changes. Many advertisers find it necessary to alter and update their objectives and strategies frequently.

Problems in Media Planning

Unfortunately, the media strategy decision has not become a standardized task. A number of problems contribute to the difficulty of establishing the plan and reduce its effectiveness. These problems include insufficient information, inconsistent terminologies, time pressures, and difficulty measuring effectiveness.

Insufficient information

While a great deal of information about markets and the media exists, media planners often require more than is available. Some data are just not measured, either because they cannot be or because it would be too expensive. For example, continuous measures of radio listenership exist, but only periodic listenership studies are reported due to sample size and cost constraints. There are problems with some measures of audience size in TV and print as well, as the examples in IMC Perspective 12–1 on page 321 show.

EXHIBIT 12–2 Activities involved in developing the media plan

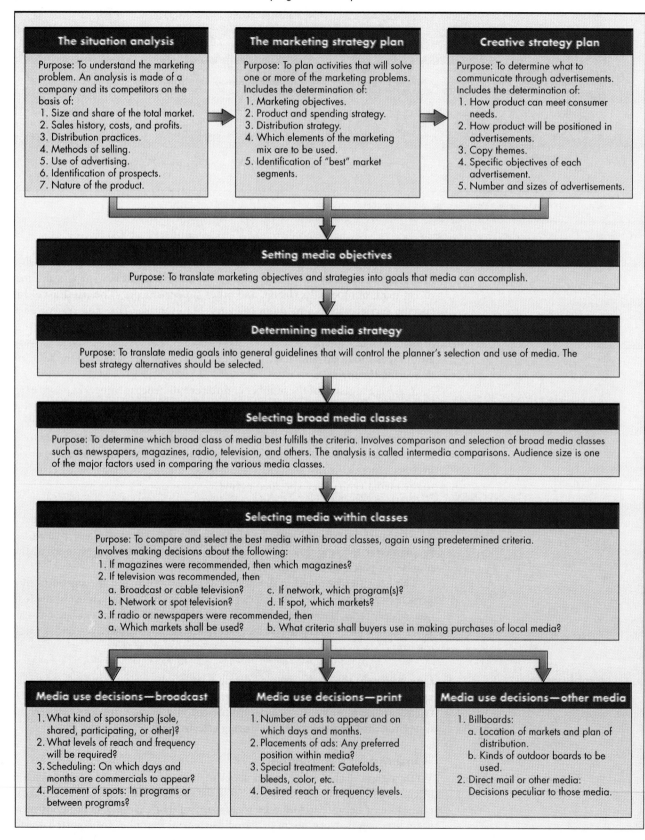

IMC Perspective 12–1
Media Services Companies Can't Seem to Agree

Advertising costs are determined by how many people can be reached through the medium. In print media, such costs are based on circulation and readership figures, while in broadcast, the basis is ratings. As in any industry, firms compete directly to provide advertisers with these services. Because so many billions of dollars are spent on advertising each year, the figures the services provide must be critical. One would expect that competing firms' information would be consistent—but it isn't.

The two primary providers of information on magazine readership are Mediamark Research Inc. (MRI) and Simmons Market Research Bureau (SMRB). Because of the importance media buyers place on these figures, they have become crucial to individual publications. As the vice president of one top ad agency noted, "If the readership numbers shift just a hair, there is a big shift in the number of ad pages." Yet MRI and SMRB's numbers rarely agree, causing many to question their validity. Differences of as much as 3 to 13 million readers have been shown for the top five magazines listed by each service, and significant differences exist in the readership profiles—yet both organizations stand by their results. Differences in research methodologies are cited as the cause of the discrepancies, and each firm believes its methods are correct.

In the TV industry, a different problem exists. Prior to 1993 there were two competing ratings services, Nielsen and Arbitron. Like MRI and SMRB, the two often provided different results. In 1993 Arbitron withdrew from the ratings game, leaving Nielsen as the sole provider of such information. To make matters even worse, Nielsen has had some irregularities in program ratings represented for ad sales. It has had to send letters to clients noting the inconsistencies. Both agency and network researchers have raised questions about the validity of the ratings and have brought pressure on Nielsen to do something about it. Nielsen has agreed to improve its research methodologies.

Radio listenership figures hardly fare better. The primary provider of market information, Arbitron, relies on the memories of listeners 12 and older as to which stations they listen to, where, and when. The service compares its results to another service called Radar, which measures network listening audiences. Unfortunately, the differences between the two services continue to increase, raising more suspicions about their validity. Since no formal basis for verification is available, no one can be exactly sure how many people listen to any given program.

If none of the media services offers verifiable figures, how do advertisers use this information? They may use the service that provides the most consistent results, the one that presents the medium in the most favorable light, or the one the buyers think offers the best methodology (from their perspective). And as they continue to use these results, they continue to clamor for improved methodologies and verifiable results—as they have for years.

Sources: Eric Schmuckler, "Second Syndicated Snafu Uncovered by A. C. Nielsen," *MediaWeek*, March 22, 1993, pp. 1–3; Joe Mandese, "Rival Ratings Don't Match Up," *Advertising Age*, Feb. 24, 1992, p. 50; Joe Mandese, "Arbitron Tries to Tune Up Ratings," *Advertising Age*, Sept. 9, 1991, p. S11; Betsy Spethmann, "Agencies Hope for Research Standard," *Advertising Age*, Sept. 9, 1991, p. S10; Joanne Lipman, "Readership Figures for Periodicals Stir Debate in Publishing Industry," *The Wall Street Journal*, Sept. 2, 1987.

The competing services provide different audience figures and readership profiles.

| | SIMMONS | | | MRI | | |
| | | Median | | | Median | |
	Total Aud. (mil.)	Age (yrs.)	HH Inc. $	Total Aud. (mil.)	Age (yrs.)	HH Inc. $
Family Circle............	17.53	43.6	35,959	26.19	42.8	33,711
Family Handyman.......	2.60	46.3	41,261	4.02	43.9	37,203
Field & Stream..........	9.91	38.4	35,360	14.01	36.9	34,212
Financial World.........	1.23	46.2	51,667	—	—	—
Flower & Garden........	—	—	—	4.01	46.2	28,674
Food & Wine...........	1.98	41.7	49,246	3.33	37.4	53,323
Forbes.................	3.39	44.5	63,342	3.67	42.3	61,382
Fortune................	3.45	41.0	58,411	4.01	37.1	53,264
Glamour...............	7.86	30.4	35,945	10.81	29.4	38,360
Golf..................	3.02	42.1	53,501	4.34	40.0	49,703
Golf Digest............	4.09	42.8	55,125	5.67	40.3	47,796
Golf Digest/Tennis (Gross)	5.70	40.9	54,003	7.63	38.5	47,853
Good Housekeeping.....	18.69	44.2	36,975	28.02	42.1	34,197
Gourmet...............	2.78	43.9	54,255	4.30	42.7	53,272
GQ...................	3.62	28.6	37,600	5.42	27.5	42,790

Source: *Marketer's Guide to Media*, Fall/Winter 1992, p. 125.

Another measurement problem involves the timing of the measurements, as some audience measures are taken only at specific times of the year. (For example, **sweeps periods** in February, May, July, and November are used for measuring TV audiences and setting advertising rates.) This information is then generalized to succeeding months, so future planning decisions must be made on past data that may not reflect current behaviors. Think about planning for TV advertising for the fall season. There are no data on the audiences of new shows, and audience information taken on existing programs during the summer may not indicate how these programs will do in the fall because summer viewership is generally much lower. While the advertisers can review these programs before they air, they do not have actual audience figures.

The lack of information is an even more pronounced problem with small advertisers, who may not be able to afford to purchase the information they require. As a result, their decisions are made on limited or out-of-date data or no data at all.

Inconsistent terminologies

Problems arise because the cost bases used by different media often vary and the standards of measurement used to establish these costs are not always consistent. For example, print media may present cost data in terms of the cost to reach a thousand people (cost per thousand, or CPM), whereas broadcast media refer to cost per ratings point (CPRP) and outdoor media to the number of showings. Audience information that is used as a basis for these costs has also been collected by different methods. Finally, terms that actually mean something different (such as reach and coverage) may be used synonymously, adding to the confusion.

Time pressures

It seems that advertisers are always in a hurry—sometimes because they need to be, other times because they *think* they need to be. Actions by a competitor—for example, the cutting of airfares by one carrier—require immediate response. But sometimes a false sense of urgency dictates time pressures. In either situation, media selection decisions may be made without proper planning and analyses of the markets and/or media.

Difficulty measuring effectiveness

Because it is so hard to measure the effectiveness of advertising and promotions in general, it is also difficult to determine the relative effectiveness of various media or media vehicles. While progress is being made in this regard (particularly in the area of direct-response advertising), the media planner must usually guess at the impact of these alternatives.

Because of these problems, not all media decisions are quantitatively determined. Sometimes managers have to assume the image of a medium in a market with which they are not familiar, anticipate the impact of recent events, or make judgments without full knowledge of all the available alternatives.

While these problems complicate the media decision process, they do not render it an entirely subjective exercise. The remainder of this chapter explores in more detail how media strategies are developed and ways to increase their effectiveness.

DEVELOPING THE MEDIA PLAN

The promotional planning model in Chapter 1 discussed the process of identifying target markets, establishing objectives, and formulating strategies for attaining them. The development of the media plan and strategies follows a similar path, except that the focus is more specifically keyed to determining the *best* way to deliver the message. The process, shown in Exhibit 12–3, involves a series of stages: (1) market analysis, (2) establishment of media objectives, (3) media strategy development and implementation, and (4) evaluation and follow-up. Each of these is discussed in turn, with specific examples. Appendix B to this chapter is an actual media plan, which we refer to throughout the remainder of the chapter to exemplify each phase further.

@ **EXHIBIT   12–3**   Developing the media plan

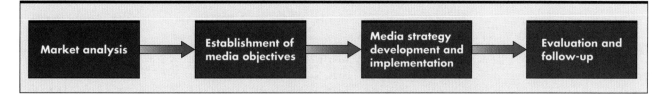

@ **MARKET ANALYSIS AND TARGET MARKET IDENTIFICATION**

The situation analysis stage of the overall promotional planning process involves a complete review of internal and external factors, competitive strategies, and the like. In the development of media strategy, a market analysis is again performed, although this time the focus is on the media and delivering the message. The key questions at this stage are these: To whom shall we advertise (who is the target market)? What internal and external factors may influence the media plan? Where (geographically) and when should we focus our efforts?

To Whom Shall We Advertise?

While a number of target markets might be derived from the situation analysis, the decision on which specific groups to go after may involve the media planner working with the client, account representative, marketing department, and creative directors. A variety of factors may be used to assist the media planners in this decision. Some will require primary research, whereas others will be available from published (secondary) sources.

The Simmons Market Research Bureau (SMRB) provides secondary information: syndicated data on audience size and composition for approximately 100 publications, as well as broadcast exposure and data on usage of over 800 consumer products and services. This information comes in the form of raw numbers, percentages, and indexes. As seen in Exhibit 12–4, information is given on (1) the number of adults in the United States by each category under consideration; (2) the number of users; (3) the percentage of users falling into each category (for example, the percentage that are female); (4) the percentage of each category that uses the product (for example, the percentage of all females using); (5) an index number; and (6) the same information classified by heavy, medium, and light users. (Both Simmons and its major competitor, Mediamark Research, Inc. (MRI), also provide lifestyle information and media usage characteristics of the population.)

In many instances, media planners are more concerned with the percentage figures and index numbers than with the raw numbers. This is primarily due to the fact that they may have their own data from other sources, both primary and secondary: the numbers provided may not be specific enough for their needs, or they believe the numbers provided may be questionable because of the methods by which they were collected. The total (raw) numbers provided by Simmons and MRI are used in combination with the media planner's own figures.

On the other hand, the **index number** is considered a good indicator of the potential of the market. This number is derived from the formula:

$$\text{Index number} = \frac{\text{Percentage of users in a demographic segment}}{\text{Percentage of population in the same segment}} \times 100$$

An index number over 100 means use of the product is proportionately greater in that segment than in one that is average (100) or less than 100. For example, the MRI data in Exhibit 12–5 on page 325 show that the age groups 45–54 and 55–64 are more likely to be heavy users of lipstick and lip gloss than those in the other age segments, as are those with a household income of $40,000+. Most occupation groups are heavy users, with the exception of those in precision crafts and in the category "other employed." Depending on their overall strategy, marketers may wish to use this information to determine which groups are now using the product and target them or to identify a group that is currently using the product less and attempt to develop that segment.

EXHIBIT 12-4 Market research profile of cola users

	TOTAL U.S. '000	ALL USERS A '000	B % DOWN	C % ACROSS	D INDX	HEAVY USERS EIGHT OR MORE A '000	B % DOWN	C % ACROSS	D INDX	BOTTLED A '000	B % DOWN	C % ACROSS	D INDX	CANNED A '000	B % DOWN	C % ACROSS	D INDX
TOTAL ADULTS	182456	107986	100.0	59.2	100	34162	100.0	18.7	100	64427	100.0	35.3	100	77735	100.0	42.6	100
MALES	87118	57364	53.1	65.8	111	19037	55.7	21.9	117	33966	52.7	39.0	110	41533	53.4	47.7	112
FEMALES	95338	50622	46.9	53.1	90	15125	44.3	15.9	85	30461	47.3	32.0	90	36202	46.6	38.0	89
18-24	25530	17961	16.6	70.4	119	7633	22.3	29.9	160	11523	17.9	45.1	128	13715	17.6	53.7	126
25-34	44118	29093	26.9	65.9	111	10646	31.2	24.1	129	17994	27.9	40.8	116	22039	28.4	50.0	117
35-44	37521	23183	21.5	61.8	104	6716	19.7	17.9	96	13883	21.5	37.0	105	17172	22.1	45.8	107
45-54	25346	14302	13.2	56.4	95	4240	12.4	16.7	89	8281	12.9	32.7	93	9798	12.6	38.7	91
55-64	21009	11029	10.2	52.5	89	2655	7.8	12.6	67	5946	9.2	28.3	80	7563	9.7	36.0	84
65 OR OLDER	28934	12419	11.5	42.9	73	2271	6.6	7.8	42	6801	10.6	23.5	67	7449	9.6	25.7	60
18-34	69647	47054	43.6	67.6	114	18279	53.5	26.2	140	29517	45.8	42.4	120	35754	46.0	51.3	120
18-49	120585	78177	72.4	64.8	110	27394	80.2	22.7	121	48074	74.6	39.9	113	58377	75.1	48.4	114
25-54	106984	66577	61.7	62.2	105	21603	63.2	20.2	108	40158	62.3	37.5	106	49009	63.0	45.8	108
35-49	50938	31123	28.8	61.1	103	9115	26.7	17.9	96	18557	28.8	36.4	103	22623	29.1	44.4	104
50 OR OLDER	61871	29810	27.6	48.2	81	6768	19.8	10.9	58	16353	25.4	26.4	75	19358	24.9	31.3	73
GRADUATED COLLEGE	35347	18823	17.4	53.3	90	4256	12.5	12.0	64	10728	16.7	30.4	86	13919	17.9	39.4	92
ATTENDED COLLEGE	35167	20303	18.8	57.7	98	6323	18.5	18.0	96	11597	18.0	33.0	93	15374	19.8	43.7	103
GRADUATED HIGH SCHOOL	70823	43928	40.7	62.0	105	15062	44.1	21.3	114	26676	41.4	37.7	107	31808	40.9	44.9	105
DID NOT GRADUATE HIGH SCHOOL	41119	24932	23.1	60.6	102	8521	24.9	20.7	111	15426	23.9	37.5	106	16634	21.4	40.5	95
EMPLOYED MALES	67846	46006	42.6	67.8	115	15993	46.8	23.6	126	27566	42.8	40.6	115	33752	43.4	49.7	117
EMPLOYED FEMALES	57394	30497	28.2	53.1	90	9317	27.3	16.2	87	18245	28.3	31.8	90	22414	28.8	39.1	92
EMPLOYED FULL-TIME	112285	69201	64.1	61.6	104	22930	67.1	20.4	109	41409	64.3	36.9	104	50475	64.9	45.0	106
EMPLOYED PART-TIME	12955	7302	6.8	56.4	95	2380	7.0	18.4	98	4402	6.8	34.0	96	5692	7.3	43.9	103
NOT EMPLOYED	57216	31483	29.2	55.0	93	8852	25.9	15.5	83	18616	28.9	32.5	92	21569	27.7	37.7	88
PROFESSIONAL/MANAGER	31819	17101	15.8	53.7	91	4515	13.2	14.2	76	10036	15.6	31.5	89	12604	16.2	39.6	93
TECHNICAL/CLERICAL/SALES	39581	22672	21.0	57.3	97	7008	20.5	17.7	95	13089	20.3	33.1	94	16905	21.7	42.7	100
PRECISION/CRAFT	14839	10235	9.5	69.0	117	4012	11.7	27.0	144	6535	10.1	44.0	125	7470	9.6	50.3	118
OTHER EMPLOYED	39001	26494	24.5	67.9	115	9775	28.6	25.1	134	16151	25.1	41.4	117	19187	24.7	49.2	115
SINGLE	40179	26098	24.2	65.0	110	10217	29.9	25.4	136	16252	25.2	40.4	115	19644	25.3	48.9	115
MARRIED	108808	64055	59.3	58.9	99	18441	54.1	17.0	91	37570	58.3	34.5	98	45904	59.1	42.2	99
DIVORCED/SEPARATED/WIDOWED	33469	17834	16.5	53.3	90	5464	16.0	16.3	87	10606	16.5	31.7	90	12188	15.7	36.4	85
PARENTS	60855	40631	37.6	66.8	113	13482	39.5	22.2	118	25180	39.1	41.4	117	30061	38.7	49.4	116
WHITE	156458	90780	84.1	58.0	98	28116	82.3	18.0	96	53093	82.4	33.9	96	65803	84.7	42.1	99
BLACK	20509	13774	12.8	67.2	113	5160	15.1	25.2	134	9041	14.0	44.1	125	9432	12.1	46.0	108
OTHER	5489	3432	3.2	62.5	106	885	2.6	16.1	86	2293	3.6	41.8	118	2500	3.2	45.5	107
NORTHEAST-CENSUS	38593	22160	20.5	57.4	97	5368	15.7	13.9	74	16028	24.9	41.5	118	14293	18.4	37.0	87
MIDWEST	44281	24898	23.1	56.2	95	7327	21.4	16.5	88	12677	19.7	28.6	81	19201	24.7	43.4	102
SOUTH	62591	39118	36.2	62.5	106	14519	42.5	23.2	124	24320	37.7	38.9	110	26905	34.6	43.0	101
WEST	36991	21811	20.2	59.0	100	6947	20.3	18.8	100	11402	17.7	30.8	87	17337	22.3	46.9	110
COUNTY SIZE A	75891	43359	40.2	57.1	97	12309	36.0	16.2	87	26324	40.9	34.7	98	30712	39.5	40.5	95
COUNTY SIZE B	54708	33119	30.7	60.5	102	10665	31.2	19.5	104	19543	30.3	35.7	101	24116	31.0	44.1	103
COUNTY SIZE C	27729	16793	15.6	60.6	102	5938	17.4	21.4	114	9674	15.0	34.9	99	12452	16.0	44.9	105
COUNTY SIZE D	24127	14715	13.6	61.0	103	5250	15.4	21.8	116	8886	13.8	36.8	104	10456	13.5	43.3	102
METRO CENTRAL CITY	57518	35162	32.6	61.1	103	11223	32.9	19.5	104	19989	31.0	34.8	98	26734	34.4	46.5	109
METRO SUBURBAN	85780	49004	45.4	57.1	97	14390	42.1	16.8	90	29956	46.5	34.9	99	34168	44.0	39.8	93
NON METRO	39158	23820	22.1	60.8	103	8549	25.0	21.8	117	14482	22.5	37.0	105	16834	21.7	43.0	101
TOP 5 ADI'S	40412	23079	21.4	57.1	96	6233	18.2	15.4	82	15097	23.4	37.4	106	15727	20.2	38.9	91
TOP 10 ADI'S	57709	32644	30.2	56.6	96	9067	26.5	15.7	84	21381	33.2	37.0	105	22081	28.4	38.3	90
TOP 20 ADI'S	83116	47625	44.1	57.3	97	13722	40.2	16.5	88	29571	45.9	35.6	101	33506	43.1	40.3	95
HSHLD. INC. $75,000 OR MORE	21409	11472	10.6	53.6	91	3137	9.2	14.7	78	6677	10.4	31.2	88	8465	10.9	39.5	93
$60,000 OR MORE	36836	20296	18.8	55.1	93	5450	16.0	14.8	79	11854	18.4	32.2	91	14883	19.1	40.4	95
$50,000 OR MORE	53155	29435	27.3	55.4	94	8401	24.6	15.8	84	17518	27.2	33.0	93	21230	27.3	39.9	94
$40,000 OR MORE	75291	42438	39.3	56.4	95	12102	35.4	16.1	86	24710	38.4	32.8	93	31064	40.0	41.3	97
$30,000 OR MORE	102396	59510	55.1	58.1	98	17769	52.0	17.4	93	35324	54.8	34.5	98	43174	55.5	42.2	99
$30,000 - $39,999	27105	17072	15.8	63.0	106	5667	16.6	20.9	112	10614	16.5	39.2	111	12111	15.6	44.7	105
$20,000 - $29,999	30317	18768	17.4	61.9	105	6373	18.7	21.0	112	10822	16.8	35.7	101	13883	17.9	45.8	107
$10,000 - $19,999	29855	18353	17.0	61.5	104	6479	19.0	21.7	116	11297	17.5	37.8	107	13108	16.9	43.9	103
UNDER $10,000	19888	11355	10.5	57.1	96	3541	10.4	17.8	95	6985	10.8	35.1	99	7571	9.7	38.1	89
HOUSEHOLD OF 1 PERSON	23383	11336	10.5	48.5	82	2915	8.5	12.5	67	6621	10.3	28.3	80	7727	9.9	33.0	78
2 PEOPLE	59547	31809	29.5	53.4	90	9263	27.1	15.6	83	17730	27.5	29.8	84	22690	29.2	38.1	89
3 OR 4 PEOPLE	72643	46028	42.6	63.4	107	15192	44.5	20.9	112	28128	43.7	38.7	110	33353	42.9	45.9	108
5 OR MORE PEOPLE	26884	18813	17.4	70.0	118	6793	19.9	25.3	135	11948	18.5	44.4	126	13965	18.0	51.9	122
NO CHILD IN HSHLD.	109702	59165	54.8	53.9	91	17626	51.6	16.1	86	33808	52.5	30.8	87	41560	53.5	37.9	89
CHILD(REN) UNDER 2 YEARS	15048	10548	9.8	70.1	118	4030	11.8	26.8	143	6875	10.7	45.7	129	7752	10.0	51.5	121
2 - 5 YEARS	25473	17985	16.7	70.6	119	6250	18.3	24.5	131	11774	18.3	46.2	131	13493	17.4	53.0	124
6 - 11 YEARS	34011	23085	21.4	67.9	115	7433	21.8	21.9	117	14221	22.1	41.8	118	17375	22.4	51.1	120
12 - 17 YEARS	33774	22170	20.5	65.6	111	7394	21.6	21.9	117	13733	21.3	40.7	115	16230	20.9	48.1	113
RESIDENCE OWNED	124747	69384	64.3	55.6	94	19886	58.2	15.9	85	40350	62.6	32.3	92	49466	63.6	39.7	93
VALUE: $70,000 OR MORE	69554	36947	34.2	53.1	90	9297	27.2	13.4	71	21652	33.6	31.1	88	26509	34.1	38.1	89
VALUE: UNDER $70,000	55193	32437	30.0	58.8	99	10588	31.0	19.2	102	18699	29.0	33.9	96	22957	29.5	41.6	98

While the index is a useful aid, it should not be used alone. Percentages and product usage figures are also needed to get an accurate picture of the market. While the index for a particular segment of the population may be very high, that doesn't always mean this is an attractive segment to target. The high index may be a result of a low denominator—that is, a very small proportion of the population in this segment. In Exhibit 12–6, the 18-to-24-year-old age segment has the highest index, but it also has both the lowest product usage and the lowest population percentage. A marketer who relied solely on the index would be ignoring a full 82 percent of product users.

@ **EXHIBIT 12-5**

Lipstick and lip gloss usage*

	Heavy Users Index	Medium Users Index	Light Users Index
Used lipstick and/or lip gloss in last 7 days	78.80%		
Number of times used in last 7 days			
Heavy—more than 10 times	23.70		
Medium—7 to 10 times	29.90		
Light—fewer than 7 times	25.2		
Base: Women			
Age			
18–24	88	116	111
25–34	83	101	107
35–44	95	98	94
45–54	128	110	75
55–64	127	95	99
65 or over	98	85	109
Employment			
Professional	116	107	96
Executive, administrative, managerial	156	84	74
Clerical, sales, technical	123	110	85
Precision, crafts, repair	64	95	103
Other employed	90	105	106
Household income			
$75,000 or more	149	104	80
$60,000–$74,999	139	98	94
$50,000–$59,999	127	98	103
$40,000–$49,999	110	103	87
$30,000–$39,999	97	104	93
$20,000–$29,999	92	103	101
$10,000–$19,999	71	107	113
Less than $10,000	57	81	120

*Mediamark Research, Spring 1993.

Further, keep in mind that while Simmons and MRI provide demographic, geographic, and psychographic information, other factors may be more useful in defining specific markets.

What Internal and External Factors Are Operating?

Media strategies will be influenced by both internal and external factors operating at any given time. *Internal factors* may involve the size of the media budget, managerial and administrative capabilities, or the organization of the agency, as demonstrated in Exhibit 12–7. *External factors* may include the economy (the rising costs of media), changes in technology (the availability of new media), competitive factors, and the like. While some of this information may require primary research, a substantial volume of information is available through secondary sources including magazines, syndicated services, and even the daily newspaper.

One service's competitive information was shown in Exhibit 9–12. The BAR/LNA Multi-Media Service provides media spending figures for various brands competing in the same market. Competitive information is also available from a variety of other sources, as shown in Appendix A to this chapter.

@ **EXHIBIT 12-6**

How high indexes can be misleading

Age Segment	Population in Segment (percent)	Product Use in Segment (percent)	Index
18–24	15.1	18.0	119
25–34	25.1	25.0	100
35–44	20.6	21.0	102
45+	39.3	36.0	91

@ **EXHIBIT   12-7**   Organizing the media buying department

While various firms and advertising agencies have different ways of organizing the media buying department, three seem to be the most common. The first form employs a product/media focus; the second places more emphasis on the market itself. The third organizes around media classes alone.

Form 1   In this organizational arrangement, the media buyers and assistant media buyers are responsible for a product or group of products and/or brands. Their media planner both plans and buys for these products/brands in whichever geographic areas they are marketed. For example, if the agency were responsible for the advertising of Hart skis, the media planners would determine the appropriate media in each area for placing the ads for these skis. The logic underlying this approach is that the planner knows the product and will identify the best media and vehicles for promoting the same.

Form 2   In this approach, the market is the focal point of attention. Media planners become "experts" in a particular market area and are responsible for planning and buying for all products/brands the firm and/or agency markets in those areas. For example, a planner may have responsibility for the Memphis, Tennessee, market. If the agency has more than one client who wishes to market in this area, media selection for all of the brands/products is the responsibility of the same

person—the logic being that his or her knowledge of the media and vehicles in the area allows for a more informed media choice. The nonquantitative characteristics of the media get more attention under this approach.

Form 3   Organizing around a specific class of media—for example, print or broadcast—is a third alternative. The purchasing and development unit handles all the agency print or broadcast business. Members of the media department become specialists who are brought in very early in the promotional planning process. Planners perform only planning functions, while buyers are responsible for all purchases. The buying function itself may be specialized with specific responsibilities for specialty advertising, national buys, local buys, etc. Knowledge of the media and the audience each serves is considered a major benefit. In addition, by handling all the media buys, they can negotiate better deals.

As to which strategy works best, who is to say? Each has been in use for some time. Discussions with media personnel in ad agencies indicate the second approach requires that the agency be of substantial size and have enough clients to support the geographic assignment. The third alternative seems to be the most common design.

Where to Promote?

The question of where to promote relates to geographic considerations. As noted in Chapter 9, companies often find that sales are stronger in one area of the country than another and may allocate advertising expenditures according to the market potential of an area. For years, Maxwell House coffee has had a much greater brand share in the East than in the West. The question is, Where will the advertising be more wisely spent? Should General Foods allocate additional promotional dollars to those markets where the brand is already the leader to maintain market share, or does more potential exist in those markets where the firm is not doing as well and there is more room to grow? Perhaps the best answer is that the firm should spend advertising and promotion dollars where they will be the most effective—that is, in those markets where they will achieve the desired objectives. Unfortunately, as we have seen so often, it is not always possible to measure directly the impact of promotional efforts. At the same time, certain tactics can assist the planner in making this determination.

Using indexes to determine where to promote

In addition to the indexes from Simmons and MRI, three other indexes may also be useful:

1. **The Survey of Buying Power Index,** published annually by *Sales and Marketing Management* magazine, is conducted for every major metropolitan market in the United States and is based on a number of factors, including population, effective buying income, and total retail sales in the area. Each of these factors is individually weighted and a buying power index is derived that charts the potential of a particular metro area, county, or city relative to the United States as a whole. The resulting index gives media planners insight into the relative value of that market, as shown in Exhibit 12–8. When used in combination with other market information, the Survey of Buying Power Index helps the marketer determine which geographic areas to target.

2. **The Brand Development Index** (BDI) helps marketers factor the rate of product usage by geographic area into the decision process.

$$\text{BDI} = \frac{\text{Percentage of brand to total US sales in the market}}{\text{Percentage of total US population in the market}} \times 100$$

@ **EXHIBIT 12–8**

Survey of buying power index

Rhode Island

POPULATION — **RETAIL SALES BY STORE GROUP**

S&MM ESTIMATES: 12/31/90

METRO AREA County City	Total Population (Thousands)	% Of U.S.	Median Age Of Pop.	18-24 Years	25-34 Years	35-49 Years	50 & Over	Households (Thousands)	Total Retail Sales ($000)	Food ($000)	Eating & Drinking Places ($000)	General Mdse. ($000)	Furniture/Furnish. Appliance ($000)	Automotive ($000)	Drug ($000)
PROVIDENCE–PAWTUCKET–WOONSOCKET	921.4	.3674	34.1	11.8	17.0	20.1	28.4	347.2	6,621,140	1,390,972	740,007	750,465	291,612	1,175,964	301,155
Bristol	49.0	.0196	35.9	10.9	15.5	20.9	30.5	17.6	239,949	66,787	27,747	2,630	6,814	53,545	13,682
Kent	162.1	.0646	35.9	8.9	16.9	22.3	29.2	62.4	1,687,207	275,155	168,616	307,478	55,278	301,666	58,221
Warwick	85.9	.0342	36.9	8.7	16.7	21.4	31.5	33.6	1,241,231	159,242	114,017	300,202	47,168	189,376	34,648
Providence	598.9	.2388	33.8	12.2	17.3	19.2	28.7	227.4	3,832,852	814,370	442,223	400,598	197,994	690,435	198,710
Cranston	76.4	.0305	37.3	9.5	17.5	20.7	32.8	29.5	513,493	116,552	55,772	21,447	43,116	94,507	34,699
East Providence	50.6	.0202	36.9	9.1	16.9	19.4	33.3	20.0	405,889	72,226	38,188	22,368	20,077	130,818	20,625
• Pawtucket	73.0	.0291	33.7	10.2	19.1	17.8	29.7	29.9	514,684	105,502	42,451	110,785	21,226	73,536	34,132
• Providence	161.4	.0644	29.6	18.0	17.6	16.5	24.0	59.1	931,996	174,406	126,906	59,502	63,388	169,702	39,520
• Woonsocket	44.1	.0176	33.3	10.9	17.9	17.9	28.9	17.7	292,009	70,461	20,413	36,712	12,715	72,514	14,174
Washington	111.4	.0444	32.6	14.2	16.2	21.9	24.3	39.8	861,132	234,660	101,421	39,759	31,526	130,318	30,542
SUBURBAN TOTAL	642.9	.2563	35.5	10.5	16.6	21.4	29.3	240.5	4,882,451	1,040,603	550,237	543,466	194,283	860,212	213,329
OTHER COUNTIES															
Newport	87.5	.0349	33.8	11.8	17.6	22.3	25.5	32.8	703,842	121,062	118,031	34,174	29,726	176,816	18,994
TOTAL METRO COUNTIES	921.4	.3674	34.1	11.8	17.0	20.1	28.4	347.2	6,621,140	1,390,972	740,007	750,465	291,612	1,175,964	301,155
TOTAL STATE	1,008.9	.4023	34.1	11.8	17.0	20.3	28.1	380.0	7,324,982	1,512,034	858,038	784,639	321,338	1,352,780	320,149

EFFECTIVE BUYING INCOME

S&MM ESTIMATES: 12/31/90

% of Hslds. by EBI Group: (A) $10,000-$19,999 (B) $20,000-$34,999 (C) $35,000-$49,999 (D) $50,000 & Over

METRO AREA County City	Total EBI ($000)	Median Hsld. EBI	A	B	C	D	Buying Power Index
PROVIDENCE–PAWTUCKET–WOONSOCKET	13,161,017	28,441	19.4	25.5	18.6	20.9	.3714
Bristol	727,359	30,275	19.2	26.8	17.6	23.9	.0182
Kent	2,422,662	30,869	17.0	27.8	21.2	21.1	.0756
Warwick	1,322,227	31,519	16.5	27.6	21.5	21.8	.0463
Providence	8,427,416	27,115	20.2	24.4	17.8	20.3	.2319
Cranston	1,237,230	31,764	17.7	24.6	19.9	25.2	.0323
East Providence	777,080	30,763	18.3	25.3	21.5	22.1	.0219
• Pawtucket	997,942	25,377	21.5	26.0	17.8	16.3	.0286
• Providence	1,924,178	20,802	24.2	23.5	13.4	14.8	.0558
• Woonsocket	566,843	23,811	22.3	24.4	16.8	15.5	.0165
Washington	1,583,580	30,461	18.6	28.1	19.4	22.3	.0457
SUBURBAN TOTAL	9,672,054	31,087	17.8	26.1	20.0	23.3	.2705
OTHER COUNTIES							
Newport	1,414,978	31,746	17.5	24.8	19.4	25.8	.0388
TOTAL METRO COUNTIES	13,161,017	28,441	19.4	25.5	18.6	20.9	.3714
TOTAL STATE	14,575,995	28,696	19.2	25.5	18.6	21.3	.4102

The BDI compares the percentage of the brand's total US sales in a given market area with the percentage of the total population in the market. The resulting BDI indicates the sales potential for that brand in that market area. An example of this calculation is shown in Exhibit 12–9. The higher the index number, the more market potential exists. In this case, the index number of 312 indicates this market has high potential for brand development.

3. **The Category Development Index** (CDI) is computed in the same manner as the BDI, except it uses information regarding the product category (as opposed to the brand) in the numerator:

$$\text{CDI} = \frac{\text{Percentage of product category total sales in market}}{\text{Percentage of total US population in market}} \times 100$$

The CDI provides information on the potential for development of the total product category, rather than specific brands. When this information is combined with the BDI, a much more insightful promotional strategy may be developed. For example, consider the market potential for coffee in the United States. One might first look at how well the product category does in a specific market area, finding that in such areas as Utah and Idaho the category potential is lower (see

@ **EXHIBIT 12–9**

Calculating BDI

$$\text{BDI} = \frac{\text{Percentage of brand sales in South Atlantic region}}{\text{Percentage of US population in South Atlantic region}} \times 100$$

$$= \frac{50}{16} \times 100$$

$$= 312$$

@ **EXHIBIT 12-10**

Using CDI and BDI to determine market potential

$$CDI = \frac{\text{Percentage of product category sales in Utah/Idaho}}{\text{Percentage of total US population in Utah/Idaho}} \times 100$$

$$= \frac{1\%}{1\%} \times 100$$

$$= 100$$

$$BDI = \frac{\text{Percentage of total brand sales in Utah/Idaho}}{\text{Percentage of total US population in Utah/Idaho}} \times 100$$

$$= \frac{2\%}{1\%} \times 100$$

$$= 200$$

Exhibit 12–10). The marketer analyzes the BDI to find how the brand is doing relative to other brands in this area. This information can then be used in determining how well a particular product category and a particular brand are performing and determining what media weight (or quantity of advertising) would be required to gain additional market share, as shown in Exhibit 12–11.

While these indexes provide important insights into the market potential for the firm's products and/or brands, this information is supplemental to the overall strategy determined earlier in the promotional decision-making process. In fact, much of this information may have already been provided to the media planner. Since it may be used more specifically to determine the media weights to assign to each area, this decision ultimately affects the budget allocated to each area as well as other factors such as reach, frequency, and scheduling.

@ **ESTABLISHING MEDIA OBJECTIVES**

Just as the situation analysis leads to establishment of marketing and communications objectives, the media situation analysis should lead to determination of specific media objectives. The media objectives are not ends in themselves. Rather, they are designed to lead to the attainment of communications and marketing objectives. Media objectives are the goals to be attained by the media program and should be limited to those that can be accomplished through media strategies. An example of media objectives is this: Create awareness in the target market through the following:

- Use broadcast media to provide coverage of 80 percent of the target market over a six-month period.
- Reach 60 percent of the target audience at least three times over the same six-month period.
- Concentrate heaviest advertising in winter and spring, with lighter emphasis in summer and fall.

@ **EXHIBIT 12-11**

Using BDI and CDI indexes

	High BDI	**Low BDI**
High CDI	High market share Good market potential	Low market share Good market potential
Low CDI	High market share Monitor for sales decline	Low market share Poor market potential

High BDI and high CDI	This market usually represents good sales potential for both the product category and the brand.
High BDI and low CDI	The category is not selling well, but the brand is; probably a good market to advertise in but should be monitored for declining sales.
Low BDI and high CDI	The product category shows high potential but the brand is not doing well; the reasons should be determined.
Low BDI and low CDI	Both the product category and the brand are doing poorly; not likely to be a good place for advertising.

@ **EXHIBIT   12–12**

Criteria considered in the
development of media plans

- Developing a media mix
- Determining target market coverage
- Determining geographic coverage
- Scheduling
- Determining reach versus frequency
- Creative aspects and mood
- Flexibility
- Budget considerations

@ DEVELOPING AND IMPLEMENTING MEDIA STRATEGY

Having determined what is to be accomplished, media planners consider *how* to achieve these objectives—that is, the development and implementation of media strategies, which media strategies evolve directly from the actions required to meet objectives and involve the criteria in Exhibit 12–12.

Developing a Media Mix

A wide variety of media and media vehicles are available to advertisers. While it is possible that only one medium and/or vehicle might be employed, it is much more likely that a number of alternatives will be used. The objectives sought, the characteristics of the product or service, the size of the budget, and individual preferences are just some of the factors that determine what combination of media will be used.

As an example, consider a promotional situation in which a product requires a visual demonstration to be communicated effectively. In this case, TV may be the most effective medium. If the promotional strategy calls for coupons to stimulate trial, print media will be necessary.

By employing a media mix, advertisers can add more versatility to their media strategies, since each of the various media contributes its own distinct advantages (as demonstrated in later chapters). By combining media, marketers can increase coverage, reach, and frequency levels while improving the likelihood of achieving overall communications and marketing goals.

Determining Target Market Coverage

The media planner determines which target markets should receive the most media emphasis. (In the Denny's plan in Appendix B, this was determined to be adults ages 25 to 54 in 28 core markets.) Developing media strategies involves matching the most appropriate media to this market by asking the question, "Through which media and media vehicles can I best get my message to prospective buyers?" The issue here is to get coverage of the market, as shown in Exhibit 12–13. The optimal goal is coverage *b*—that is, full market coverage.

But this is a very optimistic scenario. In more realistic situations, condition *c* or *d* is most likely to occur. In *c* the coverage of the media does not allow for coverage of the

@ **EXHIBIT   12–13**

Marketing coverage
possibilities

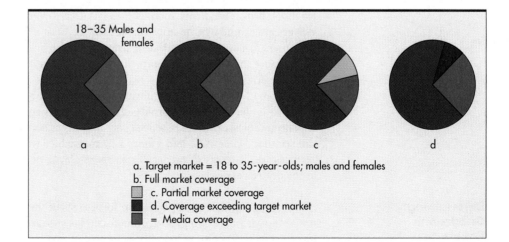

a. Target market = 18 to 35-year-olds; males and females
b. Full market coverage
c. Partial market coverage
d. Coverage exceeding target market
= Media coverage

EXHIBIT 12–14

Magazines purchased by people who do aerobics

	TOTAL U.S. '000	AEROBICS				20 OR MORE DAYS			
		A '000	B % DOWN	C % ACROSS	D INDX	A '000	B % DOWN	C % ACROSS	D INDX
REDBOOK	10533	1074	9.1	10.2	157	760	10.1	7.2	174
ROAD & TRACK	3838	*133	1.1	3.5	53	**55	0.7	1.4	35
ROLLING STONE	6154	496	4.2	8.1	124	317	4.2	5.2	124
SCIENTIFIC AMERICAN	1835	*137	1.2	7.5	115	**57	0.8	3.1	75
SELF	2957	594	5.0	20.1	310	466	6.2	15.8	381
SESAME STREET MAGAZINE	3606	444	3.8	12.3	190	292	3.9	8.1	196
SEVENTEEN	3532	259	2.2	7.3	113	*165	2.2	4.7	113
SHAPE	1664	252	2.1	15.1	234	*185	2.4	11.1	269
SKI	1764	*176	1.5	10.0	154	**102	1.4	5.8	140
SKIING	1535	*161	1.4	10.5	162	**86	1.1	5.6	135
SMITHSONIAN	6299	464	3.9	7.4	114	219	2.9	3.5	84
SOAP OPERA DIGEST	6437	756	6.4	11.7	181	433	5.7	6.7	162
SOUTHERN LIVING	7213	675	5.7	9.4	144	506	6.7	7.0	169
SPORT	3012	**153	1.3	5.1	78	**67	0.9	2.2	54
THE SPORTING NEWS	3348	*179	1.5	5.3	82	**128	1.7	3.8	92
SPORTS AFIELD	3370	**91	0.8	2.7	42	**37	0.5	1.1	27
SPORTS ILLUSTRATED	21035	1002	8.5	4.8	73	611	8.1	2.9	70
STAR	10704	814	6.9	7.6	117	470	6.2	4.4	106
SUNDAY MAGAZINE NETWORK	34831	2761	23.3	7.9	122	1828	24.2	5.2	127
SUNSET	3255	269	2.3	8.3	127	185	2.4	5.7	137
TV GUIDE	39127	2620	22.1	6.7	103	1565	20.7	4.0	97
TENNIS	1548	**102	0.9	6.6	102	**82	1.1	5.3	128
TIME	24413	1734	14.7	7.1	110	1165	15.4	4.8	115
TRAVEL & LEISURE	2520	189	1.6	7.5	116	*144	1.9	5.7	138
TRUE STORY	3060	*312	2.6	10.2	157	**234	3.1	7.6	185
USA TODAY	6199	459	3.9	7.4	114	328	4.3	5.3	128
USA WEEKEND	34618	2192	18.5	6.3	98	1369	18.1	4.0	96
U.S. NEWS & WORLD REPORT	13465	830	7.0	6.2	95	596	7.9	4.4	107
US	4059	453	3.8	11.2	172	311	4.1	7.7	185
VANITY FAIR	1974	292	2.5	14.8	228	*173	2.3	8.8	212

entire market, leaving some potential customers without exposure to the message. In *d,* the marketer is faced with a problem of overexposure—also called **waste coverage**—in which the media coverage exceeds the targeted audience. If media coverage reaches people who are not sought as buyers and are not potential users, then it is wasted. (This term is used for coverage that reaches nonpotential buyers and/or users. Consumers may not be part of the intended target market but may still be considered as potential—for example, those who buy the product as a gift for someone else.)

The goal of the media planner is to extend media coverage to as many of the members of the target audience as possible while minimizing the amount of waste coverage. The situation usually involves trade-offs. Sometimes one has to live with less coverage than desired; other times, the most effective media expose others not sought. In this instance, waste coverage is justified because the media employed are likely to be the most effective means of delivery available and the cost of the waste coverage is exceeded by the value gained from their use.

When watching football games on TV, you may have noticed a number of commercials for stock brokerage firms such as Dean Witter Reynolds and Merrill Lynch. Not all viewers are candidates for stock market services, but a very high percentage of potential customers can be reached with this strategy. So the program is considered a good media buy because the ability to generate market coverage outweighs the disadvantages of high waste coverage.

Exhibit 12–14 shows how information provided by Simmons can be used to match media to target markets. It profiles magazines read and TV shows watched by people who do aerobics. (You can practice using index numbers here.) From Exhibit 12–14, you can see that *Shape, Self,* and *Vanity Fair* magazines would likely be wise selections for aerobics ads, whereas *Road and Track, Sports Afield,* or *Sport* would be less likely to lead to the desired exposures.

Determining Geographic Coverage

Snow skiing is much more popular in some areas of the country than in others. It would not be the wisest of strategies to promote skis in those areas where interest is not high, unless you could generate an increase in interest. It may be possible to promote an interest in

@ **EXHIBIT 12–15**

Three methods of promotional scheduling

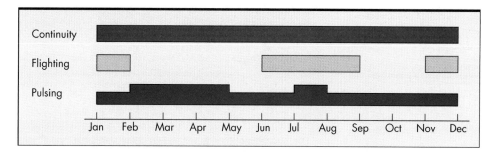

skiing in the Southeast, but a notable increase in sales of ski equipment is not very likely, given the market's distance from snow. The objective of weighting certain geographic areas more than others makes sense, and the strategy of exerting more promotional efforts and dollars in these areas follows naturally. (See Denny's overall parameters in Appendix B.)

Scheduling

Obviously, companies would like to keep their advertising in front of consumers at all times as a constant reminder of the product and/or brand name. In reality, this is not possible for a variety of reasons (not the least of which is the budget!). Nor is it necessary. The primary objective of *scheduling* is to time promotional efforts so they will coincide with the highest potential buying times. While for some products these times are not easy to identify, for others they are very obvious. Three scheduling methods available to the media planner are shown in Exhibit 12–15.

Continuity refers to a continuous pattern of advertising, which may mean every day, every week, or every month. The key is that a regular (continuous) pattern is developed without gaps or no-advertising periods. Such strategies might be used for advertising for food products, laundry detergents, or other products consumed on an ongoing basis without regard for seasonality.

A second method, **flighting,** employs a less regular schedule, with intermittent periods of advertising and nonadvertising. At some time periods there are heavier promotional expenditures, and at others there may be no advertising. Many banks, for example, spend no monies on advertising in the summer but maintain advertising throughout the rest of the year. Snow skis are advertised heavily between October and April; less in May, August, and September; and not at all in June and July.

Pulsing is actually a combination of the first two methods. In a pulsing strategy, continuity is maintained, but at certain times promotional efforts are stepped up. In the automobile industry, advertising continues throughout the year but may increase in April (income tax refund time), September (new models being brought out), and the end of the model year. The scheduling strategy depends on the objectives, buying cycles, and the budget, among other factors. There are certain advantages and disadvantages to each scheduling method, as shown in Exhibit 12–16. (Notice that in Denny's media plan in Appendix B, flighting is recommended for TV advertising strategy, but a continuous radio schedule is employed.)

Determining Reach versus Frequency

Since advertisers face a variety of objectives and have budget constraints, they usually must trade off reach and frequency. They must decide whether to have the message be seen or heard by more people or by a smaller number of people more often. To make this decision, they must know how much reach and frequency are needed, respectively. Let us explore these issues.

How much reach is necessary?

Thinking back to the hierarchies discussed in Chapter 6, you will recall that the first stage of each model requires awareness of the product and/or brand. The more people are aware, the more are likely to move to each subsequent stage. Achieving awareness requires reach—that is, exposing potential buyers to the message. New brands or products

@ **EXHIBIT 12-16**

Characteristics of scheduling
methods

Continuity	
Advantages	Serves as a constant reminder to the consumer
	Covers the entire buying cycle
	Allows for media priorities (quantity discounts, preferred locations, etc.)
Disadvantages	Higher costs
	Potential for overexposure
	Limited media allocation possible
Flighting	
Advantages	Cost efficiency of advertising only during purchase cycles
	May allow for inclusion of more than one medium or vehicle with limited budgets
Disadvantages	Weighting may offer more exposure and advantage over competitors
	Increased likelihood of wearout
	Lack of awareness, interest, retention of promotional message during nonscheduled times
	Vulnerability to competitive efforts during nonscheduled periods
Pulsing	
Advantages	All of the same as the previous two methods
Disadvantages	Not required for seasonal products (or other cyclical products)

need a very high level of reach, since the objective is to make all potential buyers aware of the new entry. High reach is also desired at later stages of the hierarchy. For example, at the trial stage of the adoption hierarchy, a promotions strategy might use cents-off coupons or free samples. An objective of the marketer is to reach a larger number of people with these samples, in an attempt to make them learn of the product, try it, and develop favorable attitudes toward it. (In turn, these attitudes may lead to purchase.)

The problem arises because there is no known way of determining how much reach is required to achieve levels of awareness, attitude change, or buying intentions, nor can we be sure an ad placed in a vehicle will actually reach the intended audience. (There has been some research on the first problem, which will be discussed in the section on effective reach.)

If you buy advertising time on "60 Minutes," does this mean everyone who is tuned to this program will see the ad? No; many will leave the room, be distracted during the commercial, and so on, as shown in Exhibit 12–17. (The exhibit also provides a good example of the difference between reach and coverage.) If I expose everyone in my target group to the message once, will this be sufficient to create a 100 percent level of awareness? The answer again is no. This leads to the next question: What frequency of exposure is necessary for the ad to be seen and to have an impact? IMC Perspective 12–2 on page 334 presents some philosophical arguments over this question.

What frequency level is needed?

With respect to media planning, *frequency* carries a slightly different meaning. (Remember when we said one of the problems in media planning is that terms often take on different meanings?) Here frequency refers to the number of times one is exposed to the media vehicle, not necessarily to the ad itself. While one study has estimated the actual audience for the commercial may be as much as 30 percent lower than that for the program, not all researchers agree.[3] Exhibit 12–17 demonstrates that depending on the program, this number may range from 12 percent to as high as 40 percent.

Most advertisers do agree that a 1:1 exposure ratio does not exist. So while your ad may be placed in a certain vehicle, the fact that a consumer has been exposed to that

⊚ EXHIBIT   12–17   Who's still there to watch the ads?

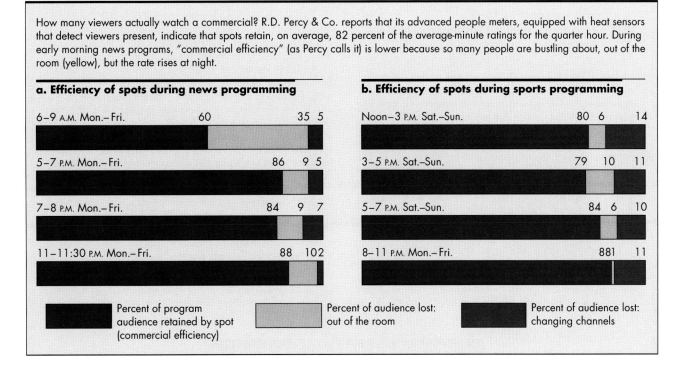

How many viewers actually watch a commercial? R.D. Percy & Co. reports that its advanced people meters, equipped with heat sensors that detect viewers present, indicate that spots retain, on average, 82 percent of the average-minute ratings for the quarter hour. During early morning news programs, "commercial efficiency" (as Percy calls it) is lower because so many people are bustling about, out of the room (yellow), but the rate rises at night.

a. Efficiency of spots during news programming

6–9 A.M. Mon.–Fri.	60	35	5
5–7 P.M. Mon.–Fri.	86	9	5
7–8 P.M. Mon.–Fri.	84	9	7
11–11:30 P.M. Mon.–Fri.	88	10	2

b. Efficiency of spots during sports programming

Noon–3 P.M. Sat.–Sun.	80	6	14
3–5 P.M. Sat.–Sun.	79	10	11
5–7 P.M. Sat.–Sun.	84	6	10
8–11 P.M. Mon.–Fri.	88	1	11

■ Percent of program audience retained by spot (commercial efficiency)   ▨ Percent of audience lost: out of the room   ■ Percent of audience lost: changing channels

vehicle does not ensure that your ad has been seen. As a result, the frequency level expressed in the media plan is an overstatement of the actual level of exposure to the ad. This overstatement has led some media buyers to refer to the reach of the media vehicle as "opportunities to see" an ad rather than actual exposure to the ad.

Because the advertiser has no sure way of knowing whether exposure to a vehicle results in exposure to the ad, the media and advertisers have adopted a compromise: one exposure to the vehicle constitutes reach, given that this exposure must occur for the viewer even to have an opportunity to see the ad. Thus, the exposure figure is used to calculate reach and frequency levels. But this compromise does not help determine the frequency required to make an impact. The creativity of the ad, the involvement of the receiver, noise, and many other intervening factors confound any attempts to make a precise determination.

At this point, you may be thinking, "If nobody knows this stuff, how do they make these decisions?" That's a good question, and the truth is that the decisions are not always made on hard data. Says Joseph Ostrow, executive vice president–director of communications services with Young and Rubicam, "Establishing frequency goals for an advertising campaign is a mix of art and science but with a definite bias toward art."[4] Let us first examine the process involved in setting reach and frequency objectives and then discuss the logic of each.

Establishing reach and frequency objectives

It is possible to be exposed to more than one media vehicle with an ad, resulting in repetition (frequency). If one ad is placed on one TV show one time, the number of persons exposed is the reach. If the ad is placed on two shows, the total number exposed once is **unduplicated reach**. Some people would see the ad twice. The reach of the two shows, as depicted in Exhibit 12–18 on page 335, includes a number of people who were reached by each show (*c*). This overlap is referred to as **duplicated reach**.

IMC Perspective 12-2
Frequency versus Propinquity: Is More Better?

One of the more spirited debates among media planners involves the number of exposures necessary to make an effective impression. It's like arguing politics or religion—no one ever wins. Abbott Wool, senior vice president and media director at Siboney Advertising, claims one exposure may be enough. Wool stresses the theory of propinquity, which states that the message received closest to the purchase decision is the one that affects brand sales the most. Thus, if we could reach the consumer with the ad very close to purchase time, we could lower the frequency levels required and save advertising dollars. Wool advises studying the geographic concentration of prospects, the seasonality of purchases, purchase times and dates, and demographics to time ads optimally.

On the other side is Jack Myers, president of Myers Reports and a media consultant. According to Myers, Krugman's work "Why Three Exposures May Be Enough" was valid 20 years ago but is not any more. Myers notes that when Krugman conducted his research the consumer was exposed to *only* 1,000 ads per day. Now that exposure is probably 3,000 to 5,000 ads per day. Throw in the fragmentation of television, the increase in the number of magazines, and the new alternative media options now being used, and Myers argues that there is less chance of one ad being noticed. He argues that 12 times may be the bare minimum frequency required to achieve the equivalent of Krugman's three exposures. Myers suggests that a new movie release, for example, may require exposures of 24 to 36 times during a 10-day period to duplicate the impact of 6 to 10 ads in 1980. He expects that in the future, brand marketers will establish average frequency levels of 24 to 36 ads, with exposure levels exceeding 100 during the course of a one-year campaign.

The two do agree on a couple of points. Wool agrees that the difficulty in reaching the consumer close to the purchase decision makes it unlikely that one exposure will be effective. Myers agrees that the timing of the presentation is critical, and the closer to the action the exposure takes place the more likely it is to be effective. So what are they all arguing about?

Sources: Abbott Wool, "Frequency vs. Propinquity," *MediaWeek*, July 26, 1993, p. 19; Jack Myers, "More Is Indeed Better," *MediaWeek*, Sept. 6, 1993, pp. 14–18.

Both unduplicated and duplicated reach figures are important. Unduplicated reach indicates potential new exposures, while duplicated reach provides an estimate of frequency. Most media buys include both forms of reach. Let us consider an example.

A measure of potential reach in the broadcast industry is the TV (or radio) **program rating**. This number is expressed as a percentage. For an estimate of the total number

@ **EXHIBIT 12–18**

Representation of reach and frequency

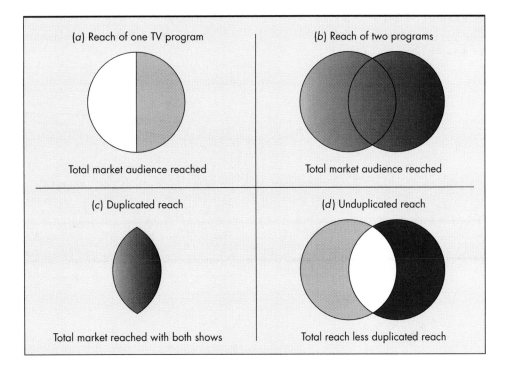

(a) Reach of one TV program

Total market audience reached

(b) Reach of two programs

Total market audience reached

(c) Duplicated reach

Total market reached with both shows

(d) Unduplicated reach

Total reach less duplicated reach

of homes reached, multiply this percentage times the number of homes with TV sets. For example, if there are 93.1 million homes with TV sets in the United States and the program has a rating of 30, then the calculation is 0.30 times 93.1, or 27.93 million homes. (We go into much more detail on ratings and other broadcast terms in Chapter 13.)

Using gross ratings points

The media buyer typically uses a numerical indicator determined by **gross ratings points (GRPs)** to know how many potential audience members might be exposed to a series of commercials. A summary measure that combines the program rating and the average number of times the home is reached during this period (frequency of exposure) is a commonly used reference point known as gross ratings points.

GRP = Reach × Frequency

GRPs are based on the total audience that might be reached by a media schedule and use a duplicated reach estimate. **Target ratings points (TRPs)** refer to the number of people in the primary target audience the media buy will reach—and the number of times. Unlike GRP, TRP does not include waste coverage.

Given that GRPs do not measure actual reach, the advertiser must ask: How many GRPs are needed to attain a certain reach? How do these GRPs translate into effective reach? For example, how many GRPs must one purchase to attain an unduplicated reach of 50 percent, and what frequency of exposure will this schedule deliver? The following example may help you to understand how this process works.

First you must know what these ratings points represent. A purchase of 100 GRPs could mean 100 percent of the market is exposed once or 50 percent of the market is exposed twice or 25 percent of the market is exposed four times, and so on. As you can see, this information must be more specific for the marketer to use it effectively. To know how many GRPs are necessary, the manager needs to know how many members of the intended audience the schedule actually reaches. The chart in Exhibit 12–19 helps make this determination.

ⓐ **EXHIBIT   12–19**

Estimates of reach
for network TRPs

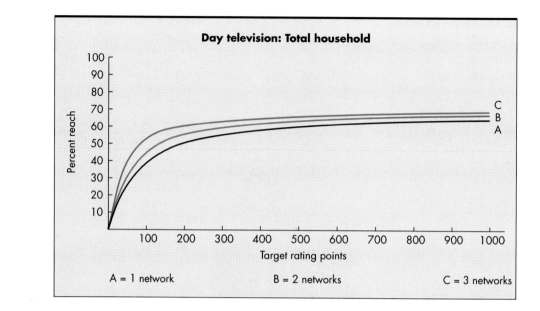

In Exhibit 12–19, a purchase of 100 TRPs on one network would yield an estimated reach of 32 percent of the total households in the target market. This figure would climb to 37.2 percent if two networks were used and 44.5 percent on three. Working backward through the formula for TRPs (GRPs), the estimate of frequency of exposure—3.125, 2.688, and 2.247, respectively—demonstrates the trade-off between reach and frequency.

As an example of a media buy, 7-Up purchased 1,400 GRPs in a four-week period to introduce a new ad campaign. This purchase employed 189 separate TV spots and was estimated to reach 96 percent of the target audience an average of 14 times. To determine if this was a wise media buy, we need to know whether this was an effective reach figure. Certainly, reaching 96 percent of the target market is attractive. But why was the frequency level so high? And was it likely to be effective? In other words, does this level of GRPs affect awareness, attitudes, and purchase intentions?

A number of researchers have explored this issue. David Berger, vice president and director of research at the Foote, Cone & Belding advertising agency, has determined that 2,500 GRPs are likely to lead to approximately a 70 percent probability of high awareness, whereas 1,000 to 2,500 would be about 33 percent likely, and less than 1,000 would result in almost no likelihood.[5] David Olson obtained similar results and further showed that as awareness increased, trial of the product would also increase, although at a significantly slower rate.[6] In both cases, it was evident that a high number of GRPs were required to make an impact.

Exhibit 12–20 summarizes the effects that can be expected at different levels of exposure, based on research in this area. A number of factors may be operating, and direct relationships may be difficult to establish.[7] In addition to those results shown in Exhibit 12–20, Joseph Ostrow has shown that while the number of repetitions increases awareness rapidly, it has much less impact on attitudinal and behavioral responses.[8]

You can imagine how expensive it was for 7-Up to purchase 1,400 gross ratings points on TV. Now that you have additional information, we will ask again, "Was this a good buy?"

Determining effective reach

Since marketers have budget constraints, they must decide whether to increase reach at the expense of frequency or increase the frequency of exposure but to a smaller audience. A number of factors will influence this decision. For example, a new product or brand introduction would attempt to maximize reach—particularly unduplicated reach—to create awareness in as many people as possible as quickly as possible. At the same time,

@ EXHIBIT 12–20

The effects of reach and
frequency

1. One exposure of an ad to a target group within a purchase cycle has little or no effect in most circumstances.
2. Since one exposure is usually ineffective, the central goal of productive media planning should be to enhance frequency rather than reach.
3. The evidence suggests strongly that an exposure frequency of two within a purchase cycle is an effective level.
4. Beyond three exposures within a brand purchase cycle or over a period of four or even eight weeks, increasing frequency continues to build advertising effectiveness at a decreasing rate but with no evidence of decline.
5. Although there are general principles with respect to frequency of exposure and its relationship to advertising effectiveness, differential effects by brand are equally important.
6. Nothing we have seen suggests that frequency response principles or generalizations vary by medium.
7. The data strongly suggest that wearout is not a function of too much frequency; it is more of a creative or copy problem.

for a high-involvement product or one whose benefits are not obvious, a certain level of frequency is necessary to achieve effective reach.

Effective reach represents the percentage of a vehicle's audience reached at each effective frequency increment. This concept is based on the assumption that one exposure to an ad may not be sufficient to convey the desired message. As we saw earlier, no one knows the exact number of exposures necessary for an ad to make an impact, although advertisers have settled on three as the minimum. Effective reach (exposure) is shown in the shaded area in Exhibit 12–21 in the range of 3 to 10 exposures. Below 3 exposures is considered insufficient reach, while beyond 10 is considered excessive exposure and thus ineffective reach. This exposure level is no guarantee of effective communication; different messages may require more or fewer exposures. IMC Perspective 12–2 provides some additional insight into effective reach.

Since they do not know how many times the viewer will actually be exposed, advertisers typically purchase GRPs that lead to more than three exposures to increase the likelihood of effective reach.

Determining effective reach is further complicated by the fact that when calculating GRPs, advertisers use a figure that they call **average frequency,** or the average number of times the target audience reached by a media schedule is exposed to the vehicle over a specified period. The problem with this figure is revealed in the scenario below.

Consider a media buy in which:
    50 percent of audience is reached 1 time.
    30 percent of audience is reached 5 times.
    20 percent of audience is reached 10 times.
    Average frequency = 4.0

In this media buy, the average frequency is 4.0, which is slightly over the number established as effective. Yet a full 50 percent of the audience receives only one exposure. Thus, the average frequency number can be misleading, and using it to calculate GRPs might result in underexposing the audience.

Although GRPs have their problems, they can provide useful information to the marketer. A certain level of GRPs is necessary to achieve awareness, and increases in GRPs are likely to lead to more exposures and/or more repetitions—both of which are necessary to have an effect on higher-order objectives. Perhaps the best advice for purchasing GRPs is offered by Ostrow, who recommends the following strategies:[9]

1. Instead of using average frequency, the marketer should decide what minimum frequency goal is needed to reach the advertising objectives effectively and then maximize reach at that frequency level.
2. To determine effective frequency, one must consider marketing factors, message factors, and media factors. (See Exhibit 12–22 on page 339.)

EXHIBIT 12–21

Graph of effective reach

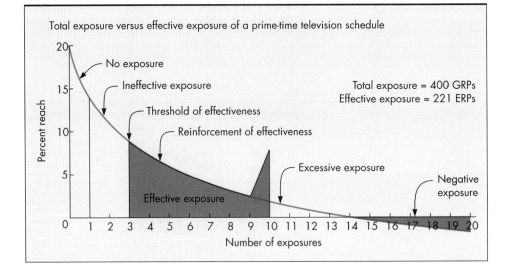

In summary, the reach versus frequency decision, while critical, is very difficult to make. A number of factors must be considered, and concrete rules do not always apply. The decision is often more of an art than a science.

Considering Creative Aspects and Mood

The context of the medium in which the ad is placed may also affect viewers' perceptions. A specific creative strategy may require certain media. Because TV provides both sight and sound, it may be more effective in generating emotions than other media; magazines may create different perceptions than will newspapers. In developing a media strategy, marketers must consider both creativity and mood factors. Let us examine each in more detail.

Creative aspects

It is possible to significantly increase the success of a product through a strong creative campaign. But to implement this creativity, you must employ a medium that will support such a strategy. For example, the Absolut vodka campaign discussed in Chapter 10 and the campaign for Obsession cologne shown in Chapter 4 used print media to communicate their messages effectively. Kodak and McDonald's, among others, have effectively used TV to create emotional appeals. In some situations, the media strategy to be pursued may be the driving force behind the creative strategy, as the media and creative departments work closely together to achieve the greatest impact with the audience of the specific media.

Mood

Certain media enhance the creativity of a message because they create a mood that carries over to the communication itself. For example, think about the mood created by the following magazines: *Gourmet, Skiing, Travel,* and *House Beautiful.* Each of these special-interest vehicles puts the reader in a particular mood. The promotion of fine wines, ski boots, luggage, and home products is enhanced by this mood. What different images might be created for your product if you advertised it in these media?

The New York Times versus *National Enquirer*

Architectural Digest versus *Reader's Digest*

A highly rated prime-time TV show versus an old rerun

The message may require a specific medium and a certain media vehicle to achieve its objectives. Likewise, certain media and vehicles have images that may carry over to the perceptions of messages placed within them.

@ EXHIBIT 12–22

Factors important in determining frequency levels

Marketing Factors

- **Brand history** Is the brand new or established? New brands generally require higher frequency levels.
- **Brand share** An inverse relationship exists between brand share and frequency. The higher the brand share, the lower the frequency level required.
- **Brand loyalty** An inverse relationship exists between loyalty and frequency. The higher the loyalty, the lower the frequency level required.
- **Purchase cycles** Shorter purchasing cycles require higher frequency levels to maintain top-of-mind awareness.
- **Usage cycle** Products used daily or oftener will quickly need to be replaced. A higher level of frequency is desired.
- **Competitive share of voice** Higher frequency levels are required when a lot of competitive noise exists and when the goal is to meet or beat competitors.
- **Target group** The ability of the target group to learn and to retain messages has a direct effect on frequency.

Message or Creative Factors

- **Message complexity** The simpler the message, the less frequency required.
- **Message uniqueness** The more unique the message, the lower the frequency level required.
- **New versus continuing campaigns** New campaigns require higher levels of frequency to register the message.
- **Image versus product sell** Creating an image requires higher levels of frequency than does a specific product sell.
- **Message variation** A single message requires less frequency; a variety of messages requires more.
- **Wearout** Higher frequency may lead to wearout. This effect must be tracked and used to evaluate frequency levels.
- **Advertising units** Larger units of advertising require less frequency than smaller ones to get the message across.

Media Factors

- **Clutter** The more advertising that appears in the media used, the more frequency is needed to break through the clutter.
- **Editorial environment** An ad that is consistent with the editorial environment needs lower levels of frequency.
- **Attentiveness** The higher the level of attention achieved by the media vehicle, the less frequency is required. Low attention-getting media will require more repetitions.
- **Scheduling** Continuous scheduling requires less frequency than does flighting or pulsing.
- **Number of media used** The fewer media are used, the lower the level of frequency required.
- **Repeat exposures** Media that allow for more repeat exposures—for example, monthly magazines—require less frequency.

Flexibility

An effective media strategy requires a degree of flexibility. Because of the rapidly changing marketing environment, strategies may need to be modified. If the plan has not built in some flexibility, opportunities may be lost and/or the company may not be able to address new threats. Flexibility may be needed to address the following:

1. **Market opportunities** Sometimes a market opportunity arises that the advertiser wishes to take advantage of. For example, the development of a new advertising medium may offer an opportunity that was not previously available.
2. **Market threats** Internal or external factors may pose a threat to the firm, and a change in media strategy is dictated. For example, a competitor may alter its media strategy to gain an edge. Failure to respond to this challenge could create problems for the firm.
3. **Availability of media** Sometimes a desired medium (or vehicle) is not available to the marketer. Perhaps the medium does not reach a particular target segment or has no time or space available. There are still some areas of this country

@ **EXHIBIT 12–23**

Cost per thousand computations—*Time* versus *Newsweek*

	Time	Newsweek
Per page cost	$135,000	$115,000
Circulation	4.0 million	3.1 million
Calculation of CPM	$\dfrac{135,000 \times 1,000}{4,000,000}$	$\dfrac{115,000 \times 1,000}{3,100,000}$
CPM	$33.75	$37.10

where certain media do not reach. Even when the media are available, limited advertising time or space may have already been sold or cutoff dates for entry may have passed. Alternative vehicles or media must then be considered.

4. **Changes in media or media vehicles** A change in the medium or in a particular vehicle may necessitate a change in the media strategy. For example, the advent of cable TV opened up new opportunities for message delivery, as will the introduction of interactive media. Likewise, a drop in ratings or a change in editorial format may lead the advertiser to use different programs or print alternatives.

Each of these factors requires that the media strategy be developed with enough flexibility to allow the manager to adapt to specific market situations.

Budget Considerations

One of the more important decisions in the development of media strategy is cost estimating. The value of any strategy can be determined by how well it delivers the message to the audience with the lowest cost and the least amount of waste. We have already explored a number of factors, such as reach, frequency, and availability, that affect this decision. The marketer tries to arrive at the optimal delivery by balancing cost with each of these. (Again, the Denny's plan in Appendix B demonstrates how this issue is addressed.) As the following discussion shows, understanding cost figures may not be as easy as it seems.

Advertising and promotional costs can be categorized in two ways. The **absolute cost** of the medium or vehicle is the actual total cost required to place the message. For example, a full-page four-color ad in *Newsweek* magazine would cost about $115,000. **Relative cost** refers to the relationship between the price paid for advertising time or space and the size of the audience delivered; it is used to compare media vehicles. Relative costs are important because the manager must try to optimize audience delivery within budget constraints. Since a number of alternatives are available for delivering the message, the advertiser must evaluate the relative costs associated with these choices. The way media costs are provided and problems in comparing these costs across media often make such evaluations difficult.

Determining relative costs of media

To evaluate alternatives, advertisers must compare the relative costs of media as well as vehicles within these media. Unfortunately, the broadcast, print, and out-of-home media do not always provide the same cost breakdowns, nor necessarily do vehicles within the print media. Following are the cost bases used.

1. **Cost per thousand (CPM)** For years the magazine industry has provided cost breakdowns on the basis of cost per thousand people reached. The formula for this computation is

$$\text{CPM} = \frac{\text{Cost of ad space (absolute cost)} \times 1,000}{\text{Circulation}}$$

Exhibit 12–23 provides an example of this computation for two vehicles within the same medium—*Time* and *Newsweek*—and shows that (all other things being

@ EXHIBIT 12–24

Comparison of cost per ratings point—"Home Improvement" versus "The Oprah Winfrey Show"

	"Home Improvement"	"The Oprah Winfrey Show"
Cost per spot ad	$6,000	$1,500
Rating	21	11
Reach (total persons)	311,000	123,000
Calculation	$6,000/21	$1,500/11
CPRP	$285.71	$136.36

equal) *Time* is a more cost-effective buy, even though the absolute cost is higher. (We come back to "all other things being equal" in a moment.)

2. **Cost per ratings point (CPRP)** The broadcast media provide a different comparative cost figure, referred to as cost per ratings point (or cost per point CPP), based on the following formula:

$$CPRP = \frac{\text{Cost of commercial time}}{\text{Program rating}}$$

An example of this calculation for a spot ad in a local TV market is shown in Exhibit 12–24. It indicates that Oprah Winfrey would be more cost effective than "Home Improvement."

3. **Daily inch rate** For newspapers, cost effectiveness is based on the daily inch rate, which is the cost per column inch of the paper. Like magazines, newspapers now use the cost per thousand formula discussed earlier to determine relative costs. As shown in Exhibit 12–25, the cost of advertising in the *Boston Globe* is significantly higher than that of the *Boston Herald* (again, all other things being equal).

As you can see, it is difficult to make comparisons across various media. What is the broadcast equivalent of cost per thousand or the column inch rate? In an attempt to standardize relative costing procedures, the broadcast and newspaper media have begun to provide costs per thousand, using the following formulas:

$$\text{Television: } \frac{\text{Cost of 1 unit of time} \times 1,000}{\text{Program rating}}$$

$$\text{Newspapers: } \frac{\text{Cost of ad space} \times 1,000}{\text{Circulation}}$$

While the comparison of media on a cost per thousand basis is important, intermedia comparisons can be misleading. The ability of TV to provide both sight and sound, the longevity of magazines, and other characteristics of each medium make it difficult to make direct comparisons. The media planner should use the cost per thousand numbers

@ EXHIBIT 12–25

Comparative costs in newspaper advertising

	Boston Globe	*Boston Herald*
Cost per page	$25,300	$11,500
Cost per inch	$211	$164.50
Circulation	476,000	324,000
Calculation	$CPM = \dfrac{\text{Page cost} \times 1,000}{\text{Circulation}}$	
Milline rate	$CPM = \dfrac{25,300 \times 1,000}{476,000}$	$\dfrac{11,500 \times 1,000}{324,000}$
	$53.15	$35.49

⊚ **EXHIBIT 12–26**

Cost per thousand estimates

Scenario A: Overestimation of Efficiency

Target market: 18–49
Magazine circulation: 4,000,000
Circulation to target market: 65% (2,600,000)
Cost per page: $135,000

$$\text{CPM} = \frac{\$135,000 \times 1,000}{4,000,000} = \$33.75$$

$$\text{CPM (actual target audience)} = \frac{\$135,000 \times 1,000}{2,600,000} = \$51.92$$

Scenario B: Underestimation of Efficiency

Target market: all age groups, male and female
Magazine circulation: 4,000,000
Cost per page: $135,000
Pass-along rate: 3* (33% of households)

$$\text{CPM (based on readers per copy)} = \frac{\text{Page cost} \times 1,000}{\text{Circulation} + 3(1,320,000)}$$

$$= \frac{\$135,000 \times 1,000}{7,960,000} = \$16.96$$

*Assuming pass-along was valid.

but must also consider the specific characteristics of each medium and each media vehicle in the decision.

The cost per thousand may overestimate or underestimate the actual cost effectiveness. Consider a situation where some waste coverage is inevitable. The circulation (using the *Time* magazine figures to demonstrate our point) exceeds the target market. If the people reached by this message are not potential buyers of the product, then having to pay to reach them results in too low a cost per thousand, as shown in scenario A of Exhibit 12–26. We must use the potential reach to the target market—the destination sought—rather than the overall circulation figure. A medium with a much higher cost per thousand may be a wiser buy if it is reaching more potential receivers.

CPM may also underestimate cost efficiency. Magazine advertising space sellers have argued for years that because more than one person may read an issue, the actual reach is underestimated. They want to use the number of **readers per copy** as the true circulation. This would include a **pass-along rate,** estimating the number of people who read the magazine without buying it. Scenario B in Exhibit 12–26 shows how this underestimates cost efficiency. Consider a family in which a father, mother, and two teenage children all read each issue of *Time* magazine. Assume such families constitute 33 percent of *Time*'s circulation base. While the circulation figure includes only one magazine, in reality there are four potential exposures in these households, increasing the total reach to 7.96 million.

While the readers per copy figure makes intuitive sense, it has the potential to be extremely inaccurate. The actual number of times the magazine changes hands is difficult to determine. How many people in a fraternity read each issue of *Sports Illustrated* or *Playboy* that is delivered? How many members of a sorority or on a dorm floor read each issue of *Cosmopolitan* or *Self?* How many of either group read each issue of *Business Week?* While research is conducted to make these determinations, pass–along estimates are very subjective and using them to estimate reach is speculative. While these figures are regularly provided by the media, managers are selective about using them. At the same time, the art of media buying enters, for many magazines' managers have a good idea how much greater the reach is than the circulation figure provided.

In addition to the potential for over- or underestimation of cost efficiencies, CPMs are limited in that they make only *quantitative* estimates of the value of media. While they may be good for comparing very similar vehicles (such as *Time* and *Newsweek*), they are less valuable in making intermedia comparisons. We have already noted some differences among media that preclude direct comparisons. The next section discusses other characteristics of media that must be considered.

You can see that the development of media strategy involves a number of factors. Ostrow may be right when he calls this process an art rather than a science, as so much of it requires going beyond the numbers.

EVALUATION AND FOLLOW-UP

All plans require some evaluation to assess their performance. The media plan is no exception.

In outlining the planning process, we stated that objectives are established and strategies developed for them. Having implemented these strategies, marketers need to know whether or not they were successful. Measures of effectiveness must consider two factors: (1) How well did these strategies achieve the media objectives? (2) How well did this media plan contribute to attaining the overall marketing and communications objectives? If the strategies employed were successful, they should be used in future plans. If not, their flaws should be analyzed.

The problem with measuring the effectiveness of media strategies is probably obvious to you at this point. At the outset of this chapter, we suggested the planning process was limited by problems with measurements and lack of consistent terminology (among others). While these problems limit the degree to which we can assess the relative effectiveness of various strategies, that does not mean it is impossible to make such determinations. Sometimes it is possible to show that a plan has worked. Even if the evaluation procedure is not foolproof, it is better than no attempt.

COMPUTERS IN MEDIA PLANNING

Attempts to improve on the media buying process through the use of computers have received a great deal of attention. While advanced planning models have been around since at least 1963, for the most part these models have met with limited success. Programs based on linear programming, simulation, and iteration have been adopted by only a few agencies.

Computers have been used, however, to automate each of the four steps involved in planning and strategy development. While the art of media strategy has not been mechanized, advances in the quantitative side have significantly improved managers' decision-making capabilities while saving substantial time and effort. Let us briefly examine some of these methods.

Computers in Market Analysis

Earlier in this chapter, we provided examples of Simmons and MRI data. In Chapter 5, we reviewed the information in Prizm, VALS, Vision, and other such systems. All these data can be accessed either through an interactive system or on the agency's own PC. For example, MRI offers its clients interactive capabilities with its mainframe or its MEMRI software database that can be used on a PC to cross-tabulate media and demographic data, estimate reach and frequency, and rank costs, in addition to numerous other applications. The interactive capabilities can also allow interface with Prizm, VALS, and Vision data. Simmons also allows access to Prizm, Acorn, VALS, and others.

Other market analysis programs are also available. ClusterPlus and Market America include demographic, geographic, psychographic, and product and media use information that can be used for media planning. Census tract information and socioeconomic data are also accessible. These systems are linked to Nielsen data for scheduling and targeting to specific groups.

◉ EXHIBIT 12–27 BAR/LNA information is also available on the PC

Company/Brand $	LNA/Arbitron Multi-Media Service January–December 1993				
			Year-to-Date Advertising Dollars (000)		
Parent Company/Brand	Class Code	10-Media Total	Magazines	Sunday Magazines	Newspapers
FORCE E					
FORCE E SPORTING GOODS	G717	44.5	44.5	–	–
FORCE FIN					
FORCE FIN DIVING EQUIPMENT	G419	47.5	47.5	–	–
FORD AUTO DEALERS ASSOCIATION					
FORD DEALERS ASSN LEASING	T119-9	1,948.1	–	–	–
FORD DEALERS ASSN VARIOUS AUTOS	T119-9	84.4	–	–	84.4
FORD DEALERS ASSOCIATION	T119-9	93,185.3	–	–	7,220.9
FORD DLRS ASSN PARTS & SERVICE	T119	499.1	–	–	–
FORD MOTOR CO DEALERS ASSN	T119-9	321.4	–	–	–
FORD-LINCOLN-MERCURY DEALERS ASSN	T119-9	19.2	–	–	19.2
LINCOLN DEALERS ASSOCIATION	T119-9	10.9	–	–	–
LINCOLN-MERCURY ASSN CAPRI	T119-9	13.5	–	–	–
LINCOLN-MERCURY DEALERS ASSN LEASING	T119-9	1,150.6	–	–	38.3
LINCOLN-MERCURY DEALERS ASSN TOWN CAR	T119-9	0.9	–	–	–
LINCOLN-MERCURY DEALERS ASSN TRACER	T119-9	1.8	–	–	–
LINCOLN-MERCURY DEALERS ASSOCIATION	T119-9	28,820.0	–	–	4,752.5
COMPANY TOTAL		126,055.2	–	–	12,115.3

Continued

In addition to customer analyses, other information used in the analysis stage is available. Exhibit 12–27 is another example of the BAR/LNA data mentioned earlier, which are also available through computers.

Analyses of these data can help planners determine which markets and which groups should be targeted for advertising and promotions. By using this information along with other data, the marketer can also define media objectives.

Computers in Media Strategy Development

In the strategy development phase, we discussed the need to make decisions regarding coverage, scheduling, costs, and the trade-off between reach and frequency, among others. Of primary benefit to media planners are the programs that assist in development of these strategies. While there are far too many of these programs to review here we will provide a small sampling to demonstrate our point.

Reach and frequency analyses on the computer

Exhibit 12–28 demonstrates one example of how software programs are being used to determine reach and frequency levels and assist in deciding which alternative is best. Various media mixes for television and radio at different TRPs are computed, with reach and frequency estimates, the number of people reached three or more times, and the costs. The program has determined that a mix of 125 TRPs on TV and 150 TRPs on radio would result in the best buy. Keep in mind that this recommendation considers only the most efficient combination of quantifiable factors and does not allow for the art of media buying.

Exhibit 12–28 shows just one of the many examples of how computer programs—in this case, the Telmar system—are being used in media strategy development. Other

@ **EXHIBIT 12–27** *Concluded*

			LNA/Arbitron Multi-Media Service January–December 1993			
			Year-to-Date Advertising Dollars (000)			
Outdoor	Network Television	Spot Television	Syndicated Television	Cable TV Networks	Network Radio	National Spot Radio
–	–	–	–	–	–	–
–	–	–	–	–	–	–
–	–	1,384.3	–	–	–	63.8
–	–	–	–	–	–	–
488.6	–	82,089.3	–	–	–	3,386.5
–	–	499.1	–	–	–	–
–	–	305.7	–	–	–	15.7
–	–	–	–	–	–	–
–	–	–	–	–	–	10.9
13.5	–	–	–	–	–	–
–	–	904.6	–	–	–	207.7
0.9	–	–	–	–	–	–
1.8	–	–	–	–	–	–
302.0	–	22,595.5	–	–	–	1,170.0
806.8	–	108,278.5	–	–	–	4,854.6

computer-based media planning programs are available. The following list is just a small sample of the many computer-based media planning programs available.

- **ADplus** provides for media planning, reach and frequency analysis, media mix information, budgeting, and more.
- **Manas** calculates cost and audience estimates for various media plans, accessing ratings data.

@ **EXHIBIT 12–28**

San Diego Trust & Savings Bank reach and frequency analyses

	Product Message		
Media Mix (A 25–54)	Reach Frequency (% / X)	3+ Level (%)	1st Quarter Weekly Cost
TV (125)	84 / 4.5	51	$21,480
TV (125) R (125)	91 / 8.2	71	29,450
TV (125) R (150)*	92 / 9.0	73	31,045
TV (150)	86 / 5.2	57	25,660
TV (150) R (125)	92 / 9.0	73	33,625
TV (150) R (150)	92 / 9.8	74	35,220
TV (175)	89 / 5.9	61	29,930
TV (175) R (125)	93 / 9.7	75	37,900
TV (175) R (150)	93 / 10.5	76	39,490
TV (200)	90 / 6.7	65	34,255
TV (200) R (125)	93 / 10.5	76	42,225
TV (200) R (150)	93 / 11.3	78	43,820

(Based on a three-week flight.)
*Recommended.

@ **EXHIBIT 12–29**

Media characteristics

Media	Advantages	Disadvantages
Television	Mass coverage High reach Impact of sight, sound, and motion High prestige Low cost per exposure Attention getting Favorable image	Low selectivity Short message life High absolute cost High production costs Clutter
Radio	Local coverage Low cost High frequency Flexible Low production costs Well-segmented audiences	Audio only Clutter Low attention getting Fleeting message
Magazines	Segmentation potential Quality reproduction High information content Longevity Multiple readers	Long lead time for ad placement Visual only Lack of flexibility
Newspapers	High coverage Low cost Short lead time for placing ads Ads can be placed in interest sections Timely (current ads) Reader controls exposure Can be used for coupons	Short life Clutter Low attention-getting capabilities Poor reproduction quality Selective reader exposure
Outdoor	Location specific High repetition Easily noticed	Short exposure time requires short ad Poor image Local restrictions
Direct mail	High selectivity Reader controls exposure High information content Opportunities for repeat exposures	High cost/contact Poor image (junk mail) Clutter

- **IMS** planning system linked to MRI, SMRB, and SRDS helps planners rank different media options according to rates and audience delivery.
- **Telmar** allows planners to analyze media data, devise media plans, and create flowcharts. It is linked to major syndicated data services.
- **Media Management Plus** ranks stations in each market according to delivery potential and costs, and calculates projected ratings.
- **AdWare** provides Arbitron and Nielsen information, calculates media costs, projects GRPs, and more.
- **Tapscan** uses syndicated data useful in radio media planning, including ratings data and reach and frequency analysis.
- **TVscan** provides information like Tapscan's for TV.
- **TV Conquest** combines Nielsen, Donnelley, and Simmons data to provide demographic, product usage, and ratings information.
- **Vanguard** is used in print, outdoor planning and buying, spot TV prebuys, and national TV data.

@ **EXHIBIT 12–30** An interactive glossary

To say there is no dominant technology in the still-forming world of interactive media is an understatement. Here is a partial list of the technologies and delivery systems — new, old and in development — likely to play a role in the electronic yellow pages.

Audiotex. These automated telephone information services are already widely used by publishers to deliver "soaps and scopes," stock quotes, sports scores, and other information to directory users. Audiotex is evolving into a more advertiser-oriented product with sponsored "tips" services and in-the-ad audiotex numbers that callers use to get more timely information on an advertiser's product or service. Many tips services are offering call completion to sponsoring advertisers, making the medium more transactional and measurable.

CD-ROM. For "compact disc–read only memory." The CD-ROM player is a computer disc drive that runs compact discs instead of magnetic floppy discs. The advantage: CDs have vastly greater storage capacity than floppies. CD-ROM is currently used to read electronic white and yellow pages listings.

Fax-on-demand. A relatively low-tech service recognized for its ease of entry and potential for widespread use, given the proliferation of fax machines. Callers can request information that is too timely for the yellow pages, such as a restaurant menu or a research report from a financial services firm. Prepared material is then faxed to callers' fax machines.

Interactive TV. This platform has gotten the most attention in the relentless hype over the information superhighway. Interactive TV, whether delivered through cable, telephone, or wireless, could revolutionize the way America shops, pays its bills, learns and entertains itself. Customers could access yellow pages listings through one of the predicted 500 cable TV channels, select listings and possibly explore multi-media ads for businesses. Transaction processing capabilities are another likely component of interactive TV. This platform offers perhaps the greatest capability to measure usage and consumer response to advertisements.

Kiosks. Available in hotels, shopping malls, and other public places, interactive kiosks are another promising delivery point for electronic directory products. Using touch-screen technology, users can menu-drive their way into directory or catalog listings.

On-line services. One of the best-known on-line services, Prodigy, delivers electronic yellow pages and classified advertising through personal computers for a joint venture of BellSouth and Cox Newspapers. Despite several years of operation, on-line services like Prodigy still reach only a limited audience. The reason: Most Americans still do not have computers in their homes.

Screen telephony. Telephones equipped (in most cases) with a keyboard and an LED display panel that permits callers to enter and access data more easily than through a regular telephone. Considered a promising delivery vehicle by many because of its ease of use and low cost of entry, it could serve as a transitional platform until interactive television gains sufficient penetration and consumer acceptance.

Source: *Link* 6, no. 1, Jan. 1994, p. 24.

The one area in which computers have not yet provided a direct benefit is in the evaluation stage of the media plan. While these programs do generate what they consider to be optimal TRP, GRP, and media mixes and allow for pre- and postbuy analyses, the true test is what happens when the plan is implemented. We reserve our discussion of the evaluation process for Chapter 20 on measuring effectiveness.

@ **CHARACTERISTICS OF MEDIA**

To this point, we have discussed the elements involved in the development of media strategy. One of the most basic elements in this process is the matching of media to markets. In the following chapters, you will see that each medium has its own characteristics that make it better or worse for attaining specific objectives. First, Exhibit 12–29 on page 346 is an overall comparison of media and some of the characteristics by which they are evaluated. This is a very general comparison, and the various media options must be analyzed for each situation. However, it provides a good starting point.

The New Interactive Media

Much has been written about the new interactive media. Articles have appeared everywhere from *Time* to *Business Week* to *MediaWeek*. *Advertising Age* now has a regular interactive section every week. When most people think of **interactive media,** they think of televison and the promise of 500 channels that range from shopping channels to news and information services to classified ads. In reality, interactive involves more media than just TV.

Interactive media move the receivers from being passive participants to active ones. Says Hanna Liebman, a writer for *MediaWeek*, these new media will "allow anybody to get information of any kind to anybody else at any time."[10] Interactive media allow the consumer to literally interact with the source, and they come in a variety of forms. While it is beyond the scope of this text to cover interactive media in depth, it is important to be acquainted with them. We describe some of these here, while Exhibit 12–30 on page 347 lists a few more.

- **Direct marketing** Home shopping services already exist. Interactive buying services like Prodigy and CompuServe have been around for years, and the number of subscribers is on the increase. General Motors now mails potential consumers interactive videodisks that allow them to view their cars, change the colors, add options, and even inquire about the purchase price. Many other companies have similar programs.
- **Internet** An international computer network, Internet has over 35 million users. A number of national companies already have ads on the network.
- **Magazines** *Newsweek* is offering CD-ROM subscriptions that combine voice, video, still photography, and animation. Others have plans to do the same.

We could expand this list, as it seems virtually all media are thinking interactive (yes, even outdoor). The important point is to recognize that interactive media will forever change the way marketers communicate with their audiences. The ability to target media will be greatly enhanced, traditional media may have to adapt, and media planners will have a lot of learning to do.

SUMMARY

This chapter has presented an overview of the determination of media objectives, development of the media strategy, and the formalization of them in the form of a media plan. In addition, sources of media information, characteristics of media, and an actual plan were provided.

The media strategy must be designed to supplement and support the overall marketing and communications objectives. The objectives of this plan are designed to deliver the message the program has developed.

The basic task involved in the development of media strategy is to determine the best matching of media to the target market, given the constraints of the budget. The media planner attempts to balance reach and frequency and to deliver the message to the intended audience with a minimum of waste coverage. At the same time, a number of additional factors affect the media decision. Media strategy development has been called more of an art than a science because while many quantitative data are available, the planner also relies on creativity and nonquantifiable factors.

This chapter discussed many factors, including developing a proper media mix, determining target market and geographic coverage, scheduling, balancing reach and frequency, and creative aspects. In addition, budget considerations, the need for flexibility in the schedule, and the use of computers in the media planning process were considered.

KEY TERMS

media planning, p. 318
media objectives, p. 318
media strategies, p. 318
medium, p. 319
media vehicle, p. 319
sweeps periods, p. 322
index number, p. 323
waste coverage, p. 330

continuity, p. 331
flighting, p. 331
pulsing, p. 331
unduplicated reach, p. 333
duplicated reach, p. 333
program rating, p. 334

gross ratings points (GRPs), p. 335
target ratings points (TRPs), p. 335
effective reach, p. 337
average frequency, p. 337
absolute cost, p. 340
relative cost, p. 340

cost per thousand (CPM), p. 340
cost per ratings point (CPRP), p. 341
daily inch rate, p. 341
readers per copy, p. 342
pass-along rate, p. 342
interactive media, p. 347

DISCUSSION QUESTIONS

1. What are sweeps periods? Why might ratings collected during sweeps periods reflect viewers' habits inaccurately?

2. What is a brand development index? A category development index? How can marketers use these indexes?

3. Discuss the various ways companies might organize the media buying department. What are some of the advantages and disadvantages of each?

4. What level of frequency is necessary to achieve an impact on the receiver?

5. Discuss some of the factors that are important in determining frequency levels. Give examples of each factor.

6. What is meant by readers per copy? How is this figure derived? What are some of the problems associated with this number?

7. Discuss the market situation being described by each of the following: high BDI and high CDI; high BDI and low CDI; low BDI and high CDI; and low BDI and low CDI.

8. The text states that flexibility is required in a media plan due to changes that may take place in the marketing environment. Describe some of these changes and how they might affect the media plan.

9. Obtain cost, circulation, and ratings information for some of your local media. Using the relative cost formulas provided in the text, compare the efficiencies of each.

10. Explain the difference between GRPs and TRPs. Many marketers argue that only TRPs are relevant. Explain why they might make this argument.

Appendixes

A. Sources of
Media Information

B. Denny's Restaurant

Appendix A Sources of Media Information:
Cross-reference guide to advertising media sources

	General Information	Competitive Activities	Market Information (geographic)	Audience Information (target groups)	Advertising Rates
Nonmedia information (general marketing)	1, 10, 15, 16, 21, 22, 23	1, 19	10, 11, 15, 16, 18, 20, 21, 24	15, 16, 21	
Multimedia or intermedia	1, 15, 16, 21	1, 13	18	2, 25	2
Daily newspapers				5, 15, 16, 21	2, 24
Weekly newspapers					24
Consumer magazines	14	13		15, 16, 21	2, 24
Farm publications				5, 26	2, 24
Business publications			6, 8	6, 26	2, 24
Network television		7, 13		4, 15, 16, 17, 21	2
Spot television		7, 13		4, 15, 16, 17, 21	2, 24
Network radio		7		12, 15, 16, 17, 21, 27	2
Spot radio				4, 5, 12, 17, 21	2, 24
Direct mail					2, 24
Outdoor		13			2, 9
Transit					2

1. *Advertising Age*
2. Advertising agency media estimating guides
3. American Business Press, Inc. (ABP)
4. Arbitron Ratings Company
5. Audit Bureau of Circulations (ABC)
6. Business/Professional Advertising Association (B/PAA) Media Data
7. Broadcast Advertisers Reports (BAR)
8. Business Publications Audit of Circulation (BPA)
9. *Buyer's Guide to Outdoor Advertising*
10. *State and Metropolitan Area Data Book*
11. *Editor & Publisher* Market Guide
12. Survey of World Advertising Expenditures, Stach/Inra/Heeper
13. Leading National Advertisers (LNA), Inc.
14. Magazine Publishers Association of America (MPA)
15. Mediamark Research, Inc. (MRI)
16. Mendelsohn Media Research, Inc. (MMR)
17. Nielsen Media Research Company
18. Prizm
19. SAMI Burke, Inc.
20. *Sales and Marketing Management Survey of Buying Power*
21. Simmons Market Research Bureau: *Study of Media and Markets*
22. *Standard Directory of Advertisers*
23. *Standard Directory of Advertising Agencies*
24. Standard Rate and Data Service
25. Telmar
26. Verified Audit Circulation Corporation (VAC)

Source: Adapted from Arnold M. Bantam, Donald W. Jugenheimer, and Peter B. Turk, *Advertising Media Sourcebook*, 3rd ed. (Lincolnwood, Ill.: NTC Business Books), pp. 8–9.

Appendix B Denny's Restaurants 1991 Media Plan*

General Overview

Denny's media plan reflects a promotion-driven marketing strategy and business development that is very geographically skewed. By focusing the available budget behind promotions in our most important geography, we believe advertising awareness levels that are well ahead of our share of voice in this heavily advertised category are achieved.

In light of the numerous promotions to be supported over the 1991 calendar year, it has been decided to focus on 28 core markets, representing 40 percent of total U.S. households and 75 percent of total sales, through the use of spot television primarily. Although national media will be considered as a base to provide some form of national presence, budget limitations prohibit any extensive use of these media vehicles; therefore, the top 28 sales markets ranked on sales volume and BDI will receive the majority of support.

The advertising programs scheduled for 1991 fall into two categories:

- Long-term equity building programs.
- Short-term price/product programs.

Both types of programs will run in all Denny's Restaurants nationally so the media will include some form of national presence with heavier emphasis in key sales markets.

Overall Parameters

- Advertising period: calendar year 1991.
- Budget: $21.2 million.
- Geography: primary—28 core markets (40 percent of United States/75 percent of Sales); secondary—National.
- Target audience: Adults 25–54 (system promotions) and kids 2–10 (Flintstones).

Long-Term Equity Programs

- Birthday.
- Grand Slam (menu introduction).
- Late Night.
- Flintstones.

General objective: Increase guest counts/customer base over a longer term period.

Birthday

In order to motivate people to come to Denny's, this program offers them a free meal on their birthday, which they can choose from the special "Birthday Menu" between breakfast, lunch, or dinner. The purpose of the promotion is not only to motivate people by giving them the "free meal," but it is also directed at increasing repeat business by them plus any potential customers they may bring.

Objective

Promote trial and repeat business via the offer of a free birthday meal.

Strategies/tactics

Use network radio over a 12-month period, recognizing:

- Cost efficiency versus television, thereby providing awareness and continuity throughout the entire year.

*Courtesy of Denny's Inc.

- Schedule flights around the beginning and end of each month to increase awareness around the new "Birthday Month."
- Ability to provide national support.

Target

Adults 25–54.

Grand Slam (Menu Introduction)

The Denny's "Grand Slam" breakfast has met considerable success since its launch and has always been one of the most popular entrees on the Denny's menu. For 1992, the "Grand Slam" concept will be expanded beyond the breakfast daypart to offer nine great new Grand Slam entrees for breakfast, lunch, and dinner.

Objective

Increase trial and repeat business via the introduction of new "Grand Slam" menu items. In addition, increase lunch and dinner business along with breakfast.

Strategies

- Use spot TV in the core 28 markets to introduce the new Grand Slam menu over three different phases/support periods:
  Phase I (introduction): 500 TRPs/4 weeks.
  Phase II: 400 TRPs/3 weeks.
  Phase III: 400 TRPs/3 weeks.
- Spot TV will provide support throughout baseball season to take advantage of the "Grand Slam" theme/tie-in with Major League Baseball.
- Use network radio (general/MLB-CBS package) for continuity throughout promotion period (baseball season):
  Cost efficient.
  Extends reach of overall campaign.
  Excellent advertising environment (CBS/MLB package).

Target

Adults 25–54.

Late Night

The Late Night promotion is Denny's marketing effort to give customers something really different from other restaurants. Since Denny's is open 24 hours a day, through advertising, promotions, in-store merchandising, and a special menu with various kinds of dishes, they offer "night owls" a better way to stay awake in a warm, comfortable, and friendly place.

Objective

To increase guest counts during the graveyard daypart. Being a 24-hour operation, Denny's has the advantage and opportunity of increasing business during this daypart.

Strategies

Use spot radio in all top sales markets to reach "night owls" owing to its:

- Ability to deliver the target without waste.
- Low out-of-pocket cost (versus television).
- Merchandising/promotional opportunities.

Executional considerations:

- Station selection: Schedules to be placed on top ranking overnight stations (Monday–Sunday; 11 P.M.–5 A.M.).
- It is recommended to purchase schedules on at least 3 stations and approximately 17 TRPs per market per week. Actual total number of spots per market per week are in the range of 40–90 but may vary depending on available ratings.
- Available research has indicated the overnight audience (11 P.M. to 5 A.M.) is approximately 10 percent that of the 6 A.M. to 7 P.M. audience. Consequently, ratings are roughly 10 percent of daytime. 17 TRPs per week in overnight should deliver the equivalent level of commercial units as the 6 A.M. to 7 P.M. time period, which typically averages roughly 150 TRPs per week.
- Commercial unit: 100 percent 60-second spots.

Target

Adults 25–54 (primary): adults 18–34 (secondary).

Flintstones

Directed to families with kids between 2 and 10 years old, this promotion attracts young families with kids by offering special Flintstones premiums. Every two months, the special premiums will be available in the restaurants (e.g., Dino Racers, Flintstone's vehicles, etc.). In addition, a special Flintstones Kid Menu has been created offering more "personable" service and ultimately increasing interest in repeat visits.

Objectives

Increase guest counts in the segment of families with kids 10 years old and under through the use of Flintstone's premiums/merchandise available to kids 2–10.

Strategies/tactics

- Use spot TV over three flights (two weeks per flight) promoting three different kids premiums in 25 markets, recognizing:
    Broad reach against target.
    High impact of television/showcase opportunity.
- Use a daypart mix of: 50 percent kids weekend/50 percent kids other (either early morning or kids afternoon, depending on market-by-market availabilities and efficiencies).
- Use national cable over three flights (two weeks per flight) to supplement the spot TV buy, recognizing:
    Opportunity for alternative programs/dayparts targeted to kids.
    Ability to provide "national" support efficiently (covers all Denny's markets).
    Low out-of-pocket cost for national support.
    Ability to extend reach against kids (basic cable share increasing versus network affiliate shares declining).
- Use top cable kids' programming on:
    TBS/TNT.
    USA.
    Nickelodeon.
    Family Channel.

Target

Kids 2–10.

Short-Term Price/ Product Promotions

General objective is to increase guest counts/sales in a more immediate, shorter-term period.

Grand Slam (Baseball Cards)

This six-week promotion is scheduled to enhance the Grand Slam menu introduction, which will be promoted during the baseball season. It consists of collectible holographic baseball cards that people can get when they order one of the special meal items on the "Grand Slam" menu. There are 26 different cards featuring a "grand slam" slugger from each Major League team.

Objective

To stimulate trial and repeat business for the Grand Slam meal concept, via the distribution of a collectible series of hologrammed baseball cards (6 million for 26 teams) distributed within the restaurants over a six-week period.

Strategies

- Target the "baseball fan" defined primarily as men 18–49.
- Utilize baseball broadcasts as the primary vehicle to reach the defined target recognizing that:
  The one behavior that separates the "core fan" from the casual fan or the general population is the need to tune in live broadcasts of the seasonal games.
  "In game" ratings invariably exceed support programming (e.g., Pre/post game, talk, anthology shows).
  Aggressive reach/frequency goals can be attained in this manner.
- Focus on local/regional versus national efforts, recognizing that baseball interest has always been "home team" oriented. Local broadcasts:
  Are higher rated than national broadcasts.
  Benefit from "the flavor" of the home team announcers (with the attendant possibilities of high awareness "value-added" opportunities).
  Can be structured to go beyond flagship stations, thereby achieving virtual national coverage.
- Utilize special "opportunistic" vehicles as available, as a means:
  To stimulate immediate broad reach relatively "early" in the promotion period.
  To "showcase" and enhance impact of the promotion.
- Utilize sports print media that collectively can provide:
  Alternative cost effective means to reach and impact the fan.
  An opportunity to explain the promotion in greater detail.
  An opportunity to reach the baseball card collector, an important subsegment within the target, and estimated to number between 7 and 10 million people (including children and teens not addressed in the adult target definitions).
  In conjunction with broadcast, an opportunity to generate a sense of "preemptive presence" that can enhance impact and sense of importance of the promotion to the baseball fan.

Target

Men 18–49/the "baseball fan."

Holiday Mug

To stimulate business during the holiday season, special "Holiday" coffee mugs will be available in all restaurants during December. They can be used for personal use and also as gifts or stocking stuffers during the holidays.

Objective

Increase sales/guest counts via the availability of a special "holiday" coffee mug.

Strategy

- Use spot television in select key sales markets, recognizing
  Visual impact, showcase opportunity.
  Budget limitations prohibit any sort of national effort.

Target

Adults 25–54.

Denny's Restaurants 1991 media flowchart

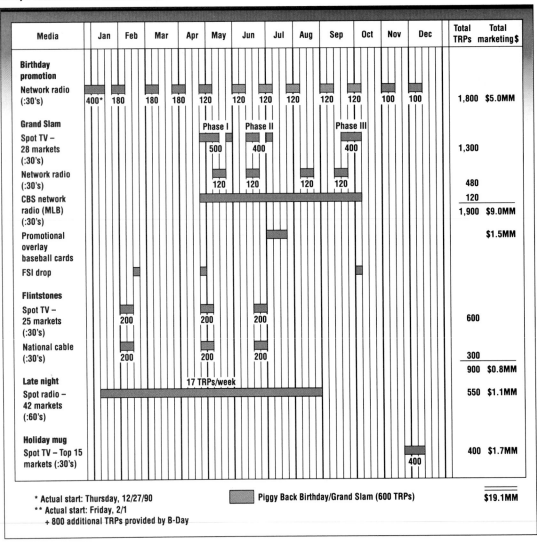

Media	Jan	Feb	Mar	Apr	May	Jun	Jul	Aug	Sep	Oct	Nov	Dec	Total TRPs	Total marketing $
Birthday promotion Network radio (:30's)	400*	180	180	180	120	120	120	120	120	120	100	100	1,800	$5.0MM
Grand Slam Spot TV – 28 markets (:30's)					500	400			400				1,300	
Network radio (:30's)					120	120		120	120				480	
CBS network radio (MLB) (:30's)													120	
													1,900	$9.0MM
Promotional overlay baseball cards														$1.5MM
FSI drop														
Flintstones Spot TV – 25 markets (:30's)		200			200	200							600	
National cable (:30's)		200			200	200							300	
													900	$0.8MM
Late night Spot radio – 42 markets (:60's)					17 TRPs/week								550	$1.1MM
Holiday mug Spot TV – Top 15 markets (:30's)												400	400	$1.7MM

Phase I, Phase II, Phase III (Grand Slam Spot TV)

* Actual start: Thursday, 12/27/90
** Actual start: Friday, 2/1
+ 800 additional TRPs provided by B-Day

Piggy Back Birthday/Grand Slam (600 TRPs)

$19.1MM

Denny's Restaurants 1991 Grand Slam promotion

Media	April	May	June	July	August	September	October	Total TRPs	Total cost $
Grand Slam - menu introduction		Phase I	Phase II			Phase III			
Spot TV (:30's)		500	400			400		1,300	
Network radio (:30's)		120	120 120 120	120 120	120 120 120			1,080	
CBS network radio (MLB) (:30's)								120 2,500	$9.0MM
- Baseball cards								Total units	
Synd. TV (MLB)								9	
CBS network TV All Star Game								1	
Regional cable fill								TBD	
ESPN MLB (Sun)								6	
Regional local/radio								14	
Print								–	

■ Denotes split copy (Birthday/Grand Slam) $1.5MM

☐ Baseball promotion copy - 16 units total   Combined total: $10.5MM

Chapter 13

Evaluation of Broadcast Media

Chapter Objectives

- To examine the structure of the television and radio industries and the role of each medium in the advertising program.
- To examine the advantages and limitations of TV and radio as advertising media.

- To explain how advertising time is purchased for the broadcast media, how audiences are measured, and how rates are determined.
- To consider future trends in TV and radio and how they will influence the use of these media in advertising.

Advertisers Learn to Drive the Information Highway

In 1941 the Bulova Watch Co. aired the first paid TV commercial. For over 50 years since, consumers have been passively receiving television programming as well as commercials. This is about to change, however; the major cable operators, telephone companies, and other firms are competing—and collaborating—to bring a comunicopia of entertainment, information, and interactive services into homes via television. Major interactive TV projects that will deliver as many as 500 channels are already under way in cities such as Orlando, Florida; Queens, New York; and Castro Valley and Cerritos, California. Industry experts predict that by 1997 two-way TV with hundreds of channels will reach 25 percent of US households.

Electronic superhighway developments will have a major impact on TV as an advertising medium. In addition to having hundreds of channels to choose from, viewers wielding souped-up, hand-held remotes will be able to actively control what they see. They can choose to watch shows when they want rather than at regularly scheduled times. For a small fee, they can view it commercial-free. One communications professor has noted that affluent consumers, a group many advertisers want to reach most, will be able to afford programs without commercials—making it even more difficult to reach them via TV.

The new media environment will have other implications for marketers. There will be even greater pressure to make commercials more creative and entertaining and target them more effectively. The proliferation of channels will contribute to the trend away from broadcasting to narrowcasting. This will be good news for some advertisers who could never afford to advertise on TV. They will be able to pinpoint prospects on one of the new cable channels such as ESPN-2, the Military Channel, or the new 24-hour Golf Channel, which is expected to begin broadcasting in early 1995. Marketers will also continue to develop media-driven creative strategies rather than a "one-sight, one-sound, one-sell" approach. Coca-Cola already uses more than two dozen commercials in different moods and styles for 20 different TV networks. MCI uses more than 50 TV commercials plus special spots for channels reaching Hispanic, Chinese, and Russian ethnic groups in the United States.

Another aspect of advertising orthodoxy that will be challenged is the allegiance to 15 and 30-second commercials. More marketers will be turning to program-length commercials known as infomercials, which have traditionally been used by direct-response advertisers. Large corporations such as Kodak, Procter & Gamble, General Motors, GTE, and Volvo are already using infomercials, and their quality will improve even more as major ad agencies become involved in producing them. Advertisers and their agencies are particularly intrigued by the possibilities of two-way television. Viewers will be able to use their TV remote control to interact with commercials, request information, and even make purchases.

The new developments in television will have implications for radio as well. As TV audiences become more fragmented and viewers use the new technologies to avoid commercials, radio will become an even more important way to reach consumers, particularly in cars. Visa doubled the radio ad budget for its credit card in 1994 because it can customize ads to reach local merchants and TV snubbers. Pepsi-Cola is also using radio very resourcefully. In the Netherlands, listeners tuning into RTL radio see the words "RTL Pepsi" glow on the display where the station number usually appears, and four times an hour the words "Be young, have fun, drink Pepsi" pop up on the display.

Advertisers must recognize that the old days of the simple sell where they could just run a commercial on network TV are gone for good. Successful marketers will be those who know how to drive the information superhighway.

Sources: Kate Maddox, "Setbacks on the Superhighway," *Advertising Age*, March 21, 1994, pp. IM 2, 4, 14; Patricia Sellers, "The Best Way to Reach Buyers," *Fortune*, Autumn/Winter 1993, pp. 14–17; Philip Elmer-Dewitt, "Take a Trip into the Future on the Information Highway," *Time*, April 2, 1993, pp. 50–55.

The development of the information highway is of tremendous importance to marketers because it affects our primary form of entertainment, the television set. TV has virtually saturated households throughout the United States and many other countries and has become a mainstay in the lives of most people. The average American household watches nearly seven hours of TV a day, and the tube has become the predominant source of news and entertainment for many people. Seventy-five percent of the TV households in the United States have a videocassette recorder (VCR), and many people have entertainment centers with large-screen TV sets, VCRs, and stereos. On any given evening during the prime-time hours of 8 to 11 PM, more than 90 million people are watching TV. Popular shows like "Home Improvement" and "Seinfeld" may have more than 40 million viewers. The large numbers of people who watch television are important to the TV networks and stations because they can sell time on these programs to marketers who want to reach that audience with their advertising messages. Moreover, the characteristics of TV that make it a great medium for news and entertainment also encourage creative ads that can have a strong impact on customers.

Radio is also an integral part of our lives. Many of us wake up to clock radios in the morning and rely on radio programs to inform and/or entertain us while we drive to work or school. For many people, radio is a constant companion in their cars, at home, or even at work. The average American listens to the radio more than three hours each day.[1] Like TV viewers, radio listeners are an important audience for marketers.

In this chapter, we examine the broadcast media of TV and radio, including the general characteristics of each as well as their specific advantages and disadvantages. We examine how advertisers use TV and radio as part of their advertising and media strategies, how they buy TV and radio time, and how audiences are measured and evaluated for each medium. We also examine the factors that have changed the role of TV and radio as advertising media and consider future developments.

TELEVISION

It has often been said that television represents the ideal advertising medium. Its ability to combine visual images, sound, motion, and color presents the advertiser with the opportunity to develop the most creative and imaginative appeals of any medium. However, TV does have certain problems that limit or even prevent its use by many advertisers.

Advantages of Television

Creativity and impact

Perhaps the greatest advantage of television is the opportunity it provides for presenting the advertising message. The interaction of sight and sound offers tremendous creative flexibility and makes possible dramatic, lifelike representations of products and services. TV commercials can be used to convey a mood or image for a brand as well as to develop emotional or entertaining appeals that help make a dull product appear interesting.

Television is also an excellent medium for demonstrating a product or service. For example, print ads are effective for showing a car and communicating information regarding its features, but only a TV commercial can put you in the driver's seat and give you the sense of actually driving, as shown by the Porsche commercial in Exhibit 13–1.

Coverage and cost effectiveness

Television advertising also makes it possible to reach large audiences. Nearly everyone, regardless of age, sex, income, or educational level, watches at least some TV. Most people do so on a regular basis. According to Nielsen estimates, over 240 million people are in TV households, 77 percent of whom are 18 or older.

Marketers selling products and services that appeal to broad target audiences find that TV lets them reach mass markets, often very cost efficiently. The average prime-time TV show reaches 11 million homes; a top-rated show such as "Rosanne" may reach nearly 20 million homes and perhaps twice that many viewers. In 1993, the average cost per thousand (CPM) was $8.37 for network evening shows and $2.50 for daytime weekly shows.[2]

Because of its ability to reach large audiences in a cost efficient manner, TV is a popular medium among companies selling mass consumption products. Companies with widespread distribution and availability of their products and services use TV to reach

@ **EXHIBIT 13-1**

This TV commercial helps demonstrate the sensation of driving a car

VO: It's the car you own before you've ever really been inside one...

The car you feel, before you've ever even driven one.

For all of you who think that maybe you've been able to put this youthful desire behind you...

we've got some bad news.

(MUSIC UP)

(MUSIC OUT)
VO: There's a new 911.

(MUSIC UP)

(MUSIC OUT)
VO: We'll be expecting your call.

the mass market and deliver their advertising messages at a very low cost per thousand. Television has become indispensable to large consumer package-goods companies, automobile manufacturers, and major retailers. Companies such as Procter & Gamble spend more than 80 percent of their media advertising budget on various forms of TV—network, spot, cable, and syndicated programs. Exhibit 13–2 shows the top 25 network TV advertisers in 1993 and their expenditures.

Captivity and attention

Television is basically intrusive in that commercials impose themselves on viewers as they watch their favorite programs. Unless we make a special effort to avoid commercials, most of us are exposed to thousands of them each year. The increase in viewing options and the penetration of VCRs, remote controls, and other automatic devices have made it easier for TV viewers to avoid commercial messages. A study of consumers' viewing habits found the audience declines an average of 17 percent from the program to the commercials.[3] However, the remaining viewers are likely to devote some attention to many advertising messages. As discussed in Chapter 6, the low-involvement nature of consumer learning and response processes may mean TV ads have an effect on consumers simply through heavy repetition and exposure to catchy slogans and jingles.

Selectivity and flexibility

Television has often been criticized for being a nonselective medium, since it is difficult to reach a precisely defined market segment through the use of TV advertising. But some selectivity is possible due to variations in the composition of audiences as a result of program content, broadcast time, and geographic coverage. For example, Saturday morning TV caters to children; Saturday and Sunday afternoon programs are geared to the sports-oriented male; and weekday daytime shows appeal heavily to homemakers.

@ **EXHIBIT 13–2**

Top 25 network TV advertisers

Rank	Advertiser	1992
1	Procter & Gamble Co.	$535.3
2	General Motors Corp.	449.5
3	Philip Morris Co.	410.3
4	PepsiCo	279.6
5	Kellogg Co.	254.1
6	Ford Motor Co.	250.7
7	McDonald's Corp.	218.4
8	Johnson & Johnson	218.2
9	Unilever	217.3
10	Chrysler Corp.	210.4
11	Sears, Roebuck & Co.	194.1
12	American Home Products Corp.	187.6
13	AT&T Co.	187.8
14	Anheuser-Busch Cos.	158.9
15	Toyota Motor Corp.	153.0
16	Nestlé SA	144.4
17	General Mills	141.7
18	Warner-Lambert Co.	134.0
19	Coca-Cola Co.	130.7
20	Eastman Kodak Co.	123.4
21	Honda Motor Co.	117.1
22	J.C. Penney Co.	116.9
23	Walt Disney Co.	107.4
24	Grand Metropolitan	105.1
25	RJR Nabisco	96.1

Numbers in millions.
Source: *Advertising Age*, Sept. 29, 1993, p. 44.

With the growth of cable TV, advertisers refine their coverage further by appealing to groups with specific interests such as sports, news, or music. The ad for Arts & Entertainment in Exhibit 13–3 promotes the value of the network for reaching more educated, upscale consumers who have a higher disposable income and thus more buying power.

Advertisers can also adjust their media strategies to take advantage of different geographic markets through local or spot ads in specific market areas. Ads can be scheduled to run repeatedly or to take advantage of special occasions. For example, Budweiser is a major sponsor during the baseball World Series, which allows it to advertise heavily to men who constitute the primary market for beer.[4]

Limitations of Television

Although television is unsurpassed from a creative perspective, the medium has several disadvantages that limit or preclude its use by many advertisers. These problems include high costs, the lack of selectivity, the fleeting nature of a television message, commercial clutter, limited viewer attention, and distrust of TV ads.

Costs

Despite the efficiency of TV in reaching large audiences, it is an expensive medium in which to advertise. The high cost of TV stems not only from the expense of buying air time but also from the costs of producing a quality commercial. Production costs for a national brand 30-second spot are approaching an average of $200,000.[5] As advertisers begin using media-driven creative strategies, they will have to produce a variety of commercials, which will drive up their costs. Even local ads can be very expensive to produce and often are not of high quality. The high costs of producing and airing commercials often price small- and medium-sized advertisers out of the market.

Lack of selectivity

Some selectivity is available in television through variations in programs and cable TV. But advertisers who are seeking a very specific, often small, target audience find the coverage of TV often extends beyond their market, reducing its cost effectiveness (as dis-

@ **EXHIBIT 13–3**

A&E promotes its ability to reach upscale consumers

cussed in Chapter 12). Geographic selectivity can be a problem to local advertisers such as retailers, since a station bases its rates on the total market area it reaches. For example, stations in Pittsburgh, Pennsylvania, reach viewers in western Pennsylvania, eastern Ohio, northern West Virginia, and even parts of Maryland. The small company whose market is limited to the immediate Pittsburgh area may find TV an inefficient media buy, since the stations cover a geographic area larger than the merchant's trade area.

Audience selectivity is improving as advertisers target certain groups of consumers through the type of program or day and/or time when they choose to advertise. However, TV still does not offer the same audience selectivity as other media such as radio, magazines, newspapers, or direct mail for reaching precise segments of the market.

Fleeting message

TV commercials usually last only 30 seconds or less and leave nothing tangible for the viewer to examine or consider. Commercials have become shorter and shorter as the demand for a limited amount of broadcast time has intensified and advertisers try to get more impressions from their media budgets. As shown in Exhibit 13–4, 30-second commercials became the norm in the mid-1970s. In September 1986, the three networks began accepting 15-second spots across their full schedules (except during children's viewing time), and, since 1987, these shorter spots have been accounting for about a third of all network commercials.

An important factor in the decline in commercial length has been the spiraling inflation in media costs over the past decade. With the average cost of a prime-time spot reaching over $100,000, many advertisers saw shorter commercials as the only way to keep their media costs in line. A 15-second spot typically sells for half the price of a 30-second spot. By using 15- or even 10-second commercials, advertisers think they can run additional spots to reinforce the message or reach a larger audience. Many adver-

EXHIBIT 13–4   Changes in percentage of network commercials by length

Commercial Length	1965	1975	1980	1985	1987	1988	1989	1990	1991	1992
15	—	—	—	10	31	36	38	35	34	32
30	23	93	96	84	65	61	57	60	62	63
60	77	6	2	2	2	2	2	2	2	2
All others	—	1	2	4	2	1	3	3	2	3

tisers believe shorter commercials can deliver a message just as effectively as longer spots for much less money.[6]

Several years ago, many advertising people predicted 15-second spots would become the dominant commercial unit by the early 1990s. However, the growth in the use of 15-second commercials peaked at 38 percent in 1989 and declined to 32 percent by 1992. The decline may be due to several factors, including creative considerations, lower prices for network time, and a desire by the networks to restrict clutter.[7]

Clutter

The problems of fleeting messages and shorter commercials are compounded by the fact that the advertiser's message is only one of many spots and other nonprogramming material seen during a commercial break, so it may have trouble being noticed. One of the greatest concerns advertisers have expressed recently with regard to TV advertising is the potential decline in effectiveness because of such *clutter*. The next time you watch TV, count the number of commercials, promotions for the news or upcoming programs, or public service announcements that appear during a station break and you will appreciate why clutter is a major concern. A 1993 study sponsored by the advertising industry found that the three major networks ran more than 13 minutes of nonprogramming material in a one-hour period during prime time; on some cable networks, the amounts exceeded 17 minutes.[8] With all of these messages competing for our attention, it is easy to understand why the viewer comes away confused or even annoyed and unable to remember or properly identify the product or service advertised.

One cause of clutter is the use of shorter commercials. Compounding this has been the use by some advertisers of **split-30s**, 30-second spots in which the advertiser promotes two different products with separate messages. Clutter also results when the networks and individual stations run promotional announcements for their shows, making more time available for commercials and redistributing time to popular programs. For many years, the amount of time available for commercials was restricted by the Code Authority of the National Association of Broadcasters to 9.5 minutes per hour during prime time and 12 minutes during nonprime time. The Justice Department suspended the code in 1982 on the grounds that it violated antitrust law. Initially, the networks did not alter their time standards, but in recent years they have increased the number of commercial minutes in their schedules. The networks argue that they must increase commercial inventory or raise already steep rates. Advertisers and agencies have been pressuring the networks to cut back on the commercials and other sources of clutter.

Limited viewer attention

When advertisers buy time on a TV program, they are not purchasing guaranteed exposure but rather the opportunity to communicate a message to the viewing audience. However, while advertisers often pay large sums for the opportunity to reach large numbers of consumers, there is increasing evidence that the size of the viewing audience during a commercial break is reduced. People leave the room to go the bathroom or to get something to eat or drink, or they are distracted in some other way during commercials.

@ **EXHIBIT 13–5**

Developing creative com-
mercials that hold viewers'
attention is one answer to
the zapping problem

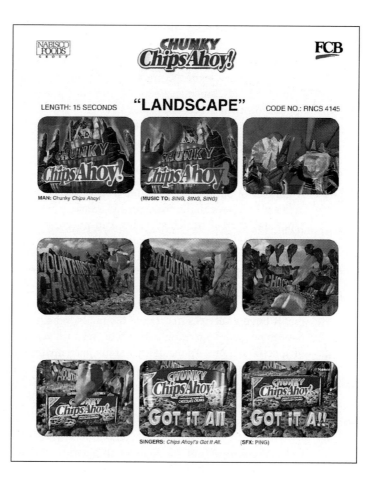

Getting consumers to pay attention to commercials has become an even greater challenge in recent years. The increased penetration of VCRs into most households and the prevalence of remote control devices have led to the problems of zipping and zapping. **Zipping** occurs when customers fast-forward through commercials during the playback of a previously recorded program. A study by Nielsen Media Research found that while 80 percent of recorded shows are actually played back, viewers zip past more than half of the commercials.[9]

Zapping refers to using the remote control to change channels and switch away from commercials. The Nielsen study found that most commercial zapping occurs at the beginning and, to a lesser extent, the end of a program. Zapping at these points is likely to occur because commercial breaks are so long and predictable. Zapping has also been fueled by the emergence of 24-hour continuous format programming on cable channels such as CNN, MTV, and ESPN. Viewers can switch over for a few news headlines, sports scores, or a music video and then switch back to the program. Research shows that young adults zap more than older adults, and men are more likely to zap than women.[10]

How to inhibit zapping? The networks use certain tactics to hold viewers' attention, such as previews of the next week's show or short closing scenes at the end of a program. Some programs start with action sequences before the opening credits and commercials. A few years ago, Anheuser-Busch began using the Bud Frame, in which the ad frames live coverage of a sporting event. The ultimate way to zap-proof commercials is to produce creative, meaningful advertising messages that will attract and hold viewers' attention. The Chips Ahoy! spot in Exhibit 13–5 is a good example. However, this is easier said than done, and as more viewers gain access to remote controls, the zapping problem is likely to continue.

Distrust and negative evaluation

To many critics of advertising, TV commercials personify everything that is wrong with the industry. Critics often single out TV commercials because of their pervasiveness and the intrusive nature of the medium. Consumers are seen as defenseless against the barrage of TV ads, since they cannot control the transmission of the message and what appears on their screens. Studies have shown that of the various forms of advertising, distrust is generally the highest for TV commercials.[11] Also, concern has been raised about the effects of television advertising on specific groups such as children or the elderly.

BUYING TELEVISION TIME

A number of options are available to advertisers that choose to use TV as part of their media mix. They can purchase time in a variety of program formats that appeal to various types and sizes of audiences. They can purchase time on a national, regional, or local basis. Or they can sponsor an entire program, participate in the sponsorship, or use spot announcements during or between programs.

The purchase of TV advertising time is a highly specialized phase of the advertising business, particularly for large companies spending huge sums of money. Large advertisers that do a lot of TV advertising generally use agency media specialists or specialized media buying services to arrange the media schedule and purchase TV time. Decisions have to be made regarding national or network versus local or spot purchases, selection of specific stations, sponsorship versus participation, different classes of time, and appropriate programs. Local advertisers may not have to deal with the first decision but do face all the others.

Network versus Spot

A basic decision for all advertisers is allocating their TV media budget to network versus local or spot announcements. Most national advertisers use network schedules to provide national coverage and supplement this with regional or local spot purchases to reach markets where additional coverage is desired.

Network advertising

A common way advertisers disseminate their messages is by purchasing air time from a **television network**. A network assembles a series of affiliated local TV stations, or **affiliates**, to which it supplies programming and services. These affiliates, most of which are independently owned, contractually agree to preempt time during specified hours for programming provided by the networks and to carry the national advertising within the program. The networks share the advertising revenue they receive during these time periods with the affiliates. The affiliates are also free to sell commercial time in nonnetwork periods and during station breaks in the preempted periods to both national and local advertisers.

The three major networks—NBC, ABC, and CBS—each have affiliates throughout the nation for almost complete national coverage. When an advertiser purchases air time from one of these three national networks, the commercial is transmitted across the nation through the affiliate station network. Network advertising truly represents a mass medium, as the advertiser can broadcast its message simultaneously throughout the country.

A major advantage of network advertising is the simplification of the purchase process. The advertiser has to deal with only one party or media representative to air a commercial nationwide. The networks also offer the most popular programs and generally control prime-time programming. Advertisers interested in reaching huge nationwide audiences generally buy network time during the prime viewing hours of 8 to 11 PM eastern time.

The major drawback is the high cost of network time. Exhibit 13–6 shows cost estimates for a 30-second spot on the three networks' prime-time shows during the 1993–94 television season. Many of the popular prime-time shows charge $200,000 or more for a 30-second spot. Thus, only advertisers with large budgets can afford to use network advertising on a regular basis.

@ **EXHIBIT 13–6**

What TV shows cost: estimated price of a 30-second spot on the three major networks

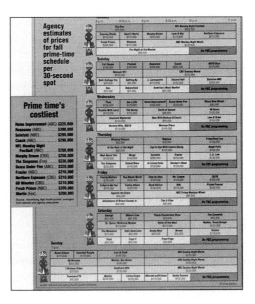

Availability of time can also be a problem as more advertisers turn to network advertising to reach mass markets. Traditionally, most prime-time commercial spots, particularly on the popular shows, are sold during the **up-front market**, a buying period that occurs before the TV season begins. Advertisers hoping to use prime-time network advertising must plan their media schedules and often purchase TV time as much as a year in advance. However, in recent years the importance of the up-front market has been declining. More television time is being purchased during the **scatter market** that runs through the TV season. Some key incentives for buying up front, such as cancellation options and lower prices, are becoming more available in the quarterly scatter market. Many media buyers believe the up-front market may be canceled in a few years.[12]

While the majority of network advertising dollars go to the three major networks, several other types of networks have evolved in recent years, including the Fox Broadcasting Co., which broadcasts its programs over a group of affiliated independent stations. Fox is rapidly becoming the fourth network, particularly among young audiences, who are attracted to popular shows such as "The Simpsons" and "Beverly Hills 90210." The network's "Power Rangers" is the top-rated show on Saturday mornings and weekdays among children ages 2 to 11. Fox also raised eyebrows in the TV industry recently when it paid $395 million for the rights to broadcast National Football League games, which had been on CBS for 38 years.[13]

Cable TV networks have developed to provide programming to local cable systems in cities throughout the country. (Cable television is discussed later in this chapter.) Network TV can also be purchased on a regional basis, making it possible for an advertiser's message to be aired in certain sections of the country with one media purchase.

Spot and local advertising

Spot advertising refers to commercials shown on local television stations, with time negotiated and purchased directly from the individual stations. All nonnetwork advertising done by a national advertiser is known as **national spot advertising**; air time sold to local firms such as retailers, restaurants, banks, and auto dealers is known as **local advertising**. Local advertisers desire media whose coverage is limited to the geographic markets in which they do business. This may be difficult to accomplish with TV, but many local businesses are large enough to make efficient use of TV advertising.

Spot advertising offers the national advertiser greater flexibility in adjusting to local market conditions. The advertiser can concentrate commercials in areas where market potential is the greatest or where additional support is needed. This appeals to advertisers with uneven distribution or limited advertising budgets, as well as those interested in test marketing or introducing a product in limited market areas. National advertisers often use spot television advertising through local retailers or dealers as part of their cooperative advertising programs and to provide local dealer support.

A major problem for national advertisers is that spot advertising can be more difficult to acquire, since the time must be purchased from a number of local stations. Moreover, there are more variations in the pricing policies and discount structure of individual stations than with the networks. However, this problem has been reduced somewhat by the use of **station reps**, individuals who act as sales representatives for a number of local stations in dealings with national advertisers.

Spot advertisements are subject to more commercial clutter, since local stations can sell time on network-originated shows only during station breaks between programs, except when network advertisers have not purchased all the available time. Viewership generally declines during station breaks, as people may leave the room, zap to another channel, attend to other tasks, or cease watching TV.

While spot advertising is mostly confined to station breaks between programs on network-originated shows, local stations sell time on their own programs, which consist of news, movies, syndicated shows, or locally originated programs. Most cities have independent stations that spot advertisers use. Local advertisers find the independent stations particularly attractive because they generally have lower rates than the major network affiliates.

The decision facing most national advertisers is how to combine network and spot advertising to make effective use of their TV advertising budget. Another factor that makes spot advertising attractive to national advertisers is the growth in syndication.

Syndication

Advertisers may also reach TV viewers by advertising on **syndicated programs**, which are shows that are sold or distributed to local stations. There are several types of syndicated programming. *Off-network syndication* refers to reruns of network shows that are bought by individual stations. Shows that are popular in off-network syndication include "M*A*S*H," "The Cosby Show," and "Cheers." The FCC prime-time access rule forbids large-market network affiliates from carrying these shows from 7 to 8 PM, but independent stations are not affected by this restriction. Other restrictions include the number of episodes that must be produced before a show is eligible for syndication and limitations on network involvement in the financing or production of syndicated shows. The FCC may ease some of the rules involving the networks' role in producing and syndicating programs.[14]

Off-network syndication shows are very important to local stations because they provide quality programming with an established audience. The syndication market is also very important to the studios that produce programs and sell them to the networks. Most prime-time network shows initially lose money for the studios, since the licensing fee paid by the networks does not cover production costs. Over four years (the time it takes to produce the 88 episodes regarded as the minimum needed to break into syndication) half-hour situation comedies often run up a deficit of nearly $12 million, and losses on a one-hour drama show can reach $30 million. However, the producers recoup their money when a show is sold to syndication. For example, "The Cosby Show" set a record a few years ago when it was sold into syndication for $800 million.[15]

First-run syndication refers to shows produced specifically for the syndication market. The first-run syndication market is made up of a variety of shows, including some that did not make it as network shows and are moved into syndication while new episodes are being produced.

Under *barter syndication*, both off-network and first-run syndicated programs are offered free or at a reduced rate to local stations, but with some advertising time presold to national advertisers. Usually, more than half of the advertising time is presold, and the remainder is available for sale by the local advertiser. Barter syndication allows national advertisers to participate in the syndication market with the convenience of a network-type media buy, while local stations get free programming and can sell the remainder of

DISCUSSION QUESTIONS

1. The vignette at the beginning of the chapter discusses the success of the new magazine *Smart Money*. Why do you think this new magazine has been so successful and been able to attract so many advertisers?

2. Discuss how the role of magazines and newspapers as advertising media differs from that of television and radio.

3. Find either a consumer or business magazine targeted to a specific audience and analyze it using information from Standard Rate and Data Service (SRDS) that should be available in your library. How might a media planner be able to use the information contained in SRDS in evaluating the value of this magazine as an advertising medium?

4. How can advertisers achieve greater selectivity in their use of magazine and newspaper advertising?

5. Explain why advertisers of products such as cosmetics or women's clothing would choose to advertise in a magazine such as *Vogue*, which devotes most of its pages to ads rather than articles.

6. Discuss some of the reasons why companies such as Ray-Ban, Sony, and Federal Express choose to publish their own magazines. Do you agree or disagree with critics who call some of these custom magazines "phony publishing"?

7. If you were purchasing magazine ad space for a manufacturer of skiing equipment, what factors would you consider? Would your magazine selection be limited to skiing publications? Why or why not?

8. Do you agree or disagree with the policy of most newspapers to charge national advertisers a higher rate than local advertisers? Do you think this policy limits the amount of advertising newspapers can generate from national advertisers? How might newspapers attract more business from national advertisers?

9. Discuss how the problem of declining readership is affecting the value of newspapers as an advertising medium. How can newspapers deal with this problem?

10. Discuss the future problems and challenges both magazines and newspapers will face from emerging media such as direct mail and interactive television.

Chapter 15

Support Media

Chapter Objectives

- To introduce the various support media available to the marketer in developing a promotional program.
- To provide an understanding of the advantages and disadvantages of support media.

- To explain how audiences for support media are measured.

Is There Anywhere Advertising Isn't?

The average consumer may be exposed to as many as 5,000 commercial messages each day, according to Jack Myers, writing in Media Week magazine. At first glance, these numbers seem inconceivable—there just can't be enough time in the day to see and hear this many ads. But if you take a few moments to look around, ads are everywhere. Besides the traditional television, radio, magazine, newspaper, and outdoor ads, consider the following examples:

- McCall's magazine places ads on manhole covers, cab doors, bus shelters, buses, and telephone kiosks. The manhole ads are life-size depictions of a construction worker reading McCall's in a manhole. The cab door ads feature a businesswoman from the neck down reading the McCall's magazine.

- FreeFone Information Network in Seattle gives advertisers access to subscribers waiting for their calls to go through. A five-second ad tells the caller where to get more information, anywhere from a 60-second commercial to coupons to a direct transfer to the marketer. Callers get paid 15¢ per call whether they listen to the ads or choose to have the call go through directly.

- 7-Up reaches kids through a medium where Coke and Pepsi haven't yet gone—videogames. Teaming up with Sega Genesis, 7-Up has developed "Cool Spot." The game begins with Cool Spot surfing up onto a beach where people are drinking 7-Up. The object is to use Cool Spot to release previously captured Spots. In the bonus round, players must collect the letters to spell "Uncola" (7-Up's long-time positioning statement). Coke is rumored to be developing a videogame featuring its famous polar bears.

- A variety of other venues have also been used to advertise products. Sambuca and Miller advertise on QB1, the channel in bars and restaurants that allows players to guess what plays will be called in NFL games. Channel One is currently in 12,000 schools, and Special Report Network is in 32,000 doctors' waiting rooms, with participating advertisers including Chrysler, Fruit of the Loom, and Paramount Pictures. The Airport Channel now reaches about 4 million people a month.

We haven't even mentioned the proposal to use lasers to light up the night sky with advertising in space. Or the ads in the bottom of golf hole cups and in toilet stalls. Maybe 5,000 ads per day isn't too high an estimate after all?

Sources: Marcy Magiera, "7-Up's Videogame Hits the Spot," Advertising Age, Jan. 10, 1994, p. 19; "Hear the Muzak, Buy the Ketchup," Business Week, June 28, 1993, pp. 70–72; Jack Myers, "More Is Indeed Better," MediaWeek, Sept. 6, 1993, pp. 14–18; Hanna Liebman, "The Future Is Nearly Now," MediaWeek, Sept. 13, 1993, pp. 54–55.

he innovative media described here are just a few of the increasing number of alternative media available to the marketer. Ads seem to be popping up everywhere, in places you never expected and in situations where you may not realize you are seeing one.

In this chapter, we review a number of support media—some that are new to the marketplace and others that have been around a while—discussing the relative advantages and disadvantages, cost information, and audience measurement of each. We refer to them as **support media** because for large advertisers, particularly national advertisers, the media reviewed in the previous chapters dominate their media strategies. Support media are used to reach those people in the target market the primary media may not have reached and to reinforce, or support, their messages.

You may be surprised at how many different ways there are to deliver the message and how often you are exposed to them. Let's begin by examining the scope of the support media industry and some of the many alternatives available to the marketer.

THE SCOPE OF THE SUPPORT MEDIA INDUSTRY

Support media are referred to by several titles, among them **alternative media, non-measured media,** and **nontraditional media.** These terms describe a vast variety of channels used to deliver communications and to promote products and services. The lead-in to this chapter discussed some of these, and the rest of this chapter will explore others. As you might imagine, it would be impossible for us to discuss them all.

Many advertisers, as well as the top 100 advertising agencies, have increased their use of nontraditional support media, and as new alternatives are developed, this use will continue to grow. Figures for nontraditional media do not include some of the more commonly used support media, such as out-of-home advertising, specialty advertising, and advertising in the Yellow Pages. Let us examine some of these in more detail.

OUT-OF-HOME MEDIA

Out-of-home advertising encompasses many advertising forms, including outdoor (billboards and signs), transit (both inside and outside the vehicle), skywriting, and a variety of other media. While outdoor advertising is the most commonly employed medium, as shown in Exhibit 15–1, the others are also increasing in use.

EXHIBIT 15–1

Estimated gross billings by media category show that outdoor ads are still the most popular

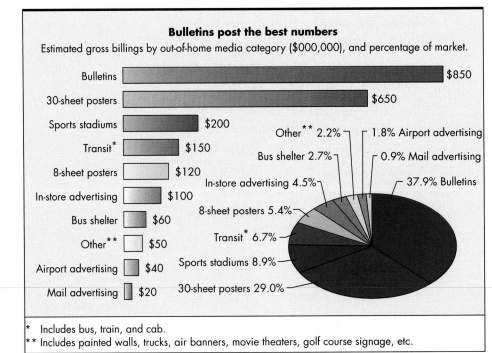

Bulletins post the best numbers

Estimated gross billings by out-of-home media category ($000,000), and percentage of market.

Category	Billings
Bulletins	$850
30-sheet posters	$650
Sports stadiums	$200
Transit*	$150
8-sheet posters	$120
In-store advertising	$100
Bus shelter	$60
Other**	$50
Airport advertising	$40
Mail advertising	$20

Other** 2.2% — 1.8% Airport advertising
Bus shelter 2.7% — 0.9% Mail advertising
In-store advertising 4.5% — 37.9% Bulletins
8-sheet posters 5.4%
Transit* 6.7%
Sports stadiums 8.9%
30-sheet posters 29.0%

* Includes bus, train, and cab.
** Includes painted walls, trucks, air banners, movie theaters, golf course signage, etc.

Outdoor Advertising

Outdoor advertising has probably existed since the days of cave dwellers. Both the Egyptians and the Greeks used it as early as 5,000 years ago. Outdoor certainly is one of the more pervasive communication forms, particularly if you live in an urban or suburban area.

Even though outdoor accounts for only about 2.3 percent of all advertising expenditures, and the number of billboards has decreased, the medium has grown steadily in terms of dollars billed. In 1982, approximately $888 million was spent in this area; by 1993 this figure had risen to an estimated $1.6 billion.[1] Outdoor expenditures are expected to increase in 1994.[2] Companies like McDonald's (34 percent increase), Anheuser-Busch (91 percent), and General Motors (61 percent) have compensated for decreased expenditures by the tobacco and spirits companies (the most frequent users of outdoor for many years). As shown in Exhibit 15–2, outdoor is used by a broad client base, a demonstration of its continued acceptance in the industry. The increase in the number of women in the work force has led to more advertising of products targeted to this segment. Travel companies, entertainment and amusement attractions, insurance companies, and board game companies have also discovered outdoor advertising.

A major reason for the continued success of outdoor is its ability to remain innovative through technology. As Exhibit 15–3 shows, billboards are no longer limited to standard two-dimensional boards; three-dimensional forms and extensions are now used to attract attention. In addition, electronic billboards and inflatables, like the one in Exhibit 15–4 that was used to promote Tropicana orange juice, have also opened new markets. You probably have been exposed to either sign boards or electronic billboards at sports stadiums, in supermarkets, in the campus bookstore and dining halls, in shopping malls, on the freeways, or on the sides of buildings, from neon signs on skyscrapers in New York City to Mail Pouch Tobacco signs on the sides of barns in the Midwest. This is truly a pervasive medium.

Outdoor advertising does have its critics. Ever since former President Lyndon Johnson's wife, Lady Bird, tried to rid the interstate highways of billboard advertising with

EXHIBIT 15–2

1993 outdoor spending by category

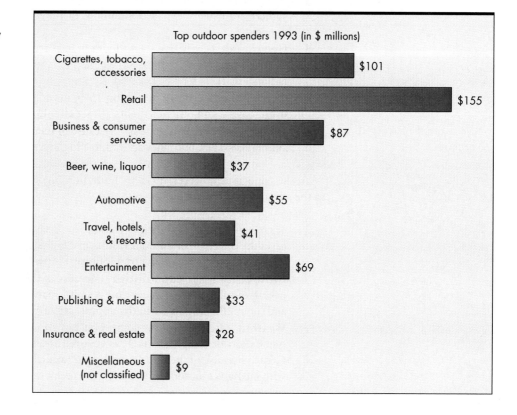

EXHIBIT 15-3 Outdoor advertising goes beyond two dimensions

the Highway Beautification Act of 1965, there has been controversy regarding its use. A number of cities and states have passed or are considering legislation limiting the use of this advertising form, considering it unsightly and obtrusive. In a study conducted by the University of Michigan Survey Research Center, 19 percent of those polled favored doing away with outdoor advertising, and 64.5 percent favored reasonable regulation.

Media buyers have not completely adopted outdoor, partially because of image problems and because of the belief that it is difficult to buy. (Approximately 80 percent of outdoor advertising is purchased by local merchants and companies.) Let us examine some of the advantages and disadvantages of the medium in more detail.

Advantages and disadvantages of outdoor

Outdoor offers the advertiser a number of advantages.

1. **Wide coverage of local markets** With proper placement, a broad base of exposure is possible in local markets, with both day and night presence. A 100 GRP showing (the percentage of duplicated audience exposed to an outdoor poster daily) could yield possible exposure to an equivalent of 100 percent of the marketplace daily, or 3,000 GRPs over a month. This level of coverage is likely to yield high levels of reach.
2. **Frequency** Because purchase cycles are typically for 30-day periods, consumers are usually exposed a number of times, resulting in high levels of frequency.
3. **Geographic flexibility** Outdoor can be placed along highways, near stores, or on mobile billboards, almost anywhere that laws permit. Local, regional, or even national markets may be covered.
4. **Creativity** As shown in Exhibit 15–3, outdoor ads can be very creative. Large print, colors, and other elements attract attention.
5. **Ability to create awareness** Because of its impact (and the requirement of a simple message), outdoor can lead to a high level of awareness.

At the same time, however, there are limitations to outdoor, many of which are related to the advantages cited earlier.

1. **Waste coverage** While it is possible to reach very specific audiences, in many cases the purchase of outdoor results in a high degree of waste coverage. It is not likely that everyone driving by a billboard is part of the target market.
2. **Limited message capabilities** Because of the speed with which most people pass by outdoor ads, exposure time is short, so messages are limited to a few words and/or an illustration. Lengthy appeals are not likely to be effective.
3. **Wearout** Because of the high frequency of exposures, outdoor may lead to a quick wearout. People are likely to get tired of seeing the same ad numerous times.
4. **Cost** Because of the decreasing signage available and the higher cost associated with inflatables, outdoor advertising is expensive in both an absolute and a relative sense.

◎ **EXHIBIT 15–8**

Posting space rates, San Diego market (per-month basis)

Showing Size	1 Month	3 Months	6 Months	12 Months
#25 (15 posters)	$10,650	$10,350	$10,050	$ 9,750
#50 (30 posters)	21,300	20,700	20,100	19,500
#75 (45 posters)	31,950	31,050	30,150	29,250
#100 (60 posters)	37,200	35,700	33,000	30,600

- Scarborough publishes local market studies providing demographic data, product usage, and outdoor media usage.
- Computer packages like Telmar, Donnelly, TAPSCAN, and IMS also provide information comparing outdoor with other media.

One of the weaknesses associated with outdoor advertising is audience measurement. Space rates are usually based on the number of desired showings, as shown in Exhibit 15–8. For example, a 100 showing would theoretically provide coverage to the entire market. In San Diego, this would mean coverage of nearly 2 million people for a monthly rate of $30,600 to $37,200. Along with rate information, the companies offering outdoor billboards also provide reach and frequency estimates. Unfortunately, there is no valid way to verify that the showings are performing as promised. The buyer is somewhat at the mercy of the selling agent when making a purchase.

Because of criticism evolving about this problem, the industry has implemented a gross ratings point system similar to that employed in the television industry. While the system has helped, problems associated with the use of GRPs discussed earlier in this text are also present here and limit the usefulness of this information. Many experts think the new service provided by Harris Media Systems is a significant improvement over the AMMO system, resulting in more credible information.[5]

Transit Advertising

A second form of out-of-home advertising is **transit advertising**. While similar to outdoor in the sense that it uses billboards and electronic messages, transit is targeted to the millions of people who are exposed to commercial transportation facilities, including buses, taxis, commuter trains, elevators, trolleys, airplanes, and subways.

Transit advertising has been around for a long time, but recent years have seen a renewed interest in this medium. Due in part to the increased number of women in the work force (they can be reached on their way to work more easily than at home), audience segmentation, and the rising cost of TV advertising, transit ad spending has increased from $43 million in 1972 to over $225 million.[6] Much of this spending has come from package-goods companies such as Colgate, H. J. Heinz, Kraft–General Foods, and Weight Watchers, which cite lower costs and improved frequency of exposures as motivations to buy transit. Other retail advertisers, clothing stores, movie studios, and business-to-business companies have also increased expenditures in this area.

Types of transit advertising

There are actually three forms of transit advertising: (1) inside cards, (2) outside posters, and (3) station, platform, or terminal posters.

Inside cards

If you have ever ridden a commuter bus, you have probably noticed the **inside cards** placed above the seats and luggage area advertising restaurants, TV or radio stations, or a myriad of other products and services. An innovation is the electronic message boards that carry current advertising information. The ability to change the message and the visibility provide the advertiser with a more attention-getting medium.

Transit cards can be controversial. For example, in the New York subway system, many of the ads for chewing gum, soup, and Smokey the Bear have given way to public

⊚ EXHIBIT 15-9

Airline ticket holders are used to promote a variety of products

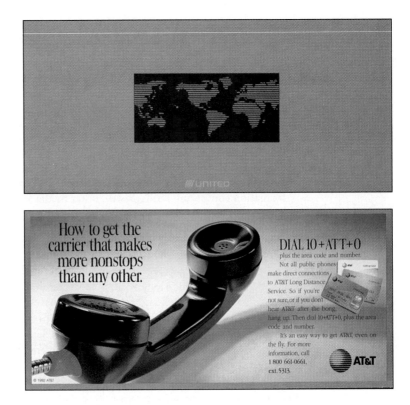

service announcements about AIDS, unwanted pregnancies, rape, and infant mortality. While subway riders may agree that such issues are important, many of them complain that the ads are depressing and intrusive.

A variation on inside transit advertising is shown in Exhibit 15–9. The airline ticket holder is a very effective form of advertising communication. It takes advantage of a captive audience and keeps the message in front of the passenger the whole time he or she is holding the ticket.

Outside posters

Advertisers use various forms of outdoor transit posters to promote products and services. These **outside posters** may appear on the sides, backs, and/or roofs of buses, taxis, trains, and subway and trolley cars. Some examples are shown in the ad for Transportation Displays, Inc., a leading outdoor and transit advertising company (Exhibit 15–10).

⊚ EXHIBIT 15-10

Outside transit posters are used on a variety of vehicles

The increased sophistication of this medium was demonstrated in a test market in Barcelona, Spain, during the 1992 Summer Olympics. Viatex—a joint venture among Atlanta-based Bevilaqua International (a sports marketing company), Saatchi & Saatchi Lifestyle Group, and Warrec Co., a Connecticut-based international business firm— mounted electronic billboards on the sides of buses. These monitors flashed Olympic news and ads that could change at scheduled times. Electronic beacons located throughout the city were activated as the buses drove by, changing the message for the various locations.

Station, platform, and terminal posters

Floor displays, island showcases, electronic signs, and other forms of advertising that appear in train or subway stations, airline terminals, and the like are all forms of transit advertising. As Exhibit 15–11 shows, **terminal posters** can be very attractive and attention getting. Shelters often provide the advertiser with expanded coverage where

@ **EXHIBIT   15–11**

Terminal posters can be used
to attract attention

other outdoor boards may be restricted. Gannett Transit has recently introduced electronic signs on subway platforms in New York.

Advantages and disadvantages of transit advertising

Advantages of using transit advertising include the following.

1. **Exposure**   Long length of exposure to an ad is one major advantage of indoor forms. The average ride on mass transit is 30 to 44 minutes, allowing for plenty of exposure time.[7] Likewise, as with airline tickets, the audience is essentially a captive one, with nowhere else to go and nothing much to do. As a result, they are likely to read the ads—and read them more than once. A second form of exposure transit advertising provides is the absolute number of persons exposed. About 9 million people ride mass transit every year, providing a substantial number of potential viewers.[8]

2. **Frequency**   Because our daily routines are standard, those who ride buses, subways, and the like are exposed to the ads repeatedly. If you rode the same subway to work and back every day, in one month you would have the opportunity to see the ad 20 to 40 times. The locations of station and shelter signs also afford high frequency of exposure.

3. **Timeliness**   Many shoppers use mass transit to reach their destinations. An ad promoting a product or service at a particular shopping area could be a very timely communication.

4. **Geographic selectivity**   For local advertisers in particular, transit advertising provides an opportunity to reach a very select segment of the population. A purchase of a location in a particular neighborhood would lead to exposure to people of specific ethnic backgrounds, demographic characteristics, and so on.

5. **Cost**   Transit advertising tends to be one of the least expensive media in terms of both absolute and relative costs. An ad on the side of a bus can be purchased for a very reasonable CPM.

Some disadvantages are also associated with transit.

1. **Image factors**   To many advertisers, transit advertising does not carry the image they would like to represent their products or services. Some advertisers may think having their name on the side of a bus or on a bus stop bench does not reflect well on the firm.

2. **Reach**   While an advantage of transit advertising is the ability to provide exposure to a large number of people, this audience may have certain lifestyles and/or behavioral characteristics that are not true of the target market as a whole. For example, in rural or suburban areas, mass transit is limited or nonexistent. As a result, the medium is not as effective for reaching these people as it might be in metropolitan areas.

3. **Waste coverage**   While geographic selectivity is a possible advantage, not everyone who rides a transportation vehicle or is exposed to transit advertising is a potential customer. For products that do not have specific geographic segments, this form of advertising incurs a good deal of waste coverage.

    Another problem is that the same bus may not run the same route every day. To save wear and tear on the vehicles, some companies alternate city routes (with much stop and go) with longer suburban routes. Thus, a bus may go downtown one day and reach the desired target group, but spend the next day in the suburbs, where there may be little market potential.

4. **Copy and creative limitations**   With respect to creativity, it may be very difficult to place colorful, attractive ads on cards or benches. And while much copy can be provided on inside cards, on the outside of buses and taxis the message will be much more fleeting, and short copy points will be necessary.

5. **Mood of the audience**   Sitting or standing on a crowded subway may not be conducive to reading advertising, let alone creating the mood the advertiser would like. Controversial ad messages may contribute to this less than positive feeling. Likewise, hurrying through an airport may create anxieties that limit the effectiveness of the ads placed there.

In summary, transit advertising has advantages as well as disadvantages, and an advantage for one product or service advertiser may be a disadvantage to another. Transit advertising can be an effective medium, but one must understand its strengths and weaknesses to use it properly.

Audience measurement in transit advertising

As with outdoor advertising, the cost basis for transit is the number of showings. In transit advertising, a 100 showing means one ad appears on or in *each vehicle* in the system; a showing of 50 means half of the vehicles carry the ad. If you are placing such ads on taxicabs, it may be impossible to determine who is being exposed to them.

Rate information comes from the sellers of transit advertising, and audience information is very limited. So much of the information marketers need to purchase transit ads does not come from purely objective sources.

PROMOTIONAL PRODUCTS MARKETING

According to the Promotional Products Association International, **promotional products marketing** is "the advertising or promotional medium or method that uses promotional products, such as ad specialties, premiums, business gifts, awards, prizes, or commemoratives." Promotional products marketing is the more up-to-date name for what has been previously termed specialty advertising. **Specialty advertising** has now been provided with a new definition: "A medium of advertising, sales promotion, and motivational communication employing imprinted, useful, or decorative products called advertising specialties, a subset of promotional products."

"Unlike premiums, with which they are sometimes confused (called advertising specialties), these articles are always distributed free—recipients don't have to earn the specialty by making a purchase or contribution."[9]

As can be seen by these descriptions, specialty advertising is often considered both an advertising and a sales promotion medium. In our discussion, we treat it as a supportive advertising medium.

There are over 20,000 *advertising specialty* items, including ballpoint pens, coffee mugs, key rings, calendars, T-shirts, and matchbooks. Unconventional specialties such as plant holders, wall plaques, and gloves with the advertiser's name printed on them

4. **Recall**   Research indicates that the next day about 87 percent of viewers can recall the ads they saw in a movie theater. This compares with a 20 percent recall rate for television.[25]

5. **Clutter**   The *lack* of clutter is another advantage offered by advertising in movie theaters. Most theaters limit the number of ads.

Disadvantages of movie and video advertising

Some of the disadvantages associated with movies and videos as advertising media are given below.

1. **Irritation**   Perhaps the major disadvantage is that many people do not wish to see advertising in these media. A number of studies suggest these ads may create a high degree of *irritability*.[26] This dissatisfaction could carry over to the product itself, to the movies, or to the theaters.

2. **Cost**   While the cost of advertising in local theaters has been cited as an advantage because of the low rates charged, ads exposed nationally cost up to $425,000 per minute to reach 25 million viewers. This rate is 20 percent higher than an equal exposure on television. CPMs also tend to be higher than in other media.

While only two disadvantages of theater advertising have been mentioned, the first is a strong one. Many persons believe that because they have paid to see a movie (or rent a video), advertising is an intrusion. In a study by Michael Belch and Don Sciglimpaglia, many moviegoers stated that not only would they not buy the product advertised, but they would consider boycotting it. So advertisers should be cautious in their use of this medium. If they want to use movies, an alternative—placing products in the movies—might be considered.

Product Placements in Movies and TV

An increasingly common way to promote a product is by showing the actual product or an ad for it as part of a movie or television show. While such **product placement** does not constitute a major segment of the advertising and promotions business, it has proved effective for some companies. (Note: Like specialty advertising, product placement is sometimes considered a promotion rather than an advertising form. This distinction is not a critical one, and we have decided to treat it as a form of advertising.)

A number of companies pay to have their products used in movies and music videos. For example, Exhibit 15–15 shows how Cheer was able to get its product featured in the movie *Wayne's World II*. Essentially, this form is advertising without an advertising medium in the sense that the audience doesn't realize a product promotion is going on, yet the impact is real. For example, when Reese's Pieces were used in the movie *ET*, sales rose 70 percent and the candies were added to the concessions of 800 movie theaters where they had previously not been sold.[27]

The move to place products on TV programs is also on the increase. In 1988, CBS broke its long-standing tradition of not mentioning brand names in its programs. Coca-Cola (a Coke machine on "TV 101") and Pine Sol (a sweepstakes on the soap "All My Children") are just two of the companies employing product tie-ins. IMC Perspective 15–1 discusses the increase in product placements, and free "plugs."

Advantages of product placements

A number of advantages of product tie-ins have been suggested.

1. **Exposure**   A large number of people see movies each year (approximately 1 billion admissions in 1993).[28] The average film is estimated to have a life span of three and one-half years (with 75 million exposures), and most of these moviegoers are very attentive audience members. When this is combined with the increasing home video rental market and network and cable TV (for example, HBO, Showtime, the Movie Channel), the potential for exposure for a product placed in a movie is enormous. And this form of exposure is not subject to zapping, at least not in the theater.

⊚ **EXHIBIT   15–15**

Many companies use movies to promote their products

IMC Perspective 15–1
Free Ad Plugs on the Rise

It probably started long before *E.T.*, but the success experienced by Reese's when its product was placed in that movie made a lot of marketers notice the potential of product placements. Since then product placements have appeared in dozens of movies, including *Sleepless in Seattle* (Keds and Evian), *Rookie of the Year* (*Sports Illustrated* and Gatorade) and *Free Willy* (Nike), among others. This form of advertising has also increased on television.

For a mere $5,000 (most of it in beer shipped to the film crew) Red Stripe beer was able to have its product shown and mentioned in *The Firm*. (Avery Tolar [Gene Hackman] told Mitch McDeere [Tom Cruise] to "grab a Red Stripe out of the fridge.") Potential exposures? An estimated 7 million people saw the movie the first weekend alone. Millions more saw it later and are still watching it on videotape.

The $5,000 paid by Red Stripe was a steal. Other companies have paid upwards of $50,000 just to have a verbal mention or hands-on placement, and Red Stripe's brand manager was much less successful in getting his import beer Moretti into the Sharon Stone movie *Sliver*. The bottle was seen, but only at a distance and not too clearly.

Ad plugs on TV are also on the increase, according to a study conducted for *Ad Age* by Northwestern University. As with movies, these plugs can take on a variety of forms. Jay Leno mentioning a Big Mac on the "Tonight Show," Kramer and Jerry on "Seinfeld" discussing Calvin Klein fragrances, and Bruce Springsteen on "Saturday Night Live" wearing blue jeans with a distinctive Levi's label are somewhat subtle approaches, while Sweet 'N Low packages not so subtly lie on a table on "One Life to Live."

Do the free ad plugs work? A lot depends on the nature of the plug—how long it is shown, how casually it is mentioned, and how familiar viewers are with the brand (popular brands are more recognizable). According to Mark Weiner, managing partner of PR Data Systems, you can determine the value by comparing the length of exposure to the cost of a one-minute spot. So in the Seinfeld discussion, Calvin Klein racked up $347,044 in free ad time for every minute the conversation lasted. Stories on the top-selling Christmas toys are often perceived as "endorsements" says Weiner. Once again, advertising appears inescapable!

Sources: Adrienne Ward Fawcett, "Free TV 'Ad Plugs' Are on the Rise," *Advertising Age*, July 12, 1993, p. 21; Laura Bird, "A Star Is Brewed as Obscure Beer Scores with Role in Hit Movie," *The Wall Street Journal*, July 8, 1993, p. B3.

Where and who gets the ad plugs

Percentage of 1,035 ad plugs measured over a recent 24-hour period

Type of Plug

Brand name shown	49.8%
Brand name spoken	34.8%
Label/logo shown	9.5%
Design identifiable	6.0%

How Clear Was It?

Very clear	74.9%
Somewhat clear	20.7%
Not very clear	4.4%

Where Are They?

Evening news	39.9%
Morning news	15.5%
Talk show	15.2%
Hour dramatic series	7.1%
News magazine	6.8%
Half-hour sitcom	4.8%
Game show	2.7%
Daytime soap opera	2.5%
Non-fictional drama	2.4%
Movie	1.7%
Feature news	1.1%
Children's	0.3%

Which Network?

ABC	31.6%
NBC	30.8%
CBS	24.9%
Fox	12.7%

Who Gets Plugs?

Autos	18.3%
Businesses	14.5%
Movies & plays	13.4%
Print media	10.4%
Beverages	7.8%
Apparel	6.2%
Sports	5.7%
Food	5.0%
Restaurants	3.9%
Universities	3.5%
Appliances	3.3%
HBA	2.6%
Music	1.7%

Context of Plugs

Editorial	48.1%
All other	51.9%

Sources: Northwestern University; *Advertising Age*, July 12, 1993, p. 21.

High exposure numbers are also offered for TV tie-ins, based on the ratings and (at least in the case of soaps) the possibility to direct the ad to a defined target market.

2. **Frequency**   Depending on how the product is used in the movie (or program), there may be ample opportunity for *repeated exposures* (many, if you like to watch a program or movie more than once). For example, if you are a regular watcher of "Seinfeld," you will be exposed to the products placed therein a number of times.

@ **EXHIBIT 15–16**

CPM for movie advertising

Title of Film	Theater Box Office	Audience[1]	Weeks in Release	Cost per Thousand[2]
Batman Returns	145,480,492	29,750,600	4	.16
Beauty and the Beast	141,838,563	29,000,500	35	.17
Lethal Weapon 3	135,799,341	27,770,820	9	.18
Wayne's World	121,115,040	24,767,900	22	.20
Hook	118,965,084	24,328,240	24	.21
The Addams Family	113,379,166	23,185,920	22	.22
Basic Instinct	110,987,913	22,696,910	17	.22

[1] Audience figure is based on an average ticket price of $4.89 from Motion Picture Association of America, Inc., data and statistics, published in June 1992.
[2] CPM is the cost for reaching 1,000 consumers with an ad multiplied by 1,000, divided by the total audience (the average cost of a product placement is $5,000).

3. **Support for other media** Ad placements may support other promotional tools. For example, Mirage Resorts ran four minutes of commercials promoting its Treasure Island Resort on an NBC special titled "Treasure Island: The Adventure Begins," a story about a boy's adventures at the Treasure Island Resort. Kimberly-Clark Corp. created a sweepstakes, coupon offer, and TV-based ad around its Huggies diapers, featured in the movie *Baby Boom*.

4. **Source association** In Chapter 7, we discussed the advantages of source identification. When many potential consumers see their favorite movie star wearing Keds, drinking Evian, or driving a Mercedes, this association may lead to a favorable product image. The purple dinosaur Barney achieved tremendous sales success as a result of its PBS show "Barney & Friends." Thomas the Tank Engine never used paid commercials, yet it rivals the sales of Teenage Mutant Ninja Turtles and G.I. Joe, thanks to its appearance on PBS.[29]

5. **Cost** While the cost of placing a product may range from free samples to a million dollars, these are extremes. As shown in Exhibit 15–16, the CPM for this form of advertising can be very low, owing to the high volume of exposures it generates.

6. **Recall** A number of firms have measured the impact of product placements on next-day recall. Results ranged from Johnson's Baby Shampoo registering 20 percent to Kellogg's Corn Flakes registering 67 percent (in the movie *Raising Arizona*). Average recall is approximately 38 percent. Again, these scores are better than those reported for TV viewing.

Disadvantages of product placements

Some disadvantages are also associated with product placements.

1. **High absolute cost** While the CPM may be very low for product placement in movies, the absolute cost of placing the product may be very high, precluding its use for some advertisers. The cost of placing a product in the movies averages approximately $7,500, with many placements being substantially higher.[30]

2. **Time of exposure** While the way some products are exposed to the audience has an impact, there is no guarantee viewers will notice the product. Some product placements are more conspicuous than others. When placements do not result in a prominent featuring of the product, the advertiser runs the risk of not being seen (although it must be remembered the same risk is present in all forms of media advertising).

3. **Limited appeal** The appeal that can be made in this media form is limited. There is no potential for discussing product benefits or providing detailed information. Rather, appeals are limited to source association, use, and enjoyment.

EXHIBIT 15–17

In-flight magazines are available on most carriers

The endorsement of the product is indirect, and the flexibility for product demonstration is subject to its use in the film.

4. **Lack of control**   In many movies, the advertiser has no say over when and how often the product will be shown. Miller beer, for example, found its placement in the movie *Dragnet* did not work as well as expected. Fabergé developed an entire Christmas campaign around its Brut cologne and its movie placement, only to find the movie was delayed until February.

5. **Public reaction**   Many TV viewers and moviegoers are incensed at the idea of placing ads in the programs (movies). These viewers want to maintain the barrier between program content and commercials. The FTC is currently exploring options for limiting placements without consumer notification.

Audience measurement for product placements

To date, no audience measurement other than that available from the providers is available. The potential advertiser may often have to make a decision based on his or her own creative insights as to potential effectiveness or rely on the credibility of the source. However, at least one study has demonstrated the potential effectiveness of product placements. In a study by Eva Steortz, they had an average recall of 38 percent.[31] Research companies like PR Data Systems (mentioned earlier) compare the amount of time a product is exposed in the program/movie to a one-minute ad spot cost to measure value. (As you will see in Chapter 20, however, we have problems with this measure of effectiveness.)

In-Flight Advertising

Another rapidly growing medium is **in-flight advertising**. As the number of flying passengers increases (to over 5 million per month on American, United, and Delta alone), so too does the attractiveness of this medium. In-flight advertising includes three forms:

- **In-flight magazines**   Free magazines (like the one in Exhibit 15–17) published by the airlines are offered on almost every plane in the air. Delta distributes over 500,000 of its *Sky* magazines per month and estimates potential exposures at 1.7 million.[32]
- **In-flight videos**   In-flight videos have been common on international flights for some time and are now being used on domestic flights. Commercials were not originally included in these videos. In 1990, about $18 million in commercials was booked on flights ($12 million on international flights), and advertisers expect a 25 percent growth rate throughout the 1990s.[33] While not all airlines offer in-flight commercials, companies such as Japan Air Lines, Delta, TWA, and British Airways are participating.

@ **EXHIBIT 16–2**

A variety of companies employ direct marketing

Adolph Coors

Coors is now advertising on PC on-line services such as Prodigy. The ads appear on a program called "Coors Light Fan Picks Poll," in which sports fans vote for the number one college football team. A full menu of scores and odds is presented, along with Coors Light ads and Coors logos.

Avon

Avon, a company in trouble in the 1980s, has turned business around by offering consumers four ways to order their products: by fax, phone, catalog, or sales representative. The company is also exploring the use of infomercials.

Pepsi

Having established a strong database, Pepsi is leveraging its files with its sister companies Frito-Lay, Pizza Hut, Kentucky Fried Chicken, and Taco Bell. The company has established a frequent customer program, targeted promotions to existing customers, and wooed new customers by mailing sample cases to 1 million households of Coke drinkers.

Xerox

Programs featuring direct mail followed by a telemarketing call expedite the sales process for Xerox. Telemarketers give the direct salespeople lists of what prospects are calling and the materials prospects receive.

AT&T

Moving monies away from television advertising, AT&T has doubled its telemarketing and direct mail efforts and upgraded its consumer database. Targeting its huge residential customer base, the company has offered a record number of combination phone/credit card sales. The company expects to increase its direct marketing efforts in 1994.

- **Direct-marketing syndicates**   Companies specializing in list development, statement inserts, catalogs, and sweepstakes have opened many new opportunities to marketers. The number of these companies continues to expand, creating even more new users.
- **The changing structure of American society and the market**   Perhaps one of the major factors contributing to the success of direct marketing is that America is now a land of "money-rich and time-poor" people.[5] The rapid increase in dual-income families (in 1993 an estimated 57.5 percent of women were in the work force) has meant more income.[6] At the same time, trends toward physical fitness, do-it-yourself crafts and repairs, and home entertainment have reduced the time available for shopping and have increased the attractiveness of direct purchases.
- **Technological advances**   The rapid technological advancement of the electronic media (discussed later in this chapter) and of computers has made it easier for consumers to shop and for marketers to be successful in reaching the desired target markets. In 1993, 117 million television homes received home shopping programs, and home channel purchases totaled over $2.55 billion.[7]
- **Miscellaneous factors**   A number of other factors have contributed to the increased effectiveness of direct marketing, including changing values, more sophisticated marketing techniques, and the improved image of the industry. Those factors will also assure the success of direct marketing in the future. The variety of companies employing direct marketing (see Exhibit 16–2) demonstrates its potential.

@ **DIRECT-MARKETING DECISIONS**

To successfully implement direct-marketing programs, companies must make a number of decisions. As in other marketing programs, decisions involve determining (1) what the program's objectives will be; (2) which markets to target (determined through the use of a list or marketing database); (3) what direct marketing strategies will be employed; and (4) how to evaluate the effectiveness of the program.

@ **EXHIBIT 16-3**

Lexus is just one of the many car companies now using direct marketing

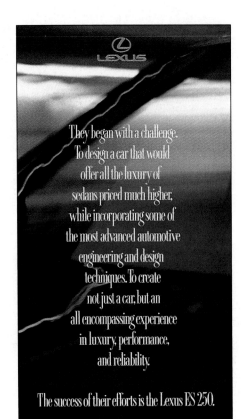

They began with a challenge. To design a car that would offer all the luxury of sedans priced much higher, while incorporating some of the most advanced automotive engineering and design techniques. To create not just a car, but an all encompassing experience in luxury, performance, and reliability.

The success of their efforts is the Lexus ES 250.

Direct-Marketing Objectives

The direct marketer seeks a direct response. The objectives of the program normally seek a behavior—for example, test drives, votes, contributions, and/or sales. A typical objective for these programs would be defined through a set response, perhaps, a 2 to 3 percent response rate.

Not all direct marketing seeks a behavioral response, however. Many organizations use direct marketing to build an image, maintain customer satisfaction, and inform and/or educate customers in an attempt to lead to future actions (see Exhibit 16–3).

Developing a Marketing Database

As we have discussed throughout this text, market segmentation and targeting are critical components of any promotional program. To segment and target their markets, direct marketers use a **database**, a listing of customers and/or potential customers. At the very least, this list contains names, addresses, and ZIP codes; more sophisticated databases include information on demographics and psychographics, purchase transactions and payments, personal facts, neighborhood data, and even credit histories. This database serves as the foundation from which the direct-marketing programs evolve. Databases might be used to perform the following functions.[8]

- **Improving the selection of market segments**   Some consumers are more likely to be potential purchasers, users, voters, and so on than others. By analyzing the characteristics of the database, a marketer can target a higher potential audience. For example, catalog companies have become very specialized, targeting only those who are most likely to purchase their products. Companies such as Lands' End, Lilly's Kids, and Johnson & Murphy have culled their lists and become much more efficient.
- **Stimulating repeat purchases**   Once a purchase has been made, the customer's name and other information are entered into the database. These people are proven direct-marketing users who offer high potential for repurchase. Magazine companies, for example, routinely send out renewal letters and/or phone subscribers be-

Global Perspective 16-1
The Global Database

Database marketing continues to demonstrate its worth. As companies continue to compile an extensive array of information about their current and potential customers, users of databases now include an international domain. A seemingly endless number of companies now spend millions of dollars on marketing to their databases, including Pepsi, IBM, Silicon Graphics, Waldenbooks, Liz Claiborne, and a multitude of auto companies.

At least one company has taken its database marketing strategies to the global market. Nestlé, headquartered in Vevey, Switzerland, believes that by using its database to pursue relationship marketing strategies, it can avoid discounting advertised brands. The company creatively marketed its Sopad-Nestlé baby food in Paris by helping mothers care for their babies while driving on European highways. Hostess-staffed rest stops where mothers can change their babies in a clean, relaxing environment put Nestlé directly in touch with its target market. Names are gathered from the rest stops and from maternity records to create a 220,000-name database that is constantly updated. Follow-up direct mail waves are then implemented. The first wave includes a business reply card asking for the baby's name and whether the mother would like to receive further mailings. If she says yes, six direct mail packages are sent, personalized with the baby's name, at key stages of development. The packages include information cards, samples of baby foods, coupons, and cutouts of the Nestlé teddy bear. The strategy has resulted in an astonishing 24-point gain in market share.

In the United Kingdom, Nestlé repositioned its Buitoni brand of pasta. Heavy TV advertising invited viewers to call for a free 2-page recipe booklet. Respondents became members of the Casa Buitoni Club, which led to the development of a 100,000-name database. Club members receive a magazine filled with recipes, articles, and features as well as opportunities to win trips to Casa Buitoni for free cooking lessons.

Europeans are not as bombarded with direct mail as Americans. Belgians receive the most (an average of 78 pieces per year) and Ireland the least (11 pieces per year). So direct strategies may have a greater chance of success in Europe. Reaching a specific target market with what Nestlé calls its individualized strategies also enhances the likelihood of success.

Sources: Stan Rapp and Thomas L. Collins, "Nestlé's Banks of Databases," *Advertising Age*, Oct. 25, 1993, pp. 16–18; Beverly Martin, "Machine Dreams," *Brandweek*, April 26, 1993, pp. 17–24.

---

fore the expiration date. Other companies, ranging from window cleaners to carpet cleaners to car dealers, build a base of customers and contact them when they are "due" to repurchase.

- **Cross-selling**   Customers who demonstrate a specific interest also constitute strong potential for other products of the same nature. For example, the National Geographic Society has successfully sold globes, maps, videos, travel magazines, and an assortment of other products to subscribers who obviously have an interest in geography and/or travel. Likewise, companies like Victoria's Secret have expanded their clothing lines primarily through sales to existing customers.

Numerous other companies have established comprehensive databases on existing and potential customers both in the United States and internationally. Global Perspective 16–1 discusses some of these efforts. Database marketing has become so ubiquitous that many people are concerned about the potential for invasion of privacy. Direct marketers are concerned as well. The Direct Marketing Association (DMA), the trade association for direct marketers, has asked its members to adhere to ethical rules of conduct in their marketing efforts. It points out that if the industry does not police itself, the government will.

Sources of database information

There are many sources of information for direct-marketing databases.

- **The US Census Bureau**   The 1990 census data provide information on almost every household in the United States. Data include household size, demographics, income, and other information.
- **The US Postal Service**   Postal ZIP code and the extended four-digit code provide information on both household and business locations.
- **List services**   Many providers of lists are available (one such provider is shown in Exhibit 16–4). The accuracy and timeliness of the lists vary.
- **Standard Rate and Data Service**   SRDS provides information regarding both consumer and business lists. These lists are published in two volumes entitled *Direct Mail List Rates and Data* and provide over 50,000 list selections in hundreds of classifications.

@ **EXHIBIT   16–4**   An example of the variety of mail response lists available

Quantity		Price		Quantity		Price
	Automotive				**Contributors**	
15,000,000	American Car Buyers/ Foreign/or USA Models	Inquire		435,000	American Museum Natural History	$75/M
208,000	AutoWeek Subscribers	$60/M		400,000	Animal Welfare Donors	$65/M
146,000	Babcox Business Leaders	$65/M		437,000	Greenpeace	$65/M
160,000	Beverly Hills Motoring Accessories Buyers	$95/M		4,000,000	Health	$65/M
165,000	4 Wheel & Off Road Subs	$60/M		1,313,000	Humanitarian	$65/M
48,000	Hearst Motor Bookbuyers	$50/M		226,000	National Foundation Cancer Research	$60/M
49,500	Hot Rod Magazine	$60/M		148,000	National Glaucoma Research	$75/M
328,000	Classic Motor Books	$55/M		1,497,000	Political	$65/M
218,000	Auto/Truck Do-It-Yourselfers	$60/M		248,000	Political/Conservative	$65/M
74,000	Cars & Parts Magazine	$70/M		162,000	Political/Liberal	$65/M
				4,000,000	Religious	$65/M
	Beauty/Health/Diet			586,000	Hands Across America Donors	$55/M
800,000	American Health Magazine	$65/M				
1,000,000	Bio-Energetics Research Buyers	$70/M			**Computers/Data Processing**	
339,000	Comfortably Yours	$85/M		2,800,000	Personal Computer Owners/Type of Brand	Inquire
1,700,000	Cosmetique Beauty Buyers	$55/M		700,000	Business Computer Owners/Type of Brand	Inquire
32,000	Cardiac Alert Subs	$85/M		260,000	Professionals Using Computers	Inquire
33,000	Executive Fitness Letter	$75/M		665,000	Brandon Computer Professionals	$75/M
912,000	Health Magazine	$60/M		255,000	Byte Magazine	$100/M
480,000	Health Conscious Americans	$50/M		113,000	Computerworld Magazine	$125/M
224,000	Tufts University Newsletter	$65/M		70,000	Computer Systems News	$87/M
550,000	University of California— Berkeley Wellness Letter	$70/M		137,580	Computel Magazine	$80/M
135,000	Vegetarian Times	$65/M		160,000	Datamation	$80/M
200,000	Weider Health and Fitness	$65/M		400,000	Family and Home Office Computing	$80/M
2,400,000	Prevention Magazine	$60/M		135,000	MIS Week	$110/M
821,000	Weight Watchers Magazine	$65/M		453,000	PC Magazine	$100/M
	Bookbuyers				**Consumer Magazines**	
2,200,000	Better Homes & Gardens	$60/M		250,000	Americana Magazine	$65/M
642,000	Barnes & Noble	$70/M		93,000	Art & Antiques Magazine	$80/M
840,000	Boardroom Bookbuyers	$85/M		380,000	Atlantic Monthly	$80/M
330,000	Warren, Gorham & Lamont	$90/M		148,000	American History Illustrated	$70/M
	Bantam Bookbuyers	Inquire		73,000	Birdwatchers Digest	$60/M
	Book of the Month Club	Inquire		110,000	Collectors Mart	$60/M
	CMG (College Bookbuyers)	Inquire		1,160,000	Contest Newsletter	$70/M
	Doubleday Bookbuyers	Inquire		1,100,000	Davis Publications	$55/M
	Literary Guild	Inquire		295,000	Early American Life	$70/M
	MacMillan Bookbuyers	Inquire		110,000	Fate Magazine	$65/M
	Prentice Hall, Inc.	Inquire		919,000	Insight Magazine	$55/M
	Time-Life—INQUIRE BY SUBJECT	Inquire		1,000,000	Life Magazine	$70/M
				112,000	New Age Journal	$75/M
				346,000	National Audubon Society	$70/M
				2,700,000	Newsweek	$60/M

Many types of **privately owned** specialty lists of people are available, such as:

- **MAIL ORDER BUYERS** of various direct mail, TV or magazine products
- **SUBSCRIBERS** to magazines, newsletters
- **CONTRIBUTORS** to fund-raising campaigns
- **CREDIT CARD HOLDERS,** charge customers

These lists can be related to your specific product or purpose. If your offer is not in competitive conflict with such lists, the owner will authorize the use of his names for your mailing. **A SAMPLE MAILING PIECE MUST BE SUBMITTED WITH YOUR ORDER FOR APPROVAL.** These **RESPONSE LISTS** are an additional tool to target specific segments of your direct mail market.

PRICES, QUANTITIES, AND MINIMUMS (usually 5,000—Inquire) for such lists are completely at the discretion of the list owner, and are subject to change. *Please inquire for details and current prices before placing your order.* Orders for RESPONSE LISTS are not commissionable and cannot be charged on credit cards.

These two pages are a *representative* group of such private response lists. Many, many more are available.

- **Simmons Market Research Bureau**   SMRB conducts an annual study of customers who buy at home via mail or telephone (see Exhibit 16–5). It compiles information on total orders placed, type of products purchased, demographics, and purchase satisfaction, among others.
- **Direct Marketing Association, Inc.**   This trade organization promotes direct marketing and provides statistical information on direct-marketing use. The DMA publishes a *Fact Book of Direct Marketing* containing information regarding use, attitudes toward direct marketing, rules and regulations, and so forth.

Consumer goods manufacturers, banks, credit bureaus, retailers, charitable organizations, and other business operations also sell lists and other selected information. Companies can build their own databases through completed warranty cards, surveys, and so on.

@ EXHIBIT 16–5

SMRB provides information on consumers who ordered merchandise by mail and phone

	Total U S '000	Ordered by mail or phone			
		A '000	B % Down	C Across %	D Indx
Total adults	185,822	97,715	100.0	52.6	100
Males	88,956	42,488	43.5	47.8	91
Females	96,866	55,227	56.5	57.0	108
Principal shoppers	112,018	60,697	62.1	54.2	103
18–24	23,965	9,846	10.1	41.1	78
25–34	42,832	22,434	23.0	52.4	100
35–44	39,908	23,902	24.5	59.9	114
45–54	27,327	16,047	16.4	58.7	112
55–64	21,238	10,939	11.2	51.5	98
65 or older	30,552	14,547	14.9	47.6	91
18–34	66,798	32,280	33.0	48.3	92
18–49	121,918	65,339	66.9	53.6	102
25–54	110,067	62,383	63.8	56.7	108
35–49	55,120	33,059	33.8	60.0	114
50 or older	63,905	32,376	33.1	50.7	96
Graduated college	36,463	23,374	23.9	64.1	122
Attended college	44,294	24,904	25.5	56.2	107
Graduated high school	66,741	34,408	35.2	51.6	98
Did not graduate high school	38,324	15,028	15.4	39.2	75
Employed males	65,500	32,228	33.0	49.2	94
Employed females	55,910	34,804	35.6	62.3	118
Employed full-time	110,363	60,402	61.8	54.7	104
Employed part-time	11,047	6,630	6.8	60.0	114
Not employed	64,412	30,682	31.4	47.6	91
Professional/manager	31,718	19,851	20.3	62.6	119
Technical/clerical/sales	37,895	22,703	23.2	59.9	114
Precision/craft	13,954	6,930	7.1	49.7	94
Other employed	37,843	17,548	18.0	46.4	88
Single	41,284	17,744	18.2	43.0	82
Married	109,023	62,594	64.1	57.4	109
Divorced/separated/widowed	35,515	17,376	17.8	48.9	93
Parents	62,342	35,701	36.5	57.3	109
White	158,841	87,327	89.4	55.0	105
Black	21,122	7,896	8.1	37.4	71
Other	5,859	2,492	2.6	42.5	81
Hshld. inc. $75,000 or more	24,165	14,731	15.1	61.0	116
$60,000 or more	40,979	24,220	24.8	59.1	112
$50,000 or more	57,996	34,185	35.0	58.9	112
$40,000 or more	80,078	47,018	48.1	58.7	112
$30,000 or more	106,838	62,069	63.5	58.1	110
$30,000–$39,000	26,759	15,051	15.4	56.2	107
$20,000–$29,000	30,669	15,147	15.5	49.4	94
$10,000–$19,999	29,083	13,069	13.4	44.9	85
Under $10,000	19,232	7,430	7.6	38.6	73

Direct-Marketing Strategies and Media

As with all other communications programs discussed throughout this text, decisions must be made as to the message to be conveyed, the size of the budget, and so on. Perhaps the major difference between direct-marketing programs and other promotional mix programs regards the use of media.

EXHIBIT 16–6

Porsche used direct mail to target high-income physicians

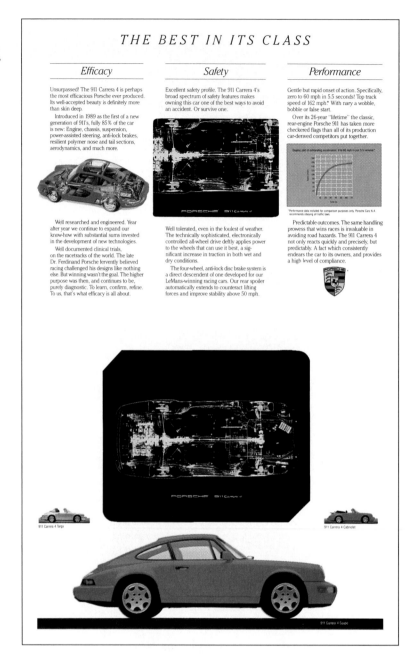

As shown in Exhibit 16–1, direct marketing employs a number of media, including direct mail, telemarketing, direct-response broadcasting, and print. Each medium is used to perform specific functions, although they generally follow what direct marketers refer to as a one- or two-step approach.

In the **one-step approach,** the medium is used directly to obtain an order. You probably have seen TV commercials for products like wrench sets, workout equipment, or magazine subscriptions in which the viewer is urged to phone a toll-free number to place an order immediately. Usually these ads allow for the use of a credit card or COD and give an address. Their goal is to generate an immediate sale when the ad is shown.

The **two-step approach** may involve the use of more than one medium. The first effort is designed to screen or qualify potential buyers. The second effort generates the response. For example, many companies use telemarketing to screen on the basis of interest, then follow up to interested parties with more information designed to achieve an order or use personal selling to close the sale.

Direct mail

Direct mail is often called junk mail—the unsolicited mail you find in your mailbox. The amount of advertising dollars spent in direct mail continues to be one of the highest of all advertising media, with an estimated $25.45 billion spent in this area in 1992.[9] Mail-order sales exceeded $234.2 billion in 1993.[10] Direct mail is not restricted to small companies seeking our business. Well-respected companies such as General Electric, American Express, and Citicorp have increased their expenditures in this area, as have many others.

While many advertisers shied away from direct mail in the past, fearful of the image it might create or harboring the belief that direct mail was useful only for low-cost products, this is no longer the case. For example, Porsche Cars North America, Inc., uses direct mail to target high-income, upscale consumers who are most likely to purchase its expensive sports cars. Exhibit 16–6 shows a direct mail piece that was sent to a precisely defined target market: physicians in specialties with the highest income levels. This list was screened to match the demographics of Porsche buyers and narrowed further to specific geographic areas. This direct mail piece was an X ray of a Porsche 911 Carrera 4 written in the language of the medical audience. This creative direct mail campaign generated one of the highest response rates of any mailing Porsche has done in recent years.[11]

Keys to the success of direct mail are the **mailing list**, which constitutes the database from which names are generated, and the ability to segment markets. Lists have become more current and more selective, eliminating waste coverage. Segmentation on the basis of geography (usually through ZIP codes), demographics, and lifestyles has led to increased effectiveness. The most commonly used lists are of individuals who are past purchasers of direct mail products.

The importance of the list has led to a business of its own. In 1990 there were an estimated 38 billion names on lists, and many companies have found it profitable to sell the names of purchasers of their products and/or services to list firms. Companies like A. B. Zeller and Metromail provide such lists on a national level, and in most metropolitan areas there are firms providing the same service locally. In 1993, the list business accounted for $1.3 billion in sales of names.

Catalogs

Major participants in the direct-marketing business are catalog companies. The number of catalogs mailed and the number of catalog shoppers have increased significantly since 1984. While a slight decline in the number of catalogs mailed occurred in the early 1990s, that decline was a result of companies culling their lists to target more effectively. Companies like Sears have abandoned their large mass-targeted catalogs and have begun to develop specialty books in alliances with Spiegel, Hanover, and other apparel, furniture, and appliance companies. Overall, the catalog industry experienced record growth in 1993, as catalog sales reached an estimated $50 to 60 billion.[12]

Many companies use catalogs in conjunction with their more traditional sales and promotional strategies. For example, companies like Sears, Nordstrom, and J. C. Penney sell directly through catalogs but also use them to inform consumers of product offerings available in the stores. Some companies (for example, L. L. Bean) rely solely on catalog sales, while others that started out exclusively as catalog companies have branched into retail outlets, among them The Sharper Image, Lands' End, and Banana Republic. Exhibit 16–7 shows some of the many companies that market through catalogs.

In addition to the traditional hard copies, catalogs are now available through on-line services such as Prodigy, Genie, and CompuServe. The Merchant Co. in San Francisco offers an interactive CD-ROM catalog service with as many as 25 different mail-order catalogs on one disk. Spiegel, Lands' End, Brooks Brothers, and Books on Tape (among others) are all available through this medium.

@ **EXHIBIT   16–7**

A few of the many companies
that market through catalogs

@ **EXHIBIT   16–7**

A few of the many companies
that market through catalogs

Broadcast media

The success of direct marketing in the broadcast industry is truly remarkable. Direct-response TV is estimated to have generated over $2 billion in sales in 1993, and some believe this figure should be higher.[13] For example, one company in California sold almost $50,000 a day in a diet program at $19.95 per order; others have successfully sold products that cost hundreds of dollars. Perhaps the most amazing thing about these sales figures is that the advertising time purchased to sell these products was among the least expensive available in the medium. (Direct advertisers often purchase advertising time at the last moment to obtain a discount. They also buy time on programs with low ratings or reruns, because consumers are less likely to leave an interesting show or event to place a phone order.)

Two broadcast media are available to the direct marketer, television and radio. While radio was used quite extensively in the 1950s, its use and effectiveness have dwindled substantially in recent years. Thus, the majority of direct-marketing broadcast advertising now occurs on TV, which receives the bulk of our attention here.

Direct marketing in the broadcast industry involves both direct-response advertising and support advertising. In **direct-response advertising**, the product or service is offered and a sales response is solicited, through either the one- or two-step approach previously discussed. Examples include ads for Soloflex, Nordic Track, CDs and tapes, and tips on football or basketball betting. **Support advertising** is designed to do exactly that—support other forms of advertising. Ads for Publishers Clearing House or *Reader's Digest* or other companies telling you to look in your mailbox for a sweepstakes entry are examples of support advertising.

@ **EXHIBIT   16–8**

The top infomercials, 1993*

1. Flowbee (hair cutter)
2. Battery Supercharger (battery charger)
3. Decosonic Prolock (vacuum sealer)
4. Meyer Duralon (cookware)
5. Jet Aire (hairstyler)
6. Popeil Pastamaker (pasta machine)
7. Microcrisp (microwave cooking sheets)
8. Jetstream oven (oven)
9. The Juiceman (juice extractor)

*Based on airings on national cable and selected broadcast markets.

@ **EXHIBIT   16–9**

Volvo uses the infomercial to
attract buyers

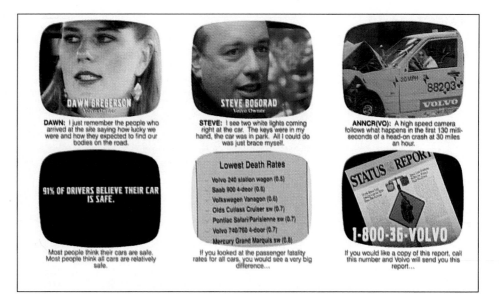

EXHIBIT   16–9

Volvo uses the infomercial to attract buyers

Infomercials

The lower cost of commercials on cable and satellite channels has led advertisers to a new form of advertising. An **infomercial** is a long commercial that ranges from 3 to 60 minutes. Most are 30 minutes long. Many infomercials are produced by the advertisers and are designed to be viewed as regular TV shows. Consumers dial a toll-free 800 or 900 number to place an order. Programs such as "Liquid Luster," "Amazing Discoveries," and "Stainerator" (the so-called miracle products shows) were the most common form of infomercial in the 1980s. While this form of show is still the most popular (Exhibit 16–8), the infomercial industry is changing to welcome many big, mainstream marketers. As demonstrated in Exhibit 16–9, the infomercial is no longer the private domain of miracle products.

As to their effectiveness, studies indicate that infomercials get watched and sell products. Exhibit 16–10 shows the results of a study by Bruskin/Goldring Research profiling infomercial viewers and buyers. It demonstrates that this advertising medium is indeed effective with a broad demographic base.[14] Infomercial sales in 1993 were expected to exceed $1 billion.[15]

However, some people are not sold on the idea of advertisements disguised as programs. Consumer complaints are on the rise, and the FTC has already levied fines for deceptive endorsements against infomercial sponsors. Four consumer groups (the Consumer Federation of America, Center for the Study of Commercialism, Center for Media Education, and Telecommunications Research and Action Center) have asked the FCC to require all infomercials to display a symbol that indicates a "paid ad" or "sponsored by" so viewers won't confuse them with regular television programming.[16]

Print media

Magazines and newspapers are difficult media to employ for direct marketing. Because these ads have to compete with the clutter of other ads, and because the cost of the space is relatively expensive, response rates and profits may be lower than in other media. This does not mean these media are not used (as evidenced by the fact that expenditures totaled over $41 billion in 1992).[17] Exhibit 16–11 on page 467 shows a direct ad that appeared in *Time* magazine. You can find many more in specific interest areas like financial newspapers or sports, sex, or hobby magazines.

⊚ **EXHIBIT 16–10**

Here's who is watching (and buying from) infomercials

Americans are becoming more familiar with half-hour program-length advertising. In new research commissioned by Hudson Street Partners, more than half the respondents said they had seen an infomercial in the past 12 months, nearly one in 10 had experience ordering infomercial products by 800-number, and nearly 2 in 10 said they had purchased products in a store based on information from an infomercial. Percentages shown below are percentages of the total survey sample.

	Seen an infomercial in the past year?	Ever purchased anything using 800-number at the end of an infomercial?	Ever purchased anything in a store based on information provided in an infomercial?
Sex			
Male	57%	8.0%	20.0%
Female	54%	9.0%	19.0%
Age			
18–24	70%	4.0%	19.0%
25–34	63%	9.0%	19.0%
35–49	58%	12.0%	20.0%
50–64	55%	10.0%	26.0%
65+	33%	3.0%	13.0%
Income			
under $15,000	53%	4.5%	22.5%
$15,000–$20,000	52%	11.0%	24.0%
$20,000–$30,000	62%	8.0%	21.0%
$30,000–$40,000	63%	9.0%	25.0%
$40,000+	60%	11.0%	16.0%
Region			
Northeast	56%	7.0%	24.0%
North Central	52%	9.0%	14.0%
South	57%	8.0%	21.0%
West	55%	10.0%	17.0%
Total	55%	8.5%	19.0%

Data are based on a national telephone survey commission by Hudson Street Partners and conducted by Bruskin/Goldring Research in August 1992. The sample was 1,005 men and women ages 18 and older.
Source: "The New Era for Infomercials," *Advertising Age*, Jan. 25, 1993, p. M3.

Telemarketing

If you have a telephone, you probably do not have to be told about the rapid increase in the use of **telemarketing**, or sales by telephone. Both profit and charitable organizations have employed this medium effectively in both one- and two-step approaches. Over 118 million Americans receive nearly 3 billion telemarketing phone calls each year; approximately 6 percent of these result in a completed transaction.[18] While 6 percent may seem low, the fact is that telemarketing is a very big industry that continues to grow. Over 5 million people are now employed in the telemarketing industry, with sales exceeding $300 billion.[19] Business-to-business marketers like Hewlett-Packard, DuPont, and Xerox use this direct-marketing medium effectively.

As telemarketing continues to expand in scope, a new dimension referred to as **audiotex** or **telemedia** has evolved. Tom Eisenhart defines telemedia as the "use of telephone and voice information services (900, 800, and 976 numbers) to market, advertise, promote, entertain, and inform."[20] Many telemedia programs are interactive. While many people still think of 900 and 976 numbers as ripoffs or "sex, lies, and phone lines," over 7,000 programs are carried on 900 networks alone. Companies such as Tele-Lawyer, a legal information services organization; Bally's Health & Tennis Corp., the nation's largest health-club chain; and NutraSweet constitute over 75 percent of these. Exhibit 16–12 on page 468 shows more specifically where such calls are going.

Telemarketing and telemedia programs have responded to public criticisms. Dial-a-Porn and its ilk hold a diminishing share of 800, 900, and 976 offerings. As more and

@ **EXHIBIT 16-11**

A direct response print ad

more large companies increase their use of these services, their tarnished image will likely brighten up.

Electronic media

Over the past few years, technological advances have opened up a number of new media for marketers. While these alternatives vary in many respects, they can all be classified as electronic media. A review of some of these follows.

Teleshopping

The development of the toll-free 800 telephone number, combined with the widespread use of credit cards, has led to a dramatic increase in the number of people who shop via their TV sets. Jewelry, kitchenware, insurance, and a variety of other companies have now employed this medium to promote (and sell!) their products. In 1992, there were five home shopping channels in the United States, accounting for over $2.55 billion worth of sales. A study conducted by Deloitte & Touche indicates that home shoppers have slightly lower than average incomes and spend slightly more time watching TV than the market average. In all other demographic categories, the markets are almost identical, though home shoppers are much more likely to shop through catalog and direct mail (44 percent versus 12 percent).[21]

Electronic teleshopping

Unlike infomercials and home shopping channels, which rely on broadcast or cable video channels, **electronic teleshopping** is an on-line shopping and information retrieval service accessed through one's personal computer.

With only a minimal knowledge of computers, home shoppers can select the information they want as if using a book index. Shoppers can purchase products, buy services such as airline tickets, play games, get stock market reports, view the latest headlines, and pay bills. Advertisers may provide their messages in the form of logos or names or in longer segments, depending on the costs they wish to assume and the message they wish to convey.

The country's leading information retrieval services companies—CompuServe, America Online, and Prodigy—have increased their information offerings over the years, making this medium more attractive to marketers. As of 1994, these three services

⊚ EXHIBIT 16-12

I'd pay to find out! (percentage of total 900 calls made to specific applications)

	1991	1992*
Information	35.6%	32.5%
Entertainment	20.1	18.4
Messaging	11.6	8.4
Ordering	7.1	8.6
Sweepstakes	5.9	6.0
Fund raising	5.4	6.4
Polling/surveying	3.5	4.6
Lead generation	2.9	3.4
Couponing	2.1	3.2
Dealer locators	1.6	1.8
Customer services	0.9	1.1
Other	3.3	5.6

*Estimate

had over 3.5 million subscribers and featured such advertisers as Sharp Electronics, KLM Royal Dutch Airlines, Oldsmobile, Holiday Inn, and Panasonic.[22] The sales dollar volume is growing at 30 to 40 percent per year.[23] Prodigy has established a joint venture with *USA Today* to sell consumers classified advertising.[24] A variety of other companies are exploring the potential use of this medium.

Advantages and disadvantages of electronic media

Given the lack of time experienced by so many dual working families, the ability of the new electronic media to offer an alternative shopping medium holds great potential. The visual aspects of TV allow for demonstrations and product representations not available through catalogs and give potential consumers much more information for decision making. The information retrieval systems offer an almost unlimited opportunity for marketers.

Despite the growth in this industry, some marketers are still skeptical. They theorize that sales are not as high as projections because:

- Computers have not been adopted at the rate expected for home use.
- Many people are still not comfortable with shopping without being able to handle the merchandise. They prefer to feel the material, see the colors, try on the product, and so on.
- Shopping may be a form of relaxation. To many people, a day in the mall or downtown is a form of entertainment. It gets them out of the house, takes their mind off work, and provides them with an opportunity to interact socially. Some people feel that since they work hard to enjoy their money, at least they can take the time to enjoy spending it!
- Many consumers prefer to get their news in the traditional manner—TV, radio, and newspapers. It's hard to change people's behaviors and habits.
- Pricing is based on the minute rather than monthly contracts, making it less attractive to advertisers.
- Information offerings are still limited.

According to Jon Berry, consumers just don't feel that they need this high-tech form of shopping and prefer to stick with their traditional shopping behaviors.[25] Michael J. Major notes that many of these problems have been corrected and projections for electronic media are much more optimistic. In France, over 5.5 million videotext screens are in use (60 percent of phone subscribers) and the future for this service appears to be rosy.[26]

Another area in which on-line services continue to increase in use is the *industrial sector*. When companies are bidding on government or private industry contracts that require meeting specifications, the electronic media offer a distinct advantage over existing

Tupperware is one of the many companies using direct selling to market its products

LEARN MORE IN A FREE CLASS!

TUPPERWAVE™ COOKWARE SYSTEM

methods. For example, where specifications previously had to be mailed to prospective bidders, these specs are now available immediately through the video screen. Changes in specs can be noted almost immediately, saving valuable time and effort for all parties involved.

In sum, while the electronic media may not be the answer for all marketers or for all shoppers, they do satisfy the needs of a particular segment of society. The commitment made by the companies offering such services and the success experienced by many of those who have advertised in these media, suggest that there is a bright future for advertisers in this area.

@ **DIRECT SELLING**

One final element of the direct-marketing program involves **direct selling**, the direct, personal presentation, demonstration, and sales of products and services to consumers in their homes. Avon, Amway, Mary Kay Cosmetics, and Tupperware are some of the best-known US direct-selling companies (Exhibit 16–13). In 1993 Chesebrough-Pond's started a direct-selling division for its facial skin–care line. Close to 5 million people engage in direct selling throughout the world; 98 percent of them are independent contractors (not employees of the firm they represent). These 5 million generate approximately $12 billion in sales.[27]

The three forms of direct selling are

1. **Repetitive person-to-person selling**   The salesperson visits the buyer's home, job site, or other location to sell frequently purchased products or services (for example, Amway).
2. **Nonrepetitive person-to-person selling**   The salesperson visits the buyer's home, job site, or other location to sell infrequently purchased products or services (for example, *Encyclopedia Britannica*).
3. **Party plans**   The salesperson offers products or services to groups of people through home or office parties and demonstrations (for example, Tupperware and PartyLite Gifts, Inc.).

@ **EVALUATING THE EFFECTIVENESS OF DIRECT MARKETING**

Because they generate a direct response, measuring the effectiveness of direct-marketing programs is not difficult. Using the **cost per order (CPO)**, advertisers can evaluate the relative effectiveness of an ad in only eight minutes based on the number of calls generated. If the advertiser targets a $5 return per order and a broadcast commercial

⊚ **EXHIBIT   16–14**

A high-quality direct mail
video

costs $250, the ad is considered effective if it generates 50 orders. Similar measures can
be developed for print and direct mail ads.

For direct-marketing programs that do not have an objective of generating a behavioral response, traditional measures of effectiveness can be applied. (We discuss these measures in Chapter 20.)

Advantages and Disadvantages of Direct Marketing

Many of the advantages of direct marketing have already been presented. A review of these and some additions follow.

1. **Selective reach**   Direct marketing lets the advertiser reach a large number of people and reduces or eliminates waste coverage. Intensive coverage may be obtained through broadcast advertising or through the mail. While not everyone drives on highways where there are billboards or pays attention to TV commercials, virtually everyone receives mail. A good list allows for minimal waste, as only those consumers with the highest potential are targeted. For example, a political candidate can direct a message at a very select group of people (those living in a certain ZIP code or members of the Sierra Club); a music club or compact disc manufacturer can target recent purchasers of CD players.

2. **Segmentation capabilities**   Marketers can purchase lists of recent product purchasers, bank card holders, recent car buyers, and so on. These lists may allow segmentation on the basis of geographic area, occupation, demographics, and job title, to mention a few. Combining this information with the geo-coding capabilities of PRIZM or VISION (discussed in Chapter 5), marketers can develop effective segmentation strategies.

3. **Frequency**   Depending on the medium utilized, it may be possible to build *frequency* levels. The program vehicles used for direct-response TV advertising are usually the most inexpensive available, so the marketer can afford to purchase repeat times. Frequency may not be so easily accomplished through the mail, as consumers may be annoyed when they receive the same mail repeatedly.

4. **Flexibility**   Direct marketing can take on a variety of creative forms. The direct mail video for the Subaru SVX in Exhibit 16–14 is a high-quality message that attracts the consumer's attention. Direct mail pieces also allow for detailed copy that provides a great deal of information. The targeted mailing of videotapes containing product information has increased dramatically, as companies have found

this a very effective way to provide potential buyers with product information. Black & Decker, Steamboat Springs Ski Resort, and the auto companies have successfully employed this medium.

5. **Timing**   While many media require long-range planning and long closing dates, direct-response advertising can be much more *timely*. Direct mail, for example, can be put together very quickly and distributed to the target population. TV programs typically used for direct-response advertising are older, less sought programs that are much more likely to appear on the station's list of available spots. Another common strategy is to purchase available time at the last possible moment to get the best price.

6. **Personalization**   No other advertising medium can personalize the message as well as direct mail. Parents with children at different age levels can be approached, with their child's name included in the appeal. Automobile owners are mailed letters congratulating them on their new car purchase and offering them accessories. Recent computer purchasers are sent software solicitations. Graduating college students receive very personalized information that recognizes their specific needs and offers solutions (such as credit cards).

7. **Costs**   While the CPM for direct mail may be very high on an absolute and a relative basis, one must keep in mind the ability of direct mail to specifically target the audience and eliminate waste coverage. This reduces the actual CPM. The ads used on TV are often among the lowest-priced available, and videotapes can be delivered to the home for less than $1 (including postage).

   A second factor contributing to the cost effectiveness of direct-response advertising is the **cost per customer purchasing**. Because of the low cost of media, each sale generated is very inexpensive.

8. **Measures of effectiveness**   No other medium can measure the effectiveness of its advertising efforts as well as direct response. Feedback is often immediate and always accurate.

Disadvantages of direct marketing include the following.

1. **Image factors**   As we noted earlier, the mail segment of this industry is often referred to as junk mail. Many people believe the unsolicited mail they receive is promoting junk products, and others dislike the idea they are being solicited. Even some senders of direct mail, including Motorola, GM, and Air Products & Chemicals, say they throw out the majority of junk mail they receive. This problem is particularly relevant given the increased volume of mail being sent. (One study estimates the typical American receives 14 pieces of junk mail per week.)[28] Likewise, the ads on television are often low-budget ads for lower-priced products, which contributes to the image that something less than the best products are marketed in this way. (Some of this image is being overcome by the home shopper channels, which promote some very expensive products.) As shown in Ethical Perspective 16–1, several other factors have created image problems for the direct marketing industry.

2. **Accuracy**   One of the advantages cited for direct mail and telemarketing was targeting potential customers specifically. But the effectiveness of both of these methods is directly related to the accuracy of the lists used. People move, change occupations, and so on, and if the lists are not kept current, selectivity will decrease. Computerized lists have greatly improved the currency of lists and reduced the incidence of bad names.

3. **Content support**   In our discussion of media strategy objectives in Chapter 12, we said the ability of magazines to create mood contributes to the overall effectiveness of the ads they carry. In direct-response advertising, mood creation is limited to broadcast and print methods (those surrounded by program and/or editorial content). Direct mail and on-line services are unlikely to create a desirable mood.

〰️ **Ethical Perspective 16–1**
Direct Marketing's Image Woes

It seems that every time the direct marketing industry takes a step forward, someone comes along and makes it look bad. While the vast majority of direct marketers are legitimate, ethical practitioners, a small minority damages the image of the entire industry. These image problems derive from several sources:

- *The right of privacy.* The privacy issue actually involves two subissues: (1) whether consumers should have to deal with pitches flooding their telephones and mailboxes; and (2) the sophisticated database marketers who know everything about you from the kind of underwear you prefer to your bank account balance. In a recent Harris-Equifax Consumer Privacy Survey, 78 percent of the respondents were concerned about threats to personal privacy and over half thought that the problem would get worse by the year 2000.
- *History.* Going back to the days of junk mail, early infomercials, and the original direct-response television ads, direct marketers became labeled as the small business guys who were out to get your money any way they could. Even though many of the largest corporations in the world now use direct marketing, to some the image remains. In fact, many industry practitioners were upset at the DMA awards banquet when the best-of-show prize went to a maritime museum's promotion "Treat a shark to dinner."

- *Fraud and deception.* One company recently sent a direct mail piece informing consumers that they had won a 25-foot boat. If they sent in their $100 registration fee, the boat would be delivered to their home in three weeks. Those who replied received a small plastic boat with 25 footprints on it! While this is an exception, many people think the majority of infomercials are deceptive. The hard-sell techniques for weight loss products, impotence remedies, and baldness treatments don't add to their credibility. Nor do those that offer cancer cures. A number of organizations have joined the fight to clean up the direct marketing industry. The Direct Marketing Association has developed a list of guidelines. The FDA and the Postal Service have closed in on deceptive advertisers and telemarketers, and the FTC recently extracted a $550,000 settlement from the Magic Wand handheld mixer company for a deceptive demonstration in its infomercial. Other groups like the Better Business Bureau are also becoming more involved.

All things considered, the image of the direct marketing business has improved from the early years. And, like it or not, the industry will be around for some time to come. It just hopes it can get rid of the small minority who continue to harm its reputation.

Sources: Joshua Levine, "Entertainment or Deception?" *Forbes*, Aug. 2, 1993, p. 102; Cyndee Miller, "Privacy versus Direct Marketing," *Marketing News*, March 1, 1993, pp. 1–14; Gary Levin, "Direct Marketers' Image Is Latest Hot Issue," *Advertising Age*, Nov. 8, 1993, p. 46.

SUMMARY

This chapter has introduced you to the rapidly growing field of direct marketing, which involves a variety of methods and media beyond direct mail and telemarketing. The number of ways direct marketing can be employed offers many different types of companies and organizations a powerful promotional and selling tool.

The growth of direct marketing continues to outpace other advertising and promotional areas, with many of the Fortune 500 companies now employing sophisticated direct marketing strategies. Database marketing has become a critical component of many marketing programs.

Advantages of direct marketing include the ability to specifically target and reach one's market, flexibility, frequency, and timing. The ability to measure program effectiveness, costs, and personalized and custom messages are also advantages of direct-marketing programs.

At the same time, a number of disadvantages are associated with the use of direct marketing. Image problems, the intrusive nature of the medium, and the proliferating sale and use of databases make some marketers hesitant to use direct-marketing tools. However, self-policing of the industry and involvement by large, sophisticated companies have led to significant changes and improvements. As a result, the use of direct marketing has increased and will continue to do so.

KEY TERMS

direct marketing, p. 454
direct-response media, p. 454
database, p. 458
one-step approach, p. 462
two-step approach, p. 462
mailing list, p. 463
direct-response advertising, p. 464
support advertising, p. 464
infomercial, p. 465
telemarketing, p. 466
audiotex, p. 466
telemedia, p. 466
electronic teleshopping, p. 467
direct selling, p. 469
cost per order (CPO), p. 469
cost per customer purchasing, p. 471

◉ DISCUSSION QUESTIONS

1. What factors have contributed to the growth of direct marketing? Why?

2. Describe what is meant by a database. What functions do databases perform?

3. Explain how business-to-business marketers might employ direct marketing.

4. Discuss the evolution of infomercials. How are today's infomercials different from those of 10 years ago?

5. What is meant by on-line media? Give examples.

6. Discuss some of the reasons direct marketing has been receiving more attention from marketers.

7. What are some of the problems associated with direct marketing?

8. Why do you think home shopping channels have been so successful? What is the profile of the home shopping channel user?

9. Name some companies that currently employ direct selling methods. What form of direct selling do they employ?

10. How is the effectiveness of a direct marketing program measured?

Chapter **17**

Sales Promotion

Chapter Objectives

- To understand the role of sales promotion in a company's integrated marketing communications program and to examine why it is increasingly important.
- To examine the various objectives of sales promotion programs.
- To examine the types of consumer- and trade-oriented sales promotion tools and factors to consider in using them.

- To understand how sales promotion is coordinated with advertising.
- To consider potential problems and abuse by companies in their use of sales promotion.

Concert Sponsorships Have Marketers Singing Profitable Tunes

When people think of Sears Roebuck, rock and roll usually isn't the first thing that comes to mind. But the retailing giant is adamant about changing its stodgy image and getting its name and message out to a new audience. So it decided to do what many other companies are doing in the 90s—use event sponsorship by becoming the exclusive sponsor of Phil Collins's 1994 US summer concert tour.

There was a heavy Sears presence at each concert, including banners near the stage and posters throughout the various venues. The sponsorship plan also had Collins appear in some Sears stores during the tour and included contests with concert tickets as the prizes. Sears sold Collins's new albums at value prices and developed tie-ins with local homelessness charities, an important concern of Collins's. Sears used both national and local advertising to promote the tour.

It is becoming common for companies to sponsor concert tours and leverage them into integrated marketing communication programs. Visa sponsored Paul McCartney's US tour a few years ago in a deal that included his appearance in Visa TV ads. Pepsi-Cola sponsored several of Michael Jackson's worldwide tours and used him in commercials around the globe to appeal to the new generation of Pepsi drinkers. PepsiCo.'s Frito-Lay snack foods division sponsored the 1993 tour of country music heartthrob Billy Ray Cyrus.

One of the reasons why many companies are sponsoring these tours is that they can leverage local concerts to drive store traffic and sales. Retailers often boost in-store support, sometimes shelling out their own marketing dollars to promote the concerts in local ads. Companies also develop tie-ins with local radio and TV stations that add free media support and give them additional exposure.

Many firms are using companies that specialize in event marketing to set retail strategy and sell local retailers on participation. One such company is PS Productions of Chicago, which uses incentives like concert tickets, local charity fund-raisers, and celebrity appearances to persuade retailers to buy into an event. When PS promoted the Beach Boys tour for Dial Corp.'s Tone soap, the group went to supermarkets, accompanied Dial salespeople on calls to major retailers, and appeared at backstage parties in all 23 cities on the tour. Twenty-five top retailers in each city got free tickets to the parties and about 300 front-row tickets were given to retailers who ordered large quantities of Tone and other Dial products. Customers could get $3 off concert tickets with each purchase of a multipack of Tone soap, and there were sweepstakes for tickets and other prizes.

PS calculates sales goals for each market based on the cost of the event and the value of extras such as donated media, customized displays and ads for key retailers, and tickets given away. Many marketers use IRI or Nielsen scanner data to track sales when the concert's in town and compare them to non-event market sales. Companies like Dial Corp. and Colgate-Palmolive use sales tracking data to calculate how much to pay for an event and choose the cities for a tour. For example, Dial chose the 23 cities on the 1993 Beach Boys tour based on what markets it thought needed special attention.

Companies are finding that concert sponsorship can have a tremendous impact on their sales. The Beach Boys concert sponsorship helped pump new life into Tone soap as many retailers gave the brand end-aisle displays and bought two to four times their normal volume. The program was so successful that Dial signed the Beach Boys to promote Premier Cruise lines, a Dial subsidiary, on their next concert tour.

Sources: Betsy Spethmann, "Sponsors Sing a Profitable Tune in Concert with Event Promos," BrandWeek, Jan. 24, 1994, pp. 20–22; Kevin Goldman, "Sears, Seeking to Change Image, Plans to Sponsor Phil Collins Tour," The Wall Street Journal, Jan. 4, 1994, p. B4; Phyllis Gillespie, "Dial Corp. Takes New Approach to Marketing," Arizona Republic, Sept. 24, 1993, p. D1.

arketers have come to recognize that advertising alone is not always enough to move their products off store shelves and into the hands of consumers. Companies are increasingly turning to sales promotion methods targeted at both consumers and the wholesalers and retailers that distribute their products to stimulate demand. Most companies' integrated marketing communication programs include consumer and trade promotions that are coordinated with advertising, direct marketing, and publicity/public relations campaigns as well as sales force efforts.

This chapter focuses on the role of sales promotion in a firm's integrated marketing communications program. We examine how marketers use both consumer- and trade-oriented promotions to influence the purchase behavior of consumers as well as wholesalers and retailers. We explore the objectives of sales promotion programs and the various types of sales promotion tools that can be used at both the consumer and trade level. We also consider how sales promotion can be integrated with other elements of the promotional mix and look at problems that can arise when marketers become overly dependent on consumer and trade promotions, particularly the latter.

THE SCOPE AND ROLE OF SALES PROMOTION

Sales promotion has been defined as "a direct inducement that offers an extra value or incentive for the product to the sales force, distributors, or the ultimate consumer with the primary objective of creating an immediate sale."[1] Several important aspects of sales promotion should be kept in mind as you read this chapter.

First, sales promotion involves some type of inducement that provides an *extra incentive* to buy. This incentive is usually the key element in a promotional program; it may be a coupon or price reduction, the opportunity to enter a contest or sweepstakes, a money-back refund or rebate, or an extra amount of a product. The incentive may also be a free sample of the product, given in hopes of generating a future purchase, or a premium, which serves as a reminder of the brand and reinforces its image, such as the Trix hypnotic sunglasses offer (Exhibit 17–1). Most sales promotion offers attempt to add some value to the product or service. While advertising appeals to the mind and emotions to give the consumer a reason to buy, sales promotion appeals more to the pocketbook and provides an incentive for purchasing a brand.

Sales promotion can also provide an inducement to marketing intermediaries such as wholesalers and retailers. A trade allowance or discount provides retailers with a financial incentive to stock and promote a manufacturer's products. A trade contest directed toward wholesalers or retail personnel gives them extra incentive to perform certain tasks or meet sales goals.

A second point regarding sales promotion is that it is essentially an *acceleration tool*, designed to speed up the selling process and maximize sales volume.[2] By providing an extra incentive, sales promotion techniques can motivate consumers to purchase a larger quantity of a brand or shorten the purchase cycle of the trade or consumers by encouraging them to take more immediate action.

EXHIBIT 17–1

Trix offers a premium to provide extra incentive to purchase a brand

Companies also use limited time offers such as price-off deals to retailers or a coupon with an expiration date to accelerate the purchase process. Sales promotion attempts to maximize sales volume by motivating customers who have not responded to advertising. The ideal sales promotion program generates sales that would not be achieved by other means such as advertising. However, as we shall see later, many sales promotion offers end up being used by current users of a brand rather than attracting new users.

A final point regarding sales promotion activities is that they can be targeted to different parties in the marketing channel. As shown in Exhibit 17–2, sales promotion can be broken into two major categories: consumer-oriented and trade-oriented promotions. Activities involved in **consumer-oriented sales promotion** include sampling, couponing, premiums, rebates, contests, sweepstakes, bonus packs, price-offs, and event sponsorship. These promotions are directed at the consumers who purchase goods and services and are designed to induce them to purchase the marketer's brand.

As discussed in Chapter 2, consumer-oriented promotions are part of a promotional pull strategy; they work along with advertising to encourage consumers to purchase a particular brand and thus create demand for it. Consumer-oriented promotions are also used by retailers to encourage consumers to shop in their particular stores. Many grocery stores use their own coupons or sponsor contests and other promotions to increase store patronage.

Trade-oriented sales promotion includes promotional allowances, dealer contests and incentives, point-of-purchase displays, cooperative advertising, trade shows, and other programs designed to motivate distributors and retailers to carry a product and make an extra effort to promote or push it to their customers. Nearly two-thirds of all sales promotional dollars are spent on trade promotions. Many marketing programs include both trade- and consumer-oriented promotions, since motivating both groups maximizes the effectiveness of the promotional program.

 **THE GROWTH OF SALES PROMOTION**

While sales promotion has been around for a long time, its role and importance in manufacturers' marketing programs have increased dramatically. Not only has the total amount of money spent on sales promotion increased, but the percentage of marketers' budgets allocated to promotion has also risen dramatically. Annual studies by Donnelley Marketing track the marketing spending of major package-goods companies in three categories: trade promotion, consumer promotion, and media advertising. Exhibit 17–3 shows the long-term trend of allocations to each category. The percentage of the marketing budget spent on consumer promotions has held steady over the past decade, while the allocation to trade promotions has increased dramatically.

EXHIBIT 17–2

Types of sales promotion activities

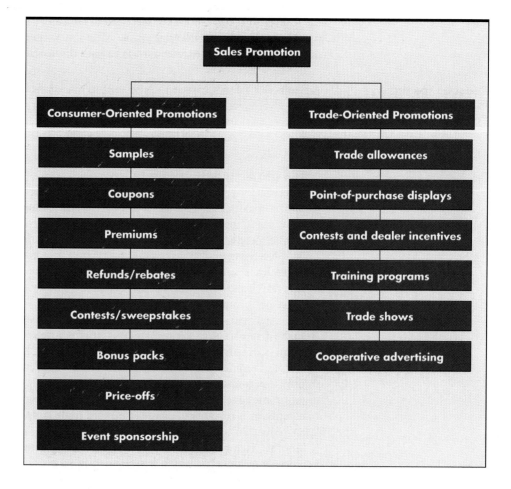

@ **EXHIBIT   17–3**   Long-term allocations to trade promotion, advertising, and consumer promotion

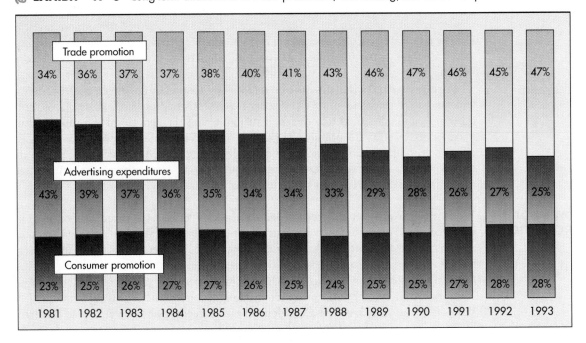

This increase in trade promotion spending has come almost totally at the expense of media advertising. Marketers say they expect trade spending to decline somewhat in the future, with corresponding increases in consumer promotions and media advertising. However, many marketing people believe it will be difficult to reverse the flow of marketing dollars to the trade, for the reasons discussed below.

Reasons for the Increase in Sales Promotion

A number of factors have led to the shift in marketing dollars to sales promotion from media advertising. Among them are the growing power of retailers, declining brand loyalty, increased promotional sensitivity, brand proliferation, fragmentation of the consumer market, short-term focus, increased accountability, competition, and clutter.

The growing power of retailers

One reason for the increase in sales promotion is the power shift in the marketplace from manufacturers to retailers. For many years, manufacturers of national brands had the power and influence, and retailers were just passive distributors of their products. Consumer products manufacturers created consumer demand for their brands by using heavy advertising and some consumer-oriented promotions, such as samples, coupons, and premiums, and exerted pressure on retailers to carry the products. Retailers did very little research and sales analysis; they relied on manufacturers for information regarding the sales performance of individual brands.

In recent years, however, several developments have resulted in power transferring from the manufacturers to the retailers. With the advent of optical checkout scanners and computers, retailers gained access to data concerning how quickly products turn over, which sales promotions are working, and which products make money. Retailers use this information to analyze sales of manufacturers' products and then demand discounts and other promotional support from manufacturers of lagging brands. Companies that fail to comply with retailers' demands for more trade support often face having their shelf space reduced or even their product dropped.

Another factor that has increased the power of retailers is the consolidation of the grocery store industry, which has resulted in larger chains with greater buying power and clout. These large chains have become accustomed to trade promotions and can pressure manufacturers to provide deals, discounts, and allowances.

Declining brand loyalty

Another major reason for the increase in sales promotion is that consumers have become less brand loyal in recent years and are purchasing more on the basis of price, value, and convenience. You may recall from Chapter 4 (Exhibit 4–18) that the percentage of consumers who are brand loyal is under 50 percent for most product categories.[3] Many consumers switch back and forth among a set of brands they view as essentially equal. These brands are all perceived as being satisfactory and interchangeable, and consumers purchase whatever brand is on special or for which they have a coupon.

Increased promotional sensitivity

Marketers are making greater use of sales promotion because consumers respond favorably to it. The percentage of purchases made in conjunction with some sort of promotional offer has increased sharply over the past decade.[4] In one recent study, consumers said 54 percent of their purchases were made under some promotional inducement, with price promotions, coupons, and point-of-purchase displays being the most important.[5] A national survey of 7,500 households found that over 90 percent of consumers had taken advantage of some form of promotion in the past month. Coupons were particularly popular among consumers as a way to get greater value.[6]

An obvious reason for consumers' increased sensitivity to sales promotion offers is that they save money. Another reason is that many purchase decisions are made at the point of purchase by consumers who are increasingly time sensitive and facing too many choices.[7] When consumers make purchase decisions in the store, they are likely to respond to promotional deals. Buying a brand that is on special or being displayed can simplify the decision-making process and deal with the problem of overchoice. Professor Leigh McAlister has described this process:

> As consumers go down the supermarket aisle they spend 3 to 10 seconds in each product category. They often don't know the regular price of the chosen product. However, they do have a sense of whether or not that product is on promotion. As they go down the aisle, they are trying to pensively fill their baskets with good products without tiresome calculations. They see a "good deal" and it goes in the cart.[8]

Brand proliferation

A major aspect of many firms' marketing strategies over the past decade has been the development of new products. Over 10,000 new products were introduced to the marketplace in 1993 (compared with only 2,689 in 1980). The market has become saturated with new brands that often lack any significant advantages that can be used as the basis of an advertising campaign. Thus, companies increasingly depend on sales promotion to encourage consumers to try these brands. In Chapter 4, we saw how sales promotion techniques can be used as part of the shaping process to lead the consumer from initial trial to repeat purchase at full price. Marketers are relying more on promotional tools such as samples, coupons, rebates, premiums, and other innovative promotions to achieve trial usage of their new brands and encourage repeat purchase (Exhibit 17–4).

Promotions are also important in getting retailers to allocate some of their precious shelf space to new brands. The competition for shelf space allocation for new products in supermarkets and other stores is enormous. Retailers are more open to new brands with strong sales promotion support that will bring in more customers and boost their sales and profits.[9] Many retailers require special discounts or allowances from manufacturers just to handle a new product. These slotting fees or allowances, which are discussed later in the chapter, can make it expensive for a manufacturer to introduce a new product.

@ **EXHIBIT 17–4**

Sales promotion tools are often used to encourage trial of a new brand

Fragmentation of the consumer market

As the consumer market becomes more fragmented and traditional mass media–based advertising less effective, marketers are turning to more segmented, highly targeted approaches. With the increasing focus on regional marketing, more major companies are tailoring their promotional efforts to specific geographic markets and even to certain retail chains.[10] Sales promotion tools have become one of the primary vehicles for doing this, through programs tied into local flavor, themes, or events. For example, Burger King spends nearly half of its advertising budget on local tie-ins and promotions designed to build traffic in its restaurants.

Marketers are also shifting more of their promotional efforts to direct marketing, which often includes some form of sales promotion incentive. Many marketers use information they get from premium offers, trackable coupons, rebates, and sweepstakes to build databases for future direct-marketing efforts. As marketers continue to shift from media advertising to direct marketing, promotional offers will probably be used to help build databases.

Short-term focus

Many businesspeople believe the increase in sales promotion is motivated by marketing plans and reward systems geared to short-term performance and the immediate generation of sales volume.[11] Some think the package-goods brand management system has contributed to marketers' increased dependence on sales promotion. Brand managers use sales promotions routinely, not only to introduce new products or defend against the competition, but also to meet quarterly or yearly sales and market share goals. Brand managers are not the only people who champion the use of sales promotion. The sales force may have short-term quotas or goals to meet and may also receive requests from retailers and wholesalers for promotions. Thus, reps may pressure marketing or brand managers to use promotions to help them move the products into the retailers' stores.

Consumer and trade promotions are viewed by many managers as the most dependable way of generating short-term sales, particularly when they are price related. The reliance on sales promotion is particularly high in mature and slow-growth markets, where it is difficult to stimulate consumer demand through advertising. This has led to concern that managers have become too dependent on the quick sales fix that can result from a promotion and that the brand franchise may be eroded by too many deals.

Increased accountability

In addition to pressuring their marketing or brand managers and sales force to produce short-term results, many companies are demanding to know what they are getting from their promotional expenditures. Sales promotion is more economically accountable than advertising. In companies struggling to meet their sales and financial goals, top management is demanding measurable, accountable ways to relate promotional expenditures to sales and profitability. For example, Philip Morris's Kraft General Foods unit and other companies have begun using computerized sales information from checkout scanners in determining compensation for marketing personnel. Part of the pay managers receive depends on the sales a promotion generates relative to its costs.[12]

Managers who are being held accountable to produce results often use price discounts or coupons, since they produce a quick and easily measured jump in sales. It takes longer for an ad campaign to show some impact and the effects are more difficult to measure. Also, marketers are feeling pressure from the trade as powerful retailers demand sales performance from their brands.

Competition

Another factor that led to the increase in sales promotion is manufacturers' reliance on trade and consumer promotions to gain or maintain competitive advantage. The markets for many products are mature and stagnant, and it is increasingly difficult to boost sales through advertising. Exciting, breakthrough creative ideas are difficult to come by, and consumers' attention to mass media advertising continues to decline. Rather than allocating large amounts of money to run dull ads, many marketers have turned to sales promotion.

Many companies are tailoring their trade promotions to key retail accounts and developing strategic alliances with retailers that include both trade and consumer promotional programs. However, retailers may use a promotional deal with one company as leverage to seek an equal or better deal with its competitors. Consumer and trade promotions are easily matched by competitors, and many marketers find themselves in a promotional trap where they must continue using promotions or be at a competitive disadvantage. (We discuss this problem in more detail later in the chapter.)

Clutter

The increasing problem of advertising clutter has led many advertisers to turn to promotions to attract consumers' attention to their ads. A promotional offer in an ad can break through the clutter that is prevalent in most media today. A premium offer may help attract attention to an ad, as will a contest or sweepstakes. Some studies have shown that readership scores are higher for print ads with coupons than for ads without them.[13] However, more recent studies by Starch INRA Hooper, Inc., suggest that magazine ads with coupons do not generate higher readership.[14]

Concerns over the Increased Role of Sales Promotion

Many factors have contributed to the increased use of sales promotion by consumer product manufacturers. Marketing and advertising executives are concerned about how this shift in the allocation of the promotional budget affects brand equity. As noted in Chapter 2, *brand equity*, or *consumer franchise*, is an intangible asset of added value or goodwill that results from consumers' favorable image, impressions of differentiation, and/or strength of attachment to a brand.

Some critics argue that sales promotion increases come at the expense of brand equity and every dollar that goes into promotion rather than advertising devalues the brand.[15] They say trade promotions in particular contribute to the destruction of brand franchises and equity as they encourage consumers to purchase primarily on the basis of price. Studies conducted by ad agency DDB Needham Worldwide show that the percentage of consumers who say they purchase well-known brands has declined from 77 percent in 1975 to 62 percent.[16]

Proponents of advertising argue that marketers must maintain strong franchises if they want to differentiate their brands and charge a premium price for them. They say advertising is still the most effective way to build the long-term franchise of a brand as it informs consumers of a brand's features and benefits, creates an image, and helps build and maintain brand loyalty. However, many marketers are not investing in their brands as they take monies away from media advertising to fund short-term promotions. If this trend continues, brands may lose the equity that advertising helped create and be forced to compete primarily on the basis of price.

Many of these concerns are justified, but not all sales promotion activities detract from the value or equity of a brand. It is important to distinguish between consumer-franchise-building and nonfranchise-building sales promotions.

Consumer-Franchise-Building versus Nonfranchise-Building Promotions

Sales promotion activities that communicate distinctive brand attributes and contribute to the development and reinforcement of brand identity are **consumer-franchise-building (CFB) promotions**.[17] Consumer sales promotion efforts cannot make consumers loyal to a brand that is of little value or does not provide them with a specific benefit. But they can make consumers aware of a brand and, by communicating its specific features and benefits, contribute to the development of a favorable brand image. Consumer-franchise-building promotions are designed to build long-term brand preference and help the company achieve the ultimate goal of full-price purchases that do not depend on a promotional offer.

For years, franchise or image building was viewed as the exclusive realm of advertising, and sales promotion was used only to generate short-term sales increases. But now marketers are recognizing the image-building potential of sales promotion and paying attention to its CFB value. A 1993 survey of senior marketing executives found that 88 percent believe consumer promotions can help build a brand's equity and 58 percent think trade promotions can contribute.[18] One sales promotion expert says:

> Today's marketers who appreciate the potential of sales promotion as an ongoing strategy that works to build a brand's franchise recognize that promotion's potential goes well beyond mere quick-fix, price-off tactics. The promotion professional is familiar with a variety of approaches to generating consumer involvement—that is, sweepstakes, special events, premiums, or rebates—and understands that the given campaign must work in harmony with long-term goals and brand positioning.[19]

Companies can use sales promotion techniques in a number of ways to contribute to franchise building. Rather than using a one-time offer, many companies are developing promotional programs that encourage repeat purchases and long-term patronage. Many credit cards have promotional programs where consumers earn bonus points every time they use their card to charge a purchase. These points can then be redeemed for various items. Most airlines and many hotel chains offer frequent flyer or guest programs to encourage repeat patronage. Fast-food chains such as McDonald's, Arby's, and Hardee's have begun testing frequency programs to build loyalty and encourage repeat purchases by their patrons.[20]

Companies also can use sales promotion to contribute to franchise building by developing an offer consistent with the image or positioning of the brand. One successful consumer-franchise-building promotion is the bone china sweepstakes for Palmolive dishwashing liquid and dishwasher detergent shown in Exhibit 17–5. For many consumers, an important factor in choosing a dishwashing product is that it does not harm dishes. The "Trust your best with our best" association with expensive Royal Doulton bone china helps to position the Palmolive products as being gentle enough to use on even the best dishes. Colgate-Palmolive has run this successful promotion for several years.

Nonfranchise-building (non-FB) promotions are designed to accelerate the purchase decision process and generate an immediate increase in sales. These activities do not communicate information about a brand's unique features or the benefits of using it, so they do not contribute to the building of brand identity and image. Price-off deals, bonus packs, and rebates or refunds are examples of non-FB sales promotion techniques.

◎ EXHIBIT 17–5

The bone china sweepstakes is an excellent example of a consumer-franchise-building promotion

Trade promotions receive the most criticism for being nonfranchise building—for good reason. First, many of the promotional discounts and allowances given to the trade are never passed on to consumers. Most trade promotions that are forwarded through the channels reach consumers in the form of lower prices or special deals and lead them to buy on the basis of price rather than brand equity.

Many specialists in the promotional area stress the need for marketers to use sales promotion tools to build a franchise and create long-term continuity in their promotional programs.[21] Whereas non-FB promotions merely borrow customers from other brands, well-planned CFB activities can convert consumers to loyal customers. Short-term non-FB promotions have their place in a firm's promotional mix, particularly when competitive developments warrant such activities. But their limitations must be recognized when a long-term marketing strategy for a brand is developed.

◎ CONSUMER-ORIENTED SALES PROMOTION

In this section, we examine the various sales promotion tools and techniques marketers can use to influence consumers. We study the various consumer-oriented promotions shown in Exhibit 17–2 and discuss their advantages and limitations. First, we consider some objectives marketers have for sales promotion programs targeted to the consumer market.

Objectives for Consumer-Oriented Sales Promotion

As the use of sales promotion techniques continues to increase, companies must consider what they hope to accomplish through their consumer promotions and how they interact with other promotional activities such as advertising, direct marketing, and personal selling. When marketers implement sales promotion programs without considering their long-term cumulative effect on the brand's image and position in the marketplace, they often do little more than create short-term spikes in the sales curve.

Not all sales promotion activities are designed to achieve the same objectives. As with any promotional mix element, marketers must plan consumer promotions by conducting a situation analysis and determining sales promotion's specific role in the integrated marketing communications program. Attention must be given to what the promotion is designed to accomplish and to whom it should be targeted. By having clearly defined objectives and measurable goals for their sales promotion programs, managers are forced to think beyond the short-term sales fix (although this can be a goal).

While the basic goal of most consumer-oriented sales promotion programs is to induce purchase of a brand, the marketer might have a number of different objectives for both new and established brands—for example, obtaining trial and repurchase, increasing consumption of an established brand, defending current customers, or enhancing advertising and marketing efforts.

@ EXHIBIT 17–6

Arm & Hammer used this FSI to promote a specific use for the product

Obtaining trial and repurchase

One of the most important uses of sales promotion techniques is to encourage consumers to try a new product or service. While thousands of new products are introduced to the market every year, as many as 90 percent of them fail within the first year. Many of these failures are due to the fact that the new product or brand lacks the promotional support needed either to encourage initial trial by enough consumers or to induce enough of those trying the brand to repurchase it. Many new brands are merely new versions of an existing product without benefits so unique that advertising alone can induce trial. Sales promotion tools have become an important part of new brand introduction strategies; the level of initial trial can be increased through techniques such as sampling, couponing, and refund offers.

The success of a new brand depends not only on getting initial trial but also on inducing a reasonable percentage of those who try the brand to repurchase it and establish ongoing purchase patterns. Promotional incentives such as coupons or refund offers are often included with a sample to encourage repeat purchase after trial. For example, when Lever Brothers introduced its Lever 2000 brand of bar soap, it distributed millions of free samples along with a 75-cent coupon. The samples allowed consumers to try the new soap, while the coupon provided an incentive to purchase it.

Increasing consumption of an established brand

Many marketing managers are responsible for established brands competing in mature markets, against established competitors, where consumer purchase patterns are often well set. Awareness of an established brand is generally high as a result of cumulative advertising effects, and many consumers have probably tried the brand. These factors can create a challenging situation for the brand manager who hopes to increase sales of the product or defend its market share against a competitor. Sales promotion can generate some new interest in an established brand to help increase sales or defend market share against competitive threats.

Marketers attempt to increase sales for an established brand in several ways, and sales promotion can play an important role in each. One way to increase product consumption is by identifying new uses for the brand. Sales promotion tools like recipe books or calendars that show various ways of using the product are often used to accomplish this. One of the best examples of a brand that has found new uses is Arm & Hammer baking soda. Exhibit 17–6 shows a clever free-standing insert (FSI) that promotes the brand's new Fridge-Freezer Pack, which absorbs more odors in refrigerators and freezers.

Another strategy for increasing sales of an established brand is to use promotions that attract nonusers of the product category or users of a competing brand. Attracting nonusers of the product category can be very difficult, as consumers may not see a need for the product. However, sales promotions can be designed to appeal to nonusers by providing them with an extra incentive to try the product. A more common strategy

EXHIBIT   17–7   The Pepsi Challenge was a very successful promotion for attracting users of a competitive brand

ANNCR: All across America people are taking the Pepsi Challenge. In California here's what they are saying.

TRACY KUERBIS: Pepsi really is the better drink.

DAVE JOHNSON: I've proven to myself now that I like Pepsi better.

ANNCR: Nationwide more people prefer the taste of Pepsi over Coca-Cola.

CHERIE BOOTH: I think today's test was very honest.

DAVE: Pepsi has a better product and that's probably why they are running a test like this because it's obvious how many people over here have picked Pepsi.

SUZANNE MACK: Being able to compare the two, I'd pick Pepsi.

CHERIE: If someone offered me either or, I choose the Pepsi.

ANNCR: What will you say? Take the Pepsi Challenge and find out.

for increasing sales of an established brand is to attract consumers who use a competing brand. This can be done by giving them an incentive to switch such as a coupon, premium offer, bonus pack, or price deal. Marketers can also get users of a competitive brand to try another brand through sampling or other types of promotional programs.

One of the most successful promotions ever used to attract users of a competing brand was the Pepsi Challenge. In this campaign, Pepsi took on its archrival, industry leader Coca-Cola, in a hard-hitting comparative promotion that challenged consumers to taste the two brands in blind taste tests (Exhibit 17–7). The Pepsi Challenge promotion included national and local advertising, couponing, and trade support as part of a fully integrated promotional program. The campaign was used for several years and was instrumental in helping Pepsi move ahead of Coke to become the market share leader in supermarket sales. As a result of the campaign, Coke launched a variety of counterattacks, including the controversial decision to change its formula and launch New Coke in 1986.

Defending current customers

With more new brands entering the market every day and competitors attempting to take away their customers through aggressive advertising and sales promotion efforts, many companies are turning to sales promotion programs to hold present customers and defend their market share. A company can use sales promotion techniques in several ways to retain its current customer base. One way is to load them with the product, taking them out of the market for a certain time. Special price promotions, coupons, or bonus packs can encourage the consumer to stock up on the brand. This not only keeps consumers using the company's brand but also reduces the likelihood they will switch brands in response to a competitor's promotion.

Enhancing advertising and marketing efforts

A final objective for consumer trade promotions is to enhance or support the advertising and marketing effort for the brand. Sales promotion techniques such as contests or sweepstakes are often used to draw attention to an ad and increase the consumer's involvement with the message and the product. Sales promotion programs can also encourage retailers to stock, display, and promote a brand during the promotional period. Cooperation from the trade is important to the success of a promotional program.

@ **EXHIBIT 17–8**

Types of consumer promotions used by large and small firms

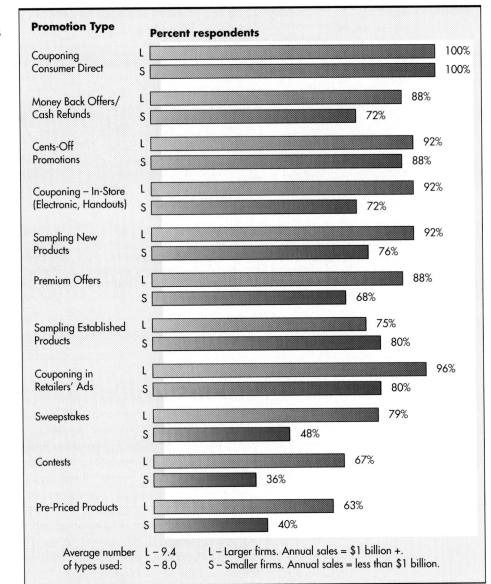

Promotion Type		Percent respondents
Couponing Consumer Direct	L	100%
	S	100%
Money Back Offers/ Cash Refunds	L	88%
	S	72%
Cents-Off Promotions	L	92%
	S	88%
Couponing – In-Store (Electronic, Handouts)	L	92%
	S	72%
Sampling New Products	L	92%
	S	76%
Premium Offers	L	88%
	S	68%
Sampling Established Products	L	75%
	S	80%
Couponing in Retailers' Ads	L	96%
	S	80%
Sweepstakes	L	79%
	S	48%
Contests	L	67%
	S	36%
Pre-Priced Products	L	63%
	S	40%

Average number of types used: L – 9.4   L – Larger firms. Annual sales = $1 billion +.
S – 8.0   S – Smaller firms. Annual sales = less than $1 billion.

@ **CONSUMER-ORIENTED SALES PROMOTION TECHNIQUES**

In this section, we examine the various sales promotional techniques used by marketers and the role they play in meeting the objectives discussed above. Exhibit 17–8 shows the extent to which these consumer promotions are used by package-goods companies of all sizes.

Sampling

Sampling involves a variety of procedures whereby consumers are given some quantity of a product for no charge to induce trial. Sampling is generally considered the most effective way of generating trial, although it is also the most expensive. As a sales promotion technique, sampling is often used to introduce a new product or brand to the market. However, as Exhibit 17–8 shows, sampling is also used for established products—particularly by large companies. Some companies do not use sampling for established products since samples may not induce satisfied users of a competing brand to switch and may just go to the firm's current customers, who would buy the product. This may not be true when significant changes (new and improved) are made in a brand.

Manufacturers of package-goods products such as food, health-care items, cosmetics, and toiletries are heavy users of sampling since their products meet the three criteria for an effective sampling program:

1. The products are of relatively low unit value, so samples do not cost too much.
2. The products are divisible, which means they can be broken into small sample sizes that are adequate for demonstrating the brand's features and benefits to the user.
3. The purchase cycle for these products is relatively short, so the consumer will consider an immediate purchase or will not forget about the brand before the next purchase occasion.

Benefits and limitations of sampling

Samples are an excellent way to induce a prospective buyer to try a product or service. One expert estimates approximately 75 percent of the households receiving a sample will try it.[22] The trial rates generated by a sampling program are much higher than those produced by advertising or other sales promotion techniques.

Getting people to try a product leads to a second benefit of sampling—consumers experience the brand directly, gaining a greater appreciation for its benefits. This can be particularly important when a product's features and benefits are difficult to describe through advertising. Many foods, beverages, and cosmetics are products whose subtle features are most appreciated when experienced directly.

The marketer must believe the brand has some unique or superior benefits for a sampling program to be worthwhile. Otherwise, the sampled consumers revert back to other brands and do not become repeat purchasers. The costs of a sampling program can be recovered only if it gets a number of consumers to become regular users of the brand at full retail price.

Another possible limitation to sampling is that the benefits of some products are difficult to gauge immediately, and the learning period required to appreciate the brand may require supplying the consumer with larger amounts of the brand than are affordable. For example, an expensive skin cream that is promoted as preventing or reducing wrinkles would have to be used for an extended period before any effects might be noticed.

Sampling methods

One basic decision the sales promotion or brand manager must make concerns the method by which the sample will be distributed. The sampling method chosen is important not only in terms of costs but also in terms of influencing the type of consumer who receives the sample. The best sampling method gets the product to the best prospects for trial and subsequent repurchase. Some basic distribution methods include door-to-door, direct mail, in-store, and on-package approaches.

Door-to-door sampling, in which the sample is delivered directly to the prospect's residence, is used when it is important to control where the samples are delivered. While virtually any type of product samples can be delivered this way, this method is on the decline because of the labor expense involved. Some companies have their samples delivered directly as part of a cooperative effort where several product samples are sent to a household together or through services such as Welcome Wagon, which calls on new residents in an area.

Sampling through the mail is common for small, lightweight, nonperishable products such as those shown in Exhibit 17–9A. A major advantage of this method is that the marketer has control over where and when the product will be distributed and can target the sample to specific market areas. Many marketers are using information from companies such as Claritas's PRIZM target marketing programs or Equifax/National Decision System's Microvision to better target their sample mailings. The main drawbacks to mail sampling are postal restrictions and increasing postal rates.

In-store sampling is increasingly popular, particularly for food products. The marketer hires temporary demonstrators who set up a table or booth, prepare small samples of the product, and pass them out to shoppers. The in-store sampling approach can be very effective for food products, since consumers get to taste the item and the demonstrator can give them more information about the product while it is being sampled. Demonstrators may also give consumers a cents-off coupon for the sampled item to encourage

⊚ EXHIBIT   17–9A

Product samples sent through the mail

IMC Perspective 17-1
The Resurgence in Sampling

Marketers have long recognized that the best way to get consumers to try their products is to give them a free sample. Many companies cut back on their sampling programs in recent years because they felt they were too expensive, wasteful, and fraught with distribution problems. Sampling became a tool for megabrands looking to blanket the country or smaller brands trying to reach a smaller crowd at the beach or county fair. But now sampling is undergoing a renaissance of sorts. A variety of marketers are showing new interest in this sales promotion technique.

There are a number of factors behind the resurgence of sampling. First, big companies like Advo Inc. and Time-Warner have entered the sampling business, which creates more competition and helps keep sampling costs down. Also, a combination of technology and creativity is driving new sampling methods that offer marketers greater targeting and efficiency. Yet another factor may be the everyday low pricing strategies that have prompted some companies to move away from coupons and other price promotions in favor of samples.

A number of creative new sampling programs have been introduced recently. For example, the Skiing Co., which is a marketing arm of Times-Mirror Magazines, joined forces with Resorts Marketing to fill a goody bag of samples for sponsor *Ski* magazine's Ski-Wee program. Nearly 300,000 sample bags were given to parents when they retrieved their kids from Ski-Wee classes. The program was supported with print and TV spots featuring a toll-free number and exposure at 10 consumer ski shows. Advo Inc. recently bought Samplicity, a direct mail sample vehicle that can reach 53 million households a week. The company also acquired Marketing Force, an in-store merchandising firm that can now put its 13,000 field reps to work handing out samples for Advo clients.

Sampling is also becoming popular because marketers recognize that it can help introduce new products. For example, Kendall-Futuro, the marketer of Curad adhesive strips, inserted kid-size bandage sample packs and coupons into 7.5 million McDonald's Happy Meals. The sampling promotion created so much exposure for the new brand, which was decorated with images of McDonald's characters, that the subsequent retail sell-in exceeded projections by 30 percent.

Sampling can also create awareness for complementary products. Hires root beer partnered with Hood ice cream in a "How do you make a black cow float" promotion. A sampling firm set up shop outside more than 40 supermarkets and handed out root beer floats and recipe booklets containing coupons for a free two-liter bottle of Hires with the purchase of a half-gallon of Hood ice cream. The two companies split the coupon redemption costs and were both happy, as the sampling program generated additional retail displays and increased sales for both brands.

The ultimate value of a sampling is, of course, the conversion of the consumer to a regular user following trial. However, marketers are finding that sampling meets the complementary goals of introducing consumers to their products and getting retailers to support their promotional programs.

Source: Glenn Heitsmith, "Something for Nothing," *Promo,* Sept. 1993, pp. 30–36, 78–80; and "Still Bullish on Promotion," *Promo,* July 1994, p. 40.

---

immediate trial purchase. While this sampling method can be very effective, it can also be expensive and requires a great deal of planning, as well as the cooperation of retailers.

On-package sampling, where a sample of a product is attached to another item, is another common sampling method (see Exhibit 17–9B). This procedure can be very cost effective, particularly for multiproduct firms that attach a sample of a new product to an existing brand's package. However, since the sample is distributed only to consumers who purchase the item to which it is attached, the sample will not reach nonusers of the carrier brand. Marketers can expand this sampling method by attaching the sample to multiple carrier brands and including samples with products not made by the company.

Other methods of sampling

The four sampling methods just discussed are the most common, but several other methods are also used. Marketers may insert packets in magazines or newspapers (particularly Sunday supplements). Some tobacco and cereal companies send samples to consumers who call toll-free numbers to request them or mail in sample request forms. As discussed in Chapter 16, these sampling methods are becoming popular because they can help marketers build a database for direct marketing.

Many companies also use specialized sample distribution services such as Advo Inc., Donnelley Marketing, and D. L. Blair. These firms help the company identify consumers who are nonusers of a product or users of a competing brand and develop appropriate procedures for distributing a sample to them. As college students, many of you probably received sample packs at the beginning of the semester that contained trial sizes of such products as mouthwash, toothpaste, headache remedies, and deodorant. IMC Perspective 17–1 discusses the resurgence in sampling that is taking place as more creative distribution options offer more targeted, cost–efficient distribution.

EXHIBIT 17-9B

Armor All uses on-package samples for related products

EXHIBIT 17-10

Doubling couponing is common in the supermarket industry

Couponing

The oldest, most widely used, and most effective sales promotion tool is the *cents-off coupon*. Coupons have been around since 1895, when the C. W. Post Co. started using the penny-off coupon to sell its new Grape-Nuts cereal. In recent years, coupons have become increasingly popular with consumers, which may explain their explosive growth among manufacturers and retailers who use them as sales promotion incentives. As Exhibit 17–8 shows, coupons are the most popular sales promotion technique and are used by all the package-goods firms in the Donnelley survey.

The number of coupons distributed by marketers increased from 16 billion in 1968 to 298 billion in 1993.[23] Coupon distribution rose dramatically during the 1980s and into the 90s, with an average annual growth rate of 11 percent. According to studies by NCH Promotional Services, nearly 80 percent of U.S. households use coupons and 39 percent use five or more coupons per week. The average face value of coupons increased from 21 cents in 1981 to 58 cents in 1993.[24]

Adding additional fuel to the coupon explosion is the vast number of coupons distributed through retailers that are not even included in the aforementioned figures. In most markets, a number of grocery stores make manufacturers' coupons even more attractive to consumers by doubling their face value (Exhibit 17–10).

Advantages and limitations of coupons

Coupons have a number of advantages that make them popular sales promotional tools for both new and established products. First, coupons make it possible to offer a price reduction to those consumers who are price sensitive without having to reduce the price for everyone. Price-sensitive consumers generally purchase *because* of coupons,

EXHIBIT   17–11

Percentage of purchases made with coupons in various product categories

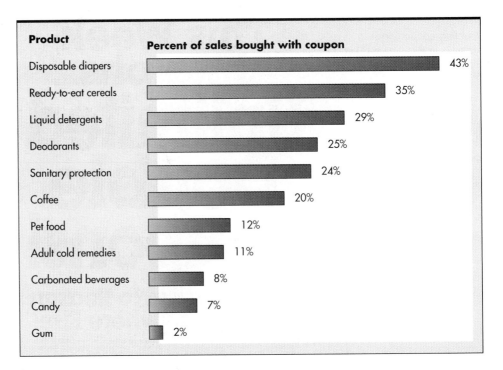

while those who are not as concerned about price buy the brand at full value. Coupons also make it possible to reduce the retail price of a product without relying on retailers for cooperation, which can often be a problem. Coupons are generally regarded as second only to sampling as a promotional technique for generating trial. Since a coupon lowers the price of a product, it reduces the consumer's perceived risk associated with trial of a new brand. Coupons can encourage repurchase after initial trial. Many new products include a cents-off coupon inside the package to encourage repeat purchase.

Coupons can also be useful promotional devices for established products. They can encourage nonusers to try a brand, encourage repeat purchase among current users, and get users to try a new, improved version of a brand. Coupons may also be helpful in getting users of a product to trade up to more expensive brands. In product categories such as disposable diapers, cereals, and detergents, coupons have become very popular. Exhibit 17–11 shows the most popular product categories for coupon users.

A number of problems are associated with the use of coupons. First, it can be difficult to estimate how many consumers will use a coupon and when. Response to a coupon is rarely immediate; the average time taken to redeem one is anywhere from two to six months. While redemption may be expedited through the use of an expiration date, coupons are generally not as effective as sampling for inducing initial product trial in a short period.

A problem associated with using coupons to attract new users to an established brand is that it is difficult to prevent the coupons from being used by consumers who already use the brand. For example, General Foods decided to reduce its use of coupons for Maxwell House coffee when research revealed the coupons were being redeemed primarily by current users.[25] Rather than attracting new users, coupons can end up reducing the company's profit margins among consumers who would probably purchase the product anyway.

Another problem with coupons is the cost. Couponing program expenses include the face value of the coupon redeemed plus costs for production, distribution, and handling of the coupons. Exhibit 17–12 shows the calculations used to determine the costs of a couponing program. The marketer should track costs closely to ensure the promotion is economically feasible.

EXHIBIT 17–12

Calculating couponing costs

Cost per Coupon Redeemed: An Illustration	
1. Distribution cost 10,000,000 circulation × $8/M	$ 80,000
2. Redemptions at 3.1%	310,000
3. Redemption cost 310,000 redemptions × $.25 face value	$ 77,500
4. Handling cost 310,000 redemptions × $.08	$ 24,800
5. Total program cost Items 1 + 3 + 4	$182,300
6. Cost per coupon redeemed Cost divided by redemptions	58.8¢
7. Actual product sold on redemption (misredemption estimated at 20%) 310,000 × 80%	$248,000
8. Cost per product moved Program cost divided by product sold	73.5¢

Another problem with coupon promotions is misredemption or the cashing of a coupon without purchase of the brand. Coupon misredemption or fraud occurs in a number of ways, including:

- Redemption of coupons by consumers for brands not actually purchased.
- Redemption of coupons by salesclerks in exchange for cash.
- Gathering and redemption of coupons by store managers or owners without the accompanying sale of the product.
- Gathering or printing of coupons by criminals who sell them to unethical merchants, who in turn redeem them.

Estimates of coupon misredemption costs are as high as $500 million. Marketers must allow a certain percentage for misredemption when estimating the costs of a couponing program. Ways to deal with the coupon misredemption, such as improved coding, are being developed, but it still remains a problem.

Coupon distribution

Coupons can be disseminated to consumers in a number of ways, including newspapers and magazines, direct mail, and packages. Distribution through newspaper free-standing inserts (FSIs) is by far the most popular method for delivering coupons to consumers. FSIs accounted for over 80 percent of all coupons distributed in 1993. This growth has come at the expense of vehicles such as manufacturers' ads in newspapers (newspaper ROP), newspaper co-op ads, and magazines.

A major advantage of media-delivered coupons is the brand exposure that results, particularly from newspapers. Many consumers actively search the newspaper for coupons, especially on Sundays or "food days" (when grocery stores advertise their specials). This enhances the likelihood of the consumer at least noticing the coupon. Distribution of coupons through magazines can take advantage of the selectivity of the publication to reach specific target audiences. Finally, coupons can be distributed through the media at reasonable costs, particularly through the free-standing inserts.

The increased distribution of coupons through FSIs has led to a clutter problem. Consumers are being bombarded with too many coupons, and although each FSI publisher offers product exclusivity in its insert, this advantage may be negated when there are three inserts in a Sunday paper. Redemption rates of FSI coupons have declined from the 7 percent range to only 2.5 percent and even lower for some products (Exhibit 17–13). These problems are leading many marketers to look at ways of delivering coupons that will result in less clutter and higher redemption rates, such as direct mail. Over the long term, many marketers will probably switch out of FSIs and into other coupon delivery methods.[26]

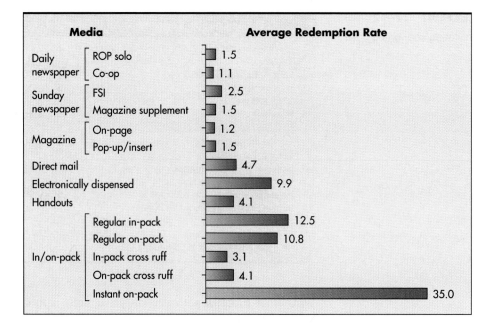

Media		Average Redemption Rate
Daily newspaper	ROP solo	1.5
	Co-op	1.1
Sunday newspaper	FSI	2.5
	Magazine supplement	1.5
Magazine	On-page	1.2
	Pop-up/insert	1.5
Direct mail		4.7
Electronically dispensed		9.9
Handouts		4.1
In/on-pack	Regular in-pack	12.5
	Regular on-pack	10.8
	In-pack cross ruff	3.1
	On-pack cross ruff	4.1
	Instant on-pack	35.0

Direct mail accounts for about 4 percent of all coupons distributed. Most are sent by local retailers or through co-op mailings where a packet of coupons for many different products is sent to a household. These couponing programs include Donnelley Marketing's Carol Wright, Metromail's Red Letter Day, Advo Systems' Mailbox Values, and Val-Pak Direct Marketing Systems.

Direct mail couponing has several advantages. First, the mailing can be sent to a broad audience or targeted to specific geographic or demographic segments. Some co-op coupon programs such as Donnelley's Carol Wright have special-market mailings to teenagers, senior citizens, Hispanics, and other segments. The firm that mails its own coupons can be quite selective about recipients. Another important advantage of direct mail couponing is a redemption rate of nearly 5 percent, much higher than for FSIs. Direct mail couponing is a more effective way to gain the attention of consumers.

The major disadvantage of direct mail coupon delivery is the expense relative to other distribution methods. The cost per thousand for distributing coupons through co-op mailings ranges from $10 to $15, and a solo mailing can have a CPM as high as $100. Also, the higher redemption rate of mail-delivered coupons may result from the fact that many recipients are already users of the brand who take advantage of the coupons sent directly to them.

Placing coupons either inside or outside the package is another method for distributing them. The in/on package coupon has virtually no distribution costs and a much higher redemption rate than other couponing methods. An in/on pack coupon that is redeemable for the next purchase of the same brand is known as a **bounce-back coupon**. This type of coupon provides consumers with an inducement to repurchase the brand.

Bounce-back coupons are often used with product samples to encourage the consumer to purchase the product after sampling. They may be included in or on the package during the early phases of a brand's life cycle to encourage repeat purchase, or they may be a defensive maneuver for a mature brand that is facing competitive pressure and wants to retain its current users. The main limitation of bounce-back coupons is that they go only to purchasers of the brand and thus do not attract nonusers. Exhibit 17–14 shows a bounce-back coupon placed on the package for Kellogg's Eggo brand waffles.

Another type of in/on pack coupon is the **cross-ruff coupon**, which is redeemable on the purchase of a different product, usually one made by the same company but occasionally through a tie-in with another manufacturer. Cross-ruff coupons have a redemp-

@ **EXHIBIT 17–14**

An example of an on-package coupon

tion rate of 3.1 to 4.1 percent and can be effective in encouraging consumers to try other products or brands. Companies with wide product lines, such as cereal manufacturers, are common users of these coupons.

Yet another type of package coupon is the **instant coupon**, which is attached to the outside of the package so the consumer can rip it off and redeem it at the checkout stand. Instant coupons have redemption levels of 35 percent and give consumers an immediate point-of-purchase incentive. Some companies prefer instant coupons to price-off deals because the latter require more cooperation from retailers and can be more expensive since every package must be reduced in price.

Couponing trends

Marketers are continually searching for more effective couponing techniques. Some companies are introducing in-store coupon distribution techniques through vending machines, electronic dispensers, or personal distributors at which consumers can request and receive coupons. These distribution methods are preferred by companies that believe coupons are most effective if given to consumers when they are ready to make a purchase. These techniques allow consumers to choose coupons they are interested in and remove the need to clip coupons from print ads and then remember to bring them to the store.

Companies are also seeking ways of using coupons to attract their competitors' customers. Since 65 percent to 85 percent of a manufacturer's coupons are used by current customers, marketers are attempting to target their coupons to users of competitive brands. For example, Catalina Marketing Corp. developed "Checkout Coupon," a way to distribute coupons at supermarkets by identifying a customer's purchases through bar codes and printing coupons for a competitor's product for use on a future shopping trip (Exhibit 17–15). Companies are also using this system to link purchases of products that are related. For example, a consumer who purchases a caffeine-free cola might be issued a coupon for a decaffeinated coffee.

EXHIBIT   17–15

Catalina Marketing promotes its checkout coupons

Premiums

Premiums are a sales promotion device used by many marketers. A **premium** is an offer of an item of merchandise or service either free or at a low price that is used as an extra incentive for purchasers. Many marketers are eliminating toys and gimmicks in favor of value-added premiums that reflect the quality of the product and are consistent with its image and positioning in the market. The two basic types of offers are the free premium and the self-liquidating premium.

Free premiums

Free premiums are usually small gifts or merchandise included in the product package or sent to consumers who mail in a request along with a proof of purchase. In/on package free premiums include toys, balls, trading cards, or other items included in cereal packages, and samples of one product included with another (Exhibit 17–16). A recent survey found that in/on package premiums are consumers' favorite type of promotion.[27]

Package-carried premiums have high impulse value and can provide an extra incentive to the consumer to use the product. However, several problems are associated with their use. First, there is the cost factor, which results from the premium itself as well as from extra packaging that is sometimes needed. Finding desirable premiums at reasonable costs can be difficult, particularly for adult markets, and using a poor premium may do more harm than good.

Another problem with these premiums is possible restrictions from regulatory agencies such as the Federal Trade Commission and the Food and Drug Administration or from industry codes regarding the type of premium used. The National Association of Broadcasters has developed strict guidelines regarding the advertising of premium offers to children. There is a danger that premium offers will entice children to request a brand to get the promoted item and then never consume the product.

Since most free mail-in premium offers require the consumer to send in more than one proof of purchase, they encourage repeat purchase and reward brand loyalty. But

@ **EXHIBIT 17–16**

Colgate toothpaste is used as an in-package premium for Life cereal

a major drawback of mail-in premiums is that they do not offer immediate reinforcement or reward to the purchaser, so they may not provide enough incentive to purchase the brand. Few consumers take advantage of mail-in premium offers; the average redemption rate is only 2 to 4 percent.[28]

Self-liquidating premiums

Self-liquidating premiums require the consumer to pay some or all of the cost of the premium plus handling and mailing costs. The items used as self-liquidating premiums are usually purchased in large quantities by the company and offered to consumers at lower than retail prices. The marketer usually does not attempt to make a profit on the premium item but only wants to cover costs and offer a value to the consumer.

In addition to cost savings, self-liquidating premiums offer several advantages to marketers. Offering values to consumers through the premium products can create interest in the brand and goodwill that enhances the brand's image. These premiums can also encourage trade support and gain in-store displays for the brand and the premium offer. Also, self-liquidating premiums are often tied in directly to the advertising campaign, so they extend the advertising message and contribute to consumer-franchise building for a brand. For example, Marlboro cigarettes offers Western wear and various outdoor items through its "Marlboro Country" catalog, which reinforces the brand's positioning theme.

Self-liquidating premium offers have the same basic limitations as mail-in premiums: a very low redemption rate. Fewer than 10 percent of US households have ever sent for a premium, and fewer than 1 percent of self-liquidating offers are actually redeemed.[29] Low redemption rates can leave the marketer with a large supply of items with a logo or some other brand identification that makes them hard to dispose of. Thus, it is important to test consumers' reaction to a premium incentive and determine whether they perceive the offer as a value. Another option is to use premiums with no brand identification, but that detracts from their consumer-franchise-building value.

Contests and Sweepstakes

Contests and sweepstakes are an increasingly popular consumer-oriented promotion. These promotions seem to have an appeal and glamour that tools such as cents-off coupons lack. Contests and sweepstakes are exciting because, as one expert has noted, consumers have a "pot of gold at the end of the rainbow mentality" and think they can win the big prizes being offered.[30]

There are differences between contests and sweepstakes. A **contest** is a promotion where consumers compete for prizes or money on the basis of skills or ability, and winners are determined by judging the entries or ascertaining which entry comes closest to some predetermined criteria (e.g., picking the winning teams and number of total points in the Super Bowl or NCAA basketball tournament). Contests usually provide a purchase incentive by requiring a proof of purchase to enter or an entry form that is available from a dealer or advertisement.

A **sweepstakes** is a promotion where winners are determined purely by chance; it cannot require a proof of purchase as a condition for entry. Entrants need only submit their names for the drawing for prizes. While there is often an official entry form, handwritten entries must also be permitted. Another form of a sweepstakes is a **game**, which also has a chance element or odds of winning. Scratch-off cards with instant winners are a popular promotional tool. Some games occur over a longer period and require more involvement by consumers. Bingo-type games, for example, are popular among retailers and fast-food chains as a way of building store traffic and repeat purchases.

Because they are easier to enter, sweepstakes attract more entries than contests. They are also easier and less expensive to administer since every entry does not have to be checked or judged. Choosing the winning entry in a sweepstakes requires only the random selection of a winner from the pool of entries or generation of a number to match those held by sweepstakes entrants.

Contests and sweepstakes can get the consumer involved with a brand by making the promotion product relevant. For example, contests that ask consumers to suggest a name for a product or to submit recipes that use the brand can increase involvement levels. Some contests require consumers to read an ad or package or visit a store display to gather information needed to enter. Marketers must be careful not to make their contests too difficult to enter, as this may discourage participation among key prospects in the target audience.

Sweepstakes and games can also be used to generate excitement. For example, Keebler used an interactive phone game and a tie-in with the hit movie *The Shadow* to promote its snack products (Exhibit 17–17).

Problems with contests and sweepstakes

While the use of contests and sweepstakes continues to increase, there are some problems associated with these types of promotions. Many sweepstakes and/or contest promotions do little to contribute to consumer-franchise building for a product or service and may even detract from it. The sweepstakes or contest often becomes the dominant focus rather than the brand, and little is accomplished other than giving away substantial amounts of money and/or prizes. Many promotional experts question the effectiveness of contests and sweepstakes. Some companies have cut back or even stopped using them because of concern over their effectiveness and fears that consumers might become dependent on them.[31]

Numerous legal problems and considerations affect the design and administration of contests and sweepstakes. These promotions are regulated by several federal agencies,

@ **EXHIBIT 17-17**

This Keebler promotion featured a unique interactive game and a movie tie-in

and each of the 50 states has its own rules. The regulation of contests and sweepstakes has helped clean up the abuses that plagued the industry in the late 1960s and has improved perceptions of these promotions among consumers. But companies must still be careful in designing a contest or sweepstakes and awarding prizes. Most firms use consultants that specialize in the design and administration of contests and sweepstakes to avoid any legal problems. However, companies can still run into problems. Global Perspective 17–1 describes the tremendous problems Pepsi encountered in the Philippines when a bottle-cap promotion went awry.

A final problem with contests and sweepstakes is the presence of professionals or hobbyists who submit many entries but have no intention of purchasing the product or service. Because most states make it illegal to require a purchase as a qualification for a sweepstakes entry, consumers can enter as many times as they wish. Professional players sometimes enter one sweepstakes several times, depending on the nature of the prizes and the number of entries the promotion attracts. Newsletters are even available that inform them of all the contests and sweepstakes being held, the entry dates, estimated probabilities of winning for various numbers of entries, how to enter, and solutions to any puzzles or other information that might be needed. The presence of these professional entrants not only defeats the purpose of the promotion but may also discourage entries from consumers who think their chances of winning are limited.

Refunds and Rebates

Refunds or rebates are offers by the manufacturer to return a portion of the product purchase price, usually after the consumer supplies some proof of purchase. Consumers are generally very responsive to refund or rebate offers, particularly as the size of the savings increases. Refunds and rebates are used by all types of companies, ranging from package-goods companies to manufacturers of major appliances and automobiles.

Package-goods marketers often use refund offers to induce trial of a new product or encourage users of another brand to switch. The savings offered through a cash refund offer may be perceived by the consumer as an immediate value that lowers the cost of the item, even though those savings are realized only if the consumer redeems the refund or rebate offer. Redemption rates for refund offers typically range from 1 to 3 percent for print and point-of-purchase offers to 5 percent for in/on package offers.[32]

Refund offers can also encourage repeat purchase. Many offers require consumers to send in multiple proofs of purchase. The size of the refund offer may even increase

Global Perspective 17-1
Pepsi's "Number Fever" Promotion Causes a Furor in the Philippines

Contests, sweepstakes, and other types of promotions are often used by marketers to give consumers an extra incentive to buy their products. However, these promotions don't always go as planned and can embarrass a company or even create legal problems. Several major companies known for their marketing excellence have experienced major promotional blunders in recent years. Coca-Cola lost millions of dollars in the summer of 1991 when its "Magi-can" promotion went awry and had to be canceled. The Beatrice Co. ran into major legal problems when a computer buff cracked the contest code of a promotion tied to ABC's "Monday Night Football" and turned in 4,000 scratch-off cards worth $21 million in prize money. Beatrice contended that the entrant violated the rules of the game in obtaining some tickets and the contest's defect nullified all prize claims, so it canceled the contest. Millions of dollars in lawsuits were filed, although the case was eventually settled out of court.

Kraft also found out how expensive it can be when a promotion is not executed properly. A newspaper FSI containing game pieces for a sweepstakes was printed incorrectly, making everyone a winner. Hundreds of consumers had matching pieces indicating they had won a Dodge minivan and thousands more won cash prizes. Kraft declared the contest null and void but still had to spend nearly $3.8 million to compensate the winners— versus the $36,000 budgeted for prizes.

These botched promotions were embarrassing for the companies and resulted in the loss of goodwill as well as money. But these consequences are mild compared to PepsiCo's problems with a recent bottle-cap promotion that went wrong in the Philippines. The problem began when the local Pepsi bottler launched a "Number Fever" promotion in May of 1992 that offered a grand prize of one million pesos (about $36,000) to holders of bottle caps with the number 349 printed on them. However, as a result of what Pepsi called a computer glitch, the winning number appeared on more than 500,000 bottle caps, making the company liable for more than $18 billion in prize money.

When the error was discovered, Pepsi announced the problem and quickly offered to pay $19 apiece for each winning cap. While more than 500,000 Filipinos have collected nearly $10 million from the company, thousands of others pursued the full amount in civil and criminal courts. The Filipino justice department found that Pepsi was not criminally liable and dismissed 7,000 lawsuits, but others are still pending. The furor caused by the botched promotion prompted anti-Pepsi rallies, death threats against Pepsi executives, and attacks on Pepsi trucks and bottling plants, including one involving a grenade.

The "Number Fever" promotion started out as an attempt to take sales away from market leader Coca-Cola, which has nearly 78 percent of the Filipino market. However, after the bottle-cap fiasco, Pepsi's market share dropped 9 points. While Pepsi is slowly regaining its market share, it may be a while before the company resorts to any promotions to take on Coke. And it's a pretty sure bet that Coke won't be using any Magi-cans to defend its market share!

Sources: Glenn Heitsmith, "Botched Pepsi Promotion Prompts Terrorist Attacks," *Promo*, Sept. 1993, p. 10; Bob Drogin, "Bottle Cap Flap Riles the Masses," *Los Angeles Times*, July 26, 1993, pp. A1, 8; Bruce Horowitz, "The Pratfalls in Promotions," *Los Angeles Times*, April 28, 1991, pp. D1, 8; "Kraft Snafu Could Cost $4 Million," *Advertising Age*, July 10, 1989, p. 53.

as the number of purchases gets larger. Some package-goods companies are switching away from cash refund offers to coupons or cash/coupon combinations. Using coupons in the refund offer enhances the likelihood of repeat purchase of the brand.

Refunds (or, as they are more commonly referred to, rebates) have become a widely used form of promotion for consumer durables. Products such as cameras, sporting goods, appliances, televisions, audio and video equipment, computers, and cars frequently use rebate offers to appeal to price-conscious consumers. The use of rebates for expensive items like cars was begun by Chrysler Corp. in 1981 to boost sales and generate cash for the struggling company. Rebates are now common not only in the auto industry and other durable products but for package-goods products as well.

Evaluating refunds and rebates

Rebates can help create new users and encourage brand switching or repeat purchase behavior, or they can be a way to offer a temporary price reduction. The rebate may be perceived as an immediate savings even though many consumers do not follow through on the offer. This perception of a price reduction can influence purchase even though the consumer may fail to realize the savings, so the marketer can reduce price for much less than if it used a direct price-off deal.

Some problems are associated with refunds and rebates. Many consumers are not motivated by a refund offer because of the delay and the effort required to obtain the savings. They do not want to be bothered saving cash register receipts and proofs of purchase, filling out forms, and mailing in the offer.[33] A study of consumer perceptions found a negative relationship between the use of rebates and the perceived difficulties associated with the redemption process.[34] It also found that consumers perceive manufacturers as offering rebates to sell products that are not faring well. Nonusers of rebates were particularly likely to perceive the redemption process as too complicated and to suspect manufacturers' motives for offering rebates. This implies that companies using rebates must simplify the redemption process and use other promotional elements such as advertising to retain consumer confidence in the brand.

When small refunds are being offered, marketers may find other promotional incentives such as coupons or bonus packs more effective. They must be careful not to overuse rebate offers and confuse consumers over the real price and value of a product or service. Also, consumers can become dependent on rebates and delay their purchases or purchase only brands for which a rebate is available. Many retailers have become disenchanted with rebates and the burden and expense of administering these programs.[35]

Bonus Packs

Bonus packs offer the consumer an extra amount of a product at the regular price by providing larger containers or extra units (Exhibit 17–18). Bonus packs result in a lower cost per unit for the consumer and provide extra value, as well as more product for the money. There are several advantages to bonus pack promotions. First, they give marketers a direct way of providing extra value to the consumer without having to get involved with complicated coupons or refund offers. The additional value of a bonus pack is generally obvious to the consumer and can have a strong impact on the purchase decision right at the time of purchase.

Bonus packs can also be an effective defensive maneuver against a competitor's promotion or introduction of a new brand. By loading current users with large amounts of its product, a marketer can often remove these consumers from the market and make them less susceptible to a competitor's promotional efforts. Bonus packs often receive favorable response from retailers and may result in larger purchase orders and favorable display space in the store as well.

Bonus pack promotions can be particularly effective when relationships with retailers are favorable. They do, however, usually require additional shelf space without providing any extra profit margins for the retailer, so the marketer can encounter problems with bonus packs if trade relationships are not favorable. Another problem is that bonus packs may appeal primarily to current users who probably would have purchased the brand anyway or to promotion-sensitive consumers who may not become loyal to the brand.

Price-Off Deals

Another consumer-oriented promotion technique is the direct **price-off deal**, which reduces the price of the brand. Price-off reductions are typically offered right on the package through specially marked price packs, as shown in Exhibit 17–19. Typically, price-offs range from 10 to 25 percent off the regular price, with the reduction coming out of the manufacturer's profit margin, not the retailer's. Keeping the retailer's margin during a price-off promotion maintains its support and cooperation.

Marketers use price-off promotions for several reasons. First, price-offs are controlled by the manufacturer, so it can make sure the promotional discount reaches the consumer rather than being kept by the trade. Like bonus packs, price-off deals usually present a readily apparent value to shoppers, particularly when they have a reference price point for the brand and thus recognize the value of the discount.[36] So price-offs can be a strong influence at the point of purchase when price comparisons are being made. Price-off promotions can also encourage consumers to purchase larger quantities, preempting competitors' promotions and assisting in obtaining trade support.

@ **EXHIBIT 17-18**

Bonus packs provide more value for consumers

@ **EXHIBIT 17-19**

Examples of price-off packages

Price-off promotions may not be favorably received by retailers, since they can create pricing and inventory problems. Most retailers will not accept packages with a specific price shown on the package, so the familiar X amount off the regular price must be used. Also, like bonus packs, price-off deals often appeal primarily to regular users instead of attracting nonusers. Finally, the Federal Trade Commission has regulations regarding the conditions that price-off labels must meet and the frequency and timing of their use.

Event Sponsorship

Another type of consumer-oriented promotion that has become popular in recent years is **event sponsorship,** in which a company develops sponsorship relations with a particular event. An estimated 4,500 companies spent $4.2 billion on event sponsorships in 1994, more than double the amount spent in 1988 (Exhibit 17–20). Sports receive two-thirds of the event sponsorship monies. Among the more popular sporting events for sponsorship are golf and tennis tournaments, auto racing, and running events.[37] Bicycle racing, beach volleyball, skiing, and various water sports are also attracting corporate sponsorship. Traditionally, cigarette, beer, and car companies have been among the largest sports event sponsors, but a number of other companies have become involved, including Coca-Cola and PepsiCo, airlines, and financial services companies.[38] Exhibit 17–21 shows companies that spend over $10 million annually on event sponsorships in the United States.

Many marketers are attracted to event sponsorship because it gets their company and/or product names in front of consumers. By choosing the right events for sponsorship, companies can get visibility among their target market. For example, RJR Nabisco is heavily involved in sponsorship of automobile racing under its Winston and Camel cigarette brands. The company's market research showed that racing fans fit the demographic profile of users of these brands and consumers would purchase a product that sponsored their favorite sport.[39] For tobacco companies, which are prohibited from advertising on radio and television, event sponsorship is also a way to have their brand names seen on TV.

@ **EXHIBIT 17–20**   Breakdown of spending on event sponsorship

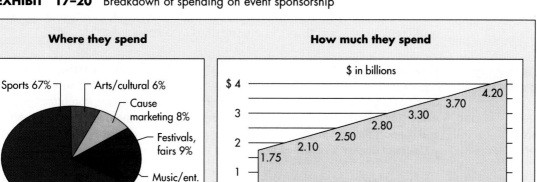

As noted in the vignette at the beginning of the chapter, many companies are attracted to event sponsorships because effective integrated marketing communications programs can be built around them and promotional tie-ins can be made to local and regional markets. For example, stock-car races are an effective way to reach consumers in Southern states. Event sponsorships are also good public relations tools that let companies become involved with local communities. As traditional media advertising becomes more crowded and expensive and local and regional marketing trends increase, it is likely that more companies will turn to event sponsorship.

A number of challenges face the event sponsorship industry, including charges that it is weak on research. As marketers become interested in targeted audiences, they will want more evidence of an event's effectiveness. The sponsorship industry also faces a

@ **EXHIBIT 17–21**

Companies spending over $10 million on event sponsorships in the United States

- **$110–$115 million**
  Philip Morris Cos.
- **$90–$95 million**
  Anheuser-Busch Cos.
- **$70–$75 million**
  The Coca-Cola Co.
- **$35–$40 million**
  Eastman Kodak Co.
  General Motors Corp.
  IBM Corp.
  RJR Nabisco, Inc.
- **$30–$35 million**
  PepsiCo, Inc.
- **$25–$30 million**
  AT&T
  Du Pont Co.
  McDonald's Corp.
  The Quaker Oats Co.

- **$20–$25 million**
  The Procter & Gamble Co.
  Sara Lee Corp.
- **$15–$20 million**
  Bausch & Lomb Inc.
  Visa U.S.A. Inc.
- **$10–$15 million**
  American Airlines
  Coors Brewing Co.
  Delta Air Lines, Inc.
  The Gillette Co.
  The Home Depot
  MasterCard Int'l, Inc.
  NationsBank Corp.
  Nestlé USA, Inc.
  Time Warner Inc.
  Xerox Corp.

potential problem as the Internal Revenue Service considers changing its guidelines on taxing corporate sponsorships of nonprofit organizations. This change in the tax code could result in major cutbacks in sponsorships by corporations.[40]

TRADE-ORIENTED SALES PROMOTION

Objectives for Trade-Oriented Sales Promotion

Like consumer-oriented promotions, sales promotion programs targeted to the trade should be based on well-defined objectives and measurable goals and a consideration of what the marketer wants to accomplish. Typical objectives for promotions targeted to marketing intermediaries such as wholesalers and retailers include obtaining distribution and support for new products, maintaining support for established brands, encouraging retailers to display established brands, and building retail inventories.

Obtain distribution and support for new products

Trade promotions are often used to encourage retailers to give shelf space to new products. Manufacturers recognize that only a limited amount of shelf space is available in supermarkets, drugstores, and other major retail outlets. Thus, they provide retailers with financial incentives to stock new products. For example, Lever Brothers used heavy sampling and high-value coupons in the successful introduction of Lever 2000 bar soap. However, in addition to these consumer promotions, the company used discounts to the trade to encourage retailers to stock and promote the new brand.

While trade discounts or other special price deals are used to encourage retailers and wholesalers to stock a new brand, marketers may use other types of promotions to get them to push the brand. Merchandising allowances can get retailers to display a new product in high-traffic areas of a store, while incentive programs or contests can encourage wholesaler or retail store personnel to push a new brand.

Maintain trade support for established brands

Trade promotions are often designed to maintain distribution and trade support for established brands. Brands that are in the mature phase of their product life cycle are vulnerable to losing wholesale and/or retail distribution, particularly if they are not differentiated or face competition from new products. Trade deals induce wholesalers and retailers to continue to carry weaker products because the discounts increase their profit margins. Brands with a smaller market share often rely heavily on trade promotions, since they lack the funds required to differentiate themselves from competitors through media advertising.

Even if a brand has a strong market position, trade promotions may be used as part of an overall marketing strategy. For example, H. J. Heinz Co. increased its marketing spending by $100 million recently and allocated virtually all of the money to trade promotions while cutting back substantially on advertising. A Heinz executive said the move was made in response to the weak economy and noted, "Price elasticity is what it's all about, and no amount of advertising will sell as well as price in this environment."[41] He also said the increased trade promotion had resulted in substantial sales volume and market share increases for Heinz brands.

Encourage retailers to display and promote established brands

Another objective of trade-oriented promotions is to encourage retailers to display and promote an established brand. An important goal is to obtain retail store displays of a product away from its regular shelf location. A typical supermarket has approximately 50 display areas at the ends of aisles, near checkout counters, and elsewhere. Marketers want to have their products displayed in these areas to increase the probability shoppers will come into contact with them. Even a single display can increase a brand's sales significantly during a promotion.

Manufacturers often use multifaceted promotional programs to encourage retailers to promote their products at the retail level. For example, Exhibit 17–22 shows a brochure

EXHIBIT   17–22   Multifaceted promotional programs encourage retail participation and support for a brand

for a promotion the Van Camp Seafood Co. used for its Chicken of the Sea tuna brand. The promotion included a variety of promotional tools designed to increase retailer participation: manufacturer-sponsored advertising in local newspapers, display cards, and even free shoes for purchasing a specified number of cases. The program also encouraged retailers to participate by showing promotional offers targeted toward consumers, such as coupons and rebate offers.

Build retail inventories

Manufacturers often use trade promotions to build the inventory levels of retailers or other channel members. There are several reasons manufacturers use trade promotions to load a retailer with their products. First, wholesalers and retailers are more likely to push a product when they have high inventory levels rather than storing it in their warehouses or back rooms. Building channel members' inventories also ensures they will not run out of stock and thus miss sales opportunities.

Also some manufacturers of seasonal products offer large promotional discounts so retailers will stock up on their products before the peak selling season begins. This enables the manufacturer to smooth out seasonal fluctuations in its production schedule and passes on some of the inventory carrying costs to retailers or wholesalers. Moreover, when retailers stock up on a product before the peak selling season, they often run special promotions and offer discounts to consumers to reduce excess inventories.

Types of Trade-Oriented Promotions

Manufacturers use a variety of trade promotion tools as inducements for wholesalers and retailers. We examine some of the most frequently used types of trade promotions and some factors marketers must consider in using them.

EXHIBIT 17-23

This contest was targeted toward food-service distributors

Contests and incentives

Manufacturers may develop contests or special incentive programs to stimulate greater selling effort and support from reseller management or sales personnel. Contests or incentive programs can be directed toward managers who work for a wholesaler or distributor as well as toward store or department managers at the retail level. Manufacturers often sponsor contests for resellers and use prizes such as trips or valuable merchandise as rewards for meeting sales quotas or other goals. Exhibit 17–23 shows a contest Van Camp sponsored for food-service distributors who call on restaurants.

Contests or special incentives are often targeted at the sales personnel of the wholesalers, distributors/dealers, or retailers. These salespeople are an important link in the distribution chain because they are likely to be very familiar with the market, more frequently in touch with the customer (whether it be another reseller or the ultimate consumer), and more numerous than the manufacturer's own sales organization. Manufacturers often devise incentives or contests for these sales personnel. These programs may involve cash payments made directly to the retailer's or wholesaler's sales staff to encourage them to promote and sell a manufacturer's product. These payments are known as **push money** (pm's) or *spiffs*. For example, an appliance manufacturer may pay a $25 spiff to retail sales personnel for selling a certain model or size. In sales contests, salespeople can win trips or valuable merchandise for meeting certain goals established by the manufacturer. As shown in Exhibit 17–24, these incentives may be tied to product sales, new account placements, or merchandising efforts.

While contests and incentive programs can generate reseller support, they also can be a source of conflict between retail sales personnel and management. Some retailers want to maintain control over the selling activities of their sales staff. They don't want their salespeople devoting an undue amount of effort to trying to win a contest or receive incentives offered by the manufacturer. These programs can also result in retail sales personnel becoming too aggressive in pushing consumers to buy certain products.

@ **EXHIBIT 17–24**

Three forms of promotion targeted to reseller sales-people

•*Product or Program Sales*
  Awards are tied to the selling of a product, for example:
    Selling a specified number of cases
    Selling a specified number of units
    Selling a specified number of promotional programs
•*New Account Placements*
  Awards are tied to:
    The number of new accounts opened
    The number of new accounts ordering a minumum number of cases or units
    Promotional programs placed in new accounts
•*Merchandising Efforts*
  Awards are tied to:
    Establishing promotional programs (such as theme programs)
    Placing display racks, counter displays, and the like

Rather than selling the product or model that is best for the customer, salespeople may push products that serve their own interests.

Many retailers refuse to let their employees participate in manufacturer-sponsored contests or to accept incentive payments. Retailers that do allow them often have strict guidelines and require management approval of the program.

Trade allowances

Probably the most common trade promotion is some form of trade allowance, a discount or deal offered to retailers or wholesalers to encourage them to stock, promote, or display the manufacturer's products. Types of allowances offered to retailers include buying allowances, promotional or display allowances, and slotting allowances.

Buying allowances

A buying allowance is a deal or discount offered to resellers in the form of a price reduction on merchandise ordered during a fixed period. These discounts are often in the form of an **off-invoice allowance**, which means a certain per-case amount or percentage is deducted from the invoice. A buying allowance can also take the form of *free goods*; the reseller gets extra cases with the purchase of specific amounts (for example, one free case with every 10 cases purchased).

Buying allowances are used for several reasons. They are easy to implement and are well accepted, and sometimes expected, by the trade. They are also an effective way to encourage resellers to buy the manufacturer's product, since they will want to take advantage of the discounts being offered during the allowance period. Manufacturers offer trade discounts expecting wholesalers and retailers to pass the price reduction through to consumers, resulting in greater sales. However, as discussed below, this is often not the case.

Promotional allowances

Manufacturers often give retailers allowances or discounts for performing certain promotional or merchandising activities in support of their brands. Sometimes referred to as merchandising allowances, they can be given for providing special displays away from the product's regular shelf position, running in-store promotional programs, or including the product in an ad. The manufacturer generally has guidelines or a contract specifying the activity to be performed to qualify for the promotional allowance. The allowance is usually as a fixed amount per case or a percentage deduction from the list price for merchandise ordered during the promotional period.

Slotting allowances

In recent years, retailers have been demanding a special allowance for agreeing to handle a new product. Also called stocking allowances, introductory allowances, or street money, these are fees that must be paid to retailers to provide a slot or position to accommodate the new product. Retailers justify these fees due to the costs associated with taking on a new product, such as redesigning store shelves, entering the product into their computers, finding warehouse space, and informing store employees of the new product.[42] They also note they are assuming some risk in taking on a new product, since so many new product introductions fail.

Slotting fees can range from a few hundred dollars per store to $50,000 or more for an entire retail chain. Manufacturers that want to get their products on the shelves nationally can face several million dollars in slotting fees. Many marketers believe slotting allowances are a form of blackmail or bribery and say some 70 percent of these fees go directly to retailers' bottom lines.

Retailers can continue charging slotting fees because of their power and the limited availability of shelf space in supermarkets relative to the large numbers of products introduced each year. Some retailers have even been demanding **failure fees** if a new product does not hit a minimum sales level within a certain time. The fee is charged to cover the costs associated with stocking, maintaining inventories, and then pulling the product.[43] Large manufacturers with popular brands are less likely to pay slotting fees than smaller companies that lack leverage in negotiating with retailers.

Problems with trade allowances

Many companies are concerned about the abuse of trade allowances by wholesalers, retailers, and distributors. Marketers give retailers these trade allowances so the savings will be passed through to consumers in the form of lower prices, but companies such as Procter & Gamble claim that only 30 percent of trade promotion discounts actually reach consumers in the form of lower prices because 35 percent is lost in inefficiencies and another 35 percent is pocketed by retailers and wholesalers. Moreover, many marketers believe that the trade is taking advantage of their promotional deals and misusing promotional funds.

For example, many retailers and wholesalers engage in a practice known as **forward buying,** where they stock up on a product at the lower deal or off-invoice price and resell it to consumers after the marketer's promotional period ends. Another common practice is **diverting,** where a retailer or wholesaler takes advantage of the promotional deal and then sells some of the product purchased at the low price to a store outside its area or to a middleman who will resell it to other stores.

Forward buying and diverting are widespread practices. Industry studies show that nearly 40 percent of wholesalers' and retailers' profits come from these activities. In addition to not passing discounts on to consumers, forward buying and diverting create other problems for manufacturers. They lead to huge swings in demand that cause production scheduling problems and leave manufacturers and retailers always building toward or drawing down from a promotional surge. Marketers also worry that the system leads to frequent price specials and consumers make purchases on the basis of what's on sale rather than developing any loyalty to their brands.

The problems created by retailers' abuse have led Procter & Gamble, one of the country's most powerful consumer products marketers, to take action. In 1991, P&G adopted a policy of **everyday low pricing (EDLP)**; it lowers the list price of over 60 percent of its product line by 10 to 25 percent, while cutting promotional allowances to the trade. The price cuts leave the overall cost of the product to retailers at about the same level it would have been with the various trade allowance discounts. P&G hopes the EDLP program will eliminate problems such as deal buying, lead to regular low prices at the retail level, and help build brand loyalty among consumers. However, as discussed in IMC Perspective 17–2, manufacturers and retailers are still undecided on the merits of EDLP.

Displays and point-of-purchase materials

The next time you are in a store, take a moment to examine the various promotional materials used to display and sell products. Point-of-purchase displays are an important promotional tool because they can help a manufacturer obtain more effective in-store

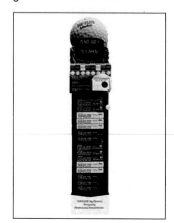

@ **EXHIBIT 17–25**

Spalding uses point-of-purchase displays for Top-Flite golf balls to generate in-store sales

IMC Perspective 17–2
The Battle over Everyday Low Pricing

Consumer product manufacturers and retailers have been battling for years over the allocation of promotional dollars. The retailers' goal is to get more money from the manufacturers in the form of trade promotions. Over the past decade, retailers have been winning the battle, demanding and getting a wealth of promotional subsidies from manufacturers such as trade allowances and discounts.

The heavy reliance on trade promotions has created problems for marketers. While they provide these promotional subsidies in hopes that the savings will be passed through to consumers, most of these discounts end up being pocketed by retailers and wholesalers rather than lowering shelf prices. Moreover, the discounts that are passed on make consumers very price sensitive. For example, a brand of dish detergent may be priced at 99 cents during the week of a promotion but $1.69 the next. When the brand goes back to its regular price, deal-conscious consumers look for another brand that has a special price.

To combat these problems, Procter & Gamble took a bold step in the fall of 1991 when it moved many of its brands to an everyday low pricing (EDLP) strategy. EDLP is designed to deliver one consistent base price to consumers and eliminate wild price fluctuations. P&G has reduced the trade allowance, discounts, coupons, and other short-term incentives on more than 60 percent of its product line, including brands such as Pringles potato chips, Vidal Sassoon shampoo, and Dawn dishwashing detergent. By cutting out price promotions and smoothing out production schedules, P&G claims the EDLP strategy will save the company $175 million annually. These savings can be used to offer consistently lower prices and invest in equity-building advertising to create greater brand loyalty.

The EDLP strategy has caused great controversy in the trade, which is heavily dependent on promotions to attract consumers. Some retailers took P&G products off the shelf, while others cut their ads and displays of the company's brands. Retailers prefer to operate on a "high-low" strategy of frequent price specials and argue that EDLP puts them at a disadvantage against the warehouse stores and mass merchandisers that already use everyday low pricing. They also say that some products, such as those that are bought on impulse, thrive on promotions and don't lend themselves to EDLP. Retailers rely on promotions like end-of-aisle displays and price discounts to create excitement and generate incremental sales and profits from products such as soft drinks, cookies, and candy.

Pricing experts also argue that the success of EDLP depends on the brand's market share, its consumer image, the level of promotional activity in the category, and the presence of store brands. While the strategy may work well for market leaders whose brands enjoy high loyalty, it is not effective for marketers trying to build market share or prop up lagging products. Moreover, many consumers are still motivated more by promotional deals and specials than by advertising claims from retailers promoting everyday low prices.

P&G says EDLP is paying off, as volume is growing faster in the more than 70 percent of its brands that have switched to the new pricing strategy. And it claims that market share in 21 of 31 product categories has increased. However, the debate over EDLP is likely to continue as other manufacturers and retailers try to decide whether to embrace or avoid it.

Source: Melissa Campanelli, "What's in Store for EDLP," *Sales & Marketing Management*, Aug. 1993, pp. 56–59; "Procter & Gamble Hits Back," *Business Week*, July 19, 1993, pp. 20–22; "Not Everyone Loves a Supermarket Special," *Business Week*, February 17, 1992, pp. 64–68; Eric Hollreiser, "Laying It Out on the Table," *AdWeek's Marketing Week*, April 27, 1992, pp. 18–20.

merchandising of products. Point-of-purchase materials include end-of-aisle displays, banners, posters, shelf cards, motion pieces, stand-up racks, and a number of other materials. Exhibit 17–25 shows an award-winning point-of-purchase display for Top-Flite golf balls.

Many manufacturers help retailers by providing more efficient shelf space planning through **planograms**, which are configurations of products that occupy a shelf section in a store. Some manufacturers are developing computer-based programs that allow retailers to input information from their scanner data and determine the best shelf layouts by experimenting with product movement, space utilization, profit yields, and other factors.[44]

Sales training programs

Another form of manufacturer-sponsored promotional assistance is sales training programs for reseller personnel. Many products sold at the retail level require knowledgeable salespeople who can provide consumers with information about the features, benefits, and advantages of various brands and models. Cosmetics, appliances, computers, consumer electronics, and sporting equipment are examples of products for which consumers often rely on well-informed retail sales personnel for assistance.

Manufacturers provide sales training assistance to retail salespeople in a number of ways. They may conduct classes or training sessions that retail personnel can attend to increase their knowledge of a product or a product line. These training sessions present information and ideas on how to sell the manufacturer's product and may also include

@ **EXHIBIT 17-26**

An example of sales training
material provided to retail
sales personnel

motivational components. Sales training classes for retail personnel are often sponsored by companies selling high-ticket items or complex products such as personal computers, automobiles, or ski equipment.

Another way manufacturers provide sales training assistance to retail employees is through their own sales force. Sales reps educate retail personnel about their product line and provide selling tips and other relevant information. The sales force can provide ongoing sales training as they come into contact with retail sales staff on a regular basis and can update them on changes in the product line, market developments, competitive information, and the like.

Manufacturers also give resellers detailed sales manuals, product brochures, reference manuals, and other material. Many companies provide videocassettes for retail sales personnel that include product information, product-use demonstrations, and ideas on how to sell their product. Many of these selling aids can be used as sales tools to provide information to customers as well. Exhibit 17–26 shows an example of sales training material that Honda provides for its dealers.

Trade shows

Another important promotional activity targeted to resellers is the **trade show**, a forum where manufacturers can display their products to current as well as prospective buyers. In many industries, trade shows are a major opportunity to display one's product lines and interact with customers. They are often attended by important management personnel from large retail chains as well as by distributors and other reseller representatives.

A number of promotional functions can be performed at trade shows, including demonstrating products, identifying new prospects, gathering customer and competitive information, and even writing orders for a product. Trade shows are particularly valuable for introducing new products, because resellers are often looking for new merchandise to stock. Shows can also be a source of valuable leads to follow up on through sales calls or direct marketing. The social aspect of trade shows is also important. Many companies use them to entertain key customers and to develop and maintain relationships with the trade.

Cooperative advertising

The final form of trade-oriented promotion we examine is **cooperative advertising**, where the cost of advertising is shared by more than one party. There are three types of cooperative advertising. Although the first two are not trade-oriented promotion, we should recognize their objectives and purpose.

Horizontal cooperative advertising refers to advertising sponsored in common by a group of retailers or other organizations providing products or services to the market.

@ **EXHIBIT 17–27**

Horizontal cooperative
advertising is reflected in this
ad for Colorado ski resorts

Exhibit 17–27 is an ad representing a cooperative effort among ski resorts in **Summit County, Colorado.**

Ingredient-sponsored cooperative advertising is supported by raw materials manufacturers; its objective is to help establish end products that include the company's materials and/or ingredients. An example is the "Intel Inside" program sponsored by Intel Corp., which makes the microprocessors found in most personal computers. Intel provides personal computer manufacturers with cooperative advertising monies based on the number of microprocessors they buy. In exchange, the computer companies display the "Intel Inside" logo in their ads.

The most common form of cooperative advertising is the trade-oriented form, **vertical cooperative advertising**. In co-op advertising, a manufacturer pays for a portion of the advertising a retailer runs to promote the manufacturer's product and its availability in the retailer's place of business. Manufacturers generally share the cost of advertising run by the retailer on a percentage basis (usually 50–50) up to a certain limit.

The amount of cooperative advertising funds the manufacturer provides to the retailer is usually based on a percentage of dollar purchases made from the manufacturer. If a retailer purchases $100,000 of product from a manufacturer, it might receive 3 percent, or $3,000 of cooperative advertising money. Large retail chains often combine their co-op budgets across all of their stores, which gives them a larger sum to work with and more media options.

Cooperative advertising can take on several forms. Retailers may advertise a manufacturer's product in, say, a newspaper ad featuring a number of different products, and the individual manufacturers reimburse the retailer for their portion of the ad. Or the ad may be prepared by the manufacturer and placed in the local media by the retailer. Exhibit 17–28 shows a cooperative ad format that retailers in various market areas can use by just inserting their store name and location.

Once a cooperative ad is run, the retailer requests reimbursement from the manufacturer for its percentage of the media costs. Manufacturers usually have specific requirements the ad must meet to qualify for co-op reimbursement, such as size, use of trademarks, content, and format. Verification that the ad was run is also required, in the form of a tearsheet (print) or an affidavit from the radio or TV station (broadcast) and an invoice.

As with other types of trade promotions, manufacturers have been increasing their cooperative advertising expenditures in recent years.[45] Some companies have been moving money out of national advertising into cooperative advertising because they believe they can have greater impact with ad campaigns in local markets. There is also a trend toward more cooperative advertising programs initiated by retailers, who approach

@ **EXHIBIT   17–28**

An example of vertical
cooperative advertising

manufacturers with catalogs, promotional events they are planning, or advertising programs they have developed in conjunction with local media and ask them to pay a percentage of the cost. Manufacturers often go along with these requests, particularly when the retailer is large and powerful.[46]

@ **COORDINATING
SALES PROMOTION
AND ADVERTISING**

Those involved in the promotional process must recognize that sales promotion techniques usually work best in conjunction with advertising and that the effectiveness of an ad campaign can be enhanced by consumer-oriented sales promotion efforts. Rather than separate activities competing for a firm's promotional budget, advertising and sales promotion should be viewed as complementary tools. When properly planned and executed to work together, advertising and sales promotion can have a *synergistic effect* much greater than that of either promotional mix element alone.

Proper coordination of advertising and sales promotion is essential if the firm wants to take advantage of the opportunities offered by each tool and get the most out of its promotional budget. Successful integration of advertising and sales promotion requires decisions concerning not only the allocation of the budget to each area but also the coordination of the ad and sales promotional themes, the target audience reached, and the timing of the various promotional activities.

Budget Coordination

While many companies are spending more money on sales promotion than on media advertising, it is difficult to say just what percentage of a firm's overall promotional budget should be allocated to advertising versus consumer- and trade-oriented promotions. This allocation depends on a number of factors, including the specific promotional objectives of the campaign, the market and competitive situation, and the stage of the brand in its life cycle.

Consider, for example, how allocation of the promotional budget may vary according to a brand's stage in the product life cycle. In the introductory stage, a large amount of the budget may be allocated to sales promotion techniques such as sampling and couponing to induce trial. In the growth stage, however, promotional dollars may be used primarily for advertising to stress brand differences and keep the brand name in the minds of consumers.

@ **EXHIBIT 17–29**

This Taster's Choice contest is tied to the brand's advertising campaign theme

When a brand moves to the maturity stage, advertising is primarily a reminder to keep consumers aware of the brand. Consumer-oriented sales promotions such as coupons, price-offs, premiums, and bonus packs may be needed periodically to maintain consumer loyalty, attract new users, and protect against competition. Trade-oriented promotions are needed to maintain shelf space and accommodate retailer demands for better margins as well as encourage them to promote the brand. A study on the synergistic effects of advertising and promotion examined a brand in the mature phase of its life cycle and found that 80 percent of its sales at this stage were due to sales promotions. When a brand enters the decline stage of the product life cycle, most of the promotional support will probably be removed and expenditures on sales promotion are unlikely.

Coordination of Ad and Promotional Themes

To integrate the advertising and sales promotional programs successfully, the theme of consumer promotions should be tied in with the advertising and positioning theme wherever possible. Sales promotion tools should attempt to communicate a brand's unique attributes or benefits and to reinforce the sales message or campaign theme. In this way, the sales promotion effort contributes to the consumer-franchise-building effort for the brand. An example of this is the contest promotion for Taster's Choice coffee in Exhibit 17–29. Notice how this promotion is tied to the developing romance theme used in the TV campaign for Taster's Choice, which was discussed in Global Perspective 11–1.

Media Support and Timing

Media support for a sales promotion program is critical and should be coordinated with the media program for the advertising campaign. Media advertising is often needed to deliver the sales promotional materials such as coupons, sweepstakes, contest entry forms, premium offers, and even samples. It is also needed to inform consumers of a promotional offer as well as to create prior awareness, interest, and favorable attitudes toward

◉ EXHIBIT 17–30

Creative advertising was coordinated with sales promotion in the successful introduction of Lever 2000

the brand. By using advertising in conjunction with a sales promotion program, marketers can make consumers aware of the brand and its benefits and increase their responsiveness to the promotion. Consumers are more likely to redeem a coupon or respond to a price-off deal for a brand they are familiar with than one they know nothing about. Moreover, product trial created through sales promotion techniques such as sampling or high-value couponing is more likely to result in long-term use of the brand when accompanied by advertising.[47]

Using a promotion without prior or concurrent advertising can limit its effectiveness and risk damaging the image of the brand. Consumers may perceive the brand as being promotion dependent or of lesser quality, so they are not likely to develop favorable attitudes and long-term loyalty. Conversely, the effectiveness of an ad can be enhanced by a coupon, a premium offer, or an opportunity to enter a sweepstakes or contest.

An example of the effective coordination of advertising and sales promotion is the introductory campaign Lever Brothers Co. developed for its new Lever 2000 bar soap. As noted earlier in the chapter, Lever Brothers used high-value coupons, sent samples to half of US households, and offered discounts to retailers as part of its introductory marketing blitz. These sales promotion efforts were accompanied by heavy advertising in print and TV, with the theme "Presenting some of the 2000 body parts you can clean with Lever 2000" (Exhibit 17–30).

Sales promotion was important in inducing trial for Lever 2000 and continued after introduction in the form of couponing. But it was the strong positioning created through effective advertising that converted consumers to regular users. Repeat sales of the brand were at about 40 percent, even after heavy discounting ended. Just six months after its introduction, Lever 2000 became the number two deodorant soap in dollar volume, with an estimated 8.4 percent of the $1.5 billion bar soap market.[48]

EXHIBIT 17–31

Shifting role of the promotion agency

Traditional	New Improved
1. Primarily used to develop short-term tactics or concepts.	1. Used to develop long- and short-term promotional strategies, as well as tactics.
2. Hired/compensated on a project-by-project basis.	2. Contracted on annual retainer, following formal agency reviews.
3. Many promotion agencies used a mix— each one hired for best task and/or specialty.	3. One or two exclusive promotion agencies for each division or brand group.
4. One or two contact people from agency.	4. Full team or "core group" on the account.
5. Promotion agency never equal to ad agency— doesn't work up front in annual planning process.	5. Promotion agency works on equal basis with ad agency— sits at planning table up front.
6. Not directly accountable for results.	6. Very much accountable— goes through a rigorous evaluation process.

To coordinate their advertising and sales promotion programs more effectively, many companies are getting their sales promotion agencies more involved in the advertising and promotional planning process. Rather than hiring agencies to develop individual, nonfranchise-building types of promotions with short-term goals and tactics, many firms are having their sales promotion and advertising agencies work together to develop more fully integrated promotional strategies and programs. Exhibit 17–31 shows how the role of sales promotional agencies is changing.

SALES PROMOTION ABUSE

The increasing use of sales promotion in the marketing program is more than a passing fad. It is a fundamental change in strategic decisions about how companies market their products and services. The value of this increased emphasis on sales promotion has been questioned by several writers, particularly with regard to the lack of adequate planning and management of sales promotional programs.[49]

As the use of sales promotion techniques increases, an important factor to consider is whether marketers are becoming too dependent on this element of the marketing program. Consumer and trade promotions can be a very effective tool for generating short-term increases in sales, and many brand managers would rather use a promotion to produce immediate sales than invest in advertising and build the brand's image over an extended time. As the director of sales promotion services at one large advertising agency noted:

> There's a great temptation for quick sales fixes through promotions. It's a lot easier to offer the consumer an immediate price savings than to differentiate your product from a competitor's.[50]

Overuse of sales promotion can be detrimental to a brand in several ways. A brand that is constantly promoted may lose perceived value. Consumers often end up purchasing a brand because it is on sale, they get a premium, or they have a coupon, rather than basing their decision on a favorable attitude they have developed. When the extra promotional incentive is not available, they switch to another brand.

Alan Sawyer and Peter Dickson have used the concept of *attribution theory* to examine how sales promotion may affect consumer attitude formation.[51] According to this theory, people acquire attitudes by observing their own behavior and considering why they acted in a certain manner. Consumers who consistently purchase a brand because of a coupon or price-off deal may attribute their behavior to the external promotional incentive rather than to a favorable attitude toward the brand. However, when no external incentive is available, consumers are more likely to attribute their purchase behavior to favorable underlying feelings about the brand.

Another potential problem with consumer-oriented promotions is that a **sales promotion trap** or spiral can result when a number of competitors use promotions extensively.[52] Often a firm begins using sales promotions to differentiate its product or service from the competition. If the promotion is successful and leads to a differential

EXHIBIT 17–32
Sales promotion dilemma

All other firms	Our firm	
	Cut back promotions	Maintain promotions
Cut back promotions	Higher profits for all	Market share goes to our firm
Maintain promotions	Market share goes to all other firms	Market share stays constant; profits stay low

advantage (or even appears to do so), competitors may quickly copy the promotional program. When all the competitors are using sales promotions, it not only lowers profit margins for each firm but also makes it difficult for any one firm to hop off the promotional bandwagon.[53] This dilemma is shown in Exhibit 17–32.

A number of industries have fallen into this promotional trap. In the cosmetics industry, gift-with-purchase and purchase-with-purchase promotional offers were developed as a tactic for getting buyers to sample new products. But they have become a common, and costly, way of doing business.[54] In many areas of the country, supermarkets have gotten into the trap of doubling or even tripling manufacturers' coupons, which cuts into their already small profit margins.

Marketers must consider both the short-term impact of a promotion and its long-term effect on the brand. The ease with which competitors can develop a retaliatory promotion and the likelihood of their doing so should also be considered. Marketers must be careful not to damage the brand franchise with sales promotions or to get the firm involved in a promotional war that erodes the brand's profit margins and threatens its long-term existence. Marketers are often tempted to resort to sales promotions to deal with declining sales and other problems rather than examining such other aspects of the marketing program as channel relations, price, packaging, product quality, or advertising.

SUMMARY

For many years, advertising was the major promotional mix element for most consumer product companies. Over the past decade, however, marketers have been allocating more of their promotional dollars to sales promotion. There has been a steady increase in the use of sales promotion techniques to influence consumers' purchase behavior. The growing power of retailers, erosion of brand loyalty, increase in new product introductions, fragmentation of the consumer market, short-term focus of marketing and product managers, and increase in advertising clutter are some of the reasons for this increase.

Sales promotions can be characterized as either franchise-building or nonfranchise-building promotions. The former contribute to the development and reinforcement of brand identity and image; the latter are designed to accelerate the purchase process and generate immediate increases in sales.

Sales promotion techniques can be classified as either trade or consumer oriented. A number of consumer-oriented sales promotion techniques were examined in this chapter, including sampling, couponing, premiums, contests and sweepstakes, rebates and refunds, bonus packs, price-off deals, and event sponsorship. The characteristics of these promotional tools were examined, along with their advantages and limitations. Various trade-oriented promotions were also examined, including trade contests and incentives, trade allowances, displays and point-of-purchase materials, training programs, trade shows, and cooperative advertising.

Advertising and sales promotion should not be viewed as separate activities but rather as complementary tools. When planned and executed properly, advertising and sales promotion can produce a synergistic effect that is greater than the response generated from either promotional mix element alone. To accomplish this, marketers must coordinate advertising and promotional themes, target audiences, and media scheduling and timing.

Sales promotional abuse can result when marketers become too dependent on the use of sales promotion techniques and sacrifice long-term brand position and image for short-term sales increases. In many industries, sales promotion traps develop when a number of competitors use promotions extensively and it becomes difficult for any single firm to cut back on promotion without risking a loss in sales. Overuse of sales promotion tools can not only lower profit margins but threaten the image and viability of a brand.

KEY TERMS

sales promotion, p. 476
consumer-oriented
   sales promotion,
   p. 476
trade-oriented sales
   promotion, p. 477
consumer-franchise-
   building (CFB)
   promotions, p. 482
nonfranchise-building
   (non-FB) promotions,
   p. 482

sampling, p. 486
bounce-back coupon,
   p. 492
cross-ruff coupon, p. 492
instant coupon, p. 493
premium, p. 494
self-liquidating
   premiums, p. 495
contest, p. 496
sweepstakes, p. 496
game, p. 496
bonus packs, p. 499

price-off deal, p. 499
event sponsorship, p. 500
push money, p. 504
off-invoice allowance,
   p. 505
failure fees, p. 506
forward buying, p. 506
diverting, p. 506
everyday low pricing
   (EDLP), p. 506
planograms, p. 507
trade show, p. 508

cooperative advertising,
   p. 508
horizontal cooperative
   advertising, p. 508
ingredient-sponsored
   cooperative
   advertising, p. 509
vertical cooperative
   advertising, p. 509
sales promotion trap,
   p. 513

DISCUSSION QUESTIONS

1. What are the differences between consumer-oriented and trade-oriented sales promotions? Discuss the role of each in a firm's integrated marketing communications program.

2. Discuss the various reasons sales promotion has become so important and is receiving an increasing portion of marketers' promotional budgets. Do you think the allocation trend toward sales promotion will continue? Why or why not?

3. It has been argued that the increase in sales promotion by consumer products companies is having a negative impact on brand equity. Why is this so? Do you agree or disagree with this argument?

4. What are the differences between consumer-franchise-building and nonfranchise-building promotions? Find an example of a promotion you believe contributes to the franchise of the brand and explain why.

5. Discuss the various ways sampling can be used as part of a company's integrated marketing communications program. What are some of the reasons sampling is becoming so popular among marketers?

6. Procter & Gamble recently cut back sharply on the use of coupons for its Pampers and Luvs brands of disposable diapers. Given that disposable diapers are one of the most popular product categories for coupon users, do you agree with this strategy? How might P&G compete without coupons in this product category?

7. How might marketers measure the effectiveness of an event sponsorship promotion such as a golf or tennis tournament or a concert?

8. Evaluate the everyday low pricing instituted a few years ago by Procter & Gamble. Do you think other companies will follow P&G's lead? Why or why not?

9. Why is it important that marketers use advertising in conjunction with sales promotion in introducing a new product?

10. What is meant by a sales promotion trap? What are the options for a company involved in such a situation?

Chapter 18

Public Relations, Publicity, and Corporate Advertising

Chapter Objectives

- To demonstrate the roles of public relations, publicity, and corporate advertising in the promotional mix.

- To differentiate between public relations and publicity and demonstrate the advantages and disadvantages of each.

- To examine the reasons for corporate advertising and its advantages and disadvantages.

- To examine methods for measuring the effects of public relations, publicity, and corporate advertising.

The Wonders of WD-40

WD-40, an industrial spray lubricant, has found its way into the consumer market in a big way. According to Craig Wilson, writing in USA Today, the product is achieving cult status as a cure-all for everything from stuck parakeets to arthritis—not to mention its intended uses as a lubricant and rust remover. In fact, there are so many uses for the product, the company (as a result of a suggestion from its public relations agency) ran a contest to determine the most unique application. The contest dubbed the "Most Unusual Uses Promotion" ran for a period of two months and drew over 1,200 entries. Users submitted their most unique uses for the product—regardless of how unusual they might be. Some of the entries submitted:

- Police wrote in to tell of a nude burglary suspect who had wedged himself into a vent at a Denver cafe, and was extracted with a large dose of WD-40.
- Dog owners claim it cures mange.
- Fishermen use it to spray on nightcrawlers (worms) to cover up the smell of human hands so the fish will bite.
- Glenn Palmer, 82, of Mission, Texas, claims it keeps his joints limber so he can go dancing two to three times a week.

Others have used it to clean oil from car engines, free toes stuck in soda bottles, and even keep squirrels from climbing metal poles to bother the birds.

There were so many interesting entries that two winners were selected. One winner—David Howland, a country and western guitarist from Ft. Worth, Texas—sprays WD-40 on his guitar strings to "increase action and maneuverability." According to David, "WD-40 makes [his] strings play faster." Winner number two was 78-year-old Agnes Saunders—the oldest carrier for the Blade-Citizen Tribune in Vista, California. Agnes's pet parakeet happened to get stuck on a sheet of mouse trap glue. When Agnes went to free the poor bird, she too got stuck. Both Agnes and her pet parakeet were ultimately freed by her veterinarian. The trick—using WD-40!

For their prizes both winners were awarded trips to San Diego (the home of WD-40) to attend the WD-40 gala even held in honor of the promotion. We know that David played the guitar, but we don't know if the parakeet sang or not.

There are so many uses for WD-40 that over a million gallons per year are manufactured and distributed to over 100 countries around the world. Sales in 1992 reached $99.9 million, and 79 percent of all of the homes in the US stock WD-40. All of this success stems from an invention that started as a product designed to prevent corrosion on airplanes and the early Atlas missiles, and was being snuck out of the factory by employees. (At the gala, company president Jerry Schleif issued an announcement that all of the "sneakers" have been forgiven!)

And how did USA Today get wind of all of this? Well, WD-40 also has a very good advertising and public relations agency that promotes the product by advertising, promotions, and public relations activities like the press release that led to this story in the USA International Edition!

Source: Craig Wilson, "A Little Spray Can Save the Day," USA Today, Feb. 16, 1993, p. B1.

he WD-40 story is just one example of the many ways organizations integrate public relations programs with other elements of the promotional mix to market their products more effectively. Besides the increased sales these programs generate, the positive publicity also provides long-term benefits.

Publicity, public relations, and corporate advertising all have promotional program elements that may be of great benefit to the marketer. They are integral parts of the overall promotional effort that must be managed and coordinated with the other elements of the promotions mix. However, these three tools do not always have the specific goals of product and service promotion as objectives, nor do they always involve the same methods you have become accustomed to as you have read this text. Typically, these activities are more involved in changing attitudes toward an organization or issue than in promoting specific products or affecting behaviors directly (though you will see that this role is changing in some organizations). In this chapter, we explore the roles of public relations, publicity, and corporate advertising, the advantages and disadvantages of each, and the process by which they are employed. Examples of such efforts—both successful and unsuccessful—are also included.

⊚ PUBLIC RELATIONS

What is public relations? How does it differ from other elements discussed thus far? Perhaps a good starting point would be to define what the term public relations has traditionally meant and then to introduce its new role.

The Traditional Definition of PR

While a variety of books define **public relations**, perhaps the most comprehensive definition is that offered by the *Public Relations News* (the weekly newsletter of the industry):

> the management function which evaluates public attitudes, identifies the policies and procedures of an organization with the public interest, and executes a program of action (and communication) to earn public understanding and acceptance.[1]

Public relations is indeed a management function. The term *management* should be used in its broadest sense; it is not limited to business managements but includes other types of organizations as well and extends to nonprofit institutions.

In this definition, public relations requires a series of stages, including:

1. The determination and evaluation of public attitudes.
2. The identification of policies and procedures of an organization with a public interest.
3. The development and execution of a communications program designed to bring about public understanding and acceptance.

This process does not occur all at once. An effective public relations programs continues over months or even years.

Finally, this definition reveals that public relations involves much more than activities designed to sell a product or service. The PR program may involve some of the promotional program elements previously discussed but use them in a different way. For example, press releases may be mailed to announce new products or changes in the organization. Special events may be organized to create goodwill in the community, and advertising may be used to state the firm's position on a controversial issue.

The New Role of Public Relations

In an increasing number of marketing-oriented companies, new responsibilities have been established for public relations. It takes on a much broader—and more marketing-oriented—perspective, designed to promote the organization as well as its products and/or services.

Exhibit 18–1 demonstrates four relationships that marketing and public relations can assume in an organization. These relationships are defined by the degree of use of each function.

@ **EXHIBIT 18–1**

Four classes of marketing and
public relations use

@ **EXHIBIT 18–1**

Four classes of marketing and
public relations use

		Public Relations	
		Weak	Strong
Marketing	Weak	1 Example: Small social service agencies	2 Example: Hospitals and colleges
	Strong	3 Example: Small manufacturing companies	4 Example: Fortune 500 companies

Class 1 relationships are characterized by a minimal use of either function. Organizations with this design typically have very small marketing and/or public relations budgets and devote little time and effort to them. Small social service agencies and nonprofit organizations are typically class 1.

Organizations characterized by a *class 2* relationship have a well-established public relations function but do very little in the way of formalized marketing. Colleges and hospitals typically have such a design, although in both cases marketing activities are increasing. Both of these groups have moved in the direction of class 4 organizations in recent years, though PR activities still dominate.

Many small companies are typified by a *class 3* organization in which marketing dominates and the public relations function is minimal. Private companies (without stockholders) and small manufacturers with little or no public to appease tend to employ this design.

Class 4 enterprises have both strong marketing and strong public relations. These two departments often operate independently. For example, public relations may be responsible for the more traditional responsibilities described earlier, while marketing promotes specific products and/or services. Both groups may work together at times, and both report to top management. Many Fortune 500 companies employ multiple ad agencies and PR firms.

The new role of public relations might best be characterized as class 4, although with a slightly different relationship. Rather than each department operating independently, the two now work closely together, blending their talents to provide the best overall image of the firm and its product or service offerings. Public relations departments increasingly position themselves as a tool to both supplant and support traditional advertising and marketing efforts and as a key part of the IMC program.

William N. Curry notes that organizations must use caution in developing class 4 relationships because PR and marketing are not one and the same, and when one becomes dominant, the balance required to operate at maximum efficiency is lost.[2] He says losing sight of the objectives and functions of public relations in an attempt to achieve marketing goals may in the long run operate to the organization's detriment. Others take an even stronger view that if public relations and marketing distinctions continue to blur, the independence of the public relations function will be lost, and it will be much less effective.[3] In this book, we take the position that in a truly integrated marketing communications program, public relations must play an integral role.

Integrating PR into the Promotional Mix

Given the broader responsibilities of public relations, the issue is how to integrate it into the promotional mix. Philip Kotler and William Mindak suggest a number of alternative organizational designs: either marketing or public relations can be the dominant

@ **EXHIBIT 18–2**

MPRs add value to marketing program

Cabbage Patch Kids The success of the Cabbage Patch Kids dolls was the result of a sophisticated public relations effort that saw the dolls featured on every major TV station, newspaper, and general-interest magazine in the United States.

Ford Motor Co. Ford achieved 50 percent brand awareness and orders of 146,000 Tauruses and Sables before they were ever advertised or released for sale, due to a strong MPR campaign.

Cuisinart An article in *Gourmet* magazine led to the launch of the food processor category and more orders for Cuisinart than the company could handle.

Saucony Hyde Athletic Industries doubled its sales when *Consumer Reports* awarded the Saucony Jazz 3000 running shoe with its top rating.

Goodyear Through an effective publicity campaign, the company sold 150,000 Aquatread tires before the first ads broke.

Source: Thomas L. Harris, "How MPR Adds Value to Integrated Marketing Communications," *Public Relations Quarterly* 38, no. 2 (Summer 1993), pp. 13–19.

---

function; both can be equal but separate functions; or the two can perform the same roles.[4] While each of these designs has its merits, in this text we consider public relations a promotional program element. This means that its broader role must include traditional responsibilities.

Whether a traditional role or a more marketing-oriented one is assumed, public relations activities are still tied to specific communications objectives. Assessing public attitudes and creating a favorable corporate image is no less important than strategies designed to promote products or services directly.

Marketing Public Relations (MPR) Functions

Thomas L. Harris has referred to public relations activities designed to support marketing objectives as **marketing public relations (MPR) functions**.[5] Marketing objectives that may be aided by public relations activities include raising awareness, informing and educating, gaining understanding, building trust, giving consumers a reason to buy, and motivating consumer acceptance. MPR adds value to the integrated marketing program in a number of ways:

- Building marketplace excitement before media advertising breaks. The announcement of a new product, for example, is an opportunity for the marketer to obtain publicity and dramatize the product, thereby increasing the effectiveness of ads.
- Creating advertising news where there is no product news. Ads themselves can be the focus of publicity. Pepsi, Apple Computers, and others have received millions of dollars of free exposure through their public relations activities surrounding Michael Jackson, Madonna, Ray Charles, and the Apple Macintosh.
- Introducing a product with little or no advertising. You will see later in this chapter that this strategy has been implemented successfully by No Excuses Jeans. Crayon manufacturer Crayola has also used this strategy to its advantage.
- Providing a value-added customer service. Butterball Turkey established a phone line where people can call in to receive personal advice on how to prepare their turkeys. The company handled 25,000 calls during the holiday season in 1993.
- Building brand-to-customer bonds. The Pillsbury Bake-off has led to strong brand loyalty among Pillsbury customers, who compete by submitting baking entries.
- Influencing the influentials—that is, providing information to opinion leaders.
- Defending products at risk and giving consumers a reason to buy. By taking constructive actions to defend a company's products, PR can actually give consumers a reason to buy. Harris notes that Heinz and McDonald's have worked with environmental groups and have been rewarded by consumers for their activities. As shown in Exhibit 18–2, a number of companies have successfully employed these strategies.

EXHIBIT 18–3

Exxon apologizes for the Alaskan oil spill

AN OPEN LETTER TO THE PUBLIC

On March 24, in the early morning hours, a disastrous accident happened in the waters of Prince William Sound, Alaska. By now you all know that our tanker, the Exxon Valdez, hit a submerged reef and lost 240,000 barrels of oil into the waters of the Sound.

We believe that Exxon has moved swiftly and competently to minimize the effect this oil will have on the environment, fish and other wildlife. Further, I hope that you know we have already committed several hundred people to work on the cleanup. We also will meet our obligations to all those who have suffered damage from the spill.

Finally, and most importantly, I want to tell you how sorry I am that this accident took place. We at Exxon are especially sympathetic to the residents of Valdez and the people of the State of Alaska. We cannot, of course, undo what has been done. But I can assure you that since March 24, the accident has been receiving our full attention and will continue to do so.

L. G. Rawl
Chairman

THE PROCESS OF PUBLIC RELATIONS

The actual process of conducting public relations and integrating it into the promotional mix involves a series of both traditional and marketing-oriented tasks.

Determining and Evaluating Public Attitudes

You've learned that public relations is concerned with attitudes toward the firm or specific issues beyond those directed at a product or service. The first question you may ask is why. Why is the firm so concerned with the public's attitudes?

One reason is that these attitudes may affect sales of the firm's products. A number of companies have experienced sales declines as a result of consumer boycotts. Procter & Gamble, Coors, Nike, and Bumblebee Tuna are just a few companies that responded to organized pressures. The oil spill that occurred in Prince William Sound, Alaska, when the tanker *Exxon Valdez* hit a submerged reef resulted in very unfavorable attitudes toward Exxon (the owner of the ship), which led to a number of protests, a boycott of Exxon products, and the return of thousands of the company's credit cards. Exhibit 18–3 shows an ad run by Exxon apologizing for the catastrophe and responding to the public relations problem it created.

Second, no one wants to be perceived as a bad citizen. Corporations exist in communities, and their employees may both work and live there. Negative attitudes carry over to employee morale and may result in a less than optimal working environment internally and in the community.

Due to their concerns about public perceptions, many privately held corporations, utilities, and publicly held companies conduct surveys of public attitudes. The reasons for conducting this research are many.

1. It provides input into the planning process. Once the firm has determined public attitudes, they become the starting point in the development of programs designed to maintain favorable positions or change unfavorable ones.

@ **EXHIBIT 18–4**

10 questions to evaluate public relations plans

1. Does the plan reflect a thorough understanding of the company's business situation?
2. Has the PR program made good use of research and background sources?
3. Does the plan include full analysis of recent editorial coverage?
4. Do the PR people fully understand the product's strengths and weaknesses?
5. Does the PR program describe several cogent, relevant conclusions from the research?
6. Are the program objectives specific and measurable?
7. Does the program clearly describe what the PR activity will be and its benefits to the company?
8. Does the program describe how its results will be measured?
9. Do the research, objectives, activities, and evaluations tie together?
10. Has the PR department communicated to marketing throughout the development of the program?

2. It serves as an early warning system. Once a problem exists, it may require substantial time and money to correct. By conducting research, the firm may be able to identify potential problems and handle them effectively before they become serious issues.
3. It secures support internally. If research shows a problem or potential problem exists, it will be much easier for the public relations arm to gain the support it needs to address this problem.
4. It increases the effectiveness of the communication. The better it understands a problem, the better the firm can design communications that will deal with it in the proper manner.[6]

Establishing a Public Relations Plan

In a survey of 100 top and middle managers in the communications field, over 60 percent said their PR programs involved little more than press releases, press kits for trade shows, and new product announcements.[7] Further, these tools were not formulated into a formal public relations effort but rather were used only as needed. In other words, no structured program was evident in well over half of the companies surveyed! As we noted earlier, the public relations process is an ongoing one, requiring formalized policies and procedures for dealing with problems and opportunities. Just as you would not develop an advertising and/or promotions program without a plan, you should not institute public relations efforts haphazardly. Moreover, the PR plan needs to be integrated into the overall marketing communications program. Exhibit 18–4 provides some questions marketers should ask to determine whether their PR plan is an appropriate one.

Cutlip, Center, and Broom suggest a four-step process for developing a public relations plan: (1) define public relations problems; (2) plan and program; (3) take action and communicate; and (4) evaluate the program.[8] These questions and the four-step planning process tie in with the promotional planning process stressed throughout this text.

Developing and Executing the PR Program

Because of the broad role that public relations may be asked to play, the PR program may need to extend beyond promotion. A broader definition of the target market, additional communications objectives, and different messages and delivery systems may be employed. Let us examine this process.

Determining relevant target audiences

The targets of public relations efforts may vary, with different objectives for each. Some may be directly involved in selling the product; others may affect the firm in a different way (e.g., they may be aimed at stockholders or legislators). These audiences may be internal or external to the firm or, as Global Perspective 18–1 demonstrates, international.

Global Perspective 18–1
Public Relations around the World

We are probably all familiar with some form of public relations activities carried out in the United States. These activities range from local sponsorships of Little League baseball teams to support of charities to sponsorships of the Olympics. All of these are made possible by a capitalist society. But public relations activities are carried out throughout the world—in some places and ways that might surprise you. Consider:

In Brazil, entrance into the public relations profession requires a university degree in PR and a professionally awarded license. Because of the large bureaucratic government, public relations is little more than a government lobbying effort. Corporate activities are almost nonexistent.

In Turkey, the PR business is flourishing due to the desire of business and government to enter the United States and the European Community. While the government still censors, unfavorable articles are tolerated.

In Russia, even though the government owns and controls the media, many nongovernment organizations successfully employ public relations techniques to get the word out. In fact, the effectiveness of their actions has contributed to the more liberal government policies there. The same is true in other former Eastern Bloc countries and Cuba.

Public relations activities in Ghana use less traditional channels of communications. Dance, songs, and storytelling are the most commonly employed PR tools for getting information to small towns and communities.

While the sophistication of public relations programs varies around the world, Ray E. Hiebert believes that the old ways of theorizing about these systems may be obsolete. (In the old system, the range was from total freedom of the press—in the United States, Canada, and the United Kingdom—to government censorship—in Russia, Cuba, and other communist countries.) Hiebert believes that the development of effective PR techniques, coupled with advances in communications technologies, requires new thinking. He thinks both extremes have moved more toward the center. Citing Russia and Cuba as examples, he notes that government can no longer control communications activities. On the other hand, Western countries have passed laws that place more restrictions on the press's freedoms. The way the media reported on Watergate and Vietnam would not be permitted now. Which raises the question: "Who is headed in the right direction here?"

Sources: Melvin L. Sharpe, "The Impact of Social and Cultural Conditioning on Global Public Relations," *Public Relations Review*, Summer 1992, pp. 103–108. Ray E. Hiebert, "Global Public Relations in a Post-Communist World: A New Model," *Public Relations Review*, Summer 1992, pp. 117–27.

Internal audiences may include the employees of the firm, stockholders and investors, members of the local community, suppliers, and current customers. Why are community members and customers of the firm considered internal rather than external? According to John Marston, it's because these groups are already connected with the organization in some way and the firm normally communicates with them in the ordinary routine of work.[9] **External audiences** are those people who are not closely connected with the organization (e.g., the public at large).

It may be necessary to communicate with these groups on an ongoing basis for a variety of reasons, ranging from ensuring goodwill to introducing new policies, procedures, or even products. A few examples might help.

Employees of the firm
Maintaining morale and showcasing the results of employees' efforts are often prime objectives of the public relations program. Organizational newsletters, notices on bulletin boards, paycheck envelope stuffers, direct mail, and annual reports are some of the methods used to communicate with these groups. Exhibit 18–5 shows an example of one such internal organization communication used by Brunswick Corporation.

Personal methods of communicating may be as formal as an established grievance committee or as informal as an office Christmas party. Other social events such as corporate softball or bowling teams are also used to create goodwill.

Stockholders and investors
You may think an annual report like the one in Exhibit 18–6 just provides stockholders and investors with financial information regarding the firm. While this is one purpose, annual reports also provide a communications channel for informing this audience about why the firm is or is not doing well, future plans, or other information that goes beyond numbers.

@ **EXHIBIT 18–5**

An example of a newsletter used for internal corporate communication

For example, McDonald's has successfully used annual reports to fend off potential public relations problems. One year the company ran a report on McDonald's recycling efforts to alleviate consumers' concerns about waste; another report included a 12-page spread on food and nutrition. Other companies have employed similar strategies. Shareholders' meetings, video presentations, and other forms of direct mail may be employed for this purpose. General Motors' annual public interest report is sent out to shareholders and community members to detail the company's high standards of corporate responsibility. Companies have used these approaches to generate additional investments, to bring more of their stocks "back home" (i.e., become more locally controlled and managed), and to produce funding to solve specific problems, as well as to promote goodwill.

Community members

People who live and work in the community where a firm is located or doing business are often the target of public relations efforts. Such efforts may involve ads informing the community of activities that the organization is engaged in—for example, reducing air pollution, cleaning up water supplies or, as shown in Exhibit 18–7, protecting wildlife. (As you can tell from Exhibit 18–7 on page 526, the community can be defined very broadly!) Demonstrating to the public that the organization is a good citizen with their welfare in mind may also be a reason for communicating to these groups.

Suppliers and customers

An organization wishes to maintain a level of *goodwill* with its suppliers as well as its consuming public. Consumers are less likely to buy from a company that they do not think is socially conscious, and they may take their loyalties elsewhere. Suppliers may be inclined to do the same.

@ **EXHIBIT 18–6**

Annual reports serve a
variety of purposes

Sometimes sponsoring a public relations effort results in direct evidence of success. For example, the "Just say no" to drugs campaign was a boon to companies manufacturing drug testing kits, hospitals offering drug rehabilitation programs, and TV news programs' ratings.[10] Indirect indications of the success of PR efforts may include more customer loyalty, less antagonism, or greater cooperation between the firm and its suppliers or consumers.

Sometimes a public relations effort may be targeted to more than one group. For example, San Diego Gas & Electric (SDGE), the public utility company for the San Diego area, has suffered from extreme negative attitudes among its customers due to high utility rates. This problem was aggravated when a series of management blunders resulted in even higher rates and plans were announced to build a nuclear plant in one of the lagoons near the ocean, resulting in protests from consumers and environmentalists. Stockholders and potential investors lacked trust, and employee morale was low. (Company cars with the SDGE logo on the doors were vandalized and drivers were threatened to the point where the identifying logos had to be removed.)

The public relations plan developed to deal with these problems targeted a variety of publics and employed a number of channels. Television spots showed consumers how to save energy. Print ads explained the reasons for the energy purchases made by management, and PR programs designed to foster more community interaction were developed. These programs have led to much more favorable attitudes among all the publics targeted. (At least employees can put the SDGE logo back on their cars!)

Relevant audiences may also include people not directly involved with the firm. The press, educators, civic and business groups, governments, and the financial community can be external audiences.

@ **EXHIBIT 18–7**

Chevron demonstrates public concern

The media

Perhaps one of the most critical external publics is the media, which determine what you will read in your newspapers or see on TV, what is news, and how this news will be presented. Because of the media's extreme power, they should be informed of the firm's actions. Companies issue press releases and communicate through conferences, interviews, and special events. The media are generally receptive to such information so long as it is handled professionally; reporters are always interested in good stories.

In turn, the media are concerned about how the community perceives them. Exhibit 18–8 is a public relations piece distributed by a San Diego television station that describes a variety of programs the station offers to benefit the community.

Educators

A number of organizations provide educators with information regarding their activities. The Direct Marketing Association, the Promotional Products Association, and the American Association of Yellow Pages Publishers (shown in Exhibit 18–9 on page 528), among others, keep educators informed in an attempt to generate goodwill as well as exposure for their causes. These groups, as well as major corporations, provide information regarding innovations, state-of-the-art research, and other items of interest.

Educators are a target audience because, like the media, they control the flow of information to certain parties—in this case, people like you.

Civic and business organizations

The local Jaycees, Kiwanis, and other nonprofit civic organizations also serve as gatekeepers of information to those in their spheres of influence. Speeches at organization functions, financial contributions to the groups, and sponsorships are all designed to

EXHIBIT 18-8

The media employs public relations to enhance their image in the community

create goodwill. Corporate executives' service on the boards of nonprofit organizations also generates positive public relations.

Governments

Public relations often attempts to influence government bodies directly at both local and national levels. Successful *lobbying* may mean immediate success for a product, while regulations detrimental to the firm may cost it millions. Imagine for a moment what FDA approval of NutraSweet meant to Searle or what could happen to the beer and wine industries should television advertising be banned. The bicycle helmet industry sometimes experiences sales increases of 200 to 400 percent when a helmet law is passed in a state.

Financial groups

In addition to current shareholders, potential shareholders and investors may be relevant target markets. Financial advisers, lending institutions, and others must be kept abreast of new developments, as well as the financial information typically provided, since they offer the potential for new sources of funding. Press releases and corporate reports play an important role in providing information to these publics.

Implementing the PR program

Once the research has been conducted and the target audiences identified, the public relations program must be developed and delivered to the receivers. A number of public relations tools are available for this purpose, including press releases, press conferences, exclusives, interviews, and community involvement.

@ EXHIBIT 18–9

The Yellow Pages distribute information to college professors, in part through *Link* magazine.

The press release

One of the most important publics is the press. To be used by the press, information must be factual, true, and of interest to the medium as well as to its audience. As shown in Exhibit 18–10, the source of the **press release** can do certain things to improve the likelihood that the "news" will be disseminated.

The information in a press release needs to be of interest to the readers of the medium it's sent to. For example, financial institutions may issue press releases to business trade media and to the editor of the business section of a general-interest newspaper. Information on the release of a new rock album is of more interest to radio disk jockeys than to TV newscasters; sports news also has its interested audiences.

Press conferences

We are all familiar with press conferences held by political figures. While used less often by organizations and corporations, this form of delivery can be very effective. The topic must be of major interest to a specific group before it is likely to gain coverage. Usually major accomplishments (such as the awarding of the next Super Bowl or Olympics location), major breakthroughs (such as medical cures), emergencies, or catastrophes warrant a national press conference. On a local level, community events, local developments, and the like may receive coverage. Companies often call press conferences when they have significant news to announce, such as the introduction of a new product or advertising campaign. Pepsi held a press conference to announce the termination of its contract with Michael Jackson when the rock star was accused of child molestation.

Exclusives

Although most public relations efforts seek a variety of channels for distribution, an alternative strategy is to offer one particular medium exclusive rights to the story if that medium reaches a substantial number of people interested in that area. Offering an **exclusive** may enhance the likelihood of acceptance. As you watch television over the next few weeks, look for the various networks' and local stations' exclusives. Notice how the media actually use these exclusives to promote themselves.

Interviews

When you watch TV or read magazines, pay close attention to the personal interviews being conducted. Usually someone will raise specific questions and a spokesperson provided by the firm answers them. For example, when four people died from eating tainted

⊚ **EXHIBIT 18–10**

Getting the public relations story told

Jonathan Schenker of Ketchum Public Relations, New York, suggests four new technological methods to make life easier for the press and to increase the likelihood of getting one's story told:

1. *Telephone press conferences*   Since reporters cannot always get to a press conference, use the telephone to call them for coverage.
2. *In-studio media tours*   Satellite communications providing a story, and a chance to interview, from a central location such as a TV studio save broadcast journalists time and money by eliminating their need to travel.
3. *Multicomponent video news releases (VNR)*   A five-component package consisting of a complete script in print and on tape, a video release with a live reporter, a local contact source at which to target the video, and a silent video news release that allows the station to fill in with its own news reporter lend an advantage owing to their budget-savings capabilities.
4. *Targeted newswire stories*   When the sender targets the public relations message, reporters are spared the need to read through volumes of news stories to select those of interest to their target audiences.

hamburgers at Jack-in-the-Box restaurants, the company's president gave personal interviews with the press to detail the corrective actions the company would take. Earvin (Magic) Johnson granted personal interviews when he announced his retirement as a player and then later his resignation as coach of the Los Angeles Lakers basketball team.

Community involvement

Many corporations enhance their public images through involvement in the local community. This involvement may take a variety of forms, including membership in local organizations like the Kiwanis or Jaycees and contributions to or participation in community events. For example, after the great flood created so much damage in the Midwest in 1993, Maytag issued press releases on how to deal with waterlogged appliances, Sara Lee provided frozen bagels and cheesecake, and Principal Mutual Life offered volunteer lawyers and actuaries to assess damages. Exhibit 18–11 is just one example of how companies pitched in to help Los Angeles residents after the January 1994 earthquake.

Other methods of distributing information include photo kits, bylined articles (signed by the firm), speeches, and trade shows. Of course, the specific mode of distribution is determined by the nature of the story and the interest of the media and its publics.

Advantages and Disadvantages of Public Relations

Like the other program elements, public relations has both advantages and disadvantages.

Advantages include the following.

- **Credibility**   Because public relations communications are not perceived in the same light as advertising—that is, the public does not realize the organization either directly or indirectly paid for them—they tend to have more credibility. The fact that the media are not being compensated for providing the information may lead receivers to consider the news more truthful and credible. For example, an article in newspapers or magazines discussing the virtues of aspirin may be perceived as much more credible than an ad for the same product.

  Automotive awards presented in magazines such as *Motor Trend* have long been known to carry clout among potential car buyers. Now marketers have found that even lesser media mean a lot as well. General Motors' Pontiac division played up an award given to Pontiac as "the best domestic sedan" by *MotorWeek* in a 30-minute program carried by about 300 public broadcasting stations. Likewise, Chrysler trumpeted the awards given to its Jeep Cherokee by *4-Wheel & Off Road Magazine.*[11]

  News about a product may in itself serve as the subject of an ad. Exhibit 18–12 on page 531 demonstrates how Toyota used favorable publicity from a variety of sources to promote its Supra. A number of auto manufacturers have also taken

@ **EXHIBIT 18–11**

Sears ad offering assistance
to earthquake victims

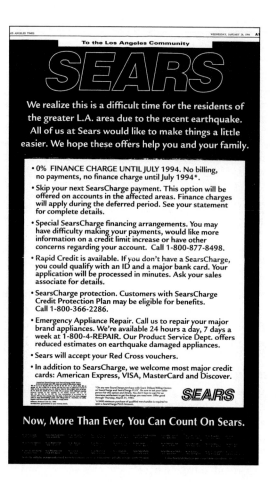

advantage in their ads of high customer satisfaction ratings reported by J. D. Powers & Associates, an independent research firm specializing in automotive research.

- **Cost**   In both absolute and relative terms, the cost of public relations is very low—particularly when the possible effects are considered. While a firm can employ public relations agencies and spend millions of dollars in this area, for smaller companies this form of communication may be the most affordable alternative available. Many public relations programs require little more than the time and expenses associated with putting the program together and getting it distributed, yet they still accomplish their objectives.

- **Avoidance of clutter**   Because they are typically perceived as *news items*, public relations messages are not subject to the clutter of ads. A story regarding a new product introduction or breakthrough is treated as a news item and is likely to receive attention. When Steven Jobs (the founder of Apple Computers) announced the introduction of the NeXT computer, all the networks covered it, as did major newspapers and magazines. Some (like CNN) devoted two- to three-minute segments to the story.

- **Lead generation**   Information about technological innovations, medical breakthroughs, and the like almost immediately results in a multitude of inquiries. These inquiries may give the firm some quality sales leads. For example, when John Daly—the longest driver on the PGA tour—was seen playing in the internationally televised Skins Game using a Cobra golf club, the club manufacturer received inquiries from all over the United States and as far away as Europe and Japan.

- **Ability to reach specific groups**   Because some products appeal to only a small market segment, it is not feasible to engage in advertising and/or promotions to reach this group. If the firm does not have the financial capabilities to engage in

@ **EXHIBIT 18-12**

Toyota capitalizes on positive publicity in its advertising

promotional expenditures, the best way to communicate to these groups is through public relations.

- **Image building**   Effective public relations leads to development of a positive image for the organization. A strong image is insurance against later misfortunes. For example, in 1982, seven people in the Chicago area died after taking Extra Strength Tylenol capsules that had been laced with cyanide (after they reached the store). Within one week of the poisonings, Tylenol's market share fell from 35 to only 6.5 percent. Strong public relations efforts combined with an already strong product and corporate image helped the product rebound (despite the opinions of many experts that it had no chance of recovering!). A brand or firm with a lesser image would never have been able to come back. The ad shown in Exhibit 18–13 demonstrates the power of a strong image.

Perhaps the major disadvantage of public relations is the potential for not completing the communications process. While public relations messages can break through the clutter of commercials, the receiver may not make the connection to the source. Many firms' public relations efforts are never associated with their sponsors in the public mind.

One way public relations may misfire is through mismanagement and a lack of coordination with the marketing department. When marketing and public relations departments operate independently, the potential exists for inconsistent communications, redundancies in efforts, and so on.

The key to effective public relations is to establish a good program, worthy of public interest, and manage it properly. To determine if this program is working, the firm must measure the effectiveness of the public relations effort.

Measuring the Effectiveness of Public Relations

As with the other promotional program elements, it is important to evaluate the effectiveness of the public relations efforts. In addition to determining the contribution of this program element to attaining communications objectives, the evaluation offers other advantages:

1. It tells management what has been achieved through public relations activities.
2. It provides management with a quantitative means of measuring public relations achievements.
3. It gives management a way to judge the quality of public relations achievements and activities.

@ **EXHIBIT 18–13**

This *Wall Street Journal* ad stresses the value of a strong brand and/or corporate image

WHY A STRONG BRAND IMAGE GIVES YOU AN ALMOST UNFAIR ADVANTAGE.

[In a world of parity products and services, nothing can tilt things more dramatically in your favor than powerful brand and corporate advertising.]

A brand or corporate image is not something that can be seen, touched, tasted, defined, or measured. Intangible and abstract, it exists solely as an idea in the mind. Yet it is often a company's most precious asset.

When in the 1980s, corporations laid out billions for the companies that owned brands like Kraft, Jell-O, Del Monte, Maxwell House and Nabisco, it wasn't the products themselves they were after, but the enduring power of warm images, feelings, and impressions associated with the brand names. In fact, when the dust finally settles, it will become clear that the megamergers, takeovers, and leveraged buyouts of that decade were primarily about the acquisition of brands.

Yet despite their enormous value, brands are not immune to neglect, and in the face of a tough economy and strong competition, companies are often tempted to sacrifice brand and corporate advertising for short-term promotion. While such strategies can yield immediate results, over time they can weaken and tarnish the brand.

Studies conducted on the PIMS (Profit Impact on Market Strategy) data base prove that companies that put

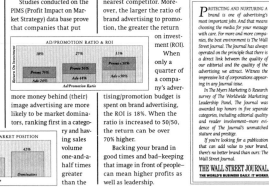

more money behind (their) image advertising are more likely to be market dominators, ranking first in a category and having sales volume one-and-a-half times greater than the nearest competitor. Moreover, the larger the ratio of brand advertising to promotion, the greater the return on investment (ROI). When only a quarter of a company's advertising/promotion budget is spent on brand advertising, the ROI is 18%. When the ratio is increased to 50/50, the return can be over 70% higher.

Backing your brand in good times and bad–keeping that image in front of people– can mean higher profits as well as leadership.

PROTECTING AND NURTURING A brand is one of advertising's most important jobs. And that means choosing the media for your message with care. For more and more companies, the best environment is The Wall Street Journal. The Journal has always operated on the principle that there is a direct link between the quality of our editorial and the quality of the advertising we attract. Witness the impressive list of corporations appearing in any Journal issue.

In The Myers Marketing & Research survey of The Worldwide Marketing Leadership Panel, The Journal was awarded top honors in five separate categories, including editorial quality and reader involvement–more evidence of The Journal's unmatched stature and prestige.

If you're looking for a publication that can add value to your brand, there's no better brand than ours: The Wall Street Journal.

THE WALL STREET JOURNAL.
THE WORLD'S BUSINESS DAILY. IT WORKS.

© 1991 Dow Jones & Company, Inc. All Rights Reserved. Source: Myers Marketing & Research. 6A292

As shown in Exhibit 18–14, a number of criteria may be used to measure the effects of PR programs. Raymond Simon suggests additional means for accomplishing this evaluation process, including the following.

- **Personal observation and reaction**   Personal observation and evaluation by one's superiors should occur at all levels of the organization.
- **Matching objectives and results**   Specific objectives designed to attain the overall communications objectives should be related to actions, activities, or media coverage. For example, placing a feature story in a specific number of media is an objective, quantitative, and measurable goal.[12]

EXHIBIT 18–14

Criteria for measuring
the effectiveness of public
relations

A system for measuring the effectiveness of the public relations program has been developed by Lotus HAL. The criteria used in the evaluation process include:

- The total number of impressions over time
- The total number of impressions on the target audience
- The total number of impressions on specific target audiences
- Percentage of positive articles over time
- Percentage of negative articles over time
- Ratio of positive to negative articles
- Percentage of positive/negative articles by subject
- Percentage of positive/negative articles by publication or reporter
- Percentage of positive/negative articles by target audience

- **The team approach**   Harold Mendelsohn suggests that one way to achieve attitude and behavior modification through public information campaigns is the **team approach**, whereby evaluators are actually involved in the campaign.[13] By using research principles and working together, the team develops—and accomplishes—assumed intents.
- **Management by objectives**   Executives and their managers act together to identify goals to be attained and the responsibilities of the managers. These goals are then used as a standard to measure accomplishments.
- **Public opinion and surveys**   Research in the form of public opinion surveys may be used to gather data to evaluate program goal attainment.
- **Audits**   Both internal and external audits may be used. **Internal audits** involve evaluations by one's superiors or peers within the firm to determine the performance of the employee (or his or her programs). **External audits** are conducted by consultants, the client (in the case of a public relations agency), or other parties outside the organization.

A number of other bases for evaluation can be used. Walter Lindenmann says three levels of measures are involved: (1) the basic, which measures the actual PR activities undertaken; (2) the intermediate, which measures audience reception and understanding of the message; and (3) the advanced, which measures the perceptual and behavioral changes that result.[14]

Some organizations may use a combination of measures, depending on their specific needs. For example, Hewlett-Packard uses impression counts, awareness and preference studies, in-house assessments, press clippings counts, and tracking of studies.[15]

In summary, the role of public relations in the promotional mix is changing. As PR has become more marketing oriented, the criteria by which the programs are evaluated have also changed. At the same time, nonmarketing activities will continue to be part of the public relations department and part of the basis for evaluation.

PUBLICITY

Publicity refers to the generation of news about a person, product, or service that appears in broadcast or print media. To many marketers, publicity and public relations are synonymous. In fact, publicity is really a subset of the public relations effort.

But there are several major differences. First, publicity is typically a *short-term* strategy, while public relations is a concerted program extending over a period of time. Second, public relations is designed to provide positive information about the firm and usually is controlled by the firm or its agent. Publicity, on the other hand, is not always positive and is not always under the control of, or paid for by, the organization. Publicity, both positive and negative, often originates from sources other than the firm.

In most organizations, publicity is controlled and disseminated by the public relations department. In this section, we discuss the role publicity plays in the promotional program and some of the ways marketers use and react to these communications.

The Power of Publicity

One of the factors that most sets off publicity from the other program elements is the sheer *power* this form of communication can generate. Unfortunately for marketers, this power is not always realized in the way they would like it to be. Publicity can make or break a product or even a company, as evidenced by the following examples.

- After Buick LeSabre received very favorable customer satisfaction ratings in J. D. Power's initial quality survey, sales jumped 81.5 percent in the next month (compared to the same month the previous year).[16]
- Sales of Perrier dropped by 40 percent when it was announced that the natural water drink contained benzene.[17]
- Sales of Cabernet Sauvignon increased an average of 45 percent in the four-week period following a CBS "60 Minutes" report that daily moderate consumption of red wine can reduce the risks of heart disease.
- The Suzuki Samurai is no longer marketed aggressively and the Audi 5000 is no longer marketed at all in the United States as a result of sales losses incurred after negative publicity in *Consumer Reports* and on "60 Minutes," respectively.

Earlier we discussed the substantial drop in Tylenol sales resulting from extensive media coverage of the tampering with its products while on store shelves. The Johnson & Johnson marketing efforts (including a strong public relations emphasis) designed to aid recovery were a model in proficiency that will be studied by students of marketing (in both the classroom and the boardroom) for many years. By January 1983, almost 100 percent of the original brand share had been regained. Unfortunately, a marketer cannot always capitalize on positive publicity or control the effects of negative publicity.

Why is publicity so much more powerful than advertising or sales promotions—or even other forms of public relations? First, publicity is highly *credible*. Unlike advertising and sales promotions, publicity is not usually perceived as being sponsored by the company (in the negative instances, it never is). So consumers perceive this information as more objective and place more confidence in it. In fact, *Consumer Reports*—the medium responsible for one of the examples previously cited—recently ran an advertising campaign designed to promote its credibility by noting it does not accept advertising and therefore can be objective in its evaluations.

Publicity information may be perceived as endorsed by the medium in which it appears. For example, publicity regarding a breakthrough in the durability of golf balls will go far to promote them if it is reported by *Golf* magazine. *Car & Driver's* award for car of the year reflects the magazine's perception of the quality of the auto selected.

Still another reason for publicity's power is its *news value* and the frequency of exposure it generates. When basketball stars Larry Bird and Kareem Abdul-Jabbar appeared together in a commercial for Lay's potato chips, the ad appeared on every major TV network and many cable sports programs, both as a paid commercial and free as the media publicized the campaign. When Lay's introduced its new campaign for Doritos Tortilla Thins featuring comedian Chevy Chase, television reporters aired 1,734 stories about the ads using footage provided by Frito-Lay.[18]

The bottom line is that publicity is *news*, and people like to pass on information that has news value. Publicity thus results in a significant amount of free, credible, word-of-mouth information regarding the firm and its products.

The Control and Dissemination of Publicity

In some of the examples cited earlier, the control of publicity was not in the hands of the company. While in some instances it is the firm's own blunder to allow the information to leak out, Suzuki and Audi could do nothing to stop the media from releasing the information. When publicity becomes news, it is reported by the media, sometimes despite the efforts of the firm. In these instances, the organization needs to react to the potential threat created by the news.

A good example of one company's efforts to respond to adverse publicity is shown in Exhibit 18–15. Tree Top's problems began when all the major news media reported that the chemical alar, used by some growers to regulate the growth of apples, might

@ **EXHIBIT 18–15**

Tree Top responds to the
threat of negative publicity

EXHIBIT 18–15

Tree Top responds to the threat of negative publicity

cause cancer in children. Despite published denials by reliable scientific and medical authorities (including the Surgeon General) that Alar does not cause cancer, a few special-interest groups were able to generate an extraordinary amount of adverse publicity, causing concern among consumers and purchasing agents. A few school districts took apples off their menus, and even applesauce and juice were implicated. To state its position, Tree Top ran the ad in Exhibit 18–15 to alleviate consumers' fears. It also sent a direct mailing to nutritionists and day care operators. The campaign was successful in assuring consumers of the product's safety and rebuilding their confidence.

In other instances, however, publicity must be managed like any other promotional tool. For example, when the FDA instructed P&G to stop using "fresh" claims in its Citrus Hill orange juice, the company refused to do so. After a lengthy confrontation, the FDA eventually impounded thousands of gallons of the product, and the resulting publicity reflected negatively on both the brand and the organization.

Publicity can also work for the marketer. The Cabbage Patch Kids, Cuisinart, and Saucony examples cited earlier are prime examples of the positive impact publicity can have.

Marketers like to have as much control as possible over the time and place where information is released. One way of doing this is the **video news release**, a publicity piece produced by publicists so that stations can air it as a news story. The videos almost never mention that they are produced by the subject organization, and most news stations don't mention it either. The Doritos Tortilla Thins ad was a subject of a video news release, as were stories about Elizabeth Taylor's 60th birthday party at Disneyland, the making of a Pepsi commercial featuring Shaquille O'Neal, and Jessica Little—a child who got lost at night in Ripley, Tennessee, and was found when searchers saw the lights on her L.A. Gear shoes.[19] Many other companies have made significant use of video news releases.

In their efforts to manage publicity and public relations, marketers are continuously learning more about these activities. Courses are offered and books written on how to manage publicity. These books cover how to make a presentation, whom to contact, how to issue a press release, and specific information for each medium addressed—including TV, radio, newspapers, magazines, and direct-response advertising. They discuss such alternative media as news conferences, seminars, events, and personal letters, as well as insights on how to deal with government and other legislative bodies. Because this information is too extensive to include as a single chapter in this text, we suggest you pursue one of the many books available on this subject for additional insights.

Advantages and Disadvantages of Publicity

Publicity offers the advantages of credibility, news value, significant word-of-mouth communications, and a perception of being endorsed by the media. Beyond the potential impact of negative publicity, two major problems arise from the use of publicity: timing and accuracy.

Timing

Timing of the publicity is not always completely under the control of the marketer. Unless the press thinks the information has very high news value, the timing of the communication release is entirely up to the media—if it gets released at all. Thus, the information may be released earlier than desired or too late to make an impact.

Accuracy

One of the major ways to get publicity is the press release. Unfortunately, the information sometimes gets lost in translation—that is, it is not always reported the way the provider wishes it to be. As a result, inaccurate information, omissions, or other errors may result. Sometimes when you see a publicity piece that was written based on a press release, you wonder if they are even talking about the same topic!

Measuring the Effectiveness of Publicity

The methods for measuring the effects of publicity are essentially the same as those discussed earlier under the broader topic of public relations. Rather than reiterate them here, we thought it would be more interesting to show you an actual example. Exhibit 18–16 is a model developed by Ketchum Public Relations for tracking the effects of publicity. (I guess we just provided Ketchum with some free publicity.)

⊚ CORPORATE ADVERTISING

One of the more controversial forms of advertising is corporate advertising. Actually an extension of the public relations function, **corporate advertising** does not promote any one specific product or service. Rather, it is designed to promote the firm overall, by enhancing its image, assuming a position on a social issue or cause, or seeking direct involvement in something. Why is corporate advertising controversial? A number of reasons are offered:

1. **Consumers are not interested in this form of advertising**   A Gallup and Robinson study reported in *Ad Age* found consumers were 35 percent less interested in corporate ads than in product-oriented advertising.[20] This may be because consumers do not understand the reasons behind such ads. Of course, much of this confusion results from ads that are not very good from a communications standpoint.
2. **A costly form of self-indulgence**   Firms have been accused of engaging in corporate image advertising only to satisfy the egos of top management. This argument stems from the fact that corporate ads are not easy to write. The message to be communicated is not as precise and specific as one designed to position a product, so the top managers often dictate the content of the ad, and the copy reflects their ideas and images of the corporation.

@ EXHIBIT 18–16 The Ketchum publicity tracking model

Paul H. Alvarez, chairman and chief executive officer of Ketchum Public Relations, describes his firm's publicity tracking model as follows:

We have done a pretty good job in educating clients on what publicity programs can and cannot do, and what can be realistically expected. But true accountability requires *measured* results. Is publicity *measurable?*

Up to now, perhaps not. But Ketchum Public Relations has been working for three years on "The Ketchum Publicity Tracking Model," the first computer-based measurement system designed specifically to evaluate publicity programs. It goes beyond traditional accounting methods such as reporting to the client the number of column inches or the amount of broadcast time obtained, and the total audiences reached... It evaluates, via a publicity exposure index, the amount of target audience exposure received and the degree to which planned messages were delivered to the target audience.

In planning a campaign to be evaluated by the model, the client and the firm agree upon standards of performance in two areas: the number of gross impressions to be achieved within the target audience, and the key messages to be delivered to that audience. The firm's computer is programmed with audience statistics from media in 120 top national markets. Performance standards for a given program are also programmed into the computer along with campaign results.

Results are then printed out by media category, target audience reached, and the quality (based on numerical values assigned to various "selling" points in the copy) of the message delivered to the audience. The computer then produces two evaluative numbers: an overall exposure index and an overall value index. Taking 1.00 as a standard index for the campaign, the degree to which the index is above or below this figure shows to what extent performance was above or below the norm.

In the accompanying "Sample Tracking Report," based on a campaign in Orlando, Florida, the exposure index (1.08) and the value index (1.48) indicate that the program overall met expectations and exceeded the established norms.

The first column of figures in the report shows media exposure among designated market area (DMA) audiences. The second column records average size/length of exposure for each medium, which is translated into average media units (based on a norm of 1.00) and publicity exposure units.

The columns for average impact factor and publicity value units indicate the degree to which key "selling" points in the copy were mentioned in the exposures. Note that the average impact factor for network television is low (0.81). The reason is that although the subject of the campaign (a special event) was mentioned fairly often (1.93 average media units), mention of specific dates and other key copy points did not meet expectations.

The tracking model also demonstrates in advance what a publicity program will do. Thus it is a tool for deciding whether or not a program is worth carrying out. If the decision is "go," it then reports how well objectives were met. Instead of guesswork, we now have a method for placing accountability to the client on a factual basis.

Sample Tracking Report

Placement Type	DMA Target Audience (thousands)	Average Size/ Length	Average Media Units	Publicity Exposure Units (thousands)	Average Impact Factor	Publicity Value Units (thousands)
Newspapers	4,552	1/9 page	0.93	4,233	1.26	5,334
Magazines	268	1/2 page	1.66	455	1.47	656
Television (network)	95	5:10 min	1.93	183	0.81	149
Television (local)	504	6:05 min	2.13	1,073	1.81	1,946
Radio (local)	200	10:00	2.60	520	1.40	728
Totals	5,619		1.15	6,454	1.37	8,813

Publicity exposure norm = 5,960,000
Publicity exposure index (6,454/5,960) = 1.08
Publicity value index (8,813/5,960) = 1.48

The publicity exposure norm is established by estimating the target audiences (adults 18–49, weighted 60 percent male, 40 percent female) and an exposure of a "good" hypothetical placement schedule.
The publicity exposure index suggests the campaign's exposure was 1.08, as good as expected on a normal (= 1.00) basis.
The publicity value index suggests the impact value of the campaign was 1.48 times as good as expected on a normal (= 1.00) basis.

3. **A belief that the firm must be in trouble**   Some critics believe the only time firms engage in corporate advertising is when they are in trouble—either in a financial sense or in the public's eye—and are advertising to attempt to remedy the problem. There are a number of forms of corporate advertising, each with its own objectives. These critics argue that these objectives have become important only because the firm has not been managed properly.

4. **Corporate advertising is a waste of money**   Given that the ads do not directly appeal to anyone, are not understood, and do not promote anything spe-

◎ **EXHIBIT 18-17**

3M promotes its image as an innovative company

cific, critics say the monies could be better spent in other areas. Again, much of this argument has its foundation in the fact that corporate image ads are often intangible. They typically do not ask directly for a purchase; they do not ask for investors; rather, they present a position or try to create an image. Because they are not specific, many critics believe their purpose is lost on the audience and these ads are not a wise investment of the firm's resources.

Despite these criticisms and others, corporate advertising has increased in use. It has been estimated that more than 7 percent of all advertising dollars spent are for corporate advertising, meaning billions of dollars are spent on this form of communication.[21]

While corporate advertising has generally been regarded as the domain of companies such as USX, Kaiser Aluminum, and Boise Cascade—that is, companies with no products to sell directly to the consumer market—this is no longer the case. Beatrice Foods, BASF, and Procter & Gamble are just a few consumer products companies running corporate image ads, and IBM and AT&T have also increased expenditures in this area.

Since the term corporate advertising has been used as a catchall for any type of advertising run for the direct benefit of the corporation rather than its products or services, much advertising falls into this category. For purposes of this text (and to attempt to bring some perspective to the term), we use it to describe any type of advertising designed to promote the organization itself rather than its products or services.

Objectives of Corporate Advertising

Corporate advertising may be designed with two goals in mind: (1) creating a positive image for the firm and (2) communicating the organization's views on social, business, and environmental issues. More specific applications include:

- Boosting employee morale and smoothing labor relations.
- Helping newly deregulated industries ease consumer uncertainty and answer investor questions.
- Helping diversified companies establish an identity for the parent firm, rather than relying solely on brand names.[22]

As these objectives indicate, corporate advertising is targeted at both internal and external audiences and involves the promotion of the organization as well as its ideas.

⊙ EXHIBIT 18-18

VISA advertises its sponsorship of the Winter Olympics

Types of Corporate Advertising

Attainment of corporate advertising's objectives is sought through implementing image, advocacy, or cause-related advertising. Each form is designed to achieve specific goals.

Image advertising

One form of corporate advertising is devoted to promoting the organization's overall *image*. **Image advertising** may accomplish a number of objectives, including creating *goodwill* both internally and externally, creating a position for the company, and generating resources—both human and financial. A number of methods are used.

1. **General image or positioning ads**   As shown in Exhibit 18–17, ads are often designed to create an image of the firm in the public mind. The exhibit shows how 3M is attempting to create an image of itself as an innovative company making life safer, easier, and better for people.

    Other companies have used image advertising to attempt to change an existing image. The American Medical Association (AMA), responding to its less than positive image among many Americans who perceived doctors as inattentive money-grubbers, ran a series of ads portraying doctors in a more sensitive light. The AMA spent over $1.75 million to highlight the caring, sharing, and sensitive side of AMA members.[23] *Penthouse* magazine attempted to change its image with advertisers by running ads in trade magazines that showed *Penthouse* was not just a magazine with pictures of nude females.

2. **Sponsorships**   A firm often runs corporate image advertising on programs or television specials. For example, the Hallmark or IBM specials and documentaries on network TV and Mobil and Gulf Oil program sponsorships on public TV are designed to promote the corporation as a good citizen. By associating itself with high-quality or educational programming, the firm hopes for a carryover effect that benefits its own image.

    Other examples of sponsorships include those run by Dutch Boy Paints and the NBA to raise funds to fight child abuse, *Family Circle* magazine and JC Penney's support of "Sesame Street," and Budget Rent-a-Car's sponsorship of women's sports (Ladies' Professional Golf Association, Women's Tennis Association, and Women's Sports Foundation).

    Exhibit 18–18 shows a Visa ad touting the company's sponsorship of the 1994 Winter Olympics. Visa considers sponsorships an important part of its integrated

EXHIBIT 18-19

A variety of companies sponsor the Olympic games

marketing communications. It has also sponsored the US Open Tennis Championships, the 1993 Major League Baseball All-Star game, the US decathlon team, US basketball "Dream Team," and US gymnastics federation. According to John Bennett, senior VP for international marketing communications, the sponsorships are designed to fulfill specific business objectives while providing support for the recipients.[24] Exhibit 18–19 shows a few of the companies that decided an Olympic sponsorship would be good for them.

3. **Recruiting**   The promotional piece for Deloitte & Touche presented in Exhibit 18–20 is a good example of corporate image advertising designed to attract college graduates. If you are a graduating senior considering a career in accounting, this ad, promoting a corporate image for the company, will interest you.

   The Sunday employment section of most major metropolitan newspapers is an excellent place to see this form of corporate image advertising at work. Notice the ads in these papers and consider the image the firms are presenting.

4. **Generating financial support**   Some corporate advertising is designed to generate investments in the corporation. By creating a more favorable image, the firm looks attractive to potential stock purchasers and investors. More investments mean more working capital, more monies for research and development, and so on. In this instance, corporate image advertising is almost attempting to make a sale; the product is the firm.

   While there is no concrete evidence that corporate image advertising leads directly to increased investment, at least one study shows a correlation between the price of stock and the amount of corporate advertising done.[25] Firms that spent more on corporate advertising also tend to have higher-priced stocks (though keep in mind that a direct relationship is very difficult to substantiate).

⊚ EXHIBIT   18–20

Deloitte & Touche creates an image for recruitment

This thing called image is not unidimensional! Many factors affect it. Exhibit 18–21 reveals the results of a survey conducted by *Fortune* magazine. The most admired firms in *Fortune's* survey did not gain their positions merely by publicity and word of mouth (nor, we guess, did the least admired).

A positive corporate image is not likely to be created just from a few advertisements. Quality of products and services, innovation, sound financial practices, good corporate citizenship, and wise marketing practices are just a few of the factors that contribute to overall image.

Advocacy advertising

A second major form of corporate advertising addresses social, business, or environmental issues. Such **advocacy advertising** is concerned with propagating ideas and elucidating controversial social issues of public importance in a manner that supports the interests of the sponsor.[26]

While still portraying an image for the company or organization, advocacy advertising does so indirectly, by adopting a position on a particular issue rather than promoting the organization itself.

An example of advocacy advertising is shown in Exhibit 18–22 on page 543. It has increased in use over the past few years and has also met with increased criticism. The ads may be sponsored by a firm or by an industry association and are designed to tell readers how the firm operates or management's position on a particular issue.

Sometimes the advertising is a response to negative publicity or to the firm's inability to place an important message through public relations channels. In other situations, the firm may just wish to get certain ideas accepted or have society understand its concerns.

@ **EXHIBIT 18–21**

Eight key attributes of corporate reputation

Quality of Management

Most Admired	Score
Home Depot	9.31
Rubbermaid	9.02
J.P. Morgan	8.87

Least Admired	Score
Leslie Fay	2.74
Brooke Group	2.79
California Federal Bank	3.69

Quality of Products or Services

Most Admired	Score
Rubbermaid	9.15
Procter & Gamble	8.83
Walt Disney	8.81

Least Admired	Score
Southern Pacific Trans.	3.47
Brooke Group	3.89
Trans World Airlines	4.53

Financial Soundness

Most Admired	Score
J.P. Morgan	9.13
Coca-Cola	8.98
Microsoft	8.96

Least Admired	Score
Trans World Airlines	1.68
Brooke Group	1.79
Northwest Airlines	2.25

Value as Long-Term Investment

Most Admired	Score
Coca-Cola	8.78
United Parcel Service	8.73
Rubbermaid	8.65

Least Admired	Score
Trans World Airlines	1.95
Brooke Group	2.05
Northwest Airlines	2.57

Use of Corporate Assets

Most Admired	Score
Rubbermaid	8.50
Berkshire Hathaway	8.25
Microsoft	8.25

Least Admired	Score
Leslie Fay	2.24
Brooke Group	2.45
Crystal Brands	3.00

Innovativeness

Most Admired	Score
Rubbermaid	9.11
3M	8.78
Motorola	8.70

Least Admired	Score
Brooke Group	3.45
Southern Pacific Trans.	3.69
Borden	3.71

Community and Environmental Responsibility

Most Admired	Score
Rubbermaid	8.03
Corning	7.90
Johnson & Johnson	7.89

Least Admired	Score
Brooke Group	2.53
Gitano Group	3.46
Food Lion	3.73

Ability to Attract, Develop, and Keep Talented People

Most Admired	Score
Microsoft	8.69
J.P. Morgan	8.67
Home Depot	8.53

Least Admired	Score
Brooke Group	2.32
Trans World Airlines	2.95
Gitano Group	3.13

Source: *Fortune*, Feb. 7, 1994.

While advocacy advertising has been criticized by a number of sources (including consumer advocate Ralph Nader), as you can see in Exhibit 18–23 on page 544 this form of communication has been around for some time. AT&T engaged in issues-oriented advertising way back in 1908 and has continued to employ this form of communication throughout the 20th century. Critics contend that companies with large advertising dollars purchase too much ad space and time and that advocacy ads may be misleading, but the checks and balances of regular product advertising also operate in this area.

◎ **EXHIBIT 18–22**

Advocacy ads take a position on an issue

Heroes

A coffin draped in the American flag...surviving officers in dress uniforms, mourning their fallen comrade...families in black, quietly sobbing, trying to understand what cannot be understood.

We have seen it too many times, the final rites for our defenders—fallen not in foreign wars, but today, right here at home in hundreds of American cities and towns. Another kind of war—against crime—is killing one American law-enforcement officer in the line of duty every 57 hours.

Like those fallen in other wars, these men and women wear the many faces of America. They are black and they are white; they trace their roots back to Asia and Africa and Europe and the Americas. They are young and old, they are commanders, detectives, and foot soldiers in the battle against lawlessness.

Consider these numbers:
● 30,000 law-enforcement officers have been killed on duty in the history of the U.S.
● In 1987 (the most recent data available), 155 officers were killed, 21,273 were wounded and 63,842 were assaulted with a weapon.
● In the past 10 years, 1,525 police officers have been killed, 204,584 have been injured and 590,822 have been assaulted.

● Every day, 500,000 American law-enforcement officers subject themselves to these risks, on our behalf.

How do we honor them? And how do we keep their sacrifices vivid in the public consciousness? One way is through the construction of the National Law Enforcement Officers Memorial. Congress has declared that the memorial will be built on three acres of open space at Washington, D.C.'s Judiciary Square. Groundbreaking is planned for Spring 1989, and the memorial should be ready for dedication by Peace Officers' Memorial Day, May 15, 1990.

Apart from donating the land, Congress purposely allocated no money for the construction. That is to come from corporations, organizations and individual donors. The fund-raising goal for the memorial is $7.5 million; more than $1.2 million has been raised to date.

Join us in contributing to the National Law Enforcement Officers Memorial Fund, 1360 Beverly Road, Suite 305, McLean, VA 22101. Contributions are tax deductible. Your contribution also is a symbol of support for our hometown heroes, for their service and sacrifice. They deserve it. They've earned it.

Mobil®

© 1988 Mobil Corporation

For example, an ad run by the seven regional Bell operating companies that addressed the threat of Japanese technologies in the telecommunications industry was perceived by some congressmen (the group the ads were designed to influence) as Japan-bashing and offensive. When the ad backfired, the campaign was immediately halted and the agency responsible for developing it was fired.[27] The ultimate judge, of course, is always the reader.

Cause-related marketing

An increasingly popular method of image building is **cause-related marketing**, in which companies link with charities or nonprofit organizations as contributing sponsors. The company benefits from favorable publicity, while the charity receives much-needed funds. This apparent win–win situation is not always as good as it seems, however, as demonstrated in Ethical Perspective 18–1 on page 545.

Advantages and Disadvantages of Corporate Advertising

A number of reasons for the increased popularity of corporate advertising become evident when you examine the advantages of this form of communication.

1. It is an excellent vehicle for positioning the firm. Firms, like products, need to establish an image or position in the marketplace. Corporate image ads are one vehicle for accomplishing this objective. A well-positioned product is much more

EXHIBIT 18–23

Advocacy ads have been used for years

likely to achieve success than is one with a vague or no image. The same holds true of the firm. Stop and think for a moment about the image that comes to mind when you hear of IBM, Apple, Johnson & Johnson, or Procter & Gamble. Now what comes to mind when you hear the words Unisys, USX, or Navistar? How many of the consumer brands can you name that fall under Beatrice Foods' corporate umbrella? (Swiss Miss, Tropicana, Cutty Sark, and many others.) While we are not saying these latter companies are not successful—because they certainly are—we are suggesting their corporate identity (or position) is not as well entrenched as those first cited. Companies with strong positive corporate images have an advantage over competitors that may be enhanced when they promote the company overall.

2. Corporate image advertising takes advantage of the benefits derived from public relations. As the PR efforts of firms have increased, the attention paid to these events by the media has lessened (not because they are of any less value, but rather because there are more events to cover). The net result is that when a company engages in a public relations effort, there is no guarantee it will receive press coverage and publicity. Corporate image advertising gets the message out, and though consumers may not perceive it as positively as information from an objective source, the fact remains that it can communicate what has been done.

3. Corporate image advertising reaches a select target market. It should not be targeted to the general public. Corporate image advertising is often targeted to investors and managers of other firms rather than to the general public. It is not a problem if the general public does not appreciate this form of communication, as long as the target market does. In this respect, this form of advertising may be accomplishing its objectives.

≈≈≈ **Ethical Perspective 18–1**
Are Good Causes Good Marketing?

Not all advertising and public relations activities are designed to sell products and services. Or are they? While many firms engage in advocacy advertising and cause-related PR for philanthropic purposes, their critics say that the real objective is always to make money.

One of the more controversial examples of this difference in opinions surrounds the Benetton ads. For years, Benetton has placed provocative advertising promoting world peace and integration and exemplifying the plight of the disadvantaged. Its most recent campaign, shown in 25 countries, pictured simply the bloody camouflage uniform of a dead soldier in Sarajevo. Benetton claimed it ran the ad to help bring attention to the terrible war; critics claimed it was exploiting the war for profit.

Avon's support of breast cancer research is one of the most visible cause-related marketing efforts ever undertaken by a Fortune 500 firm. The five-year program was initiated with 415,000 Avon sales reps wearing pink ribbons and distributing over 15 million brochures on the topic. The company co-sponsored a prime-time TV special on the disease and has underwritten a PBS special. Avon's TV ads stress the advantages of early detection. The campaign offers Avon some distinct marketing advantages: the ability to cut through the clutter of competing messages, free publicity, and an enhanced corporate image among women, just to cite a few.

A variety of other companies have also engaged in cause-related activities, including Sears, Ben & Jerry's, Kraft General Foods, Sara Lee, and Estée Lauder. All stress the benefits to society, and all expect to improve their image in the process.

But is helping others good business? Avon seems to think so. AmEx credits its antihunger campaign with boosting US charge volume by 9.4 percent, McDonald's believes its stores were not damaged in the L.A. riots because of local community support, and Midas attributes its increase in women customers to its cause-related campaign. But Star-Kist believes its promotion of dolphin-safe tuna actually hurt sales, as consumers switched to cheaper brands. A number of European countries banned the Benetton ads, and boycotts were urged (yet Benetton sales and net income continue to increase).

Research indicates confusion. In a study by Roper Starch Worldwide, 66 percent of consumers claimed they would switch brands to back a cause they supported. But 58 percent believed that cause-related efforts were designed for the sole purpose of enhancing the company's image. Only 12 percent said that helping a cause was an important factor in their purchase decision. The confusion and the controversy go on.

Sources: Geoffrey Smith and Ron Stodghill, "Are Good Causes Good Marketing?" *Business Week*, March 21, 1994, pp. 64–65; Peter Gumbel, "Benetton Is Stung by Backlash over Ad," *The Wall Street Journal*, March 24, 1994, p. B1; Suein Hwang, "Linking Products to Breast Cancer Fight Helps Firms Bond with Their Customers," *The Wall Street Journal*, Sept. 21, 1993, p. B1.

Some of the disadvantages of corporate advertising were alluded to earlier in the chapter. To these criticisms, we can add the following.

1. **Questionable effectiveness**   There is no strong evidence to support the belief that corporate advertising works. Many think the data cited earlier that demonstrated a correlation between stock prices and corporate image advertising has little meaning. A study by Bozell & Jacobs Advertising of 16,000 ads concluded that corporate advertising contributed to only 4 percent of the variability in the company's stock price, compared with a 55 percent effect attributable to financial factors.[28] A second study also casts doubts on earlier studies that concluded that corporate advertising worked.[29]

2. **Constitutionality and/or ethics**   Some critics contend that since larger firms have more money, they can control public opinion unfairly. This point was resolved in the courts in favor of the advertisers. Nevertheless, many consumers still see such advertising as unfair and immediately take a negative view of the sponsor.

As you can see, a number of valid points have been offered for and against corporate advertising. Two things are certain: (1) No one knows who is right and (2) the use of this communications form continues to increase.

Measuring the Effectiveness of Corporate Advertising

As you can tell from our discussion on the controversy surrounding corporate advertising, there needs to be some method for evaluating whether or not such advertising is effective.

- **Attitude surveys**   One way to determine the effectiveness of corporate advertising is conducting attitude surveys to gain insights into both the public's and investors' reactions to ads. The Phase II study conducted by Yankelovich, Skelly & White (a market research firm in Connecticut) is perhaps one of the best-known applications of this measurement method.[30] The firm measured recall and attitudes toward corporate advertisers and found that corporate advertising is more efficient in building recall for a company name than is product advertising alone. Frequent corporate advertisers rated better on virtually all attitude measures than those with low corporate ad budgets.

- **Studies relating corporate advertising and stock prices**   The Bozell & Jacobs study is one of many that have examined the effect of various elements of corporate advertising (position in the magazine, source effects, etc.) on stock prices. These studies have yielded conflicting conclusions, indicating that while the model for such measures seems logical, methodological problems may account for at least some of the discrepancies.

- **Focus group research**   Focus groups have been used to find out what investors want to see in ads and how they react after the ads are developed. As with product-oriented advertising, this method has limitations, although it does allow for some effective measurements.

While the effectiveness of corporate advertising has been measured by some of the methods used to measure product-specific advertising, research in this area has not kept pace with that of the consumer market. (One study reported that only 35 of the Fortune 500 companies ever attempted to measure performance of their annual reports.[31]) The most commonly offered reason for this lack of effort is that corporate ads are often the responsibility of those in the highest management positions in the firm, and these parties do not wish to be held accountable. Interestingly, those who should be most concerned with accountability are the most likely to shun this responsibility!

@ SUMMARY

This chapter examined the role of the promotional elements of public relations, publicity, and corporate image advertising. We noted that these areas are all significant to the marketing and communications effort and are usually considered differently from the other promotional elements. The reasons for this special treatment stem from the facts that (1) they are typically not designed to promote a specific product or service and (2) in many instances it is harder for the consumer to make the connection between the communication and its intent.

Public relations was shown to be useful in its traditional responsibilities as well as in a more marketing-oriented role. In many firms, PR is a separate department operating independently of marketing; in others, it is considered a support system. Many large firms have an external public relations agency, just as they have an outside advertising agency.

In the case of publicity, another factor enters the equation: lack of control over the communication the public will receive. In public relations and corporate image advertising, the organization remains the source and retains much more control. Publicity often takes more of a reactive than a proactive approach. Publicity may be more instrumental or detrimental to the success of a product or organization than all other forms of promotion combined.

While not all publicity can be managed, the marketer must nevertheless recognize its potential impact. Press releases and the management of information are just two of the factors under the control of management. Proper reaction and strategy to deal with uncontrollable events are also responsibilities.

Corporate advertising was described as controversial, largely because the source of the message is top management, so the rules for other advertising and promoting forms are often not applied. This element of communication definitely has its place in the promotional mix. But to be effective, it must be used with each of the other elements, with specific communications objectives in mind.

Finally, we noted that measure of evaluation and control are required for each of these program elements as they are for all others in the promotional mix. We presented some methods for taking such measurements and some evidence why it is important to use them. As long as the elements of public relations, publicity, and corporate image advertising are considered integral components of the overall communications strategy, they must respect the same rules as the other promotional mix elements to ensure success.

KEY TERMS

public relations, p. 518
marketing public
  relations (MPR)
  functions, p. 520
internal audiences,
  p. 523

external audiences,
  p. 523
press release, p. 528
press conference, p. 528
exclusive, p. 528
team approach, p. 533
internal audits, p. 533

external audits, p. 533
publicity, p. 533
video news release,
  p. 535
corporate advertising,
  p. 536

image advertising, p. 539
advocacy advertising,
  p. 541
cause-related
  marketing, p. 543

DISCUSSION QUESTIONS

1. Explain what is meant by the terms cause-related marketing and advocacy advertising. Cite some organizations that have used this strategy. Does it work?

2. Discuss the difference between the traditional role of public relations and its new role.

3. What are MPR's functions? How might they benefit the organization's marketing program?

4. Why is publicity so powerful? Give examples of how it has worked for and against companies.

5. Some people believe firms should not adopt the new marketing-oriented role for public relations. Argue for and against this position.

6. How do public relations programs differ in various countries around the world? Give examples.

7. What are some reasons for conducting public relations research activities?

8. Describe some of the problems that might result from boycotts. Discuss strategies for combating boycotts.

9. Discuss some strategies used to implement the public relations program. Give examples.

10. We mentioned Exxon's reaction to the Alaskan oil spill. Using the concepts presented in this chapter, discuss some of the things Exxon might have done to better remedy the negative publicity the spill generated.

Chapter *19*

Personal Selling

Chapter Objectives

- To examine the role of personal selling in the integrated marketing communications program.
- To examine the advantages and disadvantages of personal selling as a promotional program element.

- To demonstrate how personal selling is combined with other program elements in an integrated marketing communications program.
- To consider ways to determine the effectiveness of the personal selling effort.

Does Your Sales Department Have a Leak?

Kenichi Ohmae, in his book Mind of the Strategist, differentiates between sales loss and sales leakage. Perhaps the clearest distinction is that leakage refers to lost potential sales rather than the loss of existing customers. The difference between leaks and losses is not as important as the understanding that both have a detrimental effect on the organization.

Ohmae cites three reasons for sales leakages: (1) markets and customers are not covered or found; (2) customers are competed for and lost; and (3) the product/model is not offered. James Obermayer adds four more reasons: (4) sales productivity is wasted (too much driving time or paperwork); (5) incentive compensation has weaknesses; (6) follow-up on sales inquiries and leads is poor or nonexistent; and (7) there is a lack of marketing intelligence (not knowing the market, customers, and competitors).

Sales losses stem from many sources, ranging from lack of customer satisfaction to changes in the buyer-seller relationship. Says Albert Wertheimer, dean of pharmacy at the Philadelphia College of Pharmacy and Science, "It used to be you would go to the office, bring some samples, and schmooze. Now you have to sit down with some MBA or a committee staring at you."

Because the marketing environment is changing so rapidly and so dramatically, other elements of the integrated marketing program must now help stop the leaks and the outright bursts. Nowhere has this been felt more than in the pharmaceutical industry, where a variety of strategies has been pursued. For example, Merck sent its president to Group Health in Seattle to mend fences and determine how the company might remain competitive. SmithKline has used price discounts and promotional allowances to stop the sales slide of Tagamet, an ulcer medication. Other companies are supplanting traditional personal selling visits with telemarketing, direct mail, database management strategies, and toll-free numbers to provide information and handle complaints. Advertising effectiveness is being improved through a thorough analysis of competitors' advertising practices such as dollars spent, media used, and claims made. Improved inquiry follow-ups and more specific targeting have also improved the advertising program. Last but not least is increased attention to public relations activities. Salespeople are no longer just peddlers but partners, all the way from problem solving to supporting clients' charities to sponsorships. The personal selling business has certainly changed!

Sources: Joseph Weber and Sunita W. Bhargava, "Drugmakers Get a Taste of Their Own Medicine," *Business Week*, April 26, 1993, pp. 104–5; James W. Obermayer, "Looking Out for Sales Leakage," *Sales & Marketing Management*, Nov. 1991 (reprint).

PERSONAL SELLING

The above examples demonstrate just a few of the ways organizations are integrating the personal selling function into the overall marketing communications program. They also reflect the complementary role of each of these elements in a field previously dominated by personal sales. In Chapter 1, we stated that while we recognize the importance of personal selling and the role it plays in the overall marketing and promotions effort, it is not emphasized in this text. Personal selling is typically under the control of the sales manager, not the advertising and promotions department. But personal selling does make a valuable contribution to the promotional program. To develop a promotional plan effectively, a firm must integrate the roles and responsibilities of its sales force into the communications program. A strong cooperative effort between the departments is also necessary.

This chapter focuses on the role personal selling assumes in the integrated marketing communications program, the advantages and disadvantages of this program element, and the basis for evaluating its contributions to attaining communications objectives. In addition, we explore how personal selling is combined with other program elements, both to support them and to receive support from them.

The Scope of Personal Selling

Personal selling involves selling through a person-to-person communications process. The emphasis placed on personal selling varies from firm to firm depending on a variety of factors, including the nature of the product or service being marketed, size of the organization, and type of industry. Personal selling often plays the dominant role in industrial firms, while in other firms, such as low-priced consumer nondurable goods firms, its role is minimized. In many industries, these roles are changing to a more balanced use of promotional program elements. In an integrated marketing communications program, personal selling is used as a partner with, not a substitute for, the other promotional mix elements.

Exhibit 19–1 shows the results of a survey of marketing managers' perceptions of how the various elements of the promotional mix will change in the near future. The managers interviewed expect sales management and personal selling to increase in importance more than any other element of the promotional mix. Note, however, that other elements are expected to gain in importance as well, indicating an enhanced overall promotional program.

THE ROLE OF PERSONAL SELLING IN THE PROMOTIONAL MIX

Manufacturers may promote their products *directly* to consumers through advertising and promotions and/or direct-marketing efforts or *indirectly* through resellers and salespeople. (A sales force may call on customers directly—for example, in the insurance industry or real estate. But this chapter focuses on the personal selling function as it exists in most large corporations or smaller companies—that is, as a link to resellers or dealers in business-to-business transactions.) Depending on the role defined by the organization, the responsibilities and specific tasks of salespeople may differ, but ultimately these tasks are designed to help attain communications and marketing objectives.

Personal selling differs from the other forms of communication presented thus far in that messages flow from a sender (or group of senders) to a receiver (or group of receivers) directly (usually face to face). This *direct* and *interpersonal communication* lets the sender immediately receive and evaluate feedback from the receiver. This communications process, known as **dyadic communication** (between two people or groups), allows for more specific tailoring of the message and more personal communications than do many of the other media discussed. The message can be changed to address the receiver's specific needs and wants.

In some situations, this ability to focus on specific problems is mandatory, as a standard communication would not suffice. Consider an industrial buying situation in which the salesperson is an engineer. To promote the company's products and/or services, the salesperson must understand the specific needs of the client. This may mean understanding the tensile strength of materials or being able to read blueprints or plans to understand the requirements. Or say a salesperson represents a computer graphics firm. Part of

@ **EXHIBIT 19–8**

Research and consulting
companies offer businesses
direct-marketing services

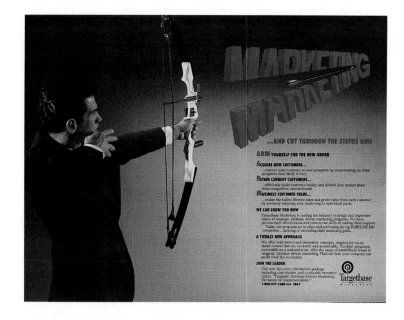

time to getting customers and noncustomers back on-line. Coors provided free water in its cans to residents of Pittsburgh when a barge break contaminated the drinking water. After the 1993 riots in Los Angeles, a number of organizations helped rebuild the ravaged community. These actions result in goodwill toward both the company and its products while at the same time benefiting society.

Combining Personal Selling and Direct Marketing

Companies have found that integrating direct marketing, specifically telemarketing, into their field sales operations makes their sales efforts more effective. The cost of a sales call and the cost associated with closing the sale are already very high and on the increase. Many marketers have reduced these costs by combining telemarketing and sales efforts (a typical telesales call costs about $15).[12] A number of companies now offer consulting services to help organizations in that endeavor, as shown in Exhibit 19–8.

The telemarketing department is used to screen leads and—after qualifying potential buyers on the basis of interest, credit ratings, and the like—pass them on to the sales force. The net result is a higher percentage of sales closings, less wasted time by the sales force, and a lower average cost per sale. For example, IBM has teamed up with Zacson Corp. to open an integrated Teleservices Center to manage and service its Northern California territory. The group handles inquiries, lead generation, and qualification; develops promotional campaigns; distributes public relations materials; and does problem solving for IBM clients. The new relationship reduced IBM's customer contact costs by 97 percent, lowered sales visit costs from $500 to $15, and exceeded customer expectations 78 percent of the time.[13]

As shown in Exhibit 19–9, there has been a rapid growth in the use of the telemarketing–sales combination for other firms as well. They have determined the phone can be used effectively for service and follow-up functions as well as for growth-related activities. Supplementing personal selling efforts with phone calls frees the sales force to spend more time selling.

In addition to selling and supporting the sales efforts, the telemarketing staff provides a public relations dimension. Communicating with buyers more often creates goodwill, improving customer satisfaction and loyalty.

In addition to telemarketing, other forms of direct marketing have been combined successfully with personal selling. For example, many companies send out lead cards to screen prospective customers. The salesperson follows up on those who express a genuine interest, saving valuable time and increasing the potential for a sale.

@ **EXHIBIT 19–9**

The growth of telemarketing as a sales function: reasons for growth (in percent)

	Telephone Sales and Service	Field Sales
Total growth related	58.0	61.8
Overall business growth or expansion	44.7	43.1
Adding product lines	10.2	8.0
Adding territories	3.1	10.7
Total system related	20.8	7.5
Added centralized telemarketing dept.	11.5	1.8
Added/changed computer system	6.2	4.4
Centralized sales and marketing	3.1	1.3
Customer demand	10.5	10.2
Cost efficiencies	1.4	0
Other	2.0	2.2
Can't tell/no response	9.8	18.2

Note: Adds to more than 100 percent owing to multiple mentions.

Combining Personal Selling and Sales Promotion

The program elements of sales promotion and personal selling also support each other. For example, many of the sales promotions targeted to resellers are presented by the sales force, who will ultimately be responsible for removing or replacing them as well.

While trade sales promotions are designed to support the reseller and are often targeted to the ultimate consumer, many other promotional tools are designed to assist the sales staff. Flip charts, leave-behinds, and specialty ads may be designed to assist salespeople in their presentations, serve as reminders, or just create goodwill. The number of materials available may range from just a few to hundreds, depending on the company. (If you ever get the chance, look into the trunk of a consumer products salesperson's car. You will find everything from pens to calendars to flip charts to samples to lost baseball mitts—all but the last of which are used in the selling effort.)

Likewise, many sales promotions are targeted at the sales force itself. Incentives such as free trips, cash bonuses, or gifts are often used to stimulate sales efforts. And, as we saw with resellers, contests and sweepstakes may also be used.

It is important that the elements of the promotional program work together, as each has its specific advantages and disadvantages. While personal selling is valuable in accomplishing certain objectives and supporting other promotional tools, it must be supported by the other elements. Ads, sales promotions, and the like may be targeted to the ultimate user, resellers, or the organization's sales force.

@ **EVALUATING THE PERSONAL SELLING EFFORT**

Like all other elements of the promotional mix, personal selling must be evaluated based on its contribution to the overall promotional effort. The costs of personal selling are often high, but the returns may be just as high.

Because the sales force is under the supervision of the sales manager, evaluations are typically based on sales criteria. Sales may be analyzed by total sales volume, territories, product line, customer type, or sales rep.[14] Other sales-related criteria such as new account openings and personal traits are also sometimes considered, as shown in Exhibit 19–10.

From a promotional perspective, sales performance is important, as are the contributions of individuals in generating these sales. On the other hand, the promotions manager is charged with evaluating the performance of personal selling as one program element contributing to the overall promotional program. So he or she needs to use different criteria in determining its effectiveness.

Criteria for Evaluating Personal Selling

A number of criteria may be used to evaluate the contribution of the personal selling effort to the promotional program. They include the following.

- **Provision of marketing intelligence** The ability of the sales force to feed back information regarding competitive programs, customer reactions, market trends, and other factors that may be important in the development of the promotional program.

@ **EXHIBIT 19–10**

Criteria used to evaluate sales forces

Quantitative Measures	
Sales Results	**Sales Efforts**
Orders Number of orders obtained Average order size (units or dollars) Batting average (orders ÷ sales calls) Number of orders canceled by customers **Sales volume** Dollar sales volume Unit sales volume By customer type By product category Translated into market share Percentage of sales quota achieved **Margins** Gross margin Net profit By customer type By product category **Customer accounts** Number of new accounts Number of lost accounts Percentage of accounts sold Number of overdue accounts Dollar amount of accounts receivable Collections made of accounts receivable	**Sales calls** Number made on current customers Number made on potential new accounts Average time spent per call Number of sales presentations Selling time versus nonselling time Call frequency ratio per customer type **Selling expenses** Average per sales call As percentage of sales volume As percentage of sales quota By customer type By product category Direct selling expense ratios Indirect selling expense ratios **Customer service** Number of service calls Displays set up Delivery cost per unit sold Months of inventory held by customer type Number of customer complaints Percentage of goods returned
Qualitative Measures	

Selling skills
Knowing the company and its policies
Knowing competitors' products and sales
  strategies
Use of marketing and technical backup
  teams
Understanding of selling techniques
Customer feedback (positive and negative)
Product knowledge
Customer knowledge
Execution of selling techniques
Quality of sales presentations
Communication skills
	Sales-related activities
	Territory management: sales call
	  preparation, scheduling, routing, and
	  time utilization
	Marketing intelligence: new product
	  ideas, competitive activities, new
	  customer preferences
	Follow-ups: use of promotional brochures
	  and correspondence with current and
	  potential accounts
	Customer relations
	Report preparation and timely submission
	Personal charateristics
	Cooperation, human relations,
	  enthusiasm, motivation, judgment, care
	  of company property, appearance,
	  self-improvement efforts, patience,
	  punctuality, initiative, resourcefulness,
	  health, sales management potential,
	  ethical and moral behavior

- **Follow-up activities**   The use and dissemination of promotional brochures and correspondences with new and existing customers; providing feedback on the effectiveness of various promotional programs.
- **Program implementations**   The number of promotional programs implemented; the number of shelf and/or counter displays used and so forth; the implementation and assessment of cooperative advertising programs.
- **Attainment of communications objectives**   The number of accounts to whom presentations were made (awareness, evaluation), the number of trial offers accepted, and the like.

Combining these criteria with those used by the sales department, the promotions manager should achieve an accurate assessment of the effectiveness of the personal selling program. The ability to make these evaluations requires a great deal of cooperation between the departments.

SUMMARY

This chapter discussed the nature of personal selling and the role this program element plays in the promotional mix. The role of personal selling in the integrated marketing communications program varies depending on the nature of the industry, competition, and market conditions. In many industries (for example, industrial markets) the personal selling component may receive the most attention, while in others (for example, consumer nondurables) it plays a minor role. However, managers in most industries believe the importance of this program element will continue to increase over the next few years.

Personal selling offers the marketer the opportunity for a dyadic communications process—that is, a two-way exchange of information. The salesperson can instanta-

neously assess the situation and the effects of the communication and adapt the message if necessary.

While this exchange lets the sales rep tailor the message specifically to the needs and wants of the receiver, it also offers the disadvantage of a nonstandardized message, since the final message communicated is under the salesperson's control. In an attempt to develop a standard communication, marketers provide their reps with flip charts, leave-behinds, and other promotional pieces.

Evaluation of the personal selling effort is usually under the control of the sales department, as sales is the most commonly used criterion. The promotions manager must assess the contribution of personal selling with nonsales-oriented criteria as well.

KEY TERMS

personal selling, p. 550
dyadic communication,
    p. 550
provider stage, p. 552
persuader stage, p. 552
prospector stage, p. 552

problem-solver stage,
    p. 552
procreator stage, p. 553
relationship marketing,
    p. 553

order taking, p. 554
creative selling, p. 554
missionary sales, p. 554
prospecting, p. 554
leads, p. 555

prospects, p. 555
qualified prospects,
    p. 555
close, p. 555
cross sell, p. 555

DISCUSSION QUESTIONS

1. Discuss some of the advantages and disadvantages of using personal selling as part of the promotional program.
2. What is relationship marketing? Give examples of how companies might employ this strategy.
3. What are some criteria typically used by marketers to evaluate personal selling's contribution to the promotional program?
4. In what situations, and for what types of products, might personal selling be effective? Give examples.
5. What questions must a company ask to determine the role of personal selling in integrated marketing communications?

6. Describe the five stages in the evolution of selling. Explain the salesperson's role at each stage.
7. Explain the responsibilities of these sales jobs: creative selling, order taking, missionary sales.
8. Describe the situations in which the sales force becomes a major part of the communications mix.
9. Explain why the sales force might be one of the more vulnerable areas of the firm in respect to ethics. Discuss some of the problems that might arise from unethical behaviors.
10. Explain why the salesperson's ability to tailor the message to the receiver can be both an advantage and a disadvantage.

PART VI

MONITORING, EVALUATION, AND CONTROL

20
Measuring the Effectiveness of the Promotional Program

"Give up my Pepsi? Don't even think about it."

BE YOUNG HAVE FUN DRINK PEPSI!

Chapter **20**

Measuring the Effectiveness of the Promotional Program

Chapter Objectives

- To discuss reasons for measuring promotional program effectiveness.
- To examine the various dependent measures used in assessing promotional program effectiveness.
- To evaluate alternative methods for measuring promotional program effectiveness.
- To review the requirements of proper effectiveness research.

Good Advertising Results in Good Sales—Or Does It?

It seems logical that good ads result in increased sales. That's why we advertise in the first place, isn't it? Unfortunately, the ads that consumers like best may not translate into increased sales at the checkout counter. Consider these facts:

1. Seven of the 25 package-goods brands identified by Video Storyboard Tests, Inc., as the best remembered commercials of 1993 had flat or declining sales.

2. Pepsi's ad featuring basketball star Shaquille O'Neal finished second in the Video Storyboard survey, but Pepsi's sales declined by 1.6 percent. (The carbonated beverage market saw a 4.2 percent growth rate.)

3. Sales for the Energizer battery were up 3.8 percent, but category growth was up 5 percent—although the Energizer bunny campaign was the thirteenth most popular in the survey.

Does this mean that advertising isn't effective? Not necessarily. Some of the other top finishers showed significant sales increases. Kodak film (up 4.5 percent), Doritos (16 percent), and Coke (8 percent) lend support to the advertising–sales relationship. Nestlé's Taster's Choice showed a 2.7 percent sales decrease, but the category sales were down even more, by 5.8 percent.

Some experts believe that the problem may be that we expect too much from advertising. Pepsi and its ad agency say that judging the effectiveness of an ad by sales is just too simplistic, because it fails to take into account other factors such as shelf space and promotions. David Badehra, president of Video Storyboard Tests, thinks ad campaigns need to be measured over time because they may take years to catch on. Others say advertising may have other objectives. They cite some of the Effie winners (the American Marketing Association's awards for the most effective advertising campaigns). For example:

- The Beef Council's primary demand campaign increased positive attitudes by 50 percent and purchase intent by 12 percent.
- The Kool-Aid international campaign increased brand awareness by 31 percent.
- The Partnership for a Drug-Free America's campaign has significantly changed teenagers' attitudes toward cocaine.

Perhaps marketers are using the wrong criteria to evaluate their advertising programs. Or maybe they just expect too much. On this point, Pepsi and Coke agree. In response to the lack of sales effectiveness of the Video Storyboard ads, senior vice president of Pepsi Jeff Campbell said, "Advertising has become a spectator sport, and the tendency is to overplay its importance." A spokesperson for Coke said, "We would assume that certainly the advertising had a positive effect on sales, . . . but I can't say it equates to 8 percent. There are so many other things going on." Indeed there are.

Sources: Laura Bird, "Loved the Ad. May (or May Not) Buy the Product," *The Wall Street Journal*, April 7, 1994, p. B1; "The 1993 Effies," *BrandWeek*, June 14, 1993, p. 1–29.

he search for ways to measure the effectiveness of advertising is constant, and as you can see by the lead-in to this chapter, not everyone agrees what should be measured or how to do it. Both clients and agencies are continually striving to determine whether their communications are working. Unfortunately, there seems to be little agreement on the best measures to use. Almost everyone agrees that research is required, but they disagree on how it should be conducted and how the results are used.

Measuring the effectiveness of the promotional program is a critical element in the promotional planning process. Research allows the marketing manager to evaluate the performance of specific program elements and provides input into the next period's situation analysis. It is a necessary ingredient to a continuing planning process, yet it is often not carried out.

In this chapter, we discuss some reasons firms should measure the effectiveness of their advertising and promotional programs and why many decide not to. We also examine how, when, and where such measurements can be conducted. Most of our attention is devoted to measuring the effects of advertising because much more time and effort have been expended developing evaluation measures in advertising than in the other promotional areas. (In some of these areas, the measures are more directly observable—for example, direct marketing and personal selling.) You should also remember that we addressed the methods used to evaluate many of the other promotional elements in previous chapters.

It is important to understand that in this chapter we are concerned with research that is conducted in an evaluative role—that is, to measure the effectiveness of advertising and promotion and/or to assess various strategies before implementing them. This is not to be confused with research discussed earlier in the text that serves as input into the development of the promotional program. While evaluative research may occur at various times throughout the promotional process (including the development stage), it is conducted specifically to assess the effects of various strategies. We begin our discussion with the reasons effectiveness should be measured as well as some of the reasons firms do not do so.

ARGUMENTS FOR AND AGAINST MEASURING EFFECTIVENESS

Almost any time one engages in a project or activity, whether for work or fun, some measure of performance occurs. In sports you may compare your golf score against par or your time on a ski course to others'. In business, employees are generally given objectives to accomplish, and their job evaluations are based on their ability to achieve these objectives. Advertising and promotion should not be an exception. It is important to determine how well the communications program is working and to measure this performance against some standards.

Reasons to Measure Effectiveness

Assessing the effectiveness of ads both before they are implemented and after the final versions have been completed and fielded offers a number of advantages.

1. **Avoiding costly mistakes** The top three advertisers in the United States spent over $5 billion in advertising and promotion in 1993. The top 100 spent a total of over $35 billion. This is a lot of money to be throwing around without some understanding of how well it is being spent. If the program is not achieving its objectives, the marketing manager needs to know so he or she can stop spending (wasting) money on it.

    Just as important as the out-of-pocket costs is the *opportunity* loss that accrues from poor communications. If the advertising and promotions program is not accomplishing its objectives, not only is the money spent lost but so too is the potential gain that could result from an effective program. Thus, measuring the effects of advertising is not just a savings of money but an opportunity to make money.

2. **Evaluating alternative strategies** Typically a firm has a number of strategies under consideration. For example, there may be some question as to which

@ **EXHIBIT 20–7**
Rough testing terminology

A rough commercial is an unfinished execution that may fall into three broad categories:

Animatic rough	Live-action rough
Succession of drawings/cartoons	Live motion
Rendered artwork	Stand-in/nonunion talent
Still-frames	Nonunion crew
Simulated movement:	Limited props/minimal opticals
Panning/zooming of frame/rapid sequence	Location settings
Photomatic rough	Finished
Succession of photographs	Live motion/animation
Real people/scenery	Highly paid union talent
Still-frames	Full union crew
Simulated movements:	Exotic props/studio sets/special effects
Panning/zooming of frame/rapid sequence	

Slides of the artwork posted on a screen or animatic and photomatic roughs may be used to test at this stage. (See Exhibit 20–7 for an explanation of terminology.) Because such tests can be conducted for about $3,000, research at this stage is becoming ever more popular.

But cost is only one factor. The test is of little value if it does not provide relevant, accurate information. Rough tests must provide an indication of how the finished commercial would perform. Some studies have demonstrated that these testing methods are reliable and the results typically correlate well with the finished ad.[10]

Most of the tests conducted at the rough stage involve lab settings, although some on-air field tests are also available. Popular tests include comprehension and reaction tests and consumer juries.

1. **Comprehension and reaction tests**   One key concern to the advertiser is whether the ad or commercial conveys the meaning intended. The second concern is the reaction the ad generates. Obviously, the advertiser does not want an ad that evokes a negative reaction or offends someone. **Comprehension and reaction tests** are designed to assess these responses (which makes you wonder why some ads are ever brought to the marketplace).

   Tests of comprehension and reaction employ no one standard procedure. Personal interviews, group interviews, and focus groups have all been used for this purpose, and sample sizes vary according to the needs of the client: they typically range from 50 to 200 respondents.

2. **Consumer juries**   Using consumers representative of the target market to evaluate the probable success of an ad is the basis of this method. Consumer juries may be asked to rate a selection of layouts or copy versions presented in pasteups on separate sheets. (The verdict is the final outcome.) The objectives sought and methods employed in **consumer juries** are shown in Exhibit 20–8,[11] and sample questions asked of jurists are shown in Exhibit 20–9 on page 579.

   While the jury method offers the advantages of control and cost-effectiveness, serious flaws in the methodology limit its usefulness.

- *The consumer may become a self-appointed expert.* One of the benefits sought from the jury method is the *objectivity* and *involvement* in the product or service that the targeted consumer can bring to the evaluation process. It is possible, however, that knowing they are being asked to critique ads, participants try to become more *expert* in their evaluations, paying more attention and being more critical than usual. The result may be a less than objective evaluation or an evaluation on elements other than those intended.
- *The number of ads that can be evaluated is limited.* Whether *order of merit* or *paired comparison methods* are used, the ranking procedure becomes tedious as the number of alternatives increases. Consider the ranking of 10 ads. While the top two and the

ⓐ EXHIBIT 20–8

Consumer juries

Objective:	Potential viewers (consumers) are asked to evaluate ads and give their reactions to and evaluation of them. When two or more ads are tested, viewers are usually asked to rate or rank order the ads according to their preferences.
Method:	Respondents are asked to view ads and rate them according to either (1) the order of merit method or (2) the paired comparison method. In the former, the respondent is asked to view the ads, then rank them from one to *n* according to their perceived merit. In the latter, ads are compared only two at a time. Each ad is compared to every other ad in the group, and the winner is listed. The best ad is that which wins the most times. Consumer juries typically employ 50 to 100 participants.
Output:	An overall reaction to each ad under construction as well as a rank ordering of the ads based on the viewers' perceptions.

bottom two may very well reveal differences, those ranked in the middle may not yield much useful information.

In the paired comparison method, the number of evaluations required is calculated by the formula

$$\frac{n(n-1)}{2}$$

In a situation where six alternatives are considered, 15 evaluations must be made. As the number of ads increases, the task becomes even more unmanageable.

- *A halo effect is possible.* Sometimes participants rate an ad good on all characteristics because they like a few and overlook specific weaknesses. This tendency, called the **halo effect**, distorts the ratings and defeats the ability to control for specific components. (Of course, the reverse may also occur—rating an ad bad overall due to only a few bad attributes.)
- *Preferences for specific types of advertising may overshadow objectivity.* Ads that involve emotions or pictures may receive higher ratings or rankings than those employing copy, facts, and/or rational criteria. Even though the latter are often more effective in the marketplace, they may be judged less favorably by jurists who prefer emotional appeals.

Some of the problems noted here can be remedied by the use of ratings scales instead of rankings. But ratings are not always valid either. Thus, while consumer juries have been used for years, questions of bias have led researchers to question their validity. As a result, a variety of other methods (discussed later in this chapter) are more commonly employed.

Pretesting Finished Ads

Exhibit 20–3 showed that pretesting finished ads received the most attention and participation among marketing researchers and their agencies. At this stage, a finished advertisement or commercial is used; however, it has not been presented to the market, so changes can still be made.

Many researchers prefer to test at this stage since the ad is in final form, which they believe provides a better test. Several test procedures are available for print and broadcast ads, including both laboratory and field methodologies.

Print methods include portfolio tests, analyses of readability, and dummy advertising vehicles. Broadcast tests include theater tests and on-air tests. Both print and broadcast may use physiological measures.

Pretesting finished print messages

A number of methods for pretesting finished print ads are available, one of which is *Diagnostic Research Inc.'s Copytest System*, described in Exhibit 20–10. The most common of these methods are portfolio tests, readability tests, and dummy advertising vehicles.

@ **EXHIBIT 20–9**

Questions asked in a
consumer jury test

1. Which of these ads would you most likely read if you saw it in a magazine?
2. Which of these headlines would interest you the most in reading the ad further?
3. Which ad convinces you most of the quality or superiority of the product?
4. Which layout do you think would be most effective in causing you to buy?
5. Which ad did you like best?
6. Which ad did you find most interesting?

Portfolio tests

Portfolio tests are a laboratory methodology designed to expose a group of respondents to a portfolio consisting of both control and test ads. Respondents are then asked to indicate what information they recall from the ads. The assumption is that the ads that yield the *highest recall* are the most effective.

While portfolio tests offer the opportunity to compare alternative ads directly, a number of weaknesses limit their applicability.

1. Factors other than advertising creativity and/or presentation may affect recall. Interest in the product or product category, the fact that respondents know they are participating in a test, or interviewer instructions (among others) may account for more differences than the ad itself.
2. Recall may not be the best test. Some researchers argue that for certain types of products—those of low involvement—ability to recognize the ad when shown may be a better measure than recall.

One way to determine the validity of the portfolio method is to correlate its results with readership scores once the product is placed in the field. Whether such validity tests are being conducted or not is not readily known, although the portfolio method continues to remain popular in the industry.

Readability tests

The communications efficiency of the copy in a print ad can be tested without reader interviews. This test uses the **Flesch formula**, named after its developer, Rudolph Flesch, to assess readability of the copy by determining the average number of syllables per 100 words. Human interest appeal in the material, length of sentences, and familiarity with certain words are also considered and correlated with the educational background of target audiences. Test results are compared to previously established norms for various target audiences. The test suggests that copy is best comprehended when sentences are short, words are concrete and familiar, and personal references are drawn.

This method eliminates many of the interviewee biases associated with other tests and avoids gross errors in understanding. The norms that have been established offer an attractive standard for comparison.

Disadvantages are also inherent, however. The copy may become too mechanical, and direct input from the receiver is not available. Without this input, contributing elements like creativity cannot be addressed. To be effective, this test should be used only in conjunction with other pretesting methods.

@ **EXHIBIT 20–10**

Reflections: Diagnostic
Research Inc.'s print test

Objective:	Tests recall and readers' impressions of print ads.
Method:	Mall intercepts in two or more cities are used to screen respondents and have them take home "test magazines" for reading. Participants are phoned the next day to determine opinions of the ads, recall of ad contents, and other questions of interest to the sponsor. Approximately 225 persons constitute the sample.
Output:	Scores reported include related recall of copy and visual elements, sales messages, and other nonspecific elements. Both quantitative (table) scores and verbatim responses are reported.

@ **EXHIBIT 20–11**

Alternative theater
methodologies

- Advertising Research Services (ARS) runs theater tests in four cities, on a total sample of 400 to 600 people. Precommercial brand preferences are taken, and respondents are asked to choose from pictures of packages of brands—resulting in a recognition test rather than recall.

  Viewers then watch a 30-minute TV program with three sets of two commercials embedded in the program. Questions are then asked about the program. A second program of 30 minutes is then shown, with six additional commercials included. Any of the 12 commercials may be the test commercial. Brand preference change is measured after the second program.

  After approximately 72 hours, half of the sample is phoned to obtain a measure of recall. These results are compared against norms established from previous tests.

- Advertising Control for Television (ACT), a lab procedure of the McCollum/Spielman Co., uses approximately 400 respondents representing four cities. It measures initial brand preference by asking participants which brands they most recently purchased. Respondents are then divided into groups of 25 to view a 30-minute program with seven commercials inserted in the middle. Four are test commercials; the other three are control commercials with established viewing norms. After viewing the program, respondents are given a recall test of the commercials.

  After the recall test, a second 30-minute program is shown, with each test commercial shown again. The second measure of brand preference is taken at this time, with persuasion measured by the percentage of viewers who switched preferences from their most recently purchased brand to one shown in the test commercials.

Dummy advertising vehicles

In an improvement on the portfolio test, ads are placed in "dummy" magazines developed by an agency or research firm. The magazines contain regular editorial features of interest to the reader, as well as the test ads, and are distributed to a *random sample* of homes in predetermined geographic areas. Readers are told the magazine publisher is interested in evaluations of editorial contents and asked to read the magazines as they normally would. Then they are interviewed on their reactions to both editorial content and ads. Recall, readership, and interest-generating capabilities of the ad are assessed.

The advantage of this method is that it provides a more natural setting than the portfolio test. Readership occurs in the participant's own home, the test more closely approximates a natural reading situation, and the reader may go back to the magazine, as people typically do.

But the dummy magazine shares the other disadvantages associated with portfolio tests. The testing effect is not eliminated, and product interest may still bias the results. Thus, while this test offers some advantages over the portfolio method, it is not a guaranteed measure of the advertising's impact.

Pretesting finished broadcast ads

A variety of methods for pretesting broadcast ads are available. The most popular are theater tests, on-air tests, and physiological measures.

Theater tests

One of the most popular laboratory methods for pretesting finished commercials is **theater testing**, in which participants are recruited by telephone, mall intercepts, and/or the mailing of tickets and invited to view pilots of proposed TV programs. In some instances, the show is actually being tested, but more commonly a standard program is used so audience responses can be compared with normative responses established by previous viewers. Sample sizes range from 250 to 600 participants.

On entering the theater, viewers are told a drawing will be held for gifts and asked to complete a product preference questionnaire asking which products they would prefer if they win. This form also requests demographic data. Participants may be seated in specific locations in the theater to allow observation by age, sex, and so on. The program and commercials are viewed, and a form asking for evaluations is distributed. Participants are then asked to complete a second form for a drawing, so that changes in product preference can be noted. In addition to product/brand preference, the form may request other information:

@ **EXHIBIT 20–20**

Sales impact of concert sponsorships (average 4–6 weeks)

Product	Market	Sales during Event (dollar or volume)	Percent Change from Average Sales
Snacks	Louisville	$119,841	+52%
	Salt Lake City	135,500	+47%
	Indianapolis	347,940	+105%
Soap	Atlanta	950 cases	+375%
	Minneapolis	880 cases	+867%
	Cleveland	972 cases	+238%
	Portland, Or.	580 cases	+580%
	St. Louis	1,616 cases	+1,454%
Salad dressing	Atlanta	NA	+175%
	Salt Lake City	NA	+143%

Sources: Betsy Spethmann, "Sponsors Sing a Profitable Tune in Concert with Event Promos," *BrandWeek*, Jan. 1, 1994, pp. 21–22.

- **Effectiveness of ski-resort based media**   In Chapter 15, we discussed advertising on ski chair lifts and other areas to attempt to reach selective demographic groups. Now the Traffic Audit Bureau (TAB) is tracking the effectiveness of this form of advertising to give advertisers more reliable criteria on which to base purchase decisions. The TAB data verify ad placements, while the media vendors have employed Simmons Market Research Bureau and Nielsen Media Research to collect ad impressions and advertising recall information.[27] These measures are combined with sales tracking data to evaluate the medium's effectiveness.

Measuring the Effectiveness of Sponsorships

One of the more difficult promotional tools to evaluate is sponsorships. But as pressure increases to make promotional expenditures accountable, the billions of dollars spent annually to sponsor events will receive attention.

At least two companies now measure the effectiveness of sports sponsorships. Events Marketing Research of New York specializes in custom research projects that perform sales audits in event areas, participant exit surveys, and economic impact studies. Joyce Julius & Associates of Ann Arbor, Michigan, assigns a monetary value to the amount of exposure the sponsor receives during the event. The company reviews broadcasts and adds up the number of seconds a sponsor's product name or logo can be seen clearly (for example, on signs or shirts). A total of 30 seconds is considered the equivalent of a 30-second commercial.[28] (Such a measure is of questionable validity.)

PS Productions, a Chicago-based research organization, provides clients with a measure of event sponsorships based on increased sales. PS calculates sales goals based on the cost of the event and the value of extras like donated media, customized displays, ads for key retailers, and tickets given away. An event's success is measured by its ability to bring in at least that amount in additional sales (Exhibit 20–20).

Measuring Other Program Elements

Many of the organizations mentioned earlier in this chapter offer research services to measure the effectiveness of promotional program elements. While we do not have the space to discuss them all, Exhibit 20–21 mentions a few just to make you aware of the fact that these options exist.

All the advertising effectiveness measures discussed here have their inherent strengths and weaknesses. They offer the advertiser some information that may be useful in evaluating the effectiveness of promotional efforts. While not all promotional efforts can be evaluated effectively at this time, at least the first step has been taken.

EXHIBIT 20–21

A sampling of measures of effectiveness of promotional program elements

Company	Effectiveness Measure Provided
Perception Research Services, Inc.	Package design, out-of-home; point-of-purchase displays; logos; corporate identity
McCollum Spielman Worldwide	Impact of celebrity presenters
Competitive Media Reporting	Business-to-business advertising; media effects
The PreTesting Company, Inc.	Package design; point-of-purchase displays; billboards; direct mail
Gallup & Robinson	Radio advertising recall; trade show exhibit measures
TransWestern Publishing	Telephone directory advertising effectiveness

SUMMARY

This chapter introduced you to issues involved in measuring the effects of advertising and promotions. These issues included reasons for testing, reasons companies do not test, and the review and evaluation of various research methodologies. We arrived at a number of conclusions: (1) advertising research to measure effectiveness is important to the promotional program, (2) not enough companies test their ads, and (3) problems exist with current research methodologies. In addition, we reviewed the criteria for sound research and suggested some ways to accomplish effective studies.

All marketing managers want to know how well their promotional programs are working. This information is critical to planning for the next period, since program adjustments and/or maintenance are based on evaluation of current strategies. Problems often result when the measures taken to determine such effects are inaccurate or improperly used. This chapter demonstrated that testing must meet a number of criteria (defined by PACT) to be successful. These evaluations should occur both before and after the campaigns are implemented.

A variety of research methods were discussed, many provided by syndicated research firms such as ASI, MSW, Arbitron, and A. C. Nielsen. Many companies have developed their own testing systems.

Single-source research data such as BehaviorScan, ERIM, and AdTel were discussed as a source of data for measuring the effects of advertising. These single-source systems offer strong potential for improving the effectiveness of ad measures in the future, as commercial exposures and reactions may be correlated to actual purchase behaviors.

KEY TERMS

vehicle option source effect, p. 572
pretests, p. 573
posttests, p. 573
laboratory tests, p. 574
testing bias, p. 574
field tests, p. 575
PACT (Positioning Advertising Copy Testing), p. 575

concept testing, p. 576
comprehension and reaction tests, p. 577
consumer juries, p. 577
halo effect, p. 578
portfolio tests, p. 579
Flesch formula, p. 579
theater testing, p. 580
on-air test, p. 581

day-after recall scores, p. 581
pupillometrics, p. 582
electrodermal response, p. 582
eye tracking, p. 582
EEG measures, p. 582
alpha activity, p. 583
hemispheric lateralization, p. 583

inquiry tests, p. 583
split-run tests, p. 583
recognition method, p. 584
recall tests, p. 585
single-source tracking methods, p. 587
tracking studies, p. 589

DISCUSSION QUESTIONS

1. Discuss some of the reasons agencies and firms do not measure advertising effectiveness and why they should do so.
2. Discuss the differences between a pretest and a posttest and between a lab test and a field test.
3. The bottom line for advertisers is to evoke some behavior—for example, sales. Explain why it may be difficult to use sales to measure advertising effectiveness.
4. Describe some of the effectiveness measures that are used to measure the value of sponsorships. Give examples of companies that might benefit from these measures.

5. Describe some of the methods used to test other elements of the promotional mix.
6. What are some of the problems associated with recognition tests?
7. Discuss how tracking studies might be tied into the hierarchy of effects models.
8. Describe some physiological measures of advertising effectiveness. Give examples of companies that might find these measures useful.
9. What is a theater test? What measures do these tests provide?
10. Discuss the concept of single-source research. What advantages does it offer the marketer?

PART VII
SPECIAL TOPICS
AND PERSPECTIVES

Better performance across the board.

How do you get a better-performing PC? Start with the best-performing PC processor. And then build a great system around it.

Today's Pentium™ processor-based systems are built to run circles around whatever you're using now. In addition to enhancements such as more RAM and larger hard drives, many feature important design improvements like the PCI local bus. So

demanding applications using pictures and graphics don't just crawl onto your screen, they jump.

All the leading manufacturers have already

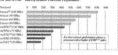

introduced designs based on the Pentium processor, giving you a wide range of choices in Pentium processor-based systems. And many of them are surprisingly affordable.

Whichever one you choose, you can be assured it's compatible with all the software written for the PC, now, and in the future. Whether it's everyday word processing, CD-ROM multimedia applications, or even Intel's new ProShare™ document and video conferencing software.

So stop by your favorite PC reseller and ask

to see the new Pentium processor-based systems. You'll find they start with the best-performing processor. But that's not where they end.

For more information and a list of the Pentium processor-based systems currently available, call 1-800-395-7009, Ext. 116.

© 1994 Intel Corporation. *Source: ICOMP™ A Simplified Measure of Relative Intel Microprocessor Performance, Intel Corp, 1992.

Chapter **21**

Business-to-Business Communications

Chapter Objectives

● *To understand the differences between business-to-business and consumer product advertising and promotions.*

● *To understand the objectives of business-to-business communications.*

● *To recognize the roles of various program elements in the business-to-business promotional program.*

● *To examine the methods for evaluating promotional program effectiveness in business-to-business communications.*

@ **EXHIBIT 21–18**

A sampling of trade publications

Publication	Industry
Industry Specific	
Banking Industry	Banking
Beverage Industry	Bottling
American Cemetery	Cemetery and monuments
Interior Textiles	Drapery
Dairy Field	Dairy
Library Journal	Education
Product Marketing	Cosmetics
Executive Jeweler	Jewelry
Coal Age	Coal mining
Appliance	Appliances
Automotive News	Cars
Construction Products	Construction
Pollution Equipment News	Pollution control
General Industry	
Advertising Age	Advertising
Sales & Marketing Management	Sales/marketing
Forbes	Financial/business
Computer World	Computers
BrandWeek	Marketing
Database Marketing	General business
Business Marketing	Business-to-business
PC World	Computer owners

@ **EXHIBIT 21–19**

Research studies used by business-to-business marketers

	Percent Responding
Market position studies	56%
Readership studies	46
Customer attitude studies	42
Focus groups	37
New product feasibility studies	37
Competitive environment analyses	35
Brand preference studies	33
Market potential studies	31
Company image studies	27
Prospect feedback studies	20

Note: Response adds to more than 100% due to multiple mentions.

Dun & Bradstreet

Dun & Bradstreet publishes a plant list index based on SIC codes. While the government lists the products made by plants, it does not carry the reverse information—that is, the names and number of plants manufacturing SIC code products.

MCC Media Data Form

The MCC Media Data Form provides information regarding an industry publication's circulation as well as its universe, or number of companies engaged in the business this medium is addressing.

Census of Manufactures

The Census of Manufactures provides reports on 452 SIC manufacturing industries in the United States, including the number of establishments, employment, payrolls, hours worked, value added by manufacturing, quantity and value of products shipped, materials consumed, and capital expenditures.

U.S. Industrial Outlook

U.S. Industrial Outlook is a yearly report from the US government detailing sales, shipments, and forecasts for selected industries. The report also identifies key trends, innovations, and foreign impacts on the market.

Trade publications

Business-to-business marketers also rely on an estimated 3,000 trade publications. Each provides information of interest to its own specific audience, as shown in Exhibit 21–18. Some trade magazines have a more general appeal.

@ **EXHIBIT   21–20**   A sampling of effectiveness measures available to business-to-business advertisers

Ad-Sell Performance Study	McGraw-Hill telephone survey of 100 magazine readers. Scores: established contact; created awareness; aroused interest; built preference; kept customers sold
Ad-Chart	Chilton Marketing Research Co. survey of 100 readers. Scores: percentage who noticed ad; % started to read; % read half or more; total readership index; informativeness index; cost-effectiveness index
Beta Research	Conducts studies in health care field. Scores: likelihood of reading; changes in opinion of product as a result of ad; informativeness of ad; believability of ad
Fosdick Ad Evaluation	Surveys 100 respondents. Scores: buyers who read ad; buyers who did not read ad; nonbuyers who read ad; nonbuyers who did not read ad
Gallup & Robinson	Reports on 150 respondents. Scores: proved name registration; idea communication; favorable attitude
Starch Readership Reports	Readership of ads. Scores: noted; associated; read most
Advalue	Readership by 100 persons. Scores: recall seeing; readership; ad effect; action taken; future purchase; salesperson contact; ad comparisons
Ad Lab	Mail survey sent to 750 to 1,500 subscribers. Scores: total sample noting; total sample who started to read; total sample reading more than half; total finding ad informative/useful; buyers noting/specified; buyers/specifiers starting to read; buyers/specifiers reading more than half; buyers/specifiers finding ad or editorial informative/useful

Of course, business-to-business marketers also engage in *primary* research, which may serve as input to the planning process or a measure of effectiveness. Many of the methodologies used in the consumer market have also been adopted by business marketers, including focus groups, interviewing, and surveys.

Evaluating Promotional Efforts

While nine out of 10 business-to-business marketers consider marketing research important in their communications programs, Exhibit 21–19 on page 613 suggests this importance is based on research input more than evaluation. None of the top 10 research studies used is specifically oriented to measuring the effects of advertising and promotions. (While focus groups are also cited, these groups are primarily used to provide in-depth views of sales prospects' attitudes rather than to evaluate ads.) Of the 5 percent or so of the promotional budget spent specifically on advertising research, approximately 23 percent is used to pretest ads or follow up the effects once the ad campaign has begun.[13] The remaining 77 percent is again used as input into the advertising program.

Interestingly, even though the amount spent on evaluative research appears low, a number of research services are available to business-to-business advertisers, as shown in Exhibit 21–20. These services provide a variety of effectiveness measures.

Throughout this chapter, we have repeatedly mentioned that business-to-business marketers tend to use advertising and promotional tools to assist in the sales support effort. It should come as no surprise, then, that the measures most commonly employed to evaluate the effectiveness of these programs also assess contribution to the selling effort. In addition to criteria often used in the general-interest and/or consumer market (read most, awareness, attention, recall), more behavioral (and sales-oriented) items such as readership by purchase decision, built preference, kept customers sold, referred ad to someone else, and specified or purchased product are measured.

In Exhibit 21–21, the criteria used by Copy Chasers—a panel of experts who evaluate business-to-business ads for *Business Marketing* magazine—provide insight into what is considered necessary to communicate effectively in this market. As you can see, the role advertising is expected to play is somewhat different in the business-to-business market from the consumer market. Should advertising be expected to generate such results? Or is this one reason so little is spent on measuring advertising effectiveness in the business-to-business market?

In sum, marketing and advertising research in business markets tends to be oriented to providing input into the marketing and promotional programs. As the role of advertising continues to change in this area, the amount and types of research used may follow.

@ EXHIBIT 21-21

The Copy Chasers criteria for
evaluating business-to-business
ads

1. The successful ad has a high degree of visual mag-
   netism.
2. The successful ad selects the right audience.
3. The successful ad promises a reward.
4. The successful ad backs up the promise.
5. The successful ad talks person to person.
6. The successful ad presents the selling proposition in
   logical sequence.
7. The successful ad invites the reader into the scene.
8. Successful advertising is easy to read.
9. Successful advertising has been purged of nonessentials.
10. Successful advertising emphasizes the service, not the
    source.

@ SUMMARY

Business-to-business advertisers view the role of advertising and promotions somewhat differently from those in the consumer products industries. While the latter may perceive the role of advertising and promotions to meet communications objectives, in the business-to-business sector it is generally considered a sales support aid.

Because of the role advertising and promotions are asked to assume, the message and media strategies designed to accomplish the sales support objectives are again different from those in the consumer products market. Messages tend to be more information laden, more straight to the point, and designed to elicit inquiries or answer questions. Illustrations, humor, and/or sex appeals are much less commonly employed.

The media employed by industrial advertising are also different. No less than 3,000 trade journals exist in the area, and the vast majority of firms use the ones in their field. Trade shows and sales incentives are also frequently employed. Interactive electronic media—somewhat of an infant in the consumer products market—has found a great reception in the industrial sector.

Finally, the measures used to determine the effectiveness of business-to-business strategies are sales-support oriented. Criteria such as number of inquiries generated, referrals, and actual purchases are often used to determine the relative effectiveness of alternative strategies.

@ KEY TERMS

business-to-business
   communications,
   p. 598

derived demand, p. 599
buying center, p. 599

social style model, p. 600
CUBE model, p. 600

multiple buying
   influences, p. 612

@ DISCUSSION QUESTIONS

1. Explain why *business-to-business communications* has replaced the term *industrial advertising*.
2. What are some of the factors that may underlie business-to-business advertisers' attempts to instill more creativity into their advertising? What are some of the reasons many continue to use more rational, informative appeals?
3. Explain some of the reasons why business-to-business advertisers have increased their use of direct marketing.
4. Discuss some of the criteria used to evaluate business-to-business ads. How do they differ from those used in the consumer products market?
5. Find examples of business-to-business ads that reflect service sector and industrial sector products. Discuss the appeals used in each.

6. Why has the use of mass media such as TV and consumer magazines for advertising business-to-business products and services been increasing?
7. Why would corporate image advertising be important to business-to-business advertisers? Cite examples of companies using this strategy.
8. Give examples of how business-to-business advertisers might employ an integrated marketing communications program.
9. Discuss nine differences between consumer and business-to-business communications.
10. Explain how a business-to-business marketer might employ sales promotions similar to those used in the consumer market as part of the integrated marketing communications mix.

Chapter 22

International Advertising and Promotion

Chapter Objectives

- To examine the importance of international marketing and the role of international advertising and promotion.
- To examine the various factors in the international environment and how they influence advertising and promotion decisions.

- To consider the pros and cons of global versus localized marketing and advertising.
- To examine the various decision areas of international advertising.
- To understand the role of other promotional mix elements in the international marketing program.

Just Doing It Globally

Most athletes or companies would give anything to have the hot streak that Nike, Inc., enjoyed during the 1980s and early 90s. Nike took advantage of the fitness boom in the US market with innovative products like its Air Trainers and Air 180 running shoes, cross-training shoes, and Air Jordans for basketball. The Nike ethos of pure, brash performance was captured in the "Just do it" slogan, which became a catchphrase for the sports world and was personified in advertising featuring Michael Jordan, Bo Jackson, and many other star athletes.

Nike quadrupled its sales from 1987 to 1993 and ran past all of its competitors to become the world's largest shoe company, with nearly $4 billion in annual sales. It leads the US market with a 32 percent share (versus 24 percent for archrival Reebok). However, like many other companies, Nike has found that it cannot rely on the US market to sustain its strong growth. Many of the teenagers and twenty-somethings responsible for Nike's growth over the past few years have turned away from sneakers in droves. Since Generation Xers seem not to be responding well to ads featuring overmarketed athletes, companies are looking for something fresh and less commercial.

Nike is responding to the changing US market by selling hiking boots and other rugged footwear through its outdoor division. However, Nike is also focusing attention on global markets; international expansion is a key element of the company's corporate strategy. In Europe, Nike has overcome 30 percent European Community duties and is stealing sales from Adidas and Puma, the German companies that dominated the European market for decades.

Nike has used nearly $100 million in advertising, appealing designs, and European youth's fascination with American products to surge to a 25 percent market share in Europe, versus less than 5 percent a decade ago. Along with Reebok, it has also helped expand the overall market by taking sneakers from the playing field into the street and making them fashionable footwear.

Nike has also exploited basketball's surging popularity in Europe, which was helped by the 1992 Olympic dream team. NBA star Charles Barkley and the recently retired Michael Jordan appear in Nike ads as well as company-sponsored basketball clinics and other promotional events in Europe. While these promotions are targeted to Nike's core teen-through–21 consumer base, a pan-European ad campaign has also been created for a market of 22- to 35-year-olds. This campaign, begun in late 1993, includes vignettes of ordinary individuals in somewhat extraordinary fitness pursuits, including running, soccer, and hiking. Each spot encourages Europeans to "Just do it" with a hint that there is a natural marriage between intellectual and physical pursuits. The director of marketing at Nike Europe said the goal of the campaign is to convey the message of "Just do it" without coming off as pushy Americans.

Nike recognizes that by 1996 nearly half of its business will be done overseas, mostly in Europe. The company is also working to expand its business in China, Mexico, and Japan. Advertising in these countries will be more tightly focused on sports and Nike will launch market-specific sneakers such as badminton shoes for Asia. While Nike realizes that it still has a long way to go in many countries, it appears to be getting consumers around the world to "Just do it."

Sources: "Can Nike Just Do It?" *Business Week*, April 18, 1994, pp. 86–90; Matthew Grimm, "Euro-Swoosh," *BrandWeek*, Aug. 2, 1993, pp. 1, 6; Joseph Pierrra, "Pushing US Style, Nike and Reebok Sell Sneakers to Europe," *The Wall Street Journal*, July 22, 1993, pp. A1, 8.

he primary focus of this book so far has been on integrated marketing communications programs for products and services sold to the US market. Many American companies have traditionally devoted most of their marketing efforts to the domestic market, since they often lack the resources, skills, or incentives to go abroad. This is changing rapidly, however, as US corporations recognize the opportunities that foreign markets offer for new sources of sales and profits as well as the need to market their products internationally. Many companies are striving to develop *global brands* that can be advertised and promoted the same way the world over.

In this chapter, we look closely at international advertising and promotion and the various issues marketers must consider in communicating with consumers around the globe. We examine the environment of international marketing and how companies often must adapt their promotional programs to conditions in each country. We look at the debate over whether a company should use a global marketing and advertising approach or tailor it specifically for various countries.

We also examine how firms organize for international advertising, select agencies, and consider various decision areas such as research, creative strategy, and media selection. While the focus of this chapter is on international advertising, we also consider other promotional mix elements in international marketing, including sales promotion, personal selling, and publicity/public relations. Let's begin by discussing some of the reasons international marketing has become so important to companies. .

THE IMPORTANCE OF INTERNATIONAL MARKETING

US companies are focusing on international markets for a number of reasons. Many recognize that the US market offers them limited opportunity for expansion because of slow population growth, saturated markets, intense competition, and an unfavorable marketing environment. For example, US tobacco companies face declining domestic consumption as a result of restrictions on their marketing and advertising efforts and the growing antismoking sentiment in this country. Companies such as R. J. Reynolds and Philip Morris are turning to Asia and South America, where there are fewer restrictions and cigarette consumption is growing.[1] Many US-based brewers, among them Anheuser-Busch, Miller Brewing Co., and Coors, are looking to international markets to sustain growth as beer sales in this country decline and regulatory pressures increase.[2]

Companies are also noticing international markets because of the opportunities they offer for growth and profits. The dramatic economic, social, and political changes around the world in recent years have opened markets in Eastern Europe and China. The growing markets of the Far East, Latin America, and other parts of the world present tremen-

EXHIBIT 22-1

Kentucky Fried Chicken is familiar to consumers around the world

dous opportunities to marketers of consumer products and services as well as business-to-business marketers.

The importance and potential profitability of international marketing have long been recognized by many US companies. IBM, Ford, General Motors, Exxon, Du Pont, and Colgate Palmolive generate much of their sales and profits from foreign markets. Gillette sells over 800 products in more than 200 countries, while Procter & Gamble markets 165 products overseas and had international sales of $15.8 billion in 1993. Kellogg earns 35 percent of its profits outside the United States and has nearly 50 percent of the European cereal market. Coca-Cola, Pepsi, IBM, Reebok, Kentucky Fried Chicken, McDonald's, and many other US companies and brands are known all over the world (Exhibit 22–1).

Many US-based companies have entered joint ventures or formed strategic alliances with foreign companies to market their products internationally. For example, General Mills and Swiss-based Nestlé entered into a joint venture to create Cereal Partners Worldwide (CPW), taking advantage of General Mills' popular product line and Nestlé's powerful distribution channels in Europe, Asia, Latin America, and Africa.[3] Nestlé has also entered into joint ventures with Coca-Cola to have the beverage giant distribute its instant coffee and tea throughout the world. Häagen-Dazs entered into a joint venture in Japan with Suntory Ltd., and its sales in Asia have doubled since 1989.[4]

International markets are important to small and mid-size companies as well as the large multinational corporations. Many of these firms can compete more effectively in foreign markets, where they may face less competition or appeal to specific market segments or where products have not yet reached the maturity stage of their life cycle. For example, the WD-40 Co. has saturated the US market with its lubricant product and now gets much of its sales growth from Europe, Canada, and Japan (Exhibit 22–2).

Another reason it is increasingly important for US companies to adopt an international marketing orientation is that imports are taking a larger and larger share of the domestic market for many products. The United States has been running a continuing **balance-of-trade deficit**; the monetary value of our imports exceeds that of our exports. American companies are realizing that we are shifting from being an isolated, self-sufficient, national economy to being part of an interdependent *global economy*. This means US corporations must defend against foreign inroads into the domestic market as well as learn how to market their products and services to other countries.

While many US companies are becoming more aggressive in their pursuit of international markets, they face stiff competition from large multinational corporations from other countries. Some of the world's most formidable marketers are European companies

@ **EXHIBIT 22–2**

The WD-40 Co. gets much of its sales growth from foreign markets

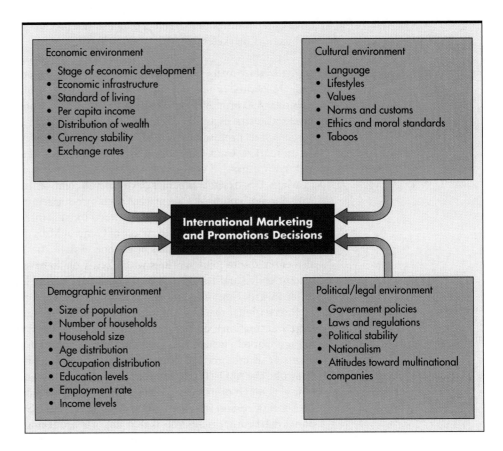

EXHIBIT 22-3

Forces in the international marketing environment

such as Unilever, Nestlé, Siemens, Phillips, and Renault, as well as the various Japanese car and electronic manufacturers and package-goods companies such as Suntory, Shiseido, and Kao.

THE ROLE OF INTERNATIONAL ADVERTISING AND PROMOTION

Advertising and promotion are important parts of the marketing program of firms competing in the global marketplace. While more than $130 billion is spent on advertising in the United States each year, advertising expenditures outside the United States have increased dramatically over the past decade and now exceed $170 billion annually.[5] More and more companies recognize that an effective promotional program is important for companies competing in foreign markets. As Vern Terpstra notes in his book *International Marketing:*

> Promotion is the most visible as well as the most culture bound of the firm's marketing functions. Marketing includes the whole collection of activities the firm performs in relating to its market, but in other functions the firm relates to the market in a quieter, more passive way. With the promotional function, however, the firm is standing up and speaking out, wanting to be seen and heard.[6]

Many companies are realizing the difficulties they face in developing and implementing advertising and promotion programs for international markets. Companies that promote their products or services abroad face an unfamiliar marketing environment and customers with different sets of values, customs, consumption patterns, and habits, as well as differing purchase motives and abilities. Languages vary from country to country and even within a country, such as India or Switzerland. Media options are quite limited in many countries, owing to lack of availability or limited effectiveness. These factors demand different creative and media strategies as well as changes in other elements of the advertising and promotional program for foreign markets.

@ **EXHIBIT 22–17**

Häagen-Dazs' sexy ads have
worked well in Britain

It is the

intense

flavour of
the finest ingredients
combined with

fresh

cream that is
essentially Häagen-Dazs

Häagen-Dazs

FRESH CREAM ICE CREAM

Dedicated to Pleasure

Marketers must also figure out what type of advertising appeal or execution style will be most effective in each market. Emotional appeals such as humor may work well in one country but not in another because of differences in cultural backgrounds and consumer perceptions of what is or is not funny. While humorous appeals are popular in the United States and Britain, they are not used often in Germany, where consumers do not respond favorably to them.

Countries such as France, Italy, and Brazil are more receptive to sexual appeal and nudity in advertising than are other societies. Grey Advertising found that an ad it developed for Camay soap in the United States, which featured a man touching a woman's skin while she bathed, would be a disaster in Japan. Even the idea of a man being in the bathroom with a female would be considered taboo.[52]

International marketers sometimes find they can change consumer purchasing patterns by taking a creative risk. For example, Häagen-Dazs broke through cultural barriers in Britain, where ice cream consumption is only a third as great as the United States and consumers usually purchase low-grade, low-priced local brands. A sexy advertising campaign showing seminude couples feeding the ice cream to one another helped get British consumers to pay premium prices for Häagen-Dazs (Exhibit 22–17). The company also used an avant-garde billboard campaign in Japan showing a young couple kissing in public—a near-taboo. The posters were so popular that many were stolen.[53]

Media Selection

One of the most difficult decision areas for the international advertiser is media strategy and selection. US firms generally find major differences in the media outside the United States, and media conditions may vary considerably from one area to another, particularly in developing countries. Media planners face a number of problems in attempting to communicate advertising messages to consumers in foreign countries.

First, the types of media available in each country are different. Many homes in developing countries do not have television sets. In some countries, TV advertising is not accepted or the amount of commercial time is severely limited. For example, in Germany, TV advertising is limited to 20 minutes a day on each of the government-owned channels, restricted to four five-minute breaks, and banned on Sundays and holidays.

Germany's two privately owned television stations, however, are permitted to devote up to 20 percent of airtime to commercials. In the Netherlands, TV spots are limited to 5 percent of air time and must be booked up to a year in advance. Programs also do not have fixed time slots for ads, making it impossible to plan commercial buys around desired programs.

The number of TV sets in places like India and China is increasing tremendously, but there is still controversy over TV advertising. In India, for example, commercials are restricted to only 10 percent of programming time and must appear at the beginning or end of a program.[54]

The characteristics of media differ from country to country in terms of coverage, cost, quality of reproduction, restrictions, and the like. Another problem international advertisers face is obtaining reliable media information such as circulation figures, audience profiles, and costs. In some countries, media rates are negotiable or may fluctuate owing to unstable currencies and economic conditions.

The goal of international advertisers is to select media vehicles that reach their target audience most effectively and efficiently. Media selection is often localized even for a centrally planned, globalized campaign. Local agencies or media buyers generally have more knowledge of local media and better opportunities to negotiate rates, and it gives subsidiary operations more control and ability to adapt to media conditions and options in their market. Media planners have two options: using national or local media or using international media.

Local media

Many advertisers choose the local media of a country to reach its consumers. Print is the most used medium worldwide, since television commercial time and the number of homes with TV sets are limited in many countries. Many countries have magazines that are circulated countrywide as well as national or regional newspapers that carry advertising directed to a national audience. Most countries also have magazines that appeal to special interests or activities, allowing for targeting in media selection.

Although restrictions and regulations have limited the development of TV as a dominant advertising medium in many countries, it is a primary medium for obtaining nationwide coverage in most developed countries and offers tremendous creative opportunities. Restrictions on television may be lessening in some countries, and time availability may increase. For example, the number of TV stations and television advertising in Italy have exploded in the past decade since government restrictions against private broadcasting were lifted.[55] Advertising groups are using economic, legal, and political pressure to get more television commercial time from reluctant European governments. The increase in TV channels through direct broadcasting by satellite to many European households, which is discussed below, may hasten this process.[56]

In addition to print and television, local media available to advertisers include radio, direct mail, billboards, cinema, and transit advertising. These media give international advertisers greater flexibility and the opportunity to reach specific market segments and local markets within a country. Most international advertisers rely heavily on national and local media in their media plans for foreign markets.

International media

The other way for the international advertiser to reach audiences in various countries is through international media that have multimarket coverage. The primary focus of international media has traditionally been magazines and newspapers. A number of US-based consumer-oriented publications have international editions, including *Time, Cosmopolitan, Reader's Digest,* and *National Geographic* and the newspaper *USA Today. Newsweek* publishes six international editions that reach over 3 million readers in 160 countries (Exhibit 22–18). US-based business publications with foreign editions include *Business Week, Fortune, Harvard Business Review,* and *The Wall Street Journal.*

International publications offer advertisers a way to reach large audiences on a regional or worldwide basis. Readers of these publications are usually upscale, high-income

@ **EXHIBIT 22-18**

Newsweek is published in 160 countries

individuals who are desirable target markets for many products and services. There are, however, several problems with these international media that can limit their attractiveness to many advertisers. Their reach in any one foreign country may be low, particularly for specific segments of a market. Also, while they deliver desirable audiences to companies selling business or upscale consumer products and services, they do not cover the mass consumer markets or specialized market segments very well. Other US-based publications in foreign markets do offer advertisers ways to reach specific market segments.

While print remains the dominant medium for international advertising, many companies are turning their attention to international commercial TV. Package-goods companies in particular, such as Gillette, McDonald's, Pepsi, and Coca-Cola, view television advertising as the best way to reach mass markets and effectively communicate their advertising messages. Satellite technology has helped spread the growth of cable TV in other countries and made global television networks a reality.

A number of satellite networks operating in Europe beam entertainment programming across several countries. For example, British Sky Broadcasting (BSkyB), which was formed by the merger of Sky Television and British Satellite Broadcasting, reaches 13 percent of all TV households in the United Kingdom and is expected to reach 36 percent by 1995.[57]

The main incentive to the growth of these satellite networks has been the severely limited program choices and advertising opportunities on government-controlled stations in most of Europe. However, many European countries are planning new channels as governments move to preserve cultural values and protect advertising revenues from going to foreign-based networks.

A major development affecting broadcasting in Europe and Asia is **direct broadcast by satellite (DBS)** to homes and communities equipped with small, low-cost receiving dishes. The first DBS satellite was launched by then West Germany in 1987, and Britain and Scandinavian countries are expected to have DBS satellites soon. In 1993 media baron Rupert Murdoch's News Corp. purchased Satellite Television Asian Region (STAR TV), which beams the BBC and many American shows and movies to 17 million Asian households, hotels, and restaurants equipped with satellite dishes. Although the current audience size is not large, STAR TV has a potential market of 3 billion people—two-thirds of the world's population, as satellite dishes become more common in this region.[58]

Advances in satellite and communications technology, the expansion of multinational companies with global marketing perspectives, and the development of global advertising agencies mean advertisers' use of television as a global medium is likely to increase.

◎ THE ROLE OF OTHER PROMOTIONAL MIX ELEMENTS

This chapter has focused on advertising, since it is usually the primary element in the promotional mix of the international marketer. However, as in domestic marketing, promotional programs for foreign markets generally include such other elements as personal selling, sales promotion, and public relations. The role of these other promotional mix elements varies depending on the firm's marketing and promotional strategy in foreign markets.

Sales promotion and public relations may be used to support and enhance advertising efforts; the latter may also be used to create or maintain favorable images for companies in foreign markets. For some firms, personal selling may be the most important promotional element and advertising may play a support role. This final section considers the roles of these other promotional mix elements in the international marketing program.

Sales Promotion

As we saw in Chapter 17, sales promotion is one of the fastest-growing areas of marketing in the United States. Companies increasingly rely on consumer- and trade-oriented sales promotion to help sell their products in foreign markets as well. Many of the promotional tools that are effective in the United States, such as free samples, premiums, event sponsorships, contests, coupons, and trade promotions, are also used in foreign markets. For example, Häagen-Dazs estimates it gave out more than 5 million free tastings of its ice cream as part of its successful strategy for entering the European market. Since taste is the major benefit of this premium product, sampling was an appropriate sales promotion tool for entering foreign markets.

A form of sales promotion that has become very popular in foreign markets is event sponsorship. Many companies sponsor sporting events, concerts, and other activities in foreign countries to promote their products and enhance corporate image. For example, Pepsi has sponsored concerts for rock stars such as Michael Jackson and Tina Turner in numerous countries, and Coke set up a pan-European sponsorship department to oversee its music-related marketing efforts.[59]

Unlike advertising, which can be done on a global basis, sales promotions must be adapted to local markets. Kamran Kashani and John Quelch noted several important differences among countries that marketers must consider in developing a sales promotion program.[60] They include the stage of economic development, market maturity, consumer perceptions of promotional tools, trade structure, and legal restrictions and regulations.

- **Economic development** In highly developed countries such as the United States, Canada, Japan, and Western European nations, marketers can choose from a wide range of promotional tools. However, in developing countries, they must be careful not to use promotional tools such as in- or on-package premiums that would increase the price of the product beyond the reach of most consumers. Free samples and demonstrations are widely used, effective promotional tools in developing countries. But coupons, which are so popular with consumers in the United States, are rarely used because of problems with distribution and resistance from retailers. In the United States and Britain, most coupons are distributed through newspapers (including FSIs) or magazines. Low literacy rates in some countries make print media an ineffective coupon distribution method, so coupons are delivered door to door, handed out in stores, or placed in or on packages. Exhibit 22–19 shows the number of coupons redeemed per household each year in various countries.

@ **EXHIBIT 22–19**

Coupon redemption in various countries

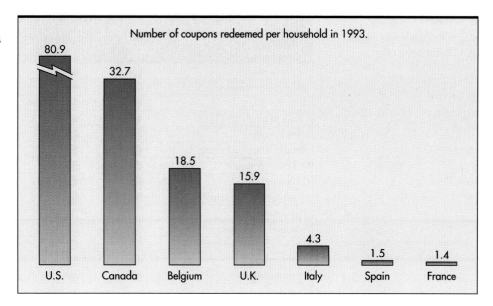

Number of coupons redeemed per household in 1993.

- **Market maturity**   Marketers must also consider the stage of market development for their product or service in various countries in designing sales promotions. To introduce a product to a country, consumer-oriented promotional tools such as sampling, high-value coupons, and cross promotions with established products and brands are often effective.

    The competitive dynamics of a foreign market are also often a function of its stage of development. More competition is likely in well-developed mature markets, which will influence the types of sales promotion tools used. For example, there may be competitive pressure to use trade allowances to maintain distribution or consumer promotions that will maintain customer loyalty, such as bonus packs, price-off deals, or coupons.

- **Consumer perceptions**   An important consideration in the design of sales promotion programs is how they are perceived by consumers as well as the trade. Consumer perceptions of various sales promotion tools vary from market to market. For example, Japanese women are less likely to take advantage of contests, coupons, or other promotions than are women in the United States.[61] Premium offers in particular must be adapted to the tastes of consumers in various markets.

- **Trade structure**   In areas with highly concentrated retailing systems such as northern Europe, the trade situation is becoming much like the United States and Canada as pressure grows for more price-oriented trade and in-store promotions. In southern Europe, the retail industry is highly fragmented and there is less trade pressure for promotions. Consideration must also be given to the willingness and ability of channel members to accommodate sales promotion programs. Retailers in many countries do not want to take time to process coupons, post promotional displays, or deal with premiums or packaging that require special handling or storage. In countries such as Japan or India, where retailing structures are highly fragmented, the small store size precludes the use of point-of-purchase displays, or in-store sampling.

- **Regulations**   An important factor affecting the use of sales promotion in foreign countries is the presence of legal restrictions and regulations. Laws affecting sales promotion are generally more restrictive in other countries than in the United States. Some countries ban contests, games, or lotteries, while others restrict the size or amount of a sample, premium, or prize. For example, fair-trade regulations in Japan limit the maximum value of premiums to 10 percent of the retail price, while

Promotion	U.K.	Spain	West Germany	France	Italy
In-pack premiums	●	●	●	▲	●
Multiple-purchase offers	●	●	▲	●	●
Extra product	●	●	▲	●	●
Free product	●	●	●	●	●
Mail-in offers	●	●	●	●	●
Purchase-with-purchase	●	●	●	●	●
Cross-promotions	●	●	●	●	●
Contests	●	●	▲	●	●
Self-liquidating premiums	●	●	●	●	●
Sweepstakes	▲	▲	●	▲	▲
Money-off coupons	●	●	●	●	▲
Next-purchase coupons	●	●	●	●	▲
Cash rebates	●	●	▲	●	●
In-store demos	●	●	●	●	●

● Permitted   ● Not permitted   ▲ May be permitted

in France the limit is 5 percent. In some countries, a free premium must be related to the nature of the product purchased. Many countries have strict rules when it comes to premium offers for children, and some ban them altogether. Exhibit 22–20 shows how restrictions on promotions vary among five European countries.

Variations in rules and regulations mean marketers must often develop separate consumer sales promotion programs for each country. Many companies have found it difficult to do any promotions throughout Europe because sales promotion rules are so different from one country to another. While the Treaty on European Union may result in a more standardized legal environment in Europe, laws regarding sales promotion are still likely to vary. To deal with problems in the design of sales promotion programs for foreign markets, many companies use local agencies or international sales promotion companies to develop them.

Management of sales promotion in foreign markets

Although sales promotion programs of multinational companies have traditionally been managed locally, this is changing somewhat as marketers create global brands. Many global marketers recognize the importance of giving local managers the autonomy to design and execute their own sales promotion programs. However, the ways local promotions influence and contribute to global brand equity must also be considered.

Kashani and Quelch developed a framework for analyzing the role of centralized (headquarters) versus local management in sales promotion decisions based on various stages of globalization (Exhibit 22–21). This model suggests headquarters' influence will be greatest for global brands and least for local brands. Since global brands require uniformity in marketing communications, the promotional program should be determined at the headquarters level. Decisions regarding overall promotional strategy—including international communication objectives, positioning, allocation of the communications budget to sales promotion versus advertising, and weight of consumer versus trade promotions—are made at the headquarters level.[62]

While the promotional strategy for global brands is determined by global product managers at headquarters, implementation of the programs should be left to local management. It is important to make the promotional strategy broad enough to allow for differences in diverse local markets. Headquarters is also responsible for encouraging

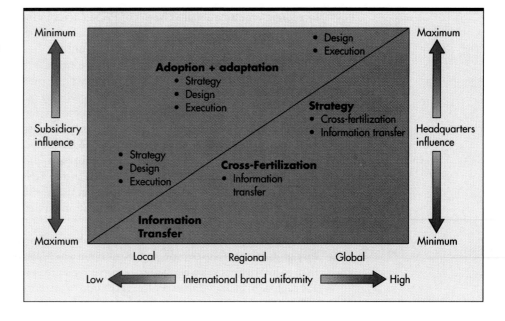

EXHIBIT 22–21

Influences and roles in international sales promotion

the cross-fertilization of ideas and practices among local managers and facilitating the transfer of information.

Regional brands usually do not require the same level of standardization as global brands, and the promotional strategy can be developed by regional offices and carried out at the local level. However, regional promotions should avoid contradictory brand communications and promotional activities that might upset local activities in nearby markets. The role of national-level brand managers is *adoption* and *adaptation*. They determine what promotional ideas to adopt from the region and adapt them to local conditions.

For local brands, decisions regarding promotional strategy, program design, and execution are left to local managers. Of course, local managers may benefit from information about the promotions used in other local markets.

Personal Selling

As a company's most direct contact with its customers in foreign markets, personal selling is an important part of the marketing and promotional process. Companies selling industrial and high-technology products generally rely heavily on personal selling as the primary method for communicating with their customers, internationally as well as domestically. Consumer products firms may also use personal selling to call on distributors, wholesalers, or major retailing operations in foreign markets. Due to low wages in many developing countries, some companies hire large sales staffs to perform missionary activities and support selling and advertising efforts.

Because it involves personal contact and communication, personal selling is generally even more culture bound than advertising. So most companies use sales reps from the host country and adapt personal selling activities and sales programs to each market. Management of the sales force is usually decentralized to the local subsidiaries, although the international marketer sets the general sales policy and advises foreign managers on the role personal selling should play in their market, the development of the sales program, and various aspects of sales management.

Public Relations

Many companies involved in international marketing are recognizing the importance of using public relations to support and enhance their marketing and advertising efforts.[63] Public relations activities are needed to deal with local governments, media, trade associations, and the general public, as all these groups may feel threatened by the presence of a foreign multinational. The job of PR agencies in foreign markets is not only to help the company sell its products or services but also to present the firm as a good corporate citizen concerned about the future of the country.

Companies generally must have a favorable image if they are to be successful in foreign markets. Those perceived negatively may face pressure from the media, local governments, or other relevant publics, or even boycotts by consumers. Often, public relations is needed to deal with specific problems a company faces in international markets. For example, the G. D. Searle Co. had problems getting its NutraSweet low-calorie sweetener into some markets because of strong sugar lobbies in Australia, Canada, and Europe. These lobbies encouraged the foreign press to pick up on some of the unfavorable news about the product that was published in the US media. Searle retained Burson-Marsteller, the second-largest PR company in the world, to help design factual ads about the product and to conduct other public relations activities to counter the problems and get the facts out about NutraSweet.

Public relations can play an important role in helping companies pursue business in foreign markets. Acustar, Inc., a US automotive component manufacturer, used its PR firm to increase its visibility before negotiating contracts with Japanese automakers. The PR campaign included an executive reception to introduce the company and its products, press interviews, and presentations to senior executives of several Japanese car manufacturers. The PR firm also distributed a news release to Japanese news media before the Acustar executives' visit and arranged interviews with the company's chairman for the leading business and trade publications in Japan. Stories about Acustar appeared in more than 10 national and regional newspapers, *The Asian Wall Street Journal*, two TV networks, and several domestic publications. The PR campaign helped the company win contracts with several Japanese auto manufacturers.[64]

Like advertising, public relations is becoming more of a global activity. Like ad agencies, PR firms are merging with and/or acquiring overseas offices so clients can use one firm to communicate with appropriate parties all over the world.

ⓐ SUMMARY

Many US companies are recognizing not only the opportunities but also the necessity of marketing their products and services internationally because of saturated markets and intense competition from both domestic and foreign competitors. Advertising and promotion are important parts of the international marketing program of a multinational corporation. Advertising is generally the most cost-effective way to communicate with buyers and create a market in other countries.

International marketers must carefully analyze the major environmental forces in each market where they compete, including economic, demographic, cultural, and political/legal factors. These factors are important not only in assessing the potential of each country as a market but also in designing and implementing advertising and promotional programs.

In recent years, much attention has focused on global marketing, where a standard marketing program is used in all markets. Part of global marketing is global advertising, where the same basic advertising approach is used in all markets. Opponents of the global (standardized) approach argue that differences in culture, market and economic conditions, and consumer needs and wants make a universal approach to marketing and advertising impractical. Many companies use an in-between approach by standardizing their basic marketing strategy but localizing advertising messages to fit each market.

There are a number of important decision areas in the development of advertising and promotional programs for international markets. These include organization, agency selection, advertising research, creative strategy and execution, and media strategy and selection.

Sales promotion, personal selling, and public relations are also part of the promotional mix of international marketers. Sales promotion programs usually must be adapted to local markets. Various factors must be considered, including stage of market development, market maturity, consumer perceptions of promotional tools, trade structure, and legal restrictions and regulations. Personal selling is the most important element of some companies' international marketing programs, since it is their main form of contact with foreign customers. Public relations programs are also important to international marketers to help them develop and maintain favorable relationships with governments, media, and consumers in foreign countries.

@ KEY TERMS

balance-of-trade
  deficit, p. 619
economic
  infrastructure, p. 621

global marketing, p. 627
global advertising, p. 627

pattern advertising,
  p. 632
localized advertising
  strategy, p. 640

direct broadcasting by
  satellite (DBS), p. 643

@ DISCUSSION QUESTIONS

1. Why are international markets becoming so important to companies like Anheuser-Busch and Nike? Discuss the role of advertising and promotion in these firms' international marketing program.

2. What are some of the major challenges facing companies as they develop advertising and promotional programs for international markets?

3. Choose two foreign countries and discuss the problems a US consumer package-goods company might encounter in developing an advertising and promotion program in these markets.

4. Discuss how cultural factors influence the development of advertising and promotional programs for foreign markets.

5. Find examples of two companies that are in a position to take advantage of the global teen market. Can these companies approach teens as a global market? Why or why not?

6. Over a decade ago, Theodore Levitt put forth his argument that the worldwide marketplace is becoming homogenized and the basic needs, wants, and expectations of consumers transcend geographic, national, and cultural boundaries. Do you think the global village has arrived and a single advertising campaign can be used for all countries?

7. Discuss the pros and cons of global advertising. What types of products and services lend themselves to global advertising?

8. In May 1994, IBM announced that it was consolidating all of its advertising from more than 40 agencies worldwide to one agency, Ogilvy & Mather of New York. Evaluate the pros and cons of this move.

9. What are some of the problems multinational companies face in developing media strategies for foreign markets?

10. Discuss the various factors involved in developing a sales promotion program in foreign markets. How would the planning and implementation of a sales promotion program differ for global brands versus regional or local brands?

Chapter 23

Regulation of Advertising and Promotion

Chapter Objectives

- To examine how advertising is regulated including the role and function of various regulatory agencies.

- To examine self-regulation of advertising and evaluate its effectiveness.

- To examine how advertising is regulated by federal and state government agencies.

- To examine how the Federal Trade Commission regulates advertising.

- To examine rules and regulations that affect sales promotion and direct marketing.

The FTC Takes on the Weight-Loss Industry

I n the fight against the "battle of the bulge," US consumers, every year, arm themselves with more than $2 billion worth of diet programs and special foods. However, the diet industry itself is under siege. It has been under investigation for a number of years by the Federal Trade Commission (FTC), which has focused on advertising claims that various low-calorie diet programs are safe and effective.

The FTC's sweep of the industry began with promoters of very low-calorie liquid diets. In 1992 the FTC settled false advertising charges against the marketers of several brands including Medifast, Optifast, and Ultra-Fast. In early 1993, the FTC extended its investigations to five large and well-known diet program marketers including Physicians Weight Loss Centers of America, Weight Watchers International, Jenny Craig, Diet Center, and Nutri/System. In March of 1993 the FTC announced that it was investigating the companies for false and misleading advertising claims and denied their joint request for the commission to develop industrywide advertising rules instead of investigating companies on a case-by-case basis.

The FTC complaints said none of the five companies had sufficient evidence to back up claims that their customers achieved their weight-loss goals or maintained the loss. The agency also charged the companies with misleading consumers about the cost and superiority of their programs, and about the speed of weight loss consumers could expect. By the fall of 1993, three of the companies, Diet Center, Nutri/System, and Physicians Weight Loss Center, settled the federal false-advertising charges. They did not admit guilt but agreed to publicize the fact that most weight loss is temporary and to disclose how long their customers keep off the weight they lose. The agreement also requires the companies to back up their weight-loss claims with scientific data and to document claims that their customers keep off the weight by monitoring a group of them for two years.

Weight Watchers International and Jenny Craig refused to settle. Weight Watchers' chairman stated that his company never misled the public by promising permanent weight loss and stressed the need to stick with the program. He noted that the company's decision to fight the FTC in court was "a matter of principle." Jenny Craig's president stated that his company's ads were forthright and complied with all advertising regulations. He also criticized the FTC for charging individual companies instead of adopting industrywide advertising standards for diet programs.

John Calfee, a former FTC staff member, suggests that the FTC prefers the case-by-case approach to avoid the burden of public hearings, public comments, arguments, and counter-arguments. However, Calfee does argue that the FTC approach misconceives the weight-loss market: "Would the average consumer responding to a Weight Watchers ad really be surprised to learn that most people who lose weight gain it back?... In such a market, advertising claims are more an invitation to investigate, perhaps a promise to provide a viable option, rather than a guarantee of success." While consumers will always find it difficult to lose weight and keep it off, the FTC wants to make sure they at least find it easy to understand the advertising claims of weight-loss companies.

Sources: John E. Calfee, "FTC's Hidden Weight-Loss Ad Agenda," *Advertising* Age, Oct. 25, 1993, p. 29; Jeanne Saddler, "Three Diet Firms Settle False-Ad Case; Two Others Vow to Fight FTC Charges," *The Wall Street Journal*, Oct. 1, 1993, p. B8; Steven W. Colford, "FTC Probes Claims of 5 Diet Programs," *Advertising Age*, March 29, 1993, p. 2.

Suppose you are the advertising manager for a consumer products company and have just reviewed a new commercial your agency created. You are very excited about the ad. It presents new claims about your brand's superiority that should help differentiate it from the competition. However, before you approve the commercial you need answers. Are the claims verifiable? Did researchers use proper procedures to collect and analyze the data and present the findings? Do research results support the claims? Were the right people used in the study? Could any conditions have biased the results?

Before approving the commercial, you have it reviewed by your company's legal department and examined by your agency's attorneys. If both reviews are acceptable, you send the ad to the major networks, who have their censors examine it. They may ask for more information or send the ad back for modification. (No commercial can run without approval from a network's Standards and Practices Department.)

Even after approval and airing, your commercial is still subject to scrutiny from such state and federal regulatory agencies as the state attorney general's office and the Federal Trade Commission. Individual consumers or competitors who find the ad misleading or have other concerns may file a complaint with the National Advertising Division of the Council of Better Business Bureaus. Finally, disparaged competitors may sue if they feel your ad distorts the facts and misleads consumers. If you lose the litigation, your company may have to retract the claims and pay the competitor damages, sometimes running into millions of dollars.

After considering all these regulatory issues, you must ask yourself if the new ad can meet all these challenges and is worth the risk. Maybe you ought to continue with the old approach that made no specific claims and simply said your brand was great.

Regulatory concerns can play a major role in the advertising decision-making process. Advertisers operate in a complex environment of local, state, and federal rules and regulations. Additionally, a number of advertising and business-sponsored associations, consumer groups and organizations, and the media attempt to promote honest, truthful, and tasteful advertising through their own self-regulatory programs and guidelines. The legal and regulatory aspects of advertising are very complex. Many parties are concerned about the nature and content of advertising and its potential to offend, exploit, mislead, and/or deceive consumers.

Numerous guidelines, rules, regulations, and laws constrain and restrict advertising. These rules and regulations primarily influence individual advertisers, but they can also affect advertising for an entire industry. For example, cigarette advertising was banned from the broadcast media in 1970, and many groups are pushing for a total ban on the advertising of tobacco products.[1] Legislation now being considered would further restrict the advertising of alcoholic beverages, including beer and wine.[2]

Advertising is controlled by internal self-regulation and by external state and federal regulatory agencies such as the Federal Trade Commission (FTC), the Federal Communications Commission (FCC), the Food and Drug Administration (FDA), and the US Post Office. And recently state attorneys general have become more active in advertising regulation. While only government agencies (federal, state, and local) have the force of law, most advertisers also abide by the guidelines and decisions of internal regulatory bodies. In fact, internal regulation from such groups as the media or National Advertising Review Board probably has more influence on advertisers' day-to-day operations and decision making than government rules and regulations.

Decision makers both on the client and agency side must be knowledgeable about these regulatory groups including the intent of their efforts, how they operate, and how they influence and affect advertising and other promotional mix elements. In this chapter, we examine the major sources of advertising regulation including efforts by the industry at voluntary self-regulation and external regulation by government agencies. We also examine regulations involving sales promotion and direct marketing.

SELF-REGULATION

For many years, the advertising industry has practiced and promoted voluntary **self-regulation**. Most advertisers, their agencies, and the media recognize the importance of maintaining consumer trust and confidence. Advertisers also see self-regulation

@ **EXHIBIT 23–1**

The Kinney & Lange firm specializes in advertising law

IF YOU THINK IT'S TOO MUCH TROUBLE SHOWING YOUR ADS TO A LAWYER, TRY SHOWING THEM TO A JUDGE.

It happens more often than you might think. With today's tough laws, advertising is increasing its reach and frequency in the courtroom.
 That's why an ad agency like yours needs a law firm like ours: Kinney & Lange.
 Advertising law is one of the areas we limit our practice to. So there's no limit to the help we can give you.
 Often, we can suggest small changes in art or copy that may prevent big legal problems later on.
 We're easy to work with, too. We have ad agency experience.
 In fact, one of our attorneys is a former agency account executive. So you'll find us extraordinarily sensitive to your creative concerns and efforts.

We understand that great advertising can break the rules. We just try to keep it from breaking the law.
 We'd like to make our case in person. With a fast-moving, fascinating presentation on advertising law.
 We'll swear under oath that it's so entertaining, many people in your agency will actually enjoy it.
 So call Stephen Bergerson or Bill Braddock today at 339-1863. And set up a time for Kinney & Lange to appear in your agency.
 Believe us, it's a lot simpler than having your agency appear in court.

KINNEY & LANGE – ADVERTISING LAW

Kinney & Lange, P.A. 625 Fourth Avenue South, Suite 1500, Minneapolis. Practice limited to Patent, Trademark, Unfair Competition, Copyright, Franchise and Advertising Law.

as a way to limit government interference, which, they believe, results in more stringent and troublesome regulations. Self-regulation and control of advertising emanate from all segments of the advertising industry including individual advertisers and their agencies, business and advertising associations, and the media.

Self-Regulation by Advertisers and Agencies

Self-regulation begins with the interaction of client and agency when creative ideas are generated and submitted for consideration. Most companies have specific guidelines, standards, and policies to which their ads must adhere. Recognizing that their ads reflect the company, advertisers carefully scrutinize all messages to ensure they are consistent with the image the firm wishes to project. Companies also review their ads to be sure any claims made are reasonable and verifiable and do not mislead or deceive consumers. Ads are usually examined by corporate attorneys to avoid potential legal problems and their accompanying time, expense, negative publicity, and embarrassment.

Internal control and regulation also come from advertising agencies. Most have standards regarding the type of advertising they either want or are willing to produce, and they try to avoid ads that might be offensive or misleading. Agencies are responsible for verifying product claims made by the advertiser and for ensuring that adequate documentation or substantiation is available. Agencies can be held legally responsible for fraudulent or deceptive claims and in some cases have been fined when their clients are found guilty of engaging in deceptive advertising. Many agencies have a creative review board or panel composed of experienced personnel who examine ads for content and execution as well as for their potential to be perceived as offensive, misleading, and/or deceptive. Additionally, most agencies either employ or retain lawyers who also review the ads for potential legal problems. Exhibit 23–1 shows an ad for a legal firm specializing in advertising law.

Self-Regulation by Trade Associations

Just like advertisers and their agencies, many industries have also developed self-regulatory programs. This is particularly true in industries whose advertising is prone to controversy, such as liquor and alcoholic beverages, drugs, and various products marketed to children. Many trade and industry associations develop their own advertising guidelines or codes that member companies are expected to abide by.

The Wine Institute, the US Brewers Association, and the Distilled Spirits Council of the United States all have guidelines that member companies are supposed to follow in advertising alcoholic beverages. For example, no specific law prohibits the advertising

EXHIBIT 23-2 Advertising by lawyers has become more common as a result of a 1977 Supreme Court ruling

Man:
We were being strangled by our debts. We couldn't sleep, our work suffered... We'd heard about bankruptcy, but didn't know much about it.

Lawyer:
By the time the Brill's came to Jacoby & Meyers, they were being harrassed by their creditors, their wages were attached and their home was in forclosure. We stopped all that.

Man:
We figured, our creditors were using lawyers to protect their rights. Why shouldn't we?

Lawyer: The Brill's just needed a chance to get a fresh start.

Jacoby & Meyers
When it's time to call a lawyer about a bankruptcy.

of hard liquor on radio or television. However, such ads have been effectively banned for over five decades as a result of a code provision of the National Association of Broadcasters and by agreements of liquor manufacturers and their self-governing body, the Distilled Spirits Council. Other industry trade associations with advertising guidelines and programs include the Toy Manufacturers Association, Motion Picture Association of America, the Pharmaceutical Manufacturers Association, and the Proprietary Association (the trade association for nonprescription drug makers).[3]

Many professions also maintain advertising guidelines through local, state, and national organizations. For years professional associations like the American Medical Association and the American Bar Association restricted advertising by their members on the basis that such promotional activities lowered members' professional status and led to unethical and fraudulent claims. However, such restrictive codes have been attacked by both government regulatory agencies and consumer groups. They argue that the public has a right to be informed about a professional's services, qualifications, and background and that advertising will improve professional services as consumers become better informed and are better able to shop around.[4]

In 1977, the Supreme Court held that state bar associations' restrictions on advertising are unconstitutional and that attorneys have First Amendment freedom of speech rights to advertise.[5] Many professional associations subsequently removed their restrictions, and advertising by lawyers and other professionals is now common (Exhibit 23–2).[6] In 1982, the Supreme Court upheld an FTC order permitting advertising by dentists and physicians.[7]

Research shows that consumers generally favor increased use of professional advertising. However, professionals continue to have reservations. They worry that advertising has a negative impact on their image, credibility, and dignity and see benefits to consumers as unlikely.[8] Advertising by professionals is gaining popularity, particularly among newcomers to medicine, dentistry, and law. Associations such as the American Medical Association and the American Bar Association developed guidelines for members' advertising to help maintain standards and guard against misleading, deceptive, or offensive ads. However, as discussed in Ethical Perspective 23–1, the issue is still hotly debated.

Although industry associations are concerned with the impact and consequences of members' advertising, they have no legal way to enforce their guidelines. They can only rely on peer pressure from members or other nonbinding sanctions to get advertisers to comply.

Ethical Perspective 23-1
Does Advertising Hurt the Image of the Legal Profession?

For many years, advertising by attorneys was considered unethical and was prohibited by state and local bar associations. However, in the 1977 case, *Bates v. The State Bar of Arizona*, the US Supreme Court ruled that state bar associations' restrictions on advertising are unconstitutional and violated attorneys' First Amendment rights to commercial free speech. Since this ruling, advertising by attorneys has become commonplace as many law firms try to generate new business and promote their services.

Jacoby & Myers, a New York–based law firm, believes in the value of advertising. With offices nationwide, it was the first law firm to advertise on television. Recently Jacoby & Myers broke new ground with a series of TV ads targeted to consumers who took the recalled asthma drug Albuterol. Legal experts say they are the first television ads that invite people to explore litigation against a specific company with a problem product.

The Jacoby & Myers solicitations are unique because they appear on television rather than in print. Stephen Myers, a partner of the firm, noted that the firm turned to TV in order to act quickly because of widespread confusion about the recall. He also indicated that his firm felt Copley Pharmaceutical, the drug's manufacturer, had done a poor job of informing the public when it discovered potentially harmful bacteria in Albuterol, which prompted the recall. Experts on legal advertising had few ethical concerns about the Jacoby & Myers ads so long as they didn't prompt an avalanche of frivolous lawsuits.

Some traditional law firms resist using advertising, particularly on television, over concern that it might hurt the profession's image. Many attorneys worry that ads soliciting personal injury victims only worsen the public's perception of attorneys. They think TV spots and print ads of the "1-800-INJURED" variety reinforce the image of attorneys as greedy ambulance chasers.

A sizable faction within the American Bar Association (ABA) blame the legal profession's worsening image problem on sleazy ads. In March of 1994 the ABA's Commission on Advertising began a series of public hearings to investigate what, if any, restrictive measures to recommend to state ethics panels. Some states, such as Iowa and Florida, already restrict the content of attorney ads and the way they can be delivered. For example, Iowa lawyers are limited to "tombstone" print ads that merely list their name, location, and objective qualifications. And all ads require a disclaimer urging consumers not to base their attorney selection on an advertisement. Florida attorneys cannot use testimonials or endorsements, dramatizations, self-laudatory statements, illustrations, or photos.

Many attorneys are incensed over efforts to restrict their rights to promote themselves because they use advertising to help build their practices. As a result, several cases are currently being litigated. Ultimately the Supreme Court may have to decide just how far states can go in curtailing advertising.

Sources: Charles Laughlin, "Ads on Trial," *Link*, May 1994, pp.18–22; Milo Geyelin and Tom Knudson, "Law Firm's Ads Pursue Users of Recalled Drug," *The Wall Street Journal*, Feb. 3, 1994, B1, 6.

Self-Regulation by Businesses

A number of self-regulatory mechanisms have been established by the business community in an effort to control advertising practices. The largest and best known is the **Better Business Bureau** (BBB), which promotes fair advertising and selling practices across all industries. The BBB was established in 1916 to handle consumer complaints about local business practices and particularly advertising. Local BBBs are located in principal cities throughout the United States and supported entirely by dues of the more than 100,000 member firms.

Local BBBs receive and investigate complaints from consumers and other companies regarding the advertising and selling tactics of businesses in their area. Each local office has its own individual operating procedures for handling complaints; however, all offices generally contact the violator and, if the complaint proves true, request that the practice be stopped or changed. If the violator does not respond, negative publicity may be used against the firms or the case may be referred to appropriate government agencies for further action.

While BBBs provide effective control over advertising practices at the local level, the parent organization, the **Council of Better Business Bureaus**, plays a major role at a national level. The council assists new industries in developing advertising codes and standards, and it provides information about advertising regulations and legal rulings to advertisers, agencies, and the media. The council also plays an important self-regulatory role through its National Advertising Division (NAD) and Children's Advertising Unit. The NAD works closely with the **National Advertising Review Board** (NARB) to sustain truth, accuracy, and decency in national advertising. The NAD/NARB has become the advertising industry's primary self-regulatory mechanism.

@ **EXHIBIT 23-3**

Sources of NAD cases and decisions, 1993

Decisions	No.	Percent	Sources	No.	Percent
Substantiated	31	36	NAD monitoring	21	24
Modified/discontinued	50	57	Competitor challenges	47	54
Referred to government agency*	2	2	Local BBBs	3	3
No substantiation received*	4	4	Consumer complaints	12	14
			Other	4	5
Total	87	100%	Total	87	100%

*These two headings were introduced in 1991. Four cases were initially reported under the "No substantiation received" heading during 1993 and one in 1992.

NAD/NARB

In 1971 four associations—the American Advertising Federation (AAF), the American Association of Advertising Agencies (AAAA), the Association of National Advertisers (ANA), and the Council of Better Business Bureaus—joined forces to establish the **National Advertising Review Council** (NARC). The NARC's mission is to sustain high standards of truth, accuracy, and social responsibility in national advertising. The council has two operating arms, the National Advertising Division of the Council of Better Business Bureaus and the National Advertising Review Board. The NAD/NARB is the advertising industry's most effective self-regulatory mechanism.

The NAD's advertising monitoring program is the source of many of the cases it reviews. It also reviews complaints from consumers and consumer groups, local BBBs, and competitors (Exhibit 23–3). The NAD acts as the investigative arm of the NARC and, after initiating or receiving a complaint, determines the issue, collects and evaluates data, and makes the initial decision on whether the advertiser's claims are substantiated. The NAD may ask the advertiser to supply appropriate substantiation for the claim in question. If this is done, the case is deemed substantiated. If the substantiation is unsatisfactory, the NAD negotiates with the advertiser to modify or discontinue the advertising. For example, in 1993 ConAgra agreed to modify advertising for its Healthy Choice fatfree cheese after competitor Kraft General Foods challenged five ConAgra claims. The claims included "So Healthy Choice took out the fat by pouring in skim milk, for more flavor" and "Never settle for less." Since ConAgra failed to provide consumer perception studies, comparative taste tests, or nutritional analysis, the NAD ruled the claims could not be substantiated, except for "Never settle for less," which was interpreted as permissible puffery.[9]

If the NAD and the advertiser fail to resolve the controversy, either can appeal to a five-person panel from the National Advertising Review Board. The NARB is composed of 70 executives including 40 national advertisers, 20 advertising agency representatives, and 10 representatives from the public sector. If the NARB panel agrees with the NAD and rules against the advertiser, the advertiser must discontinue the advertising. If the advertiser refuses to comply, the NARB refers the matter to the appropriate government agency and indicates the fact in its public record. Exhibit 23–4 shows a flowchart of the steps in the NAD/NARB review process.

Although the NARB has no power to order an advertiser to modify or stop running an ad and no sanctions it can impose, advertisers who participate in an NAD investigation and NARB appeal rarely refuse to abide by the panel's decision.[10] Most cases do not even make it to the NARB panel. For example, in 1993, of the 87 NAD investigations, 31 ad claims were substantiated, 2 were referred to the government, and 50 were modified or discontinued (Exhibit 23–3). Of the 50 cases where the advertising claims were modified or discontinued, 10 were appealed to the NARB for resolution.[11]

In 1993, for the first time in its history, the NARB referred a matter to the Federal Trade Commission following an advertiser's refusal to modify a commercial in accordance with an NARB decision The case involved advertising for Eggland's Best eggs and is discussed in IMC Perspective 23–2 later in this chapter.[12]

The NAD/NARB is a valuable and effective self-regulatory body. Cases brought to the NAD/NARB are handled at a fraction of the cost (and with much less publicity) than

@ **EXHIBIT   23–4**   Council of Better Business Bureaus, National Advertising Division resolution process

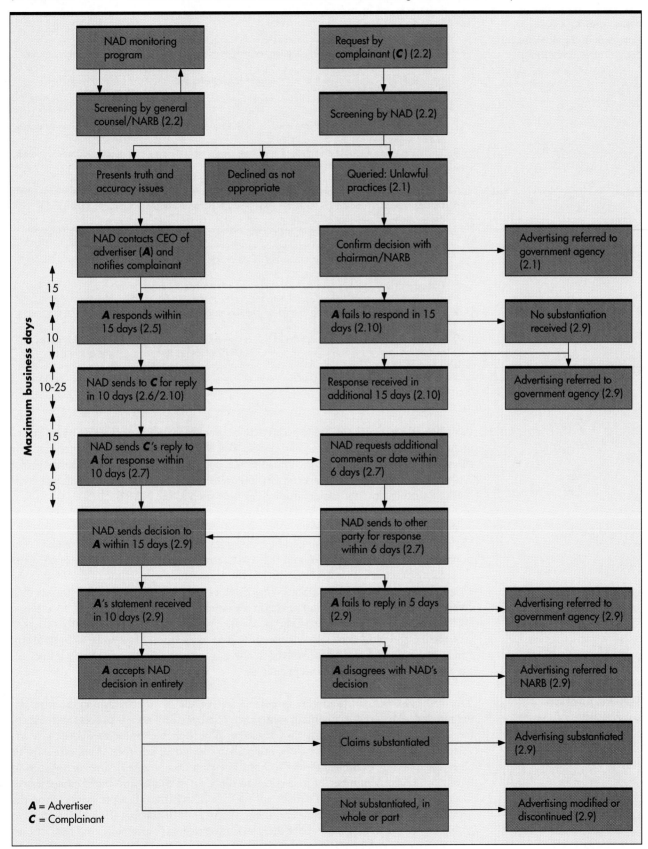

EXHIBIT 23–5

American Association of Advertising Agencies policy statement and guidelines for comparative advertising

The Board of Directors of the American Association of Advertising Agencies recognizes that when used truthfully and fairly, comparative advertising provides the consumer with needed and useful information.

However, extreme caution should be exercised. The use of comparative advertising, by its very nature, can distort facts and, by implication, convey to the consumer information that misrepresents the truth.

Therefore, the Board believes that comparative advertising should follow certain guidelines:

1. The intent and connotation of the ad should be to inform and never to discredit or unfairly attack competitors, competing products, or services.
2. When a competitive product is named, it should be one that exists in the marketplace as significant competition.
3. The competition should be fairly and properly identified but never in a manner or tone of voice that degrades the competitive product or service.
4. The advertising should compare related or similar properties or ingredients of the product, dimension to dimension, feature to feature.
5. The identification should be for honest comparison purposes and not simply to upgrade by association.
6. If a competitive test is conducted, it should be done by an objective testing source, preferably an independent one, so that there will be no doubt as to the veracity of the test.
7. In all cases the test should be supportive of all claims made in the advertising that are based on the test.
8. The advertising should never use partial results or stress insignificant differences to cause the consumer to draw an improper conclusion.
9. The property being compared should be significant in terms of value or usefulness of the product to the consumer.
10. Comparatives delivered through the use of testimonials should not imply that the testimonial is more than one individual's thought unless that individual represents a sample of the majority viewpoint.

those brought to court and are expedited more quickly than those reviewed by a government agency such as the FTC. The system also works because judgments are made by the advertiser's peers, and most companies feel compelled to comply. Firms may prefer self-regulation rather than government intervention because they can challenge competitors' unsubstantiated claims through groups such as the NARB. [13]

Advertising associations

Various groups in the advertising industry also favor self-regulation. The two major national organizations, the AAAA and the AAF, actively monitor and police industrywide advertising practices. The AAAA, which is the major trade association of the advertising agency business in the United States, has established standards of practice and its own creative code. The organization also issues guidelines for specific types of advertising such as comparative messages (Exhibit 23–5). The AAF consists of advertisers, agencies, media, and numerous advertising clubs. The association has standards for truthful and responsible advertising, is involved in advertising legislation, and actively influences agencies to abide by its code and principles.

Self-Regulation by Media

The media also constitute another important self-regulatory mechanism in the advertising industry. Most media maintain some form of advertising review process and, except for political ads, may reject any they regard as objectionable. Some media exclude advertising for an entire product class, others ban individual ads they think offensive or objectionable. For example, *Reader's Digest* does not accept advertising for tobacco or liquor products. A number of magazines in the United States and other countries refused to run some of Benetton's shock ads (discussed in Ethical Perspective 10–1) on the grounds that their readers would find them offensive or disturbing (Exhibit 23–6).

Newspapers and magazines have their own advertising requirements and restrictions, which often vary depending on the size and nature of the publication. Large, established publications, such as major newspapers or magazines, often have strict standards

@ **EXHIBIT 23-6**

A number of magazines
refused to run this Benetton ad

regarding the type of advertising they accept. Some magazines, such as *Parents* or *Good Housekeeping*, regularly test the products they advertise and offer a "Seal of Approval" and refunds if the products are later found to be defective. Such policies are designed to enhance the credibility of the publication and increase the reader's confidence in the products it advertises.

Advertising on television and radio has been regulated for years through codes developed by the industry trade association, the National Association of Broadcasters (NAB). Both the radio code (established in 1937) and the television code (1952) provided standards for broadcast advertising for many years. Both codes prohibit the advertising of certain products, such as hard liquor, and they also affect the manner in which products can be advertised. However, in 1982, the NAB suspended all of its code provisions after the courts found that portions (dealing with time standards and required length of commercials in the television code) were in restraint of trade. While the NAB codes are no longer in force, many individual broadcasters, such as the major television networks, have adopted major portions of the code provisions into their own standards.[14]

The three major television networks have the most stringent review process of any media. All three networks maintain Standards and Practices divisions, which carefully review all commercials submitted to the network or individual affiliate stations. Advertisers must submit for review all commercials intended for airing on the network or an affiliate.

A commercial may be submitted for review in the form of a script, storyboard, animatic, or finished commercial (when the advertiser believes there is little chance of objection). Network reviewers consider whether the proposed commercial meets acceptable standards and is appropriate for certain audiences. For example, different standards are used for ads designated for prime-time versus late-night spots or for children's versus adults' programs (see Exhibit 23–7). Although most of these guidelines remain in effect, ABC and NBC are currently reconsidering their position on celebrity endorsements.[15]

The three major networks receive over 50,000 commercials a year for review; nearly two-thirds are accepted and only 3 percent are rejected. Most problems with the remaining 30 percent are resolved through negotiation, and the ads are revised and resubmitted.[16]

Network standards regarding acceptable advertising change constantly. In 1987, the networks allowed lingerie advertisers to use live models rather than mannequins, and advertising for contraceptives is now appearing on some stations. The networks also revised their guidelines and loosened long-standing restrictions on endorsements and compet-

@ **EXHIBIT 23–7**

A sampling of the TV Network's guidelines for children's advertising

Each of the major television networks has its own set of guidelines for children's advertising, although the basics are very similar. A few rules, such as the requirement of a static "island" shot at the end, are written in stone; others, however, occasionally can be negotiated.

Many of the rules below apply specifically to toys. The networks also have special guidelines for kids' food commercials and for kids' commercials that offer premiums.

	ABC	CBS	NBC
Must not overglamorize product	✔	✔	✔
No exhortative language, such as "Ask Mom to buy..."	✔	✔	✔
No realistic war settings	✔		✔
Generally no celebrity endorsements	✔	Case-by-case	✔
Can't use "only" or "just" in regard to price	✔	✔	✔
Show only two toys per child or maximum of six per commercial	✔		✔
Five-second "island" showing product against plain background at end of spot	✔	✔	✔ (4 to 5)
Animation restricted to one-third of a commercial	✔		✔
Generally no comparative or superiority claims	Case-by-case	Handle w/care	✔
No costumes or props not available with the toy	✔		✔
No child or toy can appear in animated segments	✔		✔
Three-second establishing shot of toy in relation to child	✔	✔ (2.5 to 3)	
No shots under one second in length		✔	
Must show distance a toy can travel before stopping on its own		✔	

Source: "Kid Advertising Guidelines: Double Standard for Kid's TV Ads," *The Wall Street Journal*, June 10, 1988, p. 25.

itive advertising claims.[17] Network standards will continue to change as society's values and attitudes toward certain issues and products change. Also, many advertising people believe these changes are a response to competition from independent and cable stations, which tend to be much less stringent. However, television is probably the most carefully scrutinized and frequently criticized of all forms of advertising, and the networks must be careful not to offend their viewers and detract from advertising's credibility.

Appraising Self-Regulation

The three major participants in the advertising process—advertisers, agencies, and the media—work individually and collectively to encourage truthful, ethical, and responsible advertising. The advertising industry views self-regulation as an effective mechanism for controlling advertising abuses and avoiding the use of offensive, misleading, or deceptive practices, and it prefers this form of regulation to government intervention. Self-regulation of advertising has been effective and in many instances probably led to the development of more stringent standards and practices than those imposed by or beyond the scope of legislation.

In a recent speech to the American Advertising Federation, FTC Commissioner Mary Azuenaga commented on the fact that the Eggland's Best eggs case marked the first time in its 22-year history the NARB referred a matter to the FTC. She noted, "Although it was unfortunate that such a referral was necessary, the very novelty of the referral underscores the important contribution of NARB and other self-regulatory groups in addressing questions of deceptive advertising."[18]

There are, however, limitations to self-regulation, and the process has been criticized in a number of areas. For example, the NAD may take six months to a year to resolve a complaint, during which time a company often stops using the commercial anyway. Budgeting and staffing constraints may limit the NAD/NARB system's ability to investigate more cases and complete them more rapidly.[19] And some critics believe that self-regulation is self-serving to the advertisers and advertising industry and lacks the power or authority to be a viable alternative to federal or state regulation.

Many do not believe advertising can or should be controlled solely by self-regulation. They argue that regulation by government agencies is necessary to ensure that consumers get accurate information and are not misled or deceived. Moreover, since advertisers do not have to comply with the decisions and recommendations of self-regulatory groups, it is sometimes necessary to turn to the federal and/or state government.

FEDERAL REGULATION OF ADVERTISING

The government controls and regulates advertising through federal, state, and local laws and regulations enforced by various government agencies. The federal government, through the **Federal Trade Commission** (FTC), is the most important source of external regulation.

Background on Federal Regulation of Advertising

Federal regulation of advertising originated in 1914 with the passage of the **Federal Trade Commission Act** (FTC Act), which created the FTC, the agency that is today the most active in, and has primary responsibility for, controlling and regulating advertising. The FTC Act was originally intended to help enforce antitrust laws, such as the Sherman and Clayton acts, by helping to restrain unfair methods of competition. The main focus of the first five-member commission was to protect competitors from one another; the issue of false or misleading advertising was not even mentioned. In 1922, the Supreme Court upheld an FTC interpretation that false advertising was an unfair method of competition, but in the 1931 case (*FTC v. Raladam Co.*), the Court ruled the commission could not prohibit false advertising unless there was evidence of injury to a competitor.[20] This ruling limited the power of the FTC to protect consumers from false or deceptive advertising and led to a consumer movement that resulted in an important amendment to the FTC Act.

In 1938, Congress passed the **Wheeler-Lea Amendment**. It amended section 5 of the FTC Act to read: "Unfair methods of competition in commerce and unfair or deceptive acts or practices in commerce are hereby declared to be unlawful." The amendment empowered the FTC to act if there was evidence of injury to the *public*; proof of injury to competition was not necessary. The Wheeler-Lea Amendment also gave the FTC the power to issue cease and desist orders and levy fines on violators. It extended the FTC's jurisdiction over false advertising of foods, drugs, cosmetics, and therapeutic devices. And it gave the FTC access to the injunctive power of the federal courts, initially only for food and drug products but expanded in 1972 to include all products in the event of a threat to the public's health and safety.

In addition to the FTC, numerous other federal agencies are responsible for, or involved in, advertising regulation. The authority of these agencies is limited, however, to a particular product area or service, and these agencies often rely on the FTC to assist in handling false or deceptive advertising cases.

The Federal Trade Commission

The FTC has responsibility for protecting both consumers and businesses from anticompetitive behavior and unfair and deceptive practices. The major divisions of the FTC include the Bureaus of Competition, Economics, and Consumer Protection (Exhibit 23–8). The Bureau of Competition enforces antitrust laws. The Bureau of Economics aids and advises the commission on the economic aspects of its activities and prepares economic reports and surveys. The Bureau of Consumer Protection investigates and litigates cases involving acts or practices alleged to be deceptive or unfair to consumers. The National Advertising Division of the Bureau of Consumer Protection enforces those provisions of the FTC Act that forbid misrepresentation, unfairness, and deception in national advertising.

The FTC has had the power to regulate advertising since passage of the Wheeler-Lea Amendment. However, not until the early 1970s—following criticism of the commission in a book by "Nader's Raiders" and a special report by the American Bar Association

● **EXHIBIT   23–8**   The Federal Trade Commission organization

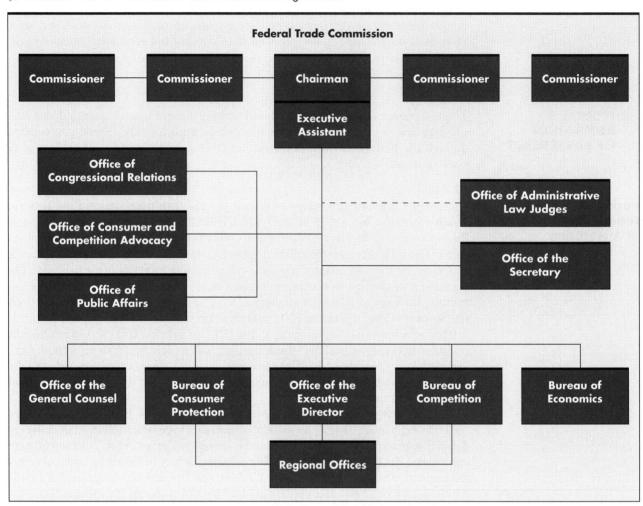

citing its lack of action against deceptive promotional practices—did the FTC become active in regulating advertising.[21]

The authority of the FTC was increased considerably throughout the 1970s. The Magnuson-Moss Act of 1975, a particularly important piece of legislation, dramatically broadened the FTC's powers and substantially increased its budget. The first section of the act dealt with consumers' rights regarding product warranties; it allowed the commission to require restitution for deceptively written warranties where the consumer lost more than $5. The second section, the FTC Improvements Act, empowered the FTC to establish **trade regulation rules** (TRRs), industrywide rules that defined unfair practices before they occurred.

During the 1970s, the FTC made enforcement of laws regarding false and misleading advertising a top priority. Several new programs were instituted, budgets were increased, and the commission became a very powerful regulatory agency. However, many of these programs, as well as the expanded powers of the FTC to develop regulations on the basis of "unfairness," became controversial. At the source of this controversy is the fundamental issue of what constitutes unfair advertising.

The Concept of Unfairness

Under Section 5 of the FTC Act, the Federal Trade Commission has a mandate to act against unfair and deceptive advertising practices. However, this statute does not define the terms *unfair* and *deceptive*, and the FTC has been criticized for not doing so itself.

While the FTC has taken steps to define and clarify the meaning of *deception*, people have been concerned for years over the vagueness of the term "unfair."

Controversy over the FTC's authority to regulate unfair advertising practices began in 1978 when the agency relied on this mandate to formulate its controversial "kid vid" rule restricting advertising to children.[22] This interpretation caused widespread concern in the business community that the term *unfair* could be used to encompass anything FTC commissioners might find objectionable. For example, in a 1980 policy statement the FTC noted that "the precise concept of consumer unfairness is one whose precise meaning is not immediately obvious." Consequently, in 1980 Congress responded by suspending the children's advertising rule and banning the FTC from using unfairness as a legal basis for advertising rulemaking.

The FTC responded to these criticisms in December of 1980 by sending Congress a statement containing an interpretation of *unfairness*. According to FTC policy the basis for determining **unfairness** is that a trade practice (*a*) causes substantial physical or economic injury to consumers, (*b*) could not reasonably be avoided by consumers, and (*c*) must not be outweighed by countervailing benefits to consumers or competition. The agency also stated that a violation of public policy (such as of other government statutes) could, by itself, constitute an unfair practice or could be used to prove substantial consumer injury. Practices considered unfair are claims made without prior substantiation, claims that might exploit such vulnerable groups as children and the elderly, and instances where consumers cannot make a valid choice because the advertiser omits important information about the product or competing products mentioned in the ad.[23]

The FTC's statement was intended to clarify its interpretation of unfairness and reduce ambiguity over what might constitute unfair practices. However, efforts by the FTC to develop trade regulation rules, whereby the commission could establish industrywide rules that would define unfair practices and have the force and effect of law, were limited by Congress in 1980 with the passage of the FTC Improvements Act. Recently there have been calls to end the 14-year-old stalemate over the FTC's regulation of unfair advertising by having the agency work with Congress to define its advertising authority. In early 1994 Congress and the advertising industry were near agreement on a definition of unfair advertising that is very similar to the FTC's 1980 policy statement discussed earlier. However, the new agreement requires that before the FTC can initiate any industrywide rule, it has to have reason to believe that the unfair or deceptive acts or practices are prevalent.[24]

The FTC does have specific regulatory authority in cases involving deceptive, misleading, or untruthful advertising. The vast majority of advertising cases that the FTC handles concern deception and advertising fraud, which usually involve knowledge of a false claim.

Deceptive Advertising

In most economies, advertising provides consumers with information they can use to make consumption decisions. However, if this information is untrue or misleads the consumer, advertising is not fulfilling its basic function. But what constitutes an untruthful or deceptive ad? Deceptive advertising can take a number of forms, ranging from an intentionally false or misleading claim to ads that, although true, leave some consumers with a false or misleading impression.

The issue of deception, including its definition and measurement, receives considerable attention from the FTC and other regulatory agencies. One of the problems regulatory agencies deal with in determining deception is distinguishing between false or misleading messages and those that, rather than relying on verifiable or substantiated objective information about a product, rely on subjective claims or statements, a practice known as puffery. **Puffery** has been legally defined as "advertising or other sales presentations which praise the item to be sold with subjective opinions, superlatives, or exaggerations, vaguely and generally, stating no specific facts."[25] The use of puffery in advertising is common. For example, Bayer aspirin calls itself the "Wonder drug that works wonders," Nestlé claims "Nestlé makes the very best chocolate," and Healthy Choice foods tell consumers to "Never settle for less." Superlatives such as *greatest*, *best*, and/or *finest* are frequently used puffs.

Puffery has generally been viewed as a form of poetic license or allowable exaggeration. The FTC takes the position that because consumers expect exaggeration or inflated claims in advertising, they recognize puffery and don't believe it. But some studies show that consumers may believe puffery and perceive such claims as true.[26] One study found that consumers could not distinguish between a verifiable fact-based claim and puffery and were just as likely to believe both types of claims.[27] Ivan Preston argues that puffery has a detrimental effect on consumers' purchase decisions by burdening them with untrue beliefs and refers to it as "soft core deception" that should be illegal.[28]

Since unfair and deceptive acts or practices have never been precisely defined, the FTC is continually developing and refining a "working definition" in its attempts to regulate advertising. The traditional standard used to determine deception was whether a claim had the "tendency or capacity to deceive." However, this standard was criticized for being vague and all-encompassing.

In 1983, the FTC, under Chairman James Miller III, put forth a new working definition of **deception**: "The commission will find deception if there is a misrepresentation, omission, or practice that is likely to mislead the consumer acting reasonably in the circumstances to the consumer's detriment."[29] Under this definition, the representation, omission, or practice must be a "material" one, meaning it is likely to affect the consumer's conduct or decision with regard to a product or service. If so, consumer injury is likely because the consumer may have chosen differently but for the deception.[30]

The goal of then Chairman Miller, who drafted this definition, was to help the commission determine which cases were worth pursuing and which were trivial. Miller argued that for an ad to be considered worthy of FTC challenge, it should be seen by a substantial number of consumers, it should lead to significant injury, and the problem should be one that market forces are not likely to remedy. However, the revised definition may put a greater burden on the FTC to prove that deception occurred and that the deception influenced the consumers' decision-making process in a detrimental way.

Determining what constitutes deception is still a gray area. However, two of the factors the FTC considers in evaluating an ad for deception are (1) whether there are significant omissions of important information and (2) whether advertisers can substantiate the claims made for the product or service. The FTC has developed several programs to address these issues.

Affirmative disclosure

An ad can be literally true yet leave the consumer with a false or misleading impression if the claim is true only under certain conditions or circumstances or if there are limitations to what the product can or cannot do. Thus, under its **affirmative disclosure** requirement, the FTC may require advertisers to include certain types of information in their ads so consumers will be aware of all the consequences, conditions, and limitations associated with the use of a product or service. The goal of affirmative disclosure is to give consumers sufficient information to make an informed decision. An ad may be required to define the testing situation, conditions, or criteria used in making a claim. For example, fuel mileage claims in automobile ads are based on Environmental Protection Agency (EPA) ratings since they offer a uniform standard for making comparisons. And cigarette ads must contain a warning concerning the health risks associated with smoking.

An example of an affirmative disclosure ruling involves the FTC's 1989 case against Campbell Soup for making deceptive and unsubstantiated claims. Campbell's ads, run as part of its "Soup is good food" campaign, linked the low fat and cholesterol content of its soup with a reduced risk of heart disease. However, the advertising failed to disclose that the soups are high in sodium, which may increase the risk of heart disease. In a consent agreement accepted in 1991, Campbell agreed that, for any soup containing more than 500 milligrams of sodium in an eight-ounce serving, it will disclose the sodium content in any advertising that directly or by implication mentions heart disease in connection with the soup. Campbell also agreed it would not imply a connection between soup and a reduction in heart disease in future advertising.[31]

Advertising substantiation

A major area of concern to regulatory agencies is whether advertisers can support or substantiate their claims. For many years, there were no formal requirements concerning substantiation of advertising claims. Many companies made claims without any documentation or support such as laboratory tests and clinical studies. In 1971, the FTC's **advertising substantiation** program required advertisers to have supporting documentation for their claims and to prove the claims are truthful.[32] Broadened in 1972, this program now requires advertisers to substantiate their claims *before* an ad appears. Substantiation is required for all claims involving safety, performance, efficacy, quality, or comparative price.

The FTC's substantiation program has had a major effect on the advertising industry, because it shifted the burden of proof from the commission to the advertiser. Before the substantiation program, the FTC had to prove that an advertiser's claims were unfair or deceptive.

Ad substantiation seeks to provide a basis for believing advertising claims so consumers can make rational and informed decisions and to deter companies from making claims they cannot adequately support. The FTC takes the perspective that it is illegal and unfair to consumers for a firm to make a claim for a product without having a "reasonable basis" for the claim. In their decision to require advertising substantiation, the commissioners made the following statement:

> Given the imbalance of knowledge and resources between a business enterprise and each of its customers, economically it is more rational and imposes far less cost on society, to require a manufacturer to confirm his affirmative product claims rather than impose a burden on each individual consumer to test, investigate, or experiment for himself. The manufacturer has the ability, the know-how, the equipment, the time and resources to undertake such information, by testing or otherwise, . . . the consumer usually does not.[33]

Many advertisers express considerable concern and respond negatively to the FTC's advertising substantiation program. They argue it is too expensive to document all their claims and most consumers either won't understand or aren't interested in the technical data and information used. Some advertisers threaten to avoid the substantiation issue by using puffery claims, which do not require substantiation.

Generally, advertisers making claims covered by the substantiation program should have available prior substantiation of all claims. However, in 1984, the FTC issued a new policy statement that suggested after-the-fact substantiation might be acceptable in some cases and it would solicit documentation of claims only from advertisers that are under investigation for deceptive practices.

In a number of cases, the FTC orders advertisers to cease making inadequately substantiated claims. In December 1993, the FTC obtained relief against Union Oil of California and its agency for making unsubstantiated claims in advertising for Unocal's 89 and 92 octane gasoline. According to the FTC complaint, Unocal lacked adequate scientific evidence for its claims that the higher octane gasolines increased engine performance and longevity. The FTC argued that a large percentage of consumers believe that higher-octane gasoline improves an engine's performance and the advertising played into this belief. In settling with the FTC, Unocal and its agency agreed that, lacking better scientific evidence, they would stop making claims that drivers could get better performance by exceeding auto manufacturers' recommendations for fuel use.[34]

The FTC's Handling of Deceptive Advertising Cases

Consent and cease and desist orders

Allegations of unfair or deceptive advertising come to the FTC's attention from a variety of sources including competitors, consumers, other governmental agencies, or the commission's own monitoring and investigations. Once the FTC decides a complaint is justified and warrants further action, it notifies the offender, who then has 30 days to respond. The advertiser can agree to negotiate a settlement with the FTC by signing a **consent order,** which is an agreement to stop the practice or advertising in question. This agreement is for settlement purposes only and does not constitute an admission of guilt by the advertiser. Most FTC inquiries are settled by consent orders because they save the advertiser the cost and possible adverse publicity that might result if the case were to go further.

If the advertiser chooses not to sign the consent decree and contests the complaint, a hearing can be requested before an administrative law judge employed by the FTC but not under its influence. The judge's decision may be appealed to the full five-member commission by either side. The commission either affirms or modifies the order or dismisses the case. If the complaint has been upheld by the administrative law judge and the commission, the advertiser can appeal the case to the federal courts.

The appeal process may take some time, during which the FTC may want to stop the advertiser from engaging in the deceptive practice. The Wheeler-Lea Amendment empowers the FTC to issue **cease and desist orders.** The cease and desist order requires that the advertiser stop the specified advertising claim within 30 days and prohibits the advertiser from engaging in the objectionable practice until after the hearing is held. Violation of a cease and desist order is punishable by a fine of up to $10,000 a day. Firms that violated the terms of a cease and desist order have had to pay substantial fines, although most firms usually comply. Exhibit 23–9 summarizes the FTC complaint procedure.

Corrective advertising

By using consent and cease and desist orders, the FTC can usually stop a particular advertising practice it believes is unfair or deceptive. However, even if an advertiser ceases using a deceptive ad, consumers may still remember some or all of the claim. To address the problem of residual effects, in the 1970s the FTC developed a program known as **corrective advertising.** Under this program, an advertiser found guilty of deceptive advertising can be required to run additional advertising designed to remedy the deception or misinformation contained in previous ads.

The impetus for corrective advertising was a case involving the Campbell Soup Company. Marbles were placed in the bottom of a bowl of vegetable soup to force the solid ingredients to the surface, creating a false impression that the soup contained more vegetables than it really did. (Campbell Soup argued that if the marbles were not used, all the ingredients would settle to the bottom, leaving an impression of fewer ingredients than actually existed!) While Campbell Soup agreed to stop the practice, a group of law students calling themselves SOUP (Students Opposed to Unfair Practices) argued to the FTC that this would not remedy false impressions created by prior advertising and contended Campbell Soup should be required to run advertising to rectify the problem.

Although the FTC did not order corrective advertising in the Campbell case, it did so in a number of subsequent cases. Profile Bread ran ads stating each slice contained fewer calories than other brands. However, the ad did not mention that slices of Profile bread were thinner than those of other brands. Ocean Spray cranberry juice was found guilty of deceptive advertising because it claimed to have more "food energy" than orange or tomato juice but failed to note it was referring to the technical definition of food energy, which is calories. In each case, the advertisers were ordered to spend 25 percent of their annual media budget to run corrective ads. The STP Corporation was required to run corrective advertising for claims regarding the ability of its oil additive to reduce oil consumption. Many of the corrective ads run in the STP case appeared in business publications to serve notice to other advertisers that the FTC was enforcing the correc-

 **EXHIBIT   23–9** FTC complaint procedure

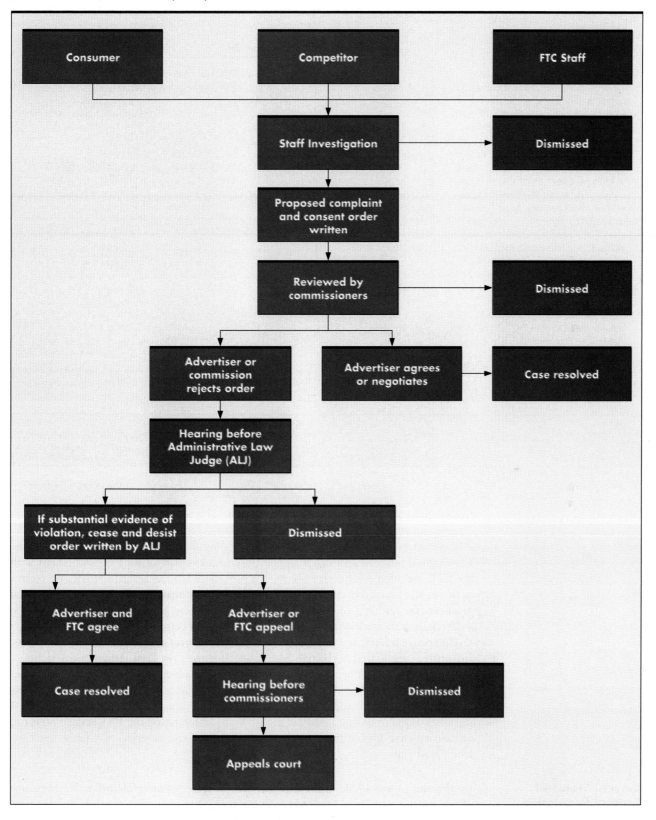

EXHIBIT 23-10 Examples of corrective advertising messages

Profile Bread	Ocean Spray	STP
"Hi, (celebrity's name) for Profile Bread. Like all mothers, I'm concerned about nutrition and balanced meals. So, I'd like to clear up any misunderstanding you may have about Profile Bread from its advertising or even its name. "Does Profile have fewer calories than any other breads? No. Profile has about the same per ounce as other breads. To be exact, Profile has seven fewer calories per slice. That's because Profile is sliced thinner. But eating Profile will not cause you to lose weight. A reduction of seven calories is insignificant. It's total calories and balanced nutrition that count. And Profile can help you achieve a balanced meal because it provides protein and B vitamins as well as other nutrients. "How does my family feel about Profile? Well, my husband likes Profile toast, the children love Profile sandwiches, and I prefer Profile to any other bread. So you see, at our house, delicious taste makes Profile a family affair." (To be run in 25 percent of brand's advertising, for one year.)	"If you've wondered what some of our earlier advertising meant when we said Ocean Spray Cranberry Juice Cocktail has more food energy than orange juice or tomato juice, let us make it clear: we didn't mean vitamins and minerals. Food energy means calories. Nothing more. "Food energy is important at breakfast since many of us may not get enough calories, or food energy, to get off to a good start. Ocean Spray Cranberry Juice Cocktail helps because it contains more food energy than most other breakfast drinks. "And Ocean Spray Cranberry Juice Cocktail gives you and your family Vitamin C plus a great wake-up taste. It's... the other breakfast drink." (To be run in one of every four ads for one year.)	As a result of an investigation by the Federal Trade Commission into certain allegedly inaccurate past advertisements for STP's oil additive, STP Corporation has agreed to a $700,000 settlement. With regard to that settlement, STP is making the following statement: "It is the policy of STP to support its advertising with objective information and test data. In 1974 and 1975 an independent laboratory ran tests of the company's oil additive which led to claims of reduced oil consumption. However, these tests cannot be relied on to support the oil consumption reduction claim made by STP. "The FTC has taken the position that, in making the claim, the company violated the terms of a consent order. When STP learned that the test did not support the claim, it stopped advertising containing that claim. New tests have been undertaken to determine the extent to which the oil additive affects oil consumption. Agreement to this settlement does not constitute an admission by STP that the law has been violated. Rather, STP has agreed to resolve the dispute with the FTC to avoid protracted and prohibitively expensive litigation."

tive advertising program. The texts of the corrective messages required in each of these cases are shown in Exhibit 23–10.

Corrective advertising has also been ordered by the FTC in some very recent cases. For example, the consent order signed by Unocal as part of its 1993 settlement with the FTC included a corrective advertising provision. Unocal agreed to mail a corrective notice to all of its active credit card customers in its primary marketing area stating that most cars do not need a high octane gasoline to perform properly and reminding them to check their owner's manual for the recommended octane level of fuel.

Corrective advertising is probably the most controversial of all the FTC programs. Advertisers argue that corrective advertising infringes on First Amendment rights of freedom of speech. The effectiveness of corrective advertising campaigns is also being questioned, as is the FTC's involvement in the business of creating advertisements through requiring particular content in corrective messages.[35] IMC Perspective 23–1 discusses a case involving Listerine mouthwash, which tested the FTC's legal power to order corrective advertising, as well as a more recent controversial case involving Eggland's Best eggs.

Current Status of Federal Regulation by the FTC

By the end of the 1970s, the FTC had become a very powerful and active regulator of advertising. However, Congress became very concerned over the FTC's broad interpretation of unfairness, which led to the restrictive legislation of the 1980 FTC Improvements Act. During the 1980s, the FTC became less active and cut back its regulatory efforts. This change was in large part due to the laissez-faire attitude of

IMC Perspective 23–1
The Debate over Corrective Advertising Continues

One of the most publicized corrective advertising cases ever, and the first to test the FTC's legal power to order corrective messages, involved Warner Lambert Company's Listerine mouthwash. For more than 50 years, Warner-Lambert advertised that gargling with Listerine helped prevent colds and sore throats or lessened their severity because it killed the germs that caused these illnesses. However, in 1975, the FTC ruled these claims could not be substantiated and ordered Listerine to stop making them. In addition the FTC argued that corrective advertising was needed to rectify the erroneous beliefs Listerine had created with its large advertising expenditures over the prior 50 years.

Warner Lambert argued that the advertising was not misleading and, further, that the FTC did not have the power to order corrective advertising. However, after months of hearings the commission ordered corrective advertising. Listerine appealed the FTC decision all the way to the Supreme Court, which rejected the argument that corrective advertising violates advertisers' First Amendment rights. The powers of the FTC in the areas of both claim substantiation and corrective advertising were upheld. Warner-Lambert was required to run $10 million worth of corrective ads over a 16-month period stating, "Listerine would not help prevent colds or sore throats or lessen their severity."

The "Warner Lambert test" was used in a 1993 FTC decision to order corrective advertising. The case involved ads for Eggland's Best eggs claiming "You can eat eggs again . . . and not increase your serum cholesterol" and "They're special eggs from specially fed hens." The FTC argued that the company's ads and promotional materials deceptively represented that Eggland's eggs do not increase consumers' serum cholesterol and are superior to regular eggs in this respect. In a settlement with the FTC, Eggland's Best agreed not to misrep-

resent the absolute or comparative amount of cholesterol, total fat, saturated fat, or any other nutrient or ingredient or to make any claims about the health benefits of its eggs.

The settlement also included a provision for corrective advertising. The commissioners, by a 3 to 2 margin, voted to require Eggland's Best to place a "clear and prominent" notice on the package label for its eggs specifying that "There are no studies showing that these eggs are different from other eggs in their effect on serum cholesterol." The corrective notice was to continue for one year and cover 28 specified geographic areas where the ads were shown for 12 weeks or more.

The two dissenting commissioners argued that corrective advertising was unwarranted under the Warner Lambert test. One noted there was no direct evidence, as there was in Warner Lambert, that Eggland's ads created a lingering false impression about its eggs' effects on serum cholesterol. The other commissioner argued that there was no evidence that Eggland's campaign was so similarly saturated or that a substantial portion of the public would continue to believe the challenged claims in the absence of corrective advertising.

However, the commissioner whose vote broke the 2-2 tie noted that Eggland's ability to charge about 200 percent of the typical price per dozen eggs constituted strong evidence that the company's ads had been successful in creating consumer beliefs that Eggland's eggs were meaningfully superior. He argued that "common sense tells me that this belief is not going to disappear overnight simply because the advertising making the claim ceases."

Some legal experts feel that despite the closeness of the vote in this case, the FTC will place more emphasis on corrective advertising in the future.

Sources: "Settlement of FTC Charges over Deceptive Cholesterol Claims Sparks Corrective Advertising Controversy," *WR&F Advertising Law Update 7*, no. 1, pp. 3, 7; *Warner Lambert Co. v. Federal Trade Commission*, CCH P61,563A-D.C., August 1977 and CCH P61, 646 CA-D.C., September 1977.

the Reagan administration toward the regulation of business in general. Concern was expressed that the FTC had become too narrow in its regulation of national advertising, forcing companies and consumer groups to seek relief from other sources such as state and federal courts or through self-regulatory groups such as the NAD/NARB.[36]

In 1988–89, an 18-member panel chosen by the American Bar Association undertook a study of the FTC as a 20-year follow-up to the 1969 report used by President Richard Nixon to overhaul the commission. The report filed by the panel expressed strong concern over the FTC's lack of sufficient resources and staff to regulate national advertising effectively, and it called for more funding.

After more than a decade of relative inactivity, the Federal Trade Commission has once again become active in the regulation of advertising. The commission has shown particular interest in cracking down on misleading advertising in areas such as health, nutrition, weight loss, and environmental claims as well as advertising telemarketing, 900 numbers, and advertising directed to children and the elderly.[37] The FTC has also become more involved with potential fraud and deception through various other promotional methods such as telemarketing, 900 numbers, and infomercials.

While the Federal Trade Commission is the major regulator of advertising for products sold in interstate commerce, various other federal agencies and departments also regulate advertising and promotion.

Additional Federal Regulatory Agencies

The Federal Communications Commission

The FCC, founded in 1934 to regulate broadcast communication, has jurisdiction over the radio, television, telephone, and telegraph industries. The FCC has the authority to license broadcast stations as well as to remove a license or deny renewal to stations not operating in the public's interest. The FCC's authority over the airways gives it the power to control advertising content and to restrict what products and services can be advertised on radio and television. The FCC can eliminate obscene and profane programs and/or messages and those it finds in poor taste. While the FCC can eliminate ads that are deceptive or misleading, it generally works closely with the FTC in the regulation of advertising.

Many of the FCC's rules and regulations for television and radio stations have been eliminated or modified. The FCC no longer limits the amount of television time that can be devoted to commercials. However, on October 1, 1991, the Children's Television Act went into effect. The act limits advertising during children's programming to $10\frac{1}{2}$ minutes an hour on weekends and 12 minutes an hour on weekdays. Under the Reagan administration, the controversial *Fairness Doctrine,* which required broadcasters to provide time for opposing viewpoints on important issues, was also repealed on the grounds that it was counterproductive. It was argued that the Fairness Doctrine resulted in a reduction in the amount of discussion of important issues because a broadcaster might be afraid to take on a paid controversial message on the grounds it might subsequently be required to provide equal free exposure for opposing viewpoints.

It was under this doctrine that the FCC required stations to run commercials about the harmful effects of smoking before passage of the Public Health Cigarette Smoking Act of 1970, which banned broadcast advertising of cigarettes. Many stations still provide time for opposing viewpoints on controversial issues on the basis that this is consistent with the station's public service requirement and not necessarily directly related to fairness.

Several pieces of legislation passed in recent years involve the FCC and have an impact on advertising and promotion. The Cable Television Consumer Protection and Competition Act was passed in 1992 and places new controls on the cable TV industry. The bill allows the FCC and local governments to regulate basic cable rates and forces cable operators to pay licensing fees for local broadcast programming they now retransmit for free. One of the purposes of this bill is to improve the balance between cable rates and rapidly escalating advertising revenue.

FCC rules affecting telemarketing will be discussed at the end of this chapter.

The Food and Drug Administration

Now under the jurisdiction of the Department of Health and Human Services, the FDA has authority over the labeling, packaging, branding, ingredient listing, and advertising of packaged foods and drug products. The FDA is authorized to require caution and warning labels on potentially hazardous products and also has limited authority over nutritional claims made in food advertising. This agency has the authority to set rules for promoting these products and the power to seize food and drugs on charges of false and misleading advertising.

Like the FTC, the Food and Drug Administration has become a very aggressive regulatory agency in recent years, particularly since David A. Kessler took over as commissioner in early 1991. The FDA has been cracking down on a number of commonly used descriptive terms it believes are often abused in the labeling and advertising of food products—e.g., *natural, light, no cholesterol,* and *fat free.* The FDA has also become tougher on nutritional claims implied by brand names that might send a misleading message to consumers. For example, Great Foods of America was not permitted to continue using the HeartBeat trademark under which it sells most of its foods. The FDA argued the trademark goes too far in implying the foods have special advantages for the heart and overall health.[38]

@ **EXHIBIT 23-11**

The Nutritional Labeling and Education Act requires that labels be easy for consumers to understand

Many changes in food labeling are a result of the Nutritional Labeling and Education Act, which Congress passed in 1990. Under this law the FDA established legal definitions for a wide range of terms (such as *low fat*, *light*, and *reduced calories*) and required straightforward labels for all foods beginning in early 1994 (Exhibit 23–11). In its current form the act applies only to food labels, but it may soon affect the advertising of food products as well. The FTC would be asked to ensure that food ads comply with the new FDA standards.

The US Postal Service

A large number of marketers use the US mail to deliver advertising and promotional messages. The US Postal Service has control over advertising involving the use of the mail and ads involved with lotteries, fraud, and obscenity regulations. The postmaster general has the power to impose legal sanctions for violations of these statutes as well as for fraudulent use of the mail. The fraud order under US Postal Service regulations has been used frequently to control deceptive advertising by numerous direct-response advertisers. These firms advertise on television or radio or in magazines and newspapers and use the US mail to receive orders and payment. Many have been prosecuted by the Post Office Department for use of the mail in conjunction with a fraudulent or deceptive offer.

Bureau of Alcohol, Tobacco, and Firearms

The Bureau of Alcohol, Tobacco, and Firearms (BATF) is an agency within the Treasury Department that enforces laws, develops regulations, and is responsible for tax collection for the liquor industry. The BATF regulates and controls the advertising of alcoholic beverages. The agency determines what information can be provided in ads as well as what constitutes false and misleading advertising. It is also responsible for the inclusion of warning labels on alcohol advertising and the banning of the use of active athletes in beer commercials. The BATF can impose strong sanctions for violators.

The Lanham Act

While most advertisers rely on self-regulatory mechanisms and the FTC to deal with deceptive or misleading advertising by their competitors, many companies are filing lawsuits against competitors they believe are making false claims. One piece of federal legislation that has become increasingly important in this regard is the Lanham Act. This act was originally written in 1947 as the Lanham Trade-Mark Act to protect words, names, symbols, or other devices adopted to identify and distinguish a manufacturer's products. The **Lanham Act** was amended to encompass false advertising by prohibiting "any false description or representation including words or other symbols tending falsely to describe or represent the same." While the FTC Act did not provide individual advertisers with the opportunity to sue a competitor for deceptive advertising, civil suits are permitted under the Lanham Act.

More and more companies are using the Lanham Act to sue competitors for their advertising claims, particularly since comparative advertising has become so common. For example, a US district court fined Jartran a record $20 million in punitive damages on top of the $20 million awarded to U-Haul International to compensate for losses resulting from ads comparing the companies' prices and equipment that were ruled deceptive. In several recent cases, companies have sued a competitor for damages resulting from false advertising claims. In late 1991, a court ordered Ralston Purina to pay Alpo Petfoods $12 million for damages caused by making false claims that its Purina Puppy Chow dog food could ameliorate and help prevent joint disease. The court ruled that the claim was based on faulty data and that the company continued the campaign after learning its research was in error. Alpo was awarded the money as compensation for lost revenue and for the costs of advertising it ran in response to the Puppy Chow campaign.[39]

In 1992 Wilkinson Sword and its advertising agency were found guilty of false advertising and ordered to pay $953,000 in damages to the Gillette Company. Wilkinson had run TV and print ads claiming its Ultra Glide razor and blades produced shaves "six times smoother" than Gillette's Atra Plus blades. This case is particularly significant in that it marked the first time an agency was held liable for damages in connection with false claims made in a client's advertising.[40] Although the agency was subsequently found not to be liable, the case served as a sobering reminder to agencies that they can be drawn into litigation over advertising they create for their clients. To deal with this problem many agencies insist on indemnification clauses in contracts with their clients.

The ease of suing competitors for false claims was facilitated even more with passage of the Trademark Law Revision Act of 1988. According to this law, anyone is vulnerable to civil action who "misrepresents the nature, characteristics, qualities, or geographical origin of his or her or another person's goods, services, or commercial activities." This wording closed a loophole in the Lanham Act, which prohibited only false claims about one's own goods or services. While many disputes over comparative claims are never contested or are resolved through the NAD, more companies will turn to lawsuits for several reasons: the broad information discovery powers available under federal civil procedure rules, the speed with which a competitor can stop the offending ad through a preliminary injunction, and the possibility of collecting damages.[41]

STATE REGULATION

In addition to the various federal rules and regulations, advertisers must also concern themselves with numerous state and local controls. An important development in state regulation of advertising was the adoption, in 44 states, of the Printer's Ink Model Statutes as a basis for advertising regulation. These statutes were drawn up in 1911 by *Printers Ink*, for many years the major trade publication of the advertising industry. Many states have since modified the original statutes and adopted laws similar to those of the Federal Trade Commission Act as a basis for dealing with false and misleading advertising.

In addition to recognizing decisions by the federal courts regarding false or deceptive practices, many states have special controls and regulations governing the advertising of specific industries or practices. As the federal government became less involved in the regulation of national advertising during the 1980s, many state attorneys general began to enforce state laws regarding false or deceptive advertising. For example, the attorneys general in New York and Texas initiated investigations of Kraft ads claiming the pasteurized cheese used in Cheez Whiz was real cheese.[42] IMC Perspective 23–2 discusses a well-publicized deceptive advertising case involving Volvo and its advertising agency that was initiated by the attorney general's office in the state of Texas.

The **National Association of Attorneys General** (NAAG) moved against a number of national advertisers as a result of inactivity by the FTC during the Reagan administration. In 1987, the NAAG developed enforcement guidelines on airfare advertising that were adopted by more than 40 states. The NAAG is also involved in other regulatory areas including car rental price advertising as well as advertising dealing with nutrition and health claims in food ads.[43] In 1991, a group of attorneys general from various states reached an agreement with Pfizer Corporation and its advertising agency to stop making deceptive claims regarding the ability of Pfizer's Plax mouthwash to reduce plaque.[44]

The NAAG's foray into regulating national advertising raises the issue of whether the states working together can create and implement uniform national advertising stan-

IMC Perspective 23-2
Volvo Recovers from the Monster Truck Ad Controversy

For nearly three decades, Swedish automaker Volvo spent millions of dollars advertising the safety and durability of its cars to US consumers, often going to great lengths to demonstrate how well its cars were built. One classic ad showed a Volvo with six others stacked on top of it, while another showed a six-ton truck being lowered onto the roof of a Volvo. However, a few years ago Volvo's ad agency went too far in its efforts to demonstrate the strength of the car's roof and body and ended up involving the company in one of the most publicized advertising controversies in decades.

In October 1990, Volvo aired its infamous "Bear Foot" monster truck ad showing a pickup truck with huge, oversized tires driving over the top of a row of cars, crushing the roofs of all of them except the Volvo. The commercial was produced in Texas where a local resident, who had been invited to watch the filming, noticed the cars used in the ad had been tampered with. He contacted the Texas Attorney General's Office, which investigated and found the ad was deceptive. The roof of the Volvo used in the ad was reinforced with steel and plywood while the rival vehicles had their roof supports weakened.

The monster truck ad created a major controversy for both Volvo and its advertising agency, Scali, McCabe, Sloves, which had handled the automaker's advertising for 23 years. In November 1990, the agency resigned the $40 million account, noting it had the ultimate responsibility for the rigged commercial. In addition to Volvo losing credibility and the agency losing its largest account, the misleading commercial also cost the two parties money. Volvo and the agency each agreed to pay a $150,000 penalty as part of a settlement with the Federal Trade Commission. However, Volvo did not admit to any guilt in its settlement with the FTC stating that it was unaware of the changes made to the cars.

Many advertising experts speculated that it would take years for Volvo to rebound from the "Bear Foot" controversy. In addition to image problems, Volvo had to contend with the fact that many of its competitors were also promoting the safety features of their cars. The company's new agency, Messmer Vetere Berger McNamee Schmetterer, sized up the situation and decided that Volvo had to reclaim the safety issue as its own. However, the agency was faced with the challenge of reclaiming Volvo's safety heritage while restoring credibility in its advertising claims.

The agency addressed the problem with a series of emotional, safety-oriented TV spots featuring members of the "Volvo Saved My Life Club," an exclusive membership organization, formalized in 1991, of people who credit Volvo safety features for their surviving horrendous wrecks. The commercials show some of the group's members doing simple, everyday things, such as a father and son playing basketball and two sisters strolling along the beach. The voiceover then tells the viewer, "The people you've been looking at all share a common belief: that a car saved their lives." The commercial won top honors in *Advertising Age's* annual Best Advertising Awards for 1993.

The copywriter noted that the skittishness caused by the "Bear Foot" ad actually helped create a better commercial. The original line in the voiceover was "these people all have something in common: a car saved their lives." However the lawyers would not allow language implying an invulnerability claim that might result in a product-liability suit if someone failed to survive a crash in a Volvo. The copywriter feels the reworked language makes for a better ad and was a safer choice. The new campaign may also have consumers viewing Volvo as a safe choice again as well.

Sources: Bob Garfield, "Best of Show," *Advertising Age,* May 9, 1994, p. 32; Bruce Horowitz, "Volvo, Agency Fined $150,000 Each for TV Ad," *Los Angeles Times,* August 22, 1991, p. D2; Steven W. Colford and Raymond Serafin, "Scali Pays for Volvo Ad: FTC," *Advertising Age,* August 26, 1991, p. 4.

---

dards that will, in effect, supersede federal authority. However, an American Bar Association panel concluded that the Federal Trade Commission is the proper regulator of national advertising and recommended the state attorneys focus on practices that harm consumers within a single state.[45] This report also called for cooperation between the FTC and the state attorneys general.

Advertisers are concerned over the trend toward increased regulation of advertising at the state and local levels because it could mean that national advertising campaigns would have to be modified for every state or municipality. However, the FTC takes the position that businesses that advertise and sell nationwide need a national advertising policy. While the FTC recognizes the need for greater cooperation with the states, the agency feels that regulation of national advertising should be its responsibility.[46] However, the advertising industry is still keeping a watchful eye on changes in advertising rules, regulations, and policies at the state and local level.

REGULATION OF OTHER PROMOTIONAL AREAS

So far we've focused on the regulation of advertising. However, other elements of the promotional mix also come under the surveillance of federal, state, and local laws and various self-regulatory bodies. In this section, we examine some of the rules, regulations, and guidelines that affect sales promotion and direct marketing.

@ **EXHIBIT 23–12**

Marketers are required to provide consumers with full details of a contest or sweepstakes

Sales Promotion

Both consumer- and trade-oriented promotions are subject to various regulations. The Federal Trade Commission regulates many areas of sales promotion through the Marketing Practices Division of the Bureau of Consumer Protection. Many promotional practices are also policed by state attorney general offices and local regulatory agencies. Various aspects of trade promotion, such as allowances, are regulated by the Robinson-Patman Act, which gives the FTC broad powers to control discriminatory pricing practices.

Contests and sweepstakes

As was noted in Chapter 17, numerous legal considerations affect the design and administration of contests and sweepstakes, and these promotions are regulated by a number of federal and state agencies. There are two important considerations in developing contests (including games) and sweepstakes. First, marketers must be careful to ensure their contest or sweepstakes is not classified as a *lottery,* which is considered a form of gambling and violates the Federal Trade Commission Act and many state and local laws. A promotion is considered a lottery if a prize is offered, if winning a prize depends on chance and not skill, and if the participant is required to give up something of value in order to participate. The latter requirement is referred to as *consideration* and is the basis on which most contests, games, and sweepstakes avoid being considered a lottery. Generally, as long as consumers are not required to make a purchase as a condition for entering a contest or sweepstakes, consideration is not considered to be present, and the promotion is not considered a lottery.

The second important requirement in the use of contests and sweepstakes is that the marketer provide full disclosure of the promotion. FTC, as well as many state and local government regulations, require marketers using contests, games, and sweepstakes to make certain all of the details are given clearly and to follow prescribed rules to ensure the fairness of the game.[47] Disclosure requirements include the exact number of prizes to be awarded and the odds of winning, the duration and dates of termination of the promotion, and making available lists of winners of various prizes (Exhibit 23–12). The FTC also has specific rules governing the way games and contests are conducted such as requirements that game pieces be randomly distributed, that a game not be terminated before the distribution of all game pieces, and that additional pieces not be added during the course of a game.

Premiums

Another sales promotion area subject to various regulations is the use of premiums. A common problem associated with premiums is a misrepresentation of their value. Marketers that make a premium offer should list its value as the equivalent price at which the merchandise is usually sold when offered for sale on its own. Marketers must also be careful in the use of premium offers to special audiences such as children. While premium offers for children are legal, their use is controversial; many critics argue that they encourage children to request a product for the premium rather than its value. The National Advertising Division's Children's Advertising Review Unit (CARU) has voluntary guidelines concerning the use of premium offers. However, a recent study of children's advertising commissioned by CARU found the single most prevalent violation involved devoting virtually an entire commercial message to information about a premium. CARU guidelines state advertising targeted to children must emphasize the product rather than the premium offer.[48]

Trade allowances

Marketers using various types of trade allowances must be careful not to violate any stipulations of the Robinson-Patman Act, which prohibits price discrimination. Certain sections of the Robinson-Patman Act prohibit a manufacturer from granting wholesalers and retailers various types of promotional allowances and/or payments unless they are made available to all customers on proportionally equal terms.[49] Another form of trade promotion regulated by the Robinson-Patman Act is vertical cooperative advertising. The FTC monitors cooperative advertising programs to ensure that co-op funds are made available to retailers on a proportionally equal basis and that the payments are not used as a disguised form of price discrimination.

Direct Marketing

As we saw in Chapter 16, direct marketing is growing rapidly. Many consumers now purchase products directly from companies in response to television and print advertising or direct selling. The Federal Trade Commission enforces laws related to direct marketing including mail-order offers, the use of 900 telephone numbers, and direct-response television advertising. In addition to the FTC, the US Postal Service enforces laws dealing with the use of the mail to deliver advertising and promotional messages or receive payments and orders for items advertised in print or broadcast media.

A number of laws govern the use of mail-order selling. The FTC and Postal Service police direct-response advertising closely to ensure the ads are not deceptive or misleading or misrepresent the product or service being offered. Laws also forbid mailing unordered merchandise to consumers, and rules govern the use of "negative option" plans whereby a company proposes to send merchandise to consumers and expects payment unless a notice of rejection or cancellation is sent by the consumer.[50] FTC rules also encourage direct marketers to ship ordered merchandise promptly. Companies that cannot ship merchandise within the time period stated in the solicitation (or 30 days if no time is stated) must provide buyers with an option to cancel the order and receive a full refund.[51]

Another area of direct marketing facing increased regulation is telemarketing. With the passage of the Telephone Consumer Protection Act of 1991, marketers who use telephones to contact consumers must follow a complex set of rules developed by the Federal Communications Commission. Under these rules, telemarketers are required to maintain an in-house list of residential telephone subscribers who do not want to be called. Consumers who continue to receive unwanted calls can take the telemarketer to state court for damages of up to $500. The rules also ban telemarketing calls to homes before 8 AM and after 9 PM, automatic dialer calls, and recorded messages to emergency phones,

EXHIBIT 23–13   The Direct Selling Association has a Code of Ethics for companies engaged in direct selling

PREAMBLE

The Direct Selling Association, recognizing that companies engaged in direct selling assume certain responsibilities toward consumers arising out of the personal-contact method of distribution of their products and services, hereby sets forth the basic fair and ethical principles and practices to which member companies of the association will continue to adhere in the conduct of their business.

INTRODUCTION

The Direct Selling Association is the national trade association of the leading firms that manufacture and distribute goods and services sold directly to consumers. The Association's mission is "to protect, serve and promote the effectiveness of member companies and the independent businesspeople marketing their products and to assure the highest level of business ethics and service to consumers." The cornerstone of the Association's commitment to ethical business practices and consumer service is its Code of Ethics. Every member company pledges to abide by the Code's standards and procedures as a condition of admission and continuing membership in the Association. Consumers can rely on the extra protection provided by the Code when they purchase products or services from a salesperson associated with a member company of the Direct Selling Association. For a current list of Association members, contact DSA, 1776 K St., N.W., Washington, DC 20006, (202) 293-5760.

A. CODE OF CONDUCT

1. Deceptive or Unlawful Consumer Practices

No member company of the Association shall engage in any deceptive or unlawful consumer practice.

2. Products or Services

The offer of products or services for sale by member companies of the Association shall be accurate and truthful as to price, grade, quality, make, value, performance, quantity, currency of model, and availability.

3. Terms of Sale

A written order or receipt shall be delivered to the customer at the time of sale, which sets forth in language that is clear and free of ambiguity:

A. All the terms and conditions of sale, with specification of the total amount the customer will be required to pay, including all interest, service charges and fees, and other costs and expenses as required by federal and state law;

B. The name and address of the salesperson or the member firm represented.

4. Warranties and Guarantees

The terms of any warranty or guarantee offered by the seller in connection with the sale shall be furnished to the buyer in a manner that fully conforms to federal and state warranty and guarantee laws and regulations. The manufacturer, distributor and/or seller shall fully and promptly perform in accordance with the terms of all warranties and guarantees offered to consumers.

5. Pyramid Schemes

For the purpose of this Code, pyramid or endless chain schemes shall be considered consumer transactions actionable under this Code. The Code Administrator shall determine whether such pyramid or endless chain schemes constitute a violation of this Code in accordance with applicable federal, state and/or local law or regulation.

---

health care facilities, and numbers for which the call recipient may be charged. This law also bans unsolicited "junk fax" ads and requires that fax transmissions clearly indicate the sender's name and fax number.[52]

The direct-marketing industry is also scrutinized by various self-regulatory groups, such as the Direct Marketing Association and the Direct Selling Association, that have specific guidelines and standards member firms are expected to adhere to and abide by. Exhibit 23–13 shows part of the Code of Ethics of the Direct Selling Association.

SUMMARY

Regulation and control of advertising stem from internal or self-regulation as well as from external control by federal, state, and local regulatory agencies. For many years the advertising industry has promoted the use of voluntary self-regulation to regulate advertising and limit interference with, and control over, advertising by the government. Self-regulation of advertising emanates from all segments of the advertising industry, including advertisers and their agencies, business and advertising associations, and the media.

The NAD/NARB, the primary self-regulatory mechanism for national advertising, has been very effective in achieving its goal of voluntary regulation of advertising. Various media also have their own advertising guidelines. The major television networks maintain the most stringent review process and restrictions.

Traditionally, the federal government has been the most important source of external regulation, with the Federal Trade Commission serving as the major watchdog of advertising in the United States. The FTC protects both consumers and businesses from unfair and deceptive practices and anticompetitive behavior. The FTC became very active in the regulation of advertising during the 1970s when several new programs and policies were initiated, including affirmative disclosure, advertising substantiation, and corrective advertising. Since 1980 the FTC has not been allowed to implement industrywide rules that would define unfair advertising practices. However the advertising industry and Congress are nearing agreement on a definition of unfairness, and this power may be restored to the FTC.

In 1983, the FTC developed a new working definition of deceptive advertising. Recently, the FTC has become more active in policing false and deceptive advertising. Under the Lanham Act, many companies are taking the initiative by suing competitors that make false claims.

Many states, as well as the National Association of Attorneys General, are also active in exercising their jurisdiction over false and misleading advertising.

A number of laws also govern the use of other promotional mix elements, such as sales promotion and direct marketing. The Federal Trade Commission regulates many areas of sales promotion as well as direct marketing. Various consumer-oriented sales promotion tools such as contests, games, sweepstakes, and premiums are subject to regulation. Trade promotion practices, such as the use of promotional allowances and vertical cooperative advertising, are regulated by the Federal Trade Commission under the Robinson-Patman Act. The FTC also enforces laws in a variety of areas that relate to direct marketing and mail-order selling, while the FCC has rules governing telemarketing companies.

KEY TERMS

self-regulation, p. 652
Better Business Bureau, p. 655
Council of Better Business Bureaus, p. 655
National Advertising Review Board, p. 655
National Advertising Review Council, p. 656
Federal Trade Commission, p. 661
Federal Trade Commission Act, p. 661
Wheeler-Lea Amendment, p. 661
trade regulation rules, p. 662
unfairness, p. 663
puffery, p. 663
deception, p. 664
affirmative disclosure, p. 664
advertising substantiation, p. 665
consent order, p. 666
cease and desist orders, p. 666
corrective advertising, p. 666
Lanham Act, p. 671
National Association of Attorneys General, p. 672

DISCUSSION QUESTIONS

1. Analyze the arguments given by the FTC for charging marketers of diet programs with false and misleading advertising. Do you agree with the position of the FTC? How might a company such as Jenny Craig defend itself against these charges?
2. Discuss the pros and cons of self-regulation of advertising through organizations such as the NAD/NARB. What are the incentives for advertisers to cooperate with self-regulatory bodies?
3. Although it is legal, do you think advertising by professionals, such as doctors, lawyers, and dentists, is ethical? Defend your position.
4. Discuss the FTC definition of unfairness. Why do you think there has been so much opposition to having the FTC use unfairness as a legal foundation for regulating advertising?
5. What is meant by deceptive advertising? How does it differ from unfairness?
6. Campbell Soup was accused of running deceptive ads, not because of any claims it made for the product but because its advertising did not warn consumers that Campbell soups are high in sodium. Should advertisers be found guilty of

deceptive advertising for what they do not say, or should their responsibility be limited to the claims they do make?
7. What is meant by puffery? Find examples of several ads that use puffery. Should advertisers be permitted to use puffery? Why or why not?
8. What is meant by advertising substantiation? Should advertisers be required to substantiate their claims before running an ad, or is it acceptable to provide documentation in response to a challenge of their advertising claims?
9. Evaluate the arguments for and against the need for corrective advertising in the case involving Eggland's Best discussed in IMC Perspective 23–1. How could the FTC determine whether corrective advertising has accomplished its purpose?
10. Discuss some rules and regulations that affect the use of nonadvertising elements of the promotional mix, such as sales promotion and direct marketing. Do these promotional areas require as much regulatory attention as advertising? Why or why not?

WHEN ADVERTISING DOES ITS JOB, MILLIONS OF PEOPLE KEEP THEIRS.

Good advertising doesn't just inform. It sells. It helps move product and keep businesses in business. Every time an ad arouses a consumer's interest enough to result in a purchase, it keeps a company going strong. And it helps secure the jobs of the people who work there.

Advertising. That's the way it works.

INTERNATIONAL ADVERTISING ASSOCIATION

The global partnership of advertisers, agencies and media

Chapter **24**

Evaluating the Social, Ethical, and Economic Aspects of Advertising and Promotion

Chapter Objectives

● *To consider various perspectives concerning the social, ethical, and economic aspects of advertising and promotion.*

● *To evaluate the social criticisms of advertising.*

● *To examine the economic role of advertising and its effects on consumer choice, competition, and product costs and prices.*

Telling Consumers around the World about the Value of Advertising

The use of advertising and other forms of promotion is increasing around the world. The former communist countries of Eastern Europe are striving to develop Western-style free market economies, and even China is trying to develop more of a capitalist system, albeit state controlled.

Governments and companies are recognizing that advertising plays an important role in a free and open marketplace of ideas and products and makes important contributions to their economic well-being. However, not everyone is sold on the value of advertising. Consumers in the United States and many other countries view advertising as a social menace that promotes materialism, encourages them to buy products they don't really need, and insults their intelligence. Some believe advertising for many, if not all, products and services should be banned.

The advertising industry in the United States continually promotes the value of advertising. Trade associations such as the American Association of Advertising Agencies and the American Advertising Federation have run campaigns highlighting advertising's contributions to the economy as well as consumers' social well-being. As advertising becomes more prevalent globally, there is also a need to remind consumers in other countries that advertising isn't so bad. In 1992 the International Advertising Association (IAA) began a global campaign to convince the general public of the value of advertising. The IAA has more than 3,200 members in 87 countries that account for 97 percent of global ad expenditures.

The IAA campaign uses two approaches, depending on how developed the market is. In markets such as China and Russia, where the concept of advertising is still unfamiliar, the tagline is "Advertising—That's the way it works." In markets such as France or the United States, where the role of advertising is understood, the campaign theme is "Advertising. The right to choose." In addition to print messages in publications around the world, the IAA campaign includes 10 television spots that are shown all over the world. When the campaign first broke, CNN ran a 12-day blitz showing the commercials in 122 countries. One TV spot shows how limiting corporate sponsorships of sports events could hurt fans: As a voice-over says, "It would be, as they say, a whole new ball game," one of two teams playing a soccer match vanishes.

In 1993, Gallup International conducted a global study to provide the IAA with baseline information for its campaign. The study surveyed 22,000 consumers in 22 countries about their attitudes toward advertising. Individuals in former communist countries were among the most enthusiastic supporters of advertising, which may reflect their desire to embrace consumer-oriented Western capitalism. Consumers in the former East Germany were more negative toward advertising than those in either West Germany or other former communist countries.

Consumers in Japan, Uruguay, and Bulgaria had the most favorable attitudes toward advertising. The Japanese were the least inclined to believe that advertising insults consumers' intelligence and the most likely to say they would miss advertising if it were banned. Egypt was the only country where respondents were consistently anti-advertising, an attitude IAA officials attributed to the rise of religious fundamentalism there.

According to Norman Vale, the director general of the IAA, the campaign is not a magic bullet that will make everyone love advertising. However, it may reassure people in healthy and emerging economies that advertising has value and is not a social menace.

Sources: Laurel Wentz, "Major Global Study Finds Consumers Support Ads," Advertising Age International, Oct. 11, 1993, pp. 11, 21; Cyndee Miller, "The Marketing of Advertising," Marketing News, Dec. 7, 1992, pp. 1, 2.

f I were to name the deadliest subversive force within capitalism, the single greatest source of its waning morality—I would without hesitation name advertising. How else should one identify a force that debases language, drains thought, and undoes dignity?[1]

The primary focus of this text has been on the role of advertising and other promotional variables as marketing activities used to convey information to, and influence the behavior of, consumers. We have been concerned with examining the advertising and promotion function in the context of a business and marketing environment and from a perspective that assumes these activities are appropriate. However, as you can see in the above quote from economist Robert Heilbroner, not everyone shares this viewpoint. Advertising is the most visible of all business activities and is prone to scrutiny by those who are concerned over the methods advertisers use to sell their products and services.

Proponents of advertising argue that it is the lifeblood of business as it provides consumers with information about products and services and encourages them to improve their standard of living. They say advertising produces jobs and helps new firms enter the marketplace. Companies employ people who make the products and provide the services that advertising sells. Free market economic systems are based on competition, which revolves around information, and nothing delivers information better and at less cost than advertising.

Not everyone, however, is sold on the value of advertising. Critics argue that most advertising is more propaganda than information; it creates needs and faults consumers never knew they had. Ads suggest that children won't succeed without a computer, that our bodies should be leaner, our faces younger, and our houses cleaner. They point to the sultry, scantily clad bodies used in ads to sell everything from perfume to beer to power tools and argue that advertising promotes materialism, insecurity, and greed.

Because of its high visibility and pervasiveness, along with its persuasive character, advertising has been the subject of a great deal of controversy and criticism. Numerous books are critical of not only advertising's methods and techniques but also its social consequences. Various parties, including scholars, economists, politicians, sociologists, government agencies, social critics, special-interest groups, and consumers have attacked advertising for a variety of reasons—including its excessiveness, the way it influences society, the methods it uses, its exploitation of consumers, and its effect on our economic system.

Advertising is a very powerful force, and this text would not be complete without considering the criticisms regarding its social and economic effects as well as some defenses against these charges. We consider the various criticisms of advertising from an ethical and societal perspective and then appraise the economic effects of advertising.

ADVERTISING ETHICS

In the previous chapter, we examined the regulatory environment in which advertising and promotion operate. While many laws and regulations determine what advertisers can and cannot do, not every issue is covered by a rule. Advertisers must often make decisions regarding appropriate and responsible actions based on ethical considerations rather than on what is legal or within industry guidelines. **Ethics** are moral principles and values that govern the actions and decisions of an individual or group.[2]

A particular action may be within the law and still not be ethical. A good example of this is the issue of target marketing, which we discussed in Ethical Perspective 5–1. No laws restrict tobacco companies from targeting advertising and promotion for new brands to African-Americans. However, given the high level of lung cancer and smoking-related illnesses among the black population, many people would consider this an unethical business practice.

Throughout this text we have presented a number of ethical perspectives to show how various aspects of advertising and promotion often involve ethical considerations. Ethical issues must be considered in integrated marketing communications decisions. And advertising and promotion are areas where a lapse in ethical standards or judgment can result in actions that are highly visible and often very damaging to a company. The con-

Ethical Perspective 24-1
Tobacco Companies Find New Ways to Promote Cigarettes

The advertising of tobacco products has been a source of controversy for many years. Cigarette advertising was banned from the broadcast media in 1970, and recently a number of groups have been calling for a total ban on the advertising of all tobacco products as well as restrictions on the use of other types of promotional campaigns. These groups are concerned that tobacco companies are getting around the ban on tobacco advertising by shifting their emphasis away from print advertising to various other forms of promotion such as event sponsorships, stadium signage, and merchandise offers—backdoor ways to get brand names on TV or on people's clothes.

Tobacco companies sponsor a number of sporting events such as NASCAR races, skiing races, and tennis tournaments. Signage promoting tobacco products can be found in many stadiums and sports arenas around the country. For example, a large Marlboro Man sign towers above an outfield wall in New York's Shea Stadium and is a frequent TV backdrop.

Philip Morris Cos. has given away millions of caps, T-shirts, sunglasses, and other merchandise displaying Philip Morris brands names and logos. The company also has a Marlboro Adventure Team promotional catalog program; coupons attached to packs of Marlboro cigarettes can be exchanged for Adventure Team merchandise. RJR Nabisco is pursuing a similar strategy with its Camel Cash promotion program. In addition to promoting their products, the tobacco companies use these programs to collect detailed personal information that can build a database of smokers who can be reached by direct mail.

Antismoking activists and legislators claim these promotions are exploiting a loophole in the federal law that requires health warning labels on cigarette ads. They are also concerned that much of the free promotional merchandise, like fanny packs, coolers, and sleeping bags, is targeted at youth. A 1992 national survey of teenagers and tobacco use by the George H. Gallup International Institute found that 25 percent of nonsmoking teens had received at least one merchandise item

> **TRY SECONDHAND SMOKE! GET ALL THE EFFECTS OF SMOKING, WITHOUT THOSE PESKY FILTERS!**
>
> SECONDHAND SMOKE KILLS.
> CALIFORNIA DEPARTMENT OF HEALTH SERVICES

from a tobacco company. The tobacco companies adamantly deny that their promotions are designed to appeal to underage smokers and say the giveaways reward adult smokers for buying brand-name cigarettes.

While tobacco companies are changing the ways they promote their products, the forces fighting the tobacco industry are stronger than ever. Legislation designed to sharply restrict promotional campaigns by tobacco companies has been introduced in Congress, and there are proposals to regulate cigarettes as a drug and to ban smoking from workplaces and even bars and restaurants. In early 1994, the city of Baltimore voted to forbid outdoor advertising for cigarettes. Organizations such as the American Cancer Society run antismoking ads that focus on the long-term health hazards of smoking, as do various government agencies. For example, the California Department of Health Services spends nearly $13 million a year on antismoking ads (funded by a tax of 25 cents per pack).

Many advertising and tobacco experts predict that tobacco advertising will ultimately be banned by the government in all forms. Until then, the advertising and promotional battle for and against cigarettes will continue.

Sources: Laura Bird, "Baltimore Clamps Down on Tobacco Ads," *The Wall Street Journal*, March 2, 1994, p. B6; John Helyar, "Signs Sprout at Sports Arenas as a Way to Get Cheap TV Ads," *The Wall Street Journal*, Feb. 8, 1994, pp. B1, 3; Eben Shapiro, "Cigarette Makers Outfit Smokers in Icons, Eluding Warning and Enraging Activists," *The Wall Street Journal*, Sept. 21, 1993, pp. B1, 8.

troversy over Volvo's Bear Foot monster truck commercial discussed in IMC Perspective 23–2 is an example of this.

The role of advertising in society is controversial and has sometimes resulted in attempts to restrict or ban advertising and other forms of promotion to various groups or for certain products. College students are an example of one such group. A 1994 study by Columbia University's Center on Addiction and Substance Abuse concluded that America's colleges are witnessing a major increase in binge drinking, particularly among women, and as many as one in three students abuses alcohol. The study advocated a ban on alcohol-related advertising and promotions—a recommendation that may be considered by Congress.[3] Ethical Perspective 24–1 discusses how tobacco companies are creating a new controversy by shifting from print advertising to promotional campaigns, which is leading many antismoking activists to call for a total ban on tobacco promotion.

Decisions to ban the advertising of alcohol or tobacco involve very complex economic considerations as well as social issues. Companies such as Joseph E. Seagram & Sons, Inc., recognize the need to reduce alcohol abuse and drunken driving, particularly among young people. The company has produced a number of ads designed to address this

EXHIBIT 24–1

Joseph E. Seagram & Sons uses ads such as this to encourage responsible drinking and the use of designated drivers

problem. (See Exhibit 24–1.) The ads promote responsible behavior among adults of legal drinking age and are intended for that audience.

Criticism often focuses on the actions of specific advertisers. Groups such as the National Organization for Women and Women Against Pornography have been critical of advertisers such as Calvin Klein for promoting sexual permissiveness and using erotic ads (Exhibit 24–2). As we will see later in this chapter, a number of advertisers have been criticized for running ads that are insensitive to certain segments of society.

As you read this chapter, remember that the various perspectives presented reflect judgments of people with different backgrounds, values, and interests. You may see nothing wrong with the advertising of cigarettes, beer commercials on TV, or the sexually suggestive ads run by Calvin Klein and others. Other students, however, may oppose these actions on moral and ethical grounds. While we attempt to present the arguments on both sides of these controversial issues, you will have to draw your own conclusions as to who is right or wrong.

SOCIAL AND ETHICAL CRITICISMS OF ADVERTISING

Much of the controversy over advertising stems from the ways many companies use it as a selling tool and from its impact on society's tastes, values, and lifestyles. The specific techniques used by advertisers are criticized as deceptive or untruthful, offensive or in bad taste, and exploitative of certain groups, such as children. Each of these criticisms is discussed, along with advertisers' responses. We then turn our attention to criticisms concerning the influence of advertising on values and lifestyles, as well as charges that it perpetuates stereotyping and that advertisers exert control over the media.

Advertising as Untruthful or Deceptive

One of the major complaints against advertising is that many ads are misleading or untruthful and deceive consumers. Attempts by industry and government to regulate and control deceptive advertising were discussed in the previous chapter. We noted that advertisers should have a reasonable basis for making a claim about product performance and may be required to provide evidence to support their claims. However, deception can occur more subtly as a result of how consumers perceive the ad and its impact on their beliefs.[4] The difficulty of determining just what constitutes deception, along with the fact that advertisers have the right to use puffery and make subjective claims about their products, tends to complicate the issue. But a concern of many critics is the extent to which advertisers are *deliberately* untruthful or misleading.

@ **EXHIBIT 24–2**

Ads by Calvin Klein have been the target of criticism by women's groups and others

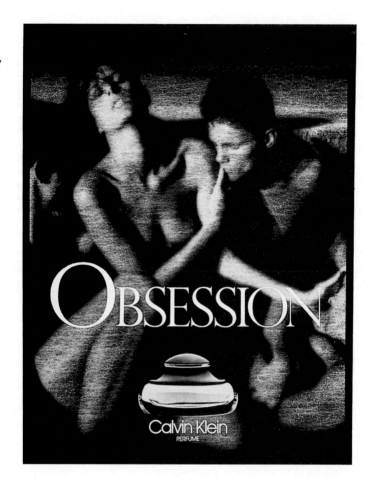

Sometimes advertisers have made overtly false or misleading claims or failed to award prizes promoted in a contest or sweepstakes. However, these cases usually involve smaller companies and represent a tiny portion of the hundreds of billions of dollars spent on advertising and promotion each year. Most advertisers do not design their messages with the intention of misleading or deceiving consumers or run sweepstakes with no intention of awarding prizes. Not only are such practices unethical, but the culprits would damage their reputation and risk prosecution by regulatory groups or government agencies. National advertisers in particular invest large sums of money to develop loyalty to, and enhance the image of, their brands. These companies are not likely to risk hard-won consumer trust and confidence by intentionally deceiving consumers.

The problem of untruthful or fraudulent advertising and promotion exists more at the local level and in specific areas such as mail order, telemarketing, and other forms of direct marketing. However, there have been many cases where large companies were accused of misleading consumers with their ads or promotions. Some companies test the limits of industry and government rules and regulations to make claims that will give their brands an advantage in highly competitive markets.

While many critics of advertising would probably agree that most advertisers are not out to deceive consumers deliberately, they are still concerned over whether consumers are receiving enough information to make an informed choice. They say advertisers usually present only information that is favorable to their position and do not always tell consumers the whole truth about a product or service.

Many believe advertising should be primarily informative in nature and should not be permitted to use puffery or embellished messages. Others argue that advertisers have the right to present the most favorable case for their products and services and should not be restricted to just objective, verifiable information.[5] They note that consumers can protect themselves from being persuaded against their will and that the various industry

@ **EXHIBIT 24-3**

Advertising principles of the American Advertising Federation (AAF)

1. **Truth** Advertising shall reveal the truth, and shall reveal significant facts, the omission of which would mislead the public.
2. **Substantiation** Advertising claims shall be substantiated by evidence in possession of the advertiser and the advertising agency prior to making such claims.
3. **Comparisons** Advertising shall refrain from making false, misleading, or unsubstantiated statements or claims about a competitor or his products or service.
4. **Bait advertising** Advertising shall not offer products or services for sale unless such offer constitutes a bona fide effort to sell the advertised products or services and is not a device to switch consumers to other goods or services, usually higher priced.
5. **Guarantees and warranties** Advertising of guarantees and warranties shall be explicit, with sufficient information to apprise consumers of their principal terms and limitations or, when space or time restrictions preclude such disclosures, the advertisement shall clearly reveal where the full text of the guarantee or warranty can be examined before purchase.
6. **Price claims** Advertising shall avoid price claims that are false or misleading, or savings claims that do not offer provable savings.
7. **Testimonials** Advertising containing testimonials shall be limited to those of competent witnesses who are reflecting a real and honest opinion or experience.
8. **Taste and decency** Advertising shall be free of statements, illustrations, or implications that are offensive to good taste or public decency.

and governmental regulations suffice to keep advertisers from misleading consumers. Exhibit 24–3 shows the advertising principles of the American Advertising Federation, which many advertisers use as a guideline in preparing and evaluating their ads.

Advertising as Offensive or in Bad Taste

Another common criticism of advertising, particularly by consumers, is that ads are offensive, tasteless, irritating, boring, obnoxious, and so on. In a study by the Ogilvy & Mather advertising agency, half of the consumers surveyed considered most ads to be in poor taste.[6]

Sources of distaste

Consumers can be offended or irritated by advertising in a number of ways. Some object when a product or service like contraceptives or personal hygiene products is advertised at all. Only in the last few years have publications begun accepting ads for condoms, as the AIDS crisis forced them to reconsider their restrictions (Exhibit 24–4). The major TV networks gave their affiliates permission to accept condom advertising in 1987, but the first condom ad did not appear on network TV until November 1991, when Fox broadcast a spot.

In 1994 the US Department of Health's Centers for Disease Control and Prevention (CDC) began a new HIV prevention campaign that includes radio and TV commercials urging sexually active young people to use latex condoms. The commercials prompted a strong protest from conservative and religious groups who argue that the government should stress abstinence in preventing the spread of AIDS among young people. NBC and ABC agreed to broadcast all the commercials, while CBS said it would air certain spots.[7]

A study of prime-time TV commercials found a strong product class effect with respect to the types of ads consumers perceived as distasteful or irritating. The most irritating commercials were for feminine hygiene products; ads for women's undergarments and hemorrhoid products were close behind.[8] Another study found that consumers are more likely to dislike ads for products they do not use and for brands they would not buy.[9] Ads for personal products have become more common on television and in print, and the public is more accepting of them.[10] However, advertisers must still be careful of how these products are presented and the language and terminology used. There are still many rules, regulations, and taboos advertisers must deal with to have their TV commercials approved by the networks.[11]

Another way advertising can offend consumers is by the type of appeal or the manner of presentation. For example, many people object to appeals that exploit consumer

@ **EXHIBIT 24–4**

Many magazines and
television stations now
accept ads for condoms

anxieties. Fear appeal ads, particularly for products such as deodorants, mouthwash, and dandruff shampoos, are criticized for attempting to create anxiety and using a fear of social rejection to sell these products. Some ads for home computers were also criticized for attempting to make parents think that if their young children couldn't use a computer, they would fail in school.

Sexual appeals

The advertising appeals that have received the most criticism for being in poor taste are those using sexual appeals and/or nudity. These techniques are often used to gain consumers' attention and may not even be appropriate to the product being advertised. Even if the sexual appeal relates to the product, people may be offended by it. Concern has been expressed over both nudity in advertising and sexually suggestive ads.

Many advertising critics are particularly concerned over the use of sexual appeals to glorify the image of cigarettes, liquor, and beer or to suggest they can enhance one's own attractiveness. For example, the Center for Science in the Public Interest, a consumer advocacy group, gave one of its 1993 Lemon Awards to an ad for Kool cigarettes featuring attractive women dressed in provocative clothing and high heels next to the headline "Totally Kool." Center officials argued that the ad implies that smoking adds to sexual attraction.[12]

Another common criticism of sexual appeals is that they can be demeaning to women (or men) by depicting them as sex objects (Exhibit 24–5). Ads for cosmetics, lingerie, beer, and liquor are among the most criticized for their portrayal of women as sex objects. Stroh's Brewing Co. ignited a major controversy a few years ago with an ad campaign for Old Milwaukee beer featuring the Swedish Bikini Team—a group of Scandinavian-looking women wearing blue bikinis who appeared out of nowhere in front of groups of beer-drinking men. A number of consumer groups were very critical of the ads, and female employees at the company even sued Stroh's because they said the ads contributed to an atmosphere that was conducive to sexual harassment in the workplace.[13]

Many advertisers are being much more careful not to portray women as sex objects. A few years ago Anheuser-Busch announced that it was committed to portraying women with more respect and in more equal roles with men (see Exhibit 24–6 on page 687).

Sexual appeals are often criticized for portraying women as sex objects

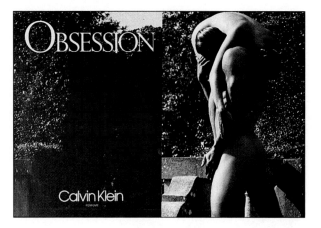

Other beer companies, such as Miller and Stroh's, are also more careful about the way they portray women in their ads.[14]

Some advertisers complain about the double standard: even the most suggestive commercials are bland compared with what is shown in many TV programs. The networks say they have to scrutinize commercials more carefully because ads encourage people to imitate behaviors, while programs are merely meant to entertain. Network executives also note the complaints of parents who are concerned about their children seeing these ads since they cannot always be there to change the channel or turn off the TV.

Because of the increasing clutter in the advertising environment, advertisers will probably continue to use sexual appeals and other techniques that offend many people but catch the attention of consumers in their target audience. How far the advertisers can go with these appeals will probably depend on the public's reactions. When consumers think they have gone too far, they are likely to pressure the advertisers to change their ads and the media to stop accepting ads that are too explicit or offensive.

Advertising and Children

One of the most controversial topics advertisers must deal with is the issue of advertising to children. TV is a vehicle through which advertisers can reach children easily. Children between the ages of 2 and 11 watch an average of 26 hours of TV a week and may see between 22,000 and 25,000 commercials a year.[15] Studies show that television is an important source of information for children about products.[16] Concern has been expressed over marketers' use of other promotional vehicles and techniques such as radio ads, point-of-purchase displays, premiums in packages, and the use of commercial characters as the basis for TV shows.

Critics argue that children, particularly young ones, are especially vulnerable to advertising because they lack the necessary experience and knowledge to understand and evaluate critically the purpose of persuasive advertising appeals. Research has shown that preschool children cannot differentiate between commercials and programs, do not perceive the selling intent of commercials, and cannot distinguish between reality and fantasy.[17] Research has also shown that children need more than a skeptical attitude toward advertising; they must understand how advertising works in order to use their cognitive defenses against it effectively.[18] Because of children's limited ability to interpret the selling intent of a message or tell the difference between a program and a commercial, critics charge that advertising to children is inherently unfair and deceptive and should be banned or severely restricted.

At the other extreme are those who argue that advertising is a part of life and children must learn to deal with it as part of the **consumer socialization process** of acquiring the skills needed to function in the marketplace.[19] They say existing restrictions are adequate for controlling children's advertising.

This issue received a great deal of attention in 1979 when the Federal Trade Commission held hearings on proposed changes in regulations regarding advertising to children. An FTC staff report recommended banning all TV advertising for any product directed

@ **EXHIBIT 24–6**

Anheuser-Busch is sensitive to the way women are portrayed in ads for the company's products

to or seen by audiences comprised largely of children under age 8 because they are too young to understand the selling intent of advertising.[20]

The FTC proposal was debated intensely. The advertising industry and a number of companies argued strongly against it, based on factors including advertisers' right of free speech under the First Amendment to communicate with those consumers who make up their primary target audience.[21] They also said parents should be involved in helping children interpret advertising and can refuse to purchase products they believe are undesirable for their children.

The FTC proposal was defeated, and changes in the political environment resulted in less emphasis on government regulation of advertising. However, parent and consumer groups such as the Center for Science in the Public Interest are still putting pressure on advertisers regarding what they see as inappropriate or misleading ads for children. One activist group, Action for Children's Television (ACT), was disbanded in 1992, but first it was instrumental in getting Congress to approve the Children's Television Act in October 1990. The act limits the amount of commercial time in children's programming to 10 1/2 minutes per hour on weekends and 12 minutes on weekdays.[22]

Children are also protected from the potential influences of commercials by network censors and industry self-regulatory groups such as the Council of Better Business Bureaus' Children's Advertising Review Unit (CARU). CARU has strict self-regulatory guidelines regarding the type of appeals, product presentation and claims, disclosures and disclaimers, the use of premiums, safety, and techniques such as special effects and animation. The five basic principles underlying the CARU guidelines for all advertising addressed to children under 12 are presented in Exhibit 24–7.

As we saw in Chapter 23, the major networks also have strict guidelines for ads targeted to children. For example, in network TV ads, only 10 seconds can be devoted to animation and special effects; the final five seconds are reserved for displaying all the toys shown in the ad and disclosing whether they are sold separately and whether accessories such as batteries are included. Networks also require three seconds of every 30-second cereal ad to portray a balanced breakfast, usually by showing a picture of toast, orange juice, and milk.[23]

Advertising to children will remain a controversial topic. A recent study found that marketers of products targeted to children believe advertising to them provides useful information on new products and does not disrupt the parent–child relationship. However, the general public did not have such a favorable opinion. Older consumers and those from households with children had particularly negative attitudes toward children's advertising.[24]

It is important to many companies to communicate directly with children. However, only by being sensitive to the naiveté of children as consumers will they be able to do so freely and avoid potential conflict with those who believe children should be protected from advertising.

EXHIBIT   24–7   Children's Advertising Review Unit principles

Five basic principles underlie these guidelines for advertising directed to children:

1. Advertisers should always take into account the level of knowledge, sophistication, and maturity of the audience to which their message is primarily directed. Younger children have a limited capability for evaluating the credibility of what they watch. Advertisers, therefore, have a special responsibility to protect children from their own susceptibilities.
2. Realizing that children are imaginative and that make-believe play constitutes an important part of the growing up process, advertisers should exercise care not to exploit that imaginative quality of children. Unreasonable expectations of product quality or performance should not be stimulated either directly or indirectly by advertising.
3. Recognizing that advertising may play an important part in educating the child, information should be communicated in a

truthful and accurate manner with full recognition by the advertiser that the child may learn practices from advertising that can affect his or her health and well-being.
4. Advertisers are urged to capitalize on the potential of advertising to influence social behavior by developing advertising that, wherever possible, addresses itself to social standards generally regarded as positive and beneficial, such as friendship, kindness, honesty, justice, generosity, and respect for others.
5. Although many influences affect a child's personal and social development, it remains the prime responsibility of the parents to provide guidance for children. Advertisers should contribute to this parent–child relationship in a constructive manner.

Social and Cultural Consequences

Concern is often expressed over the impact of advertising on society, particularly on values and lifestyles. While a number of factors influence the cultural values, lifestyles, and behavior of a society, the overwhelming amount of advertising and its prevalence in the mass media lead many critics to argue that advertising plays a major role in influencing and transmitting social values. In his book *Advertising and Social Change*, Ronald Berman says:

> The institutions of family, religion, and education have grown noticeably weaker over each of the past three generations. The world itself seems to have grown more complex. In the absence of traditional authority, advertising has become a kind of social guide. It depicts us in all the myriad situations possible to a life of free choice. It provides ideas about style, morality, behavior.[25]

While there is general agreement that advertising is an important social influence agent, opinions as to the value of its contribution are often negative. Advertising is criticized for encouraging materialism, manipulating consumers to buy things they do not really need, perpetuating stereotyping, and controlling the media.

Advertising encourages materialism

Many critics claim advertising has an adverse effect on consumer values by encouraging **materialism**, a preoccupation with material things rather than intellectual or spiritual concerns. The United States is undoubtedly the most materialistic society in the world, which many critics attribute to advertising that

- Seeks to create needs rather than merely showing how a product or service fulfills them.
- Surrounds consumers with images of the good life and suggests the acquisition of material possessions leads to contentment and happiness and adds to the joy of living.
- Suggests material possessions are symbols of status, success, and accomplishment and/or will lead to greater social acceptance, popularity, sexual appeal, and so on.

The ad shown in Exhibit 24–8 for Rolls-Royce automobiles is an example of how advertising can promote materialistic values.

The criticism of advertising on the grounds that it encourages materialistic values assumes that materialism is undesirable and is sought at the expense of other goals. Many believe materialism is an acceptable part of the **Protestant ethic**, which stresses hard work and individual effort and initiative and views the accumulation of material possessions as evidence of success. Others argue that the acquisition of material possessions has positive economic impact by encouraging consumers to keep consuming after their basic

@ **EXHIBIT 24–8**

Rolls-Royce appeals to consumers' materialism

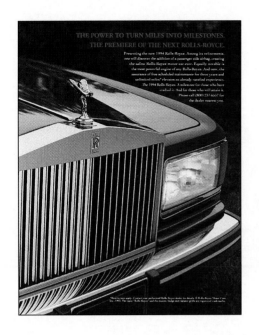

needs are met. Many Americans believe economic growth is essential and materialism is both a necessity and an inevitable part of this progress.

Economist John Kenneth Galbraith, often a vocal critic of advertising, describes the role advertising plays in industrialized economies by encouraging consumption:

> Advertising and its related arts thus help develop the kind of man the goals of the industrial system require—one that reliably spends his income and works reliably because he is always in need of more. . . . In the absence of the massive and artful persuasion that accompanies the management of demand, increasing abundance might well have reduced the interest of people in acquiring more goods. . . . Being not pressed by the need for these things, they would have spent less reliably to get more. The consequence—a lower and less reliable propensity to consume—would have been awkward for the industrial system.[26]

It has also been argued that an emphasis on material possessions does not rule out interest in intellectual, spiritual, or cultural values. Defenders of advertising say consumers can be more interested in higher-order goals when basic needs have been met. Raymond Bauer and Stephen Greyser point out that consumers may purchase material things in the pursuit of nonmaterial goals.[27] For example, a person may buy an expensive stereo system to enjoy music rather than simply to impress someone or acquire a material possession.

Even if we assume materialism is undesirable, there is still the question of whether advertising is responsible for creating and encouraging it. While many critics argue that advertising is a major contributing force to materialistic values, others say advertising merely reflects the values of society rather than shaping them.[28] They argue that consumers' values are defined by the society in which they live and are the results of extensive, long-term socialization or acculturation.

The argument that advertising is responsible for creating a materialistic and hedonistic society is addressed by Stephen Fox in his book *The Mirror Makers: A History of American Advertising and Its Creators*. Fox concludes advertising has become a prime scapegoat for our times and merely reflects society. Regarding the effect of advertising on cultural values, he notes:

> To blame advertising now for those most basic tendencies in American history is to miss the point. It is too obvious, too easy, a matter of killing the messenger instead of dealing with the bad news. The people who have created modern advertising are not hidden persuaders pushing our buttons in the service of some malevolent purpose. They are just producing an especially visible manifestation, good and bad, of the American way of life.[29]

EXHIBIT 24–9

The advertising industry argues that advertising reflects society

Exhibit 24–9 shows an ad developed by the American Association of Advertising Agencies (AAAA) that suggests advertising is a reflection of society's tastes and values, not vice versa. This ad was part of a campaign that addressed criticisms of advertising.

Advertising does contribute to our materialism by portraying products and services as symbols of status, success, and achievement and by encouraging consumption. As Richard Pollay says, "While it may be true that advertising reflects cultural values, it does so on a very selective basis, echoing and reinforcing certain attitudes, behaviors, and values far more frequently than others."[30]

The extent to which advertising is responsible for materialism and the desirability of such values are deep philosophical issues that will continue to be part of the debate over the societal value and consequences of advertising.

Advertising makes people buy things they don't need

A common criticism of advertising is that it manipulates consumers into buying things they do not need. Many critics say advertising should just provide information useful in making purchase decisions and should not persuade. They view information advertising, which reports price, performance, and other objective criteria as desirable. Persuasive advertising, however, which plays on consumers' emotions, anxieties, and psychological needs and desires such as status, self-esteem, and attractiveness, is viewed as unacceptable. Persuasive advertising is criticized for fostering discontent among consumers and encouraging them to purchase products and services to solve deeper problems. Critics say advertising exploits consumers and persuades them to buy things they don't need.

Defenders of advertising offer a number of rebuttals to these criticisms. First, they point out that a substantial amount of advertising is essentially informational in nature.[31] Also, it is difficult to separate desirable informational advertising from undesirable persuasive advertising. Shelby Hunt, in examining the *information–persuasion dichotomy*, points out that even advertising that most observers would categorize as very informative is often very persuasive.[32] He says, "If advertising critics really believe that persuasive

ⓐ EXHIBIT 24–10

The AAAA responds to the claim that advertising makes consumers buy things they do not need

advertising should not be permitted, they are actually proposing that no advertising be allowed, since the purpose of all advertising is to persuade."[33]

Defenders of advertising also take issue with the argument that it should limit itself to dealing with basic functional needs. In our society, most lower-level needs recognized in Maslow's hierarchy, such as the need for food, clothing, and shelter, are satisfied. It is natural for people to move from basic needs to higher-order ones such as self-esteem and status or self-actualization. Consumers are free to choose the degree to which they attempt to satisfy their desires, and wise advertisers associate their products and services with the satisfaction of higher-order needs.

Proponents of advertising offer two other defenses against the charge that advertising makes people buy things they do not really need. First, this criticism attributes too much power to advertising and assumes consumers have no ability to defend themselves against advertising.

Second, it ignores the fact that consumers have the freedom to make their own choices when confronted with persuasive advertising. While they readily admit the persuasive intent of their business, advertisers are quick to note it is extremely difficult to make consumers purchase a product they do not want or for which they do not see a personal benefit. For example, the green marketing movement has not gotten consumers to forgo low price for products that make environmental claims. The market research firm of Roper Starch Worldwide conducted an extensive study of 300 "green" ads that appeared in magazines between 1991 and 1994 and found that most were not effective. The study concluded that too many green ads failed to make the connection between what the company is doing for the environment and how it affects individual consumers.[34]

If advertising were as powerful as the critics claims, we would not see products with multimillion-dollar advertising budgets failing in the marketplace. The reality is that consumers do have a choice, and they are not being forced to buy. Consumers ignore ads for products and services they do not really need or that fail to interest them (see Exhibit 24–10).

EXHIBIT   24–11   Maidenform's campaign lamenting the stereotyping of women resulted in a significant increase in sales

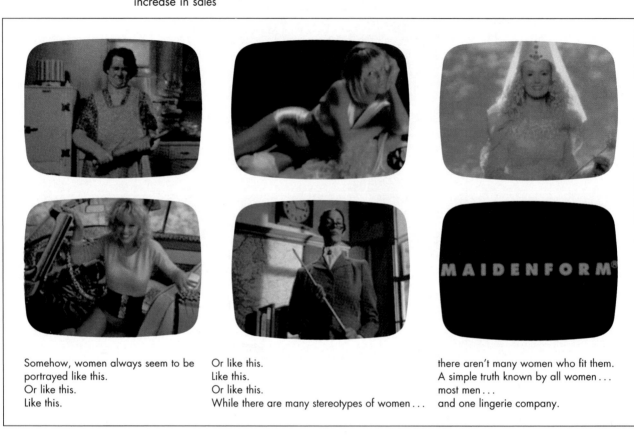

Somehow, women always seem to be portrayed like this.
Or like this.
Like this.

Or like this.
Like this.
Or like this.
While there are many stereotypes of women . . .

there aren't many women who fit them.
A simple truth known by all women . . .
most men . . .
and one lingerie company.

Advertising and stereotyping

Advertising is often accused of creating and perpetuating stereotypes through its portrayal of women, ethnic minorities, and other groups.

Women

Advertising has received much criticism for stereotyping women. Critics charge that advertising generally depicts women as homemakers or mothers and has failed to acknowledge the changing role of women in our society. Or it shows women as decorative objects or sexually provocative figures. A number of studies have examined advertising's portrayal of women. A decade ago, Alice Courtney and Thomas Whipple reviewed the findings of nearly 70 studies in this area and concluded that women are typically portrayed in traditional roles such as housewives and mothers, as dependent on men and sometimes subservient. Women are often used as sexual or decorative objects in advertising but are seldom shown in authoritative roles.[35]

While sexism and stereotyping of women still exist, advertising's portrayal of women is improving in many areas.[36] Many advertisers have begun to recognize the importance of portraying women realistically. The increase in the number of working women has resulted not only in women having more influence in family decision making but also in more single-female households, which means more independent purchasers. Many advertisers are trying to depict women in a diversity of roles that reflect their changing place in society.

Some advertisers have found that being more sensitive to women customers can have a positive influence on their purchase behavior. For example, a few years ago Maidenform began a campaign critical of negative stereotyping of women that significantly increased sales (Exhibit 24–11). Nike saw its sales to women increase 28 percent as a result of its

"Empathy" campaign, which directly targeted women and issues that are relevant to them.[37] Feminist groups such as the National Organization for Women (NOW) continually attack advertising that portrays women as sex objects, arguing that such advertising contributes to violence against women. NOW and other groups often protest to advertisers and their agencies about ads they find insulting to women and have even called for boycotts against offending advertisers.

Blacks/Hispanics

African-Americans and Hispanics have also been the target of stereotyping in advertising. For many years, advertisers virtually ignored all nonwhite ethnic groups as identifiable subcultures and viable markets. Ads were rarely targeted to these ethnic groups, and the use of blacks and Hispanics as spokespeople, communicators, models, or actors in ads was very limited.[38]

Several recent studies have examined the incidence of minorities in advertising. One study reported that 11 percent of the people in commercials were African-Americans.[39] A recent study by Robert Wilkes and Humberto Valencia found that blacks appeared in 26 percent of all ads on network TV that used live models.[40] Hispanics, however, appeared in only 6 percent of the commercials with live models. A study by Thomas Stevenson found that the number of trade journal ads depicting blacks increased from 4.9 percent in 1966 to 10.6 percent in 1976 and stayed at the same level to 1986.[41] However, this study also found that the *percentage* of blacks shown in business ads did not increase significantly over the 20 years.

In recent years, not only has the number of African-Americans in ads increased, but so has their social and role status. For example, blacks are increasingly being shown in executive positions in many ads. Federal Express said that a recent commercial featuring a black female executive beating out her white male adversaries in a conference call showdown over a high-stakes business deal was one of its most successful ads in the last 10 years.[42]

Ads are increasingly likely to be racially integrated. Recently some advertisers have begun breaking the taboo against suggesting interracial attraction. For example, a Diet Pepsi commercial placed the popular black Uh-Huh Girls in bikinis on a beach, where they were approached by two white males.[43]

While there are not many Hispanics in television advertising, the manner in which they are depicted is changing as marketers recognize they represent a very viable and expanding market. Not only are advertisers being careful to avoid ethnic stereotyping, but they are also striving to develop advertising that has specific appeals to various ethnic groups (Exhibit 24–12).

There is little question that advertising has been guilty of stereotyping women and ethnic groups in the past and, in some cases, still does so. But, as the role of women changes, advertisers must change their portrayals, to remain accurate and appeal to their target audience. Advertisers must increase the incidence of minority groups in ads while avoiding stereotypes and negative role portrayals.

Other Groups

While the focus here has been on women and ethnic minorities, some other groups feel they are victims of stereotyping by advertisers. For example, some advertisers have been criticized for portraying senior citizens as feeble, foolish, inept, or in desperate need of help.[44] Advocates for the mentally ill objected to a Nike ad campaign featuring actor Dennis Hopper, who is best known for playing eccentric and sometimes violent characters. In the commercials he plays the ultimate football fanatic—an ex-referee who is obsessed with the game—and his performance includes twitches, tics, and maniacal laughter that some suggest portray a mentally ill person.[45]

Many groups in our society are battling against stereotyping and discrimination, and companies must consider whether their ads might offend them. In the new age of political correctness, it has become increasingly difficult not to offend some segment of the public. Creative personnel in agencies are feeling restricted as their ideas are

 **EXHIBIT   24–12**

Mattel appeals to black consumers in this ad

squelched out of concern that they might offend someone or be misinterpreted.[46] However, advertisers must be sensitive to the portrayal of specific types of people in their ads.

Advertising and the media

The fact that advertising plays such an important role in financing the media has led to concern that advertisers may influence or even control the media. We consider arguments on both sides of this controversial issue.

Arguments supporting advertiser control

Some critics charge the media's dependence on advertisers' support makes them susceptible to various forms of influence, including exerting control over the editorial content of magazines and newspapers; biasing editorial opinions to favor the position of an advertiser; limiting coverage of a controversial story that might reflect negatively on a company; and influencing the program content of television.

Newspapers and magazines receive nearly 70 percent of their revenue from advertising; commercial TV and radio derive virtually all their income from advertisers. Small, financially insecure newspapers, magazines, or broadcast stations are the most susceptible to pressure from advertisers, particularly companies that account for a large amount of the medium's advertising revenue. A local newspaper may be reluctant to print an unfavorable story about a car dealer or supermarket chain on whose advertising it depends.

While larger, more financially stable media should be less susceptible to an advertiser's influence, they may still be reluctant to carry stories detrimental to companies that purchase large amounts of advertising time or space. For example, since cigarette commercials were taken off radio and TV in 1970, tobacco companies have allocated most of their budgets to the print media. The tobacco industry outspends all other national advertisers in newspapers, and cigarettes constitute the second largest category of magazine advertising (behind transportation). This has led to charges that magazines and newspapers avoid articles on the hazards of smoking to protect this important source of ad revenue.[47]

Individual TV stations as well as the major networks also can be influenced by advertisers. Programming decisions are made largely on the basis of what shows will attract the most viewers and thus be most desirable to advertisers. Critics say this often results in lower-quality television, as educational, cultural, and informative programming is usually sacrificed for shows that get high ratings and appeal to the mass markets.

@ **EXHIBIT 24–13**

This ad points out how advertising lowers the cost of newspapers for consumers

Advertisers have also been accused of pressuring the networks to change their programming. Many advertisers have begun withdrawing commercials from programs that contain too much sex and violence, often in response to threatened boycotts of their products by consumers if they advertise on these shows. For example, groups such as the American Family Association have been fighting sex and violence in TV programs by calling for boycotts.

Arguments against advertiser control

The commercial media's dependence on advertising means advertisers can exert influence on its character, content, and coverage of certain issues. However, media executives offer several reasons why advertisers do not exert undue influence over the media.

First, they point out it is in the best interest of the media not to be influenced too much by advertisers. To retain public confidence, they must report the news fairly and accurately without showing bias or attempting to avoid controversial issues. Media executives point to the vast array of topics they cover and the investigative reporting they often do as evidence of their objectivity. It is in their best interest to build a large audience for their publications or stations so they can charge more for advertising space and time.

Media executives also note that an advertiser needs the media more than they need any individual advertiser, particularly when the medium has a large audience or does a good job of reaching a specific market segment. Many publications and stations have a very broad base of advertising support and can afford to lose an advertiser that attempts to exert too much influence. This is particularly true for the larger, more established, and financially secure media. For example, a consumer products company would find it difficult to reach its target audience without network TV and could not afford to boycott a network because of disagreement over editorial policy or program content. Even the local advertiser in a small community may be dependent on the local newspaper, as it may be the most cost-effective media option available.

The media in the United States are basically supported by advertising, which means we can enjoy them for free or for a fraction of what they would cost without advertising. The alternative to an advertiser-supported media system is support by users through higher subscription costs for the print media and a fee or pay-per-view system with TV. Another alternative is government-supported media like those in many other countries, but this runs counter to most people's desire for freedom of the press. Although not perfect, the system of advertising-supported media provides us with the best option for receiving information and entertainment. The ad in Exhibit 24–13, part of the

International Advertising Association campaign discussed early in the chapter, explains how advertising lowers the cost of print media for consumers.

Summarizing Social Effects

We have examined a number of issues and have attempted to analyze the arguments for and against these concerns. Many people are concerned about the impact of advertising and promotion on society. While marketers comply with numerous rules, regulations, policies, and guidelines, they do not cover every advertising and promotional situation. Moreover, what one individual views as distasteful or unethical may be acceptable to another.

Negative opinions regarding advertising and other forms of promotion have been around almost as long as the field itself, and it is unlikely they will ever disappear. However, the industry must address the various concerns about the effects of advertising and other forms of promotion on society. Advertising is a very powerful institution, but it will remain so only as long as consumers have faith in the ads they see and hear every day. Many of the problems discussed here can be avoided if individual decision makers make ethics an important element of the integrated marketing communications planning process.

The primary focus of this discussion of the social aspects has been on the way advertising is used (or abused) in the marketing of products and services. It is important to note that advertising and other IMC tools, such as direct marketing and public relations, are also used to promote worthy causes and to deal with problems facing society such as drunk driving, drug abuse, and the AIDS crisis, among others. IMC Perspective 24–1 discusses how advertising is used in this manner.

⌾ ECONOMIC EFFECTS OF ADVERTISING

Advertising plays an important role in a free market system like ours by making consumers aware of products and services and providing them with information for decision making. Advertising's economic role goes beyond this basic function, however. It is a powerful force that can affect the functioning of our entire economic system.

Advertising can encourage consumption and foster economic growth. It not only informs customers of available goods and services but also facilitates entry into markets for a firm or a new product or brand; leads to economies of scale in production, marketing, and distribution, which in turn lead to lower prices; and accelerates the acceptance of new products and hastens the rejection of inferior products.

Critics of advertising view it as a detrimental force that not only fails to perform its basic function of information provision adequately but also adds to the cost of products and services and discourages competition and market entry, leading to industrial concentration and higher prices for consumers.

In their analysis of advertising, economists generally take a macroeconomic perspective: they consider the economic impact of advertising on an entire industry or on the economy as a whole rather than its effect on an individual company or brand. Our examination of the economic impact of advertising focuses on these broader macro-level issues. We consider its effect on consumer choice, competition, and product costs and prices.

Effects on Consumer Choice

Some critics say advertising hampers consumer choice, as large advertisers use their power to limit our options to a few well-advertised brands. Economists argue that advertising is used to achieve (1) **differentiation**, whereby the products or services of large advertisers are perceived as unique or better than competitors', and (2) brand loyalty, which enables large national advertisers to gain control of the market, usually at the expense of smaller brands.

Larger companies often end up charging a higher price and achieve a more dominant position in the market than smaller firms that cannot compete against them and their large advertising budgets. When this occurs, advertising not only restricts the choice

IMC Perspective 24-1
Using Advertising to Promote Worthy Causes

Consumers are bombarded with advertising messages designed to sell them all types of products and services. Advertising agencies make their money by creating these ads, and the media generate income by selling advertising time and space to run them. However, the advertising community also devotes considerable time, effort, services, and money to develop messages to promote worthy causes or deal with societal problems such as AIDS, drug abuse, or drunk driving. Much of this work is done through the Advertising Council, a nonprofit educational organization supported by advertisers, ad agencies, and the media that creates more than $1.2 billion of free advertising each year.

Many agencies work on these campaigns on a pro bono basis, donating the time, talent, and services of some of their creative staff. Local TV and radio stations as well as the major networks donate media time for public service announcements (PSAs), while magazines and newspapers donate space. Many pro bono campaigns address well-publicized problems. For example, the Partnership for a Drug-Free America is a nonprofit collation of professionals from the communications industry whose collective mission is to reduce demand for illicit drugs in America. To date nearly 400 commercials have been created by partnership volunteers, and more than $1 billion of media time has been donated to run the messages.

Agencies also do pro bono work for causes or groups that are not well known but are important in their own right. For example, Wieden & Kennedy, the agency best known for its outstanding creative work for Nike, does a pro bono campaign for the American Indian College Fund (AICF). The AICF was founded to raise monies to help the 27 tribal colleges in the United States that are members of the American Indian Higher Education Consortium. Most of these tribal colleges are located on Native American reservations, such as the Crow reservation in Montana, which is the home of Little Big Horn College.

The AICF campaign is somewhat different from the typical cause campaign. The ads stress the importance of a college education in helping American Indians achieve success and improve their economic opportunities. But they also focus on the preservation of Native American culture. With the theme "Help

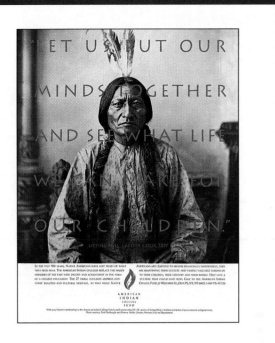

save the cultures that could save ours," the campaign promotes support for the AICF as support for the traditional values of American Indians.

In developing the campaign, Wieden & Kennedy personnel interviewed American Indians to learn stories that tell interesting aspects of the culture of various tribes. These stories were used in executing the cultural preservation theme for some of the TV commercials. Joe Pytka, who is known throughout the industry for his work on commercials for Nike, ESPN, Coca-Cola, and other advertisers, donated his time to direct the spots. Wieden & Kennedy's chairman, David Kennedy, served as the copywriter and creative director for the campaign, which includes a variety of other media, such as outdoor, radio, and magazines. Since the ads began, donations to the AICF are up significantly and *Adweek* named the series one of the best pro bono campaigns of 1993.

Sources: "The Best of Pro Bono 1993," *Adweek*, Dec. 20, 1993, p. 28; and personal communication with David Kennedy, chairman, Wieden & Kennedy.

alternatives to a few well-known, heavily advertised brands but also becomes a substitute for competition based on price or product improvements.

Heavily advertised brands dominate the market in certain product categories, such as soft drinks, beer, and cereals.[48] However, advertising generally does not create brand monopolies and reduce the opportunities for new products to be introduced to consumers. In most product categories, a number of different brands are on the store shelves and thousands of new products are introduced every year. The opportunity to advertise new brands gives companies the incentive to develop new brands and improve their existing ones. When a successful new product such as a personal computer is introduced, competitors quickly follow and use advertising to inform consumers about their brand and attempt to convince them it is superior to the original. Companies such as Virgin Atlantic Airways recognize that advertising has been an important part of their success (Exhibit 24–14).

@ **EXHIBIT 24–14**

Virgin Atlantic Airways chairman Richard Branson acknowledges the importance of advertising

"Back in 1983, the world wasn't crying out for another airline to London.

People accepted what was available. But then, they didn't know any better.

As a frequent flyer myself, I always felt being cooped up in a plane could be made more enjoyable. If you had a guest at your house you wouldn't sit him facing a blank wall and put a rubber chicken in his lap, now would you?

So I set out to create an airline people would actually enjoy flying.

"We spent over 40 million dollars to kill a rubber chicken."

Richard Branson, Chairman, Virgin Atlantic Airways.

I'd give them more space to sit in, more flight attendants to serve them, and more forms of entertainment to…entertain them.

I'd also offer 'Upper Class' passengers the only sleeper seats available in any business class to London. A Sony Video Walkman' with 25 films to choose from and free chauffeured limousine service to and from each airport. And, of course, gourmet meals and vintage wine in lieu of foul fowl.

Now, having all these niceties would have done me absolutely no good if I kept their existence to myself. So I put every available dollar into getting the word out.

The dollars were hardly momentous at first. But that didn't stop us. We applied some creativity, and over a Memorial day weekend, while everyone crowded the parks and beaches, we introduced Virgin Atlantic Airways to the people of New York. With skywriting.

Virgin is now 7 years old, serving 5 major airports and has the highest transatlantic load factor of any airline.

Print, television and radio messages have replaced skywriting. And more than 40 million advertising dollars later, no one has shed a tear for rubber chickens."

AAAA
American Association of Advertising Agencies

If you would like to learn more about the power of advertising, please write to Department D, AAAA, 666 Third Avenue, New York, New York 10017, enclosing a check for five dollars. You will receive our booklet *It Works! How Investment Spending in Advertising Pays Off.* Please allow 4 to 6 weeks for delivery. Sony Video Walkman® is a trademark of Sony. This advertisement prepared by Korey, Kay & Partners, New York.

Effects on Competition

One of the most common criticisms economists have about advertising concerns its effects on competition. They argue that power in the hands of large firms with huge advertising budgets creates a **barrier to entry**, which makes it difficult for other firms to enter the market. This results in less competition and higher prices. Economists note that smaller firms already in the market find it difficult to compete against the large advertising budgets of the industry leaders and are often driven out of business. For example, in the US beer industry, the number of national brewers has declined dramatically. In their battle for market share, industry giants Anheuser-Busch and Miller, which have over 60 percent of the market, have increased their ad budgets substantially. Anheuser-Busch alone spent nearly $600 million on advertising in 1993. However, these companies are spending much less per barrel than smaller firms, making it very difficult for the latter to compete.

Large advertisers clearly enjoy certain competitive advantages. First, there are certain **economies of scale** in advertising, particularly with respect to factors such as media costs. Firms such as Procter & Gamble and Philip Morris, which spend over $2 billion a year on advertising and promotion, are able to make large media buys at a reduced rate and allocate them to their various products.

Large advertisers usually sell more of a product or service, which means they may have lower production costs and can allocate more monies to advertising, so they can afford the costly but more efficient media like network television. Their large advertising outlays also give them more opportunity to differentiate their products and develop brand loyalty. To the extent that these factors occur, smaller competitors are at a disadvantage, and new competitors are deterred from entering the market.

While advertising may have an anticompetitive effect on a market, there is no clear evidence that advertising alone reduces competition, creates barriers to entry, and thus

@ **EXHIBIT 24–15**

The ability to advertise is important to Kia Motors as it enters the US market

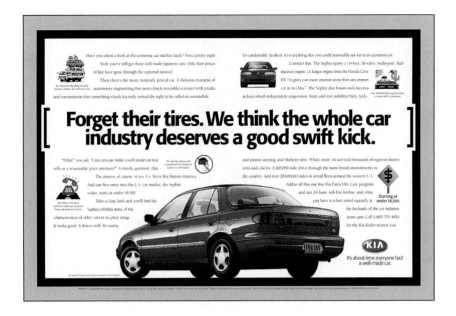

increases market concentration. Lester Telser noted that high levels of advertising are not always found in industries where firms have a large market share. He found an inverse relationship between product class advertising intensity and market share stability of the leading brands.[49] These findings run contrary to many economists' position that industries controlled by a few firms have high advertising expenditures, which result in stable brand shares for market leaders.

Defenders of advertising say it is unrealistic to attribute a firm's market dominance and barriers to entry solely to advertising. There are a number of other factors, such as price, product quality, distribution effectiveness, production efficiencies, and competitive strategies. For many years, products such as Coors beer and Hershey chocolate bars were dominant brands even though these companies spent little on advertising. Hershey did not advertise at all until 1970. For 66 years, the company relied on the quality of its products, its favorable reputation and image among consumers, and its extensive channels of distribution to market its brands. Industry leaders often tend to dominate markets because of their superior product quality and because they have the best management and competitive strategies, not simply because of the size of their advertising budgets.[50]

While market entry against large, established competitors is difficult, companies with a quality product at a reasonable price often find a way to break in. Moreover, they usually find that advertising actually facilitates their market entry by making it possible to communicate the benefits and features of their new product or brand to consumers. For example, South Korea's Kia Motors Corp. entered the US automobile market in 1994 and is using ads like the one in Exhibit 24–15 to tell consumers about the features of its low-priced compact cars.

Effects on Product Costs and Prices

A major area of debate among economists, advertisers, and consumer advocates and policy makers concerns the effects of advertising on product costs and prices. Critics argue that advertising increases the prices consumers pay for products and services. First, they say the large sums of money spent advertising a brand constitute an expense that must be covered, and the consumer ends up paying for it through higher prices. This is a common criticism from consumer advocates. Several studies show that firms with higher relative prices advertise their products more intensely than do those with lower relative prices.[51]

@ **EXHIBIT 24–16**

This ad refutes the argument that reducing advertising expenditures will lead to lower prices

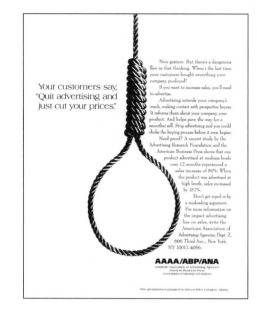

A second way advertising can result in higher prices is by increasing product differentiation and adding to the perceived value of the product in consumers' minds. Paul Farris and Mark Albion note that product differentiation occupies a central position in theories of advertising's economic effects.[52] The fundamental premise is that advertising increases the perceived differentiation of physically homogeneous products and enables advertised brands to command a premium price without an increase in quality.

Critics of advertising generally point to the differences in prices between national brands and private-label brands that are physically similar, such as aspirin or tea bags, as evidence of the added value created by advertising. They see consumers' willingness to pay a higher price for heavily advertised national brands rather than purchasing the lower-priced, nonadvertised brand as wasteful and irrational. However, consumers do not always buy for rational, functional reasons. The emotional, psychological, and social benefits derived from purchasing a national brand are important to many people. Moreover, say Albion and Farris,

> Unfortunately there seems to be no single way to measure product differentiation, let alone determine how much is excessive or attributable to the effects of advertising. . . . Both price insensitivity and brand loyalty could be created by a number of factors such as higher product quality, better packaging, favorable use experience and market position. They are probably related to each other but need not be the result of advertising.[53]

Proponents of advertising offer several other counterarguments to the claim that advertising increases prices. They acknowledge that advertising costs are at least partly paid for by consumers. But advertising may help lower the overall cost of a product more than enough to offset them. For example, advertising may help firms achieve economies of scale in production and distribution by providing information to and stimulating demand among mass markets. These economies of scale help cut the cost of producing and marketing a product, which can lead to lower prices—if the advertiser chooses to pass the cost savings on to the consumer. The ad in Exhibit 24–16, from a campaign sponsored by three major advertising trade associations, emphasizes this point.

Advertising can also lower prices by making a market more competitive, which usually leads to greater price competition. A study by Lee Benham found that prices of eyeglasses were 25 to 30 percent higher in states banning eyeglass advertising than in those that permitted eyeglass advertising.[54] Robert Steiner analyzed the toy industry and con-

@ **EXHIBIT 24–17** Two schools of thought on advertising's role in the economy

Advertising = Market Power		**Advertising = Information**
Advertising affects consumer preferences and tastes, changes product attributes, and differentiates the product from competitive offerings.	Advertising	Advertising informs consumers about product attributes but does not change the way they value those attributes.
Consumers become brand loyal and less price sensitive and perceive fewer substitutes for advertised brands.	Consumer buying behavior	Consumers become more price sensitive and buy best "value." Only the relationship between price and quality affects elasticity for a given product.
Potential entrants must overcome established brand loyalty and spend relatively more on advertising.	Barriers to entry	Advertising makes entry possible for new brands because it can communicate product attributes to consumers.
Firms are insulated from market competition and potential rivals; concentration increases, leaving firms with more discretionary power.	Industry structure and market power	Consumers can compare competitive offerings easily and competitive rivalry increases. Efficient firms remain, and as the inefficient leave, new entrants appear; the effect on concentration is ambiguous.
Firms can charge higher prices and are not as likely to compete on quality or price dimensions. Innovation may be reduced.	Market conduct	More informed consumers pressure firms to lower prices and improve quality; new entrants facilitate innovation.
High prices and excessive profits accrue to advertisers and give them even more incentive to advertise their products. Output is restricted compared with conditions of perfect competition.	Market performance	Industry prices decrease. The effect on profits due to increased competition and increased efficiency is ambiguous.

cluded advertising resulted in lower consumer prices. He argued that curtailment of TV advertising would drive up consumer prices for toys.[55] Finally, advertising is a means to market entry rather than a deterrent and helps stimulate product innovation, which makes markets more competitive and helps keep prices down.

Overall, it is difficult to reach any firm conclusions regarding the relationship between advertising and prices. After an extensive review of this area, Farris and Albion concluded, "The evidence connecting manufacturer advertising to prices is neither complete nor definitive . . . consequently, we cannot say whether advertising is a tool of market efficiency or market power without further research."[56]

However, some economists disagree. James Ferguson argues that economic theory indicates advertising cannot increase the cost per unit of quality to consumers because if it did, consumers would not continue to respond positively to advertising.[57] He believes advertising lowers the costs of information about brand qualities, leads to increases in brand quality, and lowers the average price per unit of quality.

Summarizing Economic Effects

Albion and Farris suggest that economists' perspectives can be divided into two principal schools of thought, each of which makes different assumptions regarding the influence of advertising on the economy.[58] Exhibit 24–17 summarizes the main points of the advertising equals market power and the advertising equals information perspectives.

Advertising = Market power

The belief that advertising equals market power reflects traditional economic thinking and views advertising as a way to change consumers' tastes, lower their sensitivity to price, and build brand loyalty among buyers of advertised brands. This results in higher profits and market power for large advertisers, reduces competition in the market, and leads to higher prices and fewer choices for consumers. Proponents of this viewpoint generally have negative attitudes regarding the economic impact of advertising.

IMC Perspective 24–2
Should Advertising Be Taxed?

Budget deficits are a major problem in the United States as federal and state governments search for funds to pay for health care, education, and numerous other programs. Some economists and government officials believe one way to help reduce these deficits is to eliminate the tax break for advertising and begin taxing advertising expenditures. However, the advertising industry believes such moves would have a very detrimental effect on the economy.

Advertising currently enjoys full tax deductibility as a legitimate business expense that companies can deduct from their gross income before calculating their tax liability. It has been argued that a full or partial elimination of this deduction would result in considerable tax revenue. In January 1994, the Progressive Policy Institute, a think tank with close ties to the Clinton administration, recommended that a government commission review ending or cutting 22 subsidies for US industries, one of which is advertising. The institute said the federal government would reap $17.5 billion over four years by allowing marketers to deduct only 80 percent of their ad costs and amortize the remaining 20 percent over four years.

Another way to gain revenue from advertising would be to tax it like any other purchases and charge advertisers a sales or service tax on the monies they spend to purchase media time and space. With advertising expenditures reaching nearly $140 billion per year in the United States, states could reap nearly $5 billion a year by extending a sales tax to advertising.

Those in favor of taxing advertising, such as the Center for the Study of Commercialism, argue that taxpayers are really underwriting corporate image development and helping large companies use large ad budgets to deter new competitors from entering their markets and drive up prices for brand name products. They say it does not make good economic sense to encourage companies to spend more on advertising instead of more efficient plants and equipment or research labs, which get fewer tax breaks but yield greater productivity.

As you might expect, the advertising industry is very much opposed to any form of taxation. Advocates say under our tax system, a business can deduct such ordinary and necessary expenses as rent, salaries, supplies, and so on, and advertising is an equally legitimate business expense that should not be singled out for discriminatory treatment. Moreover, they point out that limiting tax deductions for speech-related activities violates the First Amendment. A tax on advertising would result in less advertising, which would have a very negative economic impact. Advertising plays an important role in stimulating economic growth, and less advertising means fewer sales and fewer jobs.

In 1987 the state of Florida adopted a very broad sales tax on various services, including advertising. The advertising industry responded with a boycott on the placement of ads in Florida media as well as on conventions and meetings in the state. After six months of the economic revolt, the Florida legislature repealed the measure. Since then several states have considered a sales tax on services that would include advertising, but none has instituted one. There also appears to be very little congressional support for altering advertising's deductibility as a business expense. Any attempts to do so would meet stiff opposition from the advertising industry.

Sources: Steven W. Colford, "Clintonites Eye Ad Deductibility," *Advertising Age*, Jan. 31, 1994, p. 4; Michael F. Jacobson and Karen Brown, "Advertisers Should Pay Their Fair Share," and Hal Shoup, "Tax Break Pays Off as People Spend More," *The Blade Citizen*, Aug. 31, 1993, p. F1; and Steven W. Colford, "Florida Ad Tax Gets Replay," *Advertising Age*, March 2, 1992, p. 2.

Advertising = Information

The belief that advertising equals information takes a more positive view of advertising's economic effects. This model sees advertising as providing consumers with useful information, increasing their price sensitivity (which moves them toward lower-priced products), and increasing competition in the market. Advertising is viewed as a way to communicate with consumers and tell them about a product and its major features and attributes. More informed and knowledgeable consumers pressure companies to provide high-quality products at lower prices. Efficient firms remain in the market, whereas inefficient firms leave as new entrants appear. Proponents of this model believe the economic effects of advertising are favorable and think it contributes to more efficient and competitive markets.

It is unlikely the debate over the economic effects and value of advertising will be resolved soon. Many economists will continue to take a negative view of advertising and its effects on the functioning of the economy, while advertisers will continue to view it as an efficient way for companies to communicate with their customers and an essential component of our economic system. Recently the debate over the economic effects of advertising have been argued in the context of a new issue, whether companies should be allowed to deduct advertising as a business expense and whether there should be a service or sales tax placed on advertising. IMC Perspective 24–2 examines whether advertising should be taxed.

@ **EXHIBIT 24–18**

This message summarizes the viewpoint of proponents of the advertising industry regarding its economic effects

To me it means that if we believe to any degree whatsoever in the economic system under which we live, in a high standard of living and in high employment, advertising is the most efficient known way of moving goods in practically ever product class.

My proof is that millions of businessmen have chosen advertising over and over again in the operations of their business.

Some of their decisions may have been wrong, but they must have thought they were right or they wouldn't go back to be stung twice by the same kind of bee.

It's a pretty safe bet that in the next ten years many Americans will be using products and devices that no one in this room has even heard of. Judging purely by past performance, American advertising can be relied on to make them known and accepted overnight at the lowest possible prices.

Advertising, of course, makes possible our unparalleled variety of magazines, newspapers, business publications, and radio and television stations.

It must be said that without advertising we would have a far different nation, and one that would be much the poorer—not merely in material commodities, but in the life of the spirit.

Leo Burnett

This excerpt is from a speech given by Leo Burnett on the occasion of the American Association of Advertising Agencies' 50th Anniversary, April 20, 1967.

Exhibit 24–18, an excerpt from a speech given by famous adman Leo Burnett, summarizes the perspective of most advertising people on the economic effects of advertising. Perhaps the only area of agreement is that advertising has a significant effect on the functioning of our economy.

@ *SUMMARY*

Advertising is a very powerful institution and has been the target of considerable criticism regarding its social and economic impact. The criticism of advertising concerns the specific techniques and methods used as well as its effect on societal values, tastes, lifestyles, and behavior. Critics argue that advertising is deceptive and untruthful; that it is often offensive, irritating, or in poor taste; and that it exploits certain groups, such as children. Many people believe advertising should be informative only and advertisers should not use subjective claims, puffery, embellishment, or persuasive techniques.

Advertising often offends consumers by the type of appeal or manner of presentation used, with sexually suggestive ads and nudity receiving the most criticism. Advertisers say their ads are consistent with contemporary values and lifestyles and are appropriate for the target audiences they are attempting to reach. Advertising to children is an area of particular concern, as critics argue that children lack the experience, knowledge, and ability to process and evaluate persuasive advertising messages rationally. Although an FTC proposal to severely restrict advertising to children was defeated, it remains an issue.

The pervasiveness of advertising and its prevalence in the mass media have led critics to argue that it plays a major role in influencing and transmitting social values. Advertising has been charged with encouraging materialism, manipulating consumers to buy things they do not really want or need, perpetuating stereotypes through its portrayal of certain groups such as women, minorities, and the elderly, and controlling the media.

Advertising has also been scrutinized with regard to its economic effects. The basic economic role of advertising is to give consumers information that helps them make consumption decisions. Some people view advertising as a detrimental force that has a negative effect on competition, product costs, and consumer prices. Economists' perspectives regarding the effects of advertising follow two basic schools of thought: the advertising equals market power model and the advertising equals information model. Arguments consistent with each perspective were considered in analyzing the economic effects of advertising.

@ *KEY TERMS*

ethics, p. 680
consumer socialization
   process, p. 686

materialism, p. 688
Protestant ethic, p. 688

differentiation, p. 696
barrier to entry, p. 698

economies of scale,
   p. 698

DISCUSSION QUESTIONS

1. Evaluate the efforts of the International Advertising Association to convince consumers around the world of the value of advertising. Why would the advertising industry support such a campaign? Do you think it will be effective?

2. Discuss the role of ethics in advertising and promotion. How do ethical considerations differ from legal considerations?

3. Evaluate the tobacco companies' strategy of shifting promotional dollars from the print media to promotional campaigns such as premiums and event sponsorship. Do you think the use of promotional campaigns by tobacco companies should be regulated? Defend your position.

4. Should networks run commercials from the HIV prevention campaign developed by the Centers for Disease Control and Prevention that promote the use of latex condoms, or are they inappropriate for TV? Defend your position.

5. Find examples of three ads that you find irritating, offensive, or in bad taste. Discuss the basis of your objections to these ads.

6. Many advertisers complain that the TV networks scrutinize commercials more closely than the shows. Do you think that commercials should be held to higher standards than programs? Why or why not?

7. A common criticism of advertising is that it stereotypes women. Discuss how advertising might stereotype men as well. Find an example of an ad that does this.

8. With which position do you agree? "Advertising determines American consumers' tastes and values and is responsible for creating a materialistic society." "Advertising is a reflection of society and mirrors its tastes and values."

9. Discuss the role of advertising as an economic force. Include arguments for and against its effects on the economy.

10. Evaluate the arguments for and against the taxation of advertising. Do you think advertising should be taxed? Why or why not?

Glossary of Advertising and Promotion Terms

80/20 rule (5) The principle that 80 percent of sales volume for a product or service is generated by 20 percent of the customers.

5-Ws model of communication (6) A model of the communications process that contains five basic elements: who? (source), says what? (message), in what way? (channel), to whom? (receiver), and with what effect? (feedback).

A

AIDA model (6) A model that depicts the successive stages a buyer passes through in the personal selling process including: attention, interest, desire, and action.

ASI Recall Plus Test (20) A day-after recall test of television commercials (formerly known as the Burke Test).

absolute costs (12) The actual total cost of placing an ad in a particular media vehicle.

account executive (3) The individual who serves as the liaison between the advertising agency and the client. The account executive is responsible for managing all of the services the agency provides to the client and representing the agency's point of view to the client.

adjacencies (13) Commercial spots purchased from local television stations that generally appear during the time periods adjacent to network programs.

advertising (1) Any paid form of nonpersonal communication about an organization, product, service, or idea by an identified sponsor.

advertising agency (3) A firm that specializes in the creation, production, and placement of advertising messages and may provide other services that facilitate the marketing communications process.

advertising appeal (11) The basis or approach used in an advertising message to attract the attention or interest of consumers and/or influence their feelings toward the product, service, or cause.

advertising campaign (10) A comprehensive advertising plan that consists of a series of messages in a variety of media that center on a single theme or idea.

advertising creativity (10) The ability to generate fresh, unique, and appropriate ideas that can be used as solutions to communication problems.

advertising manager (3) The individual in an organization who is responsible for the planning, coordinating, budgeting, and implementing of the advertising program.

advertising specialties (15) Items used as giveaways to serve as a reminder or stimulate remembrance of a company or brand such as calendars, T-shirts, pens, key tags, and the like. Specialties are usually imprinted with a company or brand name and other identifying marks such as an address and phone number.

advertising substantiation (23) A Federal Trade Commission regulatory program that requires advertisers to have documentation to support the claims made in their advertisements.

advocacy advertising (18) Advertising that is concerned with the propagation of ideas and elucidation of social issues of public importance in a manner that supports the position and interest of the sponsor.

aerial advertising (15) A form of outdoor advertising where messages appear in the sky in the form of banners pulled by airplanes, skywriting, and on blimps.

affect referral decision rule (4) A type of decision rule where selections are made on the basis of an overall impression or affective summary evaluation of the various alternatives under consideration.

affiliates (13) Local television stations that are associated with a major network. Affiliates agree to preempt time during specified hours for programming provided by the network and carry the advertising contained in the program.

affirmative disclosure (23) A Federal Trade Commission program whereby advertisers may be required to include certain types of information in their advertisements so consumers will be aware of all the consequences, conditions, and limitations associated with the use of the product or service.

affordable method (9) A method of determining the budget for advertising and promotion where all other budget areas are covered and remaining monies are available for allocation.

agate line (14) Unit of newspaper space measurement, 1 column wide by $1/14$ inch deep. (Thus, 14 agate lines = 1 column inch.)

agency evaluation process (3) The process by which a company evaluates the performance of its advertising agency. This process includes both financial and qualitative aspects.

Note: Numbers in parentheses after term indicate chapter(s) where term is discussed.

705

alpha activity (20) A measure of the degree of brain activity that can be used to assess an individual's reactions to an advertisement.

alternative media (15) A term commonly used in advertising to describe support media.

animatic (10) A preliminary version of a commercial whereby a videotape of the frames of a storyboard is produced along with an audio soundtrack.

arbitrary allocation (9) A method for determining the budget for advertising and promotion based on arbitrary decisions of executives.

area of dominant influence (ADI) (13) A geographic survey area created and defined by Arbitron. Each county in the nation is assigned to an ADI, which is an exclusive geographic area consisting of all counties in which the home market stations receive a preponderance of viewing.

attitude toward the ad (6) A message recipient's affective feelings of favorability or unfavorability toward an advertisement.

attractiveness (7) A source characteristic that makes him or her appealing to a message recipient. Source attractiveness can be based on similarity, familiarity, or likability.

audimeter (13) An electric measurement device that is hooked to a television set to record when the set is turned on and the channel to which it is tuned.

audiotex (15) The use of telephone and voice information services to market, advertise, promote, entertain, and inform consumers.

average frequency (11) The number of times the average household reached by a media schedule is exposed to a media vehicle over a specified period.

average quarter-hour figure (AQH) (13) The average number of persons listening to a particular station for at least five minutes during a 15-minute period. Used by Arbitron in measuring the size of radio audiences.

average quarter-hour rating (13) The average quarter-hour figure estimate expressed as a percentage of the population being measured. Used by Arbitron in measuring the size of radio audiences.

average quarter-hour share (13) The percentage of the total listening audience tuned to each station as a percentage of the total listening audience in the survey area. Used by Arbitron in measuring the size of radio audiences.

B

baby boomers (2) The generation of Americans born between 1946 and 1964.

balance-of-trade deficit (22) A situation where the monetary value of a country's imports exceeds its exports.

barrier to entry (24) Conditions that make it difficult for a firm to enter the market in a particular industry, such as high advertising budgets.

barter syndication (13) The offering of television programs to local stations free or at a reduced rate but with some of the advertising time presold to national advertisers. The remaining advertising time can be sold to local advertisers.

behavioristic segmentation (5) A method of segmenting a market by dividing customers into groups based on their usage, loyalties, or buying responses to a product or service.

benchmark measures (8) Measures of a target audience's status concerning response hierarchy variables such as awareness, knowledge, image, attitudes, preferences, intentions, or behavior. These measures are taken at the beginning of an advertising or promotional campaign to determine the degree to which a target audience must be changed or moved by a promotional campaign.

benefit segmentation (5) A method of segmenting markets on the basis of the major benefits consumers seek in a product or service.

Better Business Bureau (BBB) (23) An organization established and funded by businesses that operates primarily at the local level to monitor activities of companies and promote fair advertising and selling practices.

big idea (10) A unique or creative idea for an advertisement or campaign that attracts consumers' attention, gets a reaction, and sets the advertiser's product or service apart from the competition.

billings (3) The amount of client money agencies spend on media purchases and other equivalent activities. Billings are often used as a way of measuring the size of advertising agencies.

bleed pages (14) Magazine advertisements where the printed area extends to the edge of the page, eliminating any white margin or border around the ad.

body copy (11) The main text portion of a print ad. Also often referred to as copy.

bonus packs (17) Special packaging that provides consumers with extra quantity of merchandise at no extra charge over the regular price.

bounce back coupon (17) A coupon offer made to consumers as an inducement to repurchase the brand.

brand development index (BDI) (12) An index that is calculated by taking the percentage of a brand's total sales that occur in a given market as compared to the percentage of the total population in the market.

brand extension strategy (2) The strategy of applying an existing brand name to a new product.

brand loyalty (4) Preference by a consumer for a particular brand that results in continual purchase of it.

brand manager (3) The individual in an organization responsible for planning, implementing, and controlling the marketing program for a particular brand. Brand managers are sometimes referred to as product managers.

broadcast media (14) Media that use the airwaves to transmit their signal and programming. Radio and television are examples of broadcast media.

build-up approach (9) A method of determining the budget for advertising and promotion by determining the specific tasks that have to be performed and estimating the costs of performing them. See objective and task method.

Burke test (20) A method of posttesting television commercials using a day-after recall test (now known as ASI Recall Plus Test).

business-to-business advertising (2, 21) Advertising used by one business to promote the products and/or services it sells to another business.

buying center (6, 21) A committee or group of individuals in an organization who are responsible for evaluating products and services and making purchase decisions.

C

cable television (13) A form of television where signals are carried to households by wire rather than through the airways.

carryover effect (8) A delayed or lagged effect whereby the impact of advertising on sales can occur during a subsequent time period.

category development index (CDI) (12) An index that is calculated by taking the percentage of a product category's total sales that occur in a given market area as compared to the percentage of the total population in the market.

category extension (2) The strategy of applying an existing brand name to a new product category.

category management (3) An organizational system whereby managers have responsibility for the marketing programs for a particular category or line of products.

cease and desist order (23) An action by the Federal Trade Commission that orders a company to stop engaging in a practice that is considered deceptive or misleading until a hearing is held.

central route to persuasion (6) One of two routes to persuasion recognized by the elaboration likelihood model. The central route to persuasion views a message recipient as very active and involved in the communications process and as having the ability and motivation to attend to and process a message.

centralized organizational structure (22) A method of organizing for international advertising and promotion whereby all decisions are made in a company's home office.

centralized system (3) An organizational system whereby advertising along with other marketing activities such as sales, marketing research, and planning are divided along functional lines and are run from one central marketing department.

channel (6) The method or medium by which communication travels from a source or sender to a receiver.

city zone (14) A category used for newspaper circulation figures that refers to a market area composed of the city where paper is published and contiguous areas similar in character to the city.

classical conditioning (4) A learning process whereby a conditioned stimulus that elicits a response is paired with a neutral stimulus that does not elicit any particular response. Through repeated exposure, the neutral stimulus comes to elicit the same response as the conditioned stimulus.

classified advertising (14) Advertising that runs in newspapers and magazines that generally contains text only and is arranged under subheadings according to the product, service, or offering. Employment, real estate, and automotive ads are the major forms of classified advertising.

clients (3) The organizations with the products, services, or causes to be marketed and for which advertising agencies and other marketing promotional firms provide services.

clipping service (9) A service which clips competitors' advertising from local print media allowing the company to monitor the types of advertising they are running or to estimate their advertising expenditures.

close (19) Obtaining the commitment of the prospect in a personal selling transaction.

clutter (7, 13) The nonprogram material that appears in a broadcast environment, including commercials, promotional messages for shows, public service announcements, and the like.

cognitive dissonance (4) A state of psychological tension or postpurchase doubt that a consumer may experience after making a purchase decision. This tension often leads the consumer to try to reduce it by seeking supportive information.

cognitive processing (4) The process by which an individual transforms external information into meanings or patterns of thought and how these meanings are used to form judgments or choices about behavior.

cognitive responses (6) Thoughts that occur to a message recipient while reading, viewing, and/or hearing a communication.

collateral services (3) Companies that provide companies with specialized services such as package design, advertising production, and marketing research.

combination rates (14) A special space rate or discount offered for advertising in two or more periodicals. Combination rates are often offered by publishers who own both morning and evening editions of a newspaper in the same market.

commission system (3) A method of compensating advertising agencies whereby the agency receives a specified commission (traditionally 15 percent) from the media on any advertising time or space it purchases.

communication (6) The passing of information, exchange of ideas, or process of establishing shared meaning between a sender and a receiver.

communication objectives (1, 8) Goals that an organization seeks to achieve through its promotional program in terms of communication effects such as creating awareness, knowledge, image, attitudes, preferences, or purchase intentions.

communication task (8) Under the DAGMAR approach to setting advertising goals and objectives, something that can be performed by and attributed to advertising such as awareness, comprehension, conviction, and action.

comparative advertising (7, 11) The practice of either directly or indirectly naming one or more competitors in an advertising message and usually making a comparison on one or more specific attributes or characteristics.

compensatory decision rule (4) A type of decision rule for evaluating alternatives where consumers consider each brand with respect to how it performs on relevant or salient attributes and the importance of each attribute. This decision rule allows for a negative evaluation or performance on a particular attribute to be compensated for by a positive evaluation on another attribute.

competition-oriented pricing (2)   A strategy whereby prices are set based on what a firm's competitors are charging.

competitive advantage (2)   Something unique or special that a firm does or possesses that provides an advantage over its competitors.

competitive parity method (9)   A method of setting the advertising and promotion budget based on matching the absolute level of percentage of sales expenditures of the competition.

compliance (7)   A type of influence process where a receiver accepts the position advocated by a source to obtain favorable outcomes or to avoid punishment.

computer simulation models (9)   Quantitative-based models that are used to determine the relative contribution of advertising expenditures on sales response.

concave downward function (9)   An advertising/sales response function that views the incremental effects of advertising on sales as decreasing.

concentrated marketing (5)   A type of marketing strategy whereby a firm chooses to focus its marketing efforts on one particular market segment.

concept testing (20)   A method of pretesting alternative ideas for an advertisement or campaign by having consumers provide their responses and/or reactions to the creative concept.

conditioned response (4)   In classical conditioning, a response that occurs as a result of exposure to a conditioned stimulus.

conditioned stimulus (4)   In classical conditioning, a stimulus that becomes associated with an unconditioned stimulus and capable of evoking the same response or reaction as the unconditioned stimulus.

conjunctive decision rule (4)   A type of decision rule for evaluating alternatives where consumers establish minimally acceptable levels of performance for each important product attribute and accept an alternative only if it meets the cutoff level for each attribute.

consent order (23)   A settlement between a company and the Federal Trade Commission whereby an advertiser agrees to stop the advertising or practice in question. A consent order is for settlement purposes only and does not constitute an admission of guilt.

consumer behavior (4)   The process and activities that people engage in when searching for, selecting, purchasing, using, evaluating, and disposing of products and services so as to satisfy their needs and desires.

consumer-franchise-building promotions (17)   Sales promotion activities that communicate distinctive brand attributes and contribute to the development and reinforcement of brand identity.

consumer juries (20)   A method of pretesting advertisements by using a panel of consumers who are representative of the target audience and provide ratings, rankings, and/or evaluations of advertisements.

consumer-oriented sales promotion (17)   Sales promotion techniques that are targeted to the ultimate consumer such as coupons, samples, contests, rebates, sweepstakes, and premium offers.

consumer socialization process (24)   The process by which an individual acquires the skills needed to function in the marketplace as a consumer.

contest (17)   A promotion whereby consumers compete for prizes or money on the basis of skills or ability, and winners are determined by judging the entries or ascertaining which entry comes closest to some predetermined criteria.

continuity (12)   A media scheduling strategy where a continuous pattern of advertising is used over the time span of the advertising campaign.

contribution margin (9)   The difference between the total revenue generated by a product or brand and its total variable costs.

controlled circulation basis (14)   Distribution of a publication free to individuals a publisher believes are of importance and responsible for making purchase decisions or are prescreened for qualification on some other basis.

cooperative advertising (2, 17)   Advertising programs in which a manufacturer pays a certain percentage of the expenses a retailer or distributor incurs for advertising the manufacturer's product in a local market area.

copy platform (10)   A document that specifies the basic elements of the creative strategy such as the basic problem or issue the advertising must address, the advertising and communication objectives, target audience, major selling idea or key benefits to communicate, campaign theme or appeal, and supportive information or requirements.

copywriter (3, 10)   Individuals who help conceive the ideas for ads and commercials and write the words or copy for them.

corporate advertising (18)   Advertising designed to promote overall awareness of a company or enhance its image among a target audience.

corrective advertising (23)   An action by the Federal Trade Commission whereby an advertiser can be required to run advertising messages designed to remedy the deception or misleading impression created by its previous advertising.

cost per customer purchasing (16)   A cost effectiveness measure used in direct marketing based on the cost per sale generated.

cost per order (CPO) (15)   A measure used in direct marketing to determine the number of orders generated relative to the cost of running the advertisement.

cost per ratings point (12)   A computation used by media buyers to compare the cost efficiency of broadcast programs that divides the cost of commercial time on a program by the audience rating.

cost per thousand (12)   A computation used in evaluating the relative cost of various media vehicles that represents the cost of exposing 1,000 members of a target audience to an advertising message.

cost plus system (3)   A method of compensating advertising agencies whereby the agency receives a fee based on the cost of the work it performs plus an agreed on amount for profit.

Council of Better Business Bureaus (23) The parent office of local offices of the Better Business Bureau. The council assists in the development of codes and standards for ethical and responsible business and advertising practices.

counterargument (6) A type of thought or cognitive response a receiver has that is counter or opposed to the position advocated in a message.

coverage (12) A measure of the potential audience that might receive an advertising message through a media vehicle.

creative boutique (3) An advertising agency that specializes in and provides only services related to the creative aspects of advertising.

creative execution style (11) The manner or way in which a particular advertising appeal is transformed into a message.

creative selling (19) A type of sales position where the primary emphasis is on generating new business.

creative strategy (10) A determination of what an advertising message will say or communicate to a target audience.

creative tactics (10) A determination of how an advertising message will be implemented so as to execute the creative strategy.

creativity (10) A quality possessed by persons that enables them to generate novel approaches, generally reflected in new and improved solutions to problems.

credibility (7) The extent to which a source is perceived as having knowledge, skill, or experience relevant to a communication topic and can be trusted to give an unbiased opinion or present objective information on the issue.

cross-media advertising (14) An arrangement where opportunities to advertise in several different types of media are offered by a single company or a partnership of various media providers.

cross/multimagazine deals (14) An arrangement where two or more publishers offer their magazines to an advertiser as one media package.

cross-ruff coupon (17) A coupon offer delivered on one product that is redeemable for the purchase of another product. The other product is usually one made by the same company but may involve a tie-in with another manufacturer.

cross sell (19) A term used in personal selling that refers to the sale of additional products and/or services to the same customer.

CUBE Model (21) Acronym for Comprehensive Understanding of Business Environments, a model in which values and lifestyles of corporate buying groups are detailed.

culture (4, 22) The complexity of learned meanings, values, norms, and customs shared by members of a society.

cume (13) A term used for cumulative audience, which is the estimated total number of different people who listened to a radio station for a minimum of five minutes during a particular daypart.

D

DAGMAR (8) An acronym that stands for defining advertising goals for measured advertising results. An approach to setting advertising goals and objectives developed by Russell Colley.

daily inch rate (12) A cost figure used in periodicals based on an advertisement placed one inch deep and one column wide (whatever the column inch).

database (16) A listing of current and/or potential customers for a company's product or service that can be used for direct-marketing purposes.

day-after recall scores (20) A measure used in on-air testing of television commercials by various marketing research companies. The day-after recall score represents the percentage of viewers surveyed who can remember seeing a particular commercial.

dayparts (12) The time segments into which a day is divided by radio and television networks and stations for selling advertising time.

decentralized organizational structure (22) A method of organizing for international advertising and promotion where managers in each market or country have decision-making authority.

decentralized system (3) An organizational system whereby planning and decision-making responsibility for marketing, advertising, and promotion lies with a product/brand manager or management team rather than a centralized department.

deception (23) According to the Federal Trade Commission, a misrepresentation, omission, or practice that is likely to mislead the consumer acting reasonably in the circumstances to the consumer's detriment.

decoding (6) The process by which a message recipient transforms and interprets a message.

demographics (2) Distribution of a population on selected characteristics such as age, sex, income, education, occupation, and geographic dispersion.

demographic segmentation (5) A method of segmenting a market based on the demographic characteristics of consumers.

departmental system (3) The organization of an advertising agency into departments based on functions such as account services, creative, media, marketing services, and administration.

derived demand (21) A situation where demand for a particular product or service results from the need for other goods and/or services. For example, demand for aluminum cans is derived from consumption of soft drinks or beer.

designated market area (DMA) (13) The geographic areas used by the Nielsen Station Index in measuring audience size. DMAs are nonoverlapping areas consisting of groups of counties from which stations attract their viewers.

differentiated marketing (5) A type of marketing strategy whereby a firm offers products or services to a number of market segments and develops separate marketing strategies for each.

differentiation (24) A situation where a particular company or brand is perceived as unique or better than its competitors.

direct-action advertising (2) Advertising designed to produce an immediate effect such as the generation of store traffic or sales.

direct broadcast by satellite (DBS) (22)   A television signal delivery system whereby programming is beamed from satellites to special receiving dishes mounted in the home or yard.

direct channels (2)   A marketing channel where a producer and ultimate consumer interact directly with one another.

direct headline (11)   A headline that is very straightforward and informative in terms of the message it is presenting and the target audience it is directed toward. Direct headlines often include a specific benefit, promise, or reason for a consumer to be interested in a product or service.

direct marketing (1, 16)   A system of marketing by which an organization communicates directly with customers to generate a response and/or transaction.

direct-marketing media (16)   Media that are used for direct-marketing purposes including direct mail, telemarketing, print, and broadcast.

direct-response advertising (2)   A method of direct marketing whereby a product or service is promoted through an advertisement that offers the customer the opportunity to purchase directly from the manufacturer.

direct response agencies (3)   Companies that provide a variety of direct marketing services to their clients including database management, direct mail, research, media service, and creative and production capabilities.

direct selling (1, 16)   The direct personal presentation, demonstration, and sale of products and services to consumers usually in their homes or at their jobs.

directional medium (15)   Advertising media that are not used to create awareness or demand for products or services but rather to inform customers as to where purchases can be made once they have decided to buy. The Yellow Pages are an example of a directional medium.

display advertising (14)   Advertising in newspapers and magazines that uses illustrations, photos, headlines, and other visual elements in addition to copy text.

dissonance/attribution model (6)   A type of response hierarchy where consumers first behave, then develop attitudes or feelings as a result of that behavior, and then learn or process information that supports the attitude and behavior.

diverting (17)   A practice whereby a retailer or wholesaler takes advantage of a promotional deal and then sells some of the product purchased at the low price to a store outside of their area or to a middleman who will resell it to other stores.

duplicated reach (12)   Audience members exposed to a message as a result of messages having appeared in two or more different media vehicles.

dyadic communication (19)   A process of direct communication between two persons or groups such as a salesperson and a customer.

E

economic infrastructure (22)   A country's communications, transportation, financial, and distribution networks.

economies of scale (9, 24)   A decline in costs with accumulated sales or production. In advertising, economies of scale often occur in media purchases as the relative costs of advertising time and/or space may decline as the size of the media budget increases.

effective reach (12)   A measure of the percentage of a media vehicle's audience reached at each effect frequency increment.

Elaboration likelihood model (ELM) (6)   A model that identifies two processes by which communications can lead to persuasion—central and peripheral routes.

electrodermal response (20)   A measure of the resistance the skin offers to a small amount of current passed between two electrodes. Used as a measure of consumers' reaction level to an advertisement.

electroencephalographic (EEG) measures (20)   Measures of the electrical impulses in the brain that are sometimes used as a measure of reactions to advertising.

electronic teleshopping (16)   On-line shopping and information retrieval service that is accessed through a personal computer.

emotional appeals (7, 11)   Advertising messages that appeal to consumers' feelings and emotions.

encoding (6)   The process of putting thoughts, ideas, or information into a symbolic form.

ethics (24)   Moral principles and values that govern the actions and decisions of an individual or group.

evaluative criteria (4)   The dimensions or attributes of a product or service that are used to compare different alternatives.

event sponsorship (17)   A type of promotion whereby a company develops sponsorship relations with a particular event such as a concert, sporting event, or other activity.

evoked set (4)   The various brands identified by a consumer as purchase options and that are actively considered during the alternative evaluation process.

exchange (1)   Trade of something of value between two parties such as a product or service for money. The core phenomenon or domain for study in marketing.

exclusive (18)   A public relations tactic whereby one particular medium is offered exclusive rights to a story.

expertise (7)   An aspect of source credibility where a communicator is perceived as being knowledgeable in a given area or for a particular topic.

external analysis (1)   The phase of the promotional planning process that focuses on factors such as the characteristics of an organization's customers, market segments, positioning strategies, competitors, and marketing environment.

external audiences (18)   In public relations, a term used in reference to individuals who are outside of or not closely connected to the organization such as the general public.

external audits (18)   Evaluations performed by outside agencies to determine the effectiveness of an organization's public relations program.

external search (4)   The search process whereby consumers seek and acquire information from external sources such as advertising, other people, or public sources.

eye tracking (20)   A method for following the movement of a person's eyes as he or she views an ad or commercial. Eye tracking is used for determining which portions or sections of an ad attract a viewer's attention and/or interest.

F

failure fee (17) A trade promotion arrangement whereby a marketer agrees to pay a penalty fee if a product stocked by a retailer does not meet agreed-upon sales levels.

Fairness Doctrine (23) A Federal Communications Commission program that required broadcasters to provide time for opposing viewpoints on important issues.

fear appeals (7) An advertising message that creates anxiety in a receiver by showing negative consequences that can result from engaging in (or not engaging in) a particular behavior.

Federal Trade Commission (FTC) (23) The federal agency that has the primary responsibility for protecting consumers and business from anticompetitive behavior and unfair and deceptive practices. The FTC regulates advertising and promotion at the federal level.

Federal Trade Commission Act (23) Federal legislation passed in 1914 that created the Federal Trade Commission and gave it the responsibility to monitor deceptive or misleading advertising and unfair business practices.

fee-commission combination (3) A type of compensation system whereby an advertising agency establishes a fixed monthly fee for its services to a client and media commissions received by the agency are credited against the fee.

feedback (6) Part of message recipient's response that is communicated back to the sender. Feedback can take a variety of forms and provides a sender with a way of monitoring how an intended message is decoded and received.

field of experience (6) The experiences, perceptions, attitudes, and values that senders and receivers of a message bring to a communication situation.

field tests (20) Tests of consumer reactions to an advertisement that are taken under natural viewing situations rather than in a laboratory.

financial audit (3) An aspect of the advertising agency evaluation process that focuses on how the agency conducts financial affairs related to serving a client.

first-run syndication (13) Programs produced specifically for the syndication market.

fixed-fee arrangement (3) A method of agency compensation whereby the agency and client agree on the work to be done and the amount of money the agency will be paid for its services.

flat rates (14) A standard newspaper advertising rate where no discounts are offered for large quantity or repeated space buys.

Flesch formula (20) A test used to assess the difficulty level of writing based on the number of syllables and sentences per 100 words.

flighting (12) A media scheduling pattern in which periods of advertising are alternated with periods of no advertising.

focus groups (10) A qualitative marketing research method whereby a group of 10–12 consumers from the target market are led through a discussion regarding a particular topic such as a product, service, or advertising campaign.

forward buying (17) A practice whereby retailers and wholesalers stock up on a product being offered by a manufacturer at a lower deal or off-invoice price and resell it to consumers once the marketer's promotional period has ended.

frequency (12) The number of times a target audience is exposed to a media vehicle(s) in a specified period.

full-service agency (3) An advertising agency that offers clients a full range of marketing and communications services including the planning, creating, producing, and placing of advertising messages and other forms of promotion.

functional consequences (4) Outcomes of product or service usage that are tangible and can be directly experienced by a consumer.

G

game (17) A promotion that is a form of sweepstakes because it has a chance element or odds of winning associated with it. Games usually involve game card devices that can be rubbed or opened to unveil a winning number or prize description.

gatefolds (14) An oversize magazine page or cover that is extended and folded over to fit into the publication. Gatefolds are used to extend the size of a magazine advertisement and are always sold at a premium.

general preplanning input (10) Information gathering and/or market research studies on trends, developments, and happenings in the marketplace that can be used to assist in the initial stages of the creative process of advertising.

geographical weighting (12) A media scheduling strategy where certain geographic areas or regions are allocated higher levels of advertising because they have greater sales potential.

geographic segmentation (5) A method of segmenting a market on the basis of different geographic units or areas.

global advertising (22) The use of the same basic advertising message in all international markets.

global marketing (22) A strategy of using a common marketing plan and program for all countries in which a company operates, thus selling the product or services the same way everywhere in the world.

green marketing (2, 24) The marketing and promotion of products on the basis of environmental sensitivity.

gross ratings points (GRPs) (12) A measure that represents the total delivery or weight of a media schedule during a specified time period. GRPs are calculated by multiplying the reach of the media schedule by the average frequency.

group system (3) The organization of an advertising agency by dividing it into groups consisting of specialists from various departments such as creative, media, marketing services, and other areas. These groups work together to service particular accounts.

H

halo effect (20) The tendency for evaluations of one attribute or aspect of a stimulus to distort reactions to its other attributes or properties.

headline (11) Words in the leading position of the advertisement; the words that will be read first or are positioned to draw the most attention.

hemisphere lateralization (20)   The notion that the human brain has two relatively distinct halves or hemispheres with each being responsible for a specific type of function. The right side is responsible for visual processing while the left side conducts verbal processing.

heuristics (4)   Simplified or basic decision rules that can be used by a consumer to make a purchase choice, such as buy the cheapest brand.

hierarchy of effects model (6)   A model of the process by which advertising works that assumes a consumer must pass through a sequence of steps from initial awareness to eventual action. The stages include awareness, interest, evaluation, trial, and adoption.

hierarchy of needs (4)   Abraham Maslow's theory that human needs are arranged in an order or hierarchy based on their importance. The need hierarchy includes physiological, safety, social/love and belonging, esteem, and self-actualization needs.

horizontal cooperative advertising (17)   A cooperative advertising arrangement where advertising is sponsored in common by a group of retailers or other organizations providing products or services to a market.

households using television (HUT) (13)   The percentage of homes in a given area that are watching television during a specific time period.

I

identification (7)   The process by which an attractive source influences a message recipient. Identification occurs when the receiver is motivated to seek some type of relationship with the source and adopt a similar position in terms of beliefs, attitudes, preferences, or behavior.

image advertising (10)   Advertising that creates an identity for a product or service by emphasizing psychological meaning or symbolic association with certain values, lifestyles, and the like.

image transfer (13)   A radio advertising technique whereby the images of a television commercial are implanted into a radio spot.

incentive-based system (3)   A form of compensation whereby an advertising agency's compensation level depends on how well it meets predetermined performance goals such as sales or market share.

index numbers (12)   A ratio used to describe the potential of a market. The index number is derived by dividing the percentage of users in a market segment by the percentage of population in the same segment and multiplying by 100.

indirect channels (2)   A marketing channel where intermediaries such as wholesalers and retailers are utilized to make a product available to the customer.

indirect headlines (11)   Headlines that are not straightforward with respect to identifying a product or service or providing information regarding the point of an advertising message.

industrial advertising (2)   Advertising targeted at individuals who buy or influence the purchase of industrial goods or other services.

inflight advertising (15)   A variety of advertising media targeting air travelers while they are in flight.

infomercials (13, 16)   Television commercials that are very long, ranging from several minutes to an hour. Infomercials are designed to provide consumers with detailed information about a product or service.

information processing model (6)   A model of advertising effects developed by William McGuire that views the receiver of a message as an information processor and problem solver. The model views the receiver as passing through a response hierarchy that includes a series of stages including message presentation, attention, comprehension, acceptance or yielding, retention, and behavior.

informational/rational appeals (11)   Advertising appeals that focus on the practical, functional, or utilitarian need for a product or service and emphasize features, benefits, or reasons for owning or using the brand.

ingredient sponsored cooperative advertising (17)   Advertising supported by raw material manufacturers with the objective being to help establish end products that include materials and/or ingredients supplied by the company.

inherent drama (10)   An approach to advertising that focuses on the benefits or characteristics that lead a consumer to purchase a product or service and uses dramatic elements to emphasize them.

in-house agency (3)   An advertising agency set up, owned, and operated by an advertiser that is responsible for planning and executing the company's advertising program.

ink-jet imaging (14)   A printing process where a message is reproduced by projecting ink onto paper rather than mechanical plates. Ink-jet imaging is being offered by many magazines to allow advertisers to personalize their messages.

innovation-adoption model (6)   A model that represents the stages a consumer passes through in the adoption process for an innovation such as a new product. The series of steps includes: awareness, interest, evaluation, trial, and adoption.

inquiry tests (20)   Tests designed to measure advertising effectiveness on the basis of inquiries or responses generated from the ad such as requests for information, number of phone calls, or number of coupons redeemed.

inside cards (15)   A form of transit advertising where messages appear on cards or boards inside of vehicles such as buses, subways, or trolleys.

instant coupon (17)   Coupons attached to a package that can be removed and redeemed at the time of purchase.

in-store media (15)   Advertising and promotional media that are used inside of a retail store such as point-of-purchase displays, ads on shopping carts, coupon dispensers, and display boards.

integrated information response model (6)   A model of the response process or sequence advertising message recipients go through which integrates concepts from the traditional and low-involvement response hierarchy perspectives.

integrated marketing communications (1)   A concept of marketing communications planning that recognizes the added value of a comprehensive plan that evaluates the strategic roles of a variety of communication disciplines—for example, general advertising, direct response, sales promotion, and public relations—and combines these disciplines to provide clarity, consistency, and maximum communications impact.

integrated marketing communication objectives (8) Statements of what various aspects of the integrated marketing communications program will accomplish with respect to factors such as communication tasks, sales, market share, and the like.

integration processes (4) The way information such as product knowledge, meanings, and beliefs is combined to evaluate two or more alternatives.

interactive media (12) A variety of media that allows the consumer to interact with the source of the message, actively receiving information and altering images, responding to questions, and so on.

interconnects (13) Groups of cable systems joined together for advertising purposes.

internal analysis (1) The phase of the promotional planning process that focuses on the product/service offering and the firm itself including the capabilities of the firm and its ability to develop and implement a successful integrated marketing communications program.

internal audiences (18) In public relations, a term used to refer to individuals or groups inside of the organization or with a close connection to it.

internal audits (18) Evaluations by individuals within the organization to determine the effectiveness of a public relations program.

internalization (7) The process by which a credible source influences a message recipient. Internalization occurs when the receiver is motivated to have an objectively correct position on an issue and the receiver will adopt the opinion or attitude of the credible communicator if he or she believes the information from this source represents an accurate position on the issue.

internal search (4) The process by which a consumer acquires information by accessing past experiences or knowledge stored in memory.

international media (22) Advertising media that have multicountry coverage and can be used to reach audiences in various countries.

J

jingles (11) Songs about a product or service that usually carry the advertising theme and a simple message.

L

laboratory tests (20) Tests of consumer reactions to advertising under controlled conditions.

Lanham Act (23) A federal law that permits a company to register a trademark for its exclusive use. The Lanham Act was recently amended to encompass false advertising and prohibits any false description or representation including words or other symbols tending falsely to describe or represent the same.

layout (11) The physical arrangement of the various parts of an advertisement including the headline, subheads, illustrations, body copy, and any identifying marks.

lexicographic decision rule (4) A type of decision rule where choice criteria are ranked in order of importance and alternatives are evaluated on each attribute or criterion beginning with the most important one.

line extension (2) The strategy of applying an existing brand name to another product in the same category.

local advertising (13) Advertising done by companies within the limited geographic area where they do business.

localized advertising strategy (22) Developing an advertising campaign specifically for a particular country or market rather than using a global approach.

low involvement hierarchy (6) A response hierarchy whereby a message recipient is viewed as passing from cognition to behavior to attitude change.

M

macroeconomic conditions (2) Factors that influence the state of the overall economy such as changes in gross national product, interest rates, inflation, recession, and employment levels.

macro environment (2) Uncontrollable factors that constitute the external environment of marketing including demographic, economic, technological, natural, sociocultural, and regulatory forces.

magazine networks (14) A group of magazines owned by one publisher or assembled by an independent network that offers advertisers the opportunity to buy space in a variety of publications through a package deal.

mailing list (16) A type of database containing names and addresses of present and or potential customers who can be reached through a direct-mail campaign.

major selling idea (10) The basis for the central theme or message idea in an advertising campaign.

marginal analysis (9) A principle of resource allocation that balances incremental revenues against incremental costs.

market opportunities (2) Areas where a company believes there are favorable demand trends, needs, and/or wants that are not being satisfied, and where it can compete effectively.

market segmentation (5) The process of dividing a market into distinct groups that have common needs and will respond similarly to a marketing action.

market segments (2, 5) Identifiable groups of customers sharing similar needs, wants, or other characteristics that make them likely to respond in a similar fashion to a marketing program.

marketing (1, 2) The process of planning and executing the conception, pricing, promotion, and distribution of ideas, goods, and services to create exchanges that satisfy individual and organizational objectives.

marketing channels (2) The set of interdependent organizations involved in the process of making a product or service available to customers.

marketing mix (1, 2) The controllable elements of a marketing program including product, price, promotion, and place.

marketing objectives (1, 8)   Goals to be accomplished by an organization's overall marketing program such as sales, market share, or profitability.

marketing plan (1)   A written document that describes the overall marketing strategy and programs developed for an organization, a particular product line, or a brand.

marketing public relations function (MPR) (18)   Public relations activities designed to support marketing objectives and programs.

mass media (6)   Nonpersonal channels of communication that allow a message to be sent to many individuals at one time.

materialism (24)   A preoccupation with material things rather than intellectual or spiritual concerns.

media buying services (3)   Independent companies that specialize in the buying of media, particularly radio and television time.

media objectives (12)   The specific goals an advertiser has for the media portion of the advertising program.

media organizations (3)   One of the four major participants in the integrated marketing communications process whose function is to provide information or entertainment to subscribers, viewers, or readers while offering marketers an environment for reaching audiences with print and broadcast messages.

media plan (12)   A document consisting of objectives, strategies, and tactics for reaching a target audience through various media vehicles.

media planning (12)   The series of decisions involved in the delivery of an advertising message to prospective purchasers and/or users of a product or service.

media strategies (12)   Plans of action for achieving stated media objectives such as which media will be used for reaching a target audience, how the media budget will be allocated, and how advertisements will be scheduled.

media vehicle (12)   The specific program, publication, or promotional piece used to carry an advertising message.

medium (12)   The general category of communication vehicles that are available for communicating with a target audience such as broadcast, print, direct mail, and outdoor.

message (6)   A communication containing information or meaning that a source wants to convey to a receiver.

microeconomic trends (2)   Patterns or developments in economic factors such as consumer income, savings, debt, and expenditure patterns.

missionary sales (19)   A type of sales position where the emphasis is on performing supportive activities and services rather than generating or taking orders.

mnemonics (4)   Basic cues such as symbols, rhymes, and associations that facilitate the learning and memory process.

mobile billboards (15)   An out-of-home medium in which advertisements are able to be transported to different locations (signs painted on automobiles, trailers pulling billboards, and the like).

motivation research (4)   Qualitative research designed to probe the consumer's subconscious and discover deeply rooted motives for purchasing a product.

motive (4)   Something that compels or drives a consumer to take a particular action.

multiattribute attitude model (4)   A model of attitudes that views an individual's evaluation of an object as being a function of the beliefs that he or she has toward the object on various attributes and the importance of these attributes.

multimagazine deals (14)   Arrangements whereby two or more publishers offer advertisers the opportunity to buy space in their magazines with one single media buy.

multiple buying influences (21)   The idea that a number of different individuals may influence the purchase process for a product or service within an organization.

multiplexing (13)   An arrangement where multiple channels are transmitted by one cable network.

N

narrowcasting (13)   The reaching of a very specialized market through programming aimed at particular target audiences. Cable television networks offer excellent opportunities for narrowcasting.

national advertisers (2)   Companies that advertise their products or services on a nationwide basis or in most regions of the country.

national advertising (3)   Advertising done by a company on a nationwide basis or in most regions of the country and targeted to the ultimate consumer market.

National Advertising Review Board (NARB) (23)   A part of the National Advertising Division of the Council of Better Business Bureaus. The NARB is the advertising industry's primary self-regulatory body.

National Advertising Review Council (NARC) (23)   An organization founded by the Council of Better Business Bureaus and various advertising industry groups to promote high standards of truth, accuracy, morality, and social responsibility in national advertising.

National Association of Attorneys General (23)   An organization consisting of state attorneys general that is involved in the regulation of advertising and other business practices.

national spot (13)   All nonnetwork advertising done by a national advertiser in local markets.

negotiated commission (3)   A method of compensating advertising agencies whereby the client and agency negotiate the commission structure rather than relying on the traditional 15 percent media commission.

noise (6)   Extraneous factors that create unplanned distortion or interference in the communications process.

noncompensatory integration strategies (4)   Types of decision rules used to evaluate alternatives that do not allow negative evaluation or performance on a particular attribute to be compensated for by positive evaluation or performance on some other attribute.

nonfranchise-building promotions (17)   Sales promotion activities that are designed to accelerate the purchase decision process and generate an immediate increase in sales but do little or nothing to communicate information about a brand and contribute to its identity and image.

nonmeasured media (15)   A term commonly used in the advertising industry to describe support media.

nonpersonal channels **(6)** Channels of communication that carry a message without involving interpersonal contact between sender and receiver. Nonpersonal channels are often referred to as mass media.

nonprice competition **(2)** A strategy of using factors other than price, such as advertising or product differentiation, as a basis for competition.

nontraditional media **(15)** A term commonly used in the advertising industry to describe support media.

O

objective and task method **(9)** A build-up approach to budget setting involving a three-step process: (1) determining objectives, (2) determining the strategies and tasks required to attain these objectives, and (3) estimating the costs associated with these strategies and tasks.

off-network syndication **(13)** Reruns of network shows bought by individual stations.

on-air tests **(20)** Testing the effectiveness of television commercials by inserting test ads into actual TV programs in certain test markets.

one-sided message **(7)** Communications in which only positive attributes or benefits of a product or service are presented.

one-step approach **(16)** A direct-marketing strategy in which the medium is used directly to obtain an order (for example, television direct-response ads).

open rate structure **(14)** A rate charged by newspapers in which discounts are available based on frequency or bulk purchases of space.

operant conditioning (instrumental conditioning) **(4)** A learning theory that views the probability of a behavior as being dependent on the outcomes or consequences associated with it.

order taking **(19)** A personal selling responsibility in which the salesperson's primary responsibility is taking the order.

out-of-home advertising **(15)** The variety of advertising forms including outdoor, transit, skywriting, and other media viewed outside the home.

outside posters **(15)** Outdoor transit posters appearing on buses, taxis, trains, subways, and trolley cars.

P

PACT (Positioning Advertising Copy Testing) **(20)** A set of principles endorsed by 21 of the largest US ad agencies aimed at improving the research used in preparing and testing ads, providing a better creative product for clients, and controlling the cost of TV commercials.

participations **(13)** The situation when several advertisers buy commercial time or spots on network television.

pass along rate **(12)** An estimate of the number of readers of a magazine in addition to the original subscriber or purchaser.

pass-along readership **(14)** The audience that results when the primary subscriber or purchaser of a magazine gives the publication to another person to read, or when the magazine is read in places such as waiting rooms in doctors' offices, etc.

pattern advertising **(22)** Advertisements that follow a basic global approach although themes, copy, and sometimes even visual elements may be adjusted.

payout plan **(9)** A budgeting plan that determines the investment value of the advertising and promotion appropriation.

people meter **(13)** An electronic device that automatically records a household's television viewing, including channels watched, number of minutes of viewing, and members of the household who are watching.

percentage charges **(3)** The markups charged by advertising agencies for services provided to clients.

percentage of projected future sales method **(9)** A variation of the percentage of sales method of budget allocation in which projected future sales are used as the base.

percentage of sales method **(9)** A budgeting method in which the advertising and/or promotions budget is set based on a percentage of sales of the product.

perception **(4)** The process by which an individual receives, selects, organizes, and interprets information to create a meaningful picture of the world.

perceptual map **(5)** A "map" of perceptions of the positions of brands or products as perceived by consumers.

peripheral route to persuasion **(6)** In the elaboration likelihood model, one of two routes to persuasion in which the receiver is viewed as lacking the ability or motivation to process information and is not likely to be engaging in detailed cognitive processing.

personal selling **(1)** Person-to-person communication in which the seller attempts to assist and/or persuade prospective buyers to purchase the company's product or service or to act on an idea.

persuasion matrix **(7)** A communications planning model in which the stages of the response process (dependent variables) and the communications components (independent variables) are combined to demonstrate the likely effect that the independent variables will have on the dependent variables.

phased processing strategy **(4)** An information processing strategy in which more than one decision rule is applied during the purchase decision process.

planograms **(17)** A planning configuration of products that occupy a shelf section in a store that is used to provide more efficient shelf space utilization.

portfolio tests **(20)** A laboratory methodology designed to expose a group of respondents to a portfolio consisting of both control and test print ads.

positioning **(5)** The art and science of fitting the product or service to one or more segments of the market in such a way as to set it meaningfully apart from competition.

positioning strategies **(5)** The strategies used in positioning a brand or product.

posttests **(20)** Ad effectiveness measures that are taken after the ad has appeared in the marketplace.

preferred position rate **(14)** A rate charged by newspapers that insures the advertiser the ad will appear in the position requested and/or in a specific section of the newspaper.

premium (17) An offer of an item of merchandise or service either free or at a low price that is used as an extra incentive for purchasers.

preprinted inserts (14) Advertising distributed through newspapers that is not part of the newspaper itself, but is printed by the advertiser and then taken to the newspaper to be inserted.

press release (18) Factual and interesting information released to the press.

pretests (20) Advertising effectiveness measures that are taken before the implementation of the advertising campaign.

price elasticity (2) The responsiveness of the market to changes in price.

price-off deal (17) A promotional strategy in which the consumer receives a reduction in the regular price of the brand.

primacy effect (7) A theory that the first information presented in the message will be the most likely to be remembered.

primary circulation (14) The number of copies of a magazine distributed to original subscribers.

primary demand advertising (2) Advertising designed to stimulate demand for the general product class or entire industry.

problem detection (10) A creative research approach in which consumers familiar with a product (or service) are asked to generate an exhaustive list of problems encountered in its use.

problem recognition (4) The first stage in the consumer's decision-making process in which the consumer perceives a need and becomes motivated to satisfy it.

problem-solver stage (19) A stage of personal selling in which the seller obtains the participation of buyers in identifying their problems, translates these problems into needs, and then presents a selection from the supplier's offerings that can solve those problems.

procreator stage (19) A stage of personal selling in which the seller defines the buyer's problems or needs and the solutions to those problems or needs through active buyer-seller collaboration, thus creating a market offering tailored to the customer.

product differentiation (5) The process employed in making products appear different from others.

product manager (3) The person responsible for the planning, implementation, and control of the marketing program for an individual brand.

product placement (15) A form of advertising and promotion in which products are placed in television shows and/or movies to gain exposure.

product specific preplanning input (10) Specific studies provided to the creative department on the product or service, the target audience, or a combination of the two.

product symbolism (2) The meaning that a product or brand has to consumers.

professional advertising (2) Advertising targeted to professional groups.

program rating (13) The percentage of TV households in an area that are tuned to a program during a specific time period.

promotion (1) The coordination of all seller-initiated efforts to set up channels of information and persuasion to sell goods and services or to promote an idea.

promotional management (1) The process of coordinating the promotional mix elements.

promotional mix (1) The tools used to accomplish an organization's communications objectives. The promotional mix includes advertising, direct marketing, sales promotion, publicity/public relations, and personal selling.

promotional plan (1) The framework for developing, implementing, and controlling the organization's communications program.

promotional products marketing (15) The advertising or promotional medium or method that uses promotional products, such as ad specialties, premiums, business gifts, awards, prizes, or commemoratives.

promotional pull strategy (2) A strategy in which advertising and promotion efforts are targeted at the ultimate consumers to encourage them to purchase the manufacturer's brand.

promotional push strategy (2) A strategy in which advertising and promotional efforts are targeted to the trade to attempt to get them to promote and sell the product to the ultimate consumer.

prospector stage (19) A selling stage in which activities include seeking out selected buyers who are perceived to have a need for the offering as well as the resources to buy it.

prospects (19) Those persons who may be prospective customers based on a need for the product or service.

Protestant ethic (24) A set of values that stress hard work and individual effort and initiative and view the accumulation of material possessions as evidence of success.

provider stage (19) A selling stage in which activities are limited to accepting orders for the supplier's available offering and conveying it to the buyer.

psychoanalytic theory (4) An approach to the study of human motivations and behaviors pioneered by Sigmund Freud.

psychographic segmentation (5) Dividing the product on the basis of personality and/or lifestyles.

psychosocial consequences (4) Purchase decision consequences that are intangible, subjective, and personal.

public relations (1) The management function that evaluates public attitudes, identifies the policies and procedures of an individual or organization with the public interest, and executes a program to earn public understanding and acceptance.

public relations firm (3) An organization that develops and implements programs to manage a company's publicity, image, and affairs with consumers and other relevant publics.

publicity (1) Communications regarding an organization, product, service, or idea that is not directly paid for or run under identified sponsorship.

puffery (23) Advertising or other sales presentations that praise the item to be sold using subjective opinions, superlatives, or exaggerations, vaguely and generally, stating no specific facts.

pulsing (12) A media scheduling method that combines flighting and continuous scheduling.

pupillometrics (20) An advertising effectiveness methodology designed to measure dilation and constriction of the pupils of the eye in response to stimuli.

purchase intention (4) The predisposition to buy a certain brand or product.

push money (17) Cash payments made directly to the retailers' or wholesalers' sales force to encourage them to promote and sell a manufacturer's product.

Q

qualified prospects (19) Those prospects that are able to make the buying decision.

qualitative audit (3) An audit of the advertising agency's efforts in planning, developing, and implementing the client's communications programs.

qualitative media effect (7) The positive or negative influence the medium may contribute to the message.

R

ratings point (13) A measurement used to determine television viewing audiences in which one ratings point is the equivalent of 1 percent of all of the television households in a particular area tuned to a specific program.

rational appeal (7) Communications in which features and/or benefits are directly presented in a logical, rational method.

reach (12) The number of different audience members exposed at least once to a media vehicle (or vehicles) in a given period.

readers per copy (12) A cost comparison figure used for magazines that estimates audience size based on pass-along readership.

recall tests (20) Advertising effectiveness tests designed to measure advertising recall.

receiver (6) The person or persons with whom the sender of a message shares thoughts or information.

recency effect (7) The theory that arguments presented at the end of the message are considered to be stronger and therefore are more likely to be remembered.

recognition method (20) An advertising effectiveness measure of print ads that allows the advertiser to assess the impact of an ad in a single issue of a magazine over time and/or across alternative magazines.

reference group (4) A group whose perspectives, values, or behavior is used by an individual as the basis for his or her judgments, opinions, and actions.

refutational appeal (7) A type of message in which both sides of the issue are presented in the communication, with arguments offered to refute the opposing viewpoint.

regional networks (13) A network that covers only a specific portion of the country. Regional network purchases are based in proportion to the percentage of the country receiving the message.

reinforcement (4) The rewards or favorable consequences associated with a particular response.

relationship marketing (19) An organization's effort to develop a long-term, cost-effective link with individual customers for mutual benefit.

relative cost (12) The relationship between the price paid for advertising time or space and the size of the audience delivered; it is used to compare the prices of various media vehicles.

reminder advertising (11) Advertising designed to keep the name of the product or brand in the mind of the receiver.

repositioning (5) The changing of a product or brand's positioning.

resellers (2) Intermediaries in the marketing channel such as wholesalers, distributors, and retailers.

response (6) The set of reactions the receiver has after seeing, hearing, or reading a message.

retail/local advertising (2) Advertising carried out by retailers and/or local merchants.

retail trading zone (14) The market outside the city zone whose residents regularly trade with merchants within the city zone.

ROI budgeting method (return on investment) (9) A budgeting method in which advertising and promotions are considered investments, and thus measurements are made in an attempt to determine the returns achieved by these investments.

rolling boards (15) Advertising painted or mounted on cars, trucks, vans, trailers, etc., so the exposure can be mobile enough to be taken to specific target market areas.

run of paper (ROP) (14) A rate quoted by newspapers that allows the ad to appear on any page or in any position desired by the medium.

S

S-shaped response curve (9) A sales response model that attempts to show sales responses to various levels of advertising and promotional expenditures.

sales-oriented objectives (8) Budgeting objectives related to sales effects such as increasing sales volume.

sales promotion (1) Marketing activities that provide extra value or incentives to the sales force, distributors, or the ultimate consumer and can stimulate immediate sales.

sales promotion agency (3) An organization that specializes in the planning and implementation of promotional programs such as contests, sweepstakes, sampling, premiums, and incentive offers for its clients.

sales promotion trap (17) A spiral that results when a number of competitors extensively use promotions. One firm uses sales promotions to differentiate its product or service and other competitors copy the strategy, resulting in no differential advantage and a loss of profit margins to all.

salient beliefs (4) Beliefs concerning specific attributes or consequences that are activated and form the basis of an attitude.

sampling (17) A variety of procedures whereby consumers are given some quantity of a product for no charge to induce trial.

scatter market (13) A period for purchasing television advertising time that runs throughout the TV season.

schedules of reinforcement (4) The schedule by which a behavioral response is rewarded.

script (11) A written version of the commercial that provides a detailed description of its video and audio content.

selective attention (4)   A perceptual process in which consumers choose to attend to some stimuli and not others.

selective binding (14)   A computerized production process that allows the creation of hundreds of copies of a magazine in one continuous sequence.

selective comprehension (4)   The perceptual process whereby consumers interpret information based on their own attitudes, beliefs, motives, and experiences.

selective demand advertising (2)   Advertising that focuses on stimulating demand for a specific manufacturer's product or brand.

selective exposure (4)   A process whereby consumers choose whether or not to make themselves available to media and message information.

selective learning (6)   The process whereby consumers seek information that supports the choice made and avoid information that fails to bolster the wisdom of a purchase decision.

selective perception (4)   The perceptual process involving the filtering or screening of exposure, attention, comprehension, and retention.

selective retention (4)   The perceptual process whereby consumers remember some information but not all.

selectivity (14)   The ability of a medium to reach a specific target audience.

self-liquidating premiums (17)   Premiums that require the consumer to pay some or all of the cost of the premium plus handling and mailing costs.

self-paced media (7)   Media that viewers and/or readers can control their exposure time to, allowing them to process information at their own rate.

self-regulation (23)   The practice by the advertising industry of regulating and controlling advertising to avoid interference by outside agencies such as the government.

semiotics (6)   The study of the nature of meaning.

sensation (4)   The immediate and direct response of the senses (taste, smell, sight, touch, and hearing) to a stimulus such as an advertisement, package, brand name, or point-of-purchase display.

shaping (4)   The reinforcement of successive acts that lead to a desired behavior pattern or response.

share-of-audience (13)   The percentage of households watching television in a specified time period that are tuned to a specific program.

showing (15)   The percentage of supplicated audience exposed to an outdoor poster daily.

similarity (7)   The supposed resemblance between the source and the receiver of a message.

single-source tracking (20)   A research method designed to track the behaviors of consumers from the television set to the supermarket checkout counter.

situational determinants (4)   Influences originating from the specific situation in which consumers are to use the product or brand.

sleeper effect (7)   A phenomenon in which the persuasiveness of a message increases over time.

slotting allowance (17)   Fees that must be paid to retailers to provide a "slot" or position to accommodate a new product on the store shelves.

social class (4)   Relatively homogeneous divisions of society into which people are grouped based on similar lifestyles, values, norms, interests, and behaviors.

social style model (21)   A model that suggests businesspersons' "social styles" will influence how they react on the job.

source (6)   The sender—person, group, or organization—of the message.

source bolsters (6)   Favorable cognitive thoughts generated toward the source of a message.

source derogations (6)   Negative thoughts generated about the source of a communication.

source power (7)   The power of a source as a result of his or her ability to administer rewards and/or punishments to the receiver.

specialized marketing communication services (3)   Organizations that provide marketing communication services in their areas of expertise including direct marketing, public relations, and sales promotion firms.

specialty advertising (15)   An advertising, sales promotion, and motivational communications medium that employs useful articles of merchandise imprinted with an advertiser's name, message, or logo.

split runs (14)   Two or more versions of a print ad are printed in alternate copies of a particular issue of a magazine.

split run test (20)   An advertising effectiveness measure in which different versions of an ad are run in alternate copies of the same newspaper and/or magazine.

split 30s (13)   30-second TV spots in which the advertiser promotes two different products with two different messages during a 30-second commercial.

sponsorship (13)   When the advertiser assumes responsibility for the production and usually the content of the program as well as the advertising that appears within it.

spot advertising (13)   Commercials shown on local television stations, with the negotiation and purchase of time being made directly from the individual stations.

standard advertising unit (SAU) (14)   A standard developed in the newspaper industry to make newspaper purchasing rates more comparable to other media that sell space and time in standard units.

standard learning model (6)   Progression by the consumers through a learn-feel-do hierarchical response.

station reps (13)   Individuals who act as sales representatives for a number of local stations and represent them in dealings with national advertisers.

storyboard (10)   A series of drawings used to present the visual plan or layout of a proposed commercial.

strategic marketing plan (2)   The planning framework for specific marketing activities.

subcultures (4)   Smaller groups within a culture that possess similar beliefs, values, norms, and patterns of behavior that differentiate them from the larger cultural mainstream.

subheads (11)   Secondary headlines in a print ad.

subliminal perception (4)   The ability of an individual to perceive a stimulus below the level of conscious awareness.

superagencies (3)   Large external agencies that offer integrated marketing communications on a worldwide basis.

superstations (13) Independent local stations that send their signals via satellite to cable operators that, in turn, make them available to subscribers (WWOR, WPIX, WGN, WSBK, WTBS).

support advertising (16) A form of direct marketing in which the ad is designed to support other forms of advertising appearing in other media.

support argument (6) Consumers' thoughts that support or affirm the claims being made by a message.

support media (15) Those media used to support or reinforce messages sent to target markets through other more "dominant" and/or more traditional media.

sweeps periods (12) The times of year in which television audience measures are taken (February, May, July, and November).

sweepstakes (17) A promotion whereby consumers submit their names for consideration in the drawing or selection of prizes and winners are determined purely by chance. Sweepstakes cannot require a proof of purchase as a condition for entry.

syndicated programs (13) Shows sold or distributed to local stations.

T

target marketing (5) The process of identifying the specific needs of segments, selecting one or more of these segments as a target, and developing marketing programs directed to each.

target ratings points (TRPs) (12) The number of persons in the primary target audience that the media buy will reach—and the number of times.

team approach (18) A method of measuring the effectiveness of public relations programs whereby evaluators are actually involved in the campaign.

teaser advertising (11) An ad designed to create curiosity and build excitement and interest in a product or brand without showing it.

telemarketing (16) Selling products and services by using the telephone to contact prospective customers.

tele-media (16) The use of telephone and voice information services (800, 900, 976 numbers) to market, advertise, promote, entertain, and inform.

television network (13) The provider of news and programming to a series of affiliated local television stations.

terminal posters (15) Floor displays, island showcases, electronic signs, and other forms of advertisements that appear in train or subway stations, airline terminals, etc.

testing bias (20) A bias that occurs in advertising effectiveness measures because respondents know they are being tested and thus alter their responses.

tests of comprehension and reaction (20) Advertising effectiveness tests that are designed to assess whether the ad conveyed the desired meaning and is not reacted to negatively.

theater testing (20) An advertising effectiveness pretest in which consumers view ads in a theater setting and evaluate these ads on a variety of dimensions.

top-down approaches (9) Budgeting approaches in which the budgetary amount is established at the executive level and monies are passed down to the various departments.

total audience (television) (13) The total number of homes viewing any five-minute part of a television program.

total audience/readership (14) A combination of the total number of primary and pass-along readers multiplied by the circulation of an average issue of a magazine.

tracking studies (20) Advertising effectiveness measures designed to assess the effects of advertising on awareness, recall, interest, and attitudes toward the ad as well as purchase intentions.

trade advertising (2) Advertising targeted to wholesalers and retailers.

trademark (2) An identifying name, symbol, or other device that gives a company the legal and exclusive rights to use.

trade-oriented sales promotion (17) A sales promotion designed to motivate distributors and retailers to carry a product and make an extra effort to promote or "push" it to their customers.

trade regulation rules (TRRs) (23) Industrywide rules that define unfair practices before they occur. Used by the Federal Trade Commission to regulate advertising and promotion.

trade show (17) A type of exhibition or forum where manufacturers can display their products to current as well as prospective buyers.

transformational advertising (11) An ad that associates the experience of using the advertised brand with a unique set of psychological characteristics that would not typically be associated with the brand experience to the same degree without exposure to the advertisement.

transit advertising (15) Advertising targeted to target audiences exposed to commercial transportation facilities, including buses, taxis, trains, elevators, trolleys, airplanes, and subways.

trustworthiness (7) The honesty, integrity, and believability of the source of a communication.

two-sided message (7) A message in which both good and bad points about a product or claim are presented.

two-step approach (16) A direct-marketing strategy in which the first effort is designed to screen or qualify potential buyers, while the second effort has the responsibility of generating the response.

U

undifferentiated marketing (5) A strategy in which market segment differences are ignored and one product or service is offered to the entire market.

unduplicated reach (12) The number of persons reached once with a media exposure.

unique selling proposition (10) An advertising strategy that focuses on a product or service attribute that is distinctive to a particular brand and offers an important benefit to the customer.

up-front market (13) A buying period that takes place prior to the upcoming television season when the networks sell a large part of their commercial time.

V

values and lifestyles program (VALS) (5) Stanford Research Institute's method for applying lifestyle segmentation.

vehicle option source effect (20) The differential impact the advertising exposure will have on the same audience member if the exposure occurs in one media option rather than another.

vertical cooperative advertising (17) A cooperative arrangement under which a manufacturer pays for a portion of the advertising a retailer runs to promote the manufacturer's product and its availability in the retailer's place of business.

video advertising (15) Advertisements appearing in movie theaters and on videotapes.

video news release (18) News stories produced by publicists so that television stations may air them as news.

voice-over (11) Action on the screen in a commercial that is narrated or described by a narrator who is not visible.

W

want (4) A felt need shaped by a person's knowledge, culture, and personality.

waste coverage (12) A situation where the coverage of the media exceeds the target audience.

Wheeler-Lea Amendment (23)

Wheeler-Lea Amendment (23) An act of Congress passed in 1938 that amended section 5 of the FTC Act to read that unfair methods of competition in commerce and unfair or deceptive acts or practices in commerce are declared unlawful.

word-of-mouth communications (6) Social channels of communication such as friends, neighbors, associates, co-workers, or family members.

Y

Yellow Pages advertising (15) Advertisements that appear in the various Yellow Pages–type phone directories.

Z

zapping (13) The use of a remote control device to change channels and switch away from commercials.

zero-based communications planning (8) An approach to planning the integrated marketing communications program that involves determining what tasks need to be done and that marketing communication functions should be used to accomplish them and to what extent.

zipping (13) Fast-forwarding through commercials during the playback of a program previously recorded on a VCR.

Endnotes

Chapter 1

1. Robert J. Cohen, "Ad Gain of 5.2% in 93 Marks Downturn's End," *Advertising Age,* May 2, 1994, p. 4.
2. "Insider's Report—Robert Cohen Presentation on Advertising Expenditures," *McCann Erickson Worldwide,* June 1993, p. 8.
3. Martin Fleming, "Media Spending in the 1990s," *American Demographics,* September 1991, pp. 48–53.
4. "AMA Board Approves New Marketing Definition," *Marketing News,* March 1, 1985, p. 1.
5. Richard P. Bagozzi, "Marketing as Exchange," *Journal of Marketing* 39 (October 1975), pp. 32–39.
6. Adrienne Ward Fawcett, "Integrated Marketing—Marketers Convinced: Its Time Has Arrived," *Advertising Age,* November 6, 1993, pp. S1–2.
7. Don E. Schultz, "Integrated Marketing Communications: Maybe Definition Is in the Point of View," *Marketing News,* January 18, 1993, p. 17.
8. Ibid.
9. Anthony J. Tortorici, "Maximizing Marketing Communications through Horizontal and Vertical Orchestration," *Public Relations Quarterly* 36, no. 1 (1991), pp. 20–22.
10. Joe Cappo, "Agencies: Change or Die," *Advertising Age,* December 7, 1992, p. 26.
11. Thomas R. Duncan and Stephen E. Everett, "Client Perception of Integrated Marketing Communications," *Journal of Advertising Research,* May/June 1993, pp. 30–39.
12. Faye Rice, "A Cure for What Ails Advertising?" *Fortune,* December 16, 1991, pp. 119–22.

13. Michael L. Ray, *Advertising and Communication Management* (Englewood Cliffs, N.J.: Prentice Hall, 1982).
14. Ralph S. Alexander, ed., *Marketing Definitions* (Chicago: American Marketing Association, 1965), p. 9.
15. "Trends in Media," research report by Television Bureau of Advertising, New York, July 1993.
16. "Still Bullish on Promotion," 1994 annual report on the promotion industry, *Promo,* July 1994, p. 35.
17. *Donnelley Marketing Sixteenth Annual Survey of Promotional Practices* (Stamford, Conn.: Donnelley Marketing, 1994).
18. Judann Dagnoli, "Sorry Charlie, Heinz Puts Promos First," *Advertising Age,* March 30, 1992, p. 3.
19. H. Frazier Moore and Bertrand R. Canfield, *Public Relations: Principles, Cases, and Problems,* 7th ed. (Burr Ridge, Ill.: Richard D. Irwin, 1977), p. 5.
20. Art Kleiner, "The Public Relations Coup," *Adweek's Marketing Week,* January 16, 1989, pp. 20–23.
21. Anne B. Fisher, "Spiffing Up the Corporate Image," *Fortune,* July 21, 1986, pp. 68–72.

Chapter 2

1. Spencer L. Hapoinen, "The Rise of Micromarketing," *The Journal of Business Strategy,* November/December 1990, pp. 37–42.
2. "What Happened to Advertising?" *Business Week,* September 23, 1991, pp. 66–72.
3. Judann Dagnoli, "Campbell Ups Ad $," *Advertising Age,* July 1, 1991, p. 1.
4. "Time to Rebuild Brand Muscle," *Advertising Age,* September 23, 1991, p. 20.

5. J. Paul Peter and Jerry C. Olson, *Consumer Behavior* (Burr Ridge, Ill.: Richard D. Irwin, 1987), p. 505.
6. Michael R. Solomon, "The Role of Products as Social Stimuli: A Symbolic Interactionism Perspective," *Journal of Consumer Research,* December 1983, pp. 319–29.
7. Peter H. Farquhar, "Managing Brand Equity," *Journal of Advertising Research* 30, no. 4 (August/September 1990).
8. Al Ries and Jack Trout, *Positioning: The Battle for Your Mind* (New York: McGraw-Hill, 1982).
9. Kenneth E. Runyon and David W. Stewart, *Consumer Behavior* (Columbus, Ohio: Merrill, 1987).
10. Elliot Young, "Judging a Product by Its Wrapper," *Progressive Grocer,* July 1985, pp. 10–11.
11. Peter and Olson, *Consumer Behavior,* p. 571.
12. David J. Curry, "Measuring Price and Quality Competition," *Journal of Marketing* 49 (Spring 1985), pp. 106–17.
13. Paul W. Farris and David J. Reibstein, "How Prices, Ad Expenditures, and Profits Are Linked," *Harvard Business Review,* November–December 1979, pp. 173–84.
14. Philip Kotler, *Marketing Management,* 7th ed. (Englewood Cliffs, N.J.: Prentice Hall, 1991), p. 508.
15. Francine Schwadel, "Retailers Broaden Their Ad Campaigns to Promote Image as Well as Products," *The Wall Street Journal,* June 8, 1988, p. 28.
16. J. J. Burnett and A. J. Bush, "Profiling the Yuppies," *Journal of Advertising Research,* April-May 1986, pp. 27–36.
17. Raymond Serafin, "BMW Puts $30M behind Ads to Drive Away

Yuppie Image," *Advertising Age,* June 24, 1991, pp. 3, 62.

18. Judith Waldrop, "Secrets of Age Pyramids," *American Demographics,* August 1992, p. 9

19. "Mature America in the 1990s," A publication of the AARP, 1992, The Roper Organization.

20. Lisa Fried, "Modern Maturity: When Having It All Is Too Much," *Folio,* June 1, 1991, p. 16.

21. *Statistical Abstract of the United States,* (Washington, D.C.: U.S. Bureau of Labor Statistics, 1993).

22. "Working Women More Attractive—Y&R," *Advertising Age,* January 11, 1982, p. 76.

23. "The Numbers," *Mediaweek,* July 15, 1991, p. 18.

24. Pauline Yoshihashi, "Why More Ads Aren't Targeting Asians," *The Wall Street Journal,* July 20, 1989, p. B1.

25. An excellent source for demographic information is *American Demographics* magazine which is published by American Demographics, Inc., Ithaca, N.Y.

26. "What Happened to Advertising?"

27. Judann Dagnoli, "Recession's Bleak Legacy," *Advertising Age,* July 29, 1991, p. 1.

28. *1992–1993 Nielsen Report on Television,* New York: Nielsen Media Research, 1993.

Chapter 3

1. Barry Brown, "P&G Hires 10 Shops," *Advertising Age,* October 21, 1991, p. 38.

2. Thomas J. Cosse and John E. Swan, "Strategic Marketing Planning by Product Managers—Room for Improvement?" *Journal of Marketing* 47 (Summer 1983), pp. 92–102.

3. Bradley Johnson, "Nestlè U.S. Units Join for Media Clout," *Advertising Age,* January 14, 1991, p. 3.

4. Victor P. Buell, *Organizing for Marketing/Advertising Success* (New York: Association of National Advertisers, 1982).

5. M. Louise Ripley, "What Kind of Companies Take Their Advertising In-House?" *Journal of Advertising*

Research, October/November 1991, pp. 73–80.

6. Bruce Horovitz, "Some Companies Say the Best Ad Agency Is No Ad Agency at All," *Los Angeles Times,* July 19, 1989, Sec. IV, p. 5.

7. Ibid.

8. Kevin Goldman, "GM Merging Media Buying at Interpublic," *The Wall Street Journal,* December 8, 1993, p. B3.

9. Joe Mandese, "Buyers' Boom Costs Ad Agencies," *Advertising Age,* September 16, 1991, p. 3.

10. "Achenbaum Puts His Cards on the Table," *Advertising Age,* May 9, 1988, p. 3.

11. Quote in: Patricia Sellers, "Do You Need Your Ad Agency?" *Fortune,* November 15, 1993, pp. 47–61.

12. Laurie Peterson, "Pursuing Results in the Age of Accountability," *Adweek's Marketing Week,* November 19, 1990, pp. 20–22.

13. Faye Rice, "A Cure for What Ails Advertising?" *Fortune,* December 16, 1991, pp. 119–122.

14. Melanie Wells, "Calet Will 'Guarantee Results'," *Advertising Age,* June 6, 1993, pp. 1, 44.

15. Rice, "A Cure for What Ails Advertising?"

16. Laurel Wentz, "Cost-Cutting About Face," *Advertising Age,* July 15, 1991, pp. 1, 38.

17. Nancy Giges, "Reviewing the Review: Borden Likes System of Agency Evaluation," *Advertising Age,* April 18, 1977, p. 3.

18. Joanne Lipman, "Study Shows Clients Jump Ship Quickly," *The Wall Street Journal,* May 21, 1992, p. B6.

19. Peter Doyle, Marcel Corstiens, and Paul Michell, "Signals of Vulnerability in Agency–Client Relations," *Journal of Marketing* 44 (Fall 1980), pp. 18–23; and Daniel B. Wackman, Charles Salmon, and Caryn C. Salmon, "Developing an Advertising Agency–Client Relationship," *Journal of Advertising Research* 26, no. 6 (December 1986/January 1987), pp. 21–29.

20. Cathy Taylor, "Client Conflicts Can Whipsaw Even Small Agencies," *Adweek,* August 6, 1990, p. 40.

21. William Abrams, "Big Contest for Ad Accounts Forces Agencies to Go

All Out," *The Wall Street Journal,* November 18, 1982, p. 33; and "Big Agencies Starting to Call for End to Costly Free Pitches," *The Wall Street Journal,* February 22, 1989, p. B7.

22. Bradley Johnson, "In a Millisecond, Microsoft Boots Up Marketing Database," *Advertising Age,* November 6, 1993, p. S-6.

23. Prema Nakra, "The Changing Role of Public Relations in Marketing Communications," *Public Relations Quarterly* 1 (1991) pp. 42–45.

24. "Do Your Ads Need a Superagency?" *Fortune,* April 27, 1987, p. 81.

25. Rice, "A Cure for What Ails Advertising?"

26. "Ad Firms Falter on One-Stop Shopping," *The Wall Street Journal,* December 1, 1988, p. 81; and "Do Your Ads Need a Superagency?" *Fortune,* April 27, 1987, p. 81.

27. Rice, "A Cure For What Ails Advertising?" p. 122.

28. Adrienne Ward Fawcett, "Integrated Marketing—Marketers Convinced: Its Time Has Arrived," *Advertising Age,* November 6, 1993, pp. S1-2.

29. Adrienne Ward Fawcett, "Integrated Marketing Door Open for Experts," *Advertising Age,* November 6, 1993, p. S2.

Chapter 4

1. Russell W. Belk, "Possessions and the Extended Self," *Journal of Consumer Research,* September 1988, pp. 139–68.

2. Eric N. Berkowitz, Roger A. Kerin, Steven W. Hartley, and William Rudelius, *Marketing,* 3rd ed. (Burr Ridge, Ill.: Richard D. Irwin, 1992), p. 14.

3. A. H. Maslow, "'Higher' and 'Lower' Needs," *Journal of Psychology* 25 (1948), pp. 433–36.

4. Morton Deutsch and Robert M. Krauss, *Theories in Social Psychology* (New York: Basic Books, 1965).

5. Jagdish N. Sheth, "The Role of Motivation Research in Consumer Psychology" (Faculty Working Paper, University of Illinois, Champaign: 1974); Bill Abrams, "Charles

of the Ritz Discovers What Women Want," *The Wall Street Journal*, August 20, 1981, p. 29; and Ernest Dichter, *Getting Motivated* (New York: Pergamon Press, 1979).

6. Ronald Alsop, "Advertisers Put Consumers on the Couch," *The Wall Street Journal*, May 13, 1988, p. 19.

7. For an excellent discussion of memory and consumer behavior, see James R. Bettman, "Memory Factors in Consumer Choice: A Review," *Journal of Marketing* 43 (Spring 1979), pp. 37–53.

8. Gilbert Harrell, *Consumer Behavior* (San Diego: Harcourt Brace Jovanovich, 1986), p. 66.

9. Raymond A. Bauer and Stephen A. Greyser, *Advertising in America: The Consumer View* (Boston: Harvard Business School, 1968).

10. Neal Santelmann, "Color That Yells 'Buy Me'," *Forbes*, May 2, 1988, p. 110.

11. J. Paul Peter and Jerry C. Olson, *Consumer Behavior*, 2nd ed. (Burr Ridge, Ill.: Richard D. Irwin, 1990), p. 73.

12. Gordon W. Allport, "Attitudes," in *Handbook of Social Psychology*, ed. C. M. Murchison (Winchester, Mass.: Clark University Press, 1935), p. 810.

13. Robert B. Zajonc and Hazel Markus, "Affective and Cognitive Factors in Preferences," *Journal of Consumer Research* 9 (1982), pp. 123–31.

14. Alvin Achenbaum, "Advertising Doesn't Manipulate Consumers," *Journal of Advertising Research*, April 2, 1970, pp. 3–13.

15. William D. Wells, "Attitudes and Behavior: Lessons from the Needham Lifestyle Study," *Journal of Advertising Research*, February–March 1985, pp. 40–44; and Icek Ajzen and Martin Fishbein, "Attitude-Behavior Relations: A Theoretical Analysis and Review of Empirical Research," *Psychological Bulletin*, September 1977, pp. 888–918.

16. For a review of multiattribute models, see William L. Wilkie and Edgar A. Pessemier, "Issues in Marketing's Use of Multiattribute Modlels," *Journal of Marketing Research* 10 (November 1983), pp. 428–41.

17. Joel B. Cohen, Paul W. Minniard, and Peter R. Dickson, "Information Integration: An Information Processing Perspective," in *Advances in Consumer Research*, vol. 7, ed. Jerry C. Olson (Ann Arbor: Association for Consumer Research, 1980), pp. 161–70.

18. Peter and Olson, *Consumer Behavior*, p. 182.

19. Peter L. Wright and Fredric Barbour, "The Relevance of Decision Process Models in Structuring Persuasive Messages," *Communications Research*, July 1975, pp. 246–59.

20. James F. Engel, "The Psychological Consequences of a Major Purchase Decision," in *Marketing in Transition*, ed. William S. Decker (Chicago: American Marketing Association, 1963), pp. 462–75.

21. John A. Howard and Jagdish N. Sheth, *The Theory of Consumer Behavior* (New York: John Wiley & Sons, 1969).

22. Leon G. Schiffman and Leslie Lazar Kannuk, *Consumer Behavior*, 4th ed. (Englewood Cliffs, N.J.: Prentice Hall, 1991), p. 192.

23. I. P. Pavlov, *The Work of the Digestive Glands*, 2nd ed., trans. W. N. Thompson (London: Griffin, 1910).

24. Gerald J. Gorn, "The Effects of Music in Advertising on Choice: A Classical Conditioning Approach," *Journal of Marketing* 46 (Winter 1982), pp. 94–101.

25. Brian C. Deslauries and Peter B. Everett, "The Effects of Intermittent and Continuous Token Reinforcement on Bus Ridership," *Journal of Applied Psychology* 62 (August 1977), pp. 369–75.

26. Michael L. Rothschild and William C. Gaidis, "Behavioral Learning Theory: Its Relevance to Marketing and Promotions," *Journal of Marketing Research* 45, no. 2 (Spring 1981), pp. 70–78.

27. For an excellent discussion of social class and consumer behavior, see Richard P. Coleman, "The Continuing Significance of Social Class to Marketing," *Journal of Consumer Research* 10, no. 3 (December 1983), pp. 265–80.

28. Lyman E. Ostlund, *Role Theory and Group Dynamics in Consumer Behavior: Theoretical Sources*, ed. Scott Ward and Thomas S. Robertson

(Englewood Cliffs, N.J.: Prentice Hall, 1973), pp. 230–75.

29. James Stafford and Benton Cocanougher, "Reference Group Theory," in *Perspective in Consumer Behavior*, ed. H. H. Kassarjian and T. S. Robertson (Glenview, Ill.: Scott, Foresman, 1981), pp. 329–43.

30. Jagdish N. Sheth, "A Theory of Family Buying Decisions," in *Models of Buying Behavior*, ed. Jagdish N. Sheth (New York: Harper & Row, 1974), pp. 17–33.

31. Ibid.

32. Russell Belk, "Situational Variables and Consumer Behavior," *Journal of Consumer Research*, December 1975, pp. 157–64.

Chapter 5

1. Eric N. Berkowitz, Roger A. Kerin, and William Rudelius, *Marketing*, 2nd ed. (Burr Ridge, Ill.: Richard D. Irwin, 1989).

2. Kelly Shermach, "Ski Boot Firm Targets Women," *Marketing News*, September 27, 1993, p. 6.

3. Robert Rueff, "Demographics Won't Find the Bull's Eye," *Advertising Age*, February 4, 1991, p. 20.

4. Edward M. Tauber, "Research on Food Consumption Values Finds Four Market Segments: Good Taste Still Tops," *Marketing News*, May 15, 1981, p. 17; Rebecca C. Quarles, "Shopping Centers Use Fashion Lifestyle Research to Make Marketing Decisions," *Marketing News*, January 22, 1982, p. 18; and "Our Autos, Ourselves," *Consumer Reports*, June 1985, p. 375.

5. Judith Graham, "New VALS 2 Takes Psychological Route," *Advertising Age*, February 13, 1989, p. 24.

6. Victor J. Cook and William A. Mindak, "A Search for Constants: The 'Heavy User' Revisited," *Journal of Consumer Marketing* 1, no. 4 (Spring 1984), p. 80.

7. *Ayer's Dictionary of Advertising Terms* (Philadelphia: Ayer Press, 1976).

8. David A. Aaker and John G. Myers, *Advertising Management*, 3rd ed. (Englewood Cliffs, N.J.: Prentice Hall, 1987), p. 125.

9. Jack Trout and Al Ries, "Positioning Cuts through Chaos in the Marketplace," *Advertising Age,* May 1, 1972, pp. 51–53.

10. Ibid.

11. David A. Aaker and J. Gary Shansby, "Positioning Your Product," *Business Horizons,* May–June 1982, pp. 56–62.

12. Aaker and Myers, *Advertising Management.*

13. Trout and Ries, "Positioning Cuts through Chaos."

14. Aaker and Myers, *Advertising Management.*

Chapter 6

1. Wilbur Schram, *The Process and Effects of Mass Communication* (Urbana: University of Illinois Press, 1955).

2. Ibid.

3. Joseph Ransdell, "Some Leading Ideas of Peirce's Semiotic," *Semiotica* 19 (1977), pp. 157–78.

4. Ronald Alsop, "Agencies Scrutinize Their Ads for Psychological Symbolism," *The Wall Street Journal,* June 11, 1987, p. 25.

5. For an excellent article on the application of semiotics to consumer behavior and advertising, see David G. Mick, "Consumer Research and Semiotics: Exploring the Morphology of Signs, Symbols, and Significance," *Journal of Consumer Research* 13, no. 2 (September 1986), pp. 196–213.

6. Barry L. Bayus, "Word of Mouth: The Indirect Effect of Marketing Efforts," *Journal of Advertising Research,* June-July 1985, pp. 31–39.

7. Quote by Gorden S. Bower in *Fortune,* October 14, 1985, p. 11.

8. Thomas V. Bonoma and Leonard C. Felder, "Nonverbal Communication in Marketing: Toward Communicational Analysis," *Journal of Marketing Research,* May 1977, pp. 169–80.

9. Jacob Jacoby and Wayne D. Hoyer, "Viewer Miscomprehension of Televised Communication: Selected Findings," *Journal of Marketing,* Fall 1982, pp. 12–26; Jacoby and Hoyer, "The Comprehension and Miscomprehension of Print Communications: An Investigation of Mass Media Magazines" (Advertising Education Foundation study, New York, 1987).

10. E. K. Strong, *The Psychology of Selling* (New York: McGraw-Hill, 1925), p. 9.

11. Robert J. Lavidge and Gary A. Steiner, "A Model for Predictive Measurements of Advertising Effectiveness," *Journal of Marketing* 24 (October 1961), pp. 59–62.

12. Everett M. Rogers, *Diffusion of Innovations* (New York: Free Press, 1962), pp. 79–86.

13. William J. McGuire, "An Information Processing Model of Advertising Effectiveness," in *Behavioral and Management Science in Marketing,* ed. Harry J. Davis and Alvin J. Silk (New York: Ronald Press, 1978), pp. 156–80.

14. Michael L. Ray, "Communication and the Hierarchy of Effects," in *New Models for Mass Communication Research,* ed. P. Clarke (Beverly Hills, Calif.: Sage Publications, 1973), pp. 147–75.

15. Herbert E. Krugman, "The Impact of Television Advertising: Learning without Involvement," *Public Opinion Quarterly* 29 (Fall 1965), pp. 349–56.

16. Scott A. Hawkins and Stephen J. Hoch, "Low-Involvement Learning: Memory without Evaluation," *Journal of Consumer Research,* 19, no. 2 (September 1992), pp. 212–25.

17. Harry W. McMahan, "Do Your Ads Have VIP?" *Advertising Age,* July 14, 1980, pp. 50–51.

18. Robert E. Smith and William R. Swinyard, "Information Response Models: An Integrated Approach," *Journal of Marketing* 46, no. 2 (Winter 1982), pp. 81–93.

19. Ibid., p. 90.

20. Ibid., p. 86.

21. Robert E. Smith, "Integrating Information from Advertising and Trial: Processes and Effects on Consumer Response to Product Information," *Journal of Marketing Research* 30 (May 1993) pp. 204–19.

22. Harold H. Kassarjian, "Low Involvement: A Second Look," in *Advances in Consumer Research,* Vol. 8 (Ann Arbor: Association for Consumer Research, 1981), pp. 31–34; also see Anthony G. Greenwald and Clark Leavitt, "Audience Involvement in Advertising: Four Levels," *Journal of Consumer Research* 11, no. 1 (June 1984), pp. 581–92.

23. Judith L. Zaichkowsky, "Conceptualizing Involvement," *Journal of Advertising* 15, no. 2 (1986), pp. 4–14.

24. Richard Vaughn, "How Advertising Works: A Planning Model," *Journal of Advertising Research* 20, no. 5 (October 1980), pp. 27–33.

25. Richard Vaughn, "How Advertising Works: A Planning Model Revisited," *Journal of Advertising Research* 26, no. 1 (February-March 1986), pp. 57–66.

26. Jerry C. Olson, Daniel R. Toy, and Philip A. Dover, "Mediating Effects of Cognitive Responses to Advertising on Cognitive Structure," in *Advances in Consumer Research,* Vol. 5, ed. H. Keith Hunt (Ann Arbor: Association for Consumer Research, 1978), pp. 72–78.

27. Anthony A. Greenwald, "Cognitive Learning, Cognitive Response to Persuasion and Attitude Change," in *Psychological Foundations of Attitudes,* ed. A. G. Greenwald, T. C. Brock, and T. W. Ostrom (New York: Academic Press, 1968); and Peter L. Wright, "The Cognitive Processes Mediating Acceptance of Advertising," *Journal of Marketing Research* 10 (February 1973), pp. 53–62.

28. Idem, "Message Evoked Thoughts, Persuasion Research Using Thought Verbalizations," *Journal of Consumer Research* 7, no. 2 (September 1980), pp. 151–75.

29. Scott B. Mackenzie, Richard J. Lutz, and George E. Belch, "The Role of Attitude toward the Ad as a Mediator of Advertising Effectiveness: A Test of Competing Explanations," *Journal of Marketing Research* 23 (May 1986), pp. 130–43; and Rajeev Batra and Michael L. Ray, "Affective Responses Mediating Acceptance of Advertising," *Journal of Consumer Research* 13 (September 1986), pp. 234–49.

30. Ronald Alsop, "TV Ads that Are Likeable Get Plus Rating for Persuasiveness," *The Wall Street Journal,* February 20, 1986, p. 23.

31. Andrew A. Mitchell and Jerry C. Olson, "Are Product Attribute Beliefs the Only Mediator of Advertising Effects on Brand Attitude?"

Journal of Marketing Research 18 (August 1981), pp. 318–32.

32. Julie Edell and Marian C. Burke, "The Power of Feelings in Understanding Advertising Effects," *Journal of Consumer Research* 14 (December 1987), pp. 421–33.

33. Richard E. Petty and John T. Cacioppo, "Central and Peripheral Routes to Persuasion: Application to Advertising," in *Advertising and Consumer Psychology*, ed. Larry Percy and Arch Woodside (Lexington, Mass.: Lexington Books, 1983), pp. 3–23.

34. David A. Aaker, Rajeev Batra, and John G. Myers, *Advertising Management*, 4th ed. (Englewood Cliffs, N.J.: Prentice Hall, 1992).

35. Richard E. Petty, John T. Cacioppo, and David Schumann, "Central and Peripheral Routes to Advertising Effectiveness: The Moderating Role of Involvement," *Journal of Consumer Research* 10 (September 1983), pp. 135–46.

Chapter 7

1. William J. McGuire, "An Information Processing Model of Advertising Effectiveness," in *Behavioral and Management Science in Marketing*, ed. Harry J. Davis and Alvin J. Silk (New York: Ronald Press, 1978), pp. 156–80.

2. Herbert C. Kelman, "Processes of Opinion Change," *Public Opinion Quarterly* 25 (Spring 1961), pp. 57–78.

3. William J. McGuire, "The Nature of Attitudes and Attitude Change," in *Handbook of Social Psychology*, 2nd ed., ed. G. Lindzey and E. Aronson (Cambridge, Mass.: Addison-Wesley, 1969), pp. 135–214.

4. Roobina Ohanian, "The Impact of Celebrity Spokespersons' Image on Consumers' Intention to Purchase," *Journal of Advertising Research*, February-March 1991, pp. 46–54.

5. "Business Celebrities," *Business Week*, June 23, 1986, pp. 100–107.

6. Roger Kerin and Thomas E. Barry, "The CEO Spokesperson in Consumer Advertising: An Experimental Investigation," in *Current Issues in Research in Advertising*, ed. J.

H. Leigh and C. R. Martin (Ann Arbor: University of Michigan, 1981), pp. 135–48; and J. Poindexter, "Voices of Authority," *Psychology Today*, August 1983.

7. A. Eagly and S. Chaiken, "An Attribution Analysis of the Effect of Communicator Characteristics on Opinion Change," *Journal of Personality and Social Psychology* 32 (1975), pp. 136–44.

8. For a review of these studies, see Brian Sternthal, Lynn Phillips, and Ruby Dholakia, "The Persuasive Effect of Source Credibility: A Situational Analysis," *Public Opinion Quarterly* 42 (Fall 1978), pp. 285–314.

9. Brian Sternthal, Ruby Dholakia, and Clark Leavitt, "The Persuasive Effects of Source Credibility: Tests of Cognitive Response," *Journal of Consumer Research* 4, no. 4 (March 1978), pp. 252–60; and Robert R. Harmon and Kenneth A. Coney, "The Persuasive Effects of Source Credibility in Buy and Lease Situations," *Journal of Marketing Research* 19 (May 1982), pp. 255–60.

10. For a review, see Noel Capon and James Hulbert, "The Sleeper Effect: An Awakening," *Public Opinion Quarterly* 37 (1973), pp. 333–58.

11. Darlene B. Hannah and Brian Sternthal, "Detecting and Explaining the Sleeper Effect," *Journal of Consumer Research* 11, no. 2 (September 1984), pp. 632–42.

12. H. C. Triandis, *Attitudes and Attitude Change* (New York: John Wiley & Sons, 1971).

13. J. Mills and J. Jellison, "Effect on Opinion Change Similarity between the Communicator and the Audience He Addresses," *Journal of Personality and Social Psychology* 9, no. 2 (1969), pp. 153–56.

14. Arch G. Woodside and J. William Davenport, Jr., "The Effect of Salesman Similarity and Expertise on Consumer Purchasing Behavior," *Journal of Marketing Research* 11 (May 1974), pp. 198–202; and Paul Busch and David T. Wilson, "An Experimental Analysis of a Salesman's Expert and Referent Bases of Social Power in the Buyer-Seller Dyad," *Journal of Marketing Research* 13 (February 1976), pp. 3–11.

15. Julie Liesse and Jeff Jensen, "Whole New Game without Jordan," *Advertising Age*, October 11, 1993, pp. 1, 48.

16. Bruce Horowitz, "Mazda Drops Garner to Try New Route in Commercials," *Los Angeles Times*, February 10, 1989, pt. IV, p. 1.

17. John C. Mowen and Stephen W. Brown, "On Explaining and Predicting the Effectiveness of Celebrity Endorsers," in *Advances in Consumer Research*, Vol. 8 (Ann Arbor: Association for Consumer Research, 1981), pp. 437–41.

18. "It Seemed Like a Good Idea at the Time," *Forbes*, February 28, 1987, p. 98.

19. Charles Atkin and M. Block, "Effectiveness of Celebrity Endorsers," *Journal of Advertising Research* 23, no. 1 (February-March 1983), pp. 57–61.

20. Study by Total Research Corp. cited in: Bruce Horowitz "Wishing on a Star," *Los Angeles Times*, November 7, 1993, pp. D1, 7.

21. James R. Schiffman, "PepsiCo Cans TV Ads with Madonna, Pointing Up Risks of Using Superstars," *The Wall Street Journal*, April 5, 1989, p. B11.

22. Bruce Horowitz, "It May Be Hard to Swallow Some Endorsements," *Los Angeles Times*, February 11, 1992, p. D1.

23. J. Forkan, "Product Matchup Key to Effective Star Presentations," *Advertising Age*, October 6, 1980, p. 42; and Michael A. Kamins, "An Investigation into the 'Match-up' Hypothesis in Celebrity Advertising," *Journal of Advertising* 19, no. 1 (1990), pp. 4–13.

24. Grant McCracken, "Who Is the Celebrity Endorser? Cultural Foundations of the Endorsement Process," *Journal of Consumer Research* 16, no. 3 (December 1989), pp. 310–21.

25. Ibid., p. 315.

26. For an excellent review of these studies, see W. B. Joseph, "The Credibility of Physically Attractive Communicators," *Journal of Advertising* 11, no. 3 (1982), pp. 13–23.

27. M. J. Baker and Gilbert A. Churchill, Jr., "The Impact of Physically Attractive Models on Advertising Evaluations," *Journal of*

Marketing Research 14 (November 1977), pp. 538–55.

28. Robert W. Chestnut, C. C. La Chance, and A. Lubitz, "The Decorative Female Model: Sexual Stimuli and the Recognition of the Advertisements," *Journal of Advertising* 6 (Fall 1977), pp. 11–14; and Leonard N. Reid and Lawrence C. Soley, "Decorative Models and Readership of Magazine Ads," *Journal of Advertising Research* 23, no. 2 (April-May 1983), pp. 27–32.

29. Herbert E. Krugman, "On Application of Learning Theory to TV Copy Testing," *Public Opinion Quarterly* 26 (1962), pp. 626–39.

30. C. I. Hovland and W. Mandell, "An Experimental Comparison of Conclusion Drawing by the Communicator and by the Audience," *Journal of Abnormal and Social Psychology* 47 (July 1952), pp. 581–88.

31. Alan G. Sawyer and Daniel J. Howard, "Effects of Omitting Conclusions in Advertisements to Involved and Uninvolved Audiences," *Journal of Marketing Research* 28 (November 1991), pp. 467–74.

32. Paul Chance, "Ads without Answers Make Brain Itch," *Psychology Today* 9 (1975), p. 78.

33. George E. Belch, "The Effects of Message Modality on One- and Two-Sided Advertising Messages," in *Advances in Consumer Research*, Vol. 10, ed. Richard P. Bagozzi and Alice M. Tybout (Ann Arbor: Association for Consumer Research, 1983), pp. 21–26.

34. Robert E. Settle and Linda L. Golden, "Attribution Theory and Advertiser Credibility," *Journal of Marketing Research* 11 (May 1974), pp. 181–85; and Edmund J. Faison, "Effectiveness of One-Sided and Two-Sided Mass Communications in Advertising," *Public Opinion Quarterly* 25 (Fall 1961), pp. 468–69.

35. Alan G. Sawyer, "The Effects of Repetition of Refutational and Supportive Advertising Appeals," *Journal of Marketing Research* 10 (February 1973), pp. 23–37; and George J. Szybillo and Richard Heslin, "Resistance to Persuasion: Inoculation Theory in a Marketing Context," *Journal of Marketing Research* 10 (November 1973), pp. 396–403.

36. Andrew A. Mitchell, "The Effect of Verbal and Visual Components of Advertisements on Brand Attitudes and Attitude toward the Advertisement," *Journal of Consumer Research* 13 (June 1986), pp. 12–24; and Julie A. Edell and Richard Staelin, "The Information Processing of Pictures in Advertisements," *Journal of Consumer Research* 10, no. 1 (June 1983), pp. 45–60; Elizabeth C. Hirschmann, "The Effects of Verbal and Pictorial Advertising Stimuli on Aesthetic, Utilitarian and Familiarity Perceptions," *Journal of Advertising* 15, no. 2 (1986), pp. 27–34.

37. Jolita Kisielius and Brian Sternthal, "Detecting and Explaining Vividness Effects in Attitudinal Judgments," *Journal of Marketing Research* 21, no. 1 (1984), pp. 54–64.

38. H. Rao Unnava and Robert E. Burnkrant, "An Imagery-Processing View of the Role of Pictures in Print Advertisements," *Journal of Marketing Research* 28 (May 1991), pp. 226–31.

39. William L. Wilkie and Paul W. Farris, "Comparative Advertising: Problems and Potential," *Journal of Marketing* 39 (1975), pp. 7–15.

40. For a review of comparative advertising studies, see Cornelia Pechmann and David W. Stewart, "The Psychology of Comparative Advertising," in *Attention, Attitude and Affect in Response to Advertising*, ed. E. M. Clark, T. C. Brock, and D. W. Stewart (Hillsdale, N.J.: Lawrence Erlbaum Associates, 1994), pp. 79–96.

41. Michael L. Ray and William L. Wilkie, "Fear: The Potential of an Appeal Neglected by Marketing," *Journal of Marketing* 34 (January 1970), pp. 54–62.

42. Brian Sternthal and C. Samuel Craig, "Fear Appeals Revisited and Revised," *Journal of Consumer Research* 1 (December 1974), pp. 22–34.

43. John F. Tanner, Jr., James B. Hunt, and David R. Eppright, "The Protection Motivation Model: A Normative Mode of Fear Appeals," *Journal of Marketing* 55 (July 1991), pp. 36–45.

44. Ibid.

45. Sternthal and Craig, "Fear Appeals Revisited and Revised."

46. For a discussion of the use of humor in advertising, see C. Samuel Craig and Brian Sternthal, "Humor in Advertising," *Journal of Marketing* 37 (October 1973), pp. 12–18.

47. Thomas J. Madden and Marc C. Weinberger, "Humor in Advertising: A Practitioner View," *Journal of Advertising Research*, 24, no. 4 (August-September 1984), pp. 23–26.

48. Harold C. Cash and W. J. E. Crissy, "Comparison of Advertising and Selling," *The Salesman's Role in Marketing, The Psychology of Selling* 12 (1965), pp. 56–75.

49. Marshall McLuhan, *Understanding Media: The Extensions of Man* (New York: McGraw-Hill, 1966).

50. Marvin E. Goldberg and Gerald J. Gorn, "Happy and Sad TV Programs: How They Affect Reactions to Commercials," *Journal of Consumer Research* 14, no. 3 (December 1987), pp. 387–403.

51. Peter H. Webb, "Consumer Initial Processing in a Difficult Media Environment," *Journal of Consumer Research* 6, no. 3 (December 1979), pp. 225–36.

52. Kevin Goldman, "TV Promotional Clutter Irks Ad Industry," *The Wall Street Journal*, February 11, 1994, p. B6.

53. For a review of marketing communications studies involving source, message, channel, and receiver factors, see George E. Belch, Michael A. Belch, and Angelina Villarreal, "Effects of Advertising Communications: Review of Research," in *Research in Marketing* (Greenwich, Conn.: JAI Press, 1987) 9, pp. 59–117.

Chapter 8

1. Quote by Jim Garrity cited in "A Role Model for Big Blue?" *Brandweek*, April 5, 1993, p. 18.

2. Robert A. Kriegel, "How to Choose the Right Communications Objectives," *Business Marketing*, April 1986, pp. 94–106.

3. 1993 Effies, New York Chapter of the American Marketing Association, New York, 1993, p. 10.

4. Donald S. Tull, "The Carry-Over Effect of Advertising," *Journal of Marketing*, April 1965, pp. 46–53.

5. Darral G. Clarke, "Econometric Measurement of the Duration of Advertising Effect on Sales," *Journal of Marketing Research* 23 (November 1976), pp. 345–57.

6. Philip Kotler, *Marketing Decision Making: A Model Building Approach* (New York: Holt, Rinehart & Winston, 1971), chap. 5.

7. For a more detailed discussion of this, see William M. Weilbacher, *Advertising,* 2nd ed. (New York: Macmillan, 1984), p. 112.

8. Courtland I. Bovee and William F. Arens, *Advertising,* 3rd ed. (Burr Ridge, Ill.: Richard D. Irwin, 1989).

9. 1993 Effie, p. 6.

10. Russell H. Colley, *Defining Advertising Goals for Measured Advertising Results* (New York: Association of National Advertisers, 1961).

11. Ibid., p. 21.

12. Don E. Schultz, Dennis Martin, and William Brown, *Strategic Advertising Campaigns,* 2nd ed. (Lincolnwood, Ill.: Crain Books, 1984).

13. Michael L. Ray, "Consumer Initial Processing: Definitions, Issues, Applications," in *Buyer/Consumer Information Processing,* ed. G. David Hughes (Chapel Hill: University of North Carolina Press, 1974); and David A. Aaker and John G. Myers, *Advertising Management,* 2nd ed. (Englewood Cliffs, N.J.: Prentice Hall, 1982), pp. 122–23.

14. Sandra Ernst Moriarty, "Beyond the Hierarchy of Effects: A Conceptual Framework," in *Current Issues and Research in Advertising,* ed. Claude R. Martin, Jr., and James H. Leigh (Ann Arbor: University of Michigan, 1983), pp. 45–55.

15. Aaker and Myers, *Advertising Management.*

16. Kristian S. Palda, "The Hypothesis of a Hierarchy of Effects: A Partial Evaluation," *Journal of Marketing Research* 3 (February 1966), pp. 13–24.

17. Stewart H. Britt, "Are So-Called Successful Advertising Campaigns Really Successful?" *Journal of Advertising Research* 9, no. 2 (1969), pp. 3–9.

18. Steven W. Hartley and Charles H. Patti, "Evaluating Business-to-Business Advertising: A Comparison of Objectives and Results," *Journal of Advertising Research* 28 (April/May 1988), pp. 21–27.

19. Ibid., p. 25.

20. Study cited in Robert F. Lauterborn, "How to Know If Your Advertising Is Working," *Journal of Advertising Research* 25 (February–March 1985), pp. RC 9–11.

21. Don E. Schultz, " Integration Helps You Plan Communications from Outside–In," *Marketing News,* March 15, 1993, p. 12.

22. Thomas R. Duncan, "To Fathom Integrated Marketing, Dive!" *Advertising Age,* October 11, 1993, p. 18.

Chapter 9

1. Robert L. Steiner, "The Paradox of Increasing Returns to Advertising," *Journal of Advertising Research,* February-March 1987, pp. 45–53.

2. Frank M. Bass, "A Simultaneous Equation Regression Study of Advertising and Sales of Cigarettes," *Journal of Marketing Research* 6, no. 3 (August 1969), p. 291.

3. David A. Aaker and James M. Carman, "Are You Overadvertising?" *Journal of Advertising Research* 22, no. 4 (August-September 1982), pp. 57–70.

4. Julian A. Simon and Johan Arndt, "The Shape of the Advertising Response Function," *Journal of Advertising Research* 20, no. 4 (1980), pp. 11–28.

5. Paul B. Luchsinger, Vernan S. Mullen, and Paul T. Jannuzzo, "How Many Advertising Dollars Are Enough?" *Media Decisions* 12 (1977), p. 59.

6. Paul W. Farris, "Determinants of Advertising Intensity: A Review of the Marketing Literature" (Report no. 77–109, Marketing Science Institute, Cambridge, Mass., 1977).

7. Melvin E. Salveson, "Management's Criteria for Advertising Effectiveness" (Proceedings 5th Annual Conference, Advertising Research Foundation, New York, 1959), p. 25.

8. Robert Settle and Pamela Alreck, "Positive Moves for Negative Times," *Marketing Communications,* January 1988, pp. 19–23.

9. James O. Peckham, "Can We Relate Advertising Dollars to Market Share Objectives?" in *How Much to Spend for Advertising,* ed. M. A. McNiven (New York: Association of National Advertisers, 1969), p. 30.

10. "Marketers Fuel Promotion Budgets," *Marketing and Media Decisions,* September 1984, p. 130.

11. Ibid.

12. Mary Welch, "Upbeat Marketers Wield Bigger Budgets, Shift Marketing Mix," *Business Marketing,* February 1993, p. 23.

13. John P. Jones, "Ad Spending: Maintaining Market Share," *Harvard Business Review,* January-February 1990, pp. 38–42; and James C. Schroer, "Ad Spending: Growing Market Share," *Harvard Business Review,* January-February 1990, pp. 44–48.

14. Randall S. Brown, "Estimating Advantages to Large-Scale Advertising," *Review of Economics and Statistics* 60 (August 1978), pp. 428–37.

15. Kent M. Lancaster, "Are There Scale Economies in Advertising?" *Journal of Business* 59, no. 3 (1986), pp. 509–26.

16. Johan Arndt and Julian Simon, "Advertising and Economies of Scale: Critical Comments on the Evidence," *Journal of Industrial Economics* 32, no. 2 (December 1983), pp. 229–41; and Aaker and Carman, "Are You Overadvertising?"

17. George S. Low and Jakki J. Mohr, "The Budget Allocation between Advertising and Sales Promotion: Understanding the Decision Process," *1991 AMA Educators' Proceedings: Chicago, Ill.:* Summer 1991, pp. 448–57.

Chapter 10

1. Jeanne Whalen, "BK Caters to Franchisees with New Review," *Advertising Age,* October 25, 1993, p. 3.

2. Joshua Levine, "Fizz, Fizz-Plop, Plop," *Fortune,* June 21, 1993, p. 139.

3. Bill Abrams, "What Do Effie, Clio, Addy, Andy and Ace Have in Common?" *The Wall Street Journal,* July 16, 1983, p. 1; Jennifer Pendleton, "Awards–Creatives Defend Pursuit of Prizes," *Advertising Age,*

April 25, 1988, p. 1; and David Herzbrun, "The Awards Awards," *Advertising Age*, May 2, 1988, p. 18.

4. Elizabeth C. Hirschman, "Role-Based Models of Advertising Creation and Production," *Journal of Advertising* 18, no. 4 (1989), pp. 42–53.

5. Ibid., p. 51.

6. Ronald Alsop, "TV Ads That Are Likeable Get Plus Rating for Persuasiveness," *The Wall Street Journal*, February 20, 1986, p. 23; and Cyndee Miller, "Study Says 'Likability' Surfaces as Measure of TV Ad Success," *Marketing News*, January 7, 1991, pp. 6, 14.

7. For an interesting discussion on the embellishment of advertising messages, see William M. Weilbacher, *Advertising*, 2nd ed. (New York: Macmillan, 1984), pp. 180–82.

8. David Ogilvy, *Confessions of an Advertising Man* (New York: Atheneum Publishers, 1963); and Hanley Norins, *The Compleat Copywriter* (New York: McGraw-Hill, 1966).

9. Hank Sneiden, *Advertising Pure and Simple* (New York: ANACOM, 1977).

10. Quoted in Valerie H. Free, "Absolut Original," *Marketing Insights*, Summer 1991, p. 65.

11. Cathy Taylor, "Risk Takers: Wieden & Kennedy," *Adweek's Marketing Week*, March 23, 1992, pp. 26, 27.

12. James Webb Young, *A Technique for Producing Ideas*, 3rd ed. (Chicago: Crain Books, 1975), p. 42

13. Sandra E. Moriarty, *Creative Advertising: Theory and Practice* (Englewood Cliffs, N.J.: Prentice Hall, 1986).

14. E. E. Norris, "Seek Out the Consumer's Problem," *Advertising Age*, March 17, 1975, pp. 43–44.

15. Thomas L. Greenbaum, "Focus Groups Can Play a Part in Evaluating Ad Copy," *Marketing News*, September 13, 1993, pp. 24–25.

16. William D. Wells, Clark Leavitt, and Maureen McConville, "A Reaction Profile for Commercials," *Journal of Advertising Research* 11 (December 1971), pp. 11–17.

17. Eben Shapiro, "Campbell Shifts Familiar Slogan to Back Burner,"

The Wall Street Journal, September 9, 1993, pp. B1, 5.

18. A. Jerome Jeweler, *Creative Strategy in Advertising* (Belmont, Calif.: Wadsworth, 1981).

19. John O'Toole, *The Trouble with Advertising*, 2nd ed. (New York: Random House, 1985), p. 131.

20. David Ogilvy, *Ogilvy on Advertising* (New York: Crown, 1983), p. 16.

21. Rosser Reeves, *Reality in Advertising* (New York: Knopf, 1961), pp. 47, 48.

22. Bill Abrams, "Ad Constraints Could Persist Even If the FTC Loosens Up," *The Wall Street Journal*, December 10, 1981, p. 33.

23. Alecia Swasy, "How Innovation at P&G Restored Luster to Washed-Up Pert and Made It No. 1," *The Wall Street Journal*, December 6, 1990, p. B1.

24. Ogilvy, *Confessions*.

25. Martin Mayer, *Madison Avenue, U.S.A.* (New York: Pocket Books, 1958).

26. Jack Trout and Al Ries, "The Positioning Era Cometh," *Advertising Age*, April 24, 1972, pp. 35–38; May 1, 1972, pp. 51–54; May 8, 1972, pp. 114–16.

27. David A. Aaker and John G. Myers, *Advertising Management*, 3rd ed. (Englewood Cliffs, N.J.: Prentice Hall, 1987).

Chapter 11

1. Sandra E. Moriarty, *Creative Advertising: Theory and Practice*, 2nd ed. (Englewood Cliffs, N.J.: Prentice Hall, 1991), p. 76.

2. William M. Weilbacher, *Advertising*, 2nd ed. (New York: Macmillan, 1984), p. 197.

3. William Wells, John Burnett, and Sandra Moriarty, *Advertising* (Englewood Cliffs, N.J.: Prentice Hall, 1989), p. 330.

4. For a review of research on the effect of mood states on consumer behavior, see Meryl Paula Gardner, "Mood States and Consumer Behavior: A Critical Review," *Journal of Consumer Research* 12, no. 3 (December 1985), pp. 281–300.

5. Cathy Madison, "Researchers Work Advertising into an Emotional State," *Adweek*, November 5, 1990, p. 30.

6. Christopher P. Puto and William D. Wells, "Informational and Transformational Advertising: The Different Effects of Time," in *Advances in Consumer Research*, Vol. 11, ed. Thomas C. Kinnear (Ann Arbor: Association for Consumer Research, 1984), p. 638.

7. Ibid.

8. David Ogilvy and Joel Raphaelson, "Research on Advertising Techniques That Work and Don't Work," *Harvard Business Review*, July-August 1982, p. 18.

9. *Topline, No. 4*, McCann-Erickson (September 1989) New York.

10. Jacqueline Mitchell, "New Jeep to Roll Out with 'Teaser' Ads," *The Wall Street Journal*, February 6, 1992, p. B7.

11. Martin Mayer, *Madison Avenue, U.S.A.* (New York: Pocket Books, 1958), p. 64.

12. Kevin Goldman, "Slim-Fast Ads Use Brooke Shields to Appeal to the Low-Fat Dieter," *The Wall Street Journal*, January 10, 1994, p. B7.

13. Alecia Swasy, "P&G Tries Bolder Ads—With Caution," *The Wall Street Journal*, May 7, 1990, pp. B1, 7.

14. Lynn Coleman, "Advertisers Put Fear into the Hearts of Their Prospects," *Marketing News*, August 15, 1988, p. 1.

15. Kevin Goldman, "Chips Ahoy! Ad Uses Spin on Claymation," *The Wall Street Journal*, February 9, 1994, p. B5.

16. Barbara B. Stern, "Classical and Vignette Television Advertising: Structural Models, Formal Analysis, and Consumer Effects," *Journal of Consumer Research* 20, no. 4 (March 1994), pp. 601–15; and John Deighton, Daniel Romer, and Josh McQueen, "Using Drama to Persuade," *Journal of Consumer Research* 15, no. 3 (December 1989), pp. 335–43.

17. Moriarty, *Creative Advertising*, p. 77.

18. Courtland L. Bovee and William F. Arens, *Contemporary Advertising*, 4th ed. (Burr Ridge, Ill.: Richard D. Irwin, Inc., 1992), p. 292.

19. W. Keith Hafer and Gordon E. White, *Advertising Writing*, 3rd ed. (St. Paul, Minn.: West Publishing, 1989), p. 98.

20. "How Much Should a Commercial Cost?" *Marketing Communications,* June 1983, p. 41.

21. Linda M. Scott, "Understanding Jingles and Needledrop: A Rhetorical Approach to Music in Advertising," *Journal of Consumer Research* 17, no. 2 (September 1990), pp. 223–36.

22. Ibid., p. 223.

23. Russell I. Haley, Jack Richardson, and Beth Baldwin, "The Effects of Nonverbal Communications in Television Advertising," *Journal of Advertising Research* 24, no. 4, pp. 11–18.

24. Gerald J. Gorn, "The Effects of Music in Advertising on Choice Behavior: A Classical Conditioning Approach," *Journal of Marketing* 46 (Winter 1982), pp. 94–100.

25. Swasy, "P&G Tries Bolder Ads."

26. Eva Pomice, "Madison Avenue's Blind Spot," *U.S. News & World Report,* October 3, 1988, p. 49.

27. Bruce Horowitz, "TV Spots for Light Bulbs, Diet Pepsi This Year's Big Clio Award Winners," *Los Angeles Times,* June 21, 1988, pt. IV, p. 6.

Chapter 12

1. John P. Cortez, "Flowers Flourish through Interactive Media," *Advertising Age,* July 12, 1993, p. 12.

2. Patricia Sellers, "The Best Way to Reach Buyers," *Fortune,* Autumn/Winter 1993, pp. 14–17.

3. Michael J. Naples, *Effective Frequency: The Relationship between Frequency and Advertising Effectiveness* (New York: Association of National Advertisers, 1979).

4. Joseph W. Ostrow, "Setting Frequency Levels: An Art or a Science?" *Market and Media Decisions,* 1987, p. 19.

5. David Berger, "How Much to Spend" (Foote, Cone & Belding Internal Report), in Michael L. Rothschild, *Advertising* (Lexington, Mass.: D. C. Heath, 1987), p. 468.

6. David W. Olson, "Real World Measures of Advertising Effectiveness for New Products" (Speech to the 26th Annual Conference of the Advertising Research Foundation, New York, March 18, 1980).

7. Naples, *Effective Frequency.*

8. Joseph W. Ostrow, "What Level Frequency?" *Advertising Age,* November 1981, pp. 13–18.

9. Ibid.

10. Hanna Liebman, "2002: Interactive Adland?" *Mediaweek,* May 17, 1993, p. 14.

Chapter 13

1. *Radio Marketing Guide and Fact Book for Advertisers* (New York: Radio Advertising Bureau, Inc., 1993).

2. "Trends in Television," New York: Television Bureau of Advertising, Inc., July 1993.

3. Dennis Kneale, "Zapping of TV Ads Appears Pervasive," *The Wall Street Journal,* April 25, 1988, p. 27.

4. Kevin Goldman, "Budweiser Plans World Series Ad Blitz," *The Wall Street Journal,* August 20, 1993, p. B4.

5. Janet Meyers and Laurie Freeman, "Marketers Police TV Commercial Costs," *Advertising Age,* April 3, 1989, p. 51.

6. Robert Parcher, "15-Second TV Commercials Appear to Work 'Quite Well'," *Marketing News,* January 3, 1986, p. 1.

7. Wayne Walley, "Popularity of :15s Falls," *Advertising Age,* January 14, 1991, pp. 1, 41.

8. Kevin Goldman, "TV Promotional Clutter Irks Ad Industry," *The Wall Street Journal,* February 11, 1994, p. B6.

9. Dennis Kneale, "Zapping of TV Ads Appears Pervasive."

10. Carrie Heeter and Bradley S. Greenberg, "Profiling the Zappers," *Journal of Advertising Research,* April-May 1985, pp. 9–12; and Patricia Orsini, "Zapping: A Man's World," *Spring Television Report: Adweek's Marketing Week,* April 8, 1991, p. 3.

11. Ernest F. Larkin, "Consumer Perceptions of the Media and Their Advertising Content," *Journal of Advertising* 8 (1979), pp. 5–7.

12. Jeff Jensen, "Goodbye, Upfront; but Is Client-Friendly System Next?" *Advertising Age,* May 24, 1993, p. S-8.

13. John Helyar, Meg Cox, and Elizabeth Jensen, "How Fox Stole the Football Away from CBS," *The*

Wall Street Journal, December 20, 1993, p. B1.

14. Mary Lou Carnevale, "FCC Gives Last Chance for Objections in Bitter Fight on TV Syndication Rule," *The Wall Street Journal,* March 18, 1991, p. B6.

15. John Lippman, "Too Costly for Prime Time," *Los Angeles Times,* March 22, 1992, pp. D1, 8.

16. Eric Schmuckler, "Playing the Network Game," *Adweek's Marketing Week,* January 20, 1992, pp. 17–27.

17. *1992–1993 Report on Television, Nielsen Media Research* (New York: A. C. Nielsen Co., 1993).

18. "Spot Cable Is on Target," "Cable '94, *Advertising Age,* February 28, 1994, p. C4.

19. Christine Larson, "On the Spot." *Cable Television Special Report: Adweek,* April 6, 1992.

20. John Lippman, "Merchants Begin to Shift Their Ad Focus to Cable TV," *Los Angeles Times,* February 3, 1992, pp. D1, 2.

21. Stephen Battaglio, "The Rise and Stall," *Cable Television Special Report: Adweek,* April 6, 1992, pp. 10–12.

22. "Sports on TV: Cable Is the Team to Watch," *Business Week,* August 22, 1988, pp. 66–69.

23. Gary Levin, "Arbitron Exits from Ratings Race," *Advertising Age,* October 25, 1993, p. 4.

24. Joe Mandese, "TV Ratings Monopoly Faces Changing Future," *Advertising Age,* November 15, 1993, p. S-24.

25. Quote by William Staklein, head of Radio Advertising Bureau, cited in: "More Firms Tune into Radio to Stretch Their Ad Budgets," *The Wall Street Journal,* July 17, 1986, p. 27.

26. *Radio Marketing Guide and Fact Book.*

27. Verne Gay, "Image Transfer: Radio Ads Make Aural History," *Advertising Age,* January 24, 1985, p. 1.

28. Avery Abernethy, "Differences between Advertising and Program Exposure for Car Radio Listening," *Journal of Advertising Research* 31, no. 2, (April-May 1991) pp. 33–42.

29. Lippman, "Merchants Begin to Shift Their Ad Focus to Cable TV."

30. Howard Schlossberg, "New Radio Ratings Services Zero in on Moving Cars and Smaller Markets," *Marketing News,* April 26, 1993, pp. 1, 7.

Chapter 14

1. *The Magazine Handbook* no. 59 (New York: Magazine Publishers Association, 1991); and Fred Plaff, "Trading Up," *Marketing & Media Decisions,* August 1988, pp. 77–83.
2. Herbert E. Krugman, "The Measurement of Advertising Involvement," *Public Opinion Quarterly* 30 (Winter 1966–67), pp. 583–96.
3. Jerry Schlosberg, "The Glittering City Magazines," *American Demographics,* July 1986, pp. 22–25.
4. Scott Donaton and Pat Sloan, "Ad 'Printaculars' under Scrutiny," *Advertising Age,* February 12, 1990, p. 3.
5. *Magazine Audiences 2* (New York: Mediamark Research Inc., Spring 1982).
6. Ibid.
7. Steve Fajen, "Numbers Aren't Everything." *Media Decisions* 10 (June 1975), pp. 65–69.
8. *A Study of Media Involvement 6* (New York: Magazine Publishers of America, April 1991).
9. Ibid.
10. *The Magazine Handbook.*
11. Garfield Ricketts, "The ABCs of ABC Statements," *Marketing & Media Decisions,* November 1988, p. 84.
12. Study cited in Jim Surmanek, *Media Planning: A Practical Guide* (Lincolnwood, Ill.: Crain Books, 1985).
13. "How Advertising Readership Is Influenced by A⁴ Size," (Newton, Mass.: Cahners Advertising Research Report no. 110.1) Cahners Publishing Company; and New York: McGraw-Hill Research, "Larger Advertisements Get Higher Readership," *LAP Report no. 3102.*
14. McGraw-Hill Research, "Effect of Size, Color and Position on Number of Responses to Recruitment Advertising," *LAP Report no. 3116.*
15. *The Magazine Handbook,* p. 23.
16. Eric Garland, "The Road to Recovery," *Adweek Special Report: Consumer Magazines,* February 17, 1992, pp. 4, 5.

17. Victor F. Zonana, "Hard-Pressed Magazines Push for New Image," *Los Angeles Times,* April 7, 1991, pp. D1, 10.
18. Lorne Manly, "No Gains, No Pain," *Adweek Special Report: Consumer Magazines,* February 17, 1992, p. 27.
19. Joe Mandese, "Strong Roots for Cross-Media," *Advertising Age,* October 6, 1991, pp. 34, 35.
20. Junu Bryan Kim, "Cracking the Barrier of Two Dimensions," *Advertising Age,* October 6, 1991, pp. 32, 34.
21. *Key Facts 1991: Newspapers, Advertising & Marketing* (New York: Newspaper Advertising Bureau, 1991).
22. Tamara Goldman, "Big Spenders Develop Newspaper Strategies," *Marketing Communications,* June 1988, pp. 24–29.
23. Survey by Newspaper Advertising Bureau, October 1988.
24. Hanna Liebman, "NAA Network Ready to Roll," *Mediaweek,* December 13, 1993, p. 18.
25. Amy Alson, "The Search for National Ad Dollars," *Marketing & Media Decisions,* February 1989, pp. 29–31.
26. Robert J. Cohen, "Ad Gain of 5.2 Percent in 93 Marks Downturn's End," *Advertising Age,* May 2, 1994, p. 4.
27. Thomas B. Rosentiel, "Newspapers Fear Being Bypassed by Advertisers," *Los Angeles Times,* April 27, 1989, pt. IV, p. 1.
28. Lisa Benenson, "The Data Chase," *Adweek Special Report: The Newspaper Business,* May 4, 1992, pp. 6–7.
29. Dan Cray, Tom Weisend, Michael J. McDermott, Pat Hinsberg, and Meryl Davids, "Making Change," *Newspapers: Special Supplement to Adweek's Marketing Week,* May 6, 1991, pp. 6–13.
30. Ibid.
31. Daniel Pearl, "Newspapers Strive to Win Back Women," *The Wall Street Journal,* May 4, 1992, pp. B1, 12.

Chapter 15

1. "OAAA Special Report" (New York: Outdoor Advertising Association of America, 1994).

2. Ibid.
3. John Medearis, "Ads on Wheels Run into Flak," *Los Angeles Times,* July 11, 1984, pt. IV, p. 2.
4. David Kalish, "Supermarket Sweepstakes," *Marketing & Media Decisions,* November 1988, p. 34.
5. Adam Snyder, "Outdoor Forecast: Sunny, Some Clouds," *Adweek's Marketing Week,* July 8, 1991, p. 18–19.
6. Laurie Freeman and Alison Fahey, "Package Goods Ride with Transit," *Advertising Age,* April 23, 1990, p. 28.
7. *Advertisers Take the City Bus to Work* (New York: Winston Network, 1988), p. 13.
8. *Transit Fact Book* (New York: American Public Transit Association, 1993).
9. Promotional Products Association International (Irving, Tex.: 1994).
10. Ibid.
11. George L. Herpel and Steve Slack, *Specialty Advertising: New Dimensions in Creative Marketing* (Irving, Tex.: Specialty Advertising Association, 1983), pp. 76, 79–80.
12. Ibid., p. 78.
13. Ibid., p. 75.
14. *1993 National Yellow Pages Usage Study* (Troy, Mich.: Yellow Pages Publishers Association, 1994).
15. Carol Hall, "Branding the Yellow Pages," *Marketing & Media Decisions,* April 1989, p. 59.
16. Ibid., p. 3.
17. Ibid.
18. Ibid., p. 5.
19. Ibid.
20. Ibid., p. 8.
21. Scott Hume, "Consumers Pan Ads on Video Movies," *Advertising Age,* May 28, 1990, p. 8.
22. Joanne Lipman and Kathleen A. Hughes, "Disney Prohibits Ads in Theaters Showing Its Movies," *The Wall Street Journal,* February 9, 1990, p. B1.
23. Motion Picture Association of America, 1994.
24. Betsy Baurer, "New Quick Flicks: Ads at the Movies," *USA TODAY,* March 13, 1986, p. D1.
25. Ibid.
26. Michael A. Belch and Don Sciglimpaglia, "Viewers' Evaluations of Cinema Advertising," *Pro-*

ceedings of the American Institute for Decision Sciences, March 1979, pp. 39–43.

27. "Hershey Befriends Extra-terrestrial," *Advertising Age,* July 19, 1982, p. 1.

28. Motion Picture Association of America, 1994.

29. Damon Darlin, "Highbrow Hype," *Forbes,* April 12, 1993, pp. 126–127.

30. "Consumer Products Become Movie Stars," *The Wall Street Journal,* February 29, 1988, p. 23.

31. Ibid.

32. Mendelsohn Media Research, New York, 1993.

33. Jennifer Lawrence, "In-Flight Gets above Turbulence," *Advertising Age,* August 19, 1991, p. 32.

34. Ibid.

35. Joann S. Lublin, "In-Flight TV Commercials Are Booming," *The Wall Street Journal,* September 19, 1990, p. B6.

36. Ibid.

Chapter 16

1. Stan Rapp and Thomas I. Collins, *Maximarketing* (New York: McGraw-Hill, 1987).

2. Peter D. Bennett, ed., *Dictionary of Marketing Terms* (Chicago: American Marketing Association, 1988), p. 58.

3. Direct Marketing Association, 1993.

4. *Federal Reserve Bulletin—Annual Statistical Digest,* 1993, p. 516. 1992.

5. Jagdish N. Sheth, "Marketing Megatrends," *Journal of Consumer Marketing* 1, no. 1 (June 1983), pp. 5–13.

6. *Statistical Abstracts of the U.S.* (Washington, D.C.: U.S. Bureau of Labor Statistics, 1993).

7. Joanne Cleaver, "Consumers at Home with Shopping," *Advertising Age,* January 18, 1988, pp. S16–18.

8. Herbert Kanzenstein and William S. Sachs, *Direct Marketing,* 2nd ed. (New York: Macmillan, 1992).

9. *Direct Marketing Magazine,* January 1994.

10. Paul Hughes, "Profits Due," *Entrepreneur,* February 1994, pp. 74–78.

11. Cleveland Horton, "Porsche 300,000: The New Elite," *Advertising Age,* February 5, 1990, p. 8.

12. Direct Marketing Association, 1994.

13. "Marketers, Retailers Line Up to Ride Home-Shopping Highway," *Brandweek,* March 22, 1993, p. 8.

14. "The New Era for Infomercials," *Advertising Age,* January 25, 1993, p. M3.

15. Bruce Horowitz, "The Spray-On Hair Audience," *Los Angeles Times,* March 30, 1993, p. D6.

16. Josh Levine, "Entertainment or Deception?" *Forbes,* August 2, 1993, p. 102.

17. Direct Marketing Association, 1994.

18. Peggy Moretti, "Telemarketers Serve Clients," *Business Marketing,* April 1994, pp. 27–29.

19. Ibid.

20. Tom Eisenhart, "Tele-media: Marketing's New Dimension," *Business Marketing,* February 1991, pp. 50–53.

21. "Marketers, Retailers Line Up to Ride Home-Shopping Highway," *Brandweek,* March 22, 1993, p. 8.

22. Gerry Khermooch, "Chip Connection," *Brandweek,* March 14, 1994, pp. 18–24.

23. Ibid.

24. Ibid.

25. Jon Berry, "The TV Shopping Future: It's Further Than You Think," *Brandweek,* October 4, 1993, p. 16.

26. Michael J. Major, "Videotex Never Really Left, but It's Not All Here," *Advertising Age,* November 12, 1990, p. 2.

27. Direct Selling Association, 1994.

28. Hughes, "Profits Due."

Chapter 17

1. Louis J. Haugh, "Defining and Redefining," *Advertising Age,* February 14, 1983, p. M44.

2. Scott A. Nielsen, John Quelch, and Caroline Henderson, "Consumer Promotions and the Acceleration of Product Purchases," in *Research on Sales Promotion: Collected Papers,* ed. Katherine E. Jocz (Cambridge, Mass.: Marketing Science Institute, 1984).

3. The Wall Street Journal Centennial Survey, cited in Ron Alsop, "Brand Loyalty Is Rarely Blind Loyalty," *The Wall Street Journal,* October 19, 1989, p. B1.

4. Todd Johnson, NPD Research Inc., "Declining Brand Loyalty Trends:

Fact or Fiction?" (Paper presented at the Fourth Annual AMA Marketing Research Conference, October 5, 1983).

5. Bob Schmitz and Keith Jones, "The New Retailer/Marketer: Friend or Foe?" in *Looking at the Retail Kaleidoscope, Forum IX* (Stamford, Conn.: Donnelley Marketing, 1988).

6. Scott Hume, "Coupons Score with Consumers," *Advertising Age,* February 15, 1988, p. 40.

7. Robert B. Settle and Pamela L. Alreck, "Hyperchoice in the Marketplace," *Marketing Communications,* May 1988, p. 15.

8. Leigh McAlister, "A Model of Consumer Behavior," *Marketing Communications,* April 1987, p. 27.

9. Ruth M. McMath, "Winning the Space Wars," *Marketing Communications,* May 1988, pp. 55–58.

10. Lynn G. Coleman, "Marketers Advised to Go Regional," *Marketing News,* May 8, 1989, p. 1; and Lisa Petrison, "Aiming the Pitch at the Corner Store," *Adweek's Marketing Week—Promote,* September 21, 1987, p. 6.

11. "What Happened to Advertising," *Business Week,* September 23, 1991, pp. 66–72.

12. Richard Gibson, "How Products Check Out Helps Determine Pay," *The Wall Street Journal,* August 1, 1991, p. B1.

13. *NCH Reporter, No. 1* (Nielsen Clearing House, 1983).

14. *The Magazine Handbook, Number 59* (New York: Magazine Publishers of America, 1991).

15. Judann Dagnoli, "Jordan Hits Ad Execs for Damaging Brands," *Advertising Age,* November 4, 1991, p. 47.

16. Study cited in "What Happened to Advertising," *Business Week,* September 23, 1991, pp. 66–72.

17. R. M. Prentice, "How to Split Your Marketing Funds between Advertising and Promotion Dollars," *Advertising Age,* January 10, 1977, pp. 41–42, 44.

18. Betsy Spethmann, "Money and Power," *Brandweek,* March 15, 1993, p. 21.

19. Quote by Vincent Sottosanti, president of Council of Sales Promotion

Agencies, in "Promotions that Build Brand Image," *Marketing Communications,* April 1988, p. 54.

20. "Fast Food Chains Start to Tune in on Frequency," *Brandweek,* March 21, 1994, pp. 36–38.

21. Jeffrey K. McElenea and Michael J. Enzer, "Building Brand Franchises," *Marketing Communications,* April 1986, pp. 42–64.

22. Reference cited in John P. Rossiter and Larry Percy, *Advertising and Promotion Management* (New York: McGraw-Hill, 1987), p. 360.

23. *1993 Worldwide Coupon Distribution and Redemption Trends,* Vol. 29 (Lincolnshire, Ill.: NCH Promotional Services, 1994).

24. Ibid.

25. N. Giges, "GF Trims Its Use of Coupons," *Advertising Age,* December 7, 1981, p. 22.

26. Julie Liesse Erickson, "FSI Boom to Go Bust?" *Advertising Age,* May 1, 1989, pp. 1, 82.

27. Survey by Oxtoby-Smith, Inc., cited in "Many Consumers View Rebates as a Bother," *The Wall Street Journal,* April 13, 1989, p. B1.

28. William R. Dean, "Irresistible but Not Free of Problems," *Advertising Age,* October 6, 1980, pp. S1–12.

29. William A. Robinson, "What Are Promos' Weak and Strong Points?" *Advertising Age,* April 7, 1980, p. 54.

30. "Sweepstakes Fever," *Forbes,* October 3, 1988, pp. 164–66.

31. "Catching Consumers with Sweepstakes," *Fortune,* February 8, 1982, p. 87.

32. Russell D. Bowman, *Couponing and Rebates: Profits on the Dotted Line* (New York: Lebhar-Friedman Books, 1980).

33. Survey by Oxtoby-Smith, Inc., "Many Consumers View Rebates."

34. Peter Tat, William A. Cunningham III, and Emin Babakus, "Consumer Perceptions of Rebates," *Journal of Advertising Research,* August–September 1988, pp. 45–50.

35. Martha Graves, "Mail-in Rebates Stirring Shopper, Retailer Backlash," *Los Angeles Times,* January 11, 1989, pt. IV, p. 1.

36. Edward A. Blair and E. Laird Landon, "The Effects of Reference Prices in Retail Advertisements,"

Journal of Marketing 45, no. 2 (Spring 1981), pp. 61–69.

37. Bruce Horowitz, "The Sponsorship Game," *Los Angeles Times,* January 4, 1994, pp. D1, 6.

38. Ibid.

39. Shav Glick, "Takeovers, Mergers Take Their Toll, Too," *Los Angeles Times,* March 27, 1989, pt. III, p. 14.

40. Scott Hume, "Sponsorship Up 18 Percent," *Advertising Age,* March 23, 1992, p. 4.

41. Judann Dagnoli, "Sorry Charlie, Heinz Puts Promos First," *Advertising Age,* March 30, 1992, p. 3.

42. "Want Shelf Space at the Supermarket? Ante Up," *Business Week,* August 7, 1989, pp. 60–61.

43. Ibid.

44. Tom Steinhagen, "Space Management Shapes Up with Planograms," *Marketing News,* November 12, 1990, p. 7.

45. Cynthia Rigg, "Hard Times Means Growth for Co-op Ads," *Advertising Age,* November 12, 1990, p. 24.

46. Ibid.

47. Edwin L. Artzt, "The Lifeblood of Brands," *Advertising Age,* November 4, 1991, p. 32.

48. "Everyone Is Bellying Up to This Bar," *Business Week,* January 27, 1992, p. 84.

49. Benson P. Shapiro, "Improved Distribution with Your Promotional Mix," *Harvard Business Review,* March–April 1977, p. 116; and Roger A. Strang, "Sales Promotion—Fast Growth, Faulty Management," *Harvard Business Review,* July–August 1976, p. 119.

50. Quote by Thomas E. Hamilton, director of Sales Promotion Service—William Esty Advertising, cited in Felix Kessler, "The Costly Couponing Craze," *Fortune,* June 9, 1986, p. 84.

51. Alan G. Sawyer and Peter H. Dickson, "Psychological Perspectives on Consumer Response to Sales Promotion," in *Research on Sales Promotion: Collected Papers,* ed. Katherine E. Jocz (Cambridge, Mass.: Marketing Science Institute, 1984).

52. William E. Myers, "Trying to Get Out of the Discounting Box," *Adweek,* November 11, 1985, p. 2.

53. Leigh McAlister, "Managing the Dynamics of Promotional Change,"

in *Looking at the Retail Kaleidoscope, Forum IX* (Stamford, Conn.: Donnelley Marketing, April 1988).

54. "Promotions Blemish Cosmetic Industry," *Advertising Age,* May 10, 1984, pp. 22–23, 26.

Chapter 18

1. Raymond Simon, *Public Relations, Concept and Practices,* 2nd ed. (Columbus, Ohio: Grid Publishing, 1980), p. 8.

2. William N. Curry, "PR Isn't Marketing," *Advertising Age,* December 18, 1991, p. 18.

3. Martha M. Lauzen, "Imperialism and Encroachment in Public Relations," *Public Relations Review,* 17, no. 3 (Fall 1991), pp. 245–55.

4. Philip Kotler and William Mindak, "Marketing and Public Relations," *Journal of Marketing* 42 (October 1978), pp. 13–20.

5. Thomas L. Harris, "How MPR Adds Value to Integrated Marketing Communications," *Public Relations Quarterly,* Summer 1993, pp. 13–18.

6. Simon, *Public Relations,* p. 164.

7. Bob Donath, "Corporate Communications," *Industrial Marketing,* July 1980, pp. 53–57.

8. Scott M. Cutlip, Allen H. Center, and Glenn M. Broom, *Effective Public Relations,* 6th ed. (Englewood Cliffs, N.J.: Prentice Hall, 1985), p. 200.

9. John E. Marston, *Modern Public Relations* (New York: McGraw-Hill, 1979).

10. Joe Agnew, "Marketers Find the Antidrug Campaign Addictive," *Marketing News,* October 9, 1987, p. 12.

11. Raymond Serafin, "Cars Squeeze Mileage from Awards," *Advertising Age,* June 4, 1990, p. 36.

12. Raymond Simon, *Public Relations, Concepts and Practices,* 3rd ed. (New York: John Wiley & Sons, 1984), p. 291.

13. Harold Mendelsohn, "Some Reasons Why Information Campaigns Can Succeed," *Public Opinion Quarterly,* Spring 1973, p. 55.

14. Walter K. Linermann, "An Effectiveness Yardstick to Measure Public Relations Success," *Public Relations Quarterly* 38, no. 1 (Spring 1993), pp. 7–10.

15. Deborah Holloway, "How to Select a Measurement System That's Right for You," *Public Relations Quarterly* 37, no. 3 (Fall 1992), pp. 15–18.

16. Serafin, "Cars Squeeze Mileage."

17. Gary Kurzbard and George J. Siomkos, "Crafting Damage Control Plans: Lessons from Perrier," *Journal of Business Strategy,* March/April 1992, pp. 39–43.

18. J. Lawrence, "New Doritos Gets the Star Treatment," *Advertising Age,* March 29, 1993, p. 64.

19. Adam Shell, "VNRS Are the Right Thing Uh huh!" *Public Relations Journal* 49, no. 8 (August 1993), p. 6.

20. Jaye S. Niefeld, "Corporate Advertising," *Industrial Marketing,* July 1980, pp. 64–74.

21. Tom Garbett, "What Companies Project to Public," *Advertising Age,* July 6, 1981, p. 51.

22. Bob Seeter, "AMA Hopes New Ads Will Cure Image Problem," *Los Angeles Times,* August 14, 1991, p. A-5.

23. John Burnett, "Shopping for Sponsorships? Integration Is Paramount," *Brandweek,* February 14, 1994, p. 18.

24. Ed Zotti, "An Expert Weighs the Prose and Yawns," *Advertising Age,* January 24, 1983, p. M-11.

25. Prakash Sethi, *Advertising and Large Corporations* (Lexington, Mass.: Lexington Books, 1977), pp. 7–8.

26. Janet Myers, "JWT Anti-Japan Ad Is a Bomb," *Advertising Age,* April 2, 1990, p. 4.

27. Niefeld, "Corporate Advertising," p. 64.

28. Donath, "Corporate Communications," p. 52.

29. Ibid., p. 53.

30. Ibid., p. 52.

Chapter 19

1. Carl G. Stevens and David P. Keane, "How to Become a Better Sales Manager: Give Salespeople How To, Not Rah Rah," *Marketing News,* May 30, 1980, p. 1.

2. Tom Wotruba and Edwin K. Simpson, *Sales Management* (Boston: Kent Publishing, 1989).

3. *Carr Reports No. 542.D* (Newton, Mass.: Cahners Publishing Co., 1992).

4. Thomas R. Wotruba, "The Evolution of Personal Selling," *Journal of Personal Selling & Sales Management* 11, no. 3 (Summer 1991), pp. 1–12.

5. Jonathan R. Copulsky and Michael J. Wolf, "Relationship Marketing: Positioning for the Future," *Journal of Business Strategy,* July/August 1990, pp. 16–20.

6. Ibid.

7. *Carr Reports No. 542.D* (Newton, Mass.: Cahners Publishing Co., 1992).

8. Thayer C. Taylor, "A Letup in the Rise of Sales Call Costs," *Sales & Marketing Management,* February 25, 1980, p. 24.

9. Theodore Levitt, "Communications and Industrial Selling," *Journal of Marketing* 31 (April 1967), pp. 15–21.

10. John E. Morrill, "Industrial Advertising Pays Off," *Harvard Business Review,* March–April 1970, p. 4.

11. "Salespeople Contact Fewer than 10 Percent of Purchase Decision–Makers over a Two-Month Period," *McGraw-Hill LAP Report no. 1029.3* (New York: McGraw-Hill, 1987).

12. Peggy Moretti, "Telemarketers Serve Clients," *Business Marketing,* April 1994, pp. 27–29.

13. Ibid.

14. Rolph E. Anderson, Joseph F. Hair, and Alan J. Bush, *Professional Sales Management* (New York: McGraw-Hill, 1988).

Chapter 20

1. Bruce Horowitz, "TV Ads that Public Will Never See," *Los Angeles Times,* August 3, 1988, p. 1.

2. *McGraw-Hill Lap Report, no. 3151* (New York: McGraw-Hill, 1988); and Alan D. Fletcher, *Target Marketing through the Yellow Pages* (Troy, Mich.: Yellow Pages Publishers Association, 1991), p. 23.

3. Personal interview with Jay Khoulos, president of World Communications, Inc., 1988.

4. David A. Aaker and John G. Myers, *Advertising Management,* 3rd ed. (Englewood Cliffs, N.J.: Prentice Hall, 1987), p. 474.

5. Joel N. Axelrod, "Induced Moods and Attitudes toward Products," *Journal of Advertising Research* 3 (June 1963), pp. 19–24; and Lauren E. Crane, "How Product, Appeal, and Program Affect Attitudes toward Commercials," *Journal of Advertising Research* 4 (March 1964), p. 15.

6. Robert Settle, "Marketing in Tight Times," *Marketing Communications* 13, no. 1 (January 1988), pp. 19–23.

7. "What Is Good Creative?" *Topline, No. 41* (New York: McCollum Spielman Worldwide, 1994), p. 4.

8. "21 Ad Agencies Endorse Copy-Testing Principles," *Marketing News* 15, no. 17 (February 19, 1982), p. 1.

9. Ibid.

10. John M. Caffyn, "Telepex Testing of TV Commercials," *Journal of Advertising Research* 5, no. 2 (June 1965), pp. 29–37; Thomas J. Reynolds and Charles Gengler, "A Strategic Framework for Assessing Advertising: The Animatic vs. Finished Issue," *Journal of Advertising Research,* October–November 1991, pp. 61–71; and Nigel A. Brown and Ronald Gatty, "Rough vs. Finished TV Commercials in Telepex Tests," *Journal of Advertising Research* 7, no. 4 (December 1967), p. 21.

11. Charles H. Sandage, Vernon Fryburger, and Kim Rotzoll, *Advertising Theory and Practice,* 10th ed. (Burr Ridge, Ill.: Richard D. Irwin, 1979).

12. Lymund E. Ostlund, "Advertising Copy Testing: A Review of Current Practices, Problems and Prospects," *Current Issues and Research in Advertising,* 1978, pp. 87–105.

13. Jack B. Haskins, "Factual Recall as a Measure of Advertising Effectiveness," *Journal of Advertising Research* 4, no. 1 (March 1964), pp. 2–7.

14. Paul J. Watson and Robert J. Gatchel, "Autonomic Measures of Advertising," *Journal of Advertising Research* 19 (June 1979), pp. 15–26.

15. Flemming Hansen, "Hemispheric Lateralization: Implications for Understanding Consumer Behavior," *Journal of Consumer Research* 8 (1988), pp. 23–36.

16. Hubert A. Zielske, "Does Day-After Recall Penalize 'Feeling Ads'?" *Journal of Advertising Research* 22, no. 1 (1982), pp. 19–22.

17. Terry Haller, "Day-After Recall to Persist Despite JWT Study; Other Criteria Looming," *Marketing News,* May 18, 1979, p. 4.

18. Dave Kruegel, "Television Advertising Effectiveness and Research Innovations," *Journal of Consumer Marketing* 5, no. 3 (Summer 1988), pp. 43–52.

19. Gary Levin, "Tracing Ads' Impact," *Advertising Age,* November 12, 1990, p. 49.

20. Jeffrey L. Seglin, "The New Era of Ad Measurement," *Adweek's Marketing Week,* January 23, 1988, p. 24.

21. James F. Donius, "Marketing Tracking: A Strategic Reassessment and Planning Tool," *Journal of Advertising Research* 25, no. 1 (February–March 1985), pp. 15–19.

22. Russell I. Haley and Allan L. Baldinger, "The ARF Copy Research Validity Project," *Journal of Advertising Research,* April-May 1991, pp. 11–32.

23. Glenn Heitsmith, "Something for Nothing," *Promo Magazine,* September 1993, pp. 30, 31, 93.

24. Ibid.

25. "Journeying Deeper into the Minds of Shoppers," *Business Week,* February 4, 1991, p. 85.

26. David W. Schumann, Jennifer Grayson, Johanna Ault, Kerri Hargrove, Lois Hollingsworth, Russell Ruelle, and Sharon Seguin, "The Effectiveness of Shopping Cart Signage: Perceptual Measures Tell a Different Story," *Journal of Advertising Research,* February–March 1991, pp. 17–22.

27. June Bryan Kim, "Research Makes Ski Run Easier," *Advertising Age,* August 18, 1991, p. 30.

28. Scott Hume, "Sports Sponsorship Value Measured," *Advertising Age,* August 6, 1990, p. 22.

Chapter 21

1. Business Marketing Association, 1994.

2. Yolanda Brugaletta, "What Business-to-Business Advertisers Can Learn from Consumer Advertisers," *Journal of Advertising Research* 25, no. 3 (June–July 1985), pp. 8–9.

3. Anderson & Lembke, Inc., Stamford, Conn., 1985 sales promotion literature.

4. Tom Eisenhart, "How to Really Excite Your Prospects," *Business Marketing,* July 1988, pp. 44–55.

5. Business Marketing Association, 1994.

6. *Carr Reports* (Newton, Mass.: Cahners Publishing Co., 1991).

7. Tom Eisenhart, "What's Right, What's Wrong with Each Medium," *Business Marketing,* April 1990, pp. 40–47.

8. National Telemarketing Association, 1992.

9. David Atkins, "Reeling in the Prospects," *Business Marketing,* February 2, 1994, pp. 27–31.

10. Trade Show Bureau, 1992.

11. Business Marketing Association, 1994.

12. 1986 Starmark Report, *Business Marketing,* p. 17.

Chapter 22

1. Bill Saporito, "Where the Global Action Is," *Fortune,* Special Issue, Autumn/Spring 1993, pp. 63–65.

2. "Anheuser-Busch Says Skoal, Salud, Prosit," *Business Week,* November 20, 1993, pp. 76–77.

3. Christopher Knowlton, "Europe Cooks Up a Cereal Brawl," *Fortune,* June 3, 1991, pp. 175–78.

4. "They're All Screaming for Haagen-Dazs," *Business Week,* October 14, 1991, p. 121.

5. *Insiders' Report, Robert Cohen Presentation on Advertising Expenditures* (New York: McCann-Erickson Worldwide, June 1993), p. 8.

6. Vern Terpstra, *International Marketing,* 4th ed. (New York: Holt, Rinehart & Winston–Dryden Press, 1987), p. 427.

7. "We Are the World," *Adweek's Superbrands 1990,* pp. 61–68.

8. Carla Rapoport, "Nestlè's Brand Building Machine," *Fortune,* September 19, 1994, pp. 147–56.

9. "World of Change," *Adweek's Superbrands 1991,* pp. 34–41.

10. For an excellent discussion of various elements of Japanese culture such as language and its implications for promotion, see John F. Sherry, Jr., and Eduardo G. Camargo, "May Your Life Be Marvelous: English Language Labelling and the Semiotics of Japanese Promotion," *Journal of Consumer Research* 14 (September 1987), pp. 174–88.

11. Barbara Mueller, "Reflections on Culture: An Analysis of Japanese and American Advertising Appeals," *Journal of Advertising Research,* June–July 1987, pp. 51–59.

12. Barbara Mueller, "Standardization vs. Specialization: An Examination of Westernization in Japanese Advertising," *Journal of Advertising Research,* January–February 1992, pp. 15–24; and Johny K. Johanson, "The Sense of "Nonsense: Japanese TV Advertising," *Journal of Advertising,* 23, no. 1 (March 1994) pp. 17–26.

13. Marian Katz, "No Women, No Alcohol; Learn Saudi Taboos before Placing Ads," *International Advertiser,* February 1986, pp. 11–12.

14. Dean M. Peebles and John K. Ryans, *Management of International Advertising* (Newton, Mass: Allyn & Bacon, 1984).

15. Geoffrey Lee Martin, "Tobacco Sponsors Fear Aussie TKO," *Advertising Age,* April 27, 1992, p. I–8.

16. Laurel Wentz, "Local Laws Keep International Marketers Hopping," *Advertising Age,* July 11, 1985, p. 20.

17. David Bartel and Laurel Wentz, "Danes Phase in TV Spots," *Advertising Age,* November 23, 1987, p. 65.

18. Katz, "No Women, No Alcohol; Learn Saudi Taboos."

19. Derek Turner, "Coke Pops Brazilian Comparative Ad," *Advertising Age,* September 9, 1991, p. 24.

20. J. Craig Andrews, Steven Lysonski, and Srinivas Durvasula, "Understanding Cross-Cultural Student Perceptions of Advertising in General: Implications for Advertising Educators and Practitioners," *Journal of Advertising* 20, no. 2 (June 1991), pp. 15–28.

21. J. J. Boddewyn and Iris Mohr, "International Advertisers Face Government Hurdles," *Marketing News,* May 8, 1987, pp. 21–22.

22. Ron Alsop, "Countries' Different Ad Rules Are Problem for Global Firms," *The Wall Street Journal,* September 17, 1984, p. 33.

23. Amy Haight, "EC Ad Ban May Go Up in Smoke," *Advertising Age*

International, January 17, 1994, p.
I–8.

24. Robert D. Buzzell, "Can You Standardize Multinational Marketing?" *Harvard Business Review,* November–December 1968, pp. 102–13; and Ralph Z. Sorenson and Ulrich E. Wiechmann, "How Multinationals View Marketing," *Harvard Business Review,* May–June 1975, p. 38.

25. Theodore Levitt, "The Globalization of Markets," *Harvard Business Review,* May–June 1983, pp. 92–102; and Theodore Levitt, *The Marketing Imagination* (New York: Free Press, 1986).

26. Anne B. Fisher, "The Ad Biz Gloms onto Global," *Fortune,* November 12, 1984, p. 78.

27. Keith Reinhard and W. E. Phillips, "Global Marketing: Experts Look at Both Sides," *Advertising Age,* April 15, 1988, p. 47; and Anthony Rutigliano, "The Debate Goes On: Global vs. Local Advertising," *Management Review,* June 1986, pp. 27–31.

28. Kevin Goldman, "Professor Who Started Debate on Global Ads Still Backs Theory," *The Wall Street Journal,* October 13, 1992, p. B8.

29. Example from speech by Eugene H. Kummel, chairman emeritus, McCann-Erickson Worldwide, and Koji Oshita, president and CEO, McCann-Erickson, Hakuhodo, Japan, in San Diego, California, October 19, 1988.

30. Joanne Lipman, "Marketers Turn Sour on Global Sales Pitch," *The Wall Street Journal,* May 12, 1988, p. 1.

31. Joseph M. Winski and Laurel Wentz, "Parker Pens: What Went Wrong?" *Advertising Age,* June 2, 1986, p. 1.

32. Laurie Freeman, "Colgate Axes Global Ads, Thinks Local," *Advertising Age,* November 26, 1990, pp. 1, 59.

33. Lipman, "Marketers Turn Sour."

34. Criteria cited by Edward Meyer, CEO, Grey Advertising, in Rebecca Fannin, "What Agencies Really Think of Global Theory," *Marketing & Media Decisions,* December 1984, p. 74.

35. Quote cited in Reinhard and Phillips, "Global Marketing," p. 47.

36. Salah S. Hassan and Lea P. Katsansas, "Identification of Global Consumer Segments: A Behavioral Framework," *Journal of International Consumer Marketing* 3, no. 2, pp. 11–28.

37. Goldman, "Professor Who Started Debate."

38. Fannin, "What Agencies Really Think," p. 75.

39. Gary Levin, "Ads Going Global," *Advertising Age,* July 22, 1991, pp. 4, 42.

40. Robert E. Hite and Cynthia L. Fraser, "International Advertising Strategies of Multinational Corporations," *Journal of Advertising Research,* August–September 1988, pp. 9–17.

41. Ali Kanso, "International Advertising Strategies: Global Commitment to Local Vision," *Journal of Advertising Research,* January–February 1992, pp. 10–14.

42. Sherri Shamoon, "Centralized International Advertising," *International Advertiser,* September 1986, pp. 35–36.

43. Penelope Rowlands, "Global Approach Doesn't Always Make Scents," *Advertising Age International,* January 17, 1994, pp. I–1, 38.

44. Bradley Johnson, "Tumult Ahead for IBM, Ogilvy," *Advertising Age,* May 30, 1994, pp. 36–37.

45. Terpstra, *International Marketing;* and Peebles and Ryans, *Management of International Advertising.*

46. Doris Walsh, "Demographics for Advertisers," *International Advertiser,* June 1986, p. 47.

47. John D. Furniss, "Germany Leads the Way in Special Audience Research," *International Advertiser,* October 1985, p. 30.

48. Nancy Giges, "Europeans Buy Outside Goods, but Like Local Ads," *Advertising Age International,* April 27, 1992, pp. I–1, 26.

49. Joseph T. Plummer, "The Role of Copy Research in Multinational Advertising," *Journal of Advertising Research,* October–November 1986, p. 15.

50. Yumiko Ono, "Tropicana Is Trying to Cultivate a Global Taste for Orange Juice," *The Wall Street Journal,* March 28, 1994, p. B2.

51. Ron Alsop, "Efficacy of Global Ad Projects Is Questioned in Firm's Survey," *The Wall Street Journal,* September 13, 1984, p. 31.

52. Fannin, "What Agencies Really Think."

53. "They're All Screaming for Haagen-Dazs."

54. Sheila Tefft, "India Advertising Flourishes," *Advertising Age,* December 7, 1987, p. 52.

55. James H. Rosenfield, "The Explosion of Worldwide Media," *Marketing Communications,* September 1987, p. 65.

56. Laurel Wentz, "All Eyes on Europe TV Time," *Advertising Age,* May 23, 1988, p. 71.

57. Elena Bowes, "British Sky TV Picks Up Pace," *Advertising Age International,* April 27, 1992, p. I–18.

58. Thomas McCarroll, "New Star Over Asia," *Time,* August 9, 1993, p. 53.

59. Alison Fahey, "Pepsi's Concerts vs. Coke's Games," *Advertising Age,* February 10, 1992, p. 47.

60. Kamran Kashani and John A. Quelch, "Can Sales Promotion Go Global?" *Business Horizons,* May–June 1990, pp. 37–43.

61. "What You Should Know about Advertising in Japan," *Advertising World,* April 1985, pp. 18, 42.

62. Kashani and Quelch, "Can Sales Promotion Go Global?"

63. "Foreign Ads Go Further with PR," *International Advertiser,* December 1986, p. 30.

64. Anne Roman, "Ohio Firm Breaks International Ice," *Public Relations Journal* 47, no. 5 (May 1991), pp. 40–42.

Chapter 23

1. Steven W. Colford, "Nicotine fit," *Advertising Age,* June 27, 1994, pp. 1, 8.

2. Alex M. Freedman, "Koop Urges Alcoholic-Beverage Curbs, Including Ad Restrictions and Tax Rise," *The Wall Street Journal,* June 1, 1989, p. B6.

3. Priscilla A. LaBarbera, "Analyzing and Advancing the State of the Art of Advertising Self-Regulation," *Journal of Advertising* 9, no. 4 (1980), p. 30.

4. John F. Archer, "Advertising of Professional Fees: Does the Consumer Have a Right to Know?" *South*

Dakota Law Review 21 (Spring 1976), p. 330.

5. *Bates v. State of Arizona,* 97 S.Ct. 2691. 45, *U.S. Law Week 4895* (1977).

6. Charles Laughlin, "Ads on Trial," *Link,* May 1994, pp. 18–22; and "Lawyers Learn the Hard Sell— And Companies Shudder," *Business Week,* June 10, 1985, p. 70.

7. Bruce H. Allen, Richard A. Wright, and Louis E. Raho, "Physicians and Advertising," *Journal of Health Care Marketing* 5 (Fall 1985), pp. 39–49.

8. Robert E. Hite and Cynthia Fraser, "Meta-Analyses of Attitudes toward Advertising by Professionals," *Journal of Marketing* 52, no. 3 (July 1988), pp. 95–105.

9. "NAD Slaps Kellogg over Special K Ads," *Advertising Age,* March 21, 1988, p. 70 and; *NAD Case Reports* 23, no. 4 (June 1993), p. 27.

10. Gary M. Armstrong and Julie L. Ozanne, "An Evaluation of NAD/NARB Purpose and Performance," *Journal of Advertising* 12, no. 3 (1983), pp. 15–26.

11. *NAD Case Reports: Analysis of 1993 Closings* (National Advertising Division Council of Better Business Bureaus, Inc.) 24, no. 10 (January 1994), p. 105.

12. *NAD Case Reports* 23, no. 4 (June 1993), p. 23.

13. Dorothy Cohen, "The FTC's Advertising Substantiation Program," *Journal of Marketing* 44, no. 1 (Winter 1980), pp. 26–35.

14. Lynda M. Maddox and Eric J. Zanot, "The Suspension of the National Association of Broadcasters' Code and Its Effects on the Regulation of Advertising," *Journalism Quarterly* 61 (Summer 1984), pp. 125–30, 156.

15. Joe Mandese, "ABC Loosens Rules," *Advertising Age,* September 9, 1991, pp. 2, 8.

16. Eric Zanot, "Unseen but Effective Advertising Regulation: The Clearance Process," *Journal of Advertising* 14, no. 4 (1985), p. 48.

17. Mandese, "ABC Loosens Rules."

18. Azuenga quote cited in: *Advertising Topics,* Supplement 533, March/April 1994, p. 3. Council of Better Business Bureaus, Inc. Arlington, Va.

19. Steven W. Colford, "Speed Up the NAD, Industry Unit Told," *Advertising Age,* May 1, 1989, p. 3.

20. *FTC v. Raladam Co.,* 258, U.S. 643 (1931).

21. Edward Cox, R. Fellmeth, and J. Schultz, *The Consumer and the Federal Trade Commission* (Washington, D.C.: American Bar Association, 1969); and American Bar Association, *Report of the American Bar Association to Study the Federal Trade Commission* (Washington, D.C.: The Association, 1969).

22. FTC Staff Report on Advertising to Children (Washington, D.C.: Government Printing Office, 1978).

23. Federal Trade Commission Improvements Act of 1980, P.L. No. 96-252, 94 Stat. 374 (May 28, 1980).

24. Bruce Silverglade, "Does FTC Have an 'Unfair' Future?" *Advertising Age,* March 26, 1994, p. 20.

25. Ivan L. Preston, *The Great American Blow-Up: Puffery in Advertising and Selling* (Madison: University of Wisconsin Press, 1975), p. 3.

26. Isabella C. M. Cunningham and William H. Cunningham, "Standards for Advertising Regulation," *Journal of Marketing* 41 (October 1977), pp. 91–97; and Herbert J. Rotfeld and Kim B. Rotzell, "Is Advertising Puffery Believed?" *Journal of Advertising* 9, no. 3 (1980), pp. 16–20.

27. Herbert J. Rotfeld and Kim B. Rotzell, "Puffery vs. Fact Claims— Really Different?" in *Current Issues and Research in Advertising,* ed. James H. Leigh and Claude R. Martin, Jr. (Ann Arbor: University of Michigan, 1981), pp. 85–104.

28. Preston, *The Great American Blow-Up.*

29. Federal Trade Commission, "Policy Statement on Deception," 45 ATRR 689 (October 27, 1983), at p. 690.

30. Gary T. Ford and John E. Calfee, "Recent Developments in FTC Policy on Deception," *Journal of Marketing* 50, no. 3 (July 1986), pp. 86–87.

31. Ray O. Werner, ed. "Legal Developments in Marketing," *Journal of Marketing* 56 (January 1992), p. 102.

32. Cohen, "The FTC's Advertising Substantiation Program."

33. *Trade Regulation Reporter,* Par. 20,056 at 22,033, *1970–1973 Transfer Binder,* Federal Trade Commission, July 1972.

34. Michael Parrish, "Unocal, FTC Settle over Premium Gas Claims," *Los Angeles Times,* December 31, 1993, p. D1.

35. William L. Wilkie, Dennis L. McNeill, and Michael B. Mazis, "Marketing's 'Scarlet Letter': The Theory and Practice of Corrective Advertising," *Journal of Marketing* 48 (Spring 1984), pp. 11–31.

36. "Deceptive Ads: The FTC's Laissez-Faire Approach Is Backfiring," *Business Week,* December 2, 1985, p. 136.

37. Joanne Lipman, "FTC Puts Advertisers on Notice of Crackdown on Misleading Ads," *The Wall Street Journal,* February 4, 1991, p. B6.

38. Ibid.

39. Steven W. Colford, "$12 Million Bite," *Advertising Age,* December 2, 1991, p. 4.

40. Jan Joben, "A Setback for Competitive Ads?" *Business Marketing,* October 1992, p. 34.

41. Bruce Buchanan and Doron Goldman, "Us vs. Them: The Minefield of Comparative Ads," *Harvard Business Review,* May–June 1989, pp. 38–50.

42. "Deceptive Ads: The FTC's Laissez-Faire Approach."

43. Jennifer Lawrence, "State Ad Rules Face Showdown," *Advertising Age,* November 28, 1988, p. 4.

44. "Ally in Plax Settlement," *The Wall Street Journal,* February 12, 1991, p. B4.

45. Steven Colford, "ABA Panel Backs FTC over States," *Advertising Age,* April 10, 1994, p.1.

46. S. J. Diamond, "New Director Putting Vigor Back into FTC," *Los Angeles Times,* March 29, 1991, pp. D1, 4.

47. Federal Trade Commission, "Trade Regulation Rule: Games of Chance in the Food Retailing and Gasoline Industries," 16 CFR, Part 419 (1982).

48. Steven W. Colford, "Top Kid TV Offender: Premiums," *Advertising Age,* April 29, 1991, p. 52.

49. Federal Trade Commission, "Guides for Advertising Allowances and Other Merchandising Payments and Services," 16 CFR, Part 240 (1983).
50. Federal Trade Commission, "Trade Regulation Rule: Use of Negative Option Plans by Sellers in Commerce," 16 CFR, Part 42 (1982).
51. For a more thorough discussion of legal aspects of sales promotion and mail-order practices, see Louis W. Stern and Thomas L. Eovaldi, *Legal Aspects of Marketing Strategy* (Englewood Cliffs, N.J.: Prentice Hall, 1984).
52. Mary Lu Carnevale, "FTC Adopts Rules to Curb Telemarketing," *The Wall Street Journal*, September 18, 1992, pp. B1, 10.

Chapter 24

1. Robert L. Heilbroner, "Demand for the Supply Side," *New York Review of Books* 38 (June 11, 1981), p. 40.
2. Eric N. Berkowitz et al., *Marketing*, 2nd ed. (Burr Ridge, Ill.: Richard D. Irwin, 1992), p. 90.
3. Willam J. Eaton, "College Binge Drinking Soars, Study Finds," *Los Angeles Times*, June 8, 1994, p. A21.
4. J. Edward Russo, Barbara L. Metcalf, and Debra Stephens, "Identifying Misleading Advertising," *Journal of Consumer Research* 8 (September 1981), pp. 119–31.
5. Shelby D. Hunt, "Informational vs. Persuasive Advertising: An Appraisal," *Journal of Advertising*, Summer 1976, pp. 5–8.
6. Study cited in Ron Alsop, "Advertisers Find the Climate Less Hostile Outside the U.S.," *The Wall Street Journal*, December 10, 1987, p. 29.
7. Helen Cooper, "CDC Advocates Use of Condoms in Blunt AIDS-Prevention Spots," *The Wall Street Journal*, January 5, 1994, p. B1.
8. David A. Aaker and Donald E. Bruzzone, "Causes of Irritation in Advertising," *Journal of Marketing* 5 (Spring 1985), pp. 47–57.
9. Stephen A. Greyser, "Irritation in Advertising," *Journal of Advertising Research* 13 (February 1973), pp. 3–10.
10. Ron Alsop, "Personal Product Ads Abound as Public Gets More Tolerant," *The Wall Street Journal*, April 14, 1986, p. 19.
11. Joanne Lipman, "Censored Scenes: Why You Rarely See Some Things in Television Ads," *The Wall Street Journal*, August 17, 1987, p. 17.
12. Bruce Horowitz, "Taking Aim at the Bad Ads," *Los Angeles Times*, January 28, 1994, pp. D1, 4.
13. John P. Cortez and Ira Tenowitz, "More Trouble Brews for Stroh Bikini Team," *Advertising Age*, December 9, 1991, p. 45.
14. Ira Tenowitz, "Days of 'Beer and Babes' Running Out," *Advertising Age*, October 4, 1993, p. S-5.
15. Rita Weisskoff, "Current Trends in Children's Advertising," *Journal of Advertising Research* 25, no. 1 (1985), pp. RC 12–14.
16. Scott Ward, Daniel B. Wackman, and Ellen Wartella, *How Children Learn to Buy: The Development of Consumer Information Processing Skills* (Beverly Hills, Calif.: Sage, 1979).
17. Thomas S. Robertson and John R. Rossiter, "Children and Commercial Persuasion: An Attribution Theory Analysis," *Journal of Consumer Research* 1, no. 1 (June 1974), pp. 13–20; and Scott Ward and Daniel B. Wackman, "Children's Information Processing of Television Advertising," in *New Models for Communications Research*, ed. G. Kline and P. Clark (Beverly Hills, Calif.: Sage, 1974), pp. 81–119.
18. Merrie Brucks, Gary M. Armstrong, and Marvin E. Goldberg, "Children's Use of Cognitive Defenses against Television Advertising: A Cognitive Response Approach," *Journal of Consumer Research* 14, no. 4 (March 1988), pp. 471–82.
19. For a discussion on consumer socialization, see Scott Ward, "Consumer Socialization," *Journal of Consumer Research* 1, no. 2 (September 1974), pp. 1–14.
20. *FTC Staff Report on Advertising to Children* (Washington, D.C.: Government Printing Office, 1978).
21. Ben M. Enis, Dale R. Spencer, and Don R. Webb, "Television Advertising and Children: Regulatory vs. Competitive Perspectives," *Journal of Advertising* 9, no. 1 (1980), pp. 19–25.
22. Richard Zoglin, "Ms. Kidvid Calls It Quits," *Time*, January 20, 1992, p. 52.
23. Ronald Alsop, "Watchdogs Zealously Censor Advertising Targeted to Kids," *The Wall Street Journal*, September 5, 1985, p. 35.
24. Robert E. Hite and Randy Eck, "Advertising to Children: Attitudes of Business vs. Consumers," *Journal of Advertising Research*, October–November 1987, pp. 40–53.
25. Ronald Berman, *Advertising and Social Change* (Beverly Hills, Calif.: Sage, 1981), p. 13.
26. John K. Galbraith, *The New Industrial State* (Boston: Houghton Mifflin, 1967), cited in Richard W. Pollay, "The Distorted Mirror: Reflections on the Unintended Consequences of Advertising," *Journal of Marketing*, August 1986, p. 25.
27. Raymond A. Bauer and Stephen A. Greyser, "The Dialogue that Never Happens," *Harvard Business Review*, January–February 1969, pp. 122–28.
28. Morris B. Holbrook, "Mirror Mirror on the Wall, What's Unfair in the Reflections on Advertising," *Journal of Marketing* 5 (July 1987), pp. 95–103; and Theodore Levitt, "The Morality of Advertising," *Harvard Business Review*, July–August 1970, pp. 84–92.
29. Stephen Fox, *The Mirror Makers: A History of American Advertising and Its Creators* (New York: Morrow, 1984), p. 330.
30. Richard W. Pollay, "The Distorted Mirror: Reflections on the Unintended Consequences of Advertising," *Journal of Marketing* 50 (April 1986), p. 33.
31. Jules Backman, "Is Advertising Wasteful?" *Journal of Marketing* 32 (January 1968), pp. 2–8.
32. Hunt, "Informational vs. Persuasive Advertising."
33. Ibid., p. 6.
34. Kevin Goldman, "Survey Asks Which 'Green' Ads Are Read," *The Wall Street Journal*, April 11, 1994, p. B5.
35. Alice E. Courtney and Thomas W. Whipple, "Sex Stereotyping in America: An Annotated Bibliography," *Marketing Science Institute, Report no. 80–100*, February 1980, p. v.

36. Cyndee Miller, "Liberation for Women in Ads," *Marketing News*, August 17, 1992, p. 1; Adrienne Ward-Fawcett, "Narrowcast in Past, Women Earn Revised Role in Advertising," *Advertising Age,* October 4, 1993, p. S-1.

37. Miller, "Liberation for Women in Ads."

38. Helen Czepic and J. Steven Kelly, "Analyzing Hispanic Roles in Advertising," in *Current Issues and Research in Advertising,* ed. James H. Leigh and Claude Martin (Ann Arbor: University of Michigan, 1983), pp. 219–40; R. F. Busch, Allan S. Resnik, and Bruce L. Stern, "A Content Analysis of the Portrayal of Black Models in Magazine Advertising," in *American Marketing Association Proceedings: Marketing in the 1980s,* ed. Richard P. Bagozzi (Chicago: American Marketing Association, 1980); and R. F. Busch, Allan S. Resnik, and Bruce L. Stern, "There Are More Blacks in TV Commercials," *Journal of Advertising Research* 17 (1977), pp. 21–25.

39. James Stearns, Lynette S. Unger, and Steven G. Luebkeman, "The Portrayal of Blacks in Magazine and Television Advertising," in *AMA Educator's Proceedings,* ed. Susan P. Douglas and Michael R. Solomon (Chicago: American Marketing Association, 1987).

40. Robert E. Wilkes and Humberto Valencia, "Hispanics and Blacks in Television Commercials," *Journal of Advertising* 18, no. 1 (1989), pp. 19–26.

41. Thomas H. Stevenson, "How Are Blacks Portrayed in Business Ads?" *Industrial Marketing Management* 20 (1991), pp. 193–99.

42. Leon E. Wynter, "Minorities Play the Hero in More TV Ads as Clients Discover Multicultural Sells," *The Wall Street Journal,* December 24, 1993, pp. B1, 6.

43. Ibid.

44. Kevin Goldman, "Seniors Get Little Respect on Madison Avenue," *The Wall Street Journal,* September 20, 1993, p. B8.

45. Laura Bird, "Critics Cry Foul at Nike Spots with Actor," *The Wall Street Journal,* December 16, 1993, p. B8.

46. Jon Berry, "Think Bland," *Adweek's Marketing Week,* November 11, 1991, pp. 22–24.

47. Janet Guyon, "Do Publications Avoid Anti-Cigarette Stories to Protect Ad Dollars?" *The Wall Street Journal,* November 22, 1982, pp. 1, 20; Elizabeth M. Whelan, "When *Newsweek* and *Time* Filtered Cigarette Copy," *The Wall Street Journal,* November 1, 1984, p. 3; and "RJR Swears Off Saatchi and Nabisco Is in a Sweat," *Business Week,* April 18, 1988, p. 36.

48. For a discussion of monopolies in the cereal industry, see Paul N. Bloom, "The Cereal Industry: Monopolists or Super Marketers?" *MSU Business Topics,* Summer 1978, pp. 41–49.

49. Lester G. Telser, "Advertising and Competition," *Journal of Political Economy,* December 1964, pp. 537–62.

50. Robert D. Buzzell, Bradley T. Gale, and Ralph G. M. Sultan, "Market Share—A Key to Profitability," *Harvard Business Review,* January–February 1975, pp. 97–106.

51. Robert D. Buzzell and Paul W. Farris, "Advertising Cost in Consumer Goods Industries," *Marketing Science Institute, Report No. 76,* p. 111, August 1976; and Paul W. Farris and David J. Reibstein, "How Prices, Ad Expenditures, and Profits Are Linked," *Harvard Business Review,* November–December 1979, pp. 173–84.

52. Paul W. Farris and Mark S. Albion, "The Impact of Advertising on the Price of Consumer Products," *Journal of Marketing* 44, no. 3 (Summer 1980), pp. 17–35.

53. Ibid., p. 19.

54. Lee Benham, "The Effect of Advertising on the Price of Eyeglasses," *Journal of Law and Economics* 15 (October 1972), pp. 337–52.

55. Robert L. Steiner, "Does Advertising Lower Consumer Price?" *Journal of Marketing* 37, no. 4 (October 1973), pp. 19–26.

56. Farris and Albion, "The Impact of Advertising," p. 30.

57. James M. Ferguson, "Comments on 'The Impact of Advertising on the Price of Consumer Products'," *Journal of Marketing* 46, no. 1 (Winter 1982), pp. 102–5.

58. Farris and Albion, "The Impact of Advertising."

Credits and Acknowledgments

Chapter 1

Opening photo   Permission granted courtesy Kellogg Company and NBC TV Network.

Global Perspective 1–1   Courtesy Whirlpool Corporation.

Exhibit 1–1   Courtesy Handgun Control, Inc.

Exhibit 1–2   Courtesy L'Oreal.

IMC Perspective 1–1   Courtesy Apple Computer, Inc.

Exhibit 1–4   Reprinted by permission of Philip Morris, Inc.

Exhibit 1–5   Courtesy California Raisin Advisory Board.

IMC Perspective 1–2   Courtesy Eveready Battery Company, Inc.

Exhibit 1–6   Courtesy Dell Computer Corporation.

Exhibit 1–7   Courtesy Johnson & Johnson.

Exhibit 1–8   Reprinted with permission of State Farm Insurance Companies.

Exhibit 1–9   Courtesy Hoechst Celanese Corporation.

Exhibit 1–11   Used by permission of Adolph Coors Company.

Exhibit 1–14   Courtesy Zoological Society of San Diego.

Chapter 2

Opening photo   Courtesy Major League Baseball Properties.

Exhibit 2–2   Courtesy Road Runner Sports.

Exhibit 2–3   Courtesy Michelin Tire Corporation.

Global Perspective 2–1   Reproduced with permission of PepsiCo, Inc. 1994, Purchase, New York.

Exhibit 2–4   Courtesy Guess?, Inc.

Exhibit 2–5   Courtesy of Anheuser-Busch Companies.

IMC Perspective 2–1   Courtesy The Gillette Company; Barbie® is a trademark of Mattel, Inc. Used with permission.

Exhibit 2–7   Courtesy The Procter & Gamble Company.

Exhibit 2–9   Advertisement used by permission from Godiva Chocolatier, Inc.

Exhibit 2–10   Courtesy Mendelsohn/Zien Advertising, Los Angeles, for Yonex Corporation.

Exhibit 2–11   Courtesy Ames Lawn & Garden Tools, Parkersburg, West Virginia.

Exhibit 2–12   Courtesy Sheaffer Pen.

Exhibit 2–14   Courtesy Target Stores.

Exhibit 2–15   Courtesy The Broadway.

Exhibit 2–16   Advertisement used by permission from Campbell Soup Company.

Exhibit 2–17   Courtesy National Pork Producers Council.

Ethical Perspective 2–1   Courtesy Fur Information Council of America.

Exhibit 2–18   Courtesy Xerox Corporation.

Exhibit 2–19   Courtesy VICOM FCB.

Exhibit 2–21   Courtesy Choice Hotels International.

Exhibit 2–22   Courtesy Charron, Schwartz & Partners, Inc. for Working Woman Magazine.

Exhibit 2–24   Reproduced with permission of PepsiCo, Inc. 1994, Purchase, New York.

Chapter 3

Opening photo   Courtesy The Coca-Cola Company. "Coca-Cola" and the Dynamic Ribbon device are registered trademarks of The Coca-Cola Company.

Exhibit 3–2   Courtesy *L'actualité/Maclean's*.

Exhibit 3–6   Courtesy The Procter & Gamble Company.

Exhibit 3–7   Courtesy Benetton Cosmetics Corporation. Photo by Toscani.

IMC Perspective 3–1   Courtesy MasterCard International.

Exhibit 3–12   Courtesy CKS Partners.

Exhibit 3–13   Courtesy Western International Media Corporation.

Exhibit 3–15   Courtesy Calet, Hirsch & Ferrell, Inc.

Tumbleweeds   Reprinted with special permission of NAS, Inc.

Exhibit 3–18   Courtesy J. Walter Thompson.

Global Perspective 3–1   Courtesy PNMD/Publitel.

Exhibit 3–20   Courtesy Ryan Partnership.

IMC Perspective 3–2   Courtesy Leo Burnett USA for United Airlines.

Chapter 4

Opening photos   Courtesy BMW of North America, Inc. and Martha Stewart Living.

Exhibit 4–1   Courtesy Jeep/Eagle Division, Chrysler Corporation.

Exhibit 4–3   Courtesy Oral-B Laboratories.

Exhibit 4–4   Courtesy Panasonic.

Global Perspective 4–1   Courtesy Nike, Inc.

Exhibit 4–6   Courtesy Baker Spielvogel Bates, Inc. for Campbell Soup Company.

Exhibit 4–7   Courtesy Volvo Cars of North America, Inc.

Exhibit 4–9   Courtesy Guess?, Inc.

Exhibit 4–10   © American Association of Advertising Agencies.

Exhibit 4–12   Courtesy Swarovski Jewelry U.S. Ltd. - SAVVY Brand.

Exhibit 4–13   Courtesy Hyundai Motor America.

Ethical Perspective 4–1   © American Association of Advertising Agencies.

Exhibit 4–14   Courtesy Spalding & Evenflo Companies, Inc.

Exhibit 4–15   Courtesy of International Business Machines Corporation.

Exhibit 4–16   Courtesy Geze Sport Products Inc. - Michael Furman, photographer; Richard Parker, art director; Michael Erickson, copywriter.

Exhibit 4–17   Courtesy of Anheuser-Busch Companies.

Exhibit 4–19   Courtesy Ford Motor Company.

Exhibit 4–20   Courtesy Epson America, Inc.

Exhibit 4–22   Reproduced with permission of PepsiCo, Inc. 1994, Purchase, New York.

Exhibit 4–24   Reprinted with permission of the James River Corporation.

IMC Perspective 4–1   Courtesy TYCO TOYS, Inc.

Exhibit 4–28   Courtesy North American Watch Company.

Exhibit 4–29A   Courtesy Miller Brewing Company.

Exhibit 4–29B   Courtesy The Advertising Council, Inc.

Chapter 5

Opening photo   Reproduced with permission of PepsiCo, Inc. 1994, Purchase, New York.
Exhibit 5–2   Courtesy of Anheuser-Busch Companies.
Exhibit 5–5   Courtesy Road Runner Sports.
Exhibit 5–6   Courtesy Skis Dynastar.
Exhibit 5–8   Courtesy Den-Mat Corporation.
Exhibit 5–9   Courtesy Equifax Marketing Decision Systems, Inc.
Exhibit 5–10   Courtesy Schenley Industries, Inc.
Exhibit 5–11   Courtesy Reebok International Ltd.
Exhibit 5–12   Courtesy Timex Corporation; Courtesy Samantha Advertising for Gucci.
Exhibit 5–13   Courtesy Revlon.
Exhibit 5–14   Courtesy Oneida Ltd. All rights reserved.
Exhibit 5–15   Courtesy AVIA Group International, Inc.
Exhibit 5–16   Courtesy Burson Marsteller for Church & Dwight Company, Inc.
Exhibit 5–17   Courtesy America's Dairy Farmers, National Dairy Board.
Exhibit 5–18   Courtesy of the Museum of Modern Mythology.
Exhibit 5–19   Courtesy Fallon-McElligott for *Rolling Stone.*
IMC Perspective 5–1   Courtesy Pittsburgh Brewing Company.

Chapter 6

Opening photo   Courtesy Saatchi & Saatchi Pacific for Hewlett-Packard Company.
Global Perspective 6–1   Reproduced with permission of AT&T.
Exhibit 6–2   Ad courtesy of Motorola, Inc.
Exhibit 6–3   Ad courtesy of Motorola, Inc.
Exhibit 6–4   Courtesy Estee Lauder.
Exhibit 6–5   Courtesy of Lever Brothers Company.
Exhibit 6–7   Courtesy IVAC Corporation.
Exhibit 6–9   Courtesy Johnson & Johnson.
Exhibit 6–11   Courtesy Philips Consumer Electronics Company.
Global Perspective 6–2   Courtesy Griffith & Associates for Air Canada.
Exhibit 6–13   Courtesy Heinz U.S.A.
Exhibit 6–14   Courtesy Heinz Pet Products/Leo Burnett U.S.A.
Exhibit 6–18   Courtesy Kitchen Aid.
Exhibit 6–20   Courtesy The Procter & Gamble Company.
Exhibit 6–22   Courtesy The Gillette Company.

Chapter 7

Opening photo   Courtesy New Balance Athletic Shoe, Inc.
Exhibit 7–3   Courtesy MCI.
Exhibit 7–4   Courtesy Sharp Electronics Corporation, Mahwah, New Jersey.
Exhibit 7–6   Courtesy of Lever Brothers Company.
Exhibit 7–7   Courtesy of Wendy's International.
Exhibit 7–8   Reprinted with permission of The Quaker Oats Company.
Exhibit 7–9   Used with permission of Spalding Sports Worldwide.
Exhibit 7–12   Courtesy Bristol-Myers Products.
Exhibit 7–13   Courtesy The Advertising Council, Inc.
Exhibit 7–15   Reprinted with permission of The Quaker Oats Company.
Exhibit 7–16   Courtesy Mammoth Mountain Ski Area/Thomas Bineron Advertising.
Exhibit 7–17   Courtesy California Slim, Inc.
Exhibit 7–18   © 1987 DDB Worldwide Inc. Used by permission of DDB Needham Worldwide Inc. and Partnership for a Drug Free America.
Exhibit 7–20   Courtesy Miller Brewing Company.
Exhibit 7–22   Courtesy of *TRAVEL & LEISURE.* Photography by Kenji Toma.

Chapter 8

Opening photo   © Compaq Computer Corporation.
Exhibit 8–1   Courtesy DMB&B for Dow Chemical Company.
Exhibit 8–2   Courtesy Toyota Motor Corporate Services of North America, Inc.
Exhibit 8–3   Courtesy Pace.
Exhibit 8–4   Reprinted with permission of Del Monte Foods.
IMC Perspective 8–1   Used with permission of Nissan Motor Corporation U.S.A.
Exhibit 8–6   Courtesy Johnson-Rauhoff Incorporated for Miles Inc.
Exhibit 8–7   Courtesy Cincinnati Microwave.
Exhibit 8–8   Courtesy The Broadway.
Exhibit 8–9   Courtesy Panasonic.
Exhibit 8–13   Courtesy Midwest Express Airlines.
Exhibit 8–14   © Sonance, a Division of Dana Innovations, Kevin W. Topp, art director.
IMC Perspective 8–2   Courtesy Hush Puppies Co., Division Wolverine World Wide, Inc.
IMC Perspective 8–3   Courtesy Southwest Airlines.

Chapter 9

Opening photo   Courtesy McCann/SAS for General Motors Corporation.
Exhibit 9–1   © American Association of Advertising Agencies.
Exhibit 9–3   Courtesy Lockheed Corporation.
Exhibit 9–6   Courtesy of International Business Machines Corporation.
Exhibit 9–11   Courtesy of AT&T, © Copyright William Hawkes 1993.
Exhibit 9–17   Courtesy Gift Service, Inc.
IMC Perspective 9–2   Courtesy The University of Chicago.

Chapter 10

Opening photo   Courtesy Subaru of America.
Exhibit 10–1   Courtesy Hallmark Cards, Inc.
Exhibit 10–3   Courtesy Consumer Healthcare Products, Miles Inc.
Global Perspective 10–1   Courtesy Braathens Safe Airlines.
IMC Perspective 10–1   Created by Carillon Importers, Ltd. and TBWA Advertising.
Exhibit 10–5   Courtesy Nike, Inc.
Exhibit 10–6   Courtesy Advertising Age.
IMC Perspective 10–2   Courtesy Rubin Postaer and Associates for American Honda Motor Company, Inc.
Exhibit 10–7   Used by permission of San Diego Trust & Savings Bank.
Exhibit 10–9   Army materials courtesy of the U.S. Government, as represented by the Secretary of the Army.
Exhibit 10–11   Courtesy Easterby & Associates.
Exhibit 10–12   Courtesy Castrol, Inc. Ad development by Scali, McCabe, & Sloves, Inc., New York, New York.
Exhibit 10–13   Courtesy No Fear.
Exhibit 10–14   Courtesy Kellogg Company.
Ethical Perspecitve 10–1   United Colors of Benetton advertising campaign: Concept & Photo - O. Toscani.

Chapter 11

Opening photo   Courtesy Acura Division, American Honda Motor Company, Inc.
Exhibit 11–1   Courtesy Rayovac Company.
Exhibit 11–2   Courtesy Continental Airlines, Inc.
Exhibit 11–3   Courtesy Hunt-Wesson, Inc.
Exhibit 11–4   Courtesy The Ford Motor Company.
Exhibit 11–6   Courtesy Team One Advertising for LEXUS.

Exhibit 11–8 Courtesy Hershey Foods Corporation. AMERICAN BEAUTY, HERSHEY'S, and HERSHEY'S KISSES are trademarks of Hershey Foods Corporation.

Global Perspective 11–1 Courtesy of Taster's Choice.

Exhibit 11–9 Courtesy Chrysler Corporation.

Exhibit 11–10 Courtesy Valvoline, Inc.

Exhibit 11–11 The DERMASIL print ad was reproduced courtesy of Chesebrough-Pond's USA Co.

Exhibit 11–12 Courtesy IVAC Corporation.

Exhibit 11–13 Reprinted with permission of Hewlett-Packard Company.

Exhibit 11–14 Courtesy AT&T Advertising Department.

Exhibit 11–15 Used with permission of ©Nabisco, Inc.

Exhibit 11–16 Courtesy Maytag Company.

Exhibit 11–17 Courtesy BASF Corporation.

Exhibit 11–18 Courtesy Victor Norman & Partners, Inc.

Exhibit 11–19 Courtesy Delta Air Lines, Inc.

Exhibit 11–20 Courtesy British Airways and Saatchi & Saatchi, New York, New York.

Exhibit 11–22 Courtesy Acura Division, American Honda Motor Company, Inc.

IMC Perspective 11–1 Courtesy Apple Computer, Inc.

Exhibit 11–25 Courtesy Phillips Lighting Company.

Chapter 12

Opening photo © Copyright 1994 Robbie McClaran.

IMC Perspective 12–2 Copyright ©1994 Marvel Entertainment Group, Inc.

Chapter 13

Opening photo Courtesy Interactive Network, Inc.

Exhibit 13–1 Courtesy Porsche Cars of North America.

Exhibit 13–3 Courtesy Arts & Entertainment Network.

Exhibit 13–5 Used with permission of © Nabisco, Inc.

Exhibit 13–11 MTV: MUSIC TELEVISION ®. Used by permission.

Exhibit 13–12 NICKELODEON ®. Used by permission.

Exhibit 13–13 Courtesy Group W Sports Marketing.

Global Perspective 13–1 Courtesy MTV/Latino, Inc.

IMC Perspective 13–1 Courtesy of International Business Machines Corporation.

Exhibit 13–14 Courtesy A.C. Nielsen Company.

IMC Perspective 13–2 Courtesy KCEO Radio.

Exhibit 13–18 Courtesy Radio Network Association.

Exhibit 13–16 Courtesy KHTZ-FM.

Chapter 14

Opening photo Reprinted with permission of SmartMoney; © 1994 by SmartMoney, a joint venture of the Hearst Corporation and Dow Jones & Company, Inc.

Exhibit 14–3 Courtesy Surfer Publications, Inc.

Exhibit 14–4 Courtesy *Beef* Magazine.

Exhibit 14–5 Courtesy *Newsweek* Magazine.

Exhibit 14–6 Courtesy *Newsweek* Magazine.

Exhibit 14–7 Courtesy Transamerica Corporation.

Exhibit 14–8 Used by permission of WD-40 Company.

Exhibit 14–9 Courtesy Magazine Publishers of America.

Ethical Perspective 14–1 Courtesy Bausch & Lomb Healthcare and Optics Worldwide.

Exhibit 14–11 Courtesy Audit Bureau of Circulations.

Exhibit 14–12 Courtesy Petersen Publishing Company.

Exhibit 14–13 Courtesy *Newsweek* Magazine.

Exhibit 14–14 Courtesy *Newsweek* Magazine.

Global Perspective 14–1 Courtesy *The European* Ltd.

Exhibit 14–16 Courtesy *The Daily Aztec.*

Exhibit 14–17 Courtesy Pacific Bell.

Exhibit 14–18 Courtesy *Chicago Tribune.*

Exhibit 14–19 Courtesy Union-Tribune Publishing Company.

Exhibit 14–20 Courtesy Jaguar Cars Inc.

Exhibit 14–21 Courtesy Newspaper Advertising Bureau, Inc.

Exhibit 14–22 Courtesy *Newsweek* Magazine.

Chapter 15

Opening photo Courtesy Manning, Selvage & Lee.

Exhibit 15–3 Courtesy Zoological Society of San Diego.

Exhibit 15–4 Tropicana, Pure Premium, & REP. of Girl Device are trademarks of Tropicana Products, Inc. Used in this text by permission.

Global Perspective 15–1 Courtesy The Goodyear Tire & Rubber Company.

Exhibit 15–5 Courtesy AVIAD.

Exhibit 15–9 Courtesy United Airlines, AT&T/Young & Rubicam.

Exhibit 15–10 Courtesy Transportation Displays Incorporated.

Exhibit 15–11 Courtesy Gannett Transit.

Exhibit 15–13 Courtesy Bell Atlantic Directory Services, Bell Atlantic Corporation.

Exhibit 15–15 Paramount/Shooting Star.

Exhibit 15–17 Courtesy of Halsey Publishing Co., publishers of Delta Air Lines *SKY* Magazine. Photography by Brian W. Robb.

Chapter 16

Opening photo Courtesy American Harvest.

Exhibit 16–3 Courtesy LEXUS. Photography by Doug Taub.

Exhibit 16–6 Courtesy Porsche Cars North America/Heiman & Associates.

Exhibit 16–7 Sharon Hoogstraten.

Exhibit 16–9 Courtesy Volvo Cars of North America.

Exhibit 16–11 Courtesy The GM Card.

Exhibit 16–13 Courtesy Tupperware.

Exhibit 16–14 Sharon Hoogstraten.

Chapter 17

Opening photo Courtesy Sears.

Exhibit 17–1 Courtesy General Mills, Inc.

Exhibit 17–4 Used with permission of © Nabisco, Inc.

Exhibit 17–5 Courtesy The Colgate-Palmolive Company.

Exhibit 17–6 Courtesy Burson Marsteller for Church & Dwight Company, Inc.

Exhibit 17–7 Reproduced with permission of PepsiCo, Inc. 1994, Purchase, New York.

Exhibit 17–9A Sharon Hoogstraten.

Exhibit 17–9B Courtesy ArmorAll Products Corporation.

Exhibit 17–10 Courtesy Ralph's Grocery Company.

Exhibit 17–14 Courtesy Kellogg Company. Eggo®, Common Sense®, and Kellogg's® are registered trademarks of Kellogg Company. All rights reserved.

Exhibit 17–15 Courtesy Catalina Marketing Corporation.

Exhibit 17–16 Used by permission of The Quaker Oats Company.

Exhibit 17–17 Courtesy Keebler Company/ ©1994 Universal City Studios.

Exhibit 17–18 Courtesy ArmorAll Products Corporation.

Exhibit 17–19 Courtesy Bristol-Myers Company.

Exhibit 17–22 Courtesy Van Camp Seafood Company.

Exhibit 17–23 Courtesy Van Camp Seafood Company.

Exhibit 17–25 Courtesy Spalding Sports Worldwide.

Exhibit 17–26   Courtesy American Honda Motor Company, Inc.

Exhibit 17–27   Courtesy Ski the Summit Colorado - Arapahoe Basin, Breckenridge, Copper Mountain, & Keystone.

Exhibit 17–28   Courtesy James Bunting Associates, Inc. for DuPont.

Exhibit 17–29   Courtesy of Taster's Choice.

Exhibit 17–30   Courtesy Lever Brothers Company.

Chapter 18

Opening photo   Used by permission of WD-40 Company.

Exhibit 18–3   Courtesy Exxon Corporation.

Exhibit 18–5   Courtesy Brunswick Corporation.

Exhibit 18–6   Courtesy Sprint.

Exhibit 18–7   Courtesy Chevron Corporation.

Exhibit 18–8   Courtesy KGTV.

Exhibit 18–9   Courtesy Yellow Pages Publishers Association.

Exhibit 18–11   Courtesy Sears.

Exhibit 18–12   Courtesy Toyota Motor Sales U.S.A.

Exhibit 18–13   ©1991 Dow Jones & Company, Publisher of *The Wall Street Journal*. All Rights Reserved.

Exhibit 18–15   Used by permission of Tree Top, Inc.

Exhibit 18–17   Courtesy 3M.

Exhibit 18–18   © Visa U.S.A. Inc. (1993). All Rights Reserved. Reproduced with the permission of Visa U.S.A. Inc.

Exhibit 18–19   Courtesy International Olympic Committee.

Exhibit 18–20   Courtesy Deloitte & Touche.

Exhibit 18–22   Reprinted with permission of Mobil Corporation.

Exhibit 18–23   Courtesy AT&T Advertising.

Chapter 19

Opening photo   Courtesy Brock Control Systems, Inc.

Exhibit 19–6   Courtesy Giltspur, Inc./Haddon Advertising.

Exhibit 19–7   Courtesy Gordon Publications, Inc.

Exhibit 19–8   Courtesy Targetbase Marketing.

Chapter 20

Opening photo   Reproduced with permission of PepsiCo, Inc. 1994, Purchase, New York.

Exhibit 20–1   Courtesy Chiat/Day/Mojo Inc. Advertising.

Exhibit 20–15   Courtesy Starch INRA Hooper.

IMC Perspective 20–2   Courtesy BBDO Worldwide.

Chapter 21

Opening photo   Courtesy Intel Corporation.

Exhibit 21–2   Courtesy Brock Control Systems, Inc.

Exhibit 21–6   Courtesy Mobium for R.R. Donnelley & Sons.

Exhibit 21–7   Courtesy Nomadic Display.

Exhibit 21–8   Courtesy Tektronix, Inc.

Exhibit 21–12   Courtesy Fallon-McElligott for Continental Bank.

Exhibit 21–14   Courtesy Impact Exhibits, Inc.

Exhibit 21–15   Used by permission of WD-40 Company.

Exhibit 21–16   Courtesy Norwegian Cruise Line.

Chapter 22

Opening photo   Courtesy Nike, Inc.

Exhibit 22–1   Courtesy Kentucky Fried Chicken (KFC) Corporation.

Exhibit 22–2   Used by permission of WD-40 Company.

Global Perspective 22–1   Reproduced with permission of PepsiCo, Inc. 1994, Purchase, New York.

Exhibit 22–4   Courtesy Nestlé.

Exhibit 22–5   Courtesy Heineken Breweries.

Exhibit 22–7   Coca-Cola and Coca-Cola Light are registered trademarks of The Coca-Cola Company. Permission granted by The Coca-Cola Company.

Exhibit 22–8   Courtesy The Gillette Company.

Exhibit 22–9   Courtesy Nestlé.

Exhibit 22–10   Courtesy The Colgate-Palmolive Company.

Exhibit 22–11   Courtesy Singapore Airlines.

Exhibit 22–12   Courtesy Xerox Corporation.

Global Perspective 22–2   Courtesy Brown-Forman International Ltd.

Exhibit 22–13   Courtesy Continental Airlines.

Global Perspective 22–3   Courtesy Merrill Lynch & Company, Inc.

Exhibit 22–15   Courtesy NCH Promotional Services, 1991.

Exhibit 22–17   Courtesy Häagen-Dazs.

Exhibit 22–18   Courtesy *Newsweek* magazine.

Chapter 23

Opening photo   Courtesy Jenny Craig Weight Loss Centres, Inc.

Exhibit 23–1   Reprinted with permission of Kinney & Lange. All Rights Reserved.

Exhibit 23–2   Courtesy Jamko Advertising (in-house agency for Jacoby & Meyers Law Offices).

Exhibit 23–6   Courtesy Benetton Cosmetics Corporation. Photo by Toscani.

Exhibit 23–11   Courtesy Kellogg Company. Kellogg's®, Eggo® are registered trademarks of Kellogg Company. Used with permission.

Exhibit 23–12   © 1992 Wildcraft® Herbs, Santa Cruz, CA 95060.

Exhibit 23–13   Courtesy Direct Selling Association.

Chapter 24

Opening photo   Courtesy International Advertising Association.

Exhibit 24–1   Reprinted with permission of Joseph E. Seagram & Sons, Inc.

Exhibit 24–2   Used by permission of Calvin Klein.

Ethical Perspective 24–1   Courtesy Livingston and Company.

Exhibit 24–4   Courtesy Ansell Inc.

Exhibit 24–5   Used by permission of Calvin Klein.

Exhibit 24–6   Courtesy Fleishman Hillard Inc. for Anheuser-Busch.

Exhibit 24–8   Reprinted by permission of Rolls-Royce Motor Cars Inc.

Exhibit 24–9   © American Association of Advertising Agencies.

Exhibit 24–10   © American Association of Advertising Agencies.

Exhibit 24–11   Courtesy Maidenform, Inc./Agency - Levine, Huntley, Schmidt & Beaver; Creative - Rochelle Klein, Michael Vitiello; Director - Mark Coppos, Coppos Films.

Exhibit 24–12   Courtesy Mattel.

Exhibit 24–13   Courtesy International Advertising Association.

IMC Perspective 24–1   Courtesy Weiden & Kennedy for American Indian College Fund.

Exhibit 24–14   © American Association of Advertising Agencies.

Exhibit 24–15   Courtesy Kia Motors America, Inc.

Exhibit 24–16   © American Association of Advertising Agencies.

Name/Company/Brand Index

Subject Index